ELEMENTS

OF

HISTORY,

ANCIENT AND MODERN.

BY

JOSEPH E. WORCESTER, LL.D.,
AUTHOR OF WORCESTER'S QUARTO DICTIONARY, ETC.

A NEW EDITION, REVISED AND ENLARGED.

BOSTON:
THOMPSON, BIGELOW, & BROWN,
25 AND 29 CORNHILL.
1871.

PREFACE.

The first edition of this work was published in 1826, accompanied by an *Historical Atlas*. The Elements of History and the Atlas were designed to be used together each being materially incomplete without the other. But as it is necessary that books used in most of the schools in this country should be furnished at a very low price, the expense of the Atlas was, in many cases, an obstacle to the use of the work; and after the Elements and Atlas had passed through a number of impressions, an edition of the book was prepared in such a form that it might be used without the Atlas. This was accomplished by folding in the volume the *Chart of General History*, and also by inserting a series of *Tables of History*, which, in a measure, supply the place of the Charts or Tables of History in the Atlas.

The method of using the work will be found simple and easy. After the student has attended to the three short sections on the *Uses*, *Sources*, and *Divisions of History*, it is recommended that he should study carefully the *Chart of History*, with the use of the *Description, Illustration, and Questions* (See page 333.)

By this means he will have the general outlines of history, with the periods of the rise and fall of the principal states and empires, impressed on his mind, and by having thus gained a comprehensive view of the whole ground, he will be prepared to study the particular parts with greater advantage. The Tables of Grecian, Roman, French, English, and American History are designed to be attended to in connection with the portions of the volume relating to the history of Greece, Rome, France, England, and the United States respectively.

The outlines of history may be acquired with incomparably greater facility by the use of Charts and Tables, than by the perusal of volumes, independently of such aid; and, what is of great importance, the information thus obtained will be so impressed on the mind, as to be much more durable than if acquired by any other method. By means of them one may easily trace the rise, progress, revolutions, decline, and fall of states and empires; see what states have been contemporary, and what have existed at different periods; take comprehensive views of the whole ground of history, and comparative views of the particular parts; mark the succession of the different dynasties and sovereigns in the different kingdoms and empires; learn the leading events of the several reigns and of different ages, and observe the periods when the most illustrious persons have flourished.

But for a knowledge of the internal condition and history of a state, the particular details of events, with their causes and consequences, and the exploits of individuals who have figured upon the theatre of the world, recourse must be had to other sources of information. In order, therefore, that the study of history may be pursued to the best advantage, and a proper attention be paid to the connection both of time and of subject, the use of charts should be united with that of historical narrative.

As it would be impossible, in a volume of the size of this, to trace a regular series of events relating to all the states and empires that have flourished in the world, the chief attention of the author has been paid to a few of them, — those of which the history is of the greatest importance, particularly to American students, — namely, Greece and Rome in ancient history, and France, England, and the United States, in modern Brief notices, however, of various other states have been given, and also some short treatises on topics of importance in an introduction to the study of history, and useful in preparing the student for the perusal of more extended historical works.

In the preparation of the Elements, the author has endeavored to unite so much of reflection with the details of facts, as to assist the reader in forming correct views of the causes and consequences of events; and in order to render the work more interesting, he has, in some instances, introduced short anecdotes and memorable observations of distinguished men on important occasions.

Every one, much conversant with history, must be

aware of the frequent and often great diversity in the accounts given of the characters of men and events, even by authors of reputation. This diversity is to be attributed partly to the peculiar principles and prejudices of the historians, and partly to the contradictory statements in the original sources of history.

As the line of truth is, in so many cases, obscure and difficult to be discovered, the author cannot hope that he has in no instances fallen into error. It has, however, been his object to follow the best guides, and to give true impressions of the character of persons and transactions, so far as they came under review; but as information has been derived from such a multiplicity of sources, it would be impossible for him, were it desirable, to give a complete enumeration of his authorities.

This little work has passed through numerous editions, and has received a large measure of the public approbation and patronage. It has now been revised, somewhat enlarged, better fitted to be used independently of the Atlas, and the historical information brought down to a recent date. The author hopes that it will be found, in its present form, less unworthy of the favor with which it has been received.

CONTENTS.

ELEMENTS OF HISTORY

ANCIENT HISTORY.

ELEMENTS OF HISTORY.

USES OF HISTORY.

1. HISTORY is a narrative of past events. The study of it is attractive both to the young and the old, to the unreflecting and the philosophical mind. It combines amusement of the deepest interest; the exercise and improvement of the best faculties of man; and the acquisition of the most important species of knowledge.

2. History, considered merely as a source of amusement, has great advantages over novels and romances, the perusal of which too often debilitates the mind by inflaming the imagination, and corrupts the heart by infusing what may justly be regarded as moral poison. Like works of fiction, history serves to amuse the imagination and interest the passions, not always, indeed, in an equal degree; yet it is free from the corrupting tendencies which too often belong to novels, and has a great superiority over them, inasmuch as it rests on the basis of fact.

3. The love of novelty and of excitement is natural to man; hence the general taste for history, though its details are not unfrequently painful. It affords a melancholy view of human nature, governed by the baser passions; and is to a lamentable extent, little else than a register of human crime and calamity, of war and suffering.

4. A higher use of history is, to improve the understanding and strengthen the judgment. It has been styled philosophy teaching by example, or moral philosophy exemplified by the lives and actions of men. It adds to our own experience an immense treasure of the experience of others, and thereby enable us to enter upon the business of life with the advantage of being, in a manner, acquainted with it.

5. It makes us acquainted with human nature, and enables us to judge how men will act in given circumstances, and to trace the connection between cause and effect in human affairs. It serves to free the mind from many narrow and hurtful prejudices; to teach us to admire what is praiseworthy, wherever it may be found; and to compare, on enlarged and liberal principles, other ages and countries with our own.

6. History may be regarded as the school of politics, and, as such, some knowledge of it is indispensable to rulers and statesmen; it is also highly important to every citizen of a republic, in order to enable him to perform, in a manner honorable to himself and useful to the community, the duties of a freeman. By history we gain our knowledge of the constitution of society; of the reciprocal influence of national character, laws, and government; of those causes and circumstances which have promoted the rise and prosperity, or the decline and fall, of states and empires.

7. History shows us past ages, triumphs over time, and presents to our view the various revolutions which have taken place in the world. It furnishes us with the wisdom and experience of our ancestors, exhibits their living actions, and enables us to profit by their successes and failures. It teaches us what has been done for the melioration of mankind by the wisdom of Greece and Rome, by modern literature and science, by free government, and by true religion.

8. It tends to strengthen the sentiments of virtue. In its faithful delineations, vice always appears odious, and virtue not only desirable and productive of happiness, but also favorable to true honor and solid glory. The reader of history learns to connect true glory, not with the possession of wealth and power, but with the disinterested employment of great talents in promoting the good of mankind.

9. True history has numberless relations and uses as an exhibition of the conduct of Divine Providence; and it presents numerous instances in which events, important to the welfare of the human race, have been brought about by inconsiderable means, contrary to the intentions of those who were the principal agents in them.

10. A knowledge of history has a tendency to render us contented with our condition in life, by the views which it exhibits of the instability of human affairs. It teaches us that the highest stations are not exempt from severe trials; that riches and power afford no assurance of happiness; and that the greatest sovereigns have not unfrequently been more miserable than their meanest subjects.

SOURCES OF HISTORY.

Some of the principal sources of history, independent of authentic records, or the narrative of those who were contemporary with the events which they relate, are the following: —

1. *Oral tradition.* From this source Herod'otus derived the greater part of his history. It existed before the invention of the arts of writing, carving, and painting.

2. *Historical poems.* These are common among all barbarous nations. The *Iliad* and *Od'yssey* of *Homer* were regarded by the Greeks as of historical authority; and they comprise the only history extant of what is called the heroic age of Greece.

3. *Visible monuments*, as pillars, heaps of stones, and mounds of earth, are used to perpetuate historical events among a barbarous people.

4. *Ruins*, as those of Egypt, and of the cities of Balbec, Palmy'ra, Nin'eveh and Persep'olis, are lasting memorials of the power, opulence, and taste of the builders.

5. *Giving names to countries, towns, &c.*, has been used, in all ages, as a method of perpetuating the memory of their planters or founders.

6. *Coins* and *medals* are of great use in illustrating history, chronology, geography, and mythology, as well as the manners and customs of the nations of antiquity. These, however, belong to a people of some refinement. Ancient coins have been found buried in the earth at various times, in considerable quantities. Vast numbers are now preserved belonging to different ages. The most ancient of those of which the antiquity can be ascertained belong to the 5th century before the Christian era.

7. *Inscriptions on marbles.* The most celebrated collection of marbles, made use of for the illustration of ancient history, is that which is now in the possession of the University of Oxford, in England, and which was brought from Greece by the earl of Arundel, and from him called the *Arundelian Marbles.*

8. The most important of these inscriptions is the *Chronicle of Paros*, which contains the chronology of Athens from the time of Cecrops, B. C. 1582, to B. C. 264, at which latter period it is supposed to have been compiled. The authority of this Chronicle has been called in question by a number of learned men; but it has been supported by many others, and

the chronology of Greece, at present most generally received, has been, in a great measure, founded upon it.

9. *The Hieroglyphics, Paintings, and Sculptures* which yet remain on the ruins of *Egypt* and *Assyria*, the greater part of which have been but recently discovered, and only partially deciphered, have added largely to our knowledge of the history, manners, and customs of the ancient inhabitants of those countries.

DIVISIONS OF HISTORY.

1. History, with respect to time, is divided into *Ancient* and *Modern*.

2. *Ancient History* is the history of the world from the creation, to the establishment of the *New Empire of the West* under Charlemagne, A. D. 800. *Modern History* embraces all the time subsequent to that period.

3. Some historians, however, adopt the *Christian era*, and others the subversion of the *Western Empire* of the Romans, A. D. 476, for the dividing point between Ancient and Modern History.

4. A third division of history, which is often considered as distinct from ancient and modern, is that of the *Middle Ages* This period comprises about a thousand years, from the 5th to the 15th century; or from the subversion of the *Western Empire* of the Romans to that of the *Eastern Empire*.

5. The Middle Ages embrace the time intervening between the extinction of ancient literature and the appearance of modern literature. During this period Europe was sunk in ignorance and barbarism; hence it is often styled the *Dark Ages*.

6. Ancient History is distinguished by the four great monarchies of *Assyria* or *Babylon*, *Persia*, *Greece* or *Macedonia*, and *Rome*.

7. The Middle Ages are characterized by the origin and progress of *Mahometanism* and the *Saracen Empire*, the prevalence of the *Feudal System*, the *Crusades*, and *Chivalry*.

8. Modern History is distinguished by the invention of *gunpowder*, and the consequent change in the mode of *war;* the discovery of *America*, and the extension of *commerce;* the invention of the art of *printing*, the revival of *learning*, and the diffusion of *knowledge;* also by the *reformation* in religion, and a variety of other improvements in the state of society. — The last half century has been characterized by important political

revolutions and *movements* in society, resulting in the overthrow of *absolute monarchies*, and in the establishment of *democratic* or *liberal* principles of government, in place of *arbitrary* or *despotic* principles; in the progress of various *sciences*, the multiplication of *books* and *periodical publications*, and a wide diffusion of intelligence among the masses of the people; in great improvements in the *mechanic arts*, and the application of steam-power to machinery; and in the formation of numerous *benevolent societies*, which have for their object the propagation of Christianity, the alleviation of the suffering, the amelioration of the condition and the elevation of the character of the human race.

9. History, with regard to the nature of its subjects, is divided into *Sacred* and *Profane*, *Ecclesiastical* and *Civil.*

10. *Sacred History* is the history contained in the Scriptures, and it relates chiefly to the Israelites or Jews. *Profane History* is the history of ancient heathen nations, and is found chiefly in the writings of the Greeks and Romans. *Ecclesiastical History* is the history of the Church of Christ, or of Christianity, from its first promulgation to the present time. *Civil History* is the history of the various nations, states, and empires, that have appeared in the world, exhibiting a view of their wars, revolutions, and changes.

11. Sacred History goes back to the remotest period of time, and commences with an account of the creation of the world, which, according to the Hebrew text of the Scriptures, took place 4004 years before the Christian era; according to the Samaritan text, 4700; according to the Septuagint, 5872; and according to the computation of Dr. Hales, 5411. The computation according to the Hebrew text, which gives 4004 from the creation to the Christian era, and 1656 from the creation to the deluge, is the one commonly received in English literature though the correctness of it is now generally called in question by learned men.

12. The modern science of *Geology*, which has brought to light a vast number of important and interesting facts previously unknown, has produced a conviction among men of science that the origin of the earth is to be ascribed to a period far more remote than has been heretofore supposed, and the most learned Christian divines have adopted a mode of interpreting the Mosaic account of the creation which is in accordance with this opinion.

13. The earliest profane historian, whose works are extant is *Herod'otus*, who is styled the Father of History. His history was composed about 445 years B. C., and comprises everything which he had an opportunity of learning respecting the

1*

Egyptians, Persians, Greeks, Ionians, Lydians, Lycians, and Macedonians, from about the year 713 to 479 before the Christian era.

14. With regard, therefore, to all the preceding ages of the world, which, reckoning from the creation to the time when the narrative of Herod'otus begins, comprise, according to the common chronology, nearly 3300 years, there exist no documents, with the exception of the Scriptures, really deserving the name of history. The accounts which have been given of the events of this long series of ages, comprising more than half of the time which has elapsed since the origin of the human race, were drawn up by writers who lived long after the transactions of which they treat, and were compiled from scattered records, fragments, and traditions.

15. Our knowledge, of course, of the early history of the world, the first settlement of the different portions of it, the primitive state of society, and the progress of mankind in the remotest ages, is extremely limited. The Scriptures are the only authentic source of information on these subjects. The facts which they record, though not sufficiently numerous to satisfy curiosity, are yet, in the highest degree, interesting and important.

16. Some of the most remarkable events, previous to the commencement of profane history, recorded in the Bible, are the creation of the world, the fall of man, the deluge, the dispersion of mankind at Babel, the planting of different nations, the call of Abraham, the deliverance of the Israelites out of Egypt, and their settlement in Canaan.

17. The histories of *Greece* and *Rome* are far the best known, most interesting, and most important portions of ancient profane history.

18. There is much obscurity hanging over the history of the *Middle* or *Dark Ages*.

19. The portions of history best known are those which relate to modern civilized nations, during the last three centuries.

[*The* CHART OF HISTORY, *which is found in this volume, together with the* DESCRIPTION *and* ILLUSTRATION, *beginning with the* 333*d page, may now be advantageously attended to.*]

[*For some remarks on Sacred History, and Tables of the History of the kingdoms of Israel and Judah, see pages* **343 344** *and* **345.**]

EGYPT.

1 Egypt holds a conspicuous place in history, on account of its great antiquity and early attainments in the arts. It has been styled the cradle of the sciences, and it claims the honor of the invention of the art of writing. At a period when Greece and Italy were immersed in barbarism, Egypt could boast of arts, learning, and civilization. It was the principal source from which the Greeks derived their information, and, after all its windings and enlargements, we may still trace the stream of our knowledge to the banks of the Nile.

2. It is a matter of regret that we have the means of obtaining but little knowledge respecting the ancient history of Egypt. The early dynasties of the kingdom are involved in obscurity, and history throws little light on the building of its most ancient cities, or the construction of those magnificent monuments, which show to how high a state of improvement the inhabitants, at a remote period, had carried the arts, and which still continue to be objects of admiration and astonishment.

3. The most celebrated of these works of ancient grandeur are, *Lake Mœris*, an immense artificial reservoir; the *Labyrinth*, an enormous structure of marble, built under ground; the *Catacombs*, or *Mummy-pits*, subterraneous galleries, of prodigious extent, appropriated to the reception of the dead and the *Pyramids*, a wonder both of the ancient and the modern world.

4. The glory of *Thebes*, a city of Upper Egypt, famous for its hundred gates, the theme and admiration of ancient poets and historians, belongs to a period prior to the commencement of authentic history. It is recorded only in the dim lights of poetry and tradition, which might be suspected of fable, did not such mighty witnesses to their truth remain.

5. Before the time of Herod'otus, *Memphis* had supplanted *Thebes*, and the Ptol'emies afterwards removed the seat of empire to *Alexan'dria.* Strabo and Diodo'rus described Thebes under the name of *Dios'polis*, and gave such magnificent descriptions of its monuments, as caused their fidelity to be called in question, till the observations of modern travellers proved their accounts to have fallen short of the reality.

6. The place of alphabetic writing was supplied, in ancient Egypt, by those rude pictures of visible objects, known by the name of *hieroglyphics*, a multitude of which are still found sculptured on the remains of her ancient temples, obelisks and other monuments.

7. The researches of Champollion, and various other learned men of the present century, have succeeded, to some extent, in deciphering these hieroglyphics. By means of this interpretation, great additions have been made to our knowledge of the history of Egypt and the manners and customs of its people.

8. It appears that the Egyptians were a mixture of races, differing considerably in color and organization, the lower classes having dark skins and frizzled hair, while the upper ranks possessed light complexions and agreeable features The predominant color of the population, however, seems to have been brown or yellow. The nation was divided into seven strictly defined hereditary castes, each of which had its peculiar rank and privileges. The priests and soldiers formed the two highest castes. Then followed the agriculturists, the traders, the mariners, and the artisans. The lowest caste was that of the shepherds, who were held in general detestation.

9. The government was an hereditary monarchy, in which the power of the sovereign was limited by established forms and usages, and by the influence of the priestly caste. The Kings, or Pharaohs, as they were called, belonged exclusively to the caste of soldiers, until, at a late period in the decline of the monarchy, a priest named Sethos usurped the crown.

10. The laws of Egypt appear to have been few, and generally, as far as known, founded in justice. The punishments for crimes against the person were more severe than for crimes against property. Murder was punished with death, as was also the witnessing a murder without endeavoring to prevent it. A child who killed his parent was tortured, and then burnt alive; while a parent who killed his child was only imprisoned for three days with the dead body. Debtors were not imprisoned, though the creditors could seize their goods; nor could a debt, without a written acknowledgment to prove it, be recovered at law, if the person from whom it was claimed denied it upon oath.

11. Every person, not excepting the king, was, immediately after his death, subjected to a trial, in order to determine whether he was worthy of funeral rites. His whole life passed in review, and, if pronounced virtuous, his embalmed body was, with various marks of honor, deposited in a sepulchre, which was often constructed at great expense; but if his life had been vicious, or if he had died in debt, he was left unburied, and was supposed to be deprived of future happiness.

12. The Egyptians from an early period maintained a regular standing army, a large and important portion of which consisted of warriors who fought in chariots. Their troops were well armed and organized, and were levied by conscription.

like the armies of most countries of Europe at the present day. The bow was considered the national weapon, and was used with great force and skill by the Egyptians.

13. The first king of Egypt known in history was *Menes* whose capital was the city of *This* in Upper Egypt. Under his successors, the monarchy flourished for several hundred years until it was overthrown by an invasion of the Hyksos, a race of wandering shepherds, whose origin is uncertain, though many learned men suppose them to have been Scythians. The Hyksos, or Shepherd Kings, as they are sometimes called, held possession of the greater part of Egypt for a period variously estimated at from two to nine centuries, at the expiration of which they were expelled by force of arms, and a native monarch again placed on the throne.

14. The most distinguished of the Egyptian kings was Rameses the Great, who by the Greeks was called Sesostris. He was a mighty conqueror, and subdued nearly the whole of Western Asia, with some of the adjacent countries of Europe. On returning from his foreign expeditions, he employed himself in enlarging and beautifying the chief cities of his kingdom. Some of the magnificent temples and palaces which he erected are yet standing, and on their walls are sculptured representations of his principal achievements.

15. Other celebrated kings were Osirtesen I., who is supposed by some writers to have been the Pharaoh that received Joseph; Thothmes IV., in whose reign the Hyksos were finally expelled; and Amenoph III., who conquered Nubia and erected the famous vocal statue of Memnon.

16. The next sovereign who is particularly distinguished in history was *Nechus*, or *Pharaoh-Necho.* He patronized navigation, and fitted out a fleet which sailed round Africa. He made war upon the Medes and Babylonians, and defeated *Josiah*, king of Judah, in the battle of *Megiddo.*

17. In the year B. C. 525, at the commencement of the reign of Psammeni'tus, the *Persians*, under *Camby'ses*, invaded Egypt, and laid siege to *Pelu'sium.* Taking advantage of the Egyptian superstition, the invaders placed in front of their army a variety of dogs, cats, and other animals, which were held sacred by the besieged; and the Egyptians not daring to injure the sacred animals, the Persians entered Pelusium without resistance. Soon after, Camby'ses took Memphis, and reduced Egypt to a province of the Persian monarchy.

18. It was easily wrested from the sway of Persia by *Alexander the Great;* after his death, it fell to the share of *Ptol'emy;* and under him and his successors of the same name

Egypt regained her ancient lustre, and rose to a height in science and commerce which no other part of the world then equalled.

THE PHŒNICIANS.

1. The Phœnicians were among the most remarkable and most early civilized nations of antiquity; yet there is no complete or regular history of them extant: occasional notices of them, however, are found in the Scriptures, and in the Greek historians. *Sanconi'athon*, a Phœnician historian, is supposed by some to have flourished about the time of Joshua; but of his work only a few fragments remain; and the genuineness of even these is considered as very doubtful.

2. The inhabitants of Phœnicia, who are styled *Ca'naanites* in the Scriptures, were a commercial people in the time of Abraham. *Tyre* and *Sidon*, their princial cities, were two of the most ancient we read of in history; and, in remote ages they were the most considerable seats of commerce in the world.

3. The Phœnicians were the reputed inventors of glass, purple, and coinage; the invention of letters has also been attributed to them, as well as to the Egyptians; and to *Cadmus* is ascribed the honor of having first carried letters into Greece.

4. The Phœnicians sent out a number of colonies to Cyprus Rhodes, Greece, Sicily, Sardinia, and Spain; and the foundation of *Carthage* is attributed to *Dido*, sister of *Pygma'lion*, king of Tyre, with a company of adventurers. Tyre suffered two memorable sieges and captures; the first by Nebuchadnezzar, and the second by Alexander the Great.

ASSYRIA AND BABYLON.

1. ***Assyria***, the first of the four great empires of antiquity, derived its name from *Ashur*, the son of *Shem*, and the reputed founder of *Nineveh*, its chief city. The foundation of *Babylon* is ascribed to *Nimrod*, who was the grandson of *Ham*, and considered by many the same as the *Belus* of profane historians. These two cities are supposed to have been founded near the same time, and not long after the dispersion of *Babel*. But of their history, for many ages after their foundation, very little is known with certainty, and the accounts given of them by ancient authors are inconsistent with each other.

2. It is commonly supposed that Assyria and Babylon were originally distinct kingdoms, and so continued till Ninus conquered Babylon, and annexed it to the Assyrian empire. According to Dr. Gillies, however, only one monarchy existed at the same time, but divided into three great eras; the first commencing with *Nimrod*, when *Babylon* was the seat of empire; the second with *Ninus*, whose capital was *Nineveh*; and the third beginning after the death of *Sardanapa'lus*, when *Babylon* again became the metropolis.

3. *Ninus* and *Semir'amis* are the hero and heroine of the old Assyrian and Babylonian chronicles; but the account given of them appears to partake more of fable than of credible history. So great is the uncertainty respecting them, that different historians and chronologists differ no less than a thousand years with regard to the time when they flourished.

4. *Ninus* is represented as a great and powerful sovereign, and is said to have enlarged and embellished the city of Nineveh. After having made extensive conquests, he espoused *Semir'amis*, who succeeded him in the throne. She is described not only as surpassing all her sex in wit and beauty, but also as possessing unbounded ambition, and extraordinary talents for government and war. She enlarged Babylon, and rendered it the most magnificent city in the world; and, after a reign of great splendor, was succeeded by her son *Ninyas*

5. From the time of Ninyas to the overthrow of the monarchy, under *Sardanapa'lus*, a period of several centuries, little or nothing is known respecting the history of Assyria and Babylon.

6. The name of *Sardanapa'lus* is almost a proverbial reproach. He is said to have so degraded himself as to adopt the dress and occupations of a female, and to have passed his

life in the most disgraceful effeminacy and voluptuousness, in the company of his wives and concubines. At length *Arbaces*, governor of Media, and *Bel'esis*, a priest of Babylon, disgusted with his inglorious and shameful life, excited a rebellion against him. After sustaining a defeat, Sardanapa'lus, in order to avoid falling into the hands of the conquerors, set fire to his palace, and burnt himself, together with his women and all his treasures.

7. The empire was then divided into three kingdoms, among the three conspirators, Arbaces becoming king of Media, Bel'esis of Babylon, and Pul or Phul of Assyria.

8 The successors of *Pul* were, 1st, *Tig'lath-pi-le'ser*, who took possession of that part of the kingdom of Israel which was east of the Jordan; 2d, *Shalamane'ser*, who put an end to the kingdom of Israel, and carried the inhabitants captive; 3d, *Sennach'erib*, who laid siege to Jerusalem, in the time of *Hezeki'ah*, but was compelled to return in disgrace, 185,000 men of his army being destroyed in a miraculous manner in one night; 4th, *Esarhad'don*, who defeated *Manas'seh*, king of Judah, and carried him captive to Babylon.

9. Not long after the death of Esarhad'don, *Nabopolas'sar*, or *Nebuchadnez'zar*, having got possession of Babylon, being assisted by *Cyax'ares*, king of Media, besieged and destroyed Nineveh, put an end to the Assyrian monarchy, and made Babylon the seat of empire.

10. He was succeeded by his son, *Nebuchadnezzar* II., who took Jerusalem, and carried the Jews captive to Babylon. He had a long and signal reign, some particulars of which are recorded in the book of Daniel.

11. During the reign of *Belshazzar*, who succeeded to the throne a few years after the death of Nebuchadnezzar, the Persians, under *Cyrus*, after a siege of two years, having turned the course of the Euphrates, entered the city through the dried channel, and took it while the inhabitants were engaged in feasting and riot. Belshazzar was slain, and with him ended the empire of Babylon.

12. After its conquest by the Persians, Babylon gradually declined, until in a few centuries no vestige of its grandeur remained, and even tradition was unable to point with certainty to the place where it had stood. Modern European travellers have, however, at length clearly identified its site, which, in accordance with the prophecies of Scripture, has been for ages a howling wilderness, covered with shapeless ruins, and inhabited only by wild beasts and venomous reptiles.

13. Nineveh, which, as before related, was burnt by the Medes, never revived from its ashes. In course of time, its

ruins were entirely covered with earth, so that a few huge mounds, clothed with vegetation, alone marked its site. In 1845, these mounds were explored by Layard, an English traveller, who discovered extensive remains of palaces and other edifices, which had been buried nearly 2500 years. He found also sculptures and inscriptions of great interest which throw much light on the manners and customs of its inhabitants, and on some points of its history.

PERSIA.

1. Persia was the second of the four great empires of antiquity. Its history, prior to the reign of *Cyrus the Great*, is involved in obscurity and fable. It was originally called *Elam*, and the inhabitants Elamites, who were descendants of Shem. In the earlier ages it was of small extent; but under the reign of Cyrus, who was the founder of the great Persian empire, it became the most powerful and extensive sovereignty on the globe, comprising Persia, Media, Parthia, Assyria or Babylonia Syria, and Asia Minor; and to these Egypt was added by Camby′ses.

2. For the history of Persia, from the reign of *Cyrus* to the overthrow of the empire by Alexander the Great, we are indebted chiefly to the Greeks. In the account of the same period by the writers of modern Persia, there is much of fable, and a total neglect of dates, and the names of the sovereigns are different from those given by the Greek historians. The narratives of these two classes of writers differ in many material points. The Greek authors, though they throw a veil of doubt over their records by their exaggerations, especially where the honor of their own country is concerned, are, nevertheless, esteemed as entitled to superior credit.

3. Cyrus is described as possessed of great talents, both as a warrior and a sovereign. Having subdued all the nations from the Ægæ′an sea to the Euphra′tes, he, together with his uncle, *Cyax′ares* II., king of the Medes, took Babylon, and conquered the Assyrian empire. Cyax′ares dying soon after, Cyrus reigned sole monarch over the united kingdoms, during seven years; in the first of which he published the famous edict for the return of the *Jews* and the rebuilding of *Jerusalem.*

4. Herod′otus, Xen′ophon, and Cte′sias, in their accounts of the character and history of Cyrus, differ in many particulars.

That of Xen'ophon has been followed by Rollin and other moderns; yet it is supposed to have been the design of Xen'ophon not to exhibit a faithful record of facts, but to delineate the model of a perfect prince and a well-regulated monarchy

5. Cyrus was succeeded by his son *Camby'ses*, a cruel tyrant, whose principal exploit was the conquest of Egypt On his death, *Smerdis* usurped the crown; but after a reign of seven months, he was assassinated, and *Dari'us* was elected sovereign. It was the army of the latter that invaded Greece and was defeated at Mar'athon. The history of Persia, from this time till the overthrow of the monarchy, is much connected with that of Greece.

6. Darius was succeeded by his son *Xerxes I.*, who made the second great invasion of Greece, and suffered a series of defeats, with immense losses. He left the empire to his son, *Artaxerx'es I.*, who had a long and peaceful reign.

7. The other two principal sovereigns were *Artaxerx'es II.*, during whose reign *Xen'ophon* made the famous retreat with 10,000 Greeks, and *Dari'us Codom'anus*, the last sovereign of ancient Persia. The latter was defeated by Alexander, and with his death the ancient Persian empire terminated.

Kings of Ancient Persia.

[The figures denote the commencement of the reign of each.

B.C.		B.C.	
536	Cyrus the Great.	425	**Xerxes II.**
529	Cambyses.	424.	**Sogdianus.**
522	Smerdis.	423.	**Darius Nothus.**
521.	Darius Hystaspis.	404.	**Artaxerxes Mnemon**
485	Xerxes.	358.	**Artaxerxes III. Ochus.**
464	Artabanus.	337.	**Arses.**
464.	Artaxerxes I Longimanus	336.	**Darius Codomanus.**

GREECE.

SECTION I.

Greece — the Country and the People.

1. Greece, the most celebrated country of antiquity, was of very inconsiderable extent, scarcely exceeding in size the half of the state of New York. It was bounded on all sides by the sea, except on the north, where it bordered upon Macedonia and Epi'rus.* Its general aspect is rugged, but its climate is highly propitious; and no other country of antiquity was so favorably situated for holding commerce with other ancient nations.

2. This country occupies but a speck on the map of the world, yet it fills a space in the eye of taste and philosophy incomparably greater than the mightiest empires that have overshadowed the earth. The inhabitants were renowned above all other ancient nations for genius, learning, and attainments in the arts; and they have been the teachers of all succeeding ages. Whatever, therefore, relates to Greece, is rendered peculiarly interesting by numerous associations.

3. Greece comprised numerous small, independent states, which were more commonly designated by the name of their chief city, than by that of the country or province. These states differed from each other in their forms of government, and the character and manners of the people. But, for their mutual defence, they were united in a confederacy by the council of the *Amphic'tyons*, as well as by a common language and religion, and by various public games, to which, in time of peace, they all resorted.

4. The only form of government in Greece, in the early ages, appears to have been limited monarchy; but, in process of time, monarchy was abolished, and republican forms were everywhere prevalent.

5. The history of these little republics is calculated to awaken

---

* Greece, in its most extensive sense, included *Macedonia* and *Epi rus*, countries anciently inhabited by a people of similar origin, language, and religion, but not recognized by the Greeks as a part of their body, principally on account of their less advanced civilization, and because they retained the rude monarchy of early ages, while Greece was divided into small republics. The Greeks also established colonies in Thrace, Asia Minor, Italy, Sicily, &c.; so that they were widely spread over territories beyond the limits of the country which is properly styled Greece.

perpetual and powerful interest. They underwent many revolutions, and were frequently engaged in war with each other, as well as with foreign nations; so that their history presents scenes continually new and shifting, and abounding in those strange and sudden reverses which agitate and interest the mind of man.

6. Greece was called by the natives *Hellas*, and the inhabitants *Hel-le'nes;* but, by the poets, they were often called *Dan'ai*, *Pelas'gi*, *Argi'vi*, *Achi'vi*, *Achæ'i*, &c. The original inhabitants, generally considered as the descendants of *Javan*, the son of *Japhet*, were extremely barbarous, living in caves and huts, feeding upon acorns and berries, and clothing themselves with the skins of wild beasts.

7. In this state of hopeless barbarism was Greece, when it was visited by a colony of *Egyptians* under *Cecrops*, and also by one of *Phœnicians* under *Cadmus*, who are reputed to have brought to the country the first rudiments of civilization.

SECTION II.

The History of Greece divided into Periods.

1. The history of Greece may be distinguished into two general divisions: — 1st, *the period of uncertain history*, extending from the earliest accounts of the country to the first war with Persia, in the year B. C. 490; 2d, *the period of authentic history*, extending from the Persian invasion to the final subjugation of Greece by the Romans, B. C. 146.

2. The first period, according to the most generally received chronology, reckoning from the foundation of Siç'yon, the most ancient kingdom of Greece, comprises the space of about 1600 years. This long succession of ages is involved in obscurity and fable. There are no records relating to it that really deserve the name of history; and the accounts which have been given of its events were drawn up by writers who lived long after the transactions of which they treat, and who possessed few materials for authentic history.

3. This period may be distinguished into four subdivisions, which are marked by some peculiar historical features: the 1st, reaching from the earliest accounts of Greece to the Trojan war, B. C. 1184, a period which may be termed, by way of eminence, *the fabulous age;* the 2d, extending from the expedition against Troy to the death of Homer, a period generally called *the heroic age*, of which the only history is con

tained in the poems of the Il'iad and Od'yssey, the 3d, comprising the space of time from the death of Homer to the death of Lycurgus, a period which has been denominated *the era of revolutions*, of which scarcely any species of history exists; the 4th, reaching from the death of Lycurgus to the first invasion of Greece by the Persians, a period which has been styled *the era of traditionary history*, possessing a considerable degree of credibility.

4. The second general division, *the period of authentic history*, extends from the first invasion of Greece by the Persians to its final subjugation by the Romans, a period of 344 years. The history of this portion is luminous, and connected beyond that of any other portion of pagan antiquity, having been recorded by writers of the greatest ability, who were contemporary with the events which they relate, and many of whom bore a distinguished part in them.

5. This period also may be divided into four parts, distinguished rather by political than historical characteristics: the 1st, reaching from the Persian invasion, B. C. 490, to the commencement of the Peloponnesian war, a period of 59 years, *the era of Grecian unanimity and triumphs;* the 2d, extending from the beginning of the Peloponnesian war to the accession of Philip of Macedon, B. C. 360, a period of 71 years, *the era of civil wars and intestine commotions* among the states of Greece; the 3d, reaching from the accession of Philip to the death of Alexander the Great, B. C. 324, a period of 36 years, distinguished by the *entire ascendency of Greece, or rather of Maç'edon, over Persia;* the 4th, extending from the death of Alexander to the final subjugation of Greece by the Romans, B. C. 146, a period of 178 years, *the era of degeneracy, turbulence, and ineffectual struggles for independence.* During the greater part of this period, the destinies of Greece were directed by foreign influence, and were placed successively under the protection of Macedonia, Egypt, and Rome.

SECTION III.

Fabulous Age: Foundation of Cities and Institutions. Argonautic Expedition.

1. The fabulous age comprises the period of the foundation of the principal cities, the commencement of civilization, the introduction of letters and the arts, and the establishment of the most celebrated institutions of the country.

2. *Sic'y-on*, the most ancient city, is said to have been founded by *Ægi'alus; Argos*, by *In'achus*, the last of the Titans *Ath'ens*, by *Ce'crops*, an eminent legislator, with a colony from Egypt; *Thebes*, by *Cadmus*, a Phœnician, who is said to have first introduced letters into Greece; *Cor'inth*, by *Sis'yphus*, *Myce'næ*, by *Per'seus;* and *Lacedæ'mon*, by *Lelex.*

3. Some of the memorable events of this period were the deluges of *Og'y-ges* and *Deuca'lion:* the institution of the *Olym'pic, Isth'mian, Pyth'ian*, and *Neme'an games;* of the laws of *Minos* in Crete, the court of *Areop'agus*, the *Eleusin'ian mysteries*, the *Oracle of Delphi*, and the council of the *Amphic'tyons.* This period also embraces the marvellous exploits of *Her'cules, The'seus*, and other fabulous heroes.

4. The first great enterprise recorded of the Greeks was the *Argonautic expedition*, the account of which appears to partake much more of fable than of history. It was commanded by *Jason*, the son of the king of *Iol'chos*, accompanied by about fifty of the most illustrious young men of Greece: among these heroes were *Her'cules, The'seus, Castor* and *Pollux, Or'pheus*, the physician *Æscula'pius*, and the astronomer *Chi'ron.*

5. They sailed from *Iol'chos*, in Thessaly, to *Col'chis*, on the eastern shore of the Euxine sea; and they were called *Ar'gonauts* from their sailing in the ship *Argo*, which is said to have been the first sea-vessel ever built. This famous voyage, which was probably a piratical expedition, is commonly represented to have been undertaken for the purpose of recovering the *golden fleece* of a ram, which originally belonged to their country. The fleece is pretended to have been guarded by bulls that breathed fire, and by a dragon that never slept.

SECTION IV.

The Heroic Age: Trojan War: Return of the Heraclidæ.

1. The heroic age has been compared to the age of chivalry; and there has been supposed to exist a striking resemblance between the manners and sentiments of the Greeks of that period and those of the Gothic nations of Europe in the Middle Ages, except that the latter displayed more generosity in war, and more gentleness to the female sex, than the former.

2. The history of the *Trojan war* rests on the authority of *Homer* and forms the subject of his *Iliad*, the noblest poem

of antiquity, which presents a lively picture of the Grecian character and manners at this early period.

3. *Helen*, the daughter of Tyn'darus, king of Sparta, was reputed the most beautiful woman of her age, and her hand was solicited by the most illustrious princes of Greece. Her father bound all her suitors by a solemn oath, that they should abide by the choice that Helen should make of one among them and, should she be stolen from the arms of her husband, that they would all assist, with their utmost strength, to recover her *Menela'us* was the favored individual, and, after his nuptials with Helen were celebrated, Tyn'darus resigned the crown to his son-in-law.

4. *Paris*, the son of *Priam*, king of *Troy*, a powerful city founded by Dar'danus, having adjudged the prize for superior beauty to *Venus*, in preference to *Juno* and *Minerva*, was promised by her the most beautiful woman of the age for his wife. Soon afterward he visited Sparta, and was received with every mark of respect by king Menela'us; but he abused the hospitality which was shown him by persuading Helen to elope with him to Troy, and, together with her, carried off a considerable treasure.

5. This act of treachery and ingratitude produced the Trojan war: a confederacy was immediately formed by the princes of Greece, agreeably to their engagement, to avenge the outrage. A fleet of about 1,200 open vessels conveyed an army of 100,000 men to the Trojan coast. *Agamem'non* king of Argos, brother of Menela'us, was chosen commander in-chief. Some of the other most celebrated princes, who distinguished themselves in this war, were *Achil'les*, the bravest of the Greeks, *Ajax*, *Menela'us*, *Ulys'ses*, *Nestor*, and *Diome'des*.

6. The Trojans were commanded by *Hector*, the son of Priam, assisted by *Paris*, *Deiph'obus*, *Æne'as*, and *Sarpe'don*. After a siege of ten years, the city was taken by stratagem plundered, and burnt to the ground. The venerable king Priam was slain; and his family was led into captivity.

7. About eighty years after the destruction of Troy began the *civil war of the Heracli'dæ*, usually called the *return of the Heracli'dæ* into Peloponne'sus.

8. Hercules, sovereign of Myce'næ, a city of Peloponne'sus, was banished from his country, with all his family, while the crown was seized by At'reus, the son of Pelops. After the period of a century, the Heracli'dæ, or descendants of Her'cules, returned to Peloponne'sus, and, having subdued all their enemies, took possession of the country. A part of

the inhabitants were reduced to slavery; the others being expelled, retired to Asia Minor, and possessed themselves of a country afterwards called *Ionia.*

9. This revolution in Peloponne'sus not only changed the inhabitants and government of the country, and established new divisions of the Greeks, but checked the progress of the arts and civilization.

SECTION V.

Sparta or Lacedæmon: Institutions of Lycurgus.

1. The two leading states of Greece were *Athens* and *Sparta* the latter distinguished for military valor and discipline, the former for literature and the arts. Their different characters and habits were formed, in a great degree, by the institutions of their respective legislators, *Lycurgus* of Sparta, and *Solon* of Athens.

2. Sparta, or Lacedæ'mon, was the capital of Laconia, in the southern part of Peloponne'sus. After the return of the Heracli'dæ, its government was administered by the two sons of *Aristode'mus*, who reigned jointly, and this double monarchy was transmitted to the descendants of each for many ages.

3. *Lycurgus*, the celebrated Spartan legislator, was the brother of one of the kings; and, on the death of the sovereign, he became protector. The government of Sparta being now in the greatest disorder, Lycurgus, in whom, on account of his great abilities and integrity, the highest confidence was reposed, was intrusted with the duty of reforming the constitution.

4. He wrought an entire change in the form of government, and in the manners of the people. He instituted a senate of 28 members, elected from the nobles. The two kings were continued, but were nothing more than hereditary and presiding members of the senate, generals of the army, and high priests of the nation. He divided the territory of the republic into 39,000 shares among all the free citizens.

5. Commerce was abolished, the distinction of dress annihilated, the use of gold and silver prohibited, and iron money substituted in their place. All the citizens, not excepting even the kings, were required to eat at the public tables, where all luxury and excess were to be avoided, black broth being the principal article of food.

6. Every citizen was to be wholly devoted to the service of

the state, whether in peace or war. Infants, as soon as born, were carefully inspected, and those that were well formed were delivered to public nurses; and at the age of seven years, they were introduced into the public schools, where they were all educated on the same plan. Those that were deformed or sickly, were exposed to perish.

7 Letters were taught for use, but not for ornament; and the Spartans, while they were distinguished as a shrewd and sagacious people, were never eminent for learning, and no book has been transmitted to modern times written by a genuine Spartan. Diffuseness of language and conversation was discountenanced, and the Lacedæmonians were noted for their concise or *laconic* speech.

8. The young were taught especially to respect the aged and to cherish an ardent love of their country; they were formed to a high principle of honor, and to great sensibility to applause and to shame. They were early inured to hardship, were accustomed to sleep on rushes, and were supplied with only plain and scanty food; but they were encouraged to steal whatever they could, provided they accomplished the theft without being detected.

9. The institutions of Lycurgus were well adapted to impress on the people, a character completely artificial, by stimulating some feelings and principles to excess, and almost eradicating others; but they were not calculated to promote either happiness or goodness. The system was, however, ingeniously contrived to render the Spartans a nation of soldiers; by them war was considered the great business of life, and it was their highest ambition to be terrible to their enemies. The heroic virtues or qualities, such as patriotism, public spirit, courage, fortitude, and contempt of danger, suffering, and death, were cherished; while all the softer virtues and domestic affections were sacrificed.

10. Young women, as well as young men, were trained to athletic exercises. The manners of the Lacedæmonian women were loose and indelicate. They were destitute of the virtues which most adorn the female character, modesty, tenderness, and sensibility. Their education was calculated to give them a masculine energy; to render them bold, hardy, and courageous; and to fill them with admiration of military glory. Mothers exulted when their sons fell honorably in battle. "Return with your shield, or on your shield," said a Spartan mother to her son, when he was going to meet the enemy; that is, "conquer or die."

11. The government of Lacedæ'mon acquired solidity, while the other states were torn by internal dissensions. For the

long period of 500 years, the institutions of Lycurgus continued in force, the power and influence of Sparta were felt throughout Greece; and for a considerable part of that period her glory eclipsed that of the other states.

12. But in process of time, the severe manners of her warriors were relaxed; and during the administration of some of her later kings, changes were introduced into the laws and institutions, particularly in the time of *Lysan'der*, whose conquests filled his country with wealth, and opened the sources of luxury and avarice.

SECTION VI.

Athens: Codrus: Draco: Solon and his Institutions: Pisistratus: Pisistratidæ.

1. Athens, the capital of At'tica, was the most celebrated city of Greece. It was distinguished for its commerce, wealth, and magnificence; it was the chief seat of learning and the arts; and it was the birthplace of many illustrious men.

2. The last king of Athens was *Co'drus*, who, in the war with the Heracli'dæ, sacrificed himself for the good of his country. After his death, the regal government was abolished, and the state was governed by magistrates, styled *archons*. The office was at first for life; afterward it was reduced to a period of ten years; at last it became annual, and was divided among nine persons.

3. The first code of written laws which the Athenians possessed was prepared by *Draco*, a man of stern and rigid temper. These laws punished all crimes with death; and, on account of their sanguinary character, are said to have been written in blood. Draco being asked why he was so severe in his punishments, replied, that "the smallest crimes deserved death, and he had no higher punishment for the greatest." But the great severity of these laws prevented their being fully executed.

4. The celebrated Solon, one of the seven wise men of Greece, being raised to the archonship, was intrusted with the care of framing for his country a new constitution, and a new system of laws. His disposition was mild and temporizing; and he did not, like Lycurgus, endeavor to operate a total change in the manners of his countrymen, but attempted to moderate their dissensions, restrain their passions, and open a fair field to the growth and exercise of ability and virtue

and his system, though less original and artificial, was more rational and judicious. Of his laws, he said, "If they are not the best possible, they are the best the Athenians are capable of receiving."

5 Solon vested the supreme power in an assembly of the people, composed of the freemen whose age exceeded 30 years. By them all laws were enacted, every public measure determined, all appointments made; and to them an appeal lay from all courts of justice. He instituted a senate or council of 400, afterward increased to 500; restored the Areopagus; and divided the people into four classes, according to their wealth.

6. Commerce and agriculture were encouraged; industry and economy were enforced; and ingratitude, disobedience to parents, and opprobrious language, were punished. The father who had taught his son no trade could not claim a support from him in his old age. The body of laws which Solon established has been so highly esteemed, that it has formed the basis of many subsequent systems of legislation.

7. The different laws of Athens and Sparta produced, in process of time, a corresponding difference in the character and manners of the people. At Athens, the arts were in the highest esteem; at Sparta, they were despised. At Athens, peace was the natural state of the republic, and the refined enjoyment of life the aim of the people. At Sparta, war was the great business of life, and no amusements were practised except such as were military or athletic. An Athenian was characterized by luxury; a Spartan, by frugality: the virtues of the latter were more severe; those of the former, more agreeable. They were both, however, equally jealous of liberty, and equally brave in war.

8 Before the death of Solon, *Pisis'tratus*, a citizen of great wealth and eloquence, by courting popularity in various ways, found means to raise himself to the sovereign power, which he and his sons retained for 50 years. He exercised a munificent and splendid dominion, encouraged the arts and sciences and is said to have founded the first public library known to the world, and to have first collected the poems of Homer into one volume, which before were merely repeated in detached portions.

9. Pisis'tratus transmitted the sovereignty to his sons *Hip'pias* and *Hippar'chus*, called the *Pisistrat'idæ.* They governed for some time, with wisdom and moderation; but at length an abuse of power caused a conspiracy to be formed against them and their government was overthrown by *Harmo'dius* and

Aristogi'ton. Hippar'chus was slain; and Hippias not long after fled to Darius, king of Persia, who was then meditating the conquest of Greece; and he was afterward killed in the battle of Mar'athon fighting against his countrymen.

SECTION VII

Greece invaded by the Persians under Darius: Battle of Marathon: Miltiades: Persian Invasion under Xerxes: Themistocles: Aristides: Battle of Thermopylæ: Leonidas: Battles of Salamis, Platæa, and Mycale: Cimon.— From B. C. 490 *to* 431.

1. The period from the first Persian invasion to the beginning of the Peloponnesian war is esteemed the most glorious age of Greece. The series of victories which the inhabitants obtained over the Persians are the most splendid recorded in history.

2. Persia, at this period, was far the most powerful empire in the world, embracing the territories included in modern Persia, Turkey in Asia, Egypt, a great part of Tartary, and part of Arabia. The Greek colonies in Asia Minor were subject to the Persians, who had likewise made a conquest of Thrace: Macedonia had also acknowledged subjection; so that the Persian dominion extended over a large portion of the Grecian people, and even bordered on the country of Greece.

3. The Asiatic Greeks made an attempt to throw off the Persian yoke, and were assisted by the Athenians. *Darius*, king of Persia, having reduced his revolted subjects to submission, formed a determination, in consequence of the course taken by the Athenians, to make an entire conquest of Greece; and in this design he was encouraged and assisted by the exiled tyrant Hippias.

4. Darius despatched heralds to each of the Grecian states demanding earth and water, as an acknowledgment of his supremacy. Thebes, together with a number of the other cities and most of the islands, submitted; but the Athenians and Lacedæmonians were so indignant, that, forgetting the laws of nations and of humanity, they put the heralds to death with the utmost ignominy. At one place they were thrown into a pit, at the other into a well, and told there to take their earth and water.

5. Darius began his hostile attack both by sea and land The first Persian fleet, under the command of *Mardo'nius*

was wrecked in a storm, in doubling the promontory of *Athos*, with a loss of no less than 300 vessels; a second, of 600 sail, ravaged the Grecian islands; while an immense army, consisting, according to the lowest statements of the ancient historians, of 110,000 men, commanded by *Artapher'nes* and *Datis*, invaded Attica.

6. This formidable host was met on the narrow plain of *Mar'athon* by the Athenian army, greatly inferior in number (stated by the best authorities at from 30,000 to 40,000), under the command of the celebrated *Milti'ades*, who, availing himself of an advantageous position of the ground, gained a decisive victory, and drove the routed invaders to their ships. The loss of the Persians was 6,300; that of the Athenians, only 192.

7. Miltiades, by this victory, rose to the height of popularity and influence, which, however, he lost not long afterwards by a failure in an attack on the island of *Paros*. On his return from this expedition, he was accused of treason, and though absolved from the capital charge, yet he was condemned to pay a fine of 50 talents (about 50,000 dollars). In consequence of this, he was thrown into prison, and died in a few days of the wounds which he received at Paros; but the fine was paid by his son *Cimon*.

8. The Athenians were, at this time, divided into two parties, one of which favored an aristocratical, and the other a democratical, form of government. The two leaders of these parties were the distinguished statesmen and warriors, *Aristides* and *Themis'tocles;* Aristides being the advocate of aristocracy, and Themistocles of democracy.

9. Aristides, who, on account of his stern integrity, received the surname of the *Just*, was, through the intrigues of his great rival, banished for ten years by the *ostracism*. While the people were giving their votes for his exile, it happened that a citizen, who was unable to write, and did not know him personally, brought his shell to him, and requested that he would write the name of Aristides upon it. "Why, what harm has Aristides ever done you?" said he. "No harm at all," answered the citizen, "but I cannot bear to hear him continually called the *Just*." Aristides smiled, and, taking the shell, wrote his name upon it, and quietly went into banishment; but he was recalled soon after the renewal of the war.

10. The death of Darius, and other circumstances, occasioned the discontinuance of the war for several years; but *Xerxes*, the young Persian monarch, having ascended the throne, was eager to punish Athens, and subdue Greece. Having spent four years in preparation, he collected an army

greater than the world ever saw, either before or since. According to Herod'otus, the whole number of fighting men, in the army and fleet, exceeded 2,000,000; and, including the retinue of sutlers, slaves, and women, the whole multitude is said to have exceeded 5,000,000.

11. The fleet consisted of upwards of 1,200 galleys of war, besides a greater number of transports and smaller vessels. A canal, navigable for the largest galleys, was formed across the isthmus which joins mount Athos to the continent; and, for the conveyance of the army, two bridges of boats were extended across the Hel'lespont, at a point where the width is seven furlongs.

12. Xerxes, having taken a station on an eminence, in order to gratify his vanity by viewing the vast assemblage which he had collected, — the earth covered with his troops, and the sea with his vessels, — is said to have been suddenly so much affected as to shed tears, upon reflecting that, in the space of one hundred years, not one of the many thousands would be alive.

13. The Persian army advanced directly towards Athens, and this city fortunately possessed, in *Themis'tocles*, a leader of extraordinary talents, peculiarly fitted for conducting the arduous contest. Most of the other states united in assisting Athens in repelling the invaders, Sparta taking the lead; but some of them submitted to the Persians.

14. *Leon'idas*, king of Sparta, with a small army, undertook the defence of *Thermop'ylæ*, a narrow mountain pass or defile on the coast, connecting Thessaly and Phocis. Xerxes, having approached this place, sent a herald to Leonidas, commanding him to deliver up his arms, to whom the Spartan replied, with laconic brevity, "Come and take them." For two days the Persians strove to force their way, but were repulsed with great slaughter; but having, at length, discovered a by-path over the mountains, the defence of the pass became impossible.

15. Leon'idas, foreseeing certain destruction, resolved in obedience to a law of Sparta, which forbade its soldiers, in any case, to flee from an enemy, to devote his life to the honor and service of his country; and, animated by his example, the 300 Spartans under his command determined with him to abide the event. With the fury of men resolved to sell their lives at the dearest rate, they fell upon the Persian camp, and were all cut off, after having made a dreadful havoc of the enemy. Two only of the Spartans, these having been accidentally absent, survived the battle. A monument was erected on the spot, bearing this inscription, written by Simon'ides: "O stranger! tell it at Lacedæmon, that we died here in obedience to her laws."

16. The Persians, having forced the pass of Thermopylæ poured down upon Attica, ravaging the country with fire and sword. The inhabitants of Athens, after conveying their women and children to the islands for security, betook themselves to the fleet, abandoning the city, which the Persians pillaged and burnt.

17. Preparations were now made for a great naval battle The Persian fleet consisted of 1,200 galleys; that of the Greeks, of 300, and it was commanded by *Themis'tocles* and *Aristi'des*. An engagement took place in the straits of *Sal'amis*, where it was impossible for the Persians to bring their numerous ships regularly into action, and they were defeated with immense loss. The king, who had seated himself on an eminence to witness the battle, terrified at the result, retreated, with a part of his army, to his own dominions.

18. Xerxes left *Mardo'nius*, with 300,000 men, to complete the conquest of Greece in the following summer. This army, which was joined by many Grecian auxiliaries, was met at *Platæ'a*, early in the next season, by the combined forces of Athens and Lacedæmon, consisting of 110,000 men, under the command of *Aristi'des* and *Pausa'nias*, and was defeated with tremendous slaughter, *Mardo'nius* being killed, and the most of his men being slain in the battle and the subsequent massacre.

19. On the same day of the great victory of Platæ'a, the Greeks, under *Leotych'ides* the Lacedæmonian, and *Xanthip'pus* the Athenian, engaged and destroyed the Persian fleet at the promontory of *Myc'a-le*, near Ephesus. The Persian army was now completely destroyed. Xerxes, having been entirely frustrated in all his mad schemes, was soon after assassinated, and was succeeded by his son *Artaxerxes Longim'anus*.

20 The Persian war, however, was not yet terminated The Greeks, in their turn, became the assailants and invaders. They undertook to defend the Ionians, who had thrown off the Persian yoke. The Spartans, commanded by *Pausa'nias*, and the Athenians, by *Aristi'des* and *Ci'mon*, advanced to the island of *Cyprus*, which they took, and set free; and, having taken and plundered the city of *Byzan'tium*, they returned with immense booty.

21. *Pausa'nias*, who had borne a distinguished command in this war, being at length intoxicated with glory and power aspired to hold, under Persia, the dominion of Greece, and, in a letter to Xerxes, promised to effect the subjugation of the country, on condition of his receiving his daughter in marriage. Being convicted by the ephori of this treason, he took

refuge in the temple of Minerva where, the sanctity of he place securing him from violence, he was doomed to perish by hunger.

22 *Themis'tocles*, the great Athenian commander, was accused of participating in the treason of Pausanias, and was banished by the ostracism. Proceeding to Asia, he wrote a letter to king Artaxerxes, in which he said, "I, Themistocles, come to thee, who have done thy house most ill of all the Greeks, while I was of necessity repelling the invasion of thy father, but yet more good, when I was in safety, and his return was endangered." He was permitted to live in great splendor in Persia, and there died in exile, leaving an almost unrivalled reputation as a statesman and warrior; but if to his great talents he had joined an unquestionable integrity, his fame would have been purer.

23. After the banishment of Themistocles, the affairs of Athens were, for a short time, directed by *Aristi'des;* and, upon his death, the whole power came into the hands of *Ci'mon*, the son of Milti'ades, one of the most illustrious statesmen and warriors that Greece ever produced.

24. Cimon maintained the political influence and military power of Athens, conducted the war with great success, and gained two great victories over the Persians on the same day, one by sea, and the other by land, near the mouth of the *Eurym'edon*, in Asia Minor.

25. A powerful party at length arose against Cimon, and procured his banishment by the ostracism, and *Per'icles*, a young man of noble birth, great talents, and extraordinary eloquence, succeeded him in authority.

26. But, after a banishment of five years, Cimon was recalled, restored to the command of the army, gained further important victories over the Persians, and finally died of a wound which he received at the siege of Citium, in Cyprus.

27. The Persian war, which had lasted, with little intermission, about fifty years, was now brought to a termination. Artaxerxes, finding his strength, both by sea and land, broken, sued for peace, which was granted on condition that he should give freedom to all the Grecian colonies in Asia Minor, and that the Persian fleets should be excluded from the Grecian seas.

28. After the death of Cimon, his brother-in-law *Thucyd'ides*, became the competitor of *Per'icles* for popular favor and authority. A war of eloquence ensued, and Thucydides, being worsted, was banished by the ostracism, and the lead of Pericles was, from this time till his death a period of about twenty years but little disputed

29. He governed Athens with almost arbitrary sway, adorned the city with master-pieces of architecture, sculpture, and painting, patronized the arts and sciences, celebrated splendid games and festivals, and his administration formed an era of great internal splendor and magnificence; but he exhausted the public revenue, and corrupted the manners of the people.

30. The time of the Persian war was the period of the highest military glory of the Greeks, and they owed their prosperity to their union. But after this war had ceased, this union was dissolved, and the jealousies and ambitious views of the rival states were again revived. Athens had been rebuilt, and surrounded with a strong wall. But to this Sparta had meanly objected, and Athens saw with pleasure the depopulation of Sparta by an earthquake, in which about 20,000 lives were lost. Sparta also suffered greatly about this time by the insurrection of the *Helots*, or slaves.

31. Although the *Athenians* were apparently the greatest sufferers by the invasion, their city being burnt, and their country laid waste, yet they derived the greatest benefits from its effects. In consequence of their naval superiority, and the unrivalled talents of their commanders, *Milti'ades*, *Themis'tocles*, *Aristi'des*, and *Ci'mon*, they reached the summit of political influence and military power, and attained that supremacy in Greece which the Lacedæmonians had hitherto enjoyed.

32. The politics of Greece, for a considerable time after the Persian war, turned upon the rivalry between the two leading republics, Athens and Lacedæmon. The former was powerful by sea, the latter by land. Athens was the patroness of democracy, Lacedæmon of aristocracy. It was customary for the weaker states, for their security, to ally themselves with one of the two leading ones; and, in most of them, there were two parties in continual contest, the democrats and the aristocrats: the former naturally adhered to Athens; the latter to Sparta.

33. From this period the martial and patriotic spirit began to decline. An acquaintance with Asia, and an importation of her wealth, introduced a relish for Asiatic manners and luxuries. With the Athenians, however, this luxurious spirit was under the guidance of taste and genius, and it led to the cultivation of the fine arts, which, during the age of *Pericles*, were in the most flourishing state

SECTION VIII.

PELOPONNESIAN WAR: *Pericles: Alcibiades: Battle of Ægos-Potamos: Lysander: Thirty Tyrants: Socrates Retreat of the* 10,000: *Peace of Antalcidas: Thebes Epaminondas: Battles of Leuctra and Mantinea: Agesilaus. — From B. C.* 431 *to* 360.

1. In the latter part of the administration of Per'icles, commenced the *Peloponnesian War*, which grew out of the long continued rivalship between Athens and Sparta, and was the most important and celebrated war ever carried on by the Grecian states with each other.

2. This contest partook, in a great degree, of the nature of a civil war; and through the time of its continuance, being the age of Soc'rates himself, was an era characterized by the high perfection to which the arts, philosophy, and refinement had been brought, yet it was carried on in a spirit of savage ferocity, rarely exemplified among civilized nations; a boundless scope was given to ambition and party rage; all the ties of nature were trampled upon, and Greece exhibited, during this period a perpetual scene of conflict and calamity.

3. The Athenians having assisted the inhabitants of Corcy'ra against the Corinthians, were accused by the latter of having thereby violated the treaty of the confederated states of Peloponne'sus, and an appeal to arms was immediately resolved on.

4. *Sparta* took the lead against Athens, and was joined by all the Peloponnesian states, except Argos, which remained neutral; and in Northern Greece, by the Megarians, Bœotians, Locrians, Phocians, &c. *Athens* had few allies; the principal were the Thessalians, Acarnanians, and several islands. The Peloponnesian forces, commanded by the Spartan king, Archid'amus, amounted to 60,000, while the army of the Athenians did not exceed 32,000; but the navy of the latter was much the superior.

5. In the first year of the war, the Lacedæmonians ravaged Attica, and laid siege to Athens; in the second year, the city was visited by a dreadful *plague*, which swept away multitudes, and among its victims was Pericles, who died the third year of the war, and at a time when his services were most wanted. The war, however, was not arrested by this awful calamity, but continued to rage for several years in a similar manner and with nearly equal losses on both sides.

6. After the death of Per'icles, *Cleon*, the leader of the

democratic party, had, for a time, the direction of the Athenian councils; but he was slain at *Amphip'olis*, in a battle with *Bras'idas*, the Spartan general, who was also mortally wounded. After the death of Cleon, a treaty of peace was concluded between Athens and Sparta, by means of the influence of *Ni'cias*, the leader of the aristocratic and pacific party.

7. But the war was again soon renewed through the influence of *Alcibi'ades*, who now took the lead in the government of Athens, and who was one of the most accomplished orators and generals of his age, but whose want of principle rendered his talents ruinous both to himself and his country.

8. An expedition was sent against the island of *Sicily*, under the command of *Alcibi'ades* and *Ni'cias;* but the former was accused of misconduct and recalled, and the latter totally defeated and slain. Alcibiades afterward again took the command of the army of Athens, and gained important advantages; but he at length fell into disgrace, and was banished, and the chief command of the Athenian army was given to *Conon.*

9. But *Lysan'der*, the ablest of the Lacedæmonian generals, having succeeded to the command, utterly defeated the Athenian fleet at *Æ'gos-Pot'amos*, on the Hellespont, which reduced Athens to the last extremity. The Lacedæmonians blockaded the city by land and sea, and its reduction was left to the sure operation of famine.

10. The Athenians, anxious to avoid utter extermination, were ready to accept almost any terms of peace. They were spared on condition that they should demolish their port, with all their fortifications, limit their fleet to 12 ships, and in future undertake no military enterprise, except under the command of the Lacedæmonians. Thus the Peloponnesian war terminated by the humiliating submission of Athens, and by rendering Lacedæ'mon the leading power in Greece.

11. Lysander, after the reduction of Athens, abolished the popular government, and substituted in its place an oligarchy consisting of 30 magistrates, whose power was absolute, and who, from their atrocious acts of cruelty, were styled the *Thirty Tyrants.* In the space of eight months, 1,500 citizens were sacrificed to their avarice or vengeance. At length *Thrasybu'lus*, at the head of a band of patriots, drove the tyrants from the seat of their abused power, and restored the democratical form of government.

12. But pure democracy was far from being any security, at Athens, against acts of tyranny and oppression, even in the most enlightened age of the republic. The Athenians were

characterized as fickle and capricious; and, in some of their proceedings, they were as unjust and cruel as the most lawless despots.

13. The name of *Soc'rates* is at once the glory and the reproach of Athens. This illustrious philosopher, who, on account of his high moral views, is the boast of the pagan world, and who attempted to introduce among his countrymen worthier sentiments of religion, and a better understanding of the duties of life, was accused of corrupting the youth, and condemned by the assembly of Athens to die by poison.

14. During his imprisonment, which lasted thirty days, he conducted himself with the greatest dignity; refused to escape when opportunity offered; conversed with his friends on topics of moral philosophy, particularly the immortality of the soul; and, when the appointed time arrived, drank the fatal cup of hemlock, and died with the greatest composure.

15. The philosophy of Socrates, which forms an important epoch in the history of the human mind, was wholly promulgated in conversation, not in writing; but his doctrines and character have been handed down to us by two of his most gifted pupils, *Plato* and *Xenophon.* He turned all the powers of his mind against the atheists, materialists, and sceptics. He attended but little to physical science; he ridiculed the metaphysical speculations of his predecessors; and introduced *moral philosophy*, by teaching mankind to govern their passions, and to consider their actions and their duties. From this it was said of him, that he drew down philosophy from heaven to earth.

16. About the end of the Peloponnesian war, the death of Darius left the throne of Persia to his son, Artaxerxes II.; but his brother Cyrus attempted to dethrone him, and for this purpose he employed upwards of 10,000 Grecian mercenaries, and after the battle of *Cunaxa*, near Babylon, Cyrus, and also the Grecian commander, were slain. The remainder of the Grecian army, under the command of *Xen'ophon*, made a retreat, in which they encountered incredible difficulties and dangers, in traversing an enemy's country of 1,600 miles in extent, from Babylon to the shores of the Euxine.

17. This celebrated return of the Greeks, usually called the *Retreat of the Ten Thousand*, is beautifully described by Xenophon, and is considered one of the most extraordinary exploits in military history; but it is to be regretted that the pupil and biographer of Socrates should have gathered his laurels in so vile a trade as that of a mere hireling military adventurer.

18. The Greek cities of Asia having taken part with Cyrus, the Spartans, under their king, *Agesila'us*, engaged in their defence, and thus became involved in the war with the Persians. But the king of Persia, by means of bribes, induced Athens, Thebes, Corinth, and other Grecian states jealous of the Lacedæmonians, to join in a league against them. Agesilaus was obliged to return from Asia Minor to protect his own country; and he defeated the confederates at *Corone'a*, but the Spartan fleet was soon after defeated by the Athenians under *Conon* near Cnidos.

19. After various vicissitudes, all parties became weary of the war, and a treaty of peace was concluded, called the *peace of Antal'cidas*, from the Lacedæmonian who negociated it. The conditions were, that all the Grecian cities of Asia should belong to Persia, and that all the others should be completely independent, except that the islands of Lemnos, Scyros, and Imbros should remain under the dominion of Athens.

20. While Athens and Sparta had been for some time declining, *Thebes*, emerging from obscurity, rose, for a short period, to a degree of splendor superior to that of all the other states. The Spartans, jealous of its rising greatness, took advantage of some internal dissensions, and seized upon its citadel; but it was recovered, and the independence of Thebes was again restored by the efforts of *Pelop'idas* and *Epaminon'das*, two famous Thebans, admired for their talents and exploits, and for their faithful friendship for each other.

21. A war between the two states ensued; and the Theban army of 6,000 men, commanded by *Epaminondas* and *Pelopidas*, gained the memorable battle of *Leuctra*. In this battle, the Thebans lost only 300 men, while the Spartans lost 4,000, together with their king, *Cleom'brotus;* and it was with mortification and astonishment that they saw themselves defeated by numbers greatly inferior, a thing unknown for ages.

22. The victorious Thebans, headed by *Epaminondas*, and joined by many of the Grecian states, entered the territories of Lacedæmon, and overran all Laconia with fire and sword, to the very suburbs of the capital. This country had not been ravaged by a hostile army for 600 years; and the boast of the inhabitants, "that never had the women of Sparta beheld the smoke of an enemy's camp," was now done away.

23. The Theban commander, having completely humbled the power of Sparta, returned to Thebes with his victorious army: not long after, the war being renewed, he gained another great victory over the Lacedæmonians, commanded by

Agesila'us and assisted by the Athenians, at *Mantine'a*; but he fell mortally wounded in the moment of victory.

24. *Epaminon'das* is regarded as one of the greatest characters of Greece, equally eminent as a philosopher, a statesman, a general, and a citizen. He raised his country to its highest eminence in military renown, and its power and splendor perished with him.

25. The battle of Mantine'a was followed by a peace between all the Grecian states, establishing the independence of each city. Soon afterward, the Spartans, under the command of *Agesila'us*, proceeded to Egypt, to assist Tachos, the king of that country, against Nectane'bus, who aspired to the throne. But when the Egyptians, who crowded to see the famous warrior, beheld a little, deformed, lame old man, sitting on the seashore, clad in homely attire, they could scarcely conceal their disappointment. In consequence of some personal affront received from Tachos, Agesilaus deserted him, and raised his competitor to the throne. Having set sail for Sparta, he died on the coast of Egypt, leaving a high reputation as an able statesman and warrior.

SECTION IX.

Philip of Macedon: Sacred War: Battle of Chæronea Alexander the Great: Conquest of Persia: Battles of the Granicus, Issus, and Arbela: Alexander's Death.— From B. C. 360 *to* 324.

1. After the death of Agesila'us, little occurs in the history of Greece deserving notice, till the appearance of *Philip* of Macedon. The several states were now in an abject condition, the inhabitants having greatly degenerated from the patriotism and valor of their ancestors.

2. Athens, at this time the most prominent of the republics, was sunk in luxury and dissipation; yet she was distinguished for her cultivation of literature and the arts. Sparta, weakened by the new independence of Peloponne'sus, and corrupted by the introduction of gold, had abandoned her characteristic simplicity and severity of manners, and was greatly reduced from her former greatness. Under these circumstances, Philip formed the ambitious project of bringing the whole of Greece under his dominion.

3 The kingdom of *Maç'edon*, or *Macedonia*, had existed

upwards of 400 years, but it had not risen to any considerable eminence; it had formed no part of the Greek confederacy and had had no voice in the Amphictyon'ic council. The inhabitants boasted of the same origin with the Greeks, but they had had little intercourse with the mother country, and were considered by the latter as barbarians.

4. The *Macedonian Empire*, which was commenced by Philip, and completed by his son Alexander, formed the third great empire of antiquity. It is sometimes called the *Grecian Empire*, because Greece, in its most extensive sense, included Macedonia, and because all Greece was subject to Philip and Alexander.

5. Philip, when only ten years old, was sent as a hostage to Thebes, and there enjoyed the advantage of an excellent Grecian education under Epaminondas. At the age of 24 years he ascended the throne. He possessed great military and political talents, and was eminently distinguished for his consummate artifice and address. In order to accomplish his design of bringing all the states of Greece under his dominion, he cherished dissensions among them, and employed agents or pensionaries in each, with a view of having every public measure directed to his advantage.

6. The Phocians had long cultivated a valuable tract, called the Cirrhæan plain, which, it was now maintained, had been, in a former age, consecrated to the Delphian Apollo; and it was decreed, by the council of the Amphictyons, that they should cease to use the sacred land, under the penalty of a heavy fine. From this circumstance a contest arose, called the *Sacred War*, in which almost all the states of Greece took a part, and which was carried on with spirit for ten years. The Thebans, Locrians, Thessalians, and others, undertook to punish the Phocians, who were supported by Athens, Sparta, and some other states.

7. Philip, having taken and destroyed the city of *Olynthus*, a length availed himself of the opportunity, which this war afforded, of bringing his power into full contact with the Grecian states. He proposed to act as arbitrator of the matter in dispute, and procured himself to be elected a member of the Amphictyonic council; and he was afterwards styled the *Amphictyonic general.* The Athenians, suspicious of his designs, refused to acknowledge the election, and, being now guided by the inflammatory eloquence of *Demos'thenes*, rather than by the pacific counsels of *Pho'cion*, they were plunged into a destructive contest with their powerful rival and neighbor.

8. A second *Sacred War* drew Philip again into Greece The Locrians of Amphis'sa having encroached upon the con-

secrated ground of Delphi, and having refused to obey the decrees of the Amphictyonic council, Philip was invited, as their general, to vindicate their authority by force of arms. The Athenians and Thebans, roused to the utmost enthusiasm by Demos'thenes, united to resist the growing power of this ambitious monarch. The two armies met at *Chærone'a*, and, after a most obstinate battle, Philip gained a decisive victory, which secured to him an entire ascendency in Greece.

9. It was not the policy of the conqueror to treat the several states as a vanquished people. He permitted them to retain their separate independent governments, while he directed and controlled all the public measures.

10. Philip next projected the invasion of *Persia*, and, convoking a general council of the states, laid before them his design, which was highly popular, and he was chosen commander-in-chief of the united forces of all the states of Greece. Having made formidable preparations for his expedition, and being just ready for his departure, he was assassinated by a captain of his guards, while solemnizing the nuptials of his daughter. The news of Philip's death caused the most tumultuous joy among the Athenians, who indulged the vain hope of again recovering their liberty.

11. *Alexander*, (afterward surnamed the *Great*,) the son of Philip, succeeded to the throne of Macedon, at the age of 20 years. He had been educated by *Ar'istotle*, the most eminent philosopher of his time, and, at an early age, he gave proofs of a love of learning, a generous and heroic disposition, distinguished talents, and unbounded ambition.

12. Demosthenes exerted all his eloquence to persuade his countrymen to unite against the youthful king. But Alexander, having reduced to subjection some barbarous nations to the north of Macedon, turned the whole force of his arms upon Greece. The Thebans, who had risen in rebellion, were defeated with great slaughter, their city razed to the ground, and the inhabitants, to the number of 30,000, sold for slaves These dreadful acts of severity so intimidated the other states that they immediately submitted to his dominion.

13. Alexander then assembled the deputies of the Grecian states at Cor'inth, and renewed the proposal of invading Persia, then ruled by *Dari'us Codom'anus*, and he was appointed, as his father had before been, generalissimo. He had, for his companions in arms, *Parme'nio* and other officers, who had distinguished themselves in the wars of Philip.

14. With an army of 30,000 foot and 5,000 horse, the sum of only 70 talents, and provisions merely for a single month

he crossed the Hel'lespont, in order, with means apparently so inadequate, to accomplish his arduous enterprise. He first proceeded to the site of Ilium, or Troy, and offered sacrifices to the manes of the heroes who fell in the Trojan war, particularly *Achil'les*, whom he pronounced to be the most fortunate of men, in having *Patro'clus* for his friend, and *Homer* for his panegyrist.

15. The Persian satraps who ruled the western provinces of the empire met him, on the banks of the little river *Grani'cus*, with an army of 100,000 foot, and 20,000 horse. Here an obstinate battle was fought, in which the Persians were defeated, with the loss, according to Plutarch, of 22,000 men, while the Macedonians lost only 34. In this battle Alexander escaped very narrowly with his life. Being attacked by two officers, one of whom was about to cleave his head with a battle-axe, he was preserved by *Clytus*, who prevented the blow by disabling the assailant.

16. The consequences of this victory were important to Alexander, as it put him in possession of the city of *Sardis*, with all its riches; and he soon after took *Mile'tus*, *Halicarnas'sus*, and other places of importance.

17. The next campaign opened early in the spring, when the great battle of *Issus* was fought. The Persian army, stated at about 600,000 men, commanded by the king in person, was defeated with prodigious slaughter, no less than 110,000 being killed, while the Macedonians lost only 450. The engagement took place in a narrow defile, where only a small part of the Persian army could be brought into action.

18. The mother, wife, and two daughters of Darius, fell into the hands of the conqueror, who treated his royal captives with the greatest delicacy and respect. Darius, hearing of Alexander's kindness towards his family, sent an embassy to him, offering, for their ransom, the sum of 10,000 talents (about £2,000,000 sterling), and proposing a treaty of peace and alliance, with the further offer of his daughter in marriage, and all the country between the Euphrates and the Ægæ'an Sea as her dower.

19. When the offer was laid before Alexander's council Parme'nio is reported to have said, "If I were Alexander, I would accept the terms." "And so would I," replied Alexander, "were I Parmenio." The answer which he returned to the proposal imported that he had invaded Asia to avenge the unprovoked aggressions of the Persian monarchs that, if Darius would come to him, and ask for his wife and family he would willingly deliver them to him; but if he proposed to dispute the sovereignty, he would find him ready to oppose him

20. He next directed his course towards the rich and commercial city of *Tyre*, and demanded admittance into it, in order to perform a sacrifice to the Tyrian Her'cules. But the Tyrians refusing to grant it, he was so much exasperated, that he resolved to reduce the place, which he accomplished after a siege of seven months. On this occasion he exercised a piece of wanton cruelty, by ordering 2,000 men to be crucified, in addition to all those who were put to the sword, or sold into slavery.

21. Having invested and taken the city of *Gaza*, which made an obstinate resistance, he sold 10,000 of the inhabitants for slaves, and dragged *Be'tis*, its brave defender, at the wheels of his chariot.

22. Alexander next proceeded to *Egypt*, which was then subject to Persia; but it readily submitted to his authority Amidst incredible fatigues, he led his army through the deserts of Lybia to visit the temple of *Jupiter-Ammon*, and, as the reward of his labors, was gratified by receiving the title of *the son of Jupiter*. While in Egypt, he commenced a more useful and lasting monument of his greatness, by founding the city of *Alexan'dria*, afterward the capital of Lower Egypt, the seat of the Ptolemies, and, for a long time, one of the greatest commercial cities in the world.

23. Returning from this romantic expedition, he received again advantageous proposals from Darius, who offered to surrender to him his whole dominions to the west of the Euphrates; but he haughtily rejected the offer, telling him "the world could no more admit two masters than two suns."

24. Having crossed the Euphrates, with an army of nearly 50,000 men, he met that of Darius, which is said to have amounted to about 700,000. A tremendous battle ensued, in which the Persians were entirely defeated, with a loss stated at 300,000 men, while that of Alexander was only about 500. This engagement took place near the village of *Gaugame'la*, but it is usually called the battle of *Arbe'la*, from a town farther distant.

25. This great battle decided the fate of Persia, and introduced a new era into the history of the world. From that period, Europe has maintained the superiority over Asia, which was then acquired. Darius, having first escaped into Media, and afterwards into Bactria, was there betrayed by Bessus, the satrap of the province, and murdered; and, no long after, the whole Persian empire submitted to the conqueror.

26. Alexander, not yet satiated with conquest, penetrated into India and, in a great battle defeated *Po'rus*, an illustri

ous sovereign of that country. He was projecting further achievements, when his soldiers, seeing no end to their toils refused to proceed, and demanded that they might be permitted to return to their country.

27. Finding it impossible to overcome their reluctance, he returned to the Indus, whence, sending round his fleet to the Persian gulf under Ne-ar'chus, he marched his army across the desert to *Persep'olis*, and thence proceeded to *Babylon*, which he chose for the seat of his Asiatic empire; and, having resided here some time, he was seized with a fever, brought on, according to some writers, by excessive drinking, and soon after died, in the 33d year of his age, and the 13th of his reign

28. Alexander was the most renowned hero of antiquity surpassing all others in the rapidity, extent, and splendor of his conquests. Some other conquerors have shed more blood and have waged war on a more cruel system; but no one ever bestowed such fatal brilliancy upon the hateful lust of conquest; nor has any other person, perhaps, been the cause of more misery to mankind, if, to the slaughter occasioned by his own wars, we take into the account the influence which his example has had on the career of others who have made him their model.

29. His extraordinary abilities, his romantic and daring spirit, and the unparalleled splendor of his successes, have been the more mischievous, in their example, from the amiable and generous qualities which formed a part of his character. He possessed talents which might have rendered him distinguished as a statesman and a benefactor to his species, yet it was to his military renown alone that he owed the surname of *Great.*

30. Though, in the early part of his career, he was distinguished for self-government, yet he became intoxicated by his extraordinary success; and his vanity, which was naturally excessive, being cherished by the extravagant adulations of the sycophants who surrounded him, he was, at length, induced to believe himself the son of Jupiter, and a god, that he could do no wrong, and that his will ought to be the supreme law to his subjects. With these views, he gave himself up to unbounded indulgence, and to acts of the most atrocious cruelty and ingratitude.

31. His most celebrated general, *Parme'nio*, who had assisted him in gaining all his victories, he caused to be assassinated on mere suspicion. His friend *Clytus*, who had saved his life at the Grani'cus, he ran through the body with a spear, because he contradicted him, when heated with wine. He caused the philosopher *Cal'lis'thenes* to be put to death, with

the most cruel tortures, because he refused to pay him adoration as a divinity.

32. His personal qualities and exploits were such as mankind are too much inclined to admire; and his history shows how easily uninterrupted success degrades the character and corrupts the heart; and how necessary disappointments and misfortunes are to teach us moderation, justice, and humanity

---

SECTION X.

Alexander's Successors: Demosthenes: Phocion: Demetrius Phalereus: Achæan League: Philopœmen: Subjugation of Macedonia and of Greece.—From B. C. 324 to 146.

1. Alexander named no successor, but, on his death-bed, he gave his ring to *Perdic'cas*, one of his generals; and, upon being asked to whom he left his empire, he replied, "to the most worthy." His vast empire was soon rent in pieces by the greedy soldiers who had assisted him in the acquisition of it, and a period of confusion, bloodshed, and crime ensued, to which civilized nations can scarcely furnish a parallel.

2. The generals of the army appointed *Philip Aridæ'us*, the brother of Alexander, with his infant son by *Roxa'na*, to succeed him; and *Perdic'cas* was made regent. The empire was divided into 33 governments, distributed among as many of the principal officers. Hence arose a series of intrigues and fierce and bloody wars, which resulted in the total extirpation of Alexander's family, and, after the defeat of *Antig'onus*, one of his generals, (who had obtained possession of his principal dominions in Asia,) in the famous battle of *Ipsus*, in a new division of the empire into four kingdoms, namely, that of *Egypt*, under *Ptol'emy; Macedonia*, including Greece, under *Cassan'der; Thrace*, together with Bithynia, under *Lysim'achus;* and *Syria*, &c., under *Seleu'cus*.

3. The kingdom of Thrace lasted only till B. C. 281, when Lysim'achus was defeated and slain by Seleu'cus, and that of *Macedonia* till the battle of *Pydna*, B. C. 168. The two most powerful kingdoms were *Syria* and *Egypt;* the former continued under the sceptre of the *Seleu'cidæ*, and the latter under that of the *Ptolemies*, till they were both annexed to the Roman empire.

4. During the progress of Alexander's conquests, various attempts were made by the Grecian states to throw off the

yoke of Macedonia. The Spartans, especially, excited a powerful insurrection, but they were subdued by *Antip'ater*, who had been left by Alexander to govern Macedonia in his absence.

5. The news of Alexander's death occasioned great joy at Athens, and the eloquence of *Demos'thenes* was again exerted to rouse his countrymen to secure their liberty. But he was still opposed by his former antagonist, the incorruptible and prudent *Pho'cion*, who continued a strenuous advocate for peace, and whose language was, "Since the Athenians are no longer able to fill their wonted glorious sphere, let them adopt counsels suited to their abilities, and endeavor to court the friendship of a power which they cannot provoke but to their ruin."

6. The counsels of Demosthenes prevailed so far, that the Greeks formed a confederacy, and made an effort to recover their liberty; but they were finally defeated by Antip'ater, and Athens was obliged to purchase peace by the sacrifice of her ten chief public speakers, among whom the renowned orator *Demosthenes* was included. But he put an end to his life by poison, in order to avoid falling into the hands of his enemies.

7. Antip'ater was succeeded, in the government of Macedonia by *Polysper'chon*, who restored, for a short time, the Grecian states to independence. Athens renewed its scenes of turbulence, and proceeded to put to death the friends of Antipater, and, among others, the venerable Pho'cion, who was upwards of 80 years of age. He was eminent for his public and private virtues, and had been 45 times appointed governor of Athens. To a friend, who lamented his fate, he said, "This is no more than what I expected; this treatment the most illustrious citizens of Athens have received before me."

8. Polysperchon was succeeded by Cassander, who appointed *Demetrius Phale'reus* governor of Athens. Under his wise and beneficent government, which continued 12 years, the city enjoyed quiet and prosperity, and the Athenians testified their gratitude by erecting to him 360 statues.

9. From this time, Athens never enjoyed anything more than a precarious independence. Her political power and greatness had ceased, and her citizens, formerly so distinguished for their spirit of liberty and independence, became no less so for their excessive flattery and abject servility.

10. From this period to the final subjugation of Greece by the Romans, the different states underwent a variety of revo

lutions; but they present little that is interesting, and still less that is pleasing. An immense number of Gauls, under their king *Brennus*, ravaged the country; but they were at last mostly cut off.

11. Scarcely recovering from the inroads of these barbarians, the states of Peloponnesus were involved in calamities by the invasion of the celebrated *Pyrrhus*, king of Epi'rus, the greatest general of his age. He made an unsuccessful attack on Sparta, and was afterward slain, at the siege of *Argos*, with a tile thrown by a woman from the top of a house.

12. The last effort for maintaining the liberty and independence of Greece was made by a confederacy, styled the *Achæ'an League*, which was at first formed by only four small cities of Peloponnesus; not long after, eight other cities joined, and, at last, most of the Grecian states. The government of this confederacy was committed to *Ara'tus*, with the title of *pretor*. He formed the design of establishing the independence of all Greece, but the jealousy of some of the principal states rendered the scheme abortive.

13. Aratus was succeeded by *Philopæ'men*, a man of integrity and distinguished talents, styled "the last of the Greeks," because, after him, Greece produced no leader worthy of her former glory. Having triumphed over the Spartans and Ætolians, he was taken and put to death in an expedition against the revolted Messenians.

14. The Romans, who had now become the most powerful nation in the world, being solicited by the Ætolians to afford them aid against the Macedonians, readily complied with the request: and their army, under the command of *Quin'tius Flamin'ius*, defeated *Philip*, king of Macedon, at *Cynoceph'al-e*, and proclaimed liberty to the Grecian states. Nearly 30 years afterwards, a second Roman army, commanded by *Paulus Æmil'ius*, entered Greece, in a war against *Per'seus* son of Philip, who was entirely defeated in the battle of *Pydna*, and was led captive to Rome, to grace the triumph of the conqueror, and *Macedonia* was reduced to a Roman province

15. The Romans, jealous of the power of the Achæan League, endeavored to weaken it by cherishing divisions among the states, and by corrupting the principal citizens. At length the Spartans, in a contest with the Achæan states, sought the aid of the Romans. *Metel'lus* led his legions into Greece, and gained a complete victory over the Achæan army. The remainder of the Achæan forces having shut themselves up in *Cor'inth*, the Roman consul, *Mum'mius*, completed the conquest by taking and destroying that city. The Achæan con

stitution was soon after dissolved, and the whole of *Greece* was reduced to a Roman province, under the name of *Acha'ia.*

16. But Greece, though subject to the Roman arms, acquired, by her arts of peace, her learning, genius, and taste a silent superiority over her conquerors, and was regarded with respect. The most distinguished Romans were educated in the Grecian schools of philosophy; Rome derived her learning from Athens, and the victors became the disciples of the vanquished.

17. In reviewing the history of this extraordinary people, we see much to admire, and much also to condemn. With regard to genius, taste, learning, patriotism, love of liberty, and heroism, they were unrivalled among the nations of antiquity.

18. In perusing the history of Athens, a circumstance which must forcibly impress the reader is the injustice and ingratitude which she frequently manifested towards many of her best citizens, her most illustrious patriots and philosophers. Some of the most distinguished victims of this injustice were *Milti'ades*, *Aristi'des*, *Themis'tocles*, *Ci'mon*, *Pho'cion*, and *Soc'rates.* These were all sentenced to death or banishment, yet, not long after their condemnation, the Athenians, with their characteristic fickleness and inconsistency, did ample justice to their merit, and punished their accusers.

19. In no period of Grecian history does there appear to have existed that *virtuous age* which many are accustomed to describe, more in the spirit of poetical romance, than of historical truth. The standard both of public and private morality in all the states, and at all times, was low; and the most illustrious men that figure in the history of Greece were little scrupulous in the choice of means for effecting their public objects, but seemed to think it right to secure the ascendency of their own country, to humble a rival state, or to carry on designs of conquest, at any expense of blood or of suffering.

20 "It is evident," says Mitford, "from the writings of Xenophon and Plato, that, in their age, the boundaries of right and wrong, justice and injustice, honesty and dishonesty, were little determined by any generally received principles.— That might gave right especially in public transactions, was a tenet generally avowed."

21. The earlier times were characterized by violence and rapine. In a later age, that preceding the Christian era, the philosophy of *Epicu'rus* had gained the ascendency, and the subtilties of scepticism, and corruption of manners, had reached a height of extravagance which it seemed difficult to exceed. The history of the world had demonstrated the necessity of

some better guide to man than human wisdom had been able to afford him, either as a member of society, or as a being formed for immortality.

SECTION XI.

Grecian Antiquities.

Grecian Sects of Philosophy.

Most of the ancient sects of philosophy had their origin among the Greeks. The most flourishing period of Grecian literature was in the 4th and 5th centuries B. C.

The *Ionic sect*, the most ancient school of philosophy among the Greeks, was founded by *Tha'les*, who was distinguished for his knowledge of geometry and astronomy.

The *Italian* or *Pythagore'an sect* was founded by *Pythag'oras*, who taught the transmigration of souls through different bodies.

The *Socratic school* was founded by *Soc'rates*, who was esteemed the wisest and most virtuous of the Greeks, and the father of moral philosophy.

The *Cynics*, a sect founded by *Antis'thenes*, and supported by *Diog'enes*, condemned knowledge as useless, renounced social enjoyments and the conveniences of life, and indulged themselves in scurrility and invective.

The *Academic sect* was founded by *Plato*, a philosopher who has had an extensive empire over the minds of men, owing to the sublimity of his doctrines, and the eloquence with which he has propounded them. He gave his lectures in the groves of *Acade'mus*, near Athens.

The *Peripatet'ic sect* was founded by *Ar'istotle*, who established his school in the Lyceum at Athens. His philosophy predominated over the minds of men during 16 centuries.

The *Sceptical sect* was founded by *Pyrrho*, who inculcated universal doubt as the only true wisdom.

The *Stoic sect* was founded by *Zeno*. The Stoics inculcated fortitude of mind, denied that pain is an evil, and endeavored to raise themselves above all the passions and feelings of humanity.

The *Epicure'ans*, named from their founder, *Epicu'rus*, held that man's supreme happiness consists in pleasure.

"The Greek philosophy," says Tytler, "affords little more than a picture of the imbecility and caprice of the human mind. Its teachers, instead of experiment and observation satisfied themselves with constructing theories; and these, wanting fact for their basis, have only served to perplex the understanding, and retard equally the advancement of sound morality and the progress of useful knowledge."

Philosophers and Poets

The names of the principal Greek philosophers, poets, &c., may be seen in the *Chronological Table of Grecian Literature.*

The most illustrious of the Greek poets are *Homer*, the great epic poet; *Pindar*, a lyric poet; *Æs'chylus*, *Eurip'ides*, *Soph'ocles*, *Aristoph'anes*, and *Menan'der*, dramatic poets. — The poets *Homer* and *He'siod* are supposed to have flourished 9 or 10 centuries B. C.

Artists and Historians.

Phid'ias and *Praxit'eles* were famous statuaries; *Polyg'notus*, *Parrha'sius*, *Zeuxis*, and *Apelles*, eminent painters; *Herod'otus*, *Thucyd'ides*, *Xen'ophon*, *Polyb'ius*, *Diodo'rus Sic'ulus*, and *Dionysius* of Halicarnassus, distinguished historians.

The Seven Wise Men.

The *seven wise men* of Greece were *Tha'les*, of Mile'tus; *Solon*, of Athens; *Bias*, of Prie'ne; *Chilo*, of Lacedæ'mon; *Pit'tacus*, of Mityle'ne; *Cleobu'lus*, of Lindos; and *Perian'der*, of Cor'inth. — Instead of *Perian'der*, some enumerate *My'son*, and others *Anachar'sis.*

The Council of the Amphictyons.

This council is supposed to have been instituted by *Amphic'tyon*, the son of Deuca'lion, king of Thes'saly, at an early period of the history of Greece. It was composed of deputies from the different states, and resembled the diet of the German empire. At its first institution, it is said to have consisted of 12 deputies, from 12 different cities or states; but the number of deputies was afterwards increased to 24 and to 30. They usually met twice a year; in the spring at *Delphi*, and in the autumn at *Thermop'ylæ.*

The objects of this assembly were to unite in strict amity the states which were represented; to consult for their mutual welfare and defence; to decide differences between cities; to try offences against the laws of nations; and also to protect the oracle of Delphi.

Oracles.

The Greeks were in the habit of consulting oracles on al important occasions, — as when they were about to declare war, to conclude a peace, to institute a new form of government, or to enact laws. The most celebrated oracles were those of Apollo at *Delphi* and *Delos*, the oracle of Jupiter at *Dodo'na*, and that of Tropho'nius at *Lebade'a.*

Public Games.

There were four public and solemn games in Greece, — the *Olympic*, *Pythian*, *Nemean*, and *Isthmian.*

The exercises practised at these games were leaping, running, throwing, boxing, and wrestling; also horse and chariot races, and contests between poets, orators, musicians, philosophers, and artists of different descriptions.

Running was much esteemed among the ancient Greeks. Leaping was sometimes performed with weights in the hands, or upon the head or shoulders. In boxing, the combatants held in their hands balls of stone or lead, while their arms were guarded with thongs of leather.

The *Olympic games*, which were instituted by Hercules, in honor of Jupiter Olympus, were celebrated at the town of Olympia, in the first month of every fifth year, and lasted five days. They drew together an immense concourse from all parts of Greece, and numbers even from foreign countries. No one was permitted to contend unless he had prepared himself, by continual exercises, during ten months, in the public gymnasium at Elis.

The contenders were obliged to take an oath that they would use no unlawful means to obtain the reward. The prize bestowed on the victor was a crown of *olive;* yet trifling as was this reward, it was considered as the highest honor, and was sought for with the utmost eagerness. The victor was greeted with loud acclamations, and his return home was in the style of a warlike conqueror.

The Greeks computed their time by the celebrations of these games, the space intervening between one celebration and another being called an *Olympiad.*

The *Pythian games* were celebrated every 5th year, in the second year of every Olympiad, near Delphi, in honor of Apollo. The victors were crowned with *laurel*

The *Ne'mean games* were celebrated at the town of Ne'mea every third year. The victors were crowned with *parsley.*

The *Isth'mian games* were so called from their being celebrated on the isthmus of Corinth. They were instituted in honor of Neptune; observed every 3d or 5th year; and held so sacred and inviolable, that a public calamity could not prevent their celebration. The victors were rewarded with a garland of *pine leaves.*

Government of Athens.

Classes of inhabitants. The inhabitants of Athens were divided into three classes; *citizens* or *freemen*, *foreigners* or *sojourners*, and *slaves.*

The *citizens* were the privileged class, and had the government exclusively in their hands. They were divided into 10 tribes, but they were not limited to the city, a part of them residing in the small boroughs of Attica. The privilege of citizenship was highly esteemed, and was obtained with much difficulty.

The *sojourners* were permitted to exercise trades in the city, but had no vote in the assembly, nor could they be raised to any office.

The *slaves* or *servants* were the most numerous portion of the inhabitants of Attica. They were in a state of hopeless servitude, wholly at the disposal of their masters, and performed the labor in the fields, the mines, and in private houses.

Archons and other magistrates. The supreme executive power was vested in nine *archons*, elected annually. They wore garlands of myrtle, and were protected from violence and insult.

The first, or chief of the nine, was called *the archon*, by way of eminence. He had the care of widows and minors throughout Attica, and determined all causes respecting wills. He was punished with death, if convicted of drunkenness while in office.

The *second archon*, styled *Bas'ileus*, had the superintendence of religious ceremonies, and decided all disputes among priests.

The *third archon*, called *Pol'emarch*, had originally the superintendence of military affairs; but his jurisdiction was afterwards confined to strangers and sojourners, and to the appointment of games in honor of those who fell in war, and the care of the education of their children.

The *six other archons* were called *Thesmoth'etæ.* They presided at the election of inferior magistrates, ratified public contracts or leagues, received complaints against persons guilty of various offences, and decided disputes respecting trade and commerce.

The *Athenian magistrates* were divided into three sorts; 1st, the *Chirotone'ti*, who were chosen by the people, in a lawful assembly, in which they voted by holding up their hands; 2d, the *Clero'ti*, who, after having been approved by the people, were promoted by lots drawn in the temple of Theseus; 3d, the *Ær'eti*, who were extraordinary officers appointed by particular tribes to take care of any business.

The poorer citizens were admitted to a share in the government, and might aspire to preferments; yet the higher offices were generally bestowed upon the most distinguished persons. The candidates for office were obliged to give an account of their past life in the public forum. While in office, the magistrates were liable to trial for an accusation of any failure in the discharge of their duties; and, after their office had expired, they were obliged to give an account of their management, and during 30 days every man was allowed to bring forward his complaint.

Assemblies. The assemblies of the people were composed of all the citizens or freemen of Athens; all foreigners, slaves, women, children, and such persons as had received an infamous punishment, being excluded. They were held four times in 35 days; the place of meeting was the forum, the pnyx, or the temple of Bacchus.

No business could be transacted in an assembly containing less than 6,000 citizens. When the question under consideration was sufficiently discussed, the president called for a decision, which was manifested by show of hands.

Senate The senate, which was elected annually, originally consisted of 400, but was afterwards increased to 500. It was the business of this body to examine, with care, all matters, before they were proposed to the people, and to see that nothing was submitted to them which was contrary to the public good. The senate also examined the accounts of the magistrates, took care of the fleet, and punished such offences as were not forbidden by any written law.

Areopagus. The name of this court, which signifies *Mars' Hill*, was taken from the place where it was held. This was the most distinguished and venerable court of justice in ancient times, and took cognizance of crimes, abuses, and innovations, either in religion or government. The Areop'agites were guardians of education and manners, and inspected the laws. To laugh in their assembly was an unpardonable act of levity.

Ostracism. One of the most iniquitous and absurd peculiarities in the government of Athens, and some other of the Grecian states, was the practice of the *os'tracism*, a ballot of all the citizens, in which each wrote down the name of the individual most offensive to him; and he who was marked out by the greatest number of votes, was banished from his country for 5, 10, or 20 years. It was not necessary that any crime should be alleged, and the property and honor of the exile remained unhurt.

This barbarous institution was often subservient to the worst purposes, and stained the character of the Athenians with many flagrant instances of injustice and ingratitude.

Government of Sparta.

Classes of inhabitants. The inhabitants of Sparta consisted of *citizens*, and *slaves* or *Helots*.

The citizens were divided into two classes, the *Homoii*, and the *Hypomiones;* the former alone could be elected to office; the latter, consisting of the poorer citizens, were only allowed to vote at the elections.

The *slaves* or *Helots* were much more numerous than the freemen. They performed all the servile labor in the field and in the house; also served as sailors in the fleet, and were attached to the army, every soldier being attended by one or more.

Kings. The two chief magistrates of the republic of Sparta were styled *kings;* but their power was very limited. They presided in the senate, and were high priests of the nation. One of them commanded the army, while the other usually remained at home to administer justice. They appeared in public places without any retinue, and could scarcely be distinguished from other citizens.

Senate. The senate of Sparta consisted of the two kings and 28 elective members, who were above 60 years of age, and retained their dignity till death. It constituted the supreme council of the republic, and considered all questions relating to peace and war, and other important affairs of state. None were admitted into this august assembly except such as had been distinguished from youth for prudence and virtue.

Ephori. The *Eph'ori* were five Spartan magistrates, elected annually by the people, and might be taken from every rank of citizens. It was their duty to inspect the education of youth and the administration of justice.

Assemblies. Two public assemblies met at Sparta; one called the *general assembly*, attended by all the freemen of Laconia; the other, called the *lesser assembly*, composed of the freemen of the metropolis who were above 30 years of age. The general assembly was convened when questions relating to peace or war, or other matters of general concern, were to be determined. The lesser assembly was held at every full moon, and regulated the succession of the crown, and discussed matters relating to government and religion.

B. C.		Chronological Table of Grecian History.
800	76	First *Olympiad* begins.
8th	56	*Cherops*, the first *Decennial Archon* in Athens.
	43	First *Messenian War*; — ends 724, and *Ithome* taken.
700	85	Second *Messenian War*; — ends 671, the Messenians subdued
	84	*Creon*, the first *Annual Archon* in Athens.
7th	24	*Draco* forms his bloody code of laws for Athens.
		Solar Eclipses first calculated by Thales
600	94	SOLON forms a new code of laws for Athens.
	62	*Comedy* and *Tragedy* first exhibited in Athens.
	60	*Pisistratus* tyrant of Athens; a splendid rule.
	60	*Temples* first built in Greece.
6th		*Literature* encouraged: *Homer's* poems collected into a vol ume.
	24	*Hippias* and *Hipparchus*, the *Pisistratidæ*, govern Athens
	14	*Hipparchus* slain; and (510) *Hippias* expelled.
500	90	PERSIAN WAR. — Victory gained by *Miltiades* at *Marathon*.
	80	Conflict of *Leonidas* at *Thermopylæ*.
	80	Victory gained by *Themistocles* at *Salamis*.
	79	Victories of the Greeks at *Platæa* (*Aristides*) and *Mycale*.
	70	Victory gained by *Cimon* on the *Eurymedon*.
	64	Third *Messenian War* begins.
5th	45	*Herodotus* reads his history at the Olympic games.
	31	PELOPONNESIAN WAR begins. — 430. *Plague* at Athens.
	5	*Lysander* defeats the Athenians at *Ægos Potamos*.
	3	The *Thirty Tyrants* expelled. — PHILOSOPHY and the ARTS.
		Xenophon's Retreat with the 10,000. Death of SOCRATES.
400	94	*Agesilaus* defeats the Athenians, Thebans, &c., at *Coronea*.
	87	Peace of *Antalcidas* between the Spartans and Persians.
	71	*Epaminondas* of Thebes defeats the Spartans at *Leuctra*.
	63	*Epaminondas* defeats the Spartans at *Mantinea*.
	56	First *Sacred War*. — 348. *Philip* takes *Olynthus*.
4th	39	Second *Sacred War*. — 338. *Philip's* victory at *Chæronea*.
	34	ALEXANDER invades Persia; his victory on the *Granicus*.
	33	Battle of *Issus*. — 332. *Tyre* taken, and *Egypt* conquered.
	30	Battle of *Arbela*; *Persia* conquered. — 224. *Alexander* dies.
	1	Battle of IPSUS; Alexander's empire divided.
300	98	Athens taken by Demetrius Poliorcetes.
	81	The *Achæan League* begins; also the *Ætolian League*.
	80	Greece ravaged by the *Gauls* under *Brennus*.
3d	73	*Pyrrhus*, having ravaged Greece, is killed at *Argos*.
	64	The *Arundelian Marbles* composed.
	25	*Cleomenes* reforms the government of Sparta.
	20	War between the *Achæans*, under *Aratus*, and the Ætolians.
	6	The *Achæans*, under *Philopæmen*, defeat the Ætolians.
200	97	Battle of *Cynocephale*; the Macedonians defeated by the Romans.
	68	Battle of *Pydna*; the Macedonians defeated by the Romans, and *Macedonia* reduced to a Roman province.
2d	47	The *Achæans* defeated by the Romans under Metellus.
	46	*Corinth* taken by the Romans under Mummius, and GREECE reduced to a Roman province under the name of *Achaia*.

To ascertain the date of any event mentioned in this Table, add the figures connected with the event to the century *below*. Thus, the first *Olympiad* begins 776 B. C.

CHRONOLOGICAL TABLE OF GRECIAN LITERATURE.

B. C	Statesmen and Warriors.	Philosophers.	Poets and Artists.*	Historians and Orators.	Contemporary Sovereigns.
700					
7th	Aristomenes Draco		Tyrtæus Archilochus Terpander		Numa Josiah Cyaxares
600					
6th	Periander SOLON Zaleucus Pisistratus Hippias Hipparchus Harmodius Aristogiton	Chilo, Bias Pittacus Cleobulus THALES Anacharsis Anaximander Xenophanes Anaximenes	Alcæus Sappho Æsop, *Fab.* Epimenides Stesichorus Mimnermus Thespis Susarion		Nebuchad-nezzar Serv. Tullius Crœsus Cyrus Tarquin, *Pr.* Cambyses
500					
5th	Miltiades Leonidas Aristides Pausanias Themistocles Cimon Pericles Nicias Alcibiades Critias Lysander	PYTHAGORAS Heraclitus Melissus Zeno Empedocles Anaxagoras Diagoras Meton Protagoras Cebes SOCRATES	Anacreon Simonides Æschylus PINDAR Phidias, *Art.* Cratinus Eupolis Polygnotus *A.* Parrhasius *A.* EURIPIDES SOPHOCLES	HERODOTUS Georgias, *Or.*	Darius Xerxes Hiero Artaxerxes L. Dionysius
400					
4th	Thrasybulus Conon Pelopidas Epaminondas Agesilaus Timoleon Parmenio Perdiccas Phocion Polysperchon Antigonus	Euclid, *Meg.* Phædo Antisthenes Aristippus Hippocrates Democritus PLATO Diogenes ARISTOTLE Pyrrho Euclid, *Alex.*	Aristophanes Zeuxis, *Art.* Euphranor, *Art.* Timotheus Lysippus, *A.* Apelles, *Art.* Praxiteles, *A.*	Thucydides Lysias, *Or.* Ctesias XENOPHON Isocrates, *Or.* Theopompus Hyperides, *O.* DEMOSTHENES, *Or.* Æschines, *Or.*	Artaxerxes Philip Alexander Darius Cod
300					
3d	Demetrius Antigonus G. Antigonus D. Cleomenes Aratus	Theophrastus Epicurus ZENO, *Stoic* Apollonius Arcesilaus Archimedes	Menander Theocritus Lycophron Aratus Callimachus Apollonius	Timæus Manetho	Lysimachus Cassander Seleucus I. Ptolemy I. Pyrrhus Ptolemy II.
200					
2d	Philopœmen Lycortas	Eratosthenes Heraclides Carneades Hipparchus	Bion Moschus Nicander	Polybius Apollodorus	Antiochus G Eumenes Antiochus E. Judas Mac.
100					
1st		Potamo	Archias	Diodorus Sic. Dionysius H.	Mithridates Julius Cæsar.
0					
1st		Dioscorides		Strabo, *Geog.*	Augustus Vespasian
100					
2d		Epictetus Galen, *Med.*	Lucian, *Dial.*	Plutarch, *Bio.* Arrian.	Trajan Adrian

* The poets *Homer* and *Hesiod* are supposed to have flourished 9 or 10 centuries B C

SYRIA UNDER THE SELEUCIDÆ.

1. After the death of Alexander the Great, *Antig'onus*, one of his generals, obtained possession of his principal dominions in Asia. But *Seleu'cus*, another officer of Alexander, and son of *Anti'ochus*, one of Philip's generals, revolted against Antigonus, and took possession of Babylon; and by the battle of *Ipsus*, in which *Antig'onus* was defeated and slain, *Seleucus* was confirmed in his authority. He founded the kingdom of *Syria*, or *Syro-Media*, which, reckoning from the time of his taking Babylon to the period when Syria became a Roman province, lasted 247 years. It was governed by 23 kings, who were styled the *Seleu'cidæ*, from the name of the founder.

2. Seleucus was a great general, an able and popular sovereign, and was surnamed *Nica'tor* or *Conqueror*, on account of 23 battles which he gained. He founded 16 large cities, the most famous of which were An'tioch, Seleu'cia, Apame'a, and Laodice'a. *Antioch*, which became the capital of the kingdom, was a very large and splendid city, styled "The Queen of the East," and also "The Eye of the Christian Church." The disciples of Christ were here first called *Christians;* and this city, at an early period, became the seat of a Christian patriarch.

3. Seleucus, having made war against *Lysim'achus*, king of Thrace, defeated and slew him in battle, but was himself soon after assassinated by Ptolemy Cerau'nus, who was afterwards king of Macedon. He was succeeded by his son *Anti'ochus Soter*, during whose reign the Gauls made an irruption into Asia Minor, and founded the state of Galatia.

4. The reigns of his successors, *Anti'ochus Theos* and *Seleu'cus Callini'cus*, were disturbed by conspiracies and by wars, particularly with the Parthians and Bactrians, who revolted from the government.

5. One of the most distinguished of this race of sovereigns was *Anti'ochus the Great*, who had a long reign of 36 years, and was as much distinguished for his faults and misfortunes, as for his great qualities and successes. His reign was a continued warfare, presenting alternately victories and defeats. He subdued several governors of different provinces, who revolted from him. In a war with Ptolemy, king of Egypt, after having gained many advantages, he lost a great battle at *Raphia*. He carried his victorious arms into Media, Parthia Hyrcania, and India.

6 Anti'ochus was visited by *Han'nibal*, the great Carthe

ginian general, who endeavored to persuade him to make war upon the Romans by invading Italy. Instead of this, however, he invaded Greece, but was defeated by the Romans and compelled to retire into Asia. Being pursued by a Roman army, commanded by *Scipio Asiat'icus*, he was entirely defeated in a great battle, on the plains of *Magne'sia*, and compelled to accept of peace on humiliating terms. He was afterwards put to death by his own officers.

7. The next two kings were *Seleu'cus Philop'ator* and *Anti'ochus Epiph'anes*, sons of Antiochus the Great. The latter profaned and plundered the temple of Jerusalem, and attempted to abolish the Jewish worship. But the Jews, under *Judas Maccabæ'us*, revolted, and defeated the army of Antiochus, who immediately engaged in a design to exterminate the whole nation; but before he had effected anything, he died in a sudden and signal manner.

8. The succeeding reigns of the *Seleu'cidæ* exhibit a series of assassinations, conspiracies, and contests, till Syria was finally conquered by *Pompey*, 65 B. C., and made a Roman province.

The Seleucidæ, Kings of Syria.

[The figures denote the commencement of the reign of each.]

B.C.		B.C.	
312.	Seleucus I. Nicator.	144.	Antiochus VI.
283.	Antiochus I. Soter.	143.	Tryphon.
261.	Antiochus II. Theos.	139.	Antiochus VII.
246.	Seleucus II. Callinicus.	127.	Alexander II.
226.	Seleucus III. Ceraunus.	123.	Antiochus VIII
223	Antiochus III. the Great.	112.	Antiochus IX.
185.	Seleucus IV. Philopator.	95.	Antiochus X.
175.	Antiochus IV. Epiphanes	94.	Antiochus XI.
164	Antiochus V. Eupator.	87.	Antiochus XII.
162	Demetrius I. Soter.	83	Tigranes.
150	Alexander I.	69	Antiochus XIII. Asiaticus deposed by Pompey, 65 B. C
146	Demetrius II. Nicator		

EGYPT UNDER THE PTOLEMIES.

1. Of all the conquests of Alexander the Great, Egypt enjoyed the earliest and most lasting prosperity. The dynasty of the *Ptol'emies*, which, reckoning from the death of *Alexander* to that of *Cleopa'tra*, lasted 293 years, forms a conspicuous period in the history of that country.

2. *Ptol'emy Lagus*, surnamed also *Soter*, was the reputed son of Philip, king of Macedon, by a concubine, and half-brother of Alexander the Great. At the time of Alexander's death, he was governor of Egypt, and after the division of the empire into four monarchies, he became king of the country, and had a prosperous reign of 39 years. He was a man of great abilities, eminent as a general and a statesman, and was also a man of learning, and a great patron of literature.

3. He founded the famous *library of Alexandria*, established a museum, or academy, which became the abode of learned men, and erected the celebrated watch-tower of *Pharos*, which was sometimes reckoned one of the seven wonders of the world He built a number of new cities, and caused decayed ones to emerge from their ruins, rendered the canals again navigable, encouraged commerce and agriculture, restored prosperity to Egypt, and conquered Syria.

4. Ptolemy Soter was succeeded by his second son *Ptol'emy Philadel'phus*, who followed, in a great measure, the steps of his father, and had a prosperous and splendid reign. He founded cities, erected magnificent edifices, finished the canal from Suez to the Nile, and promoted navigation and commerce. His court surpassed all others of the age as a seat of learning, politeness, and the arts, and was illustrated by *Theoc'ritus*, and other men of genius. During his reign, the celebrated version of the *Old Testament* into Greek, called the *Septuagint*, was made for the use of the *Jews*, many of whom were, at this time, settled in Alexandria.

5. *Ptolemy Ever'getes*, the son and successor of the preceding monarch, was a warlike and prosperous prince, and likewise a patron of learning. His reign commenced with a severe though successful war with *Anti'ochus*, king of Syria. While absent on one of his expeditions, his queen *Bereni'ce*, alarmed for his safety, made a vow, that, if he were restored to her wishes, she would consecrate her hair in the temple of Venus.

6. The hair was regarded as the chief ornament of Egyptian ladies that of Bereni'ce was particularly beautiful, and

the sacrifice acquired additional value, as it was a monument of her affection for her husband. By some accident, the consecrated locks were soon lost, and the keepers were rescued from punishment by the address of the astronomer Conon, who affirmed that *Bereni'ce's hair* had been translated to the firmament, and formed a constellation in the heavens.

7. Ptolemy Ever'getes was succeeded by his son *Ptolemy Philop'ator*, whose character was cruel and sanguinary, and whose reign was distinguished for an unrelenting persecution of the Jews. When he was at Jerusalem, he attempted to penetrate by force into the most holy place of the Jewish temple, into which none but the high priest, and he only once a year, was permitted to enter. Being forcibly prevented from committing this sacrilege, he returned to Egypt, frantic with rage, and resolved to wreak his vengeance on the Jewish people, who had enjoyed many indulgences under his predecessors.

8. He published a decree requiring all the Jews within his dominions to abjure their religion, and worship the gods of Egypt; but only about 900 were so base as to apostatize. He then commanded all the Jews in Alexandria to assemble in the Hip'podrome, or place of public diversion, where he collected 500 elephants for the destruction of this devoted people. But the enraged animals rushed upon the crowd of spectators, and crushed more of them to death than of the Jews; yet about 40,000 of the latter are said to have been slain in the city.

9. The reigns of the first three Ptolemies, which comprised about a century, formed far the most prosperous part of the dynasty. Most of the other reigns were unhappy, abounding in crimes and calamities.

10. The Egyptian kings of the name of Ptolemy were most of them distinguished by a surname, by which they were in some manner characterized: 1st, *Ptolemy Soter*, or *Savior*, so named by the Rhodians, in gratitude for the protection which he afforded them; 2d, *Ptolemy Philadel'phus*, or *Lover of his Brother*, so called, in derision, because he caused his two brothers to be put to death; 3d, *Ptolemy Ever'getes*, or *Benefactor*, so styled because he restored to Egypt the idols which had been carried away by Camby'ses; 4th, *Ptolemy Philop'ator*, or *Lover of his Father*, so named, in derision, because he was supposed to have put his father to death; 5th, *Ptolemy Epiph'anes*, or *Illustrious*, so styled, though his reign was weak and inglorious; 6th, *Ptolemy Philome'ter*, or *Lover of his Mother*, so called, in derision, on account of his hatred of his mother; 7th, *Ptolemy Physcon*, or *Big-bellied* so name

from his deformity; 8th, *Ptolemy Lathyrus*, or *Chick-pea*, so called from an excrescence on his nose like a pea; 9th, *Ptolemy Aule'tes*, or *Flute-player*.

11. The last was *Ptolemy Dionysius*, who succeeded to the throne at the age of 13 years. He had for his queen his sister, the celebrated *Cleopa'tra*, who, having caused him to be murdered, assumed the sole government. Her history is connected with that of Julius Cæsar and Mark Antony. She finally caused herself to be bitten by an asp, in order to avoid being led captive to Rome, to grace the triumph of Octavius. After her death, Egypt became a Roman province, 30 B. C.

12. The queens of the Ptolemies were, according to the usage of the country, for the most part, their sisters; and their names were *Arsin'oë*, *Bereni'ce*, and *Cleopa'tra*. Several of them were women distinguished for their talents and accomplishments.

The Ptolemies, Kings of Egypt.

[The figures denote the commencement of the reign of each.]

B.C.	
323	Ptolemy Lagus.
263	Ptolemy Philadelphus
246	Ptolemy Evergetes.
221	Ptolemy Philopator.
204	Ptolemy Epiphanes.
180	Ptolemy Philometer
145	Ptolemy Physcon.
117	Ptolemy Lathyrus

B.C.	
101.	Ptolemy Alexander.
81.	Cleopatra.
80.	Ptolemy Alexander II
65.	Ptolemy Auletes.
	Berenice.
51.	Ptolemy and Cleopatra
48.	Cleopatra II., *the last sovereign, died* 30 B. C.

ROME.

SECTION I.

Roman History: Foundation of Rome: Romulus: Numa Tullus Hostilius: Ancus Martius: Tarquinius Priscus: Servius Tullius: Tarquinius Superbus, — expelled, and the regal government abolished. — From B. C. 753 to 509.

1. In the delineation of ancient history, *Rome*, the last of the four great empires of antiquity, becomes, after the conquest of Greece, the leading object of attention. It rose gradually from small beginnings to almost universal empire, surpassing, in the extent of its dominions, in military power, and in the stability and strength of its government, all the great sovereignties that had preceded it. Its history is fruitful in great events and illustrious personages; and from it statesmen and philosophers, of different periods and countries, have drawn facts to support their respective speculations and theories. The history of this empire, in its progress and decline, involves a collateral account of all other nations of antiquity, which, in those periods, are particularly deserving of attention.

2. During the reign of the kings, and the early years of the republic, the Roman territories extended only about 15 or 20 miles around the capital; and, for about 400 years after the foundation of the city, the commonwealth was of very limited extent. It then made a rapid progress towards universal dominion; and, about 50 years before the Christian era, it had reduced to its authority almost all the civilized world. This universal empire continued till the 5th century, when it began to be broken; and, towards the end of that century, the *Western Empire* became extinct. The *Eastern Empire* subsisted till about the middle of the 15th century, when Constantinople was taken by the Turks.

3. The early history of the Romans, like that of other ancient nations, is mixed with fable, and what has been extensively received as an authentic account of the early ages is far from being entitled to full credit. That a considerable mixture of fiction must be blended with the history of the first three or four centuries, will appear more than probable when we consider, that the earliest writer on Roman affairs, whose works are extant, flourished nearly 600 years after the foundation of the city; that the Romans were not a literary people till the time of the conquest of Greece; that, according to their writ-

ers, the records and monuments of their early history were destroyed when the city was burnt by the Gauls, B. C. 390; and that many of the narratives, relating to the early times, have much more the air of fable than of credible history.

4. The length of time comprised in the reigns of the seven kings of Rome is justly regarded as a circumstance calculated to throw a veil of doubt over the accuracy of the account given of them. Of these kings, three or four died a violent death, and one was expelled; yet the average length of their reigns was about 35 years, nearly twice as great as the common average length of reigns in those kingdoms whose histories are most accurately known.

5. It may be remarked, with regard to those Roman Histories which treat copiously of the early ages, that although this portion of them may contain much that is true, yet the evidence on which it rests is too slender to command implicit belief, especially with respect to such narratives or statements as are in themselves highly improbable. We can by no means place the account of *Romulus* and that of *Julius Cæsar* on the same footing, with respect to authentic narrative. The history, indeed, not only of the foundation of the monarchy and also of the seven kings of Rome, but likewise of the early ages of the commonwealth, contains obviously an intermixture of fable or legendary stories; and the narrative may be regarded as often disguised by the national vanity of the Romans.

6. According to the poets, *Æne'as*, a Trojan prince, who escaped from the burning of Troy, after a variety of adventures, arrived in Italy, where he was hospitably received by *Lati'nus*, king of the Latins, whose daughter he married, and whom he succeeded in the throne. The succession is said to have continued in his family nearly 400 years, till the time of *Nu'mitor*, the 15th king in a direct line from Æne'as.

7. Rhea Sylvia, the daughter of *Nu'mitor*, was the mother of the twin brothers, *Rom'ulus* and *Remus*. The two brothers founded a city; but, having quarrelled with each other for the sovereignty, Romulus slew Remus, and proceeded with the building of the city, which he called, from his own name, *Rome*. He was elected king, made the new city an asylum for fugitives, and, by stratagem, at a public festival, his subjects seized and carried off the *Sabine women* for wives.

8. Romulus is said to have divided his people into *three tribes*, each tribe consisting of 10 *curiæ;* and into two orders, *patricians* and *plebe'ians*. He instituted a *senate* of 100 members, afterwards increased to 200. These were at first always chosen from the patricians, but the plebeians afterwards acquired an equal right to that dignity. In order to attach the two

classes, patricians and plebeians, to each other, by mutual bonds, he established the connection of *patron* and *client*. Each plebeian had the right of choosing a patrician for his patron, whose duty it was to protect him from oppression, and who received from his client certain services.

9. The king was attended by 12 lictors, with fasces, and had a guard of 300 horsemen, called *cel'eres eq'uites*, or knights.

10. *Numa Pompil'ius*, a Sabine, was elected the second king of Rome. He was a native of the town of *Cures*, whose inhabitants were styled *Quiri'tes*, a term afterwards applied to Roman citizens. Numa is represented as studious, virtuous, and pacific; and the Romans are said to have received great benefits from his government. He softened their fierce and warlike dispositions, by cherishing the arts of peace, obedience to the laws, and respect for religion. He built the temple of *Janus* which was open during war, and closed during peace.

11. *Tullus Hostil'ius*, the third king of Rome, was of a warlike disposition. His reign is memorable for the romantic story of the combat between the *Hora'tii* and *Curia'tii*, who were six in number, sons of two sisters, three at a birth. The Horatii fought for *Rome*, and the Curiatii for *Alba*. One of the Horatii survived, all the rest being slain; and, by this victory, the Romans became masters of Alba.

12. *Ancus Mar'tius*, the fourth king, was the grandson of Numa. He conquered the Latins, and built the port of Os'tia at the mouth of the Tiber.

13. *Tarquin'ius Priscus*, or *Tarquin the Elder*, the son of a merchant from Corinth, was elected successor of Ancus Martius. He embellished the city with works of utility and magnificence, built the walls of hewn stone, erected the circus, or *hip'podrome*, founded the *Capitol*, and constructed the *cloa'cæ*, those immense common sewers, or aqueducts, which conveyed into the Tiber the rubbish and superfluous waters of the city.

14. *Ser'vius Tul'lius*, the son of a captive female slave and son-in-law of Tarquin, secured his election to the vacant throne by his own address and the intrigues of his mother-in-law. He established the *census*, by which, at the end of every fifth year, the number of citizens, their dwellings, number of children, and amount of property, were ascertained. The census was closed by a *lustrum*, or expiatory sacrifice; hence the period of five years was called a *lustrum*.

15. Servius had two daughters, of whom the elder was gentle and submissive, and the younger haughty and ambitious. In order to secure the throne, he married them to the two sons

of Tarquin, the late king, whose names were *Tarquin* and *Aruns*, and whose different dispositions corresponded to those of his daughters. But he took care to cross their tempers by giving the elder to Tarquin, who was violent, and the younger Tullia, to Aruns, who was mild, hoping they would correct each other's defects. But *Tarquin* and *Tul'lia* soon murdered their consorts, married each other, and then caused Servius to be assassinated. Tarquin usurped the throne, and Tullia, in her eagerness to salute him as king, is said to have driven her chariot over the dead body of her father.

16. *Tarquin*, surnamed the *Proud*, (in Latin, *Tarquin'ius Super'bus*,) began his reign by putting to death the chief senators, and governing in the most arbitrary manner; but, by his tyranny and cruelty, he soon disgusted all classes of his subjects. *Sextus*, his son, having entered the house of *Colla-ti'nus*, a nephew of Tarquin, under the mask of friendship, did violence to his wife *Lucre'tia*, a woman distinguished for her beauty and domestic virtues. The unhappy Lucretia immediately sent for her husband and father, who came, bringing with them *Junius Brutus*, a grandson of Tarquin the Elder, and other friends. To them she related her mournful story, enjoining upon them to avenge her injury; and, being unable to survive her dishonor, plunged a dagger into her bosom, and expired.

17. Her corpse was carried to the public square; the vengeance of the people was roused; and, by the strenuous exertions of Brutus, the senate pronounced a sentence of perpetual banishment against Tarquin and his family. The tyrant, being expelled from his capital, and abandoned by his army was never able to gain a readmission into the city; and the regal government was abolished, after having continued 244 years.

SECTION II.

The Commonwealth: Consuls, Collatinus and Brutus: Valerius: Porsenna: Dictator: The Plebeians encamp on Mons Sacer: Tribunes: Coriolanus: Law of Volero: Cincinnatus: The Twelve Tables: Decemvirs: Appius Claudius. — From B. C. 509 to 449.

1. The regal authority being abolished, a republican form of government was established in its stead. The supreme power, as heretofore, belonged to the senate and people: but instead of a regent for life, two *consuls* were chosen annually

from the patrician families, as presidents of the republic, and chief directors of affairs. Their power was nearly the same as that of the kings, except that it was limited to one year The first consuls were *Bru'tus* and *Collati'nus*, who had taken so distinguished a part in the expulsion of the tyrants.

2. Tarquin was now in Etruria, where he prevailed upon two of the most powerful cities, *Ve'ii* and *Tarquin'ii*, to espouse his cause. He had also numerous partisans in Rome, particularly among the young patricians, who preferred the luxuries and splendor of a royal court to the simplicity and austerity of a republic. A plot was formed to open the gates to receive him, and, upon its being discovered, *Brutus* had the mortification to find his two sons among the conspirators. They were brought to trial before himself; he condemned them to be beheaded in his presence, and witnessed the shocking spectacle with a steady look and an unaltered countenance. "He ceased to be a father," says an ancient author, "that he might execute the duties of a consul, and chose to live childless rather than to neglect the public punishment of a crime."

3. The insurrection in the city being suppressed, Tarquin relied wholly upon external aid, and raised an army in order to regain the crown; but he was defeated by the Romans under the command of the consuls, *Vale'rius* (who was elected in place of Collatinus) and *Brutus.* In this battle *Brutus* was killed, and the Roman matrons honored his memory by wearing mourning for him a whole year. *Vale'rius*, after the victory, returned to the city, and was the first Roman who enjoyed the splendid reward of a *triumph.*

4. Valerius having become arrogant from the honors which he had received, his popularity began to decline; and, with a view to recover it, he proposed a law, termed, from him, the *Valerian law*, which granted to a citizen, condemned by a magistrate, the right of appealing to the people. This gave the first blow to the aristocracy in the Roman republic

5. For 13 years after the expulsion of Tarquin, the Romans were involved in continual hostilities on his account. Of these the most remarkable was the war with the Etrurians, under their king *Porsen'na;* a war fertile in exploits of romantic heroism, and signalized by the daring intrepidity of *Hora'tius Co'cles*, who, alone, arrested the progress of the enemy at the head of a bridge, and of *Mutius Scæv'ola*, who entered the enemy's camp in disguise, with a design to assassinate Porsenna; but hostilities were finally terminated by an amicable arrangement between the two parties.

6. Dangers from domestic disorders were soon added to those of war Tarquin had induced the Latins to enlist in his

cause and approached the city with his army. The plebeians being poor, and oppressed with debt, complained of their grievances, and refused to aid in repelling the enemy, unless the senate would grant them relief, by remitting their debts to the rich. The consuls found their authority of no avail, as the Valerian law gave to any condemned citizen the right of appealing to the people.

7. An extraordinary measure was now necessary; and a new magistrate was created, styled *dictator*, who was to continue in office only as long as the danger of the state required never exceeding the space of six months, and was vested with absolute power. He was appointed only in cases of public exigency, when quick and decisive measures were necessary. He had authority to make peace and war, to levy taxes, to appoint all public officers, and to dispense with the laws, without consulting the senate or people. *Titus Lar'tius*, one of the consuls, being elevated to this high office, raised a large army, and, by his firmness and moderation having restored tranquillity, resigned the dictatorship. War having been again excited by the Tarquins, *Posthu'mius* was appointed dictator; the Romans were completely victorious, and the sons of Tarquin were slain.

8. After the death of the *Tarquins*, and the return of peace, Rome was disturbed by domestic dissensions, and the dispute between the creditors and debtors was again revived. On an alarm of war, the plebeians refused to take up arms in defence of the republic. Their language was, "Of what consequence is it to us whether our chains are forged by our enemies or our fellow-citizens. Let the patricians, since they alone have the reward of victories, encounter the dangers of war." At length, finding no relief from their oppressions, the whole army abandoned their officers, withdrew from Rome, and encamped upon *Mons Sacer*, about three miles from the city. Here they were soon joined by the greater part of the people.

9. This resolute procedure had the desired effect. The senate, being alarmed, deputed ten of the most respectable of their order, with authority to grant a redress. *Mene'nius Agrip'pa*, one of the senators, is said to have related in his speech to the people, with great effect, the celebrated fable of the belly and the members. A reconciliation was brought about. The debts of the plebeians were abolished, and, for their future security, they were allowed the right of choosing, from their own order, magistrates, styled *trib'unes*, who should have the power of annulling, by a single *veto*, every measure which they should judge prejudicial to their interest. The tribunes were elected annually; their number at first was five,

afterwards increased to ten. By them the aristocracy was held within bounds, and the fury of the populace was regulated. Two magistrates, styled *ædiles*, were appointed to assist the tribunes, and to take charge of the public buildings.

10. The neglect of agriculture, which had arisen from the revolt of the army, brought on a famine, which caused great commotion; but the arrival of a large quantity of corn from Sicily produced a temporary relief. At this time, the resentment of the people was strongly excited against *Coriola'nus* who was a man of aristocratic principles, of talents and courage, and who had distinguished himself in a war against the Volsci. He advised that no corn should be distributed to the people, unless they would restore the rights of the senate, and abolish the office of the tribunes. In consequence of the resentment which these proposals excited, the tribunes brought charges against him, and he was sentenced by the people to perpetual banishment. He then went over to the Volsci, who appointed him their commander; and he led their army against Rome, which was, for a time, threatened with ruin; but he was at last persuaded, by the earnest entreaties of his mother and his wife, to lay down his arms.

11. The proposal of an *Agrarian law* for dividing among the people the lands which were obtained by conquest, and which were the joint property of all the citizens, proved an apple of discord thrown out between the rich and the poor. Such a division of the public lands was demanded by the plebeians, but it was strenuously opposed by the patricians. The design was repeatedly brought forward before any such law was enacted, and caused violent dissensions.

12. By the influence of the tribune *Vol'ero*, a law was enacted that the election of tribunes should be made, and the chief public business discussed, in the *comitia*, or public meetings held by tribes; and not, as before, by the centuries and curiæ. By this law, the supreme authority was taken from the patricians and placed in the hands of the plebeians, and the Roman government became a democracy.

13. Dissensions arising on account of the proposed Agrarian law, and dangers from the invasions of the *Æqui* and *Volsci*, *Cincinna'tus* was twice called from the plough to assume the government as dictator. Having completely vanquished the enemies of his country, and entered the city in a splendid triumph, he resigned his office, and returned again to his retirement, to labor upon his farm.

14. The Romans had hitherto possessed no body of written laws. Under the regal government, the kings administered justice and the consuls succeeded them in the exercise of

this high authority. But their arbitrary proceedings were frequently the subject of complaint, and the citizens became desirous of having a fixed code of laws for the security of their rights. Three commissioners were, therefore, sent to Greece in order to procure the laws of *Solon*, and such others as were deemed useful in forming a suitable code.

15. Upon the return of the commissioners, ten of the principal senators, styled *decemvirs*, were appointed to digest a body of laws, and put them in execution for one year. This was the origin of those celebrated statutes known by the name of the *Laws of the Twelve Tables*, which formed the basis of Roman jurisprudence, and continued to be of the highest authority in the most flourishing times of the republic.

16. The decemvirs were invested with absolute power; and during the time for which they were appointed, all other magistrates were suspended. Each decemvir, by turn, presided for a day, and had the sovereign authority, with its insignia and fasces. They governed with so much moderation and equity during the first year, that they obtained a new appointment; but they soon became tyrannical, and two flagrant abuses of power by *Ap'pius Clau'dius*, the leading member of their body, caused a speedy termination of the office.

17. One of these crimes was his procuring the assassination of *Sicin'ius Denta'tus*, a Roman tribune, who, on account of his extraordinary valor and exploits, was styled the *Roman Achil'les;* the other was his villany with regard to *Virginia*, a beautiful young maiden, who had been betrothed to *Icil'ius*, formerly a tribune. Having seen her as she was going to a public school, and being inflamed with a lawless passion, he employed a profligate dependent to claim her as his own property, on the pretence of her being the daughter of one of his female slaves.

18. He caused the claim to be brought for trial before himself, and pronounced an infamous decree, by which the innocent victim was torn from her parents, and placed within his own power. *Virginius*, her father, in order to prevent the dishonor of his daughter, plunged a dagger into her heart. Brandishing in his hand the bloody weapon, he exclaimed, "By this blood, Appius, I devote thy head to the infernal gods," and running wildly through the city, he roused the people to vengeance. Appius soon after died in prison by his own hand; the other decemvirs went into exile; the decemvirate, after having continued for three years, was abolished; and the consuls were restored.

SECTION III

Military Tribunes. Censors: Veii destroyed: Camillus Rome burnt by the Gauls: Brennus: Manlius: The Samnites: Pyrrhus: Conquest of Italy. — *From B. C.* **449** *to* **266.**

1. The two great barriers which still separated the patricians and plebeians were the prohibition of their intermarriage, and the limitation of the office of consul to the patricians. After a long contest, the law prohibiting intermarriages was repealed, with the hope that this concession would satisfy the people. But this success, on the contrary, stimulated them to urge their claim to be admitted to a share in the consulship; and on the occurrence of war, they had recourse to their former custom of refusing to enlist. unless their demand was granted.

2. After a long contest, it was agreed on both sides, that instead of consuls, six *military tribunes*, with the power of consuls, should be chosen, three of them from the patricians, and three from the plebeians. This institution, however, was, in a short time, laid aside; and the consuls were again restored to office.

3. The disorders of the republic prevented the survey, or enumeration, of the citizens from being regularly attended to. In order to remedy this neglect, two officers, styled *censors* were appointed; and it was made their duty, not only to take the census every five years, but also to inspect the morals and regulate the duties of all the citizens. This was an office of great dignity and importance, exercised for 100 years by patricians; in the later times of the republic, only by consular persons; and afterwards by the emperors.

4. In order to avoid the evils which arose from the people's frequently refusing to enlist in the army, the senate introduced the practice of giving *regular pay to the troops.* From this period, the Roman system of war assumed a new aspect. The senate always found soldiers at command; the army was under its control; the enterprises of the republic were more extensive, and its success more signal and important. The art of war was improved, as it now became a profession, instead of an occasional employment. The Roman dominion, hitherto confined to a territory of a few miles, soon began to be rapidly extended.

5. The inhabitants of the city of *Ve'ii*, long the proud rival of Rome, equal in extent and population, had repeatedly made

depredations on the Roman territories; and it was decreed that Veii, whatever it might cost, should be destroyed. A siege was begun, which was continued, with great exertion and various success, for ten years. At length, in order to carry it on with greater vigor, *Camillus* was created dictator; and to him was intrusted the sole management of the long protracted war.

6. He caused a passage to be opened under ground into the citadel, by means of which he filled the city with his legions, who plundered and destroyed it. Camillus was honored with a splendid triumph, in which he was drawn in a chariot by four white horses; but being afterwards accused of having appropriated to his own use a part of the plunder of Veii indignant at the ingratitude of his countrymen, he went into voluntary exile.

7. The *Gauls*, a barbarous and warlike people, had long before this opened a passage through the Alps, and had settled themselves in the northern part of Italy. Under the command of their king *Brennus*, they laid siege to *Clu'sium*, a city of Etruria, the inhabitants of which implored the assistance of the Romans. The senate sent three patricians of the *Fabian* family on an embassy to Brennus, to inquire what offence the citizens of Clusium had given him. To this he sternly replied, that "the right of valiant men lay in their swords; that the Romans themselves had no other right to the cities they had conquered." The ambassadors, having obtained leave, entered Clusium, and assisted the inhabitants against the assailants This so incensed Brennus, that he raised the siege, marched directly towards Rome, and, in a great battle near the rivulet *Allia*, defeated the Roman army with great slaughter.

8. The Gauls then entered Rome, and after a general massacre of such of the inhabitants as remained in it, and a pillage of the city, they burnt it to ashes, and razed the walls to the ground. They next besieged the capitol; but the Romans repelled their attacks with great bravery. At length, having discovered footsteps leading up to the top of the Tarpeian Rock, a body of Gauls undertook the difficult enterprise of gaining the summit in the night, which they accomplished while the Roman sentinel was asleep. At this moment, the cackling of some geese in the temple of Juno is said to have awakened *Marcus Manlius*, with his associates, who instantly threw the Gauls headlong down the precipice.

9. From this time, the hopes of the Gauls began to decline and they soon after agreed to quit the city on condition of receiving 1000 pounds weight of gold; but, after the gold was brought, the Gauls weighed with false weights, and the com-

plaints, which the Romans made of the deception were treated with insolence. At this juncture, *Camillus*, who had recently been restored to favor, and again appointed dictator, appeared a the gates with an army. Having been informed of the deception and insolence of the Gauls, he ordered the gold to be carried back into the capitol, commanded the Gauls to retire, adding that "Rome must be ransomed by steel, and not by gold." Upon this a battle ensued, in which the Gauls were entirely routed, and Camillus was honored as the father of his country and the second founder of Rome. The city, being freed from its invaders, soon began to rise again from its ashes.

10. Manlius was liberally rewarded for his heroism; but at length, envying the fame of Camillus, he abandoned himself to ambitious views; and being accused of aiming at sovereign power, he was sentenced to be thrown headlong from the *Tarpeian Rock*. Thus the place, which had been the theatre of his glory, became that of his punishment and infamy.

11. The Romans next turned their arms against the *Samnites*, a race of hardy mountaineers, inhabiting an extensive tract in the southern part of Italy. This contest lasted upwards of 50 years, and was carried on by the Samnites with great valor and skill, though they were finally subdued. They defeated the Romans at *Caudinæ Furculæ*, near Caudium, and made their whole army pass under the yoke, formed by two spears set upright, and a third bound across them. This roused the spirit of revenge on the part of the Romans, who appointed *Papir'ius Cursor* dictator; and the next year, under his command, they gained a victory over the Samnites, compelling them, in turn, to undergo the same disgrace at *Luce'ria;* and by the exertions of *Fabius Maximus* and *Decius*, they were finally subjugated.

12. During the consulship of *Manlius Torquatus*, a war broke out between the Romans and Latins. In order to prevent confusion in time of action by reason of the similarity of the two nations, Manlius issued orders that death should be inflicted on any one who should leave his ranks. When the two armies were drawn out for battle, *Metius*, a Latin commander challenged to single combat any Roman knight. *Titus Manlius*, the son of the consul, accepted the challenge, and slew his adversary; and for this act he was beheaded by the stern order of his father. The Latins were vanquished, and submitted to the Romans.

13. The *Tarentines*, who were the allies of the Samnites, sought the aid of *Pyrrhus*, king of Epi'rus, the greatest general of his age. He landed at Tarentum with an army of 30,000 men, and twenty elephants; and the Romans, under the com

mand of the consul *Lævi'nus*, not being accustomed to the mode of fighting with elephants, were at first defeated, with the loss of 15,000 men; that of Pyrrhus was nearly as great; and he was heard to confess that another such victory would compel him to return to Epirus. His admiration of the heroism of his enemy drew from him the celebrated exclamation, "O, with what ease could I conquer the world, had I the Romans for soldiers, or had they me for their king!"

14. In the progress of the war, *Fabri'cius*, who afterwards commanded the Roman army, received a letter from the physician of Pyrrhus, importing that for a proper reward he would poison the king. Fabricius, indignant at so base a proposal, gave immediate information of it to Pyrrhus, who, admiring the generosity of his enemy, exclaimed, "It is easier to turn the sun from his course, than Fabricius from the path of honor!" — and that he might not be outdone in magnanimity, he released all his Roman prisoners without ransom.

15. Pyrrhus then withdrew his army from Italy, in order to assist the Sicilians against the Carthaginians; but he again returned, and made a last effort near *Beneventum*, where he was totally defeated by *Cu'rius Denta'tus*. He then withdrew to his own dominions, and the Romans, after having gained further victories over the Samnites, became masters of all *Lower Italy*.

SECTION IV.

Carthage: Sicily.

1. As the history of Rome now becomes connected with that of *Carthage* and *Sicily*, it may be proper to introduce here a short notice of those states.

2. *Carthage* is said to have been founded, nearly 900 years before the Christian era, by *Dido*, with a colony of *Tyrians*. The government, at first monarchial, became afterwards republican, and it is commended by Aristotle as one of the most perfect of antiquity. The two chief magistrates, called *suffe'tes*, or judges, were elected annually from the first families. The religion was a cruel superstition, and human victims were offered in sacrifice.

3. In the time of the Punic wars, Carthage was the most commercial and wealthy city, and one of the most splendid in the world. It had under its dominion about 300 smaller towns in Africa, bordering on the Mediterranean, a great part of Spain, also of Sicily and other islands. The Carthagini

ans worked the gold mines of Spain they were devoted to commerce, and had the vices and characteristics of a commercial people. The Romans, who were their rivals and enemies represented them as wanting in integrity and honor; hence the ironical phrase, *Pu'nica fides* [*Punic faith*], to denote treachery.

4. History records the names of few persons among the Carthaginians eminent as philosophers, or distinguished in the arts. The *Per'iplus*, or voyage of *Hanno*, an illustrious Carthaginian, who wrote an account of his expedition, affords proof of ardent enterprise. Carthage produced several celebrated generals, among whom were *Hamil'car*, *As'drubal*, and *Hannibal:* the last was the most formidable enemy that Rome ever experienced.

5. The Phœnicians sent colonies to *Sicily* before the Trojan war, and the Greeks, at later periods, made settlements on the island. Sicily contained many large and opulent cities; of these, *Syr'acuse*, founded by the Corinthians, was the most populous and commercial, and larger than any of the cities of Greece. It was governed, in its early ages, like most of the other cities of Sicily, by a democracy, but at length it fell into the power of an individual.

6. To *Gelon*, one of its sovereigns, history ascribes every virtue; but his successors being cruel tyrants, the people took measures to rid themselves of the regal government. It was however, after 60 years, again restored in the person of *Dionysius*, a man of great talents; but he found it easier to acquire royalty than to preserve and enjoy it. His son, *Dionysius the Younger*, a weak and capricious tyrant, was dethroned by the aid of *Timo'leon*, an illustrious Corinthian, and exiled to Corinth, where he died in poverty.

SECTION V.

First Punic War; Regulus: Second Punic War; Hannibal: Conquest of Macedonia: Third Punic War; Carthage destroyed: Conquest of Greece.—From B. C. 264 to 133.

1. The Romans, having become masters of all Lower Italy were eager to extend their conquests into foreign countries. They had hitherto made no naval conquests, and possessed no fleet. *Carthage* was now their most formidable rival, and the

greatest maritime power in the world, possessing an extensive sway over all the commercial towns of the Mediterranean. The Carthaginians were rich in merchandise, in silver and gold: the Romans were comparatively poor, but preëminent in patriotism and valor, and ambitious of conquest.

2. The *Mamertines*, a people of Campa'nia, obtained assistance of the Romans in a war with *Hi'ero*, tyrant of Syracuse. The Syracusans being at first assisted by the Carthaginians, a war was brought on between the latter and the Romans, styled the *first* PUNIC WAR. The object, at first, of both parties, was merely to obtain possession of *Messa'na*, in order to command the passage of the straits, which took their name from that city; but it soon became a contest for the sovereignty of the whole island, and the dominion of the seas.

3. The Romans now earnestly applied themselves to maritime affairs. A Carthaginian vessel, which happened, in a storm, to be driven ashore, served as a model; and within two months, a fleet, consisting of upwards of 100 vessels, of a rude construction, was prepared, of which the command was given to the consul *Duil'lius*, who defeated the Carthaginians, and took 50 of their vessels. Soon after the commencement of the war, the Syracusans, changing their course, joined the Romans, and *Agrigen'tum* was taken from the Carthaginians.

4. The Romans increased their naval force to upwards of 300 galleys, and gained another great victory, off the coast of Sicily, over the Carthaginians, who then made an offer of peace; but it was rejected. The consul *Reg'ulus*, with an army, soon landed on the coast of Africa, defeated the Carthaginians, and appeared before the gates of the capital. Here, being met by the Carthaginians, under the command of *Xanthip'pus*, a Spartan, he was totally defeated, and taken prisoner. He was afterwards sent with the Carthaginian ambassadors to Rome, in order to procure peace, under an oath to return if the negotiation should fail. Regulus, thinking the terms not advantageous to his country, strenuously opposed their being accepted, and returned to Carthage, where he was put to death with the most cruel tortures.

5. The war continued to rage in Sicily with various success; but the Romans finally prevailed, and the Carthaginians were compelled to accept of humiliating terms of peace They agreed to abandon Sicily, to pay the Romans 3,200 talents, and release their captives. Sicily was now declared a Roman province, but Syracuse still maintained its independent government. After the close of this war, the Romans made a conquest of *Cisal'pine Gaul.*

6. The peace between the Romans and Carthaginians lasted

23 years; and during a part of this period, the temple of *Janus* was shut for the first time since the reign of Numa.

7. The most distinguished Carthaginian commander in the first Punic war was *Hamil'car*, who was the father of *Han'nibal*, and who trained his son to war, and made him swear, when very young, a perpetual enmity to the Roman name. Hannibal was one of the greatest generals of antiquity, and at the early age of 26 years, was raised to the chief command of the Carthaginian army. He commenced the *second Punic War* by besieging *Saguntum*, a city of Spain in alliance with the Romans. After a siege of seven months, the desperate inhabitants set fire to the city, and perished in the flames.

8. Hannibal now formed the bold design of carrying the war into Italy, and by an arduous and toilsome march, he led his army over the *Pyr'enees*, and afterwards over the *Alps*, and gained four great victories, — the first over *Scip'io*, near the *Tici'nus;* the second over *Sempro'nius*, near the *Tre'bia;* the third over *Flamin'ius*, near lake *Thrasyme'nus;* and the fourth over *Æmil'ius* and *Varro*, at *Cannæ*. The last was the most memorable defeat that the Romans ever suffered. According to Livy, 50,000, and, according to Polybius, no less than 70,000, of their troops were left dead on the field, together with the consul Æmilius. Among the slain were 5,000 or 6,000 Roman knights, the greater part of the whole body; and Hannibal is said to have sent to Carthage three bushels of gold rings, which they wore on their fingers.

9. Hannibal has been censured for not making the best use of this great victory by immediately attacking Rome, and, instead of doing this, for leading his troops into winter-quarters, at *Cap'ua*, where they were corrupted and enervated by dissipation in that luxurious city.

10. The Romans, being now guided by the counsels of the sagacious and prudent *Fa'bius Max'imus*, concentrated their strength. The chief command of their armies was given to *Fabius*, styled the *Shield*, and to *Marcellus*, the *Sword* of Rome. The good fortune of Hannibal now forsook him; and he remained 13 years in Italy, after the battle of Cannæ, without gaining any signal advantage. At the siege of *Nola*, he was repulsed by Marcellus with considerable loss, and his army was harassed and weakened by Fabius.

11. *Syracuse*, which had taken part with Carthage, was besieged by *Marcellus*, and after being defended for three years by the inventive genius of the celebrated mathematician *Archime'des*, it was at last compelled to surrender. This event put an end to the kingdom of Syracuse, which now became a

part of the Roman province of Sicily. A large army of Carthaginians was sent from Spain into Italy under the command of *As'drubal*, the brother of Hannibal, who was defeated with great slaughter by the Romans, under the command of the consuls *Livy* and *Nero*, near the small river *Metau'rus*, which empties into the Tyrrhene sea.

12. *Scip'io*, afterwards surnamed *Africa'nus*, having conquered Spain, passed over into Africa, with a Roman army, and carried havoc and devastation to the walls of Carthage. Alarmed for the fate of their empire, the Carthaginians immediately recalled Hannibal from Italy. These two great commanders, *Hannibal* and *Scipio*, at the head of their respective armies, fought on the plains of *Zama* a memorable battle, in which the Carthaginians were totally defeated. A peace soon followed, the conditions of which were, that Carthage should abandon Spain, Sicily, and all the other islands in the Mediterranean, surrender all their prisoners, give up their whole fleet, except ten galleys, and, in future, undertake no war without the consent of the Romans. Thus terminated the second Punic war, in the humiliation of Carthage, after having continued for 17 years.

13. Hannibal afterwards fled from his country, and passed the last 13 years of his life in Syria and Bithynia. During his exile, Scipio resided a while in the same country, and many friendly conversations passed between them; in one of which the Roman is said to have asked the Carthaginian "whom he thought the greatest general." Hannibal immediately replied, "Alexander; because that, with a small body of men, he had defeated very numerous armies, and had overrun a great part of the world." "And who do you think deserves the next place?" continued the Roman. "Pyrrhus," replied the other; "he first taught the method of forming a camp to the best advantage. Nobody knew better how to choose, or post guards more properly." "And whom do you place next to those?" said Scipio. "Myself," said Hannibal; at which Scipio asked, with a smile, "Where, then, would you have placed yourself, if you had conquered me?" "Above Alexander," replied the Carthaginian, "above Pyrrhus, and above all other generals."

14. While engaged in hostilities with the Carthaginians, the Romans prosecuted the first *Macedonian War*, which terminated in the defeat of king *Philip*, in the battle of *Cynoceph'ale*. Not long afterwards, a Roman army, under *Scip'io*, surnamed *Asiat'icus*, invaded Syria, and, in the battle of *Magnesia* defeated *Anti'ochus the Great*. The second *Macedonian War*

followed, which terminated in the defeat of *Per'seus*, the last king of that country, in the battle of *Pydna*, and the reduction of Macedonia to a Roman province.

15. About 50 years after the conclusion of the second Punic war, the Carthaginians attempted to repel the Numidians, who made incursions into a territory claimed by the former. The Romans, pretending this was a violation of their treaty, laid hold of it as a pretext for commencing the *third Punic War*, with a determination to effect the entire destruction of Carthage. *Por'cius Cato*, the censor, who now swayed the decisions of the senate, had long cherished this savage design, and had been in the habit of concluding his speeches with this expression; *Delenda est Carthago*, "Carthage must be destroyed."

16. The Carthaginians, conscious of their inability to resist the Romans, offered every submission, and were ready even to acknowledge themselves subjects of Rome. They yielded up, to the demand of the Romans, their ships, their arms, and munitions of war. They were then required to abandon the city, in order that it might be destroyed. This demand was heard by the inhabitants with a mixed feeling of indignation and despair; but the spirit of liberty and independence not being yet extinct, they were roused to make the most strenuous efforts, having resolved to sacrifice their lives rather than to obey the barbarous mandate.

17. After the most desperate resistance for three years, the city was at last taken by *Scipio*, the second *Africanus*, and, being set on fire, the flames continued to rage during 17 days. Thus was Carthage, with its walls and buildings, the habitations of 700,000 people, razed to its foundations. Such of the inhabitants as disdained to surrender themselves prisoners of war, were either massacred or perished in the flames. The scenes of horror were such as to force tears even from the Roman general.

18. The year in which this barbarous transaction took place was signalized by the taking of *Cor'inth*, and the reduction of *Greece* to a Roman province. And a few years afterwards, *Numan'tia*, in Spain, after a tremendous siege, fell into the hands of the Romans.

SECTION VI.

The Gracchi: Jugurtha: Social War: Mithridates: Marius and Sylla: Servile War: Conspiracy of Catiline.— From B. C. 133 to 63.

1. The Romans had hitherto been characterized by temperance, severity of manners, military enterprise, and public spirit; but they were not as yet a literary people, and the arts and sciences had been but little cultivated by them. These were now introduced from Greece; and the period of the subjugation of that country is the era of the dawn of taste and literature in Rome. Acquaintance with foreign nations, and the introduction of foreign wealth, began also, at this period, to introduce luxury and corruption of manners.

2. The power of Rome was now widely extended; her arms had been everywhere triumphant; and by the destruction of Carthage she was freed from the fear of a rival. But when there was no longer a foreign object to excite apprehension, she began to be torn by domestic dissensions, which continued, in various forms, to distract the state, till the final dissolution of the commonwealth.

3. *Tibe'rius* and *Ca'ius Grac'chus*, men of eloquence and influence, distinguished themselves by asserting the claims of the people. Tiberius, the elder of the two brothers, being a tribune, attempted to check the power of the patricians, and abridge their overgrown estates, by reviving the *Licinian law*, which ordained that no citizen should possess more than 500 acres of the public lands. A tumult was the consequence, in which Tiberius, together with 300 of his friends, was killed in the forum by the senators.

4. This fatal example did not deter his brother Caius from pursuing a similar career, in endeavoring to maintain, by force, the privileges of the people, against the encroachments of the senate. But, like his brother, he fell a victim to the attempt, with 3,000 of his partisans, who were slaughtered in the streets of Rome by the consul *Opim'ius*.

5. *Jugur'tha*, a grandson of *Masinis'sa*, attempted to usurp the crown of *Numid'ia* by destroying his cousins, Hiemp'sal and Adher'bal, grandsons also of Masinissa, and sons of the deceased king *Micip'sa*. He murdered the elder, but Adherbal, the younger, escaping, applied to Rome for aid; but the senate, being bribed by Jugurtha, divided the kingdom between the two. Jugurtha, having defeated and slain his cousin, seized the whole kingdom; but he excited against himself the vengeance of the Romans.

6. War being declared against him, the Roman army was at first commanded by *Metellus;* but the celebrated *Ma'rius* having supplanted and succeeded him in command, gained two great victories over Jugurtha, who was taken prisoner, led in chains to Rome, and, after having graced the triumph of the conqueror, was confined in a dungeon, where he was starved to death. Marius afterwards led the Roman army against the *Teu'tones* and *Cimbri*, and defeated them with great slaughter

7. A confederacy of the states of Italy against Rome, to obtain the rights of citizenship, gave rise to the *Social War*, which continued to rage for several years, and is said to have caused the destruction of about 300,000 men. It was ended by conceding the rights of citizenship to all such as should return to their allegiance.

8. *Mithrida'tes*, king of Pontus, the most powerful monarch of the East, and one of the greatest generals of the age, formed a design of uniting in a confederacy the eastern and northern nations, and, at the head of their forces, of overrunning Italy. He began the war by causing about 80,000 Romans, who dwelt in the cities of Asia Minor, to be massacred in one day; and soon after he invaded Greece. — In this celebrated contest, styled the *Mithridatic War*, the famous Roman generals, *Sylla*, *Lucullus* and *Pompey*, successively bore a distinguished part.

9. *Sylla*, a man of great talents and an able general, who had distinguished himself in the late wars, and was now at the head of an army in Campania, was appointed to the chief command in the war against Mithrida'tes. He belonged to an illustrious family, and was popular with the senate. But his great rival *Marius*, a peasant by birth, was an enemy to the aristocracy, and a favorite with the people. He was now 70 years of age, had been distinguished for his warlike genius and exploits for nearly half a century, and had been honored with two triumphs and six consulates. But his ambition was not yet satisfied; and he had the address to get the command of the army transferred from Sylla to himself.

10. Sylla, on receiving this intelligence, finding his troops devoted to him, led them immediately to Rome, which he entered sword in hand, surrounded the house of the senate, and compelled that body to issue a decree declaring Marius an enemy to his country. Marius, being obliged to flee, made his escape into Africa, and Sylla afterwards entered upon the Mithridatic war. *Cinna*, a zealous partisan of Marius, collected an army, recalled the veteran warrior, who, after gaining a bloody victory, entered Rome, and gave orders for murdering all the great senators. After a horrible massacre of their enemies, *Marius* and *Cinna* proclaimed themselves con

suls, without the formality of an election. But he career of Marius was soon terminated by death, and, not long after, Cinna was assassinated.

11. Sylla, after having had a victorious campaign in the war against Mithrida'tes, in which he gained great victories returned to Italy, and entering Rome with his army, caused another horrible massacre, in which his object was to exterminate every enemy he had in Italy. Having obtained the appointment of perpetual dictator, he caused the streets of Rome to flow with the blood of her citizens. To the surprise, however, both of his friends and of his enemies, he resigned the dictatorship, before he had completed three years in office, and retired to a villa at Pute'oli, where he spent the rest of his days in the society of licentious persons, and the occasional pursuits of literature. On his death, he was honored with a magnificent funeral, and a monument with the following epitaph, written by himself: — " I am Sylla the Fortunate, who, in the course of my life, have surpassed both friends and enemies; the former by the good, the latter by the evil I have done them." — In the civil wars carried on between Sylla and Marius, 150,000 Roman citizens were sacrificed, including 200 senators, and 33 men who had been consuls.

12. After the death of Sylla, the old dissensions again broke out between the two parties, supported respectively by the two consuls, *Cat'ulus* and *Lep'idus.* The latter favored the party of *Marius*, and was also supported by *Serto'rius*, a great general, who was now at the head of an army in Spain, where he established an independent republic, and sustained, with great ability, a war for several years against the Roman state; but he was at last murdered by *Perper'na.*

13. The commonwealth was now, for two years, harassed by the *Servile War*, excited by *Spar'tacus*, a Thracian shepherd who had been kept at Capua as a gladiator. Escaping from his confinement, he placed himself at the head of an army of slaves, laid waste the country; but he was at length totally defeated, with the loss of 40,000 men, by *Crassus.*

14. A few years after the defeat of Spar'tacus, a conspiracy threatening the destruction of Rome, was headed by *Cat'iline*, a man of extraordinary courage and talents, but of ruined fortune, and most profligate character. A plan was concerted, that there should be a simultaneous insurrection throughout Italy; that Rome should be fired in different places at once; and that Catiline, at the head of an army, should take possession of the city and massacre all the senators.

15. This sanguinary plot was seasonably detected and crushed by the vigilance and energy of the consul *Cicero*

the great Roman orator. Catiline, at the head of 12,000 men whom he had collected, was defeated and slain, together with his whole army.

SECTION VII.

First Triumvirate: Civil War of Cæsar and Pompey Second Triumvirate: Dissolution of the Commonwealth. From B. C. 60 *to* 31.

1. *Pompey*, who, on account of his military exploits, was surnamed the *Great*, was appointed to the chief command in conducting the *Mithridatic War*, which he brought to a successful termination. He defeated *Mithrida'tes*, king of Pontus, and *Tigra'nes*, king of Armenia, and reduced *Syria*, together with *Judea*, to the state of a Roman province. Returning home, after his splendid campaign, the Romans honored him with a triumph, and gazed, for three successive days, on the spoils of eastern grandeur, which preceded his chariot.

2. The two most considerable men now in Rome were *Pompey* and *Crassus;* the former distinguished for his talents, popularity, and military fame, the latter for his enormous wealth, extensive patronage, and great liberality. *Julius Cæsar* had, before this time, distinguished himself by his military achievements, and risen into public notice. When a young man, he was exceedingly profligate, and had, at an early age, excited the jealousy of Sylla, who, discerning his great talents and ambition, said of him, that "he saw many a Marius in that dissolute youth." *Pompey* and *Crassus* were hostile to each other, both of them contending for the command of the republic. *Cæsar* paid court to both, and had the address to unite them. The three formed the design of appropriating to themselves the whole power of the state, and entered into that famous league, known by the name of the *First Triumvirate.*

3. They distributed the foreign provinces among themselves: Pompey received Spain and Africa, and remained in Rome Crassus chose Syria, which was the richest; Cæsar took Gaul, and he ratified his treaty with Pompey by giving him his daughter *Julia* in marriage. Crassus, having made war against the Parthians, who were commanded by *Sure'na*, was defeated in a battle fought near *Carræ*, and was afterwards taken and slain, leaving the empire to his two colleagues. The bond of union between Cæsar and Pompey had already been dissolved by the recent death of *Julia;* the two rivals became jealous

of each other; each began to manifest hostility and to aspire to undivided dominion.

4. On the division of the provinces among the triumvirs Cæsar had proceeded immediately to take possession of *Gaul* which was inhabited by many barbarous and warlike nations, most of them yet unconquered. Here he had a most brilliant career of victory, in eight campaigns, which he conducted with extraordinary ability. He contrived to give a color of justice and humanity to his bloody operations, by professing himself the protector of the native inhabitants against the invasions of the Helvetii and the Germans. He acquired a high military reputation, and great popularity; and rendered himself the idol of his troops by sharing with them every danger, and by his great liberality, affability, and clemency.

5. Pompey, who had remained all this time in Rome, was alarmed on account of the great reputation of his rival, and endeavored to thwart his views. The term of Cæsar's government being about to expire, he applied to the senate to be continued in his authority; but this body, being devoted to Pompey, denied his demand. He now resolved to support his claim by force of arms, and a civil war was the consequence The consuls and most of the senators were the friends of Pompey. Cæsar had on his side a victorious army devoted to his cause, and the great body of Roman citizens, whom he had won by his liberality.

6. Pompey had been careful to place in the provinces governors devoted to himself; but he had no army, and took no measures to raise one. Cicero, surprised at his negligence in his preparations, asked him with what troops he expected to oppose Cæsar? "I need only stamp my foot on the ground" he replied, "and an army will arise."

7. Cæsar, having bound his army to him by an oath of fidelity, led it over the Alps, and, stopping at Ravenna, wrote to the Roman government, offering to resign all command, in case Pompey would do the same; but the senate decreed that he should lay down his government and disband his forces, within a limited time, under the penalty of being declared an enemy to the commonwealth. Cæsar marched his army to the banks of the *Ru'bicon*, a small river separating Italy from Cisalpine Gaul, and forming the limits of his command; and to pass which with an army, or even a single cohort, had been declared by the senate a sacrilege and parricide. On arriving at this famous stream, he is said to have hesitated, impressed with the greatness of the enterprise, and its fearful consequences, and to have said to Pollio, one of his generals, "If I pass this river, what miseries I shall bring on my country! and if I do not

pass it. I am undone." Soon after, he exclaimed, "The die is cast!" and, putting spurs to his horse, he passed the stream, followed by his soldiers.

8. The news of this movement excited the utmost terror in Rome. The citizens reproached Pompey with his supineness. "Where now," said a senator, in derision, "is the army that is to rise up at your command? Let us see if it will come by stamping." Pompey himself was alarmed, and aware that he was unable to resist Cæsar in Rome, where the great body of the citizens were devoted to him, he led his forces to *Capua* where he had two legions; thence he proceeded to *Brundusium* and passed over to *Dyrrach'ium*, in Macedonia. He was followed by the consuls and a great part of the senate, and took measures to levy troops both in Italy and Greece.

9. Cæsar, having made himself master of Italy in 60 days, directed his course to Rome, entered the city triumphantly amidst the acclamations of the people, seized the public treasury, and possessed himself of the supreme authority without opposition. He made great ostentation of clemency, said that he entered Italy, not to injure, but to restore the liberties of Rome and the citizens, and gradually dissipated the fears which had been generally entertained of another proscription. After staying a few days in the city, he proceeded with his army to Spain, defeated Pompey's lieutenants, made himself master of the whole country, and returned victorious to Rome, where the citizens created him dictator and consul.

10. The monarchs of the East had declared in favor of Pompey, and had sent him large supplies; and he had at this time collected a numerous army. His cause was considered that of the commonwealth; and he was daily joined by crowds of the most distinguished nobles and citizens from Rome. He had, at one time, in his camp, upwards of 200 senators, among whom were *Cicero* and *Cato*, whose approbation alone was equivalent to a host.

11. Cæsar stayed only eleven days at Rome: being anxious to bring his antagonist to a decisive engagement, he pursued him with his army, and near *Dyrrach'ium* an engagement took place, which terminated in favor of Pompey, who afterwards led his troops into the plains of *Pharsa'lia.* Cæsar did everything to provoke a general battle; and when he saw his enemy advancing, he exclaimed, "The time we have so long wished for is come; let us see how we are to acquit ourselves. The contest was now calculated to excite the deepest interest; the two armies were composed of the best soldiers in the world, and were commanded by the two greatest generals of the age; and the prize contended for was nothing less than the Roman empire.

12. Pompey's army consisted of upwards of 50,000 men Cæsar's, of less than half that number; yet the troops of the latter were far the best disciplined. On the side of Pompey, there was the most confident expectation of success; the minds of all being less occupied about the means of conquering, than about distributing the fruits of victory. The engagement, which lasted from early in the morning till noon, terminated in a decisive victory in favor of Cæsar, who lost only 200 men, while the loss of Pompey amounted to 15,000 killed, and 24,000 prisoners.

13. Cæsar, on this occasion, manifested his characteristic clemency, and the honors which he had acquired as victor were soon rendered more glorious by his humanity and moderation. He set at liberty the senators and Roman knights, and incorporated with the rest of his army the most of the prisoners. The baggage of Pompey was brought to him, containing numerous letters of his enemies; these he threw into the fire without opening them. When viewing the field strewn with his fallen countrymen, he seemed affected at the melancholy sight, and exclaimed, as if by way of justification, — "They would have it so!"

14. The fate of Pompey was wretched in the extreme. Accustomed to victory for 30 years, and master of the republic, he was in one day deprived of his power, and became a miserable fugitive. Taking with him his wife *Cornelia*, he fled with very few attendants to Egypt, to seek protection of Ptolemy, whose father he had befriended. But he was basely murdered in the presence of his wife, and his body thrown upon the sand. His freed man burnt his corpse, and buried the ashes, over which the following inscription was afterwards placed: — "He, whose merits deserve a temple, can now scarcely find a grave." In the mean time, Cæsar had instantly followed Pompey into Egypt, and the head of his rival, which had been preserved, was presented to him; but he turned his face from it with horror, shedding tears on remembering their former friendship, and he ordered a splendid monument to be erected to his memory.

15. The throne of Egypt was now possessed by *Ptolemy* and his sister, the celebrated *Cleopa'tra*. The latter aspired to undivided authority, and Cæsar, captivated by the charms of the beautiful queen, decided the contest in her favor. A war ensued, in which Ptolemy was killed, and Egypt subdued by the Roman arms. Cæsar for a while abandoned himself to pleasure, in the company of Cleopatra, but was at length called away to suppress a revolt of *Pharnaces*, the son of Mithrida'tes, who had seized upon Colchis and Armenia

Cæsar subdued him with great ease, in a battle at *Zela* and in his letter to Rome, he expressed the rapidity of his conquest in three words: *Veni, vidi, Vici;* "I came, I saw, I conquered."

16. Cæsar now hastened to Rome, which he found in a state of great disorder, by reason of the bad government of *Mark Antony*, but he soon restored tranquillity. Pompey's party had rallied their forces in Africa, under the command of *Cato* and *Scipio*, assisted by *Juba*, king of Maurita'nia. Cæsar pursued them thither, and gained a complete victory in the battle of *Thapsus*. *Cato*, who was a rigid Stoic and a stern republican, shut himself up in *Utica*, where he meditated a brave resistance; but, perceiving all was lost, he killed himself in despair.

17. The war in Africa being thus ended, Cæsar returned again to Rome, and celebrated a most magnificent triumph, which lasted four days: the first was for Gaul; the second for Egypt; the third for his victories in Asia; and the fourth for his victory over Juba. He distributed liberally rewards to his veteran soldiers and officers, and to the citizens; he treated the people with combats of elephants, and engagements between parties of cavalry and infantry; and he entertained them at a public feast, at which 20,000 couches were placed for the guests. The multitude, intoxicated by these allurements of pleasure, cheerfully yielded up their liberties to their great enslaver. The senate and people vied with each other in acts of servility and adulation. He was hailed *father of his country*, was created perpetual dictator, received the title of *imperator* or *emperor*, and his person was declared sacred.

18. After having settled affairs at Rome, he found himself obliged to go again into Spain, where *Labie'nus* and the two sons of Pompey had raised an army against him; but he completely defeated them in the obstinate and bloody battle of *Munda*, which decided the fate of the adherents of his rival

19. Having now acquired, by the force of his arms, the whole Roman empire, and subdued all who opposed his usurpation, Cæsar returned to Rome the master of the world. But no usurper ever used his power with greater wisdom and moderation. "I will not," he said, in one of his speeches, "renew the massacres of Sylla and Marius, the very remembrance of which is shocking to me. Now that my enemies are subdued, I will lay aside the sword, and endeavor, solely by my good offices, to gain over those who continue to hate me." He pardoned all who had carried arms against him, made no distinction with regard to parties, devoted himself to the pros

perity and happiness of the people, corrected abuses, extended his care to the most distant provinces, reformed the calendar, undertook to drain the Pontine marshes, to improve the navigation of the Tiber, and to embellish the city; and he conceived many noble projects which he was not destined to realize.

20. Though Cæsar had repeatedly refused the crown when offered, by Mark Antony, to his acceptance, yet a rumor was widely circulated that he aspired to the name of an office of which he enjoyed all the splendid realities; and the fresh honors which the senate continued to heap upon him were calculated to excite the envy and jealousy of a body of men who conspired against his life: nor could he, by his clemency and munificence, obliterate from the minds of the people the remembrance of their former constitution, or of the manner in which he had obtained his power. The conspiracy which was now formed against him embraced no less than 60 senators; and at the head of it were *Brutus* and *Cassius*, men whose lives had been spared by the conqueror after the battle of Pharsalia. The former, who was beloved by Cæsar, and had received from him numerous favors, was actuated by hatred, not of the tyrant, but of tyranny, and sought the equivocal reputation of sacrificing all the ties of friendship and gratitude to the love of liberty and of his country. The latter thirsted for revenge against an envied and hated superior.

21. The rumor that the crown was to be conferred upon the dictator on the ides [15th] of March, induced the conspirators to fix upon that day for the execution of their designs; and no sooner had Cæsar taken his seat in the senate-house, than he was assailed by their daggers. He defended himself for a while with vigor, till, on a sudden, seeing Brutus among the assailants, and being astonished at the desertion of his friend, he uttered the celebrated exclamation, *Et tu Brute!* "And you, too, Brutus!" when, muffling up his face with his mantle, he resigned himself to his fate, and fell pierced with 23 wounds. Thus perished *Julius Cæsar*, in the 56th year of his age, 14 years after he commenced his career of conquest in Gaul, and after having been only about five months in the undisputed possession of that power, which it had been the object of his life to obtain.

22. Cæsar was one of the most extraordinary men that have appeared in history, uniting the threefold character of the historian, the warrior, and the statesman. Although, as the subverter of the liberties of his country, he deserves only to be detested, yet he is not without claims to admiration; for, together with his unbounded ambition he possessed the most

splendid endowments of genius, and many noble qualities of the heart; and the world has scarcely seen a more able or a more amiable despot.

23. His career was indeed bloody, involving in destruction vast numbers of his species; yet he had no tendency to cruelty, except so far as it was necessary to effect his ambitious designs, nor any thirst for blood; and he was always distinguished for his clemency to a vanquished enemy. It has been said, by way of apology for him, that it was his misfortune to be born in a degenerate age: it was, however, the age in which flourished *Cicero*, *Cato*, and *Brutus*, who are ranked among the most illustrious of the Roman patriots.

24. In passing a small village among the Alps on his way to take upon himself the government of Spain, before the formation of the triumvirate, he remarked, that "he would rather be the first man in that village, than the second man in Rome." He had frequently in his mouth a verse of Eurip'ides, which expresses the image of his soul: "That if right and justice were ever to be violated, they were to be violated for the sake of reigning."

25. In his military character, he has probably never been surpassed. He was so much the idol of his troops, that in any important conjuncture, his lieutenant could say nothing more impressive to them than, "Soldiers, imagine that Cæsar beholds you!" Alexander was an heir to the throne, and carried into execution the splendid conquest which his father had projected, overrunning nations sunk in luxury and effeminacy. Cæsar, originally a private individual, appears as the framer of his own fortune, gradually rising, by well-concerted plans, to the summit of power, pursuing an uninterrupted career of victory, and finally conquering the conquerors of the world.

26. "We are now contemplating that man," says Müller, "who, within the short space of 14 years, subdued Gaul, thickly inhabited by warlike nations; twice conquered Spain; entered Germany and Britain; marched through Italy at the head of a victorious army; destroyed the power of Pompey the Great: reduced Egypt to obedience; saw and defeated Pharnaces; overpowered, in Africa, the great name of Cato and the arms of Juba; fought 50 battles, in which 1,192,000 men fell: was the greatest orator in the world, next to Cicero; set a pattern to all historians, which has never been excelled; wrote learnedly on the sciences of grammar and augury, and, falling by a premature death, left memorials of his great plans for the extension of the empire, and the legislation of the world So true it is, that it is not time that is wanting to men, but resolution to turn it to the best advantage."

27. The Roman people were struck with horror at the murder of Cæsar. Although he was a usurper, and had made himself master of their lives and fortunes, yet he was generally popular. His bleeding body was exposed in the forum; and over it Mark Antony, unfolding the bloody robe, pronounced a funeral oration; and by many eloquent appeals to the sympathy of the people, he so inflamed their feelings against his murderers, that they were obliged to escape forthwith from the city in order to avoid destruction.

28. *Mark Antony*, a man of great military talents, but of most profligate character, *Lep'idus*, who was possessed of immense riches, and *Octa'vius*, or *Octavia'nus Cæsar*, afterwards surnamed *Augustus*, (the adopted heir of Cæsar, and his sister's grandson, now only in his 18th year,) concerted a plan to divide among themselves the supreme authority, and formed the *Second Triumvirate*, the effects of whose union were, beyond measure, dreadful to the republic.

29. They stipulated that all their enemies should be destroyed, and each sacrificed his best friends to the vengeance of his associates. Antony consigned to death his uncle Lu'cius; Lepidus, his brother Paulus; and Octavius gave up the celebrated *Cicero*, to whom he was under many obligations, in order to gratify the hatred of Antony. The great orator was assassinated in his 64th year, by Popillius Lænas, whose life he had saved in a capital cause. Antony caused his head to be fixed upon the rostra, a spectacle which drew tears from all virtuous citizens. Rome was again deluged in blood: in this horrible proscription, 300 senators, 2,000 knights, and many other respectable citizens, were sacrificed.

30. *Brutus* and *Cassius*, whose object it was to restore the commonwealth, had retired to Thrace, and were at the head of an army of 100,000 men. Antony and Octavius pursued them with a still greater number of troops. The empire of the world again depended on the fate of a battle. The two armies met near *Philippi*, and, after a dreadful conflict of two days, the death-blow was given to Roman liberty, by the total defeat of the republican army. Brutus and Cassius, agreeably to a resolution which they had made before the battle, escaped the vengeance of their enemies by a voluntary death.

31. The triumvirs did not long live in harmony. Lep'idus was deposed and banished Antony having summoned Cleopa'tra to Tarsus, to answer to the charge of having given succor to the conspirators, she came decked in all the emblems of the queen of love, in a galley decorated in the most splendid style, and had the address to make a complete conquest of him. He forgot to decide upon her cause, gave up the pursuit

8

of ambition, neglected all his affairs, and abandoned himself to licentious pleasure with the Egyptian queen. He lavished on her the provinces of the empire, for which he was declared an enemy to the Roman people; and on her account he divorced his wife *Octavia*, the sister of his colleague, which was a signal for open hostilities between him and Octavius.

32. A great naval battle, fought near *Ac'tium*, decided the contest against Antony and Cleopatra, and left Octavius sole master of the empire. Antony, following the example of many celebrated Romans, fell upon his own sword; and Cleopatra in order to avoid being led captive to Rome, to grace the triumph of Augustus, procured her own death by the poison of an asp.

SECTION VIII.

Rome under the Emperors: *The Cæsars; Augustus, Tiberius, Caligula, Claudius, Nero, Galba, Otho, Vitellius Vespasian, Titus, and Domitian.— From B. C.* 31 *to A D.* 96.

1. The battle of Actium terminated the commonwealth and *Octavius*, now named *Augustus*, being the undisputed sovereign of the whole Roman empire, had attained the object of his wishes. But, though ambitious of power, he was, nevertheless, aware of its dangers; and he consulted his friends, *Agrippa* and *Mæce'nas*, respecting the course which it was advisable for him to pursue. Agrippa entreated him to restore liberty to his country; but Mæcenas represented to him the danger of renouncing his authority, advised him to govern others as he would wish to be governed if it had been his destiny to obey, and suggested to him that under the title of *Cæsar* or *Imperator*, he might enjoy all the influence of a king, without offending the prejudices of his countrymen.

2. Augustus gave the preference to the advice of Mæcenas, as it best agreed with his natural love of power. He affected an appearance of great moderation and respect for the public rights, paid particular attention to the people, and having completely gained their affections, he used every means to render permanent the attachment which already existed between him and his soldiers. It was his policy to change the nature, rather than the form of the government, and he had the address to rule as emperor, and yet preserve the appearance of a republic.

3. The reputation of Augustus, not only as a warrior, but

as a legislator and statesman, extended to the remotest kingdoms. After having arrived at sovereign power, he engaged in some successful military enterprises; but the general character of his reign was pacific: he cherished the arts of peace, embellished the city, erected public edifices, pursued the policy of maintaining order and tranquillity throughout his vast empire, and the temple of Janus was now shut for the first time since the commencement of the second Punic war, and only the third time from the foundation of the city.

4. Augustus died in the 76th year of his age, after an illustrious reign of 44 years. His talents were unquestionably great; but the many instances of treachery and cruelty by which his conduct was marked, while a member of the triumvirate, have left a stain upon his character, and have caused it to be generally believed, that the virtues which he afterwards manifested, sprung from policy, rather than principle.

5. The emperor and his minister Mæcenas were both eminent patrons of learning and the arts; and the *Augustan age* of Roman literature has been celebrated by the admiration of all succeeding ages. Some of the distinguished men who illustrated this reign were *Virgil*, *Horace*, *Ovid*, and *Livy*.

6.—The reign of Augustus was rendered memorable by the birth of our *Lord and Savior Jesus Christ*, which took place, according to the best authorities, in the 26th year of his reign, and four years before the period commonly assigned for the *Christian era*. In the 18th year of Tiberius, our Savior suffered death upon the cross.—

7. Augustus was succeeded by *Tibe'rius*, who was the son of his wife *Liv'ia*, by a former husband, and who had distinguished himself by his military talents. The new emperor commenced his reign by a show of moderation and clemency; but he soon threw off the mask, and appeared in his real character, as an odious and cruel tyrant. The specious form of the republic, which Augustus had continued, now disappeared, as well as the substance.

8. The brilliant successes of his nephew *German'icus*, in Germany, who had for his antagonist the celebrated German general *Armin'ius*, and the high favor with which he was regarded by the people, excited the jealousy of Tiberius, who is supposed to have caused him to be poisoned. He then took into his confidence *Seja'nus*, a Roman knight, who became the minister of the tyranny, rapine, and cruelty, which characterized his reign, and who persuaded him to quit Rome, and retire to the island of *Ca'preæ*, where he abandoned himself to the most infamous debaucheries. Sejanus was now in possession of almost unlimited power, and after a short career

of despotism, he was accused of treason, suddenly precipitated from his elevation, executed by the order of the senate, and his body ignominiously dragged through the streets. A few years afterwards, the death of Tiberius was hastened by strangling or poison, by one of his favorites, in the 78th year of his age, and the 22d of his reign.

9. Tiberius adopted for his heir and successor *Calig'ula*, his grand-nephew and the son of Germanicus, who commenced his reign under favorable auspices, and his first acts were beneficent and patriotic ; but his subsequent conduct was so marked by profligacy, tyranny, madness, and folly, as to give countenance to the assertion that a disorder, which took place after his accession to power, had destroyed his understanding and altered his nature. He became almost as much the object of the contempt, as of the hatred, of his subjects. He caused temples to be built, and sacrifices to be offered to himself as a divinity. He took such delight in cruelty, that he wished "that all the Roman people had but one neck, that he might despatch them at a single blow." Seneca says of him, that "nature seemed to have brought him forth to show what was possible to be produced from the greatest vice, supported by the greatest authority." He was assassinated in the 4th year of his reign, and the 29th of his age.

10. After the death of Caligula, the senate were inclined to restore the republic ; but, in the general corruption of morals, which, since the early part of the reign of Tiberius, had surpassed all former example, and extended to all classes of the people, the spirit of Roman liberty had disappeared. The army preferred an emperor, and *Claudius*, the uncle of Caligula, and the grandson of Mark Antony and Octa'via, the sister of Augustus, was raised to the throne. He was a man of weak and timid character, a dupe even of his domestics, and a slave of his infamous vices.

11. The most remarkable enterprise in the reign of Claudius was his expedition into Britain, and the conquest of a part of that island by his generals. *Carac'tacus*, a British king, after a brave resistance, was taken prisoner, and carried captive to Rome, where his magnanimity gained him admiration. On being led through the streets, and observing the splendor around him, he exclaimed, "How is it possible, that men, possessed of such magnificence at home, should envy Caractacus an humble cottage in Britain ?"

12. Claudius had five wives, of whom the fourth was *Messali'na*, whose very name is a proverbial reproach, and who, having abandoned herself to the most shameful profligacy, was put to death for her crimes. The emperor then married

Agrippi'na, who was equally practised in vice, and who poisoned him in the 14th year of his reign, and the 64th of his age, in order to make way for *Nero*, her son by a former husband.

13. *Nero* had enjoyed the advantage of a good education under the philosopher *Sen'eca*, and at the commencement of his reign, he pursued an excellent plan of government, which was laid down by Seneca and Burrhus, (the latter of whom was prefect of the pretorian guard,) and which held out the prospect of better times; but he soon got rid of his counsellors, abandoned himself to rioting and licentiousness, gained a notoriety for profligacy and cruelty above that of even all his predecessors, and rendered his name proverbial, in all succeeding ages, as a detestable tyrant. Among the numerous victims, who suffered death by his cruelty, were his mother *Agrippi'na*, his wives *Octa'via* and *Poppæ'a*, *Seneca* and *Burrhus*, also *Lucan*, the poet.

14. He is charged with having caused the city of Rome to be set on fire, in mere wantonness, that it might exhibit the representation of the burning of Troy; and he stood upon a high tower that he might enjoy the scene. The conflagration continued eight or nine days, and a great part of the city was burnt to ashes. In order to avert from himself the public odium of the crime, he charged it upon the *Christians*, who had now become numerous in Rome, and commenced against them a most dreadful persecution, in which *St. Paul* was beheaded.

15. Nero, who rendered himself no less contemptible by his follies and extravagances than hateful by his crimes, was too odious a monster to be long endured. A conspiracy, headed by *Vindex* in Gaul, and *Galba* in Spain, hurled him, at length, from the throne. Galba, in a speech, recapitulating his crimes, said: "What enormity has been too great for him? Is he not stained with the blood of his father, his mother, his wife, his preceptors, of all those who, in the senate, the city, or the provinces, were distinguished by birth, riches, courage, or virtue? The blood of these innocent victims cries for vengeance and since we are possessed of arms, and of power of using them, let us disdain to obey, not a prince, but an incendiary, a parricide, a singer, and an actor." The senate having passed sentence against him, he avoided falling into their hands by a voluntary death, in the 14th year of his reign, and the 32d of his age.

16. After the death of Nero, *Galba* was declared emperor both by the senate and by the legions under his command. He was esteemed a man of courage, talents, and virtue, and

had acquired a high reputation in the command of armies in the provinces; but he was now in the 72d year of his age, and he soon became unpopular by his severity and parsimony, and by the abuses practised by his favorites. He adopted for his successor the virtuous *Piso*, a measure which gave offence to *Otho*, his former favorite, who excited a rebellion against him, and caused the death both of the emperor and of Piso, after a reign of only seven months. Tacitus says of him, that, "Had he never ascended the throne, he would have been thought, by all, capable of reigning."

17. *Otho* was then proclaimed emperor; but he found a formidable rival in *Vitel'lius*, by whose lieutenants he was defeated, and he slew himself after a reign of 95 days. *Vitellius*, being saluted as emperor, is said to have proposed Nero for his model, and rendered himself odious to the people by his tyranny and profligacy. *Vespa'sian*, who was now at the head of the Roman army in Egypt, was proclaimed emperor by his troops; Rome was taken by one of his generals, and Vitellius was assassinated before he had completed the first year of his reign.

18. *Vespa'sian* was declared emperor by the unanimous consent of the senate and the army; and on his arrival at Rome he was received with the greatest joy. He had risen by his merit from a mean origin; was distinguished for his affability, clemency, and firmness; and he reigned with high popularity for ten years, promoting the welfare of his subjects. He restored order, built the celebrated amphitheatre or Coliseum, whose ruins still attest its grandeur, cherished the arts, and patronized learned men, among whom were *Josephus*, the Jewish historian, *Quintilian*, the orator, and *Pliny*, the naturalist.

19. The reign of Vespasian is memorable for the destruction of *Jerusalem*, which was effected by his son *Titus*, after a tremendous siege of six months, the city being taken and razed to the ground so that, according to the prediction of our Savior, "not one stone remained upon another." The number that perished in this siege, according to Josephus, amounted to upwards of a million, and the captives to almost a hundred thousand. The wretched survivors were banished, sold, and driven into various parts of the world, and have continued to this time a dispersed, yet a distinct people, and a monument of the truth of Revelation.

20. Vespasian was succeeded by his son *Titus*, who exhibited such an example of justice, humanity, and generosity, that he obtained the enviable appellation of the "*Delight of mankind*." Recollecting, one evening, that he had done no

beneficent act during that day, he made the celebrated exclamation, "My friends, I have lost a day!" During his reign happened that dreadful erŭption of *Vesu'vius*, which overwhelmed the cities of *Hercula'neum* and *Pompe'ii*, and caused the death of *Pliny*, the naturalist. Titus died in the 3d year of his reign, and the 41st of his age, not without suspicion of being poisoned by his brother *Domi'tian*, who succeeded him

21. *Domitian* was another monster of profligacy and cruelty. He caused himself to be worshipped as a god; put to death the most illustrious Romans, and took pleasure in witnessing the torture of his victims. He banished the philosophers from Rome, and raised a dreadful persecution against the Christians. When secluded from the world, he passed his time in vicious and degrading amusements. He was so much in the habit of catching flies, and piercing them through with a bodkin, that one of his servants, being asked if any one was with the emperor, answered, "Not even a fly."

22. After a reign of 15 years, Domitian was assassinated at the instigation of his wife, who had discovered that he had put her name on the list of those whom he designed to destroy. This reign was signalized by the successes of the Romans in Britain, under the command of *Agric'ola*, a great general, who had been sent into that country by Vespasian, and who made an entire conquest of all the southern part of the island.

23. Domitian was the last of those emperors who are called the *Twelve Cæsars*, *Julius Cæsar*, the dictator, being considered the first; though *Augustus* was the first that is generally styled *emperor*, and *Nero* was, in reality, the last emperor of the family of Augustus.

SECTION IX.

Nerva: Trajan: Adrian: Antoninus Pius: Marcus Aurelius Antoninus. — *From A. D.* 96 *to* 180.

1 After the death of Domitian, the senate elected for his successor *Nerva*, who was 65 years old, and venerable for his virtues, as well as for his age. He was distinguished for clemency, but did not possess energy sufficient to repress the disorders of the empire. Having adopted *Trajan* for his successor, he died after a reign of 16 months.

2. *Trajan*, who was a native of Seville, in Spain, is esteemed the greatest and most powerful, and one of the most virtuous of the Roman emperors. He has been highly commended

for his affability, his simplicity of manners, his clemency, and munificence. He was the greatest general of his age, possessed an ardent spirit of enterprise, accustomed himself to hardship, and, even after he ascended the throne, marched on foot, at the head of his troops, over extensive regions. On presenting the sword to the pretorian prefect, he gave this remarkable charge: "Make use of it *for* me, if I do my duty; if I do not, *against* me." The senate conferred on him the surname of *Optimus*, or *Best;* and for more than 200 years that body was accustomed to hail every new emperor with the exclamation, "Reign fortunately, as Augustus; virtuously, as Trajan."

3. During the reign of Trajan, the boundaries of the empire were more extensive than either before or afterwards. He subdued the *Dacians*, conquered the *Parthians*, and brought under subjection *Assyria*, *Mesopotamia*, and *Arabia Felix.* In commemoration of his victories over the Dacians, he erected a *pillar*, which bears his name, and which still remains in Rome, one of the most remarkable ancient monuments in the city.

4. He was a munificent patron of literature, and in his reign flourished *Pliny the Younger*, *Juvenal*, and *Plutarch.* He died, greatly lamented by his subjects, in the 20th year of his reign, and the 63d of his age. The character of this great prince was tarnished by a want of equity with regard to the *Christians*, whom he suffered to be persecuted.

5. Trajan was succeeded by *A'drian*, his nephew, who was an able sovereign, generally beneficent and equitable in his government; distinguished also for his eloquence and his taste in the liberal arts; but he was, nevertheless, chargeable with cruelty and licentiousness. Judging the limits of the empire too extensive, he abandoned the conquests of Trajan, declined war, devoted himself to the arts of peace, and promoted the welfare of his subjects. He undertook to visit, in person, all the provinces of the empire, in which expedition he spent 13 years. In his progress, he reformed abuses, relieved his subjects from burdens, and rebuilt cities. While in *Britain* he erected a turf wall or rampart across the island, from *Carlisle* to *Newcastle*, in order to prevent the incursions of the *Picts.*

6. He rebuilt *Jerusalem*, and changed its name to *Æ'lia Capitoli'na.* The *Jews*, incensed at the privileges which the pagan worshippers enjoyed in the new city, made a great slaughter of the Romans and Christians residing in Judea: in consequence of which, the emperor sent against them a powerful army, which destroyed upwards of 1,000 of their best towns, and slew nearly 600,000 men. Adrian adopted for his

successor *Titus Antoni'nus*, and died in the 22d year of his reign, and the 62d of his age.

7. *Titus Antoninus*, more commonly called *Antoninus Pius*, had a reign of 23 years, which was marked by few striking events; but it will ever be distinguished in the Roman annals for the public and private virtues which exalted his character. It was his favorite maxim, that "he would rather save the life of one citizen, than to put to death a thousand enemies."

8. This excellent sovereign adopted for his successor his son-in-law, *Marcus Aure'lius Antoni'nus*, surnamed the *Philosopher*. He is esteemed the best model of pagan virtue among the Roman emperors; and "appeared," says an ancient author, "like some benevolent deity, diffusing around him universal peace and happiness." He was attached, both by nature and education, to the Stoic philosophy, which he admirably exemplified in his life, as well as illustrated in his work, entitled "*Meditations.*"

9. Distinguished as the two Antonines were for justice and humanity, yet the persecution of the Christians was permitted, in some degree, during their reigns. It was to the former of the two that *Justin Martyr* presented his first "*Apology for Christianity*"; and the Roman army under the latter experienced, by means of a thunder-storm, a remarkable deliverance, which has been represented by many as miraculous, and which gave to a legion of Christians, then serving under Aurelius, the name of the *Thundering Legion.* — The name of the wife of each of these emperors was *Fausti'na*, and both of them were noted as women of the most abandoned character.

10. Aurelius died in the 19th year of his reign, and the 59th of his age. He was the last of the sovereigns styled 'The five good emperors"; and the glory and prosperity of the Roman people seemed to perish with him. From this time, we behold a succession of sovereigns, who, with few exceptions, were either weak or vicious; an empire grown too large, sinking by its own weight, surrounded by barbarous and successful enemies without, and torn by ambitious and cruel factions within; the principles of the times wholly corrupted and patriotism, virtue, and literature gradually becoming almost extinct.

SECTION X

From Commodus to Constantine. — *From A. D.* 180 *to* 306.

1. Aurelius was succeeded by his most unworthy son *Com'-modus*, who resembled his mother *Fausti'na*, and equalled even Nero in profligacy and cruelty. He was assassinated in the 13th year of his reign, and the 32d of his age; and *Per'tinax* a man of mean birth, who had risen by his merit, and who, from the various conditions through which he passed, was styled "the tennis-ball of fortune," was proclaimed his successor by the pretorian guards. But the new emperor, giving offence by his severity in correcting abuses, was, after a reign of three months, put to death by the same hands that had placed him on the throne.

2. The empire was now put up to sale by the soldiers, and was purchased by *Did'ius Julia'nus*, who was murdered in the fifth month of his reign, by order of *Septim'ius Seve'rus*, who was proclaimed emperor in his stead. He had two competitors for the empire, *Niger* and *Albi'nus*, both of whom were entirely defeated. Severus was an able warrior, and governed with ability, yet with despotic rigor. He made an expedition into Britain, and built a stone wall extending from Solway frith to the German ocean, and nearly parallel to that of Adrian. He died at York, in the 18th year of his reign.

3. Seve'rus left the empire to his two sons, *Caracal'la* and *Geta*, the former of whom murdered the latter; and after a tyrannical reign of six years, he was himself assassinated at the instigation of *Macri'nus*, who succeeded to the throne, and who, after a reign of 14 months, was supplanted by *Heliogab'-alus*, who caused him to be put to death.

4. *Heliogab'alus* succeeded to the throne when only 14 years old; yet, at this early age, he showed himself to be a monster of vice, equalling the worst of his predecessors in extravagance, profligacy, and cruelty. He was murdered in the 4th year of his reign; yet, in this short period, he had exhausted all the resources of pleasure, and had married and divorced six wives.

5. Heliogabalus was succeeded by his cousin, *Alexander Seve'rus*, a mild, beneficent, and enlightened prince, whose excellent character shines the brighter from the contrast of those who preceded and followed him. He was murdered in the 14th year of his reign, and the 29th of his age, at the instigation of *Max'imin*, the son of a herdsman of Thrace, and a Goth by nation, who succeeded to the throne, and who was

nearly eight feet and a half in height, and not less remarkable for the symmetry of his person, and his extraordinary strength, than his gigantic stature; and was also distinguished for his military talents.

6. The interval from the time of *Alexander Seve'rus* to that of *Diocle'tian* was filled by 16 reigns; those of Max'imin, Max'imus and Balbi'nus, Gor'dian, Philip, De'cius, Gal'lus, Æmilia'nus, Vale'rian, Gallie'nus, Clau'dius, Aure'lian, Tac'itus, Flo'rian, Probus, Carus, Cari'nus, and Nume'rian; a period of 49 years, which furnishes little that is pleasing or interesting. The short reigns of most of these emperors were alike disastrous to themselves and their subjects; and all of them except Claudius and Tacitus, were cut off by a violent death.

7. The emperor *Vale'rian*, in a war with *Sapor*, king of Persia, was defeated and taken prisoner. Sapor treated his captive with the greatest indignity and cruelty: he used him as a footstool in mounting his horse; afterwards ordered his eyes to be plucked out, and finally caused him to be flayed alive.

8. The reign of *Aure'lian*, which lasted only five years, was noted for military achievements. He was distinguished for great talents, as well as great severity, as a general; and for courage and promptitude, has been compared with Julius Cæsar. He defeated the *Goths* and *Germans*, who had begun to harass the Romans; but his most renowned victory was that over *Zeno'bia*, the famous queen of *Palmy'ra*, who was taken captive; and her secretary *Longi'nus*, the celebrated critic, was slain, by order of the conqueror. On his return to Rome, Aurelian was honored with one of the most splendid triumphs ever witnessed in that city. Zenobia was reserved to grace this grand show, bound in chains of gold, and overloaded with a profusion of pearls and diamonds.

9. *Diocle'tian*, who was the son of a Dalmatian slave, rose by his merit from the rank of a common soldier to that of a great commander, and, on the death of Cari'nus and Nume'rian, was acknowledged emperor. He began his reign in 284, and two years afterwards associated with himself in the government his friend *Maxim'ian;* and in 292, they took two other colleagues, *Gale'rius* and *Constan'tius*, each bearing the title of *Cæsar*. The empire was now divided into four parts, under the government of *two emperors* and *two Cæsars*, each being nominally supreme; but, in reality, under the direction of the superior talents of Diocletian.

10. In this reign happened the 10th and last great persecution against the Christians, which raged for several years. It

was more bloody than any that had preceded it, and was so nearly fatal, that the tyrants boasted that they had extinguished the Christian name.

11. Diocletian, in the latter part of his reign, experienced a series of calamities, and he and his colleague Maxim'ian, resigned the government into the hands of the two Cæsars. He then retired to his native country, Dalmatia, and built a magnificent palace near the town of Salo'na, where he lived eight or nine years, and amused himself in cultivating his garden. He declared that he here enjoyed more happiness than when adorned with the imperial purple; and was often heard to exclaim, "Now it is that I live; now I see the beauty of the sun!"

SECTION XI.

From the Accession of Constantine to the Extinction of the Western Empire. — From A. D. 306 *to* 476.

1. Constantius died at York, in Britain, having appointed his son *Constantine*, his successor; Galerius also died four years after; and *Constantine*, surnamed the *Great*, having defeated all his competitors, became sole master of the empire. One of the principal competitors for the crown was *Maxen'tius;* and historians relate that when Constantine was marching at the head of his army against this rival, he beheld in the heavens a luminous cross, with an inscription in Greek, τουτῳ νικα, "*Conquer by this*"; and that, in consequence of this vision and of the success which attended his arms, he embraced Christianity.

2. But whatever may have been the circumstance which first attracted the favorable notice of Constantine, he became the avowed friend and supporter of Christianity, and has the honor of being enrolled as the first *Christian emperor.* He put an end to the persecution of the Christians, and also to the combats of gladiators, and other barbarous exhibitions. His reign forms an important era in ecclesiastical history, as the Roman government now became the professed protector of the religion which it had repeatedly and cruelly persecuted

3. An important event in the reign of Constantine, was the removal of the seat of empire from *Rome* to *Byzan'tium*, which latter city, from him, took the name of *Constantinople.* The empire had long been verging to ruin, and this measure is thought to have hastened its downfall. Constantine died in the 31st year of his reign, and the 63d of his age. His

character has been variously represented by different writers. "It is manifest," says Müller, "that the genius of Constantine, fertile, if not happy, at least in specious ideas, gave a new direction to the course of human affairs He maintained peace by the reputation of his arms, and his name, alternately too much exalted and unjustly degraded by prejudiced historians, deserves an honorable mention among the monarchs of the Roman world."

4. Constantine divided the empire between his three sons, *Con'stantine II. Con'stans* and *Constan'tius II.*, and two nephews. In the space of a few years, all these princes were slain, except *Constantius*, the youngest of the sons, who remained sole master of the empire. He had a weak and unfortunate reign of 24 years, during which the empire was harassed and weakened by the inroads of the barbarians from the north, and the incursions of the Persians on the eastern provinces.

5. Constantius was succeeded by his cousin *Julian*, surnamed the *Apostate*, because, after having received a Christian education, he relapsed into paganism. He was possessed of considerable talents and learning, and of many heroic qualities; but was the slave of the most bigoted superstition. He restored the pagan worship, and attempted to suppress Christianity. He undertook to reassemble the Jews, and rebuild their temple; but his design is stated, by a number of ancient writers, to have been miraculously defeated by the eruption of fire-balls from the ground. Julian was killed in a war with the Persians, in the second year of his reign, and the 32d of his age.

6. Julian was succeeded by *Jo'vian*, who restored the Christian religion, and recalled *Athanasius*, who had been banished by Julian; but he died after a short reign of seven months. *Valentin'ian*, who was then chosen emperor, associated with himself his brother *Valens*, giving him the eastern provinces, which occasioned the final separation of the empire into Eastern and Western. The barbarians continued to make inroads into different parts of the empire, and the *Goths* now obtained a settlement in Thrace.

7. The successor of Valentinian was his son *Gra'tian*, who, on the death of Valens, associated with himself *Theodo'sius*, afterwards surnamed the *Great*. After the death of *Gratian*, and his brother *Valentinian II.*, *Theodosius* became sole master of the empire. His reign was signalized by the complete establishment of Christianity, and the downfall of paganism in the Roman dominions. Being an able and politic sovereign, he repelled the encroachments of the barbarians, and by his

wise administration, strengthened, in some measure, the empire, which had, for a considerable time, been hastening to its fall. He was the last sovereign who presided over both divisions of the empire; and, after a reign of 16 years, he was succeeded by his sons, *Hono'rius* in the *West*, and *Arca'dius* in the *East*.

8. Through the weakness of Honorius and Arcadius, the barbarians were enabled to establish and strengthen themselves in their territories. The *Goths*, under the conduct of the famous *Al'aric*, spread their devastations to the very walls of Constantinople, and filled all Greece with the terror of their arms Alaric then penetrated into Italy, at the head of a large army but he was defeated with great loss by the Romans, under *Stil'icho.* After the death of Stilicho, Alaric invaded the country a second time, and being joined by 300,000 auxiliaries, he took and pillaged several cities of Italy, and at length pitched his camp before the walls of Rome. This great city, which had long sat as mistress of the world, and had for ages enriched herself with the spoils of vanquished nations, was now reduced to the greatest extremities by famine and pestilence.

9. After the famine had made the most dreadful ravages, Alaric entered Rome, deprived Honorius of the imperial dignity, and gave up the city to be plundered by his soldiers. "All the riches of the world," said Alaric in addressing his army, "are here concentrated: to you I abandon them: but I command you to spill the blood of none but those whom you find in arms; and to spare such as take refuge in the churches." The fearful devastation continued for six days, during which, these fierce barbarians indulged their cruelty and ferocity without pity or restraint.

10. Alaric died immediately after this conquest; and the Goths, having elected in his stead *Ataul'phus*, for their leader, took possession of the southern part of Gaul, and likewise passed over the mountains, and founded their kingdom in Spain.

11. A few years after the sacking of Rome by Alaric, commenced the sanguinary ravages of the *Huns*, a barbarous people of Scythian origin, under the command of their ferocious king *At'tila*, styled the *Scourge of God*. Having ravaged the Eastern Empire, he invaded Gaul with an army of 500,000 men; and, on the plains of *Chalons*, was defeated by the combined forces of the *Romans*, under *Æ'tius* (who is styled by Gibbon "the last of the Romans"), and the *Goths*, under *Theod'oric*, with a loss, according to the lowest accounts, of 160,000 men. Notwithstanding this defeat he

soon after invaded Italy, extended his ravages to the gates of Rome, and compelled *Valentinian III.* to purchase a peace by an immense dowry to be given to him with the emperor's sister *Hono'ria.* But the death of Attila soon followed, and by this event the earth was delivered from a warrior who had never suffered Europe to enjoy any repose, and who had never enjoyed any himself.

12. Valentinian III. being assassinated at the instigation of *Petro'nius Max'imus*, who was saluted emperor, the empress *Eudox'ia* invited *Gen'seric*, king of the *Vandals*, to take vengeance on the murderer of her husband. He eagerly embraced the opportunity of disguising his rapacious designs landed in Italy with a numerous army of *Moors* and *Vandals* took the city of Rome, and gave it up to his soldiers to be pillaged, with implacable fury, for 11 days ; during which those monuments of art and literature, which Alaric had spared, were ransacked and destroyed.

13. From the death of Valentinian III., the Western Empire dragged on a precarious and lingering existence, under nine successive emperors, for 21 years, till it was finally terminated, in 476, by the resignation of the last emperor, *Rom'ulus Augus'tulus*, to *Odoa'cer*, the chief of the *Her'uli*, who assumed the title of *king of Italy ;* and from this period the history of Rome merges into that of Italy.

14. " Such was the end of this great empire, that had conquered the world with its arms, and instructed mankind with its wisdom ; that had risen by temperance, and that fell by luxury ; that had been established by a spirit of patriotism, and that sunk into ruin when the empire had become so extensive that the title of a Roman citizen was but an empty name."

SECTION XII.

The Kingdom of the Heruli, of the Goths, and of the Lombards in Italy. — The Eastern Empire, to its Extinction in 1453.

1. The kingdom of the *Her'uli*, in Italy, continued only about 17 years ; at the end of which period, *Theod'oric the Great*, king of the *Ostrogoths*, or *Eastern Goths*, defeated and slew Odoacer, made himself master of all Italy, was acknowledged sovereign of the country, and fixed his residence at *Raven'na.* *Theod'otus*, the third Gothic king of Italy, was

defeated and slain by *Belisa'rius*, the general of Justinian who made himself master of Rome. But the Ostrogoths under the brave *Tot'ila*, recovered their authority, but were in turn, utterly defeated, after their dominion in Italy had lasted 64 years, by *Narses*, who succeeded Belisarius, and who governed Italy 13 years.

2 *Narses* having been recalled by Justin II., the successor of Justinian, invited *Alboin*, king of the *Lombards*, or *Lon'gobards*, to avenge his injury. Alboin overran and subdued the country, was proclaimed king, and made *Pavia* the capital of his dominions. The kingdom of the Lombards, in Italy during the successive reigns of 22 kings, lasted 206 years, till 774, when *Deside'rius*, or *Didier*, was defeated by *Charlemagne*, and Italy was afterwards incorporated into the new Empire of the *West*. The period which elapsed from the death of *Theodosius the Great* to the establishment of the *Lombards* in Italy, was one of the most calamitous and distressing in the history of the world.

3. The *Goths* were originally from *Scandina'via*, and were distinguished for hospitality and heroic virtues. At the time of their taking Rome, under Alaric, they had partially embraced Christianity. The *Ostrogoths* and *Visigoths*, or *Eastern Goths* and *Western Goths*, were so called from their situation The *Her'uli* were of Gothic origin; and the *Lombards* were originally either from Scandinavia or the north of Germany.

4. The *Eastern Empire*, called also the *Greek Empire*, and the *Empire of Constantinople*, although it suffered from the ravages of the barbarous nations who overthrew the Western Empire, yet it resisted their attacks, and subsisted more than 11 centuries, from the time of its foundation by Constantine This long period furnishes but few events which are particularly interesting.

5. This empire was in the meridian of its glory in the 6th century, during the long reign of *Justin'ian*, sometimes styled the *Great*, who published a celebrated *code of laws*, prepared by *Tribo'nian*, a great lawyer of that age. This code is regarded as the foundation of the jurisprudence of modern Europe.

6. During the reign of Justinian, *Belisarius* and *Narses* the two most renowned generals of the age, defended the empire against the Persians, recovered Africa from the Vandals and Italy from the Goths, and obtained several great victories over these fierce enemies. Justinian built the church of *St. Sophia*, which is now a Mahometan mosque. He and some

of his successors patronized the arts and learning, and endeavored to revive a taste for literature and science in the dark ages; yet the majority of these emperors were weak sovereigns, debased by luxury and vice.

7. After the removal of the seat of empire, there arose a rivalship between the pope or bishop of Rome, and the patriarch of Constantinople, each contending for the precedence. This controversy, which occupies a prominent place in the history of the times, finally terminated in the entire separation of the *Western* or *Roman*, and the *Eastern* or *Greek Churches*

8. In 1204, the crusaders took and pillaged Constantinople and proclaimed their leader, *Baldwin*, count of Flanders, sovereign of the empire. They kept possession of the throne till 1261, under the reign of five French or Latin emperors. During this period, the Greek emperors made *Nice* the seat of their power.

9. In 1453, during the reign of *Constantine XII.*, Mahomet II., at the head of 300,000 Turks, besieged and took Constantinople, and gave up the city to be plundered by his soldiers. He put a final end to the Eastern Empire; and since that event, Constantinople has continued the seat of the Turkish government.

SECTION XIII.

Roman Antiquities.

1. Some account of the origin and nature of most of the principal offices, or magistracies, in the Roman government, and also of the division of the inhabitants, has already been given.

2. The whole structure of the constitution under the monarchy has, upon the authority of *Dionysius of Halicarnassus*, been attributed, by most authors, to *Romulus*, a leader of a band of shepherds or fugitives. Yet it is doubtless true, that the Roman government, like most others, was the gradual result of circumstances; the fruit of time, and of political emergency.

3. In addition to the divisions of the people, which are attributed to Romulus, into *three tribes*, each of them consisting of 10 *curiæ*, and into two orders, *patricians* and *plebeians*, further subdivisions were afterwards made. To the three tribes, into which the city was at first divided, Servius Tullius added a fourth; and the four tribes were named, from the quarters

where they dwelt, the *Pal'atine*, *Subur'ran*, *Col'latine*, and *Es'quiline.* Augustus afterwards divided the city into 14 wards.

4. Besides this local division, Servius distributed the citizens into six *classes*, and each class into several *centuries*, or portions of citizens, so called, not because they consisted of 100, but because they were obliged to furnish and maintain 100 men in time of war. The six classes were formed according to their property; the first consisting of the richest citizens, and the sixth, which was the most numerous, of the poorest. The whole number of centuries was 193.

5. To the two orders of patricians and plebeians, there was afterwards added the *equestrian order*, composed of *equites*, or knights, who were chosen under the direction of the censor and presented with a horse at the public expense, and a gold ring. They were taken promiscuously from those of the patricians and plebeians who had attained their 18th year, and whose fortune amounted to £3,229.

6. There were, besides, some other distinctions among the Roman people, as *nobiles*, the noble, including those whose ancestors had held the office of consul, pretor, censor, or curule edile, and who had a right to make images of themselves. The *homines novi*, or new men, were persons who were the first of their families that had raised themselves to any of the above offices. The *ignobiles*, or ignoble, were those who had no images of their own, or of their ancestors. Those whose parents had always been free were called *in-gen'ui;* and those who had been slaves, but had been made free, were styled *liberti*, and *libertini.*

7. The *Roman citizens* were not merely those who resided in the city and Roman territory, but the freedom of the city was granted to other parts of Italy, and afterwards to foreign cities and towns in the empire, whose inhabitants, thereby, enjoyed the same rights as the Romans.

8. The *slaves* were an unfortunate class of persons, who performed all domestic services, and were employed also in various trades and manufactures. They were considered as mere property, at the absolute disposal of their owners, and were publicly sold in a market-place. Men became slaves by being taken in war, or by being born in a state of servitude; criminals also were reduced to slavery by way of punishment

9. *Kings.* The kings of Rome were not absolute or hereditary, but limited and elective. They could neither enact laws, nor make war or peace, without the concurrence of the senate and people. Their badges were a white robe, adorned with

stripes of purple, or fringed with the same color, a golden crown, and an ivory sceptre. They sat in the *curule* chair, which was a chair of state, made or adorned with ivory ; and they were attended by 12 lictors, carrying *fasces*, which were bundles of rods with an axe [*securis*] stuck in the middle.

10. *Senate.* The senate at first consisted of 100 members, but was afterwards increased to 300 by Tarquin the Elder ; and near the dissolution of the republic, it comprised upwards of 1000. The senators were at first nominated by the kings , but they were afterwards chosen by the consuls, and at last by the censors. This body was usually assembled three times a month, but was frequently called together on other days for special business. A decree, passed by a majority of the senate, and approved by the tribunes of the people, was termed *senatûs consultum.* The senators were styled *patres*, or fathers, on account of their age, gravity, and the paternal care they had of the state. From them the *patricians* derived their designation, because the senate was, at first, composed wholly of that order.

11. *Magistrates in general.* The magistrates in the Roman republic were elective, and previous to their election they were called *candida'ti* [candidates], from a white robe which they wore while soliciting the votes of the people.

12. The Roman magistrates were divided into *ordinary*, *extraordinary*, and *provincial.* The ordinary magistrates were those who were created at stated times, and were constantly in the republic : the chief of these were the consuls, censors, tribunes, ediles, and questors. The extraordinary were such as rose out of some public disorder or emergency : these were the dictator and the master of the horse, who commanded the cavalry ; the decemvirs, the military tribunes, and the *interrex.* The provincial magistrates were those who were appointed to the government of the provinces. These were at first pretors, afterwards pro-consuls and pro-pretors, to whom were joined questors and lieutenants.

13. *Consuls.* The consuls had the same badges as the kings, with the exception of the crown ; and their authority was nearly equal, except that it was limited to one year. In dangerous conjunctures, they were clothed with absolute power, by a solemn decree, " that the consuls take care the commonwealth receive no harm." In order to be a candidate for the consulship, it was requisite to be 43 years of age.

14. *Pretors.* The pretor, who was next in dignity to the consuls, and in their absence supplied their place, was appointed to administer justice. He presided in the assemblies of the people, convened the senate upon any emergency, and exhibit

ed certain public games. There was at first but one pretor then two, afterwards more.

15. *Censors.* The office of censor was esteemed more honorable than that of consul, although attended with less power. There were two censors, chosen every five years, and their most important duty was performed every fifth year, in taking the census of the people; after which they made a solemn *lustration*, or expiatory sacrifice, in the *Campus Martius*, in the name of the people.

16. *Tribunes.* The office of the tribunes was instituted merely to protect the plebeians against the patricians; but the tribunes gradually acquired very great power.

17. *Ediles.* The ediles were so named from their office which was the care of the public edifices, baths, aqueducts, roads, markets, &c. They were of two kinds; *plebeian ediles*, who were assistants to the tribunes; and *curule ediles*, who superintended the public games.

18. *Questors.* The questors were elected by the people to take care of the public revenue. At first there were only two, but several more were afterwards added. The *military questors* accompanied the army, and took care of the payment of the soldiers. The *provincial questors* attended the consuls or pretors into their provinces, and received the taxes and tribute.

19. *Assemblies of the people.* An assembly of the whole Roman people, to give their vote on any subject, was called *comi'tia*. There were three kinds of *comi'tia*; the *curia'ta*, the *centuria'ta*, and the *tribu'ta*. The comitia were summoned, by some magistrate, to pass laws, to elect magistrates, to decide concerning peace and war, and to try persons guilty of certain heinous crimes.

20. The *comitia curiata* consisted of an assembly of the resident Roman citizens, who were divided into 30 *curiæ*, a majority of which determined all matters of importance which were laid before them.

21. The *comitia centuriata* were the principal assembly of the people, in which they gave their votes, divided into the *centuries* of their classes, according to the census. At these comitia, the consuls, pretors, and censors were created, the most important laws enacted, cases of high treason tried, and war declared. They met in the *Campus Martius*, and all Roman citizens, whether residing in the city or country, had a right to be present and vote with their respective centuries.

22. The *comitia tributa* were an assembly, in which the people voted divided into tribes, according to their regions or wards. They were held to create inferior magistrates to elect certain priests, to make laws, and hold trials

23. The comitia continued to be assembled for upwards of 700 years, when that liberty was abridged by *Julius Cæsar* and after him by *Augustus*, each of whom shared the right of creating magistrates with the people. *Tiberius* deprived the people altogether of the right of election.

24 *Priests.* The ministers of religion did not form a distinct order from the Roman citizens, but were chosen from the most honorable men in the state. Some of the priests were common to all the gods; others were appropriated to a particular deity: of the former kind, the most important were the *pontif'ices*, the *au'gures*, the *harus'pices*, the *quindecim'viri*, and the *septem'viri;* who were all subject to the *pont'ifex max'imus*, or high priest, chosen by the people.

25. The *pontifices* among the Romans were priests, 15 in number, who judged all causes relating to religion, regulated the feasts, sacrifices, and all other sacred institutions, and inspected the lives and manners of the inferior priests. The *pontifex maximus*, or high priest, was a person of great dignity and authority: he held his office for life, and all the other priests were subject to him.

26. The *augures*, or augurs, were 15 in number, and were of great authority. It was their office to foretell future events, to interpret dreams, oracles, prodigies, &c., and to say whether any action would be fortunate or not. They divined the future chiefly in five ways; — from the appearance of the heavens, as thunder and lightning; from the singing or flight of birds, from the feeding of chickens; from quadrupeds; and from uncommon accidents, as sneezing, stumbling, seeing apparitions, &c. &c.

27. The *haruspices* were priests whose business it was to look upon the beasts offered in sacrifice, and by them to divine the success of any enterprise, and to obtain omens of futurity. They derived their omens from the entrails of beasts; also from the flame, smoke, and other circumstances attending the sacrifice.

28. The *quindecimviri* were 15 priests who had the charge of the *Sibylline books*, which were three prophetic volumes, said to have been procured from a woman of extraordinary appearance, in the time of Tarquin the Proud. They were supposed to contain the fate of the Roman empire, and were kept in a stone chest under the Capitol.

29. The *septemviri* were seven priests who prepared the sacred feasts at the games, processions, and other solemn occasions; and they were also assistants to the pontifices.

30. The priests of particular deities were called *Flam'ines*:

the chief of them were the *Dia'lis*, priest of Jupiter the *Salii*, priests of Mars; the *Lupe'vii*, priests of Pan; the *Poti'tii*, priests of Hercules; the *Gal'li*, priests of Cyb'ele; and the *Vestal Virgins*, consecrated to the worship of Vesta.

31. The Romans worshipped their gods in temples consecrated by the augurs; also in groves. Their worship consisted chiefly in prayer, vows, and sacrifice.

32. *Festivals.* The Romans celebrated feasts in January in honor of Janus; in February were the *Luperca'lia*, or feasts of Pan, and the *Fera'lia*, in honor of ghosts or spirits of the deceased; in March, the *Matrona'lia*, a feast kept by the Roman matrons, and the *Quinqua'tria*, in honor of Minerva; in April, the *Cerea'lia*, in honor of Ceres; in December, the *Saturna'lia*, or the feasts of Saturn, the most famous of all the festivals. There were, besides, many other festivals.

33. *Games.* The shows exhibited in the *circus maximus* were chariot and horse-races; contests of strength and agility; mock fights on horseback; combats of wild beasts; representations of horse and foot battles; and *nauma'chiæ*, or mock naval battles.

34. *Gladiators.* The gladiators were persons who fought with weapons in a public circus or amphitheatre, for the amusement of the people. These combats were introduced about the 400th year of the city, and became a most favorite entertainment. The combatants were, at first, composed of captives, slaves, and condemned malefactors, who were regularly trained for the combat; but in the more degenerate period of the empire, free-born citizens, and even senators, engaged in this disgraceful and dangerous amusement. Great numbers of men were destroyed in these inhuman exhibitions. After the triumph of Trajan over the Dacians, spectacles were exhibited for 123 days, in which 11,000 animals of different kinds were killed, and 10,000 gladiators fought.

35. *Triumph.* A triumph was a solemn procession, in which a victorious general and his army advanced through the city to the Capitol. It was the highest military honor which could be obtained in the Roman state, and was reserved for those generals who, by hard-earned victories and glorious achievements, had added to the territories of the commonwealth, or had delivered the state from threatened danger. The procession began from the Campus Martius, and passed through the most public places in the city to the Capitol; the streets being strewed with flowers, and the altars smoking with incense. It was composed of musicians, oxen for sacrifice, carriages carrying the spoils taken from the enemy, the captive kings or leaders and their attendants, and after the whole

the triumphant general, dressed in purple embroidered with gold, with a crown of laurel upon his head, and other decorations.

36. *Dress.* The most distinguished parts of the Roman dress were the *toga* and the *tu'nica.* The toga, or gown, worn by Roman citizens only, was loose and flowing, and covered the whole body; it had no sleeves, and was disposed in graceful folds, to give the wearer a majestic appearance. The *toga viri'lis,* or manly gown, was assumed by young men at the age of 17 years. — The *tunica,* or tunic, was a white woollen vest, which came down a little below the knees before, and to the middle of the leg behind, and was fastened tight about the waist by a girdle.

37. *Meals.* The principal meal of the Romans was called *cœna* or supper, which took place about three o'clock in the afternoon, and exceeded in luxury everything known in modern times. The early Romans lived chiefly on bread and potherbs; but when riches were introduced by their conquests, luxury seized all ranks, and everything was ransacked to gratify the appetite. In the early ages, the Romans sat at meals, but afterwards they reclined on sumptuous couches. Their ordinary drink at feasts was wine, which they mixed with water, and sometimes with spices.

38. *Forum.* The Forum was the principal public place in the city. It was a large, oblong, open space, where the assemblies of the people were held, where justice was administered, and public business transacted. It was entirely surrounded with arched porticos, within which were spacious halls, called *basil'icæ,* where courts of justice might sit for the decision of private affairs.

39. *Campus Martius.* The Campus Martius, or Field of Mars, was a large plain, without the city, along the Tiber where the Roman youth practised all kinds of athletic exercises and sports, and learned the use of arms. It was adorned with the statues of famous men, and with triumphal arches, columns, porticos, and other magnificent structures.

B.C.		Chronological Table of Roman History. — *No.* 1. *From the Foundation of Rome to the end of the Commonwealth.*
800	53	Romulus, founds *Rome;* institutes the *senate;* divides the people into *tribes* and *curiæ; patricians* and *plebeians.*
8*th*	15	*Numa Pompilius*, a pacific king; regulates *religious ceremonies.*
700	72	*Tullus Hostilius.* Combat between the *Horatii* and *Curiatii.*
7*th*	40	*Ancus Martius*, builds the port of *Ostia;* conquers the *Latins.*
	16	*Tarquin the Elder*, constructs the *cloacæ;* founds the *capitol.*
600	78	*Servius Tullius*, establishes the *census*, made every 5th year.
6*th*	34	*Tarquin, the Proud*, disgusts the people by his tyranny: rape of *Lucretia* by *Sextus.* The Tarquins expelled: the *regal government* abolished (509), and the *Commonwealth* begins.
500	98	Lartius first *Dictator.* Contests between the *Patricians* and *Plebeians:* the latter retire to *Mons Sacer. Tribunes* created
	85	Dissensions respecting *Agrarian Law* begin. *Coriolanus.*
	71	Law *Volero;* the privileges of the Plebeians increased.
5*th*	56	*Cincinnatus* Dictator; defeats the *Volsci* and *Æqui.*
	51	*Decemvirs* appointed; Laws of the *Twelve Tables.*
	49	The *Decemvirs* banished. — 445. *Military Tribunes* created.
	45	*Intermarriages* of the Patricians and Plebeians.
	37	Two *Censors* appointed.—406. The troops receive *regular pay.*
400	91	*Veii* taken by *Camillus*, the Dictator.
	90	The *Gauls*, under Brennus, defeat the Romans, and burn *Rome.*
4*th*	83	*Manlius Capitolinus* thrown down the Tarpeian Rock.
	43	War with the *Samnites* begins; lasts 53 years.
	38	The *Campanians* subdued. — 332 The *Appian Way* formed.
300	80	War with the *Tarentines* and *Pyrrhus.* - 266. *Lower Italy* conq.
	64	*First* Punic War: lasts till 241. — 255. *Regulus* defeated.
	22	*Cisalpine Gaul* reduced to a Roman province.
	18	*Second* Punic War; lasts till 201.
3*d*	18	*Hannibal* defeats the Romans on the *Ticinus* and the *Trebia;* (217) on the *Thrasymenus;* and (216) at Cannæ.
	12	Romans (*Marcellus*) take *Syracuse;* and (210) conquer *Sicily.*
	7	The Romans (*Nero* and *Livy*) defeat Asdrubal at *Metaurus.*
	2	The Romans (*Scipio Africanus*) defeat *Hannibal* at *Zama.*
200	97	The Romans defeat the Macedonians at *Cynocephale.*
	68	Battle of *Pydna; Macedonia* reduced to a Roman province.
	49	*Third* Punic War; ends (146), *Carthage* being destroyed.
	46	*Corinth* taken, and all Greece reduced to a Roman province.
2*d*	33	*Numantia* taken, after a long siege.
	33	*Tiberius Gracchus* slain. — 121. *Caius Gracchus* slain.
	11	War against *Jugurtha;* — concluded (106) by *Marius* and *Sylla*
	2	Marius defeats the *Teutones* at *Aquæ Sextiæ.*
100	89	*Mithridatic War;* — lasts till 66
	88	*Civil war* between *Marius* and *Sylla.* — 82. Sylla's proscription
	73	*Servile War; Spartacus.* — 65. *Syria* conquered by *Pompey.*
	63	*Catiline's Conspiracy* suppressed by Cicero.
	60	*First Triumvirate;* formed by Pompey, Crassus, and Cæsar.
1*st*	48	*Civil war; Cæsar* and *Pompey;* battle of *Pharsalia.*
	45	Cæsar perpetual *Dictator;* — 44. Cæsar murdered.
	43	*Second Triumvirate;* Octavius, Antony, and Lepidus.
	42	Battle of *Philippi; Brutus* and *Cassius* overthrown.
	31	Battle of *Actium* gained by *Augustus*, who puts an end to the *Commonwealth*, and becomes *emperor.*

To ascertain the date of any event in this Table, add the figures connected with the event to the century below. Thus it appears that *Rome was burnt by the Gauls* B.C. 390

CHRONOLOGICAL TABLE OF ROMAN HISTORY — *No. 2.*
From the end of the Commonwealth to the extinction of the Western Empire.

B.C.	31 *Augustus*, 1st *Emperor*: golden period of *Roman Literature*.	
A.D.	14 *Tiberius*, 2, characterized by cruelty and oppression.	
	36 *Caligula*, 3, noted for profligacy and folly; is murdered.	
	41 *Claudius*, 4, a weak sovereign; invades *Britain*.	
	54 *Nero*, 5, a profligate tyrant; sets *Rome* on fire. *Peter* and *Paul* martyred.	
	68 *Galba*, 6, slain and succeeded by [69] *Otho*, 7; by *Vitellius*, 8.	
1st	70 *Vespasian*, 9, a popular emperor. *Jerusalem* taken by Titus in 70.	
	79 *Titus*, 10. *Herculaneum* and *Pompeii* overwhelmed in 79.	
	81 *Domitian*, 11, a cruel tyrant, the last of the *Twelve Cæsars*, Julius Cæsar being the first. *Britain* conquered by *Agricola*.	
	96 *Nerva*, 12, enfeebled by age; adopts Trajan for his successor.	
	98 *Trajan*, 13, a great sovereign. The empire in its greatest extent.	
100	17 *Adrian*, 14, journeys through the empire; rebuilds *Jerusalem* in 137.	
	38 *Antoninus Pius*, 15, eminent for his public and private virtues.	
	61 *Marcus Aurelius Antoninus*, 16, the virtuous *Stoic philosopher*.	
2d	80 *Commodus*, 17, profligate and cruel; is assassinated.	
	93 *Pertinax*, 18, proclaimed by the Pretorian guards; murdered.	
	93 *Didius Julianus*, 19, purchases the empire; soon put to death.	
	93 *Septimius Severus*, 20, defeats his competitors, *Niger* and *Albinus*.	
200	11 *Caracalla* and *Geta*. 21, two brothers; murdered.	
	17 *Macrinus*, 22, murdered at the instigation of Heliogabalus.	
	18 *Heliogabalus*, 23, a monster of cruelty and vice; is murdered.	
	22 *Alexander Severus*, 24, an excellent prince; defeats the *Persians*.	
	35 *Maximin*, 25, of gigantic stature. During his reign, *Gordian I.*, 26, is proclaimed by the army; unites *Gordian II.*, 27.	
	38 *Maximus* and *Balbinus*, 28; both slain.	
	38 *Gordian III.*, 29. defeats the Persians under *Sapor*.	
3d	44 *Philip*, 30, *the Arabian*, succeeded by *Decius*, 31.	
	51 *Gallus*, 32, with *Gallus Volusian*. [54] *Æmilian*, 33.	
	54 *Valerian*, 34, taken prisoner and put to death by *Sapor*, king of Persia.	
	61 *Gallienus*. 35; succeeded by [68] *Claudius*, 36.	
	70 *Aurelian*, 37, a great warrior, defeats *Zenobia*, the *Goths*, &c.	
	75 *Tacitus*, 38. [76] *Florian*, 39. [77] *Probus*, 40. [82] *Carus*, 41.	
	82 *Numerian* and *Carinus*, 42.	
	84 *Diocletian*, 43. The empire divided into four parts, under two *emperors* and two *Cæsars*. The last and greatest persecution of the *Christians*.	
300	6 *Constantine, the Great*, 44, 1st *Christian emperor*; removes the seat of empire from *Rome* to *Constantinople*.	
	36 *Constantine II.*, *Constantius*, and *Constans*, 45, three emperors.	
	61 *Julian*, 46, *the Apostate*, reëstablishes the *pagan worship*, and attempts to rebuild the *Temple* of Jerusalem.	
	63 *Jovian*, 47, restores the *Christian religion*.	
	64 *Valentinian I.*, 48, emp. of the *West*.	64 *Valens I.*, emperor of the *East*.
4th	75 *Gratian*, 49.	79 *Theodosius the Great*.
	83 *Valentinian II.*, 50; *Goths*.	
	92 *Theodosius*, 51, *the Great*, the last sole emperor of the *West* and *East*: complete establishment of *Christianity*, and downfall of *paganism*.	
	WESTERN EMPIRE.	EASTERN EMPIRE.
	ROME the *Capital*.	CONSTANTINOPLE the *Capital*.
	95 *Honorius*, 52. *Alaric*.	95 *Arcadius*.
400	24 *Valentinian III.*, 53. *Attila*.	8 *Theodosius II.* Theodosian Code. Invasion of the *Huns*, under *Attila*.
	55 *Maximus*, 54. [55] *Avitus*, 55.	
	57 *Majorian*, 56. [61] *Severus*, 57. [67] *Athenius*, 58.	50 *Marcian*.
5th	72 *Olybrius*, 59. [73] *Glucerius*, 60. [74] *J. Nepos*, 61.	57 *Leo, the Great*, first emperor crowned by the Patriarch.
	75 *Augustulus Romulus*, 62. *Odoacer* puts an end to the *Western Empire*, in 476.	74 *Zeno*, makes *Theodoric*, the Ostrogoth, his general.
		91 Anastasius.

The figures on the left hand of the *emperors* denote the *commencement* of their reigns; those on the right, the *number* of the emperor. Thus, *Constantine the Great* began to reign in 306, and was the 44th emperor.

Chronological Table of Roman Literature.

B. C.	Public Men.	Poets.	Historians.	Philosophers, Orators, &c.	Jews.
500					
5th	Coriolanus Cincinnatus				Ezra Malachi
400					
4th	Camillus Manlius				Jadua
300					
3d	Fabricius Marcellus	Livius And. Nævius			Sadoc Jesus Sirac
200					
2d	Fabius Max. Scipio Afric. Cato, *Censor*	Plautus Ennius Terence			Mattathias Judas Mac. J. Hyrcanus
100					
1st	Marius Sylla Sertorius Catiline Crassus Pompey Lucullus Cato, *Utica* Cæsar Brutus Cassius Antony	Roscius, *Drama.* Lucretius Catullus VIRGIL Propertius Tibullus HORACE	Sisenna J. CÆSAR Sallust Hirtius Pansa Cornelius Nepos	Hortensius CICERO Varro, *Literature.* Vitruvius, *Architecture.*	Shammai Hillel
0					
1st	*Emperors.*	Ovid Phædrus Persius Lucan Petronius Silius Italicus Valerius Flaccus Statius	LIVY Valerius Ma. Pomp. Mela, *Geog.* Paterculus Quintus Curtius TACITUS	Columella Seneca Pliny, *Sen.* Quinctilian, *Criticism.*	John Baptist Philo Jonathan Onkelos *Christians.* James Peter Paul Josephus, *Jew* John Clemens Ro.
100					
2d		Martial Juvenal Palladius	Pliny, *Jun.* Suetonius Florus Aulus Gellius Justin	Frontinus M. Aurelius Antoninus	Ignatius Papias Justin Mar. Polycarp Irenæus
200					
3d		Calpurnius			Tertullian Origen Cyprian
300					
4th		Ausonius	Vopiscus Lampridius Eutropius		Arius Athanasius Ambrose
400					
5th		Prudentius Claudian	V. Sequester Orosius		Chrysostom Jerome Augustine
500					
6th		Mar. Capella	Cassiodorus		Fulgentius Benedict
600					
7th			Boethius Trebonian		Gregory Isidore

The most flourishing period of *Roman Literature* comprised the century immediately preceding, and that immediately following, the Christian era.

THE MIDDLE AGES.

---

1. THE *Middle Ages* comprise a period of about a thousand years, from the 5th to the 15th century; or from the subversion of the Western Empire of the Romans to that of the Eastern Empire. During these centuries, Europe was sunk in ignorance, barbarism, and superstition; hence this period is styled the *Dark Ages*.

2. The migration of the *Goths*, *Vandals*, *Huns*, and other barbarous nations from the north of Europe, took place in the latter part of the 4th century, and the beginning of the 5th. These barbarians possessed themselves of the middle and south of Europe; and in less than one hundred years after this event, almost all learning and civilization disappeared. Literature had been gradually declining since the reign of Augustus; yet considerable remains of it existed in the Roman Empire till after the fall of the capital before the arms of the Goths. The darkest period was from the 6th century to the 12th.

3. In these dark and miserable times, the human mind was neglected and debased; books were extremely scarce, and were procured only at an immense price, the cost of a single volume being equal to that of a good house; the common people were wholly uneducated; many persons of the highest rank, and in the most important stations, were unable to read; and contracts were made verbally for the want of persons capable of writing them. The learning which existed was confined chiefly to ecclesiastics and monks; yet many priests did not understand the service which it was their duty daily to recite; and many bishops had never seen a copy of the Bible during their lives.

4. The state of morals, both among the clergy and laity, was exceedingly low; and Christianity had lost most of its original excellence, and was corrupted into a degrading superstition. The political state of Europe was also characterized by anarchy violence, and rapine.

5. The absurd modes of trial by *single combat* or *duel*, and also by *ordeal*, that is, by walking blindfold over hot bars of iron, or being thrown into the water, were commonly used as methods of discovering guilt and innocence.

6. The most considerable empire that existed in Europe during the Middle Ages was the *New Empire of the West*, which was established by *Charlemagne*, but which was not of long duration. It was during these ages that the famous and successful impostor *Ma'homet* appeared, and the *Mahometan* or *Saracen Empire* flourished. From the 8th to the 13th centuries the Saracens surpassed all their contemporaries in the cultivation of literature and science.

7. Some of the most remarkable circumstances which characterize the history of Europe and the state of society, during this period, are, the *Feudal System*, the *Crusades*, and *Chivalry*

THE ARABS OR SARACENS.

1. Before the time of *Ma'homet*, the Arabians were a rude nation, living generally in independent tribes, who traced their descent from *Ishmael*, and professed a mixed religion, compounded of Judaism and idolatry. They had had, as a nation but little intercourse with the neighboring kingdoms.

2. The *Saracens*, however, a warlike tribe of Arabs who inhabited the western part of Arabia, had, before this period, been induced, by the hope of plunder, to forsake their deserts, and had become alternately the support and terror of the tottering empires of Rome and Persia. They were in the habit of selling their services, as mercenaries, to those who would pay most liberally ; and their name was applied, by Christian authors of the Middle Ages, to the Arabian nations generally, who were the first disciples of Mahomet ; and who, within 50 years after his death, conquered a considerable part of Asia and Africa, and some portions of Europe ; but the descendents of the Arabs, who subdued and possessed themselves of Spain, have been styled *Moors*.

3. Arabia had afforded an asylum to the persecuted Christians of different sects ; and, at the end of the 6th century, Christianity had become the prevailing religion in some parts of the country. It was, however, a most corrupt form of Christianity, inculcating the worship of saints and images, with many other absurd and superstitious ceremonies ; and among

both the priests and the people, a general depravity of manners prevailed.

4. Such was the state of Arabia, when *Ma'homet* or *Mohammed*, that most extraordinary and successful impostor, appeared. He was a native of *Mecca*, a man of no education but of great natural talents. In 609, when about 40 years of age, he pretended to have received a divine commission to propagate a new religion. He withdrew to a place of retirement, where he affirmed that he held conferences with the angel Gabriel. These discourses were collected into a volume called the *Koran*, or *Alcoran*, which is the Mahometan bible. Ma'homet performed no miracles, but appealed chiefly to the excellence of the doctrine contained in the Koran, and to the elegance of its style, as proofs of its inspiration.

5. The two leading doctrines of his religion were these, namely, "*There is but one God, and Mahomet is his prophet.*" He taught that others, at various times, as Abraham, Moses, and Jesus Christ, had been divinely commissioned to teach mankind; but that he himself was the last and greatest of the prophets. He adopted much of the morality of the Gospel, and retained many of the rites of Judaism, and some of the Arabian superstitions, particularly the pilgrimage to Mecca. But he owed his success, in a great measure, to his allowing his followers great latitude in licentious indulgences, and to his promising them, as their future reward, a paradise of sensual pleasures.

6. He propagated his religion by the sword, stimulated the courage of his followers by inculcating the strictest predestinarianism or fatalism, and roused their enthusiasm by the assurance of a martyr's crown to every one who should fall in battle. It was inculcated as a fundamental doctrine, that "to fight for the faith was an act of obedience to God"; hence the Mahometans or Saracens denominated their ferocious and bloody ravages *holy wars.* — They term their religion *Islam* or *Islamism;* and call themselves *Mussulmans* or *Moslems*, that is, true believers or orthodox.

7. Mahomet, in the beginning of his efforts, had but little success in making proselytes. His first converts were his wife *Kadija*, his slave *Zeid*, his cousin and son-in-law the famous *Ali*, and his father-in-law *Abu-beker*, who was a man of influence. These, together with ten others, were all whom he had persuaded to acknowledge the truth of his mission, at the end of three years.

8. A popular tumult being raised against him at Mecca, he was compelled, in order to save his life, to escape; and he fled in disguise to *Medina.* His *flight* or *Hegira*, is the Mahom-

10 *

etan era, corresponding to the year A. D. 622. He was carried into Medina in triumph, by 500 of its richest citizens; and there he assumed the sacerdotal and regal office. He placed himself at the head of an army of his converts, and began to propagate his religion by the sword: having defeated his enemies, he entered his native city, Mecca, in 629, as a triumphant conqueror. He fought in person nine battles, subdued all Arabia, extended his conquests to Syria, and after a career of victory, died at Medina, at the age of 63, ten years after his flight from Mecca to that city.

9. Mahomet affected the most rigid austerity, and the most ostentatious piety; and he is described "as a perfect model of Arabian virtue, brave and liberal, eloquent and vigorous, noble and simple in all his dealings, and of irreproachable morals." This is the fair side of his character; but on the other hand, he is reproached with the grossest sensuality, — having married, according to some authors, eleven, and according to others, seventeen wives, — with never having hesitated to make use of the worst passions of his followers for the advancement of his purposes, and with having had frequent recourse, in the progress of his conquests, to the most wanton cruelty and the basest perfidy.

10. Mahomet was succeeded by *Abu-beker*, who is styled the first *caliph*, a subordinate title, which was assumed from respect and in reference to Mahomet, and which signifies, in Arabic, *successor* or *vicar*. He continued the career of conquest, and, with the aid of his general *Caled*, defeated a great army of the Greek emperor *Herac'lius*, took *Damascus*, and died in the third year of his reign. At his death he bequeathed the sceptre to the brave *Omar*. "I have no occasion for the place," said Omar. "But the place has occasion for you," replied the dying caliph.

11. *Omar*, with the assistance of his favorite general *Obeidah*, in one campaign, deprived the Greek empire of Syria Phœnicia, Mesopotamia, and Chaldea; and in a second campaign, he reduced to the Mussulman dominion and religion the whole empire of Persia. His army, under *Amrou*, took Alexandria, and subdued Egypt.

12. Amrou, being requested to spare the *Alexandrian library*, wrote for directions respecting it to Omar, who is said to have returned the following answer, characteristic of an ignorant barbarian and fanatic: "If these writings agree with the Koran, they are useless, and need not be preserved; if they disagree, they are pernicious, and ought to be destroyed." The sentence, as is related by numerous authors, was executed by using this vast collection of the writings of the ancients as fuel for heating the 4000 baths of the city for six months. This

was the largest library that the world had then seen, — stated at 700,000 volumes, — and its destruction is regarded as the greatest loss to literature that is recorded in history.

13. Omar, during a reign of 10 years, reduced 36,000 cities and villages to his obedience, demolished 4,000 Christian churches or temples, and erected 1,400 mosques for Mahometan worship. He was finally assassinated, and succeeded by *Othman*, who added Bactria'na and a part of Tartary to the dominion of the caliphs. On his death, *Ali*, who had married *Fat'ima*, the daughter of Mahomet, was elected to the caliphate. He is reputed the bravest and most virtuous of the caliphs, and his reign was glorious, though of only five years' duration.

14. In the space of less than half a century, the Saracens raised an empire more extensive than what then remained of the Roman; and in 100 years from the flight of Mahomet from Mecca to Medina, the dominions of his successors extended from India to the Atlantic, comprehending the widely distant regions of Persia, Syria, Asia Minor, Arabia, Egypt, the North of Africa, and Spain.

15. The reign of *Ali* forms a remarkable era in the Mussulman history, on account of a schism which then arose, and which caused the followers of Mahomet to be divided into two great parties, which still continue to exist, known by the names of *Sunnites*, or *Sonnites*, and *Shiites*, who detest and anathematize each other as heretics. The Shiites are zealous adherents of Ali, whom they regard as equal to Mahomet, but reject Abu-beker, Omar, and Othman, the first three caliphs, as usurpers. The Sunnites, or orthodox Mahometans, acknowledge the rightful authority of these caliphs, but admit no one to be equal to Mahomet; and they receive the *Sunnah*, or body of traditions concerning the prophet, as of canonical authority; but this is rejected by the Shiites. The Turks are Sunnites, and the Persians are Shiites.

16. Ali removed the seat of the Mussulman sovereigns from Mecca to *Cufa*, on the Euphrates; and in 768, it was removed by Almansor to Bagdad; hence they are styled *caliphs of Bagdad*. Next to the caliphate of Bagdad, the other caliphate most illustrious in Saracenic history was that of *Cordova* in Spain. *Walid*, who reigned at Cufa in the early part of the 8th century, was the first that founded a hospital, and built caravansaries or public inns, for the accommodation of travellers

17. The first race of caliphs were styled *Ommi'ades*, the first of whom was *Moawiyah;* of these, 19 reigned in succession; after which began the dynasty of the *Abbas'sides*, who

were descended from *Abbas*, the uncle of Mahomet *Almansor*, the second caliph of this race, built Bagdad, and made it the seat of the Saracen empire, and it became the largest and most splendid city in the world. He was a liberal patron of learning and science; and it was he who first introduced the cultivation of them among the Saracens.

18. The reign of *Haroun al Raschid*, the 25th caliph, who was contemporary with Charlemagne, was the most splendid of the whole dynasty; and it is regarded as the Augustan age of Saracen or Arabic literature. This prince rendered himself illustrious by his valor, generosity, and benevolence; by his equitable government, and his patronage of learned men. It is to these times that a great part of our proverbs and romances must be referred; and the *Thousand and one Nights* have rendered Haroun al Raschid more celebrated than his victorious march through Asia. Schools of learning were, at this period, established in the principal towns. The sciences chiefly cultivated were medicine, geometry, and astronomy: poetry and fiction also commanded attention. Some of the successors of Haroun al Raschid, particularly his son *Al Mamun*, followed his footsteps in patronizing learning. Literature was also successfully cultivated by the Saracens of Spain and Africa

19. From the time of the removal of the seat of government to Bagdad, the importance of Arabia began to decline. Many chiefs of the interior provinces rose to assert their independence, and withdrew themselves from the civil jurisdiction of the caliph, regarding him only as the head of their religion.

20. The Saracens might have established an immense empire, if they had acknowledged but one head; but as their conquests extended, their states soon became disunited. Spain, Egypt, Morocco, and India had, at an early period, their separate sovereigns, who continued to respect the caliph of Bagdad as the successor of the prophet, but acknowledged no temporal subjection to his government.

21. The house of *Abbas* furnished 37 caliphs, who reigned in succession. Bagdad continued to be the seat of the Saracen empire 490 years, during which long period it sustained several obstinate sieges, and was the scene of many a bloody revolution. At length, in the 656th year of the Hegira, A. D. 1258, Bagdad was taken by *Hulaku*, the grandson of the celebrated *Genghis Khan:* the reigning caliph, *Al Mostasem*, was put to death; the caliphate was abolished, and the Saracen empire terminated.

22 The immediate successors of Mahomet found them-

selves under the necessity of affecting that enthusiastic devotion, and rigid austerity, by which he had established his character as a prophet, and his power as a sovereign. All the time they could spare from the duties of royalty was spent in prayer or preaching before the sepulchre of the impostor Their manners were modest and unassuming; they affected great humility, practised various mortifications, and condescended to perform the meanest offices. Satisfied with the power of royalty, they affected to disdain its pomp. But when their power was confirmed beyond the fear of revolution, they forgot the real or affected virtues which their predecessors had found it necessary to practise, and became distinguished for their oppression, their love of show and magnificence, their luxury and effeminacy.

23. As the caliphs succeeded to both the regal and sacerdotal offices which Mahomet had assumed, they were the most absolute monarchs in the world. No privileged order was recognized in the Saracen empire, to impose a salutary restraint on the will of the despots. The Koran was, indeed, prescribed as the rule of their actions, and it inculcated the duties of humanity and justice; but they were themselves the interpreters and judges of that code; nor did any Mussulman dare dispute their infallibility. Their office, uniting spiritual with temporal power, bore a striking resemblance to that of the popes; nor did the resemblance fail, with regard to pomp, haughtiness, and oppression.

THE FEUDAL SYSTEM.

1. The *Feudal System* had its origin among the barbarous nations, the Goths, Vandals, Huns, Lombards, &c., that overran the countries of Europe, on the decline of the Roman empire; but it is supposed to have received its earliest improvement among the Lombards. It was adopted by Charlemagne, and eventually by most of the princes of Europe; and it is generally believed to have been first introduced into England by William the Conqueror.

2. When the northern barbarians had made a conquest of the provinces of the Roman empire, the conquered lands were distributed by lot hence they were called *allotted* or *allodial*, and they were held in entire sovereignty by the different chieftains, without any other obligation existing between them than

that of uniting, in case of war, for the common defence. The king or captain-general, who led on his respective tribes to conquest, naturally received by far the largest portion of territory for his own share; and his principal followers, to whom he granted lands, bound themselves merely to render him military services.

3. The example of the king was imitated by his courtiers, who distributed, under similar conditions, portions of their estates to their dependants. Thus a feudal kingdom became a military establishment, and had the appearance of a victorious army encamped under its officers in different parts of a country; every captain or baron considering himself independent of his sovereign, except during a period of national war.

4. Possessed of wide tracts of country, and residing at a distance from the capital, these barons or lords erected strong and gloomy castles or fortresses in places of difficult access; and not only oppressed the people, and slighted the civil magistracy of the state, but were often in a condition to set the authority of the crown itself at defiance.

5. The fundamental principle of this system was, that all the lands were originally granted out by the sovereign, and were held of the crown. The grantor was called *lord*, and those to whom he made grants were styled his *feudatories* or *vassals*. As military service was the only burden to which the feudatories were subjected, this service was esteemed honorable, and the names of freeman and soldier were synonymous.

6. The great mass of the people, who cultivated the lands, were styled *serfs* or *villains*, and were in a state of miserable servitude. They were not permitted to bear arms, nor suffered to leave the estates of their lords.

7. The feudal government, though well calculated for defence, was very defective in its provisions for the interior order of society. A kingdom resembled a cluster of confederated states under a common head; and though the barons or nobles owed a species of allegiance to the king, yet, when obedience was refused, it could be enforced only by war.

8. The bond of union being feeble, and the sources of discord innumerable, a kingdom often exhibited a scene of anarchy, turbulence, and war; and such was, in fact, the state of Europe, with respect to interior government, from the 7th to the 11th century.

9. Some of the principal causes of the gradual overthrow of the Feudal System were, the crusades, the formation of cities into communities with special privileges, the change of

the mode of war which followed the invention of gunpowder the extension of commerce, the increase and distribution of wealth, and the diffusion of knowledge. Some relics of it, however, still exist in some parts of Europe, particularly in Russia and Poland, and in some portions of Germany.

THE CRUSADES.

1. The Crusades, or Holy Wars, the first of which was commenced in 1096, and the last in 1270, were military expeditions, undertaken by the Christians of Europe, for the deliverance of Palestine, and particularly the sepulchre of our Savior, from the dominion of the Mahometans. These enterprises involved all the nations of Western Europe; yet, in most of them, the *French* took the lead. In 637, Jerusalem was conquered by the *Saracens*, who were induced, by self-interest, to permit Christian pilgrims to visit the city. But when the *Turks*, a wild and ferocious tribe of Tartars, got possession of Jerusalem, in 1065, the pilgrims were no longer safe, but were exposed to insult and robbery. The dangers of pilgrimage, painted in the most frightful colors by those who returned from the holy city, threatened the discontinuance of what was regarded, in that age of ignorance and superstition, a sacred duty.

2. *Peter the Hermit*, a native of Amiens, in France, having returned from a painful pilgrimage, conceived the design of arming the sovereigns and people of Europe, for the purpose of rescuing the holy sepulchre out of the hands of the infidels. With this view, he travelled from kingdom to kingdom, describing the sufferings of the pilgrims with the most inflammatory pathos, and calling aloud for vengeance. He exhibited in his own person, a complete specimen of monkish austerity and frantic enthusiasm. His body, which was covered with a coarse garment, seemed wasted with fasting; his head was bare; his feet naked; he bore aloft in his hand a large and weighty crucifix; and his prayers were frequent, long, and loud. He accosted every person whom he met, and entered without hesitation, the palaces of the great and the cottages of the poor.

3. *Urban II.*, the reigning pontiff, pitched upon this enthusiast as a fit person to commence the execution of a grand design, which had before been entertained by the popes, particularly *Gregory VII.* (*Hildebrand*,) of arming all Christen

dom against the Mahometans. The project was opened in two general councils, which were held at *Placentia* and *Clermont* in 1095, and attended by many thousands. The pope himself harangued the multitude, and proposed that the *cross*, which was made of red stuff attached to the right shoulder, should be the badge of the combatants; and from this badge the expeditions were termed *crusades*. Plenary indulgence and full absolution were proclaimed to all who should devote themselves to the service.

4. An immense multitude of ambitious and disorderly nobles, with their dependants, eager for enterprise and rapine, and assured of eternal salvation, immediately took the cross. Robbers, incendiaries, murderers, and thousands of inferior offenders, readily embraced the opportunity of making expiation for their sins; and their zeal was increased by the hope of plunder and of sensua gratification. *Peter the Hermit* assumed the office of general, for which he was totally unqualified, and, placing himself at the head of 80,000 recruits, commenced his march towards the East in the spring of 1096. This army was followed by a promiscuous assemblage of 200,000 persons, more like the collected banditti of Europe than a regularly constituted soldiery. The Jews of Germany were their first victims; but their outrages in Hungary and Bulgaria drew upon them a severe retaliation from the inhabitants, so that not more than a third part of this undisciplined multitude arrived with Peter at Constantinople. These were met by sultan *Solyman*, on the plain of *Nice*, and almost totally destroyed, without ever having seen Jerusalem.

5. But a more valuable part of the expedition was still in reserve, and soon after arrived at Constantinople. These were men properly trained and appointed, led by experienced and able generals. The supreme command was conferred on *Godfrey of Bouillon*, who was supported by *Baldwin* his brother, *Robert*, duke of Normandy (son of William the Conqueror of England), *Hugh*, count of Vermandois, *Raymond* count of Thoulouse, and various other distinguished princes of Europe. When reviewed in the neighborhood of Nice, they amounted to 100,000 horse, and 600,000 foot, including a train of women and followers.

6. Having taken *Nice*, and defeated *Solyman*, they proceeded eastward, conquered *Edessa*, took the city of *Antioch*, vanquished an army of 600,000 *Saracens*, and, being reduced to little more than a twentieth part of their original number, advanced to *Jerusalem*, which, after a siege of 40 days, was taken by storm, in 1099; and the whole of its Mahometan and Jewish inhabitants were barbarously massacred. The heroic

Godfrey was proclaimed *king of Jerusalem* by the troops, and he soon after defeated the sultan, with an immense army, at *Ascalon;* but, after having reigned one year, he was compelled to give up his kingdom to the pope's legate.

7. The conquerors divided Syria and Palestine into four states; and, seeing their object accomplished, they began to return to Europe. The Turks gradually recovered their strength; and the crusaders who remained in Asia, finding themselves surrounded by foes, were under the necessity of soliciting aid from Christendom. An army of adventurers, collected by *Hugh*, the brother of Philip I. of France, met with a fate similar to that of the army under Peter the Hermit, being cut off in hostilities, first with the Greeks, and afterwards with Solyman.

8. The *second crusade* was preached, in 1147, by the famous *St. Bernard*, the founder of the monastic order of the Bernardines; and *Louis VII.* of France, and *Conrad III.* of Germany, with 300,000 of their subjects, were persuaded to assume the cross. Conrad took the lead, but his army was almost entirely extirpated near *Ico'nium;* the French, under Louis, were totally defeated near *Laodice'a;* and the two monarchs, after witnessing the destruction of the finest armies which their countries had produced, returned with shame to their dominions.

9. The illustrious *Sal'adin*, who, about the year 1174, raised himself, from the condition of an attendant of the caliphs, to the sovereignty of Egypt, Arabia, Syria, and Persia, formed the design of recovering Palestine from the Christians. Having defeated their army in the battle of *Tiberias*, he besieged and took *Jerusalem*, in 1187, and made its sovereign, *Guy of Lusignan*, prisoner.

10. The reigning sovereigns of the principal states of Europe, *Philip Augustus* of France, *Richard I.* of England, and *Frederic Barbarossa* of Germany, were men of eminent talents; and by the influence of pope *Clement III.*, they were induced to unite in a *third crusade*, in 1188. The Emperor Frederic was drowned in Cilicia, in the small river Cydnus, and his army mostly destroyed. The English and French were more fortunate. they took *Ptolema'is;* but Richard and Philip quarrelled from jealousy of each other's glory, and the French monarch returned in disgust to his country.

11. Richard ably sustained the contest with the Sultan Sal'adin, whom he defeated near *As'calon:* but his army was reduced by famine, fatigue, and intestine quarrels. Returning through Germany, unaccompanied by his troops, he was arrested, and kept in prison, till an immense ransom was pro-

cured from his subjects. Before his departure from Syria, he had made a peace with Saladin, who soon after died.

12. Notwithstanding the misery which had been the uniform result of the crusades, such was the madness of the age, that fresh adventurers were ever ready to renew them. In 1202 during the pontificate of the ambitious pope *Innocent III.*, *Baldwin*, count of Flanders, collected an army to act against the Mahometans in a *fourth crusade ;* but he began, as others had done, with the Eastern Christians. Arriving at *Constantinople* at a time when there was a dispute respecting the succession, his interference tempted one claimant to assassinate his rival, and Baldwin, after despatching the other by a public execution, and indulging his followers with the plunder of the city, took possession of the imperial throne of the *Eastern Empire.* Satisfied with this splendid acquisition, he attempted nothing against the Saracens.

13. John de Brienne, a French nobleman, being appointed king of Jerusalem, made, in 1217, a descent upon Egypt, at the head of 100,000 men, with the design of destroying the power of its sultan at the seat of government. After a long siege, he took Damietta ; but, his army being subsequently surrounded by an inundation of the Nile, he was forced to give up his conquests and surrender his person as a hostage.

14. The crusading fanaticism in Europe had, at length, begun to languish ; but it was again revived by *St. Louis IX.* of France, a monarch alike distinguished for being deeply imbued with the superstition of the age, and for possessing every amiable and heroic virtue. After four years' preparation, he set out for the *Holy Land*, in 1248, with his queen, his three brothers, and all the knights of France.

15. He began his enterprise by invading *Egypt*, and, after losing one half of his numerous army by sickness, he was utterly defeated and taken prisoner by the Saracens. Having ransomed himself and his followers, he proceeded to *Palestine*, where he remained for a considerable time; and then, returning to France, he reigned wisely and prosperously for 13 years. But the same frenzy assailing him again, he embarked, in 1270, on another crusade against the *Moors* in Africa, and laid siege to *Tunis*, near which he and the greater part of his army were destroyed by a pestilence. This was the last of those mad enterprises.

16. *Effects of the Crusades.* The crusades owed their origin to the fanaticism and superstition of an ignorant and barbarous age, superadded to ambition, love of military achievement, and a desire of plunder. No other military enterprise ever commanded the attention of Europe so generally or so

long · and no other affords a more memorable monument of human folly. They assumed the sacred character of religion and were styled *Holy Wars*. Their tracks marked the three quarters of the world which were then known with blood; and for nearly two centuries they afflicted almost every family of Europe with the most painful privations. It is computed, that, during their continuance, more than *two millions* of Europeans were buried in the East. Those who survived were soon blended with the Mahometan population of Syria, and, in a few years, not a vestige of the Christian conquest remained.

17. These barbarous expeditions, though productive of so much misery, had, nevertheless, a powerful influence in producing a great and beneficial change in the aspect of society. Their effects were observable, in a greater or less degree, on the *political condition*, the *manners and customs*, the *commerce*, the *literature*, and the *religion* of Christendom.

18. At the commencement of the crusades, the *Feudal System* prevailed throughout Europe. The barons who engaged in them were obliged to sell their lands, in order to procure the means of conveying their troops to a foreign country. In this way the aristocracy was weakened, wealth more widely distributed, and the lower classes began to acquire property, influence, and a spirit of independence. Kings, likewise, raised money by selling to towns immunities and privileges, such as the right of electing their own magistrates, and being governed by their own municipal laws.

19. In the ages immediately preceding the crusades, the manners and mode of life which prevailed in Europe were gross and barbarous; and so, indeed, they continued for a long time after their termination; yet a gradual improvement was soon visible. Travelling in foreign countries has a tendency to enlarge the views, and polish the manners. In the East, particularly in Constantinople, the crusaders became acquainted with modes of life superior to what they had been accustomed to in their own countries, and of which, on their return, they were ready to recommend the adoption. The crusades gave rise to various orders of *knighthood*, especially those of *St. John of Jerusalem*, and the *Templars*. They imbued *chivalry* with religion, and brought it to maturity.

20. These enterprises had a most beneficial influence on *commerce and the arts*. Commerce had been carried on upon only a very limited scale; and European nations had never had their attention sufficiently drawn to the numerous advantages of water-transport, till the destructive disasters of the first crusaders, in attempting a march by land, forced upon the minds of their followers the expediency of conveying their

troops by water. By the consequent frequency of voyages to Palestine, the arts of navigation and ship-building were rapidly improved; and from this period may be dated the commercial prosperity of *Pisa*, *Genoa*, and *Venice*.

21. The crusades, although immediately injurious both to *literature* and *religion*, were, nevertheless, ultimately beneficial. They commenced at a time of the profoundest ignorance and the grossest superstition; — nearly all that remained of ancient art and science being, at that period, confined to *Constantinople* and the more enlightened of the *Saracens*; — during their continuance, military fame was the chief object of ambition to all who aspired to distinction; and that blind and fanatical devotion to the will of the priesthood, without which the people could never have been seduced into so wild an enterprise, continued undiminished. But after two centuries of disaster, Europe began to suspect the folly of these expeditions, and to doubt the infallibility of their promoters; and the human mind was gradually prepared for an emancipation from bigotry and servility.

22. It may be observed, that if, by the superintendence of Providence, these benefits to society grew out of the crusades they were diametrically opposite to what their projectors intended; that these were results which they had neither the wisdom to foresee, nor the virtue to design.

CHIVALRY.

1. Chivalry was an institution in which valor, gallantry, and religion were strangely blended. It constitutes one of the most remarkable features in the history of European nations in the Middle Ages; and, during several centuries, it produced a wonderful influence upon their opinions, habits, and manners, the effects of which may still be traced. Its distinguishing features were a romantic spirit of adventure; a love of arms, and of the rewards of valor; an eagerness to succor the distressed, and to redress wrongs; high sentiments of honor and religion; and a devoted and respectful attachment to the female sex.

2. The early history of chivalry is involved in obscurity; and different theories have been formed with regard to the period, the nation, and the circumstances, to which it owed its origin. But the best supported account appears to be that which fixes its origin, as a regular institution, in the 11th cen

tury. Before this period, however, the great principles of it were to be found in the manners and customs of the *Gothic* nations, among whom the profession of arms was the only employment which was esteemed honorable, and who were distinguished for their delicate and respectful gallantry to the female sex. It was embodied into form and regularity by the *Feudal System;* and was afterwards brought to maturity and splendor by the *Crusades*, and, by the change wrought upon it by these expeditions, was rendered as much a *religious* as a *military* institution. Some improvements in it are supposed also to have been derived from the *Saracens.*

3. Chivalry pervaded almost all parts of Europe; yet *Spain* and *France* appear to have been the countries in which it was first regularly formed into a system, and where it flourished in its greatest purity and splendor. In *Germany* also, at an early period, it arrived at maturity; but in *England* it was of later birth, and slower growth.

4. The sons of noblemen, who were destined for chivalry, entered, at the age of seven years, on a course of education, which was to prepare them for the performance of its duties and the enjoyment of its honors. The place of their education was the castle of their father, or of some neighboring noble. From the age of 7 to 14, the appellation given to these boys was *page* or *varlet;* in old English ballads, *child;* and at 14 they were raised to the rank, and received the title, of *esquire*, and were then authorized to bear arms.

5. They were kept in constant and active employment, and waited on the master and mistress of the castle at home and abroad, and became accustomed to obedience and courteous demeanor. They were surrounded by noble ladies and valiant knights; and the first impressions made on their minds were those of love, gallantry, honor, and bravery. They were taught to reverence chivalry as containing everything that was alluring and honorable; and that the only means of attaining the highest honors were, devotion to the female sex, and skill and courage in warfare.

6. By the ladies of the castle they were taught, at the same time, the rudiments of religion and love. "The love of God and the ladies," says Hallam, "was enjoined as a single duty He who was faithful and true to his mistress was held sure of salvation in the theology of the castles." In order that they might have opportunity to practise, in some degree, the instructions which they received, it was customary for each youth to select some young, accomplished, and virtuous lady at whose feet he displayed all his gallantry, and who undertook to polish his manners.

7. The esquires were employed in various subordinate offices in the castles, and as attendants on the knights, till they arrived at 21, which was the proper age for admitting them to the full honors of knighthood. The candidate was required to prepare himself by ablutions, by rigid fasting, by passing the night in prayer, and by making a solemn confession of his sins; and, as a type of the purity of manners which would be required of him, he was clothed in white.

8. Having performed the preliminary rites, he then entered a church, and after an examination, if he were judged worthy of admission to the order of knighthood, he received the sacrament, and took an oath, consisting of 26 articles, in which among other things, he swore that he would be a good, brave loyal, just, generous, and gentle knight, a champion of the church and the clergy, a protector of ladies, and a redresser of the wrongs of widows and orphans.

9. While upon his knees, he received from the hands of the knights and the ladies the insignia of chivalry, his spurs, cuirass, coat of mail, and the other parts of his armor, and, in the last place, his sword. The most distinguished chevalier then *dubbed* him, or bestowed on him the *accolade*, by giving him a slight blow on the shoulder or cheek with his sword, which has been interpreted as an emblem of the last affront which it was lawful for him to endure.

10. The most important part of the equipments of a knight was his horse; his distinguishing weapon was the *lance;* his other offensive arms consisted of a sword, dagger, battle-axe, and maces. His dress consisted of a long, flowing robe, which reached down to his heels.

11. "The virtues and endowments that were necessary to form an accomplished knight," says Dr. Henry, "in the flourishing times of chivalry, were such as these;—beauty, strength, and agility of body; great dexterity in dancing, wrestling, hunting, hawking, riding, tilting, and every other manly exercise; the virtues of piety, chastity, modesty, courtesy, loyalty, liberality, sobriety; and above all, an inviolable attachment to truth, and an invincible courage."

12. Such was the estimation in which knighthood was held that, for a long time, no sovereign could be crowned till he had been knighted. Whoever had been dubbed became, as it were, a citizen of universal chivalry, and possessed various privileges and dignities, which were not limited to the territory of his sovereign, but extended throughout a great part of Europe. He had a right to roam through the world in quest of adventures, which, whether just or not in their purpose, were always esteemed honorable in proportion as they were perilous.

13. He was authorized to propose a trial of skill with the lance to all those of his order whom he met, and to combat them with the utmost fury, if they did not acknowledge the lady to whom he had devoted himself, and whom they had never seen, the most beautiful in the world. When he challenged them to single combat, it was in the name of his mistress; and he established her unparalleled beauty by vanquishing his antagonist, and compelling him to acknowledge her superior charms. The portrait, the device, the livery, or even the most trifling gift of his mistress, he cherished with the utmost fondness. The crest of his helmet was ornamented with the *favors* which she had bestowed upon him. When the sovereign led his army to the attack, his never-failing injunction was, "Let every one think of his mistress."

14. The influence of chivalry was not limited to either sex. The manners of the ladies of rank were necessarily polite and courteous; for such they taught those of the chevaliers to be; and it was their highest ambition to deserve and obtain the love of a valiant knight. As the laws of the institution made it the duty of a knight to protect the chastity and honor of the ladies, and forbade his speaking ill of them, or tamely hearing them spoken ill of by others, it was incumbent on him to warn them against the commission of every thing that might lower them in his opinion.

15. Strictly decorous and respectful in his behavior towards them, he expected they would never forfeit their claim to such behavior. If, however, they transgressed the laws of modesty or prudence, he did not fail to stigmatize their failings in a way that would be keenly felt. If he passed the castle of one of this character, he marked, in such a manner as could not be mistaken, the dwelling of a lady unworthy to receive a true chevalier.

16. As the knights were ambitious to gain the esteem of the fair sex by their heroic exploits and the protection which they afforded them, so the ladies were ambitious to merit such protection by their virtue. In accordance with this is the language of *Spenser*: —

It hath been through all ages ever seen,
  That, with the praise of arms and chivalry,
The prize of beauty still hath joined been;
  And that for reason's special privity:
For either doth on other much rely;
  For he, me-seems, most fit the fair to serve,
That can her best defend from villany;
  And she most fit his service doth deserve,
That fairest is, and from her faith will never swerve.

17. Chivalry especially enjoined the virtues of hospitality

humanity, and courtesy. Every true and loyal knight was expected to have the door of his castle constantly open. As soon as one chevalier entered the castle of another, he considered himself at home, and was treated as if he were so; every thing that could contribute to his comfort and his luxury was at his command. If he arrived wounded, every possible care was taken of him by the ladies, both young and old, who were proud of having in their possession remedies proper for such occasions. To a vanquished foe the most scrupulous and delicate attention was paid: he was treated rather as a conqueror than as one who had been conquered.

18. The favorite amusement and exercise of the knights consisted in *justs* and *tournaments*, the most splendid of which were celebrated at coronations, royal marriages, and distinguished victories. "Every scenic performance of modern times," says Hallam, "must be tame in comparison of these animating scenes. At a tournament, the space inclosed within the lists was surrounded by sovereign princes and their noblest barons, by knights of established renown, and all that rank and beauty had most distinguished among the fair. Covered with steel, and known only by their emblazoned shields, or by the favors of their mistresses, a still prouder bearing, the combatants rushed forward to a strife without enmity, but not without danger.

19. "Victory at a tournament was little less glorious, and perhaps, at the moment, more exquisitely felt, than in the field; since no battle could assemble such witnesses of valor. 'Honor to the sons of the brave!' resounded, amidst the din of martial music, from the lips of the minstrels, as the conqueror advanced to receive the prize from his queen or his mistress; while the surrounding multitude acknowledged, in his prowess of that day, an augury of triumphs that might, in more serious contests, be blended with those of his country."

20. Absurd and ridiculous as the institution of chivalry appears, yet it had a powerful influence in producing a favorable change in the manners of society in a barbarous age; and was wonderfully adapted to the taste and genius of martial nobles It infused humanity into war, at a time when the disposition of the age made it almost the constant business of life, and the ruling passion of persons of every rank: it introduced courtesy of manners, when men were rude and uncultivated: it exacted and produced a scrupulous adherence to truth, at a time when its obligations were feebly felt, and the temptations to falsehood were numerous; it imparted an additional impulse and motive to a respectful and delicate attention to the female sex when such attention was particularly necessary to them.

21 As chivalry rose to splendor, and was embodied into form by the feudal system, so it fell along with it. The invention of gunpowder, and the consequent change in the mode of war; the invention of the art of printing, and the diffusion of knowledge; the extension of commerce, and the increase and distribution of wealth, gradually produced the destruction of the feudal system, and put a period to the existence of chivalry. It arose principally from the peculiar state of society, the evils of which it was calculated, in some degree, to remove or alleviate: it fell when that state of society and those evils had given way to the general diffusion of wealth and of knowledge.

22. "The wild exploits of those romantic knights," says Dr. Robertson, "who sallied forth in quest of adventures, are well known, and have been treated with proper ridicule. The political and permanent effects of the spirit of chivalry have been less observed. Perhaps the humanity which accompanies all the operations of war, the refinements of gallantry, and the point of honor, the three chief circumstances which distinguish modern from ancient manners, may be ascribed, in a great measure, to this whimsical institution, seemingly of little benefit to mankind. The sentiments which chivalry inspired had a wonderful influence on the manners and conduct during the 12th, 13th, 14th, and 15th centuries. They were so deeply rooted, that they continued to operate after the vigor and reputation of the institution itself began to decline."

23. But the actual morals of chivalry were by no means pure: its principles, like those of other institutions, were much superior to the practice of its professors; and it fell far short of establishing and preserving that purity in the intercourse of the sexes which it inculcated. The poetry of the Troubadours, and the tales and romances which describe the manners of chivalry, all afford evidence of dissolute morals.

24. The knights professed to redress wrongs, to relieve the oppressed, and to protect the defenceless; but in performing these very acts, they were not unfrequently guilty of the grossest injustice and violence. Chivalry nourished a pernicious thirst for military renown, and cherished a love of war, founded more on feelings of personal resentment than on those of public spirit. It indeed taught mankind to carry the civilities of peace into the operations of war, and to mingle politeness with the use of the sword; but it also gave birth to a punctilious refinement, and sowed the seeds of that fantastic honor, the bitterness of whose fruits is still felt in the modern practice of *duelling*.

25 The origin of the *duel* is traced to the *Gothic* nations

Under the feudal system, and during the age of chivalry, the duel was warmly patronized. It so far prevailed among the Germans, Danes, and Franks, that none were exempted from it but women, sick people, cripples, and such as were under 21 years of age, or above 60. Even ecclesiastics, priests, and monks, were obliged to find a champion to fight in their stead.

26. Laws and regulations were defined for it, in most of the kingdoms of Europe; forms of prayer were likewise prescribed; and the combatants prepared themselves by taking the sacrament. It was then resorted to as a method of discovering truth and preventing perjury, with the belief of the interference of Providence for the punishment of the guilty, and the protection of the innocent. It is now practised as a mode of private revenge; and its use is no longer supported by any plea derived from reason, religion, or superstition.

MODERN HISTORY.

1 DIFFERENT periods, as has already been mentioned, have been adopted by different historians for the commencement of Modern History, — as the Christian era, the downfall of the Western Empire of the Romans, A. D. 476, the establishment of the New Empire of the West under Charlemagne, A. D. 800, and (when considered as distinct from the history of the Middle Ages) the downfall of the Eastern Empire, in 1453.

2. But in treating of the history of the several European states, the most convenient method is to begin with the commencement of each respectively, without being confined to any one common period. The French monarchy dates from the latter part of the 5th century; but no other one of the present sovereignties of Europe traces its origin, by any authentic data, further back than the commencement of the 9th century.

3. The period that succeeded the downfall of the Eastern Empire is one of the most important and interesting in the history of man. On casting an eye back to this period, we see a flood of light suddenly bursting upon the world; mankind waking, as from profound sleep, to a life of activity and bold adventure; ignorance, barbarism, superstition, and feudal slavery, retreating before advancing civilization, knowledge religion, and freedom.

4. Some of the principal causes which produced the great and beneficial changes in the state of society which then took place, were the invention of the mariner's compass, of gunpowder, and of the art of printing; the discovery of America and of a maritime passage to India round the Cape of Good Hope; the dispersion of the literary men of Constantinople to the western parts of Europe, and the Reformation in religion.

5. In the history of European commerce, the association of the *Hanse Towns*, or *Hanseatic League*, holds a conspicuous place. This was a celebrated confederacy of commercial cities on the coasts of the Baltic and in the adjoining countries.

The League was formed before the middle of the 13th century, and among the towns which were early associated were Hamburg, Lubec, Bremen, Cologne, and Dantzic. It was soon widely extended; and it comprenended, at one period, 85 towns; and it had four principal foreign *depôts* or factories,—at London, Bruges, Novgorod, and Bergen. Regular assemblies, composed of deputies from all the cities, were held, once in three years, at Lubec, where the archives were kept.

6. In the 14th and 15th centuries the League was in its most flourishing condition; it became of high political importance, and made war and peace as a sovereign state. But when the princes of the several countries in which these towns were situated began to afford an efficient protection to their commercial operations, and when the discovery of America, and of the way to India by the Cape of Good Hope, gave an entirely new form and direction to commerce, the Hanseatic League gradually declined; and the last general assembly of the deputies from the several towns was held at Lubec in 1630, when the League was dissolved.

7. From the time of the crusades to the 15th century, the Italians, more especially the cities of Venice, Genoa, and Pisa, had the chief management of European commerce. In the maritime discoveries, and the commercial enterprise of the 15th and 16th centuries, Portugal and Spain took the lead; and on the discovery of a passage to India round the Cape of Good Hope, the commerce of Europe was turned into new channels, and the Italian cities declined.

8. Spain and Portugal have long since lost their former comparative rank in commerce, wealth, and power. They were succeeded in maritime enterprise and activity by the Netherlands, Holland, and England, which became, in turn the most commercial states in Europe.

9. The most powerful states in Europe, at the present time, are England, France, Russia, Austria, and Prussia; the last three of which are comparatively very modern. The history of England is to Americans more important than that of any other European country; and next to that in importance is the history of France.

FRANCE.

SECTION I.

Merovingian Kings: Carlovingian Kings: Charlemagne &c. — From A. D. 420 to 987.

1 The history of *France* and that of *England* are intimately connected, as they have, for many centuries, been rival states, and, during a great part of the time, engaged in war with each other. The kings of England, for a long time, assumed also the title of *King of France*, as they held possessions in that country, more or less extensive, from the time of *William the Conqueror* to that of *Queen Mary*.

2. The ancestors of the modern French were the *Gauls* or *Celts*, an enterprising and warlike people; and it has been frequently remarked, that there is a striking similitude between the descendants and their progenitors. Ancient *Gaul* comprehended, in addition to modern France, the *Netherlands*, and the western part of *Germany*. It was conquered and annexed to the Roman empire by *Julius Cæsar*, 51 years before the Christian era. It received its modern name from the *Franks*, who were originally a German tribe, inhabiting the districts on the Lower Rhine and the Weser, and who assumed the appellation of *Franks*, or *Freemen*, from their union to resist the dominion of the Romans.

3. The Franks made an irruption into Gaul about the year 420, under their leader, *Pharamond*, who is said to have been succeeded by *Clodion*, *Merovæus*, *Childeric*, and *Clovis*. The first race of the French kings is styled *Merovingian*, from *Merovæus;* but the authentic history of the monarchy commences in 481, with his grandson, *Clovis*, who is regarded as its real founder, and who achieved the conquest of France, by several victories over the Romans, the Alemanni, and the Visigoths, and by marrying *Clotilda*, a Christian princess, and daughter of the King of Burgundy. In consequence of this marriage, Clovis and his subjects embraced *Christianity*. He made *Paris* the seat of his government, and published the *Salic laws*, excluding females from the throne.

4. The *Merovingian kings*, who were generally weak sovereigns, continued to possess the throne till 751. In 690, *Pepin d'Heristel*, mayor of the palace, the first officer under the crown, acquired the chief control, which he retained for many years, and left it to his son, *Charles Martel*, who gained a great

victory over the *Saracens*, between *Tours* and *Poictiers*, and who was succeeded in office by his son, *Pepin le Bref*, or *the Short*, so called from his low stature, being only four and a half feet high.

5. Pepin governed France while the weak *Childeric III.* was nominally king; and being a man of talents and ambition he proposed the question to *Pope Zachary*, whether he himself or Childeric was the best entitled to the crown. Zachary from interested motives decided in favor of Pepin, who was accordingly crowned at Soissons, by St. Boniface, Bishop of Mentz, and became the founder of the *second* or *Carlovingian race* of French kings. Pepin recompensed the services done him by the pope, by turning his arms, during the pontificate of *Stephen II.*, who succeeded Zachary, against the *Lombards* in Italy, and by granting the exarchate of *Ravenna* and other territories to the see of Rome. In this manner the pope was, in 755, raised to the rank of a *temporal prince.*

6. Pepin was succeeded by his two sons, *Charles* and *Carloman;* but the latter dying not long after the death of his father, Charles possessed the undivided sovereignty. This distinguished monarch is known in history by the name of *Charlemagne*, or *Charles the Great.* Notwithstanding the diminutive stature of his father, he is said to have been seven feet in height, of a robust constitution and majestic appearance.

7. Charlemagne was far the greatest monarch of his age and distinguished both as a conqueror and a statesman. He was engaged in war during most of his reign, had a long and bloody contest with the *Saxons*, put an end to the kingdom of the *Lombards* in Italy, by defeating *Desiderius* or *Didier*, their last sovereign, and made extensive conquests; but he sustained a great defeat by the Spaniards, at *Roncesvalles.* In 800 he was crowned *Emperor of the West*, by the pope. His empire comprised France, the Netherlands, Germany, Switzerland, a great part of Italy, and part of Spain. He had no permanent capital, though *Aix-la-Chapelle* was, for a long time, his favorite residence.

8. Charlemagne was a luminary in a dark age, and an eminent patron of learning. "He stands alone," says Hallam, "like a beacon upon a waste, or a rock in the broad ocean." His court was frequented by *Alcuin* and other learned men; and he endeavored to dispel the profound ignorance which generally prevailed. He manifested his zeal for religion by compelling those whom he subdued to receive Christian baptism, on the pain of being either made slaves or of suffering death. Succeeding generations, impressed with a grateful sense of the services which he rendered to the church,

canonized his memory and turned this bloody warrior into an eminent saint.

9 His private character, though stained with vices, exhibited many estimable qualities. On days of ceremony, he made a great display of luxury and splendor in his apparel; but at other times he was plain in his dress, and frugal in regard to his table. The economy of his family was characteristic of an age of great simplicity. He superintended his farms, and trained his sons himself to manly exercises: the women belonging to his court made use of the needle, and managed the distaff; and he took delight in appearing ornamented with the productions of his wife and daughters.

10. Charlemagne was succeeded, in 814, by his son, *Louis the Debonair*, whose reign was inglorious and turbulent, and who divided his dominions among his sons. The quarrels of the rival brothers, which commenced before the death of their father, involved their subjects in a sanguinary war, and the family contest was decided in a great battle on the plains of *Fontenay*, where no less than 100,000 men are said to have fallen, and most of the ancient nobility of France perished. A new division of the empire followed; *Charles the Bald* receiving the western part of France, termed Aquitaine and Neustria; *Lothaire*, Italy and some of the southern provinces of France; and *Louis*, Germany. During the reign of Charles, the *Normans*, from Scandinavia, commenced their invasions of France, and burnt Paris.

11. Charles, after a weak and inglorious reign, was succeeded by his son, *Louis the Stammerer*, who, in order to insure tranquillity to his estates, made numerous grants of lands, titles, and offices to his nobles and bishops. After a short reign, he left his kingdom to his two sons, *Louis III.* and *Carloman.* After the death of these princes, the emperor *Charles the Fat* was elected to the vacant throne; but he governed with so much imbecility, that he was soon dethroned, and the imperial dignity was transferred to Germany.

12. The nobility gave the crown to *Eudes*, till *Charles the Simple* should attain to the age of manhood; and on the death of the former, the latter was raised to the throne; but he was deposed by *Robert*, the brother of Eudes; and Robert was succeeded by his son-in-law *Rodolph.* During the reign of Charles the Simple, the *Normans*, under *Rollo*, invaded and took *Neustria*, and, in 912, established themselves in the country, which from them was named *Normandy.*

13. During the succeeding reigns of *Louis IV.* and *Lothaire*, *Hugh the Great*, the most powerful nobleman in France obtained the chief direction of the government; and in the

reign of *Louis V.*, he was succeeded in his authority by his son *Hugh Capet*, who, on the death of Louis, placed himself upon the throne, and founded the *third* or *Capetian race* of French kings, in 987.

SECTION II.

Capetian Kings, from Hugh Capet to Philip VI. of Valois —From A. D. 987 *to* 1328.

1. *Hugh Capet*, an able and politic sovereign, added considerable territories to the kingdom, and made Paris his capital. He was succeeded by his son *Robert*, who was commanded by the pope to divorce his queen *Bertha*, because she was his cousin in the fourth degree. But he refused to comply, and was excommunicated. He was, in consequence, reduced to the most abject condition, being abandoned by all his courtiers, as a person infected with the plague; and was finally compelled to submit.

2. The quiet of his son and successor, *Henry I.*, was disturbed by the hostile designs of his unnatural mother, *Constantia.* During his reign a law was enacted, called *the truce of God*, prohibiting private combats between Thursday and Sunday. This was all that the ecclesiastical and civil power united could, in this age, do to check the general rage for duelling.

3. The reign of *Philip I.*, the successor of Henry, was signalized by the first *crusade*, preached by *Peter the Hermit;* and by the invasion of France, in 1087, by William the Conqueror, of England. From this event may be dated the long-continued rivalship and hostility between the *French* and *English* monarchies, which form a leading feature in their history during several centuries.

4. *Louis VI.*, surnamed *the Fat*, the son of Philip, was an able and accomplished sovereign, and had a prosperous and useful reign. On his death-bed he addressed his son, who succeeded him, in the following words: "Remember that royalty is nothing more than a public charge, of which you must render a very strict account to Him who makes kings, and who will judge them."

5. *Louis VII.*, surnamed *the Young*, having been educated in an abbey, was zealous for the religion of the age. The abbeys, at this period, produced some eminent men, among whom were *Suger*, abbot of St. Denis, a great politician; *St. Bernard*, abbot of Clairvaux, famous for his eloquence and

zeal; and *Abelard*, celebrated for his genius, and his learning in scholastic theology, and not less so for his unhappy connection with *Heloise*.

6. A civil war was excited on account of the refusal of Louis to assent to the choice of an archbishop, who was supported by the pope. The king entered the town of *Vitry* at the head of a large army, and caused the parochial church, in which the rebellious inhabitants had taken refuge, to be set on fire, and 1,300 persons perished in the flames. The remorse which Louis felt for this act of cruelty and sacrilege gave rise to the *second crusade*, which was preached by St. Bernard

7. Louis had married *Eleanor*, heiress of the great duchy of Guienne, whom he divorced for her levities and vices; and, in six weeks, she married Henry Plantagenet, Earl of Anjou, who became, the next year, *Henry II.* of England, and who, by this marriage, acquired a great addition to his possessions in France.

8. *Philip II.*, surnamed *Augustus*, on account of his exploits, surpassed, in systematic ambition and military enterprise, all the sovereigns who had reigned in France since the time of Charlemagne. He signalized the commencement of his reign by a tyrannical act, in confiscating the property of the Jews in France, and banishing them from his dominions he soon after joined Richard I. of England in the *third crusade.*

9. John, who succeeded Richard in the throne of England, was suspected of having murdered his nephew, Arthur; and for this Philip summoned him, as his vassal, to be tried by a court of his peers; but John, refusing to obey the summons, was declared guilty of felony, and his possessions were confiscated. Philip, with his troops, in 1204, invaded and made a conquest of Normandy, and reunited it to the crown of France; and the King of England then lost all his territories in that country, with the exception of Guienne.

10. Philip, who left his kingdom about twice as large as he found it, was succeeded by his son, *Louis VIII.*, who was surnamed *the Lion*, on account of his valor, and whose short reign was chiefly distinguished by a barbarous crusade against the *Albigenses.*

11. *Louis IX.*, commonly called *Saint Louis*, succeeded to the throne at the age of 12 years; and during his minority, his mother, *Blanche of Castile*, filled the office of regent with great firmness and courage. St. Louis was distinguished for his uprightness, benevolence, and piety, and with regard to the purity of intention, has, perhaps, scarcely been excelled by any sovereign that ever sat on a throne; and his long reign

was, in many respects, highly beneficial to his country. His principal weakness was superstition, which, in a great measure, effaced the good effects of his virtues, and which prompted him to engage in two disastrous *crusades*, in the second of which he died near *Tunis*.

12. St. Louis was succeeded by his son, *Philip III.*, surnamed *the Hardy*, or *Bold*, because, when a prisoner with his father in Africa, he had the boldness to punish a soldier who treated him with insolence; or, as others say, because he extricated the remains of the army in Africa, and brought the crusade, which was undertaken by his father, to a favorable issue. During this reign, an insurrection took place in Sicily which was occasioned by the tyranny of Charles of Anjou uncle of Philip, who had recently become king of that island; and 8 or 10,000 *Frenchmen* were massacred, on the evening of Easter-day, in 1282, a transaction called the massacre of the *Sicilian Vespers*.

13 *Philip IV.*, surnamed *the Fair*, from the beauty of his countenance and the elegance of his person, was distinguished for his ambition, dissimulation, perfidy, and cruelty, and was engaged in continual contests. By endeavoring to raise money from the clergy, as well as from his other subjects, he was involved in a quarrel with the ambitious and haughty Pope *Boniface VIII.*, who prohibited the clergy from paying the assessment, laid France under an interdict, and issued a bull, declaring "that the Vicar of Christ is vested with full authority over the kings and kingdoms on the earth."

14. The arrogant pontiff died during the contest, and Philip managed to get Clement V., a Frenchman devoted to his interests, elected his successor, and transferred, in 1308, the seat of the papacy from *Rome* to *Avignon*, where it continued 70 years. This removal greatly exasperated the Italians, who, in consequence, became hostile to the pope, and styled his residence at Avignon, "The Babylonish captivity of the Holy See." — The fraternity of *Knights Templars*, a religious and military order of great wealth, was abolished by Philip, and their property confiscated; but a measure more creditable to him was his instituting parliaments.

15. Philip was succeeded by his son, *Louis X.*, surnamed *Hutin*, that is, *the Stubborn*, or *Wrangler*, whose short reign was signalized by the execution of his prime minister, *Marigni*, for pretended crimes, though, in reality, for his wealth. *Philip V.*, *the Long*, on the death of *John I.*, the infant son of *Philip IV.*, succeeded to the throne. His reign is noted chiefly for a barbarous massacre and banishment of the Jews, who were accused of having poisoned the wells and fountains of water

His successor, *Charles IV., the Fair*, was the last of three brothers, whose reigns were all short, and who were always necessitous in respect to their finances, and little scrupulous with regard to their methods of improving them.

SECTION III.

Branch of Valois: — Philip VI.; John II.; Charles V.; Charles VI.; Charles VII.; Louis XI.; Charles VIII. — From A. D. 1328 *to* 1498.

1. Philip the Fair left three sons, *Louis Hutin*, *Philip the Long*, and *Charles the Fair*, who were all successively kings of France, but who all died without leaving any male heirs; and one daughter, *Isabella*, Queen of England, and mother of *Edward III.* On the death of Charles the Fair, the male succession to the throne devolved on *Philip VI. of Valois*, Charles's cousin-german; and his title was universally acknowledged and supported by the French nation.

2. But Edward III. of England was a nearer relative on the female side, and he asserted his claim in right of his mother. This claim gave rise to those contests for the French crown by the kings of England, which are so famous in the history of both countries. Edward invaded France with an army of 30,000 men, in order to enforce his claim, gained the famous battle of *Cressy*, in 1346, and besieged and took *Calais.* — In the midst of these misfortunes, Philip had the satisfaction of seeing *Dauphiny* annexed to the crown of France, by *Hubert*, the last count, on condition that the king's eldest son should bear the title of *Dauphin.*

3. Philip was succeeded by his son *John II.*, surnamed *the Good*, who was still more unfortunate than his father, being utterly defeated, in 1356, by the English, under the *Black Prince*, near *Poictiers*, and carried a prisoner to London, where he died.

4. During the captivity of John, the kingdom was thrown into the greatest disorder and confusion; but soon after his son, *Charles V.*, surnamed the *Wise*, ascended the throne, the condition of the country began to improve. This distinguished sovereign resolved to make France a match for England; and, in order to effect this object, he deemed it necessary to restore tranquillity to the people, and inspire them with confidence in the government. He raised to the office of Constable of France the celebrated *Du Guesclin*, who was one of the great-

est generals of the age, though he is represented as so illiterate that he was unable to read or write. The French, under his command, drove into Spain the banditti that had ravaged the country, routed Charles, king of Navarre, and expelled the English from all their possessions in France, except Bourdeaux, Bayonne, and Calais.

5. Charles was one of the best sovereigns that have sat on the throne of France; a sagacious statesman, a beneficent lawgiver, a patron of literature, and an excellent man in his private character. His father left him a library of only 20 volumes; to which he added 900, which rendered it one of the greatest libraries then existing; and it was an immense number for that period, when printing was not yet invented. Charles may be regarded as the founder of the royal library at Paris, which is now the largest library in the world.

6. This eminent sovereign was succeeded by his son, *Charles VI.*, styled *the Well-beloved*, a weak prince, subject to insanity, which, at last, reduced him almost to idiocy. His life and his reign were alike miserable, and all the fruits of the wisdom of his father's government were soon lost. His queen, *Isabella of Bavaria*, was of most infamous character, and the court was notorious for profligacy. The kingdom was governed by a succession of regents, whose misconduct occasioned seditions and rebellions.

7. During this calamitous state of France, *Henry V.* of England invaded the country, gained, in 1415, the memorable victory of *Agincourt*, and after obtaining other advantages, he concluded the treaty of *Troyes*, by which his succession to the throne, on the death of Charles, was acknowledged. Henry and Charles both died soon after this transaction.

8. *Charles VII.*, afterwards surnamed *the Victorious*, son of Charles VI., asserted his right to the crown; and the infant *Henry VI.* of England was also proclaimed King of France, under the regency of his uncle, the Duke of Bedford. The English undertook the siege of *Orleans*, a place of the utmost importance, and pushed their designs so successfully, that the affairs of Charles seemed almost desperate, when they were suddenly restored by one of the most marvellous transactions recorded in history.

9. An obscure country girl, 27 years of age, who had lived in the humble station of a servant at an inn, overthrew the power of England. This was that wonderful heroine, *Joan of Arc*, otherwise called *the Maid of Orleans*, who appeared at this juncture, pretending to be Divinely commissioned to deliver her oppressed country, and promising to raise

the siege of *Orleans*, and to conduct the king to *Rheims* to be crowned.

10. Her mission was pronounced by an assembly of divines to be supernatural; and, at her own request, she was armed *cap-à-pie*, dressed like a man, mounted on horseback, entered Orleans at the head of the French troops, and actually compelled the English to raise the siege (1429). Charles, in obedience to her exhortations, proceeded to Rheims, which was then in possession of the English, entered it without difficulty, and was there crowned. Joan then declared that her mission was ended, and requested leave to retire; but her presence was thought still necessary, and, being detained, she afterwards fell into the hands of the English, who condemned her for witchcraft and caused her to be burnt alive at Rouen.

11. The French gained further victories, and the English were finally expelled from all their possessions in the country except *Calais*. Charles now directed his attention to the improvement of the internal condition of his kingdom, and was a useful and popular sovereign. The latter part of his life was imbittered by the undutiful and rebellious conduct of his son the Dauphin, by whom he was in such fear of being poisoned that he is said to have died through want of sustenance.

12. *Louis XI.*, who was an odious compound of dissimulation, profligacy, cruelty, and superstition, is sometimes styled the *Tiberius* of France; yet he obtained from the pope the title of *Most Christian*, a title ever since annexed to the name of the French kings. He possessed, however, considerable talents great application to business, and affability to his inferiors and he was the author of many wise laws and excellent regulations for the encouragement of commerce, and for promoting the administration of justice.

13. It was his policy to humble the feudal nobles, who formed a confederacy against him, and engaged in a contest to preserve their authority, entitled "the war of the public good." The barbarity of the public executions during his reign is almost incredible: his own life was rendered miserable, especially towards its close, by the knowledge of his being generally hated, and by the torments of a guilty conscience.

14. *Charles VIII.*, the son of Louis, succeeded to the throne, at the age of 13 years. He was mild in his disposition and courteous in his manners, and received the surname of *the Affable*, or *Civil*. His father had acquired a claim to the kingdom of Naples; and, on coming of age, he engaged in an expedition for the conquest of that country, which was easily accomplished: but the possession of it was soon lost.

SECTION IV

Louis XII.; Francis I., Henry II., Francis II., Charles IX., Henry III. — *From A. D* 1498 *to* 1589.

1. Charles VIII., who was the last of the direct line of the house of Valois, was succeeded by *Louis XII., Duke of Orleans*, great-grandson of Charles V. He was a beneficent and popular sovereign, though injudicious and unfortunate in his enterprises. Being frugal in his policy, he diminished the taxes and burdens of his subjects, and gained the title of "the Father of his People." He retained the ministers of the late king in office, even those who had treated him ill before he came to the throne. "It is unworthy of the King of France," said he, "to punish the injuries done to the Duke of Orleans."

2. Near the commencement of his reign, he reduced *Milan* and *Genoa*, and afterwards prosecuted his claim to *Naples*, but though, by the aid of his generals, the celebrated *Chevalier Bayard* and *Gaston de Foix*, he obtained some advantages, he was ultimately unsuccessful, and became the dupe of his allies, *Ferdinand* of Spain, and the infamous *Pope Alexander VI.;* and the former, by treachery, got possession of the whole of Naples.

3. At this period, the republic of *Venice*, on account of its wealth, acquired by commerce, excited the envy and jealousy of its neighbors, particularly of the politic and ambitious *Pope Julius II.*, who projected against it the famous *League of Cambray*, in 1508, which was composed of the Pope, the Emperor of Germany, and the Kings of France and Spain. Louis entered with spirit into the war against Venice, and gained the famous victory of *Agnadello*. But the confederates afterwards quarrelled with each other, and a new league was formed against France.

4. The French, under the command of *Gaston de Foix* gained a victory over the new confederates at *Ravenna*, but it cost them the life of their commander. The death of this celebrated hero was fatal to Louis, for he soon afterwards lost all the places which he possessed in Italy, and was compelled to evacuate the country. In the midst of his preparations to recover these losses, Louis died suddenly, and the exclamation of "The good king is dead!" was heard on every side.

5. *Francis I., Duke of Angoulême*, and nephew of Louis XII., succeeded to the throne, at the age of 21 years. He was

of a romantic turn, fond of war, and eager for glory; and he departed from the frugal maxims of his predecessor, and soon distinguished himself by the conquest of the Milanese.

6. In 1519, on the death of *Maximilian*, Emperor of Germany, *Francis* and *Charles V.* (who was then King of *Spain*) became rival candidates for the imperial crown. Francis, speaking with Charles respecting the object of their competition, said, with his natural vivacity and frankness, "We are suitors to the same mistress; the more fortunate will win her, but the other must remain contented."

7. Charles was the successful candidate and Francis, whose heart was too much set upon the prize to lose it with quiet feelings, retired disappointed, and thirsting for revenge. The two rivals were now declared enemies, and their mutual claims on each other's dominions were the subject of perpetual hostility during nearly the whole of their long reigns.

8. The reign of *Charles V.* forms a distinguished period in history, — memorable not only for the wars and contests among the states of Europe, but still more so for the establishment of the Reformation, the advancement of literature, the extension of commerce, and the impulse given to the progress of society. Charles was the greatest sovereign of the age, and superior to his rival, Francis, both in policy and power. Other distinguished sovereigns of the same age were *Henry VIII.* of England, who was courted by both of the ival monarchs, and, in some degree, involved in their wars *Solyman the Magnificent*, Sultan of Turkey, a formidable enemy of Charles; *Gustavus Vasa* of Sweden; and *Pope Leo X.*

9. In the contest between the two rivals, the first hostile attack was made by Francis on the kingdom of Navarre, which was won and lost in the space of a few months. The emperor attacked Picardy, and his troops, at the same time, drove the French out of the Milanese. Francis quarrelled with his best general, the *Constable of Bourbon*, who, in revenge, deserted to the emperor, and was by him invested with the chief command of his armies. The French king marched into Italy with great success, and laid siege to *Pavia;* but was here, in 1525, defeated by Bourbon, and taken prisoner.

10. Francis was detained some time at Madrid by Charles, who compelled him to comply with disadvantageous terms of peace. After being set at liberty, and having passed the boundaries between Spain and France, he mounted his horse, and, waving his hand over his head, exultingly exclaimed, several times, "I am yet a king!" Charles had not treated him with generosity, having extorted from him more promises than a

king, restored to freedom, would be likely to perform, and more than his subjects would assent to. The violation of this treaty occasioned, between the two sovereigns, insulting challenges and new wars.

11. After war had been prosecuted with various success, a truce was at length agreed upon, and a circumstance took place, which brought the rival monarchs, who had been engaged 20 years in hostilities with each other, to a personal interview, in 1538, at *Aigues Mortes*, in the south of France. On meeting, they vied with each other in expressions of respect and friendship. The next year, Charles obtained permission of Francis to pass through France on his way to the Netherlands, and was entertained, during a stay of six days in Paris, with great magnificence.

12. Charles having afterwards refused to give up Milan to France, as he had promised, the war was again renewed with redoubled animosity; but its final issue, as had usually been the case, was unfavorable to the designs of the King of France, who died immediately after the restoration of peace.

13. Though Francis was engaged in war during the whole of his reign, and was unsuccessful in his projects, yet he left his kingdom in a flourishing condition. He was a patron of literature and the arts, which made great progress in France during his reign; and at this period, the French court acquired much of that external polish and refinement for which it has been since distinguished.

14. Francis possessed, in a high degree, those qualities which captivate the multitude, — impetuous courage, great decision and activity of mind, a frank disposition, and a generous heart; and there was a polish about his manners, an amiableness about his more common actions and his mode of performing them, and a delicacy and strictness of honor about his whole conduct, which characterize a finished gentleman. Yet he was far from being actuated by a sense of justice and good faith in his public character; nor were his private morals free from reproach. He formed his plans with too little deliberation, and was wanting in perseverance. It was his misfortune to contend with a rival, who was more than a match for him in policy and resources.

15. *Henry II.*, the son and successor of Francis, was brave affable, and polite, in some respects resembling his father, yet possessing far less talent, and easily governed by favorites. His reign, which was 13 years in duration, was spent in war chiefly with *Charles V.*, and his son, *Philip II.* of Spain. Charles sustained a great loss at the siege of *Metz*; but Philip

obtained over Henry, in 1557, the famous victory of *St. Quentin*, in commemoration of which he built the palace of the *Escurial*.

16. This war, the success of which had not been much to the satisfaction of either party, was terminated by the treaty of *Chateau Cambresis*. The reign of Henry was signalized by the recovery of *Calais* from the English, and by the increase of those persecutions of the *Calvinists*, or *Protestants* often also called *Huguenots*, which had been begun in the reign of his father, and which gave rise to the civil wars which distracted France during the three succeeding reigns.

17. The successor of Henry II. was his son, *Francis II.*, the first husband of *Mary*, afterwards Queen of Scots, who died after a reign of one year, and was succeeded by his brother, *Charles IX.*, then a boy only ten years old, who had for his guardian his mother, *Catherine de Medici*, an ambitious, intriguing, and unprincipled woman.

18. At this time, the Protestant religion had spread extensively in France, and was professed by some men of great influence at court, among whom were the *Prince of Condé* and *Admiral Coligny*.

19. At the head of the Catholics was the ambitious and powerful family of the *Guises*, consisting of five brothers, the most prominent of whom were the *Duke of Guise* and the *Cardinal of Lorraine*, who were leading men in the government. To the intolerance and cruelty of this family the Protestants attributed all their calamities; and the conspiracy of *Amboise* was formed for the destruction of the Catholic leaders. It was, however, discovered, and about 1,200 conspirators were massacred and executed.

20. In 1561, a public conference was held for discussing the points in dispute between the two parties. In this discussion, *Theodore Beza* defended the cause of the Protestants, and the *Cardinal of Lorraine* that of the Catholic church, before the king, the princes of the blood, and a number of nobles and dignified ecclesiastics. The differences, however, were not to be decided by words; but not long after, an edict was published, granting liberty to the Protestants to exercise their worship without the walls of towns. But this edict being soon violated, both parties flew to arms, and commenced the sanguinary civil war which, for a long time, harassed the kingdom.

21. The Catholics, under the command of *Guise* and *Montmorency*, defeated the Protestants, commanded by *Condé* and *Coligny*, in several engagements; but the latter were stil

powerful, and obtained, in 1570, conditions of peace, which granted them amnesty and liberty of conscience. But this treaty of peace, so far as Catherine de Medici and her party were concerned, was an act of treachery, got up for the purpose of luring the Protestant chiefs to their destruction.

22. The marriage of Henry of Navarre (afterwards *Henry IV.* of France) with Margaret, King Charles's sister, was celebrated with great pomp on the 18th of August, 1572 Most of the Protestant nobility and gentry, with Admiral Coligny at their head, were induced to attend on the occasion, and three or four days were spent in all sorts of festivities. A plan for the massacre of the Protestants having been arranged, the execution of it was intrusted to the Dukes of Guise, Anjou, and Aumale, Montpensier, and Marshal Tavannes. At a very early hour in the morning of the 24th, *St. Bartholomew's day*, the signal was given, and the work of slaughter commenced; and, before five o'clock in the morning, Admiral Coligny and his friends, without regard to age or sex, were murdered in cold blood. The court leaders, as they galloped through the streets, shouted, "Death to the Huguenots! — treason! — courage! — kill every man of them! — it is the king's orders!" The fury of the populace was excited to such a degree, that it could not easily be restrained; the slaughter was partially continued for three days; and, to gratify private hatred or revenge, many Catholics were slain by the hand of Catholic assassins.

23. This inhuman butchery, which was commenced at Paris, was extended throughout France, and the whole number murdered is stated by *Sully* at 70,000; though some state it at only 25,000. The French historian, De Thou [Thuanus], observes of this massacre, that "No example of equal barbarity is to be found in all antiquity, or in the annals of the world."

24. Charles, who is represented by some to have given his consent with reluctance to the plot, after having done it, expressed the hope that not a single Huguenot would be left alive to reproach him with the deed; and the next day he went in state to the parliament of Paris, and avowed himself the author of the massacre, claiming to himself the merit of having thereby given peace to his kingdom.

25. When the news of this horrible transaction was heard at Rome, solemn thanks were given for "the triumph of the Church militant!" Charles died soon after the massacre, for which he is said to have suffered the bitterest remorse. Notwithstanding the distractions of this unhappy reign, many wise laws were enacted through the influence of the celebrated chancellor *De l'Hôpital.*

26 Charles was succeeded by his brother *Henry III.*, a weak, fickle, and vicious monarch. The massacre of St. Bartholomew served rather to strengthen than weaken the Protestants, who were now a powerful party, and had at their head the *Prince of Condé* and the *King of Navarre*. Henry found it expedient to grant them some privileges: this measure incensed the Catholics, who, with the *Duke of Guise* at their head, formed the celebrated *League* for the purpose of extirpating the Calvinists: it had also another and more secret object, that of usurping all the powers of government.

27. The king was persuaded to unite himself with this league, and took the field against the Protestants. But he soon found himself deprived of a great part of his authority by the Duke of Guise; and after repeated contests, Henry caused the duke, and his brother, the Cardinal of Lorraine, to be put to death by the hand of assassins. This act excited an insurrection throughout France, and subjected the king to the abhorrence of his subjects; and he was soon after assassinated himself by James Clement, a Dominican friar.

SECTION V.

House of Bourbon: — *Henry IV.; Louis XIII.; Louis XIV. — From A. D.* 1589 *to* 1715.

1. As Henry III. died without children, and the house of Valois was extinct, the throne passed to the house of *Bourbon*, in the person of Henry III., King of Navarre, who now became *Henry IV.* of France, afterwards surnamed *the Great.* His mother had avowed herself the protector of the Reformed religion, in which he had been educated. He was now in his 36th year; an able general, possessed of distinguished talents and popular qualities, for the exercise of all which he soon found ample occasion, as his being a Protestant prejudiced the greater part of his people against him.

2. The army of the League was now commanded by the *Duke of Mayenne*, brother of the late Duke of Guise, who proclaimed his uncle, the *Cardinal of Bourbon*, king, by the title of *Charles X.* Henry defeated this army in the famous battle of *Ivry* (1590).

3. Meeting afterwards with various obstacles, he was induced, by views of policy, in order to conciliate the majority of his subjects, to renounce Protestantism, and declare himself a Catholic. He was then crowned at Chartres, and obtained

absolution from the Pope. To his old friends, the Calvinists, who had been his defenders, and by whose aid he ascended the throne, he granted, in 1598, the celebrated *Edict of Nantes*, by which he confirmed all their rights and privileges, giving them free admission to all offices of honor and profit.

4. After Henry was quietly seated on the throne, he turned his attention to the improvement of the internal condition of his kingdom; encouraging agriculture and commerce, causing mulberry-trees to be planted, and silk-worms to be reared; and in all his patriotic designs, he found an able assistant in his great minister, the *Duke of Sully*, in whom he possessed what kings can rarely boast of, — a true friend. The civil war, of nearly thirty years' duration, had produced the most calamitous effects: the crown was loaded with debt; the country uncultivated; the people poor and miserable: but by means of the wise and prudent measures which were adopted, the face of things was soon happily changed; and, during this reign, all the state debts were discharged.

5. Henry, with the aid of Sully, formed a romantic scheme, styled the *grand design*, for dividing Europe into 15 states, so arranged as to avoid the grounds of war, and secure perpetual peace. With regard to his real motive, there have been different opinions; but the object, whatever it might be, was to be obtained by force of arms. Having made great preparations for war, just before he was to set out to put himself at the head of his army, he was assassinated, in 1610, by *Ravaillac*, a bigoted Catholic, in the 21st year of his reign, and the 57th of his age.

6. Henry was the most popular sovereign that ever sat on the throne of France. His person and manners were prepossessing, at once inspiring affection and commanding respect: his talents were great, both as a general and a statesman; but his master virtue was his love for his people. His soldiers and his subjects regarded him with the affection of children When asked what the revenue of France amounted to, he replied, "To what I please; for, having the hearts of my people, they will give me whatever I ask. If God sees proper to spare my life, I will take care that France shall be in such a condition, that every peasant in it shall be able to have a fowl in his pot."

7. Notwithstanding his many noble qualities as a sovereign and a man, yet, as a husband, he is little to be commended; his dissoluteness rendered his domestic life unhappy, and the manners of his court were rendered profligate by the example of his libertine conduct. No less than 4,000 French gentle

men are said to have been killed in duels, chiefly arising out of amorous quarrels, during the first 18 years of his reign.

8. Henry was succeeded by his son, *Louis XIII.*, then a boy in his 9th year. *Mary de Medici*, the mother of the young king, who was appointed regent, disgusted the nobility by her partiality for Italian favorites, and the kingdom soon relapsed into the most fatal disorders. But the abilities of *Cardinal Richelieu*, who, after the king became of age, was made Prime Minister, soon effected a great change. It was his policy to promote rather the aggrandizement of the kingdom, than the true interests and happiness of the people. His three leading objects were, to subdue the turbulent spirit of the French nobility, to humble the power of the Protestants, and to curb the encroachments of the house of Austria.

9. The Protestants, alienated by persecution, attempted to throw off their allegiance, and establish an independent state, of which *Rochelle* was to be the capital. Richelieu laid siege to this city, which, after maintaining a most obstinate resistance for a year, during which 15,000 persons perished, was forced to surrender (1628). By this event, the civil war was ended, and the *Protestant* power in France finally crushed.

10. The cardinal entered deeply into foreign politics, influenced all the courts of Europe, and was continually engaged in vast projects for humbling his enemies, and extending his influence abroad, or in checking the designs which were formed against his power and his life at home. A rebellion was excited by the *Duke of Orleans*, the king's brother, supported by the *Duke of Montmorency;* but their army was defeated, and Montmorency executed for treason. Amidst all this turbulence and intrigue, the haughty and ambitious cardinal extended the glory of the French name to distant regions, commanded the respect of all the European powers, patronized literature and science, and instituted the *French Academy.*

11. Louis was so completely under the influence of Richelieu, that his character is little seen. He acquired the epithet of *Just;* but if he were entitled to it, the injustice and cruelty of some of the public measures of his reign must be imputed entirely to his minister.

12. *Louis XIV.* (sometimes surnamed *the Great*) succeeded to the throne, in 1643, in the 5th year of his age, under the regency of his mother, *Anne of Austria*, who made choice of *Cardinal Mazarin* for her minister. Mazarin was an artful Italian, whose excessive avarice rendered him odious to the people; but one of his greatest faults was his neglect of the education of the young king, who was instructed only in dan-

cing, fencing, and other superficial accomplishments. The administration of Mazarin was signalized by the defeat of the Spaniards, and by intestine commotions, particularly a civil war, called the *Fronde*, fomented by *Cardinal de Retz*, and supported by the aristocracy.

13. On the death of Mazarin, Louis, being now 22 years of age, took upon himself the entire command and direction of the affairs of government, and entered on a vigorous and splendid career. The love of glory was his ruling passion and this he pursued, not only by the terror of his arms and the splendor of his conquests, but also by his patronage of literature, science, and the arts; by his able administration of internal affairs; and by the extension and improvement of all kinds of public works. The capital was embellished, the splendid palace of *Versailles* built, commerce and manufactures encouraged, the canal of *Languedoc*, and other useful works, constructed.

14. The finances were admirably regulated by *Colbert*, one of the ablest statesmen of modern times: in the former part of his reign, his armies were commanded by *Condé* and *Turenne*, two of the greatest generals of the age; and the genius of the famous *Vauban* was employed in fortifying his towns.

15. For a long time, he was everywhere successful: he conquered *Franche Compté*, and annexed it to France; made great conquests in the *Netherlands;* overran *Alsace;* and twice laid waste the *Palatinate* with fire and sword. Such was the barbarous devastation, that, in the first instance, from the top of the castle of *Manheim*, 27 cities and towns of the Palatinate were seen, at the same time, in flames; and in the second instance, more than 40 towns and a vast number of villages were burnt, and the inhabitants reduced to the greatest extremities by hunger and cold.

16. In 1675, *Turenne* was killed by a cannon-ball; *Condé* soon after retired; and *Colbert* died. No men of equal talents arose to supply their places. The conquests of Louis had been made at such an enormous expense. that his dominions were, in a measure, exhausted. and his means of defence weakened. He had, by his unbounded ambition, by the violence and injustice of his projects, and the alarming increase of his power, gradually raised up, among the states of Europe, a formidable opposition to his authority, which gave rise to long and bloody wars.

17. By the *League of Augsburg*, which was organized in 1686, Holland, Spain, Sweden, and the Emperor and several of the princes of Germany, were united against him. In 1701 the alliance against France, by England, Germany, and Hol

land, was formed; and a series of reverses marked the latter part of his long reign. His armies had now to contend against the genius of the *Duke of Marlborough* and *Prince Eugene*, who gained over them the celebrated battles of *Blenheim*, *Ramillies*, *Oudenarde*, and *Malplaquet;* and at the peace of *Utrecht*, he lost nearly all that he had gained.

18 One of the most unjust as well as impolitic measures of Louis was the revocation (1685) of the *Edict of Nantes* granted by Henry IV., for the toleration of the Protestants. By this barbarous act, all the Reformed churches were destroyed, their ministers banished, and every individual was outlawed, or compelled to renounce his religion. They were hunted like wild beasts, and great numbers were put to death. By this measure, the kingdom lost from 500,000 to 800,000 of her most useful and industrious citizens, who were driven into exile, and carried the arts and manufactures of France, in which the Protestants greatly excelled, to other countries.

19. Louis died in the 73d year of his reign, and the 78th of his age. His reign was the longest and most brilliant in the history of France, but not the happiest for his country; and his government was more despotic than that of his predecessors. "The greater part of his reign," says Anquetil, "may be considered as a spectacle with grand machinery, calculated to excite astonishment. Towards the end, we behold nothing but the wrecks of that theatrical majesty, and the illusion vanishes."

20. Louis was one of the handsomest men in his kingdom and excelled in all the polite accomplishments. In his appearance and manners there was an extraordinary degree of dignity and majesty, which were softened and tempered by affability and politeness; so that, if he was not the greatest king he was at least, as Bolingbroke expresses it, "the best actor of majesty that ever filled a throne."

21. He possessed great vigor of mind, and good talents, which were, however, but little improved by education. His morals were dissolute, and his ambition and love of glory were insatiable, and led him to violate the duties of justice and humanity, and to sacrifice the real interests of his people He patronized every species of merit, and his reign, which is regarded as the *Augustan age* of French literature, was less illustrious for military achievements, than for the splendor of the arts and sciences.

SECTION VI.

Louis XV.; Louis XVI.: — The Revolution. — From A. D. 1715 *to* 1793.

1. *Louis XV.*, great-grandson of the late king, succeeded to the throne, in 1715, in his 6th year; and the *Duke of Orleans* was appointed regent. This regency is remarkable chiefly for the famous *Mississippi scheme* of *Law*, who formed a project to pay off the national debt by the introduction of a paper currency; — a scheme which was ruinous to the fortunes of thousands.

2. Louis, soon after he came of age, chose for his minister the mild and amiable *Cardinal Fleury*, who was then 73 years of age, and retained his vigor till near 90. By his pacific counsels, the tranquillity of France, and even of the rest of Europe, was continued, with little interruption, for nearly 20 years.

3. After the death of Fleury, France was involved in the war of the *Austrian Succession*, which was occasioned by the death of the emperor, *Charles VI.* There were two claimants to the imperial throne; *Maria Theresa*, the late emperor's eldest daughter, who was married to *Francis* of Lorraine, Grand Duke of Tuscany; and *Charles*, the Elector of Bavaria. The former was supported by England; the latter by France and Prussia. In this war, the French were defeated by the allies, under *George II.* of England, at *Dettingen;* but, under Marshal *Saxe*, they gained the battle of *Fontenoy.* Hostilities were terminated, in 1748, by the peace of *Aix-la-Chapelle*, by which the claim of Maria Theresa was acknowledged.

4. In 1755, a war broke out between France and England respecting their *American possessions*, which was terminated by the peace of *Paris*, in 1763, when Canada and the other French territories in North America were ceded by France to Great Britain. The remainder of this reign was chiefly occupied with the conquest of *Corsica*, and contests between the king and his parliaments.

5. Louis died, after a reign of 59 years, at the age of 65 He possessed nothing, as a king or a man, that entitled him to the gratitude or affection of his people. In the early part of his reign, his subjects conferred upon him the title of *Well beloved;* but a long course of rapacity, profusion, and tyranny, as a monarch, and of the most profligate debaucheries in private life, induced them to retract the appellation. His reign

resembled that of *Charles II.* of England, in its pernicious influence on the interests of religion, morality, and liberty. His own odious character; his attempts to crush the spirit of freedom; the prodigality of his government; the extreme profligacy of his court, — all conspired to loosen the bonds between the sovereign and his subjects, and prepare for the overthrow of all the ancient institutions of the kingdom; and the general uneasiness and the murmurs of the people indicated approaching storms.

6. *Louis XVI.* succeeded his grandfather, in 1774, at the age of 20 years. He was a man of correct morals, upright intentions, desirous of correcting abuses, but was wanting in decision of character. His post was one beset with great difficulty and danger from various quarters. It was difficult either to do good or to continue evil, as the privileged classes were as little disposed to submit to reforms as the people to abuses. The finances, by reason of the long course of prodigality, were in the most embarrassed condition; and the people, irritated by the tyrannical conduct of the late sovereign, were now more than ever alive to their rights.

7. One of the first measures of the new king was, to remove from office those who, by their misconduct, had become unpopular, and had contributed to the distresses of the kingdom, and to replace them by men of talents and integrity. *Turgot* was placed at the head of the finances, and *Malesherbes* was made Minister of the Interior. These enlightened statesmen attempted useful reforms, which offended the courtiers and privileged orders; and, after a short ministry, they retired from office.

8. The celebrated *Necker*, a Protestant of Geneva, and a banker, succeeded Turgot, and pursued the system of economy and reform; but, becoming unpopular with the courtiers, he was displaced. The important office of the general control of the finances had now become exceedingly difficult to fill. Two financiers having attempted, without success, to supply the place of Necker, the office was given, in 1783, to *Calonne*, who abandoned reforms, and made a boast of prodigality.

9 War between Great Britain and the American Colonies having broken out, many Frenchmen, among whom were the *Marquis de Lafayette*, and other officers and engineers, crossed the Atlantic to aid the Americans; and France soon after declared war against England. On the return of peace, in 1783, the difficulties increased; the enormous public expenses had brought the finances into the most embarrassed condition and the government was reduced to a stand for want of supplies

10. Various causes had been, for some time, at work to pro

duce a *revolution* in France, which was now about to burst forth, and convulse not only that country, but the whole civilized world. Some of the principal of these causes were, the progress of philosophy, the diffusion of information, and the freedom of thinking on subjects of government and religion; the notions and feelings in favor of liberty excited by the American revolution, and disseminated by the return of the French officers and army from the United States; the prevalence of infidelity among the literary classes; the despotism of the government, and the abuses both of the ecclesiastical and political establishments; the odious privileges of the nobility and clergy, especially their exemption from taxes; the desire of the nobility to regain those privileges of which they had been stripped by the crown; and the discontent of the mass of the people on account of their oppressed condition, being the despised portion of the state, yet bearing all its burdens. All these circumstances had an influence in preparing the way for this great event; yet the more immediate cause of the revolution was the derangement of the finances.

11. All plans for restoring the finances to order having proved ineffectual, Louis, by the advice of Calonne, convoked in 1787, an assembly of the *Notables*, a body consisting of persons selected by the king, chiefly from the higher orders of the state. To this assembly it was proposed to levy a land-tax, proportioned to property, without any exception in favor of the nobility or clergy; but being little inclined to make sacrifices, they refused to sanction the measure.

12. Calonne, finding it impossible any longer to maintain his ground, resigned his office, and was succeeded by *Brienne* Archbishop of Toulouse. But the assembly of Notables still continuing unmanageable and parsimonious, recourse was then had to the Parliament of Paris, but without success, and a convocation of the *States-General* was demanded. This body, which was composed of three orders, nobility, clergy, and the third estate, or commons, had not been assembled since 1614 and it never had a regular existence.

13. Necker was again recalled to power; and a second assembly of the Notables was convoked, in order to determine the form and composition of the States-General. Necker proposed that the deputies of the commons should equal, in number, those of the other two orders united; but the Notables refused to concur in the measure. It was, however, sanctioned by the king, and carried into effect. The commons chose able men; and on the 5th of May, 1789, the assembly of the *States-General* was opened at Versailles. This body carried forward a revolution, which was now effectually commenced.

14. The king addressed the States-General in a conciliatory speech, no longer using the language of a sovereign who expected implicit obedience to his will. But difficulties soon arose respecting the manner in which questions should be decided, whether by a majority of orders or of polls, and whether there should be a separation or union of the three branches.

15. At length the deputies of the third estate, or commons with such deputies of the nobility and clergy as were disposed to unite with them, on the motion of the *Abbé Siéyes*, declared themselves the supreme legislative body, under the title of the *National Assembly*, a body "one and indivisible." Of this assembly *Bailly* was chosen the president, and *Mirabeau*, a man of brilliant talents and great eloquence, was the popular leader. The *Duke of Orleans*, a descendant of Louis XIII., and the father of Louis Philippe, ex-king of the French, noted for his immense wealth and profligacy, was also a prominent member.

16. The first decree of the National Assembly was an act of sovereignty; and by proclaiming the indivisibility of the legislative power, it placed under its dependence the privileged orders. Thus Louis found that his authority was, in a great measure, wrested from him; and the great body of the nobility and clergy, by their refusal to unite with the commons, likewise saw themselves shut out from power, and their privileges invaded.

17. During the irritated state of the public mind, the king again dismissed Necker from office. This unpopular measure was the signal for insurrection in Paris, which was soon in a state of violent commotion. The *Bastile*, a huge state prison, was demolished by the populace; other excesses were committed in the city and elsewhere, by the furious rabble, and by mobs of frantic women of the vilest character. The army united with the people; the nobles emigrated for safety, and for foreign aid; the king, queen, and royal family, were forced, on the 6th of October, from Versailles to the capital by the ungovernable mob; but were protected from violence by the influence and efforts of *Lafayette*, who commanded the National Guard. In consequence of this removal, the Assembly adjourned its sittings to Paris.

18. The progress of the revolution was rapid, and produced the most important consequences. The seat of power was changed, and all the preliminary alterations were effected. The three orders were discontinued; the States-General converted into the Assembly of the nation; the royal authority nearly annihilated; the privileges of the nobles and clergy,

and the feudal system, in all its branches, abolished; religious liberty and the freedom of the press established; the church lands confiscated; the monasteries suppressed; and France was divided into 83 departments.

19. After these measures were accomplished, the great design of the National Assembly was the formation of a *constitution*, and from this circumstance it is denominated the *Constituent Assembly.* While engaged in its deliberations, Louis and his family, finding their situation uncomfortable, escaped from Paris, but were stopped on the frontiers of the kingdom, and brought back. A constitution, which established limited monarchy, and the equality of all ranks, was at length completed, and accepted by the king, and the assembly dissolved itself on the 30th of September, 1791.

20. The next assembly, styled the *Legislative Assembly*, met on the first of October, and was composed wholly of new members, as the members of the Constituent Assembly were, by their own act, excluded from holding seats in it. Soon after the commencement of the revolution, various political clubs were formed in Paris, of which the *Jacobin club* (so called from its meeting in a convent of suppressed *Jacobin monks*) was the most prominent, and insensibly absorbed all the rest; and, for a time, this factious association governed the capital, and controlled the Assembly.

21. On the 21st of September, 1792, a new body, styled the *National Convention*, commenced their deliberations; and, at their first sitting, they abolished the regal government, and declared France a *republic.* The king was arraigned at their bar to answer to various charges; he appeared before them with a firm and manly countenance, and looked round upon the assembly with an air of resolution.

22. Desèze, one of the defenders of the king, ended his speech with these words: "Listen to History, who will say to Fame,—Louis, who ascended the throne at the age of twenty, carried with him there an example of morals, of justice, and of economy: he had no weaknesses, no corrupting passions, and he was the constant friend of his people. The people desired that a disastrous impost should be abolished, and Louis abolished it; the people asked for the destruction of servitudes, and Louis destroyed them; they demanded reforms, he consented to them; they wished to change the laws by which they were governed, he agreed to their wish; the people required that several millions of Frenchmen should recover their rights and these he restored to them; the people asked for liberty and he gave it. No one can dispute that Louis had the glory of anticipating the demands of his people by making these

sacrifices; and it is he whom it has been proposed to.... Citizens, I cannot go on; I pause in the presence of History: remember that History will judge your judgment, and that her decision will be that of ages to come."

23. But the passions of the Convention were deaf and unmoved; and the sentence of death was pronounced by a majority of 26 out of 721 voters. The king was carried to the place of execution, and mounted the ladder of the scaffold with a firm step. "I die innocent," said he; "I forgive my enemies; and you, unfortunate people...." At this moment, the noise of the drums drowned his voice; the executioners seized him; and the axe of the guillotine separated his head from his body, on the 21st of January, 1793. Thus perished, at the age of thirty-nine, and after a most disastrous reign of eighteen years and a half, this well-disposed, but most unfortunate monarch.

SECTION VII.

The Revolution continued: — Robespierre; Bonaparte; European War: Bonaparte dethroned, and the Bourbon Family restored. — From A. D. 1793 *to* 1815.

1. In 1793, the constitution of the republic was completed by the Convention; the executive power was lodged in a Committee of Public Safety; and the revolutionary tribunal was erected under *Robespierre* and his associates, whose bloody domination is styled "*the reign of terror.*" Two factions soon arose in the National Convention, one styled the *Mountain party*, from their occupying the most elevated seats in the hall of the Convention, — these were the most violent revolutionists and advocates for the extreme of democracy; the other named *Girondists*, because some of their leaders were from the department of the *Gironde*, — these were more moderate, and more distinguished for love of order and equity. The leaders of the former were *Robespierre*, *Danton*, and *Marat*, men almost unparalleled in depravity and cruelty: of the latter, the leaders were *Brissot*, *Vergniaud*, and *Condorcet*.

2. The Mountain party, having gained the ascendency over their opponents, were instrumental in causing the most horrid massacres. They condemned and executed the *Queen Antoinette*, and guillotined *Brissot*, *Vergniaud*, and 20 others of the Girondists. That monster of vice, the *Duke of Orleans*, suffered the same fate from the hands of the very party that

he had materially contributed to bring forward to serve his own purposes.

3. The Convention abandoned themselves to the most extravagant excesses: on the motion of *Gobet*, Archbishop of Paris, they suppressed the *Christian religion;* passed a decree that the only French deities hereafter should be *Liberty Equality*, and *Reason;* established a republican calendar, abolished the *Sabbath*, and, instead of it, made every 10th day a day of rest. The churches were plundered of their gold and silver; and even their bells were melted and cast into cannon.

4. The Convention was at length divided anew into two most violent parties; *Robespierre* at the head of one and *Danton* of the other. Robespierre triumphed. and all his most active opponents were guillotined; but his own fate soon followed, being condemned and executed on a charge of tyranny, in July, 1794. The *Jacobins* were soon after suppressed by the Convention; and, during the next year (1795), the third constitution was proclaimed, the executive power being vested in *five directors.* — From 1791 to 1799, four different constitutions were formed. By the 4th, adopted in 1799, the executive power was vested in three *consuls*, of whom *Bonaparte* was elected to be first, *Cambacères* the second, and *Le Brun* the third; and, in 1802, these three were appointed consuls for life.

5. The French revolution was at first *political*, as directed against the absolute power of the court and the privileges of the higher classes; but it afterwards became *military*, because Europe attacked it. The European sovereigns, fearful of its consequences in their respective dominions, attempted to put it down; but, on the contrary, they extended its sphere. It was destined in its progress to work a change in the politics of Europe, by terminating the struggle of the kings with each other, and beginning one between the kings and the people; and in its final result, it diminished the power of the sovereigns and the privileges of the nobility and clergy, and promoted the liberty of the people and the advancement of civilization.

6. Before the execution of the king, many of the clergy and nobility, together with multitudes of persons, attached to the ancient order of things, had fled from France, through fear of personal danger, and to solicit foreign aid. A powerful body was thus collected on the frontiers, who were assisted by the surrounding nations, especially the *Prussians* and *Austrians*, in their efforts to reëstablish royalty and tranquillity. This was the origin (1792) of the *First* of that series of *coalitions* against France, into which nearly all the powers of Europe

successively entered. On the death of the king, Great Britain and Holland, and soon afterwards Russia and Spain also, declared war against France.

7. The invading army was commanded by the *Duke of Brunswick*, who injudiciously published a threatening manifesto, the effect of which was to irritate the revolutionists into greater violences, to hasten the execution of the king, and to unite all parties in the defence of the country.

8. The combined invasion under the Duke of Brunswick was completely overthrown. France in her turn became the assailant, and her army under *Dumouriez* conquered the Netherlands in the autumn of 1792; and afterwards Holland, Switzerland, and a part of Germany, yielded to her arms. The republic, having made peace with several of the German princes, turned her views towards Italy; and the command of the army was (1796) given to *Napoleon Bonaparte*, then a young man in the 27th year of his age, who had previously distinguished himself at the siege of *Toulon*. By a series of rapid victories, this extraordinary man retrieved the affairs of France, and obliged the Austrians to sign, in 1797, the treaty of *Campo Formio*, by which the conquests of the French in the Netherlands were confirmed, and the Milanese ceded to the new Cisalpine Republic; whilst the Venetian territories were given up to Austria.

9. The *Second Coalition* was formed after the defeat of the French fleet, in 1798, by that of the English, under *Nelson*, in the bay of *Aboukir*, off the mouth of the *Nile*. Before this event, Bonaparte had invaded Egypt, defeated the Mamelukes in the battle of the *Pyramids*, and taken possession of Cairo and all the Delta.

10. In the campaign of 1799, the French were very unfortunate; the Austrians, under the *Archduke Charles*, and the Russians, under *Suwarrow*, gained a number of important victories in the north of Italy, in Switzerland, and in Germany: by their united forces, the very frontiers of France were threatened; whilst the ill conduct of the *Directory* at home brought the country to the brink of ruin. At this crisis, Bonaparte, who had proceeded from Egypt to Syria, and taken Jaffa, returned to Paris, and, by the aid of *Fouché*, *Cambacères*, *Talleyrand*, *Lucien Bonaparte*, and *Siéyes*, together with a military force, he abolished the Directory, framed a new constitution, and caused himself to be elected, in 1799, *First Consul*.

11. From this moment, the affairs of the republic took a new turn. By his activity and energy, Bonaparte overcame the intrigues of all his rivals, introduced a new order of things in the different departments of state, suppressed the various

factions that had long raged in the empire, and, by the reformation of many abuses, restored order and tranquillity to the government.

12. After this, he put himself at the head of the army, and, having effected the celebrated passage of the *Alps*, defeated (1800) the Austrians under *Melas*, in the memorable battle of *Marengo*, which decided the fate of Italy. This victory, together with the defeat of the Austrians, soon afterwards, at *Hohenlinden*, by the French under *Moreau*, and other successes, led the way to the peace of *Luneville* with Austria and the German empire (1801), and afterwards to the peace of *Amiens* with England (1802). Thus Europe, for the first time since the late revolution, enjoyed the blessings of universal peace.

13. The limits of France were now greatly enlarged, and Bonaparte, as First Consul, exercised an absolute sway over almost all the continent of Europe west of the Adriatic and the Rhine. Soon after the establishment of peace, he restored the Catholic religion, concluded a *concordat* or convention with the Pope, granted toleration to all religions, and instituted the Legion of Honor.

14. He was next elected First Consul for life, with supreme power; but a conspiracy was now formed against him, in which *Moreau*, *Pichegru*, *Georges*, and other eminent men, were accused of participating. Moreau was banished to America; Pichegru was strangled; Georges, and 11 others, were guillotined; and the *Duke d'Enghien* was shot without trial. — In 1804, *Bonaparte* was proclaimed *Emperor of France*, and was crowned by the Pope: the next year, he assumed also the title of *King of Italy*.

15. The peace of Amiens was of short duration. In 1803, the war was renewed between France and England; Bonaparte seized Hanover, and threatened to invade the British isles, and in 1805, the *Third Coalition* was formed by England, Austria, Russia, Sweden, and afterwards Prussia. The emperor immediately put himself at the head of the French army; carried his rapid and victorious arms to *Ulm*, where he captured the Austrian army of 33,000 men under *Mack*; and in the memorable battle of *Austerlitz* (1805), defeated the united forces of Russia and Austria, — at which battle the *three emperors* were present. This great victory terminated the campaign, and brought about the peace of *Presburg*, by which Austria ceded to the French the Venetian territories, and submitted to other humiliating conditions.

16. A few weeks before the battle of Austerlitz, the English fleet, under *Lord Nelson*, gained a great victory off *Cape Trafalgar*, over the combined fleets of France and Spain. The

English captured 19 ships of the line, but lost their great admiral, who was slain in the action.

17. The King of Naples having permitted a British and Russian army to land in his dominions, the Emperor of France deposed the Neapolitan dynasty, and raised his brother *Joseph*, to the throne; he also compelled the Dutch to receive his brother, *Louis*, as King of Holland. He next subverted the constitution of the German empire, and formed a union of several states, under the title of "*The Confederation of the Rhine*" of which he was chosen protector. *Francis II.* solemnly resigned (1806) his title as "Emperor of Germany and King of the Romans," and retained the title which he had assumed in 1804, namely, that of *hereditary Emperor of Austria.* The electors of *Bavaria*, *Wurtemberg*, and *Saxony* joined the Confederation, and were raised, by Bonaparte, to the rank of *kings*.

18. The vast accession of power acquired by this alliance was the cause of new jealousies, and hastened the *Fourth Coalition*, formed in 1806, by which Prussia, Russia, Austria, Sweden, and England were united in the war against France. Hostilities were commenced by the Prussians, without waiting for the aid of Russia; but Bonaparte, with his usual good fortune, gained over them the great battles of *Jena* and *Auerstadt*, entered the capital of Prussia as a conqueror, and here commenced the "*Continental System*" against English commerce, by issuing the *Berlin Decree*, declaring the British islands in a state of blockade, and ordering all ports to be shut against them. The French army penetrated into Poland, and gained an advantage over the Russians, in the hard-fought battle of *Pultusk* (1806).

19. The following year (1807), Bonaparte fought with the Russians the indecisive battle of *Eylau;* defeated them at *Friedland;* and, having gained possession of *Dantzic* and *Konigsberg*, concluded the peace of *Tilsit*. Separate treaties were made with Russia and Prussia: the former gained a small acquisition of territory; but the dominions of the latter were reduced almost one half; both agreed to shut their ports against England, and thus became parties in the French emperor's favorite object of excluding British commerce from the continent. The provinces conquered from Prussia were erected into the new kingdom of *Westphalia*, of which *Jerome Bonaparte* was acknowledged king.

20. The English government, in retaliation of Bonaparte's *Berlin Decree*, issued their *Orders in Council*, by which all neutral vessels trading with France were compelled to stop at a British port and pay a duty. After the peace of *Tilsit*, the

emperor proceeded to Italy; and at Milan, in consequence of the Orders in Council, he issued (1807) his *Milan Decree*, by which every vessel which submitted to British search, or consented to any pecuniary exactions whatever, was confiscated.

21. Elated by his astonishing successes, the Emperor of France appeared now (1808) to consider himself as sovereign of Europe, and to set at defiance all principles of justice and moderation. Being ambitious of appropriating more of the thrones of Europe to his brothers and relatives, he next fixed his attention on *Spain* and *Portugal;* and so decisive was he in the execution of his plans, that, in a short time, the royal family of Portugal emigrated to Brazil.

22. Though *Charles IV.*, King of Spain, had shown himself subservient to the views of the French emperor, yet the latter was not content, but compelled the Spanish monarch to resign his crown in favor of his brother, *Joseph Bonaparte*, whom he removed from Naples, and caused to be proclaimed King of Spain; and he raised to the throne of Naples *Murat*, who had married his sister.

23. The Spaniards rose in opposition to this tyrannical measure, and, in this emergency, had recourse to England, who readily afforded her assistance. The war which was thus excited in the peninsula continued to rage from 1808 to 1813; and, in a series of engagements, the forces of England and Spain, under the command of *Wellington* and others, were, in most instances, victorious over the armies of France. Some of the principal exploits in this war were the desperate, but ineffectual, defence of *Saragossa*, by *Palafox*, and the victories of *Wellington* at *Talavera*, *Salamanca*, and *Vittoria.*

24. In 1809, while the war was raging in Spain, hostilities again broke out between France and Austria, which were prosecuted by Bonaparte with his usual success. Having gained advantages over the Austrians at *Abensberg*, *Eckmuhl*, and *Ratisbon*, he entered *Vienna;* afterwards fought, against the Archduke Charles, the indecisive battle of *Aspern* or *Essling*, and entirely defeated him at *Wagram.*

25. This war was terminated (1809) by the treaty of *Vienna* or *Schoenbrunn*, by which *Francis II.*, the Emperor of Austria, was compelled to submit to considerable losses of territory, to accede to the "continental system," and, what was more humiliating, to promise his daughter, *Maria Louisa*, in marriage to his great and victorious enemy. In consequence of this treaty, Bonaparte was divorced from his empress *Josephine*, and his marriage with the emperor's daughter was solemnized April 1, 1810; and he thus became allied to the imperial house of Austria.

26 By the treaty of Tilsit, *Alexander*, the Emperor of Russia, had acceded to Bonaparte's "continental system" against England, by agreeing to exclude British goods from his dominions but the consequences of this measure were extremely injurious to his subjects, and ruinous to his finances. The year (1811) was spent in negotiations and discussions; but as they did not promise an amicable adjustment, both parties prepared for war. Early in the spring of 1812, Bonaparte collected, in Poland, an immense army, consisting of 400,000 infantry, 60,000 cavalry, and 1,200 pieces of artillery; and on the 24th of June, crossing the Niemen, he invaded the Russian territories.

27. His march was directed towards *Moscow*, the ancient capital of the empire, and was everywhere marked with desolation and blood. He defeated the Russians at *Smolensk*; fought the tremendous battle of *Borodino*, or *Moskwa*, in which nearly 30,000 men fell on each side; proceeded afterwards to Moscow, which he found enveloped in flames, and abandoned by the inhabitants. The city had been set on fire by the Russians, in order to prevent the French from deriving any advantage from possessing it; and nearly three-fourths of it were consumed before the conflagration ceased.

28. This extraordinary transaction was the cause of the greatest mortification and disappointment to Bonaparte. He had imagined that, after obtaining possession of Moscow, he should become the arbiter of the whole Russian empire, and be able to prescribe to it such a peace as he should think proper. But his good fortune had now forsaken him; and finding himself thwarted in this object, the Russian generals concentrating their forces around him, and the horrors of a Russian winter approaching, he thought it most prudent to evacuate the city, and retreat towards the frontiers.

29. Then followed, amidst the solitudes and snows of Russia, in consequence of cold and famine, a series of disasters losses and sufferings, which are scarcely paralleled in history and which issued in the almost entire destruction of the invading army. About 30,000 horses perished by the severity of the weather in a single day; all the pieces of cannon were lost, and only about 30,000 men remained to recross the Niemen.

30. After the remnant of the French army had effected the disastrous passage of the Berezina, near the frontiers of Russia, the emperor quitted it, and fled, in disguise, through Poland and Germany, to Paris. He resolved to hazard another campaign, and raised (1813) a fresh army of 350,000 men but he was now opposed by the *Fifth Coalition*, consisting of

Russia, Prussia, Austria, some of the confederates of the Rhine, and Sweden, subsidized by England.

31. Bonaparte again put himself at the head of his army, was worsted by the Allies in the battle of *Lutzen;* defeated them in the battle of *Bautzen;* repulsed them at *Dresden*, where *Moreau* was slain; but was utterly routed in the tremendous battle of *Leipsic* (Oct. 1813), with the loss of 40,000 men in killed, wounded, and prisoners. The combatants, in this action, called the "Battle of Nations," exceeded 400,000 a greater number than has been engaged in any other battle in modern times.

32. Bonaparte made his escape from the scene of his defeat, and proceeded to Paris. In his address to the senate, he frankly acknowledged his disasters. "All Europe," said he, "was with us a year ago, — all Europe is now against us." Having attempted in vain to rouse the French people, he again joined his army. In the mean time, the Allies had crossed the Rhine, and penetrating, after a desperate struggle, into the heart of France, they *entered Paris*.

33. The situation of Bonaparte having now become hopeless, he abdicated the throne of France, and, after various deliberations, the island of *Elba* was fixed upon for his future residence; but he was allowed to retain the title of emperor. The mighty empire which he had raised was suddenly crumbled to the dust; and *Louis XVIII.* was restored (1814) to the throne of his ancestors.

34. A General Congress of European sovereigns was immediately assembled at *Vienna*, to arrange and settle the affairs of Europe, with a view to restore, yet with many variations, the ancient order of things. But while the sovereigns were deliberating on these matters, Bonaparte, dissatisfied with his situation, made another effort to regain the throne of France. Landing at Frejus, he marched with 1140 men, without opposition, through the country; presented himself in an open carriage to the royal army at Melun; was received with shouts of applause; the same evening, entered Paris in triumph, amidst the loudest acclamations; was proclaimed emperor; and Louis XVIII. fled, on his approach, to the frontiers. This progress of the exiled emperor through France, which was one of the most extraordinary exploits that he ever performed, is without a parallel in history, and evinces, in the most striking manner, his ascendency over the French nation. In 20 days from his landing at Frejus, he found himself quietly seated on the throne, without having spilled a drop of blood.

35. Aware that he had not returned to his former power, he therefore, in order to strengthen his authority, issued some

popular decrees, establishing the freedom of the press, abolishing the slave trade, and regulating the taxes which weighed most heavily on the people: he also condescended to offer them the plan of a constitution very different from the system of despotism upon which he had before acted, and containing many excellent regulations.

36. He had, however, but little time for legislative measures. As soon as his arrival in France was known at Vienna, he was declared by the Congress a traitor and an outlaw; and a new and formidable coalition was immediately formed against him among the European powers. He placed himself once more at the head of a large army, but was entirely defeated by the Allies under the command of *Wellington* and *Blucher*, in the memorable battle of *Waterloo*, which cost the French army upwards of 40,000 men in killed and wounded.

37. This battle sealed the fate of Bonaparte. He returned immediately to Paris, abdicated the throne in favor of his son and afterwards surrendered himself to *Captain Maitland*, of the Bellerophon, claiming, in a letter to the Prince Regent of England, an asylum, "like Themistocles, among the most powerful, most constant, and most generous of his enemies." By the unanimous agreement of the allied sovereigns, he was sent a prisoner to *St. Helena*, where he arrived on the 17th of October, 1815; and there died on the 5th of May, 1821, in the 6th year of his captivity, and 52d of his age.

38. The career of *Bonaparte* surpassed, in many respects, that of every great conqueror who preceded him. No other man has appeared on the theatre of the world, who has been the cause of so many and so astonishing revolutions, or whose contemporary fame has been so widely extended. In his 27th year, he was raised to the chief command of the French army; at the age of 30, he caused himself to be elected First Consul; and in his 35th year, he was proclaimed Emperor of France. During the ten years that he possessed the imperial throne, he was the most powerful potentate, not only of the age, but of modern times, and he made the world tremble by the terror of his name.

39. He may be emphatically called a *king-maker;* for he raised to the rank of kings three brothers, one brother-in-law, and three German electors; *Bernadotte*, also, one of his marshals, was raised to the throne of Sweden. The last four were recognized, by the Congress of Vienna, among the legitimate sovereigns of Europe.

40. He united in his own person, at an early period of his life, and in an advanced state of society, the conqueror, the usurper, and the lawgiver. He triumphed over civilized en

emies; legislated in a refined age; and seized upon the sceptre of a powerful and enlightened people, among powerful and enlightened rivals. To him France is indebted for an admirable code of laws, in the formation of which he was an efficient agent, in which he greatly prided himself, and with regard to which he was repeatedly heard to say, he "could wish to be buried with it in his hands."

41. He favored, in many instances, liberal principles; patronized merit independent of rank; encouraged liberally such branches of science as were useful to his purposes; granted religious toleration; removed or diminished many abuses; broke down oppressive feudal and ecclesiastical institutions and establishments; and left France, and also Europe, in many respects, in a better condition than he found them. But though he was not more unprincipled than other great conquerors have been, yet his ruling passion was evidently insatiable ambition and lust of power, to which he was ready to sacrifice every principle of justice and humanity. No man ever enjoyed a greater opportunity of benefiting his species than he; but this opportunity he cast away, except so far as it suited his own purposes of self-aggrandizement. He chose to be an Alexander or a Cæsar, rather than a Washington; a subverter, rather than a protector, of liberty; a terror and a scourge, rather than a delight and a blessing, to mankind.

42. He exercised over his own dominions a military despotism: his ambition prompted him to sacrifice, without scruple, the rights and independence of nations, and rendered him an enemy to freedom, and to the repose of the world. It was not, therefore, without reason, that the friends of liberty, of peace, and of human improvement, exulted at his downfall His eventful life, and his miserable end, furnish a most instructive lesson on the instability of human affairs, and the vanity of human glory.

SECTION VIII

Louis XVIII. · *Charles X.:* — *Revolution of* 1830; *Louis Philippe:* — *Revolution of* 1848; *Republican Constitution*, *Louis Napoleon, President.*

1. After the second dethronement of Bonaparte, *Louis XVIII.* was again (1815) placed on the throne, and a second pacification took place at Paris. France was reduced to nearly the same limits as before the revolution; she was compelled to restore much of the plunder which had been collected at

Paris, to pay £28,000,000 sterling, as a partial indemnification for the expenses of the war, and to maintain, for five years, an army of occupation, consisting of 150,000 allied troops, to be placed in 16 frontier fortresses. In 1817, the Allies consented to reduce the army of occupation to one fifth; and in 1818, it was wholly withdrawn. — Those officers who, in spite of their oaths to Louis, had sided with Bonaparte in his attempt to reascend the throne of France, were tried for treason and condemned: some of them, among whom was *Marshal Ney* were shot; and others were exiled.

2. Louis XVIII., who was a man of cultivated mind and liberal views, found his situation a difficult one, on account of the conflicts of different political parties, the ultra-royalists, Bonapartists, and liberals; and his policy was somewhat variable, though the ultra-royalist party, for the most part, had the ascendency. One of the principal events during his reign was, in concert with the northern powers of Europe (1823), an invasion of Spain, by a French army, under the *Duke d'Angoulême*, by means of which Ferdinand VII. was released from his thraldom, and restored to the plenitude of his power; and the designs of the *Constitutionalists* of that country, for establishing a more liberal system of government, were frustrated.

3. Louis XVIII. was succeeded, in 1824, by his brother, Count d'Artois, who assumed the title of *Charles X.*, and who was much inferior to Louis in talent, and in the liberality of his political views. Charles seems to have learnt little wisdom from the troubles which the Bourbon family had experienced; and he ascended the throne imbued with the exploded dogmas of a preceding age. His course of life had been very licentious; but, before he came to the throne, his morals were much improved; and he had become, and so continued as long as he lived, much under the influence of priests.

4. His reign was signalized by two enterprises of foreign war of some importance: one in favor of the Greeks, in which France united with England and Russia; the other against *Algiers*, which city, after a siege of six days, surrendered to the French army, on the 5th of July, 1830.

5. The contests between the different political parties, which had agitated the preceding reign, continued and became more violent in this. Charles sided strongly with the ultra-royalists, and promoted men of that party to the highest offices; and the government endeavored, in various ways, to check the rising spirit of liberty, by exerting an influence on the elections, by dissolving the chambers, and by restraining the liberty of the press

6. In March, 1830, the Chamber of Deputies made a strong stand against the ministry, of which *Prince Polignac* was the

head; and, in consequence of this, the chamber was dissolved by the king; new elections were ordered, and the two chambers were convoked for the 3d of August. The elections followed; and it was soon found that the liberal party had secured a large majority. In consequence of this result, the ministers made a report to the king, which was published on the 26th of July, accompanied by three ordinances: one dissolving the Chamber of Deputies, another suspending the liberty of the press, and a third altering the law of election.

7. All the liberal newspapers in Paris were suppressed; the bank refused to discount bills; the manufacturers discharged their workmen; and Paris was in a state of great commotion. On the morning of the 27th, the newspapers appeared as usual; and the seizure of the presses, and the imprisonment of the editors, were signals for revolution.

8. The citizens immediately took up arms against the government, and on the 29th, after a contest of *three days*, having obtained a complete victory over the king's guards, the liberal deputies, who had assembled in Paris, appointed General Lafayette commander-in-chief of the National Guards. The two chambers met on the 3d of August; and the Chamber of Deputies, on the 6th, declared the throne of France to be vacant adopted the new-modelled charter, and voted, on the 7th, to invite the Duke of Orleans to become King of the French The Duke accepted the crown on the 8th, and took the prescribed oath on the 9th.

9. Charles had already fled from Paris. He soon went to England, thence to Edinburgh, and resided for some time at Holyrood House. He afterwards proceeded to Austria, and died at Goritz, in Illyria, on the 4th of November, 1836, in the 80th year of his age.

10. *Louis Philippe* — (the son of the *Duke of Orleans*, who made himself infamous as the associate and dupe of the Jacobin party in the first French revolution, and who renounced his family name, and assumed that of *Egalité*) — was raised to the throne by the enemies of despotism and friends of liberty and constitutional government. The authors of this revolutionary movement cherished the expectation that he would carry out their political principles; but in this they were much disappointed. He proved himself to be a man of eminent ability, had able men for his ministers, among whom may be named Périer, Gerard, Molé, Thiers, Soult, and Guizot; and he always exerted a strong personal influence in directing the measures of the government.

11. His policy in relation to foreign states was pacific; and the condition of France was greatly improved, during his reign

with respect to education, agriculture, commerce, and manufactures; also by internal improvement, particularly by extensive lines of railroad, which connect the capital with different parts of the country. The navy was much increased; and the city of Paris was fortified at immense expense, and in a style of grandeur unequalled in modern times. Louis Philippe however, did not make himself a popular sovereign, but manifested more inclination to increase his own power and aggrandize his family, than to gratify the wishes of his subjects or increase their political privileges. By his arbitrary measures in restraining the liberty of the press and the freedom of discussing political affairs, he imitated the example of Charles X and he also shared a similar fate.

12. The most considerable foreign achievement of the French arms, during this reign, was the complete subjugation of *Algeria*, and its establishment as a French colony, which was effected after a long and sanguinary struggle with the natives. The heroic Arab leader, *Abdel Kader*, surrendered in 1847.

13. Although the government of Louis Philippe was conducted with ability, and the state of the country generally prosperous, yet great discontent prevailed among the lower classes, particularly in the capital and other large cities. These classes were deeply imbued with democratic principles, revolts and conspiracies were frequent; and no less than seven attempts were, during his reign, made upon the life of the king.

14. Care was taken by the government to promote the interest and to secure the support of the wealthy and privileged classes, which possessed the exclusive right of voting at the elections; and these classes upheld the throne, and sanctioned a system of excessive taxation, which enabled the king to strengthen himself by the maintenance of a numerous army and by the multiplication of lucrative offices, which were bestowed with an especial design of gaining support to the government.

15. The system of obtaining a venal support of the government was carried so far as, at length, to disgust all classes. The government was loudly charged with corruption in pecuniary matters, and with improper interference in elections. Great dissatisfaction was likewise excited by severe laws against the press, and against the right of public discussion.

16. These offensive measures were ascribed to the influence of the king himself, rather than to his ministers; and the impression gained ground among the people, that it was his intention to abridge the liberties of France, and that he cared more

for the welfare of his family than for that of the nation, — an impression strengthened by the eagerness which he exhibited to contract marriages and alliances with the courts which were known to be most hostile to the progress of liberal principles.

17. The popular discontent was much augmented, in 1847 by a severe commercial revulsion, which depressed trade, lowered the wages of labor, and rendered almost intolerable the heavy taxation, which had been sufficiently oppressive even in periods of the greatest prosperity. In that year, the opponents of the government began to hold, throughout the kingdom, a series of public dinners, or *reform banquets*, as they were termed for the purpose of discussion and agitation. At these meetings, which were numerously attended, speeches were made, in which the conduct and measures of the government were criticized with great severity.

18. At length it was resolved to hold a reform banquet in Paris, on Sunday, the 20th of February, 1848. The king's ministers (Guizot and his colleagues) directed the police to prohibit the meeting, on the pretence that it was of a seditious nature, and would cause disturbance of the public peace. The friends of reform, deeming this prohibition illegal, determined to disregard it, though they postponed the banquet till Tuesday, the 22d.

19. On that day, vast crowds of citizens, greatly excited by the course of the ministry, assembled in the streets of Paris and were soon engaged in conflict with the military forces which had been poured into the city to the number of nearly 80,000. The people took arms from the shops and houses, raised numerous barricades, and attacked the Chamber of Deputies and the residence of Guizot, from both of which, however, they were repulsed by the troops.

20. On the two following days, the insurrection became still more general. The National Guards refused to act, or joined the insurgents, who were everywhere victorious against the king's troops, and finally carried by storm the Palais Royal and the palace of the Tuileries; from the latter of which the throne was taken in triumph, and publicly burnt in the street. The king, after repeated unsuccessful attempts to form an acceptable ministry, abdicated in favor of his grandson, the Count of Paris, and fled, with the royal family, to England. Guizot, the prime minister, also escaped to London.

21. The revolutionists or insurgents, consisting chiefly of the people and workmen of Paris, refused all terms of conciliation or compromise, exclaiming, "It is too late!" A provisional government was immediately instituted, consisting of the following seven distinguished men: Dupont de L'Eure

Lamartine, Arago, Marie, Garnier Pagès, Ledru-Rollin and Crémieux.

22. The provisional government immediately proclaimed France a republic, with the motto, "Liberty, Equality, Fraternity!" A decree was issued abolishing all hereditary titles and distinctions of rank; also abolishing slavery in the French colonies; and ordering the election, by universal suffrage, of a national assembly of 900 members, to meet in Paris, on the 4th of May 1848, to frame a constitution.

23. The National Assembly met on the 4th of May, and the government was organized. In the succeeding month of June, a violent insurrection broke out in Paris; the city was declared in a state of siege, and, to restore order, *General Cavaignac* was appointed, by the Assembly, military dictator, or chief of the executive government.

24. After a session of six months, the National Assembly proclaimed a constitution of a very liberal and democratic character, which provided for the election of a President, by universal suffrage, for the term of four years, with a provision that he could not be reëlected; and also for the election of a single legislative body, styled the National Assembly, consisting of 750 members.

25. An election was made under this constitution in December, 1848, when *Louis Napoleon* [Charles Louis Napoleon Bonaparte] was chosen by an immense majority, having received about 5,500,000 votes out of about 7,500,000. He was to hold the office for four years, ending in May, 1852.

26. Louis Napoleon is the nephew of the late Emperor *Napoleon*, and the son of *Louis Bonaparte*, late King of Holland His mother was *Hortense*, daughter of the Empress *Josephine*, by her first marriage.

27. The Emperor Napoleon had four brothers, *Joseph*, *Lucien*, *Louis*, and *Jerome*. Joseph, the eldest, left no sons; and Lucien, the second brother, being in disgrace in 1804, when Napoleon became Emperor, he and his posterity were excluded from the succession. Louis Napoleon, therefore, claims the right of succession, not by right of primogeniture, but by the laws of the empire, as established by his imperial uncle.—Previous to his election as President, he had been chiefly distinguished by two rash and abortive attempts to place himself on the throne of Louis Philippe: one at *Strasburg*, in 1836; and the other at *Boulogne*, in 1840.

28. A new National Assembly was elected in 1849, and the party which headed the democratic revolution was defeated The Assembly was not harmonious, and there was a great want of harmony between the Assembly and the President.

29. The most important transaction, in relation to foreign

affairs, during the presidency of Louis Napoleon, was the intervention in relation to the government of the pope. In 1848, a revolution broke out at Rome; the pope, *Pius IX.*, was deprived of his temporal power; a republican government was established; and the pope fled to Gaeta, in the kingdom of Naples. In April, 1849, a French army, commanded by *General Oudinot*, was sent to Italy, and after a severe attack and bombardment, the city of Rome surrendered, and on the 3d of July, the French army entered it, overthrew the republican government, and prepared the way for the pope to return reinstated in his former power.

30. In 1851, Louis Napoleon, as the term of his presidency was drawing near its close, had recourse to different manœuvres to get the clause in the constitution, that forbade his reëlection, abrogated. After having failed to induce the Assembly to sustain his views, and having secured the support of a large part of the army, he achieved, by a *coup d'état*, one of the most extraordinary usurpations recorded in history. Early in the morning of the 2d of December, he dissolved the Assembly, seized and imprisoned such of the members as would not acquiesce in his usurpation, and also other liberal statesmen, and some of the most distinguished generals, suppressed all the newspapers, except such as were devoted to his views, and declared, not only Paris, but a great part of the departments, in a state of siege.

31. Having thus possessed himself of power, he called on the people of France to vote, by universal suffrage, yes or no, on the question whether he should be President for ten years, with dictatorial powers. To this call, the people responded, by an immense majority, in his favor. He then proclaimed a constitution, or form of government, which is one of the most despotic in Europe, and according to which the ministry are responsible only to him; and he holds the appointment of the senators and council of state, and nominates the candidates for election to the legislative body.

32. On the 7th of November, 1852, the senate, in compliance with the will of the President, adopted a measure, by 86 votes out of 87, to reëstablish the *imperial government*, and the people were called upon to ratify the measure by their votes on the 20th and 22d of that month. The vote was officially declared on the 1st of December; the whole number of votes being 8,180,660, of which 7,864,189 were in favor of the empire. Thus, in just one year after the *coup d'état*, or usurpation of the President, he was, in accordance with the vote of the people, declared Emperor of the French, under the title of *Napoleon III.*, and the hereditary title secured in his family

Chronological Table of French History. — No. 1.
From Pepin, 752, to the Death of Henry III., 1589.

A. D.		Kings.	Yrs.	
700	—		—	
				Carlovingian Race.
	52	Pepin	16	Son of *Charles Martel*, founds the *second* of *Carlovingian Race* of French kings
8*th*	68	Charlemagne	46	The greatest sovereign of the age; founds, in 800, the *Empire of the West.*
800	—		—	
	14	Louis I.	26	The empire divided into three kingdoms.
	40	Charles I.	37	Battle of *Fontenay;* invasion of the Normans
	77	Louis II.	2	Makes grants to the nobles and bishops.
9*th*	79	Louis III. } Carloman }	5	Reign jointly.
	84	Charles II.	4	The *imperial dignity* transferred to *Germany*
	88	Eudes	10	
	98	Charles III.	25	Invasion of the Normans under *Rollo.*
900	—		—	
	22	Robert	1	
	23	Rodolph	13	Defeats the Normans.
	36	Louis IV.	18	Surnamed *Outremer* or *Stranger.*
10*th*	54	Lothaire	32	*Hugh the Great,* a powerful nobleman.
	86	Louis V.	1	Governed by *Hugh Capet,* son of Hugh the Great.
				Capetian Race.
	87	Hugh Capet	9	Obtains the crown; founds the *Capetian Race.*
	96	Robert	35	A victim of papal tyranny.
1000	—		—	
11*th*	31	Henry I.	29	Prevalence of *duelling.*
	60	Philip I.	48	*First Crusade;* Peter the Hermit.
1100	—		—	
	8	Louis VI.	29	An able and useful sovereign.
12*th*	37	Louis VII.	43	*Second Crusade; St. Bernard; Abelard.*
	80	Philip II.	43	A powerful sovereign; *third Crusade.*
1200	—		—	
	23	Louis VIII.	3	*Crusade* against the *Albigenses.*
	26	St. Louis IX.	44	Engages in two *Crusades;* dies at Tunis.
13*th*	70	Philip III.	15	Massacre of the *Sicilian Vespers.*
	85	Philip IV.	29	Quarrels with *Boniface. Knights Templars*
1300	—		—	
	14	Louis X.	2	
	16	John I.		Dies an infant four days old.
	16	Philip V.	5	The *Salic Law* recognized.
	22	Charles IV.	6	Supports his sister *Isabella* of England.
14*th*				*Branch of Valois.*
	28	Philip VI.	22	Defeated at *Cressy,* &c.; gains *Dauphiny.*
	50	John II.	14	Defeated at *Poitiers,* and taken prisoner.
	64	Charles V.	16	Recovers the English possessions. *Library.*
	80	Charles VI.	42	Defeated by the English at *Agincourt.*
1400	—		—	
	22	Charles VII.	39	The siege of *Orleans* raised by *Joan of Arc.*
	61	Louis XI.	22	The *Tiberius* of France; title *Most Christian*
15*th*	83	Charles VIII.	15	Makes an expedition against Naples.
	98	Louis XII.	17	*Duke of Orleans;* League of Cambray.
1500	—		—	
	15	Francis I.	32	*Duke of Angoulême;* an able sovereign; a patron of *literature;* at war with *Charles* V.
	47	Henry II.	12	Defeated at *St. Quentin;* recovers *Calais.*
	59	Francis II.	1	Husband of *Mary, Queen of Scots.*
16*th*	60	Charles IX.	14	*Civil Wars* commence: *Guise, Condé,* and *Coligny; St. Bartholomew Massacre.*
	74	Henry III.	15	*League* formed against the Protestants; the king assassinated by James Clement.

Chronological Table of French History.—*No. 2.*

***From Henry* IV., 1589, *to the Revolution of* 1848.**

A. D.		Kings.	yrs.	
1500				
				House of Bourbon.
16th	89	Henry IV.	21	A great and popular sovereign; triumphs over the *League* in the battle of *Ivry*; renounces Protestantism and becomes Catholic; issues the *Edict of Nantes*: *Duke of Sully*.
1600				
	10	Louis XIII.	33	*Mary de Medici* regent; afterwards *Cardinal Richelieu* prime minister: *Rochelle* taken and the power of the *Protestants* crushed Revolt of the *Duke of Orleans*.
17th	43	Louis XIV.	72	Possessed of talents and unbounded ambition, his reign the longest and the most renowned for literature and the arts in French history, also distinguished for military achievements, *Colbert*, *Vauban*, *Turenne*, and *Condé*: the canal of *Languedoc* formed: the *Edict of Nantes* revoked; 500,000 Protestants exiled.
1700				
	15	Louis XV.	59	Profligate and tyrannical; *Mississippi Scheme* of Law: Pacific administration of *Cardinal Fleury*; War of the *Austrian Succession*, ended by the Peace of Aix-la-Chapelle: War with England, and loss of *Canada*.
18th	74	Louis XVI.	18	Begins his reign in a time of great difficulty and danger; *Turgot*, and afterwards *Necker*, ministers: the *Americans* assisted: the *States-General* convoked; the *National Assembly* formed; and the *Revolution* begins, 1789. France declared a *Republic*, 1792: *Louis* and *Queen Antoinette* beheaded, 1793: *War* with Prussia, Austria, Great Britain, &c.; *Robespierre*; Reign of Terror. (*Louis* XVII. dies 1795.) *Bonaparte*; victories at *Marengo*, &c.; made First Consul, 1799.
1800				
	4	Napoleon Bonaparte	10	Crowned emperor; gains the victories of *Austerlitz*, *Jena*, &c., and extends his dominion; invades *Russia*, and gains the battle of *Borodino*; retreats; defeated at *Leipsic*; deposed (1814) and sent to *Elba*; escapes, and is overthrown at *Waterloo* (1815): sent to *St. Helena*.
	14	Louis XVIII.	10	Restored. *Constitutional Charter* established: Louis displaced by Bonaparte, but again restored: Invasion of Spain.
19th	24	Charles X.	6	Arbitrary; *Villèle*, *Martignac*, and *Polignac*, successively, ministers: Despotic measures; *Revolution*; *Charles* dethroned.
	30	Louis Philippe	18	*Duke of Orleans*; able, but arbitrary: The Constitutional Charter remodelled: Algeria annexed to France: Education and Internal Improvement promoted: Censorship of the Press: Reform Banquets prohibited: *Revolution*: The King dethroned: Provisional Government: Republican Constitution.
	48	President. *Louis Napoleon*		*President of the Republic of France*; Odillon Barrot Prime Minister; Expedition against Rome.

The figures on the left hand of the *kings*, in these tables, denote the *commencement* of their reigns. Thus it appears that *Henry* IV. began to reign in 1589, and reigned 21 years

ENGLAND.

SECTION I.

The History of England: The Roman Conquest: The Saxon Conquest: The Heptarchy. — From B. C. 55 to A. D. 827.

1. The history of no country, of either ancient or modern times, is richer in various instruction, or calculated to excite deeper interest, than that of England. We here see the gradual rise of a people from a low state of barbarism to the highest rank in national power, in the arts both of peace and war, in commercial wealth, and intellectual and moral greatness.

2. In England, liberty has maintained frequent and bloody conflicts with tyranny. No nation can boast of more ardent patriots, of firmer and more enlightened friends to the rights and liberties of mankind, or men of higher excellence, or of greater intellectual endowments, than are presented to us in the eventful pages of English history.

3. To the citizens of the *United States*, the history of England is next in importance to that of their own country; for it is, to a majority of them, the history of their own ancestors as it is also of the country from which have been derived, in a great measure, their language and literature, and their civil and religious institutions.

4. We feel a peculiar interest and sympathy in the conflicts which civil and religious liberty has there maintained with despotism and bigotry; for our ancestors were, more or less, involved in them; and the first settlement and early growth of our own country were, in a great degree, owing to oppression and persecution in the parent state. We have a fellow-feeling for the English patriots of former days, and the memory of *John Hampden* is scarcely held in greater honor in his native country than in this.

5. Britain was little known to the rest of the world till the time of its conquest by the Romans. *Julius Cæsar* invaded the island 55 years before the Christian era, and conquered a part of it. In the reign of the Emperor *Claudius*, the Roman general, *Ostorius*, defeated the British king, *Carac'tacus*, and sent him a prisoner to Rome; in the reign of *Nero*, *Suetonius* defeated the Britons under their queen, *Boadiçea;* and the Roman dominion was completely established by *Agricola*, who

first landed in Britain, A. D. 78. He met with an obstinate resistance from *Galgacus*, a Caledonian chief, but in a few years made a complete conquest of all the southern parts of the island.

6. At the time of this conquest, the *Britons* were a rude and barbarous people, divided into numerous tribes. They were clothed with the skins of beasts, and their property consisted almost wholly in their arms and cattle. Their religion was *druidism*, a cruel superstition; and the *druids*, their priests, possessed great authority. They taught the transmigration of souls, and offered in sacrifice human victims, in great numbers.

7. The Romans built *three walls* across the island, in order to prevent irruptions of the inhabitants from the north the first was built of turf, by the Emperor *Adrian*, extending from Solway Frith to the mouth of the Tyne; the second, by *Antoninus*, of earth and stone, reaching from the Forth to the Clyde; and the third by *Severus*, of stone, running nearly parallel with that of Adrian. Other works were also constructed by them, the remains of which are still to be seen. In the 5th century, the Romans took their final leave of Britain, 465 years after the landing of Julius Cæsar.

8. Soon afterwards, the *Scots* and *Picts*, from the northern part of the island, invaded and ravaged the country. The Britons, in their distress, applied for assistance to the *Saxons*, a warlike people, inhabiting the north of Germany. A Saxon army of 1,600 men, commanded by two brothers, *Hengist* and *Horsa*, came (449) to their relief, and the Scots and Picts were defeated, and driven into their own territories.

9. The Saxons, finding the country much superior to their own, procured from Germany a reinforcement of 5,000 men, *Saxons*, *Angles*, and *Jutes*, took possession of Britain, and reduced the inhabitants to submission, or compelled them to leave the country or retreat to the mountains. — From the *Angles* is derived the name of *England*.

10. Violent contests afterwards took place, in which King *Arthur*, a British champion, is said to have defeated the Saxons in 12 different engagements. The whole history of this renowned prince is regarded by many as a fiction. But, with respect to him, Lord Bacon observes, that " in his acts there is enough of truth to make him famous, besides that which is fabulous." The Saxons, however, finally triumphed; and in about 150 years after their invasion, the *Heptarchy*, or *seven Saxon kingdoms*, were established, which subsisted about 200 years, exhibiting a series of dissensions and contests. At length, *Egbert*, a prince of the house of *Cerdic*, the first King of Wessex, by his prudence and valor, united them into one monarchy, under the name of *England*, in 827.

11. In 597, about 230 years previous to this event, *Augustine*, with 40 monks, had been sent to Britain by Pope Gregory the Great, to convert the Saxons to *Christianity:* the Britons had long before been partially converted. The state of society however, was still barbarous. Christianity, in the defective form in which it had been inculcated, had not banished the ignorance of the people, nor softened the ferocity of their manners.

SECTION II.

From the Foundation of the Monarchy to the Norman Conquest. — *From A. D.* 827 *to* 1066.

1. Scarcely had *Egbert* established and regulated his infant monarchy, when he found himself assailed by formidable enemies in the *Danes*, whose depredations form a prominent feature in the early history of England, and who continued, for upwards of two centuries, to be a scourge to the country.

2. The reign of *Alfred the Great*, the 6th King of England, which began in 872, forms a distinguished era in the early history of the monarchy. In one year he defeated the Danes in eight battles. But, by a new irruption, they extended their ravages, and forced him to solicit a peace. He was compelled to seek his safety, for many months, in an obscure part of the country, disguised in the habit of a peasant, and lived in a herdsman's cottage as a servant. In this humble situation, the herdsman's wife is said, on one occasion, to have ordered him to take care of some cakes that were baking by the fire; but he forgot his trust, and let them burn, for which she severely reprimanded him.

3. Success having rendered his enemies remiss, and his followers having gained some advantages, he left his retreat; and, in order to discover the state of the hostile army, he entered the Danish camp in the disguise of a harper. He excited so much interest by his musical talents, that he was introduced to *Guthrum*, the Danish prince, and remained with him some days. Having discovered the unguarded condition of the Danes, he returned to his adherents, and with a large force attacked his enemies by surprise, and defeated them with great slaughter.

4. After having restored tranquillity to his distracted kingdom, he employed himself in cultivating the arts of peace, and in raising his subjects from the depths of wretchedness, ignorance, and barbarism. According to various historians he

divided England into counties, composed a code of laws, established trial by jury, founded the University of Oxford, instituted schools, and, for the instruction of his people, translated a number of works into the Saxon language.

5. The character of Alfred shines forth with distinguished lustre in a dark age. He was one of the greatest and best sovereigns that ever sat on a throne, — equally excellent in his private and his public character. He was distinguished for his personal accomplishments both of body and mind, and is reputed the greatest warrior, legislator, and scholar of the age in which he lived.

6. He was succeeded, in 900, by his son *Edward*, surnamed *the Elder*, from his being the first English monarch of that name. He inherited the military genius of his father, and his reign was a continued, but successful, struggle against the Northumbrians and Danes, who were powerful in the north of England.

7. *Athelstan*, an able and popular sovereign, was successful in his wars with the Danes, Northumbrians, Scots, Irish, and Welsh, and he enlarged and strengthened his kingdom. He caused the *Scriptures* to be translated into the Saxon language, and enacted a law which conferred the rank of *thane*, or gentleman, on every merchant who made three voyages to the Mediterranean.

8. *Edmund*, after a short reign, was assassinated by the notorious robber, *Leolf*. *Edred* was the slave of superstition, and became the dupe of the famous *Dunstan*, who was afterwards Archbishop of Canterbury, and was canonized as a saint; and with regard to whose pretended conflicts with the devil ridiculous stories are related in history. Dunstan possessed great abilities, and, under the appearance of sanctity, veiled the most inordinate ambition; yet, in these times of superstition and barbarism, he gained a wonderful ascendency over the sovereign and the people.

9. *Edwy*, or *Edwin*, by marrying *Elgiva*, a beautiful princess nearly related to him, gave offence to Dunstan; and Archbishop *Odo* caused her to be put to death in the most cruel manner.

10. *Edgar* promoted Dunstan to the archbishopric of Canterbury, and made him his chief counsellor. His reign is remarkable for being the period in which England was freed from *wolves*. Edgar, having heard of the extraordinary beauty of *Elfrida*, daughter of the Earl of Devonshire, sent Athelwold, his favorite, to ascertain the truth of it. Athelwold, overcome by the charms of Elfrida, on his return, assured the king that the account of her beauty had been greatly exagger

ated, and obtained the king's permission to marry her himself But the king, having afterwards discovered the treachery of his favorite, put him to death, and married Elfrida.

11. Edgar was succeeded by *Edward*, his son by his first marriage, who was assassinated in the 4th year of his reign, and 19th of his age, at the instigation of his mother-in-law Elfrida; and from this circumstance he was surnamed *the Martyr*.

12. *Ethelred II.*, the son of Edgar and Elfrida, succeeded to the throne at the age of 11 years. He was a weak monarch, surnamed *the Unready*. The Danes again renewed their ravages, and, by order of the king, such of these foreigners as were settled throughout England were massacred, at the festival of *St. Brice*, without distinction of age or sex. The news of this barbarous transaction, arriving in Denmark, fired every bosom with a desire of vengeance.

13. A large army of Danes, under their king, *Sweyn*, (who was the grandson of Beatrix, the daughter of Edward the Elder,) invaded and ravaged the country. Ethelred fled to Normandy, and *Sweyn* was acknowledged (1013) sole king of England; but he survived his exaltation only a short time, and Ethelred was again restored. The latter, dying not long afterwards, was succeeded by his son, *Edmund*, surnamed *Ironside* from his strength and valor; but his abilities and courage were insufficient to save his sinking country.

14. On the death of Sweyn, his son *Canute* was proclaimed King of England by the Danes. Having expelled a younger brother who had usurped the throne of Denmark, Canute asserted his claim to the crown of England, invaded the country with a numerous army, and compelled the king to divide his dominions with him. Edmund was soon after murdered by the treachery of *Edric*, his brother-in-law, and Canute became sole monarch. He was the most powerful sovereign of his time in Europe, and was styled *the Great*, from his talents and successes. In the former part of his reign he was severe, but in the latter part mild and beneficent; and he died lamented.

15. Canute was succeeded by his son *Harold*, whose principal amusement was the chase, and who obtained the surname of *Harefoot*, from his swiftness in running. On his death, the throne was filled by his brother, *Canute II.*, or *Hardicanute*, the last of the Danish kings. The reigns of these two monarchs were short, and signalized by few important events; and both died without issue.

16. The English now shook off the Danish yoke, and restored (1041) the Saxon line in *Edward*, brother of *Edmund Ironside*, though the rightful heir of this line was *Edward*

surnamed *the Outlaw*, the son of Edmund Ironside, who was now an exile in Hungary. Edward had been educated in a monastery; and with regard to his life, says Mr. Burke, "there is little that can call his title to sanctity in question, though he can never be reckoned among the great kings." He married the daughter of *Godwin*, the Earl of Kent, an ambitious and powerful nobleman, who acted a conspicuous part during this reign. Edward was canonized by the Pope, and received the surname of *Confessor;* and it was pretended that he was favored with the special privilege of curing the *scrofula*, or *king's evil*. This power was long supposed to have descended to his successors, and the superstitious practice of touching for that disorder was continued by the kings of England from this period till the revolution of 1688.

17. Edward the Confessor, dying without children, is said to have bequeathed the crown to *William, Duke of Normandy*, though *Edgar Atheling*, the son of Edward the Outlaw, was the rightful heir. Yet *Harold*, the son of the Earl Godwin, and grandson of Esthritha, daughter of Sweyn, was elected and proclaimed king by the nobility and clergy.

18. William of Normandy resolved to maintain his claim to the crown of England by force of arms; and, having raised an army of 60,000 men, he invaded the country. *Harold*, at the head of an army about equal in number, met him, and was defeated and slain in the memorable battle of *Hastings* (1066). The Normans lost about 15,000 men, and the English the greater part of their army. The nation soon submitted to the sceptre of *William*, who was surnamed *the Conqueror*, and whose descendants have, to this day, occupied the throne of England.

SECTION III.

THE NORMAN FAMILY: — *William I., the Conqueror Wil·liam II.; Henry I.; Stephen (of Blois). — From A. D. 1066 to* 1154.

1. William possessed great abilities both as a statesman and a warrior. In his person he was tall and well proportioned, and is said to have been so strong, that scarcely any other person in that age could bend his bow or handle his arms. "He had," says Mr. Burke, "vices in his composition, and great ones; but they were the vices of a great mind; ambition, the malady of every extensive genius; and avarice, the madness of the wise: one chiefly actuated his youth, the other governed

his age. The general run of men he looked on with contempt and treated with cruelty when they opposed him."

2. He disgusted the English by promoting his Norman followers to all offices of importance. He caused the *Norman language* to be adopted in the service of the church, as well as in the courts of justice. He is said to have introduced the *feudal system*, and to have exchanged trial by jury for the pernicious one of single combat; and he compelled the people to extinguish their fires at the sound of the *curfew bell* [*the fire-covering bell*], which was rung at 8 o'clock in the evening.

3. By his forest laws he reserved to himself the exclusive privilege of killing game throughout the kingdom; and made it a greater crime to take the life of an animal than that of a man. He formed the *New Forest* by depopulating a tract of country about 30 miles in circuit, demolishing 36 parish churches, together with the houses of the inhabitants. One of the most useful acts of his reign was his compiling *Doomsday Book*, which contained a register of all the estates of the kingdom.

4. *William II.*, surnamed *Rufus*, from his red hair, inherited the ambition and talents of his father; and was, like him, tyrannical, perfidious, and cruel. After a reign of 13 years, which was disturbed by insurrections, and by quarrels with the ecclesiastics, particularly with *Anselm*, the primate, he was accidentally shot by Sir Walter Tyrrel, with an arrow aimed at a stag in the New Forest.

5. *Henry I.*, surnamed *Beauclerc*, or *the Scholar*, on account of his learning, was the younger brother of William Rufus. He took advantage of the absence of his eldest brother, *Robert*, the rightful heir, who was on a crusade to the Holy Land and secured the crown for himself. He invaded his brother's Norman dominions, and Robert, on his return, was defeated, taken prisoner, and confined in Wales till his death.

6. Henry married *Matilda* of Scotland, great granddaughter of *Edmund Ironside*, and in this way the *Saxon* and *Norman* families were united. The latter part of his life was rendered disconsolate by the loss of his only son, who was drowned on his passage from Normandy; and from that fatal moment he was never seen to smile. Henry was an able, courageous, and accomplished sovereign; but ambitious, licentious, and ungrateful.

7. On the death of Henry, the crown fell by right to his daughter, *Matilda*, or *Maud*, married first to *Henry V*, Em-

peror of Germany, and afterwards to *Geoffrey Plantagenet Earl of Anjou* By the latter she had several children, of whom the eldest bore the name of *Henry*. But *Stephen*, a nephew of the late king, the most popular nobleman in the kingdom, and distinguished for his ambition, valor, generosity. and courtesy, seized upon the crown. Matilda immediately landed in England, and, raising a small army, defeated Stephen, and took possession of the crown; but her haughty and despotic behavior caused a revolt, and Stephen, in his turn, defeated her, compelled her to quit the kingdom, and again obtained possession of the throne.

8. *Henry*, the son of Matilda, afterwards invaded England, and, during the heat of the contest, Eustace, the king's eldest son, was removed by a sudden death. Soon after this event, the jarring interests of the two parties were reconciled, Stephen being allowed to retain the crown during his life, and Henry being acknowledged as his successor; and this transaction was shortly afterwards followed by Stephen's death. — During this reign, England was harassed and desolated by a succession of civil contentions and wars, which were carried on with unrelenting barbarity by the pillage and destruction of the inhabitants, and the conflagration of the towns.

SECTION IV.

Family of Plantagenet: — *Henry II.; Richard I.; John, Henry III.; Edward I.; Edward II.; Edward III., Richard II. — From A. D.* 1154 *to* 1399.

1. *Henry II.*, the first of the *Plantagenets*, being descended by his grandmother from the *Saxon kings*, and by his mother from the *Norman family*, succeeded to the throne, to the great satisfaction of the nation. He is sometimes called *Shortmantle* because he brought the use of short cloaks out of Anjou to England. In addition to *England*, he possessed, by inheritance, and by his marriage with *Eleanor*, heiress of the duchy of Guienne, nearly one half of *France*, and, during his reign, he conquered *Ireland*; so that he had more extensive dominions than any English monarch who had preceded him, and was the most powerful sovereign of his age. Of Eleanor, his queen, Sir James Mackintosh says, "She was the firebrand of his family, in whose eyes the fair dowry of Aquitaine appeared a cover for every crime."

2. The different countries of Europe had for a century

been agitated with the contest between church and state, or the ecclesiastical and civil authority. This contest reached its height in England during Henry's reign, of which it forms a prominent feature. Thomas à Becket, the hero and martyr of the ecclesiastical party, a man of extraordinary talents and inordinate ambition, exalted his power to such a degree, that it would admit of a question, whether the king or the archbishop was the first man in the kingdom. Becket had for some time held the office of chancellor, and lived in the manner of a prince; but, on assuming the office of Archbishop of Canterbury, he dismissed his splendid train, cast off his magnificent apparel, abandoned sports and revels, and wore the habit of a monk. "Religion," says Sir James Mackintosh, "might acquire a place in his mind which she had not before; but it was so alloyed by worldly passions, that it is impossible for us to trust on any occasion to the purity of his motives."

3. During the preceding reign, the power of the clergy had increased to a most exorbitant height; they were also extremely corrupt in their morals, and committed with impunity the most enormous crimes. No less than 100 murders are said to have been proved, in the presence of the king, to have been committed by ecclesiastics since his accession; and holy orders were esteemed a sufficient protection for every species of crime.

4. Henry resolved to restrain the authority, and reform the abuses, of the clergy, and for this purpose he summoned, in 1164 a general council of the nobility and clergy at Clarendon, and submitted to them 16 propositions, which were agreed to, and are known under the title of the *Constitutions of Clarendon.* Among other things, it was enacted, that clergy men accused of any crime should be tried by temporal judges. Becket, however, made the most resolute and formidable resistance to the changes proposed by Henry; and, after a long series of contests with the haughty primate, the king was, on a certain occasion, so exasperated by his conduct, that he rashly exclaimed, "What! among all those whom I have obliged, is there none who will avenge me of that insolent priest?" The words were scarcely spoken, when four knights of distinguished rank, interpreting the king's complaints as commands, set out with a resolution to avenge the wrongs of their sovereign. They pursued the prelate into the cathedral, and assassinated him before the altar.

5. The account of this transaction filled Henry with consternation, and caused great excitement in England. Becket died a martyr to ecclesiastical authority, and the manner of his death effected the triumph of his cause. He was canonized

by the Pope as a saint, by the title of *St. Thomas of Canterbury;* and numerous miracles were pretended to be wrought at his tomb, which became a celebrated resort of pilgrims 100,000 of whom are said to have been present at a jubilee which was observed once in 50 years.

6. Henry publicly expressed his sorrow for having used the rash words which had occasioned the death of the primate, and expiated his offence by a humiliating penance at his tomb. Having approached within three miles of Canterbury, he dismounted, walking barefoot over the flinty road, which, in some places, he marked with blood, to the consecrated spot; spent there, in fasting and prayer, a day and night, and even presented his bare shoulders to be scourged by the monks with a knotted cord. The assassins did penance by a pilgrimage to Jerusalem, where they died; and this inscription, in Latin, was put on their tomb: "Here lie the wretches who murdered St. Thomas of Canterbury."

7. The latter part of Henry's life and reign presents an involved and deplorable scene of family discord and contention, sons against their father, wife against husband, and brother against brother. His three eldest sons, instigated by their mother, and assisted by Louis VII., King of France, engaged in a series of rebellions, with a design to wrest the crown from their father.

8. Queen Eleanor left her husband, and openly associated herself with the rebellion of her sons; but she was, while making her way to the court of France, taken, dressed in man's clothes, brought back to Henry, and kept in confinement during the rest of his life. The queen had been irritated against her husband by his neglect and infidelities, and particularly by his attachment to Rosamond Clifford, who, under the title of the *Fair Rosamond*, is described as a woman of extraordinary beauty, and who made a conspicuous figure in the romances and ballads of the times.

9 Henry had manifested for his children, in their more early years, an affection bordering on excess; and when he at last found that his youngest, unworthy, but favorite son, *John*, like all the rest, had joined the confederacy against him, he felt that his cup of affliction was full; gave himself up to transports of ungovernable grief; cursed the day of his birth; uttered imprecations against his sons which he could never be prevailed upon to retract; and, worn out with cares, disappointments, and sorrows, died of a broken heart.

10. The character of Henry may be regarded as a mixture of the qualities, good and bad, naturally arising out of strong intellect, a strong will, and strong passions. He was distin-

guished both as a warrior and a statesman; and he is ranked among the ablest and most useful sovereigns that have occupied the throne of England. The government was still despotic; but the power of the barons was restrained during this reign, and the laws better administered than they had been since the Conquest.

11. Henry was a patron of the arts, particularly of Gothic architecture; and his reign is remarkable for being the period when many of the sumptuous English edifices were erected and also for the introduction of various improvements with regard to the conveniences and comforts of life. The arts of luxury, however, were yet in a rude state. Glass windows were regarded as a mark of extraordinary magnificence; and the houses of the citizens of London were constructed of wood, covered with thatch, with windows of lattice or paper; they had no chimneys; and the floors were covered with straw.

12. The description of the magnificence displayed by *Becket*, while he was *chancellor* of the kingdom, will afford some idea of the rude state of the arts. Nobody, it is said by contemporary writers, equalled him in refinement and splendor. "Every day, in winter, his apartments were strewed with clean straw or hay, and, in summer, with rushes or leaves, that those who came to pay their court to him might not soil their fine clothes by sitting on a dirty floor."

13. *Richard I.*, surnamed *Cœur de Lion*, or *Lion-hearted* who succeeded his father, Henry II., commenced his reign by a cruel persecution of the Jews. The frenzy for the crusades was, at this period, at its height in Europe. To a prince of the adventurous spirit and military talents of Richard, these enterprises presented irresistible attractions; and after making preparation, he, in connection with *Philip Augustus* of France, embarked on an expedition to the Holy Land. They took *Acre* in concert; and *Richard*, especially, acquired great renown by his exploits, and defeated the heroic *Saladin* in the battle of *Ascalon*, in which about 40,000 of the Saracens were slain.

14. On his voyage homeward, being shipwrecked, he disguised himself, with an intention of travelling through Germany; but he was discovered, and imprisoned by the emperor He was ransomed by his subjects for the sum of £300,000 and, after an absence of nine years, returned to his dominions, but he died, not long after, of a wound which he received at the siege of the castle of *Chaluz*, in France, belonging to one of his rebellious vassals.

15. Richard, who has been styled the *Achilles* of modern

history, was preëminent for his valor, which was almost his only merit. Even a century after his death, his name was employed by the Saracen cavalier to chide his horse, and by the Saracen mother to terrify her children. His ambition, tyranny, and cruelty, were scarcely inferior to his valor; his laurels were steeped in blood, and his victories were purchased with the impoverishment of his people.

16. Richard was succeeded by his brother *John*, who is supposed to have murdered his nephew *Arthur*, who was the son of *Geoffrey*, an elder brother, and the rightful heir. *Philip Augustus* of France supported the claim of Arthur to the throne; and, on account of his being murdered, he stripped the English monarch of his possessions in that country. In consequence of this loss of his territories, John received the surname of *Lackland*.

17. John excited against himself the displeasure of *Innocent III.*, the haughty and tyrannical pontiff, who proceeded to lay the kingdom under an interdict, and afterwards excommunicated the king, and absolved his subjects from their allegiance. The wretched monarch was intimidated into submission, and on his knees solemnly surrendered his kingdom to the holy see, consenting to hold it as the Pope's vassal. In this manner he made peace with the church, but he brought upon himself the universal contempt and hatred of his people.

18. The barons, under the direction of *Langton*, the primate, formed a confederacy, and demanded of the king a ratification of a charter of privileges. John, bursting into a furious passion, refused their demand. They immediately proceeded to open war; and the king, finding himself deserted was compelled to yield. He met his barons at *Runny-mede*, and, after a debate of a few days, signed and sealed (1215) the famous deed of *Magna Charta*, or *the Great Charter*, which secured important liberties and privileges to every order of men in the kingdom, and which is regarded as the great bulwark of English liberty. John granted, at the same time, the *Charter of the Forest*, which abolished the exclusive right of the king to kill game all over the kingdom.

19. The character of John is represented as more odious than that of any other English monarch; debased by every vice, with scarcely a single redeeming virtue. His reign, though most unhappy and disastrous, is, notwithstanding, memorable as the era of the dawn of English freedom.

20. *Henry III.* succeeded to the throne at the age of only nine years, under the guardianship of the *Earl of Pembroke*

He was a weak monarch, timid in danger, presumptuous in prosperity, and governed by unworthy favorites. His lot was cast in a turbulent period of English history, and his long reign of 56 years consisted of a series of internal conflicts, though it was little disturbed by foreign war.

21. The incapacity of the king was more productive of inconvenience to himself than of misery to his subjects. Under his weak but pacific sway, the cause of popular freedom was advanced, and the nation grew more rapidly in wealth and prosperity than it had done under his military and more renowned predecessors.

22. Towards the latter part of the reign of Henry, the barons, with *Simon de Montfort*, *Earl of Leicester*, at their head, entered into a confederacy to seize the reins of government; and they compelled Henry to delegate the regal power to 24 of their number. These divided among themselves all the offices of government, and new-modelled the parliament, by summoning a certain number of knights, chosen from each county.

23. This measure proved fatal to the power of the barons, for the knights, indignant at Leicester's usurpation, concerted a plan for restoring the king. A civil war ensued. Leicester, at the head of a formidable force, defeated the royal army at *Lewes*, and made both the king and his son Edward prisoners. He compelled the feeble king to ratify his authority by a solemn treaty; assumed the character of regent, and called a parliament, summoning two knights from each shire, and deputies from the principal boroughs (1265). This is regarded as the era of the commencement of the *House of Commons*, being the first time that representatives to Parliament were sent from the boroughs.

24. *Prince Edward*, having at length regained his liberty, took the field against Leicester, and defeated him with great slaughter, in the famous battle of *Evesham*. In this battle, Leicester himself was killed, and Henry, by the assistance of his son, was again placed on the throne.

25. *Edward I.*, surnamed *Longshanks*, from the length of his legs, on succeeding to the throne, caused 280 Jews in London to be hanged at once, on a charge of having corrupted the coin; and 15,000 were robbed of their effects, and banished from the kingdom. He soon after undertook to subdue *Wales*, and having defeated and slain the sovereign, Prince *Llewellyn*, he annexed the country to the crown of England. He created his oldest son *Prince of Wales*, a title which has ever since been borne by the oldest sons of the English monarchs.

26. The conquest of Wales inflamed the ambition of Edward, and inspired him with the design of extending his dominion to the extremity of the island. On the death of Alexander III., who left no son, *Bruce* and *Baliol* were competitors for the throne of Scotland, and Edward was chosen umpire to decide the contest between the two rivals. He adjudged the crown to Baliol, who engaged to hold it as a vassal of the King of England.

27 Baliol, however, soon afterwards renounced his allegiance; hence arose a war between England and Scotland which lasted, with little intermission, upwards of 70 years and drenched both kingdoms with blood. Edward invaded Scotland with a large army; defeated the Scots with great slaughter in the battle of *Dunbar;* subdued the kingdom; and Baliol was carried captive to London.

28. While Edward was prosecuting a war in France, the Scots were roused to exertion, for the recovery of their independence, by their renowned hero, *Sir William Wallace;* but, after gaining a series of victories, they were at length defeated by the King of England, with immense loss, in the battle of *Falkirk. Wallace* became a prisoner of Edward, who put him to death with barbarous cruelty. The Scots found a second champion and deliverer in *Robert Bruce*, grandson of the competitor of Baliol, who, having expelled the British from the country, was raised to the throne of his ancestors. Edward prepared to make a new invasion with an immense army, but died after having advanced as far as Carlisle.

29. Edward, who was one of the greatest of the English sovereigns, was eminent as a warrior; and, on account of his wisdom as a legislator, he has been styled *the English Justinian.* But he was, in disposition, a tyrant, and, as often as he dared, trampled on the liberties or invaded the property of his subjects. He was, however, admired by his contemporaries, and his barons respected the arbitrary sway of a monarch as violent and haughty as themselves. His reign was highly advantageous to the kingdom, particularly for the improvements made in the national code, and the administration of justice He repeatedly ratified Magna Charta, and an important clause was added to secure the people from the imposition of any tax without the consent of parliament. Ever since that time, there has been a regular succession of *English parliaments.*

30. *Edward II*. surnamed *of Caernarvon*, from the place of his birth, soon after succeeding to the throne, in compliance with his father's dying injunction, invaded Scotland, with an

army of 100,000 men, which was met at *Bannockburn* by 30,000 Scots, under their king, *Robert Bruce* (1314). A great battle ensued, in which the English sustained a more disastrous defeat than they had experienced since the battle of Hastings.

31. Edward II., who possessed little of the character of his father, was of a mild disposition, weak, indolent, fond of pleasure, and governed by unworthy favorites, the most famous of whom were *Gaveston* and the two *Spencers*. His inglorious reign was characterized by the corruption of the court, and by contests and war between the king and the barons; and his life was rendered unhappy by a series of mortifications and misfortunes.

32. *Isabella*, his infamous queen, fixed her affections, which had long been estranged from her husband, upon *Mortimer*, a powerful young baron; and she, together with her paramour, formed a conspiracy against the king, and compelled him to resign the crown to his son. He was then thrown into a prison, and afterwards murdered, by order of Mortimer, in a barbarous manner.

33. *Edward III.* succeeded to the throne at the age of 14 years. A council of regency, consisting of 12 persons, was appointed, during the minority of the king; yet *Mortimer* and *Isabella* possessed the chief control. But Edward, on coming of age, could not endure the authority of a man who had caused the murder of his father, or of a mother stained with the foulest crimes. Mortimer was condemned by parliament, and hanged upon a gibbet; and Isabella was imprisoned for life at Castle Risings, and continued for 28 years a miserable monument of blasted ambition.

34. The king, soon after he was established on the throne, made war with the Scots, and defeated them with great slaughter in the battle of *Halidown Hill* (1333). On the death of *Charles IV.*, he laid claim, in right of his mother, to the crown of France, which he attempted to gain by force of arms, in opposition to Philip of Valois, who was acknowledged by the French nation as the rightful heir. This claim involved the two countries in a long and sanguinary war.

35. After having made his preparations, Edward sailed from England with a powerful armament. His fleet, consisting of 250 sail, encountered that of France, amounting to 400 ships, off the coast of Flanders, and gained one of the greatest naval victories recorded in history. The loss of the English is stated at 4,000 men and 2 ships; that of the French, at 30,000 men and 230 ships.

36. Edward then invaded France at the head of 30,000 troops, and, in the famous battle of *Cressy* (1346), gained a splendid victory over Philip, the French king, who had an army of upwards of 100,000 men, and whose loss exceeded 30,000 This battle is noted not only for the greatness of the victory, but also for being the first in English history in which cannon were made use of, and likewise for being the scene in which Edward the Black Prince, the king's eldest son, then only 16 years of age, commenced his brilliant military career. — Edward afterwards besieged and took *Calais*, which remained in the possession of the English till the time of *Queen Mary*.

37. While the English monarch was in France, the Scots under their king *David*, invaded England, and were defeated at *Neville's Cross*, near *Durham*, by *Philippa*, Edward's heroic queen, and their king was led prisoner to London. Of the four generals under the queen, three were prelates.

38. *John*, who succeeded his father in the throne of France, took the field with an army of 60,000 men, against the *Black Prince*, who, with only 16,000 troops, gained a signal victory at *Poictiers* (1356). King *John* was taken prisoner, and led in triumph, by the victorious prince, to London, where he was kept a fellow-captive with *David* of Scotland.

39. Edward, in the latter part of his reign, sunk into indolence and indulgence, and experienced a reverse of fortune and, before his death, all his conquests, with the exception of Calais, were wrested from him. His son, the *Black Prince*, (so called from the color or covering of his armor,) falling into a lingering consumption, was obliged to resign the command of the army; and *Charles V.* of France, an able sovereign, recovered most of the English possessions in that country. The death of the Black Prince, illustrious for his amiable virtues, as well as for his noble and heroic qualities, plunged the nation in grief, and broke the spirits of his father, who survived him only about a year.

40. Edward was the most powerful prince of his time in Europe; and, in personal accomplishments, is said to have been superior to any of his predecessors. His domestic administration was, in many respects, excellent, and advantageous to his subjects. The astonishing victories, which cast so much military splendor on his reign, and which are accounted the most brilliant in English history, appear to have dazzled the eyes both of his subjects and foreigners, who placed him in the first rank of conquerors. But his wars with France and Scotland were unjust in their object; and. after having caused great suffering and devastation, he at last found that the crowns of those kingdoms were beyond his reach.

41. In this reign, *chivalry* was at its zenith in England, and in all the virtues which adorned the knightly character in courtesy, munificence, and gallantry, in all the delicate and magnanimous feelings, none were more conspicuous than *Edward III.* and his son, the *Black Prince.* Their court was, as it were, the sun of that system, which embraced the valor and nobility of the Christian world.

42. *Richard II.*, the unworthy son of Edward the Black Prince, succeeded to the throne, at the age of 11 years. He was indolent, prodigal, perfidious, and a slave to pleasure. The administration of the government, during the minority of the king, was intrusted to his three uncles, the Dukes of Lancaster, York, and Gloucester, whose contests embroiled all the public measures. Of these, the *Duke of Lancaster*, *John of Gaunt*, or *Ghent*, (so named from the place of his birth,) was the most distinguished, and was possessed of great wealth and power; but he became unpopular, particularly with the courtiers and clergy; and he was noted for being (for political reasons, as is supposed) the protector of *Wickliffe*, the Reformer, whose opposition to the tyranny and corruptions of Rome commenced in the preceding reign, and gained him many adherents.

43. A *poll-tax* of three groats, imposed by Parliament upon every male and female above the age of 15 years, excited universal discontent among the lower classes, on account of its injustice in requiring as much of the poor as of the rich. One of the brutal tax-gatherers, having demanded payment for a blacksmith's daughter, whom the father asserted to be below the age specified, was proceeding to improper familiarities with her, when the enraged father dashed out his brains with a hammer. The spectators applauded the action; a spirit of sedition spread through the kingdom; and 100,000 insurgents, under *Wat Tyler*, were soon assembled upon *Blackheath.* But the leader was slain, and his followers were finally compelled to submit.

44 While the kingdom was convulsed with domestic contests, it was also engaged in hostilities with France and Scotland. At *Otterburn* (1388) was fought, between the English under *Percy* (surnamed *Hotspur*, on account of his fiery temper) and the Scotch under *Douglas*, a battle, in which Percy was taken prisoner, and Douglas was slain. — On this battle is founded the celebrated ballad of *Chevy Chace.*

45. Richard unjustly banished his cousin Henry, the eldest son and heir of John of Gaunt, Duke of Lancaster; and, on the death of the duke, he seized upon his estate: but the king

having afterwards undertaken an expedition to Ireland, in order to quell an insurrection, Henry, the young duke, took advantage of his absence, returned to England, landed at Ravenspur, soon found himself at the head of a numerous army, and compelled Richard, on his return, to resign the crown. The king being very unpopular, the parliament readily confirmed his deposition; he was then imprisoned, and afterwards murdered.

46. The Duke of Lancaster was raised to the throne with the title of *Henry IV.;* though *Edmund Mortimer* was the true heir to the crown, being descended from *Lionel*, the 3d son of Edward III., whereas Henry was the son of *John of Gaunt*, the 4th son of Edward III. — Hence began contests between the houses of *York* and *Lancaster*. — During this reign and the preceding one, flourished *Chaucer*, who has been styled the Morning Star of English poetry.

SECTION V

Branch of Lancaster. — *Henry IV.; Henry V.; Henry VI. — From A. D.* 1399 *to* 1461.

1. *Henry IV.*, surnamed *Bolingbroke*, from the place of his birth, who succeeded to the throne by the deposition and murder of the lawful king, and the exclusion of the rightful heir, soon found that the throne of a usurper is but a bed of thorns. A combination was immediately formed against him. The Scots under *Douglas*, and the Welsh under *Owen Glendower*, took part with the rebels; but their united forces were defeated in a most desperate and bloody battle at *Shrewsbury*, and their leader, *Percy* [*Hotspur*], was killed (1403).

2. While a subject, Henry was supposed to have imbibed the religious principles of his father, John of Gaunt, the patron of *Wickliffe* and his followers. But, after he was raised to the throne, he made his faith yield to his interest: as he needed the support of the clergy, he procured their favor by endeavoring to suppress the opinions which his father had supported; and he has the unenviable distinction of having his name recorded in history, as the first English monarch that burnt his subjects on account of religion.

3. Henry was distinguished for his military talents and for his political sagacity; and, had he succeeded to the throne by a just title, he might have been ranked as one of the greatest of English monarchs. He had been one of the most popular

noblemen in the kingdom; yet, although his reign was, in many respects, beneficial to the nation, he became a most unpopular sovereign. His peace of mind was destroyed by jealousy and by remorse; he was an object of pity even when seated on the throne; and he felt the truth of the language which Shakspeare puts into his mouth, — "Uneasy lies the head that wears a crown."

4. The latter part of his life was imbittered by the extreme profligacy of his son Henry, Prince of Wales. One of the prince's dissolute companions having been indicted before the chief justice, *Sir William Gascoigne*, for some misdemeanor, he was so exasperated at the issue of the trial that he struck the judge in open court. The venerable magistrate, mindful of the dignity of his office, ordered the prince to be committed to prison. Henry quietly submitted, and acknowledged his error.

5. When the circumstance was related to the king, he is said to have exclaimed, in a transport of joy, "Happy is the king who has a magistrate endowed with courage to execute the laws upon such an offender; still more happy in having a son willing to submit to such chastisement!"

6. *Henry V.*, on succeeding to the throne, immediately assembled his former riotous companions; acquainted them with his intended reformation; forbade their appearance in his presence till they should imitate his example; and dismissed them with liberal presents. He commended the chief justice for his impartial conduct, and encouraged him to persevere in a strict execution of the laws. This victory, which he gained over himself, is incomparably more honorable to him than the martial exploits which have immortalized his name.

7. The *Wickliffites*, or *Lollards*, were now numerous in England, and had for their leader the famous *Sir John Oldcastle*, *Lord Cobham*, a nobleman of distinguished talents, and high in favor with the king. But Henry, in matters of religion, being under the influence of an intolerant clergy, and particularly of Archbishop *Arundel*, gave up to the fury of his enemies the virtuous and gallant nobleman, who was condemned for heresy, hung up by the middle with a chain, and roasted alive.

8. Henry revived the claim to the crown of France, and, taking advantage of disorders in that kingdom, invaded it with an army of about 15,000 men, and defeated the French army, amounting to 60,000 men, in the memorable battle of *Agincourt* (1415). The loss of the French amounted to 11,000 killed, and 14,000 prisoners. Henry afterwards re-

duced all Normandy, was declared regent of France, and acknowledged heir to the crown. But death soon put an end to his career of victory.

9. Henry V. was one of the most heroic of the English sovereigns, eminent as a warrior, beloved and adored by military men; and his short reign is one of the most brilliant in English history for military achievement. But his conquests were of little benefit to his people.

10. *Henry VI.* succeeded to the throne when an infant only nine months old, and was proclaimed king both of England and France. His education was intrusted to *Cardinal Beaufort*, brother of his grandfather, Henry IV.; and his uncles the Dukes of *Bedford* and *Gloucester*, were appointed protectors or guardians of his dominions, the former for France, and the latter for England.

11. Charles VII., the Dauphin of France, being supported by the French people, recovered the kingdom by degrees; and the English, being compelled by that extraordinary heroine, *Joan of Arc*, to raise the siege of *Orleans*, were afterwards stripped of all their conquests in that country, except *Calais* and *Guienne*.

12. Henry, on coming of age, proved himself to be mild and inoffensive, but totally incapable of managing the reins of government: "he would have adorned a cloister, though he disgraced a crown." He married *Margaret of Anjou*, a woman whose distinguished talents, ambition, and heroism well fitted her to supply the defects of her husband in the wars which distracted his reign; but her intriguing disposition and cruelty multiplied the number of her enemies.

13. Discontents prevailing among the people, an insurrection broke out, headed by *Jack Cade*, who assumed the name of John Mortimer, and collected an army of 20,000 rebels but he was defeated and slain.

14. The *Duke of Gloucester*, a favorite of the nation, the chief pillar of the house of Lancaster, and presumptive heir to the crown [that is, heir in case the king should die without issue], had opposed the marriage of Henry with Margaret. From this circumstance, he became odious to the queen, and his death soon after took place in a suspicious manner. This event, added to the imbecility of the king, encouraged the *Duke of York* to assert his claim to the crown.

15. The houses of *York* and *Lancaster* were both descended from *Edward III.;* that of York from his third son, and that of Lancaster from his fourth: the rightful title was, of course, on the side of the former. Each party was distinguished by a particular badge or symbol; that of the house of York was a

white rose, and that of Lancaster a *red* one; hence the civil contests were styled the wars of the *Two Roses*.

16. This fatal quarrel, which now (1455) broke out into open hostilities, lasted 30 years, was signalized by 12 sanguinary pitched battles, and marked by the most unrelenting barbarity. During the contest, more than 100,000 of the bravest men of the nation, including 80 princes of the blood, fell on the field, or were executed on the scaffold.

17. In the battles of *St. Alban's* and *Northampton*, the Lancastrians were defeated, and the king was taken prisoner; but *Queen Margaret*, having collected a large army, gained the battle of *Wakefield* (1460), in which the *Duke of York* was defeated and slain. But his son and successor, at the head of a numerous army, entered London, amidst the shouts of the citizens, and was proclaimed king, by the title of *Edward IV.*

SECTION VI.

Branch of York: — *Edward IV.; Edward V.; Richard III.* — *From A. D.* 1461 *to* 1485.

1. The new king was not permitted to enjoy the crown in peace. The heroic *Margaret* again collected an army of 60,000 men, which was met by the Yorkists, to the number of upwards of 40,000, under the command of *Edward* and the *Earl of Warwick*. A tremendous battle was fought (1461) at *Towton*, in which Edward obtained a decisive victory, and upwards of 36,000 Englishmen, slain by one another's hands, were left dead on the field. — Henry, having been taken prisoner, was confined in the Tower, and there, after being liberated, and a second time imprisoned, was finally murdered (1471), as was supposed, by the Duke of Gloucester, afterwards Richard III.

2. The unfortunate queen, accompanied by her son, a boy eight years old, while flying from her enemies, was benighted in Hexham forest, and fell into the hands of ruffians, who stripped her of her jewels, and treated her with great indignity After she was liberated from them, being overcome with fatigue and terror, she sunk in despair; but was suddenly roused by the approach of a robber, with a drawn sword. Seeing no way to escape, she rose and presented to him her child: "My friend," said she, "here is your king's son, whom I commit to your protection." The man, pleased with this unexpected confidence reposed in him, afforded every assistance in his pow

and conducted the mother and son, through numerous perils, to a small seaport whence they sailed to Flanders.

3. The House of York had been hitherto supported by the important assistance of *Nevil, Earl of Warwick*, the most powerful baron in England, and the greatest general of his time. But Edward having given offence to his benefactor Warwick was induced to abandon him, and to support the Lancastrians. By his exertions, Edward was deposed, and Henry after having been a prisoner six years in the Tower, was released, and again proclaimed king. Thus Warwick, having restored Henry, whom he had deposed, and pulled down Edward, whom he had placed on the throne, obtained the title of *king-maker*.

4. But in the bloody battle of *Barnet*, Edward prevailed and the brave Warwick was slain. The intrepid Margaret having returned to England, made a last effort for the crown, in the desperate battle of *Tewkesbury* (1471), which proved fatal to her hopes. Her son was slain, and she herself was taken prisoner; but was afterwards ransomed by the King of France, and in that country she passed the remainder of her life in obscurity and neglect.

5. Edward, being now secured on the throne, gave himself up to unrestrained indulgence in acts of tyranny, cruelty, and debauchery. His brother, the *Duke of Clarence*, who had assisted him in gaining the crown, he caused, with the concurrence of his other brother, the Duke of Gloucester, to be impeached and condemned; and he is said to have been drowned in a butt of Malmsey wine. — Edward was possessed of talents, and was reputed the handsomest and most accomplished man of his time in England. The love of pleasure was his ruling passion. "His character," says an elegant writer, "is easily summed up: — his good qualities were courage and beauty; his bad qualities, every vice." — It was in his reign that the *art of printing* was introduced (1471) into England by *William Caxton.*

6. Edward IV. left two sons, the eldest of whom being only 13 years of age, was proclaimed king, by the title of *Edward V.* Richard, Duke of Gloucester, brother to Edward IV., being appointed protector, caused *Lord Hastings*, and other distinguished persons, to be executed without trial; seized the crown, on the pretence that his nephew, Edward V., and his brother, the Duke of York, were illegitimate; and procured himself to be proclaimed king, by the title of *Richard III.* After two months, the young princes disappeared, and are said to have been smothered in the Tower, by order of Richard.

7. The multiplied and detestable crimes of *Richard III.* who waded to the throne through the blood of his nearest relations, found an avenger in the *Earl of Richmond*, the only surviving heir of the house of Lancaster. The armies of the two rivals met at *Bosworth* (1485), where a desperate battle was fought, which, by reason of *Lord Stanley's* going over to Richmond, proved fatal to Richard, who was defeated and slain; and his rival was crowned on the field by the title of *Henry VII.* This battle terminated the long and bloody conflicts between the two houses of York and Lancaster, which had reduced the kingdom to a state of almost savage barbarity; laws, arts, and commerce being entirely neglected for the practice of arms.

8. Richard, who was a man of talents and courage, could conceal the most bloody projects under the mask of affection and friendship; and his insatiable ambition led him to perpetrate the most atrocious crimes. He had a harsh and disagreeable countenance, was crook backed, splay-footed, and had his left arm withered; so that the deformity of his body corresponded to that of his mind.

SECTION VII.

THE TUDOR FAMILY: — *Henry VII.; Henry VIII.; Edward VI.; Mary; Elizabeth.* — *From A. D.* 1485 *to* 1603.

1. The hereditary right of *Henry VII.* to the crown was very defective; but he strengthened his claim by marrying *Elizabeth*, daughter of Edward IV.; and in this way the two houses of York and Lancaster were united. Henry was the son of *Margaret*, great-granddaughter of John of Gaunt, and of *Edmund Tudor*. The sovereigns of the house of *Tudor* were arbitrary in their principles and character; but their reign, though disturbed by conflicts, both domestic and foreign, was, notwithstanding, less convulsed by war than that of any other family of English kings.

2. The policy of Henry was pacific, and his reign was comparatively tranquil; yet it was disturbed by several plots and conspiracies, two of which were of a singular character. One of these was the attempt of *Lambert Simnel*, the son of a baker, to counterfeit the person of the Earl of Warwick; the other was a similar attempt of *Perkin Warbeck* to counterfeit the Duke of York, who is said to have been smothered in the Tower, by the order of Richard III. By the earlier English

historians, Warbeck is uniformly represented to have been an impostor, but several later writers maintain that he was the real son of Edward IV.

3. Both of the adventurers aspired to the crown, and met with considerable support from the people. Simnel, after being proclaimed King of England and Ireland, at Dublin, was taken prisoner, and, instead of being executed, was made a scullion in the king's kitchen, and afterwards promoted to be falconer. Perkin Warbeck, who maintained his cause by force of arms for five years, was supported by many of the nobility, and acknowledged by the Kings of France and Scotland; but, being at last taken prisoner, he was executed as a traitor; and near the same time, the *real Earl of Warwick*, the son of the Duke of Clarence, and nephew of Edward IV., the last male of the *Plantagenets*, who had been imprisoned from his childhood, for no other crime than his birth, was condemned and executed on a charge of treason.

4. Henry VII. was more deficient in the feelings of the heart than in the qualities of the mind; and, though much respected, was little beloved. He was wholly devoted to business; prudent and sagacious; little susceptible of the social and generous affections; serious and reserved in his manners, suspicious in his temper, despotic in his government, and avaricious in his disposition, — the love of money being his ruling passion. He was capable of descending to the meanest artifices, and of employing the most unprincipled agents in extorting money from his subjects, to fill his own coffers. Empson and Dudley, two lawyers, gained an infamous notoriety as instruments of his rapacity and oppression. By his frugality and arbitrary exactions, he accumulated immense wealth, and is said to have left, at his death, in ready money, the sum of £1,800,000, — an enormous amount of specie for that age, equivalent to £10,000,000, or, according to some, to £16,000,000, at present.

5. His reign was prosperous at home, and respected abroad and, though not a popular sovereign, he was, perhaps, next to Alfred, the most useful prince that had hitherto sat on the throne of England. He enacted many wise and salutary laws, promoted industry; encouraged commerce; reduced to subordination a factious and insolent aristocracy; and taught the peaceful arts of civilized life to a warlike and turbulent people

6. By permitting the nobles to alienate their lands, he weakened their power, raised the respectability of the lower orders, and gave a mortal wound to the *feudal system.* He expended £14,000 in building one ship, named "*the Great Harry*," which may be considered as the beginning of the

English navy: inasmuch as the government, before this period, had no other mode of raising a fleet than by hiring or pressing the vessels of merchants.

7. No monarch ever succeeded to the throne of England with brighter prospects than *Henry VIII.* (1509.) Uniting in his person the claims of the two houses of York and Lancaster, his title was undisputed: the treasury was well stored, the nation at peace, and the state of the country prosperous. He was 18 years of age, of beautiful person, accomplished manners, frank and open in his disposition, possessed of considerable learning, and fine talents; and was regarded by the people with affection and high expectations.

8. But these fond expectations were wofully disappointed. As the character of the king developed itself, he was found to be destitute both of wisdom and virtue, and proved himself an unprincipled and cruel tyrant, rapacious and prodigal, obstinate and capricious, fickle in his friendships, and merciless in his resentments, and capable of sending a minister or a wife to the scaffold, with as little feeling or compunction as he would have shown in ordering a dog to be drowned. "If all the pictures and patterns of a merciless prince," says Sir Walter Raleigh, "were lost in the world, they might all again be painted to the life out of the story of this king."

9. His government was but little short of a despotism; and one of the greatest wonders respecting it is the degrading servility of the people and parliament in tamely submitting to his tyranny, or becoming the passive instruments of its exercise. He chose for his ministers men of eminent talents; but he made them feel the effects of his caprice and cruelty. Archbishop *Cranmer* was almost the only one of great distinction among them, who had the good fortune to retain, to the last, his confidence and regard.

10. By his profusion and expensive pleasures he soon exhausted the treasures which he inherited from his father. Though his military operations were not numerous, yet, in the early part of his reign, he made war against *Louis XII* of France, invaded the country, and, at *Guinegast*, gained the battle of *the Spurs* (so named from the rapid flight of the French); and his general, the *Earl of Surrey*, gained a bloody victory over the *Scots*, at *Flodden*, where *James IV.*, and a great part of his nobility, were slain. Henry was also, in some degree, involved in the wars of the two great rivals of the age, *Charles V.* of Germany, and *Francis I.* of France.

11. Before he arrived at the age of 30, he wrote a book on the Seven Sacraments, against *Luther*, the reformer, which pleased the pope so much that he conferred on him the title of

"Defender of the Faith," a title which his successors have ever since retained.

12. But the most memorable transactions of Henry's reign were his matrimonial alliances, and the consequences which flowed from them. His first wife was *Catharine of Arragon* widow of his elder brother *Arthur*, daughter of *Ferdinand* of Spain and aunt of *Charles V.* He had been contracted to her, at a very early age, by the influence of his father; and, after having lived with her about 18 years, he professed to feel conscientious scruples respecting the lawfulness of the marriage on account of her having been the wife of his brother; and conceiving a passion for the beautiful and accomplished *Anne Boleyn*, he applied to the pope for a divorce.

13. Having experienced various delays, and imagining that his favorite minister, the celebrated *Cardinal Wolsey*, was the chief obstacle in the way of effecting his object, the king resolved on his ruin, and ordered him to be arrested for high treason. But the haughty cardinal soon after fell sick and died, having exclaimed, in the pangs of remorse, "Had I but served God as diligently as I have served the king, he would not have given me over in my gray hairs!"

14. The opinions of various universities, favorable to Henry's views, having been obtained, and the pope failing to grant the divorce, the king caused a court to be held, under *Cranmer*, which pronounced his marriage invalid; and Lady Anne was soon after crowned queen. The papal jurisdiction in England was immediately abolished (1534); the monasteries suppressed; some alterations made in the doctrines and forms of religion; and the king was declared the Supreme Head of the English Church.

15. The separation of England from the Church of Rome was thus begun by the passions of a prince, who meant nothing in the world less than the *Reformation* of religion, which was the consequence of it; and who was a most unworthy instrument of a most important event. Though Henry ceased to be a Roman Catholic, he was far from being a Protestant. He arrogated infallibility to himself, and caused the law of the *Six Articles* of religion, termed the "bloody statute," to be enacted, and condemned to death both Catholics and Protestants who ventured to maintain opinions in opposition to his own. The venerable *Bishop Fisher* and the celebrated *Sir Thomas More*, two conscientious Catholics, were beheaded for refusing to acknowledge his supremacy.

16. In less than three years after his new marriage, he caused Anne Boleyn to be condemned and beheaded, in order to gratify a new passion for *Jane Seymour*, whom he married

the day after the execution, and who died soon after giving birth to *Prince Edward.* He next married *Anne of Cleves*, but soon discarded her, because he did not find her so handsome as she had been represented; and *Thomas Cromwell, Earl of Essex*, his prime minister, having been instrumental in bringing about this joyless marriage, lost the favor of his sovereign, and suffered death on the scaffold. *Catharine Howard*, whom he next married, was condemned and executed for adultery. But *Catharine Parr*, his 6th wife, had the good fortune to survive him.

17. Henry VIII. left three children, *Mary*, daughter of Catharine of Arragon, *Elizabeth*, daughter of Anne Boleyn and *Edward*, son of Jane Seymour. The last succeeded him, with the title of *Edward VI.*, in his 10th year, Edward Seymour Duke of Somerset, uncle of the young king, being appointed protector; and, after his fall, the Duke of Northumberland was raised to the same office. Edward's short reign was distracted by contests between those to whom the direction of public affairs was intrusted; but the Protestant influence prevailed in the government, the cause of the Reformation was promoted, and the reformed liturgy was modelled under the direction of Cranmer; yet a great part of the people were still attached to the Catholic faith.

18. Edward, a prince of great hopes and virtues, died in his 16th year, deeply lamented. So different was his character from that of his father, that he is said never to have signed an order for an execution against any person without shedding tears. Just before his death, he had been prevailed upon, by the interested influence and intrigues of the Duke of Northumberland, the protector, to set aside his sisters, Mary and Elizabeth, and bequeathe the crown to *Jane Grey*, great-granddaughter of Henry VII., who was married to Lord Guilford Dudley, a son of the protector.

19. Notwithstanding the attempt to alter the succession, *Mary*, who was educated a strict Catholic, was acknowledged the rightful heir, and succeeded to the throne (1553); and the Catholic religion was again restored. Her short reign is noted for the cruel persecution of the English Reformers; and her character is painted by Protestant writers in the darkest colors; but it may be remarked, by way of apology for her, that the treatment which both she and her mother had received from those who rejected the papal supremacy was calculated to inflame her prejudices; that she was under the influence of evil counsellors; and that she lived in an age when the principles

of religious toleration were not understood or practised by either Catholics or Protestants.

20. Immediately after the death of Edward, Jane Grey, who had been appointed successor, by the intrigues of her friends, was proclaimed queen by her adherents; but after wearing the crown ten days, she resigned it, and would gladly have returned to private life. The youth and innocence of herself and her husband (neither of them exceeding their 17th year) pleaded strongly in their favor; yet they were condemned and beheaded, as also were their principal supporters.

21 Lady Jane, who is described as a young woman of singular virtues and accomplishments, sent, on the day of her execution, a message to her husband, who desired to see her, informing him that the tenderness of their last interview would be too much for her to bear. "Tell him," added she, "that our separation will be only for a moment. We shall soon meet each other in a place where our affections shall be for ever united, and where misfortunes will never more disturb our eternal felicity."

22. A cruel persecution was now commenced against the Reformers; the men who had been most forward in establishing the Protestant religion in England, were singled out for punishment; and among the most eminent martyrs who were burnt at Smithfield (1555), were *Cranmer*, *Latimer*, *Ridley*, *Hooper*, *Ferrar*, and *Rogers*. By the cruelty of these proceedings, the feelings of the people were shocked; the excellent character of most of the sufferers, and the undaunted spirit which they exhibited, produced a strong sensation in their favor, and diminished the influence of the Church of Rome; so that these barbarities tended to forward, rather than to check, the progress of the *Reformation*.

23. Mary, in the second year after she succeeded to the throne, was married to *Philip II.* of Spain, — a union unpopular with her subjects, and productive of little happiness to herself, and, in the last year of her reign, the French took *Calais*, which had been in possession of the English 210 years. Soon after this event, the queen died, feeling bitter vexation for the loss, and for being aware that she was an object of aversion to her husband and to a great part of her subjects. She left few to lament her, and there was scarcely the semblance of sorrow for her death.

24. The accession of *Elizabeth* to the throne, in 1558, was hailed by the nation with joyful acclamations. She had a long and auspicious reign, during which tranquillity was maintained in her dominions, while the neighboring nations were convulsed

with dissensions; and England rose, from the rank of a secondary kingdom, to a level with the first states of Europe. The Protestant religion was again restored and protected; the Church of England was established in its present form; and the nation attained a higher state of prosperity than it had ever before known, in agriculture, commerce, arts, and literature This reign, which some have considered as the Augustan age of English literature, was illustrated by the great names of *Hooker*, *Bacon*, *Spenser*, and *Shakspeare*.

25. A remarkable circumstance in this period of English history relates to the repeated and sudden changes with respect to religion, in accordance with the views of the sovereign and the court. Many, who had been Protestants under Edward, became persecuting Romanists under Mary; and, under Elizabeth, they were again transformed into zealous promoters of the Reformation. Religion, it would seem, hung so loose upon a great part, that they were equally ready to conform to the Church of Rome or to Protestantism, as might best suit their temporal interests. Of 9,000 beneficed clergymen, the number of those who preferred, on the accession of Elizabeth, to quit their preferments rather than the Roman Catholic Church, was less than 200.

26. Elizabeth is charged with treachery and cruelty in her treatment of *Mary, Queen of Scots*, a woman whose extraordinary beauty and misfortunes seem, in the minds of many, to have thrown a veil over all the defects of her character. Mary was great grand-daughter of *Henry VII.*, and next heir to Elizabeth to the throne of England. She had been educated in France as a Catholic, and married, when very young, to the dauphin, afterwards *Francis II.* She had been persuaded, imprudently, to assume the title of Queen of England, — a circumstance which proved fatal to her peace.

27. On the death of Francis, she returned to Scotland, at the age of 18 years. At this period the *Reformation*, by the zealous labors of *John Knox*, had made great progress in that country; and the people regarded their Catholic queen with abhorrence, and looked to her enemy Elizabeth for support.

28 Mary married, for her second husband, her cousin *Henry Stuart* (*Lord Darnley*), who soon became disagreeable to her, and was, in less than two years, murdered: in about three months after this tragical event, she married (1567) the *Earl of Bothwell*, who was stigmatized as the murderer of Darnley. Her conduct excited against her the whole kingdom of Scotland Public indignation could no longer be restrained. The nobles rose against her and her husband, Bothwell: she was taken, confined in the castle of Lochleven and was at length compelled

to resign the crown to her infant son, who was proclaimed *James VI.;* and her illegitimate brother, the *Earl of Murray* a friend to the Reformation, was appointed regent during the young king's minority.

29. In less than a year, Mary, by the assistance of friends effected her escape from Lochleven Castle, and fled into England, hoping to secure the favor of her rival, Elizabeth. In this, however, she was disappointed. After being kept as a prisoner more than 18 years in Fotheringay Castle, she was tried on an accusation of having been accessory to a conspiracy against the Queen of England, was condemned, and beheaded in one of the rooms of her prison, in the 45th year of her age.

30. Elizabeth warmly espoused the cause of the *Netherlands*, in their revolt against the authority of *Philip II.* of Spain; and her admiral, *Sir Francis Drake*, had taken some of the Spanish possessions in South America. To avenge these offences, and to subjugate the leading Protestant power, the Spanish "*Invincible Armada*," a more formidable fleet than Europe had ever before witnessed, was fitted out for the invasion of England.

31. This armament consisted of 150 ships, 3,000 pieces of cannon, and 27,000 men. It entered the English Channel in the form of a crescent, extending its two extremities to the distance of seven miles. It was met by the English fleet, consisting of 108 ships, commanded by those distinguished maritime chiefs, *Howard*, *Drake*, *Hawkins*, *Frobisher*, and *Raleigh.* Being gradually weakened, and finally overtaken by a storm, it suffered an entire defeat. Only 50 vessels, with 6,000 men, returned to Spain.

32. The age of Elizabeth was fruitful in men of talents, and she was assisted in her government by eminent statesmen, among whom were *Bacon*, *Burleigh*, and *Walsingham*, men wholly devoted to the interests of the nation. But her chief personal favorites were unworthy. Of these, in the early part of her reign, the principal was *Robert Dudley*, *Earl of Leicester:* after his death, *Robert Devereux*, *Earl of Essex*, a young nobleman of accomplishments, talents, and high spirit, possessed the first place in her affections. The queen and Essex had many quarrels and reconciliations; at last, he broke into open rebellion, was convicted of treason, and beheaded.

33. Elizabeth, who had surprised the nations of Europe by the splendor of her course, was destined to close the evening of her life in gloom and sorrow. Some ascribe the deep depression and mental suffering which she, at this period, endured, to the neglect which she imagined she experienced on account of her age and infirmities, when, to use her own ex

pression, "men would turn their backs on the setting, to worship the rising, sun"; others to the revival of her regret for the death of Essex, whom she had given up for his invincible obstinacy, but who, she now discovered, had actually thrown himself upon her clemency, while his enemies had found means to conceal his application. The Countess of Nottingham, now upon her death-bed (according to various historians), sent for the queen, to confess to her that Essex, while under the sentence of death, had desired her to convey to Elizabeth a ring which she had given him, with the assurance that the sight of it would at any time recall her tenderness; but that she had neglected to deliver it. The queen, in a frenzy of passion, shook the dying countess, exclaiming, "God may forgive you, but I never can!" From that moment she sunk into a deep melancholy, rejected all sustenance, and died (1603) in profound grief, in the 45th year of her reign, and the 70th of her age.

34. Elizabeth was distinguished for her learning, and spoke fluently Greek, Latin, French, and Spanish. She possessed extraordinary talents for government, was great as a public character, and commanded the high respect of her subjects and of foreign nations. Her three leading maxims of policy were, to secure the affections of her subjects, to be frugal of her treasures, and to excite dissensions among her enemies. She manifested less regard for the liberty, than for the prosperity, of the people. In the former part of her reign, she was comparatively moderate and humble, but afterwards haughty and severe. Both her disposition and her principles were despotic. With regard to religion, she persecuted both Catholics and Puritans; but, like her father, she had a leaning towards Rome in almost everything except the doctrine of papal supremacy.

35. Her private character is less to be admired, being tarnished with insincerity and cruelty, and destitute of the milder and softer virtues of her sex. Her manners were haughty and overbearing, and her conversation grossly profane. Vain of her beauty, which she only could discover; delighted with the praise of her charms, even at the age of 65; jealous of every female competitor, to a degree which the youngest and silliest of her sex might despise; and subject to sallies of anger which no sense of dignity could restrain, — she furnishes a remarkable instance of great moral weaknesses united with high intellectual superiority.

SECTION VIII.

THE STUART FAMILY: — *James I.; Charles I.: — The Commonwealth; Cromwell: — Charles II.; James II., William and Mary; Anne. — From A. D.* 1603 *to* 1714.

1. Elizabeth, on the approach of death, nominated for her successor the son of her rival Mary, *James VI.* of Scotland who was the rightful heir by descent. He took the title of *James I.* of England; and in him the two crowns were united He was the first of the *Stuarts*, a family whose reign was one continued struggle for power between the monarch and the people; and who were characterized by despotic principles, injudicious conduct, and such a want of gratitude and good faith as to be proverbial for leaving their friends in distress.

2. James had scarcely arrived in England, when a conspiracy was discovered for subverting the government, and placing on the throne his cousin, *Arabella Stuart.* The celebrated *Sir Walter Raleigh*, who had been distinguished in the preceding reign, was sentenced to death on an accusation of being connected in this plot. He was, however, reprieved, cast into prison, and, 15 years after his condemnation, was, at the instigation of the king, barbarously beheaded.

3. Another conspiracy followed, of a more daring nature. This was the famous *Gunpowder Plot*, a design of some desperate Catholics to blow up the Parliament-house, and involve in one common destruction the king, lords, and commons. Just on the eve of its accomplishment, the plot was discovered, and *Guy Fawkes* was taken, having matches for firing the magazine in his pocket.

4. It was the characteristic weakness of James to attach himself to worthless favorites; such were *Carre, Earl of Somerset*, and *Villiers, Duke of Buckingham*, — men on whom he bestowed his favors with the utmost prodigality, though they were of profligate character, odious to the people, and were possessed of no merit, except external beauty and superficial accomplishments.

5. During the reign of Mary, the ***Puritans*** first made their appearance; and in the time of Elizabeth they became, in a considerable degree, conspicuous. They were strenuous advocates for freedom in the state, and a more thorough reformation in religion. At the accession of James, they cherished high hopes that their views would meet with more favor than during the reign of the late queen, inasmuch as he had been educated in Presbyterianism, but, of all persons, they were the

most disappointed. So great was their dissatisfaction, that some of them sought refuge, from their restraints and persecutions, in the wilds of America, and commenced (1620) the settlement of *New England.*

6. The leading characteristic of James was his love of arbitrary power. The divine right of kings to govern their subjects without control was his favorite topic in conversation, and in his speeches to parliament. The best part of his character was his pacific disposition; and his reign, which lasted 22 years, though ignoble to himself, was, in many respects, happy to his people, who were enriched by peace and commerce.

7. In his private character, his morals were far from being pure. He possessed considerable ingenuity, and a good deal of learning, but more pedantry. He blended a childish and degrading familiarity so incongruously with a ridiculous vanity, insufferable arrogance, and a vulgar stateliness, that he reminds us more of some mock king in a farce, than a real one on the theatre of history. He was excessively fond of flattery, which was dealt out to him with an unsparing hand by his bishops and parasites, who styled him the British Solomon; yet, in the opinion of less interested observers, he merited the appellation given him by the Duke of Sully, that of "the wisest fool in Europe." "He was," says Bishop Burnet, "the scorn of the age, a mere pedant, without true judgment, courage, or steadiness, his reign being a continued course of mean practices."

8. The increase of commerce, and consequent influx of wealth; the diffusion of information; the little respect cherished for the personal character of the king; the disappointed hopes of the Puritans, the multiplication of their numbers, the controversies in which they were engaged, and the privations to which they were subjected, — all conspired to diffuse widely the spirit of liberty. The current of public opinion was now strongly turned to an extension of the rights of the people, and to a retrenchment of the power of the sovereign; and, during this reign, the seeds were sown of that spirit of resistance to despotic power, on the part of the people, which, in the next produced a subversion of the monarchy.

9 *Charles I.* ascended the throne (1625) in his 25th year, under favorable circumstances: his title was undisputed, and the kingdom was in a flourishing condition. But within the last fifty years, public opinion in the nation had undergone a great change, and many of his subjects were extremely jealous of their civil and religious liberties, and would no longer be governed by precedents which had their origin in times of ignorance and slavery. He soon gave proof that he inherited

the same arbitrary principles with his father, and the same worthless favorite, *Buckingham*, retained his influence and authority. — He married *Henrietta Maria*, daughter of Henry IV. of France, who was a zealous Papist, and whose influence over the king is regarded as one of the principal causes of his calamities.

10. In the latter part of the reign of James, Charles, accompanied by Buckingham, had visited the court of Madrid, in order to solicit the hand of the *Infanta* in marriage. The negotiation, however, failed through the misconduct of Buckingham, and England was involved in a war with Spain. Soon after Charles ascended the throne, he was offended with the Parliament for refusing to grant him sufficient supplies in carrying on this war, and for resisting his arbitrary designs, and, having adopted the resolution to rule without their aid, he proceeded to levy money, in various ways, independent of their authority.

11. One of these methods was by a tax on merchandise, called *tonnage* and *poundage*, and another by a tax called *ship-money*. The money raised by the latter was now levied, not only on seaport towns, but over the whole kingdom; and Charles claimed the right to command his subjects, without an act of parliament, to provide and furnish ships, together with men, victuals, and ammunition, in such numbers, and at whatever time, he should think proper, — a claim which struck at the vital principle of a free government. This assessment of ship-money is the famous tax which first roused the whole nation, at length, to fix and determine, after a long continuance of an unsettled constitution, the bounds of their own freedom, and the king's prerogative.

12. A noble stand was made against the payment of this imposition by *John Hampden*, a man who, on account of his high character for talents, integrity, and patriotism, possessed the greatest influence in parliament, and in the nation. But, although the venal judges decided the cause against him, yet he obtained the end for which he sacrificed his quiet and his safety. The people, believing that the decision was unjust were roused from their lethargy, and became fully sensible of the danger to which their liberties were exposed.

13. The Duke of Buckingham having been assassinated by *Felton*, an Irish fanatic, the *Earl of Strafford*, the most able and devoted champion of the claims of the crown, and the most formidable enemy of the liberties of the people, became the chief counsellor of the king, and *Archbishop Laud* had the principal influence in ecclesiastical affairs. The current of the public sentiment was now running strongly towards

Puritanism, in favor of a simpler form of worship. But Laud, so far from countenancing this tendency, had overloaded the church with new ceremonies, which were disgusting to the people, and which he enforced with the most intolerant zeal.

14. Not satisfied with attempting to enforce conformity in England, the king undertook to establish episcopacy in Scotland also, and to impose the use of the English liturgy upon the national church. This measure excited a strong sensation among all ranks, from the peer to the peasant: even the women were not backward in manifesting opposition. In one of the churches of Edinburgh, on the day when the introduction of the liturgy was first attempted, no sooner had the service begun, than an old woman, impelled by sudden indignation, started up, and exclaiming aloud against the supposed mass, threw the stool, on which she had been sitting, at the preacher's head. The assembly was instantly in confusion, nor could the minister finish the service. The people from without burst open the doors, broke the windows, and rent the air with exclamations of " A pope ! an antichrist ! stone him, stone him !"

15. The prelates were equally unsuccessful, in most instances, throughout Scotland, in enforcing the liturgy. The *National Covenant*, which was first framed at the Reformation, and which renounced episcopacy as well as popery, was renewed, and subscribed by all ranks; and afterwards a new bond, of similar purport, but still more determined and hostile in its spirit, styled the *Solemn League and Covenant*, was formed and signed by many in England as well as in Scotland, who combined together for their mutual defence.

16. After eleven years' intermission, the king found it necessary, in 1640, to convoke a *Parliament;* but the House of Commons, instead of listening to his demands for supplies, began with presenting the public grievances, under three heads those of the broken privileges of parliament, of illegal taxes and of violence done to the cause of religion. Charles, perceiving he had nothing favorable to hope from their deliberations, soon dissolved the assembly. By another parliament which was not long afterwards assembled, *Strafford* and *Laud* were sent to the Tower on several charges of endeavoring to subvert the constitution, and to introduce arbitrary power. Strafford was brought to trial on a charge of treason, and was condemned and beheaded; and, five years afterwards, Laud suffered the same fate.

17. Charles had, in 1629, violated the privileges of parliament, by causing nine members to be imprisoned for the part which they had taken in debate; but he was now betrayed into a still greater indiscretion, which contributed much to

wards kindling the flame of civil war. This was the impeachment of *Lord Kimbolton*, and five distinguished commoners *Pym*, *Hampden*, *Hollis*, *Hazlerig*, and *Strode;* and his going himself to the House to seize them, leaving 200 armed men at the door Having entered the House, he ordered the speaker *Lenthal*, to point them out. "Sir," answered the speaker falling on his knees, "I have neither eyes to see, nor tongue to speak in this place, but as the House is pleased to direct me whose servant I am; and I humbly ask pardon that I cannot give any other answer to what your majesty is pleased to demand of me."

18. The king withdrew without effecting his object, amidst low but distinct murmurs of "Privilege, privilege." This ill-advised and abortive attempt, which was condemned both by his friends and enemies, completed the degradation of the unfortunate monarch. He afterwards apologized to parliament for this conduct, but the day of reconciliation was past; he had lost the confidence of that body and they were now prepared not only to confine his power within legal bounds, but to strip him of his constitutional authority.

19. Both parties resolved to stake the issue of the contest on the sword; and the standard of civil war was now (1642) erected. The cause of the king was supported by three fourths of the nobility and superior gentry, by the bishops and advocates of episcopacy, and by the Catholics; that of the parliament by the yeomanry of the country, the merchants and tradesmen in the towns, — by the Puritans, or opponents of episcopacy, comprising the Presbyterians, Independents, and other dissenters. The supporters of the king were styled *Cavaliers;* those of the parliament, *Roundheads*, — an appellation given to them by their adversaries, because many of them cropped their hair short

20. A religious spirit, unfortunately tinctured with fanaticism, extravagance, and party feeling, was at this period widely diffused throughout Great Britain, and it formed a prominent characteristic of most of the leaders in parliament and also of those who took up arms in defence of their liberties. The charge of license and excess fell chiefly on the royalists, a great part of whom were men of pleasure, disposed to deride the sanctity and austere morality of their opponents. "All the sober men that I was acquainted with, who were against the parliament," says the celebrated Richard Baxter, "used to say, 'The king had the better cause, but the parliament had the better men.'"

21. England had been, comparatively, but little engaged in war since the accession of Henry VII., and it had but few

men of military experience. The chief commanders in the royal army, besides the *king*, were the *Earl of Lindsey*, *Prince Rupert*, and *Sir Jacob Astley;* and, in the parliamentary army, the *Earl of Essex* had the chief command at first, then *Lord Fairfax*, and afterwards *Oliver Cromwell.* In the early part of the contest, each side lost one of their greatest and best men; *Hampden* on the part of the parliament, and *Lord Falkland* on that of the king. In the battles of *Edge-hill* (1642), and *Newbury* (1643), the royalists had the advantage; but in those of *Marston Moor* (1643), and *Naseby* (1645), they were entirely defeated.

22. After the war had raged nearly five years, the king fell into the hands of his enemies, who held him for some time a prisoner. At length, a minority of the House of Commons, after having expelled their colleagues, being under the influence of the parliamentary army, instituted a high court of justice, composed of 133 members, for trying him on a charge of treason. Of this court, Bradshaw was appointed president. The king, having been arraigned before this tribunal, received the sentence, that "the court, being satisfied that Charles Stuart is guilty of the crimes of which he has been charged, do adjudge him, as a tyrant, traitor, murderer, and public enemy to the good people of the nation, to be put to death, by severing his head from his body."

23. Charles was now no longer the man he had been before the civil war. Affliction had chastened his mind; he had sought and found strength and relief in the consolations of religion; and his conduct during his trial exalted his character, even in the estimation of his enemies. He denied the authority of the court, but declared that he forgave those who were the cause of his death, and submitted to his fate with fortitude and composure. Having laid his head on the block, one of the masked executioners severed it from his body at a blow; the other, holding it up, exclaimed, "Behold the head of a traitor!" while the sobs and lamentations of the spectators were mingled with the acclamations of the soldiery (1649).

24. Such was the end of Charles I., — an awful lesson to kings to watch the growth of public opinion, and to moderate their pretensions in conformity with the reasonable desires of their subjects. His execution, however, was contrary to the general feelings of the nation, but was the deed of comparatively a few men, actuated by ambition or the madness of the times. Even of the commissioners appointed to sit in judgment on him, only about half could be induced to attend his trial. But the manner of his death has tended to exalt his posthumous reputation; for, while it has moderated the reproaches of his

adversaries, it has enhanced the encomiums of his advocates who have styled him "the royal martyr," and, in sympathy for his sufferings and resentment against the regicides, have been disposed to overlook his misdeeds which brought him to the scaffold.

25. It was the misfortune of Charles to inherit despotic principles from his ancestors, to be educated in a servile and profligate court, and to be surrounded by wretched counsellors. He was one of the last men to learn the important lesson, which princes in all ages have been slow to learn, that the influence of authority must ultimately bend to the influence of opinion. But his greatest defect, as well as the principal cause of his ruin, was the system of duplicity and insincerity upon which he acted in his public character. Such was his want of fidelity in his engagements, that the parliament could never confide in his promises.

26. But, weak and reprehensible as he was as a king, he was by no means destitute of abilities. He was possessed of considerable learning and good talents as a speaker and writer, and, in his private character, was exemplary. In his manners he is represented as cold, stiff, and formal, preserving a state and reserve, which were calculated to alienate those who approached him. With respect to religion, he was, says Bishop Burnet, "much inclined to a middle way between Protestants and Papists."

27. The proceedings of Charles were at direct variance with every principle of civil and religious liberty; and, had they been acquiesced in on the part of the people, England might now have been a despotism. Mr. Hume, the great apologist for the Stuart family, acknowledges the services of the *Puritans*, "by whom alone," according to him, "the precious spark of liberty had been kindled and was preserved, and to whom the English owe the whole freedom of their constitution."

28. The intentions of those who first resisted the despotic and intolerant measures of the king and his court were doubtless upright and patriotic; and their exertions to secure the rights of the nation, which had been wantonly violated, entitle them to the gratitude of posterity. Yet it must be acknowledged, that those who opposed the intolerance of the king and of Laud had themselves no consistent principles of religious liberty In the progress of the contest, party spirit and fanaticism were called into powerful operation, and the leaders of the popular party, in many cases, acted on the principle that the end sanctifies the means, and appeared to think themselves absolved from all obligations of honor and honesty. Right

and justice were outraged by those who professed to have drawn the sword in their defence. But such inconsistency is characteristic of revolutions.

29. The death of the king was soon followed by the abolition both of the monarchy and the House of Lords by the Commons; and a republican government was established. It was publicly proclaimed, that the supreme authority of the nation resided in the representatives of the people; and that it should be accounted treason to give any person the title of king without the authority of parliament.

30. After the execution of Laud, *Episcopacy* had been abolished, and *Presbyterianism* substituted in its stead. But the Presbyterian interest soon began to decline, and the *Independents* gained the ascendency; and the power which the parliament had wrested from the king was at length, by the management of *Cromwell*, transferred to the army. Before the trial of Charles, measures had been taken to exclude the Presbyterians from parliament; and that part of the House which remained, distinguished by the ridiculous name of the *Rump*, was composed of Independents, under the influence of Cromwell. In this manner the Presbyterians, who had overturned the church and the throne, fell victims to the military power which they had used as the instrument for accomplishing their designs.

31. The parliament of Scotland took no part in the trial of the king, and after his death they proclaimed *Charles II.* their sovereign, on condition of his signing the Covenant. Cromwell, at the head of 16,000 men, marched into Scotland, and defeated (1650) the royalist Covenanters in the battle of *Dunbar*. The royal army, retreating into England, was pursued by Cromwell, and, in the desperate battle of *Worcester* (1651) almost the whole of the troops were killed or taken prisoners, and the victorious commander returned in triumph to London.

32. Young Charles escaped with difficulty. He assumed the disguise of a peasant, journeying in the least frequented roads, travelling only in the night, and passing the day in obscure cottages, where he was unknown, and where his food was generally a little coarse bread and milk. On one occasion he sought safety by concealing himself, for a day, in the top of a large oak. In that precarious situation, he saw and heard his pursuers, as they passed by, talking of him, and expressing a wish that they might discover the place of his concealment. After two months of romantic adventure, he found an opportunity of escaping to France.

33 The republican parliament passed (1651) the famous

Navigation Act, which, by prohibiting the importation of all foreign merchandise, except in English bottoms, or in those of the country producing the commodities, tended greatly to promote the naval superiority of Great Britain. This act, the object of which was to wrest the carrying-trade of Europe from the Dutch, was the cause of a war between England and Holland, which terminated in favor of the former, and in which the celebrated Admiral *Blake* distinguished himself, and had for his antagonists the great Dutch maritime chiefs, *Van Tromp* and *De Ruyter*.

34 The parliament, which had been in session twelve years known by the name of the *Long Parliament*, had lost the confidence of the people. It had been subservient to the views of Cromwell; but, having at length become jealous of him, it formed the design of reducing the army, intending, by that means, to diminish his power. Cromwell, perceiving their object, and being secure of the attachment of the army, resolved on seizing the sovereign power. While sitting in a council of officers, on being informed of an unfavorable reply of parliament to a petition which they had presented, he rose up on a sudden, with an appearance of fury, and, turning to Major General Vernon, cried out, that he was compelled to do a thing which made the very hairs of his head stand on end.

35. Taking with him 300 soldiers to the door, he speedily entered the house with marks of violent indignation in his countenance; and, after listening awhile to the debates, he started up, and began to load the parliament with reproaches. Then, stamping upon the floor, he gave a signal for his soldiers to enter; and, addressing himself to the members, "For shame!" said he; "get you gone; give place to honester men! I tell you, you are no longer a parliament; the Lord has done with you!" Having turned out all the members, he ordered the doors to be locked.

36. In this manner Cromwell seized the reins of government; but he was willing to give his subjects a parliament not, indeed, elected in the usual form, but modelled on principles entirely new. The ministers took the sense of the "Congregational churches" in the several counties, and returns were made containing the names of such persons as were deemed qualified for this high trust. Out of these, the council, in the presence of Cromwell, selected 163 representatives, to each of whom a writ of summons was sent, requiring his attendance; and, on the appointed day, 120 of them presented themselves in the council-chamber at Whitehall. This body, composed of men who were deeply imbued with the fanaticism of the times, is known by the name of the *Little*

Parliament, and is also often called *Barebone's Parliament*, from a leading member, a leather-dresser, whose name, given according to the taste of the age, was Praise-God Barebone.

37. The Little Parliament assembled on the 4th of July 1653, and was dissolved in the following December. At the time of its dissolution, a new constitution was published, and Cromwell assumed the title and office of *Protector*, having now obtained the great object of his ambition, the station and authority, though not the title, of king. He was assisted by a council of 21 members, and, instead of the title of *majesty*, he received that of *highness*. He afterwards aspired to the title of king, which was at length tendered to him, yet under such circumstances of opposition and danger, that he thought proper to decline it.

38. The government which he had usurped he administered with unrivalled energy and ability, and he was the most able and powerful potentate of his time in Europe. Abroad, his fleets and armies were victorious, and the island of *Jamaica* and the strong town of *Dunkirk* were taken from the Spaniards: at home, he defeated and punished the conspiracies formed against him; granted religious toleration; caused justice to be ably and impartially administered by upright and learned judges; made himself to be respected and dreaded by the neighboring nations, and his friendship to be sought by every foreign power; and the splendor of his character and exploits rendered the short period of the protectorate one of the most brilliant in English history; nor were the rights of England, under the reign of any other sovereign, more respected abroad. But, notwithstanding all his efforts, his enemies were numerous among both the royalists and republicans: he passed the last part of his life in constant fear of assassination; wore armor under his clothes; kept pistols in his pocket; and never slept more than three nights in the same chamber. At last, after having usurped the government 9 years, he died of a tertian ague (1658), in the 60th year of his age.

39. Cromwell was one of the greatest and most extraordinary men that England has produced; and, till the rise of Bonaparte, his name was without a parallel in modern Europe. Men were accustomed to look with a feeling of awe upon the individual who, without the aid of birth, wealth, or connections, was able, by the force of his talents, to seize the government of three powerful kingdoms, and impose the yoke of servitude upon the necks of the very men who had fought in his company to emancipate themselves from the arbitrary sway of their hereditary sovereign.

40. He owed his elevation to his influence with the army

and the character of that body and that of their leader were in a great measure, mutually formed by each other. The officers and soldiers made high professions of religion; religious exercises were of as frequent occurrence as those of military duty; the generals opened their proceedings in council by prayer; and among them Cromwell was preëminent in spiritual gifts, and was regarded by them as the favorite of Heaven. While eagerly toiling up the ascent to greatness, he labored to make it appear that he was involuntarily borne forward by a resistless force, by the wishes of the army, by the necessities of the state, and by the will of Providence; and, in assuming authority, he yielded, with feigned reluctance, to the advice which he had himself suggested.

41. The name of Cromwell has been subjected to the almost universal charge of unbounded ambition and deep hypocrisy; and there is scarcely to be met with, in the annals of the world, another man alike conspicuous, and possessed of equal merit in his public and private character, who has met less favor from history. This is, indeed, a natural result, as his course was alike hostile to legitimate monarchy and republican liberty, and rendered him equally odious to the two leading parties of the times, the advocates of the privileges of the people, and those of the prerogative of the king; and it may also be remarked, that, by his high professions of religion, he made himself liable to the severest judgment. His desertion from the cause of liberty, and his baseness in subverting the freedom of his country, proved fatal, at once, to his happiness and his fame.

42. Cromwell, in private life, in the several relations of a husband, a father, a neighbor, and a friend, was exemplary. From his early days to the close of his career, religion, or religious enthusiasm, formed a distinguished trait in his character; and it frequently manifested itself in the senate and in the field, and also in his domestic retirement. Some writers have maintained that he was a dissembler in religion as well as in politics; and that, for interested purposes, he condescended to act the part of a character which he despised. "But this supposition," as Dr. Lingard justly observes, "is contradicted by the uniform tenor of his life."

43. *Richard Cromwell*, after the death of his father, was proclaimed protector; but the contrast between the father and son was wonderful. Richard was neither a statesman nor a soldier, had no experience in public business, and possessed feeble talents, and little ambition; and, after a few months, he resigned the office, and retired to private life. A state of

anarchy succeeded, when *General Monk* (afterwards *Duke of Albemarle*), the military commander in Scotland, marched his army into England, and crushed the contending factions. A parliament was assembled, and on the 29th of May, 1660, *Charles II.*, now 30 years of age, was restored to the throne of his father.

44 The nation, indiscreetly trusting to the general professions of *Charles II.*, suffered him to assume the crown without imposing on him any conditions; and his reign, and that of *James II.*, exhibit a disgusting repetition of struggles, similar to those which had occurred under the two first princes of the house of Stuart. The first impressions with regard to the new king were favorable; his manners were easy and familiar, but his habits were indolent; and experience soon proved his character to be profligate and worthless.

45. The change in the public sentiment, observable at this period, is not a little remarkable. The same people, who, but a few years before, were so jealous of liberty, and exclaimed so loudly against monarchical government, are now exhibited as soliciting, with eagerness, the shackles of arbitrary power. A number of the regicides were condemned and executed, and the bodies of Cromwell, Bradshaw, and Ireton, were dug up from their graves, and hanged upon the gallows, to gratify the vindictive spirit of the king and the cavaliers. High-church or Tory principles, and the slavish doctrines of passive obedience and non-resistance, now came in vogue. An act of *uniformity* in religion was passed (1662), by which about 2,000 non-conforming ministers were deprived of their livings; and another attempt was made to establish episcopacy in Scotland.

46. The prodigality of Charles kept him always in want. *Dunkirk*, which had been acquired by Cromwell, he sold to the French for £400,000, which he soon squandered upon his pleasures. He entered into hostilities with the Dutch, which were carried on, for some time, with spirit. While this war was raging, London was visited (1665) by a tremendous *plague*, which carried off about 90,000 inhabitants; and was followed, the next year, by a *fire*, by which 13,200 houses, comprising about two thirds of the metropolis, were reduced to ashes.

47. In consequence of the unsuccessful issue of the war (which was terminated by the peace of *Breda*, 1667), and of the sale of *Dunkirk*, the government became unpopular, and the celebrated *Lord Clarendon*, on whom the odium was chiefly cast was banished, and passed the remainder of his

life in France. After the fall of Clarendon, the government became more unprincipled; and the five ministers, by whom it was conducted, have been stigmatized by the term of *Cabal* so called from the initial letters of their names.

48. The *Duke of York* (afterwards *James II.*), who had now the chief influence at court, was an avowed *Catholic* Charles, so far as he had any sense of religion, was a concealed one, and had the baseness to receive from Louis XIV of France a pension of £200,000 a year, for the purpose of establishing the Catholic religion and despotic power in England. A general consternation for the safety of the Protestant religion and of public liberty prevailed; and the latter part of Charles's reign exhibits an uninterrupted series of attacks upon the lives, liberty, and property of his subjects, and a disgusting scene of party intrigues, and of plots and conspiracies; yet it was at this period that parliament passed the *Habeas Corpus* act, a most important security to the subject against personal oppression.

49. A pretended *Popish Plot*, disclosed by the infamous *Titus Oates*, occasioned an unjust execution of *Lord Stafford*, and some other Catholics. Another pretended conspiracy, in favor of reform, was called the *Rye-House Plot*, in which those eminent patriots, *Lord Russell* and *Algernon Sydney*, were accused of being concerned, and, on testimony supposed to be perjured, were condemned and beheaded.

50. The character of the court, as well as that of the king, was notorious for its profligacy; and it had a most unhappy influence upon the nation. A general dissoluteness of manners characterized the reign. All appearance of devotion, and all regularity of morals, were regarded as puritanical, and exploded as unfashionable. Charles II. was a man of wit and good-humor, and possessed such talents as enabled him to shine among his gay and profligate companions, but he had no qualities, as a man or a king, that entitle him to the respect or gratitude of posterity.

51. *James II.*, who succeeded (1685) his brother Charles was inferior to him in talents, but much more devoted to business: like his predecessors of the Stuart family, he was arbitrary and impolitic; and his short and inglorious reign was wholly employed in attempts to establish the Catholic religion and despotic power On assuming the government, he expressed his contempt for the authority of parliament, and his determination to exercise an unlimited despotism. He made Romish priests and Jesuits his chief counsellors; and though the Catholics, at this time, composed but a very small propor

tion of the people of England, yet he undertook the desperate attempt to set aside the Protestant religion, and, instead of it to establish the Roman Catholic faith.

52. The *Duke of Monmouth*, a natural son of Charles II. who, during the preceding reign, had defeated the Scottish Covenanters at *Bothwell Bridge*, having now excited a rebellion, with a view to seize the crown, was defeated, taken prisoner, and beheaded. The most inhuman rigor was exercised against those who favored him. The atrocious chief justice, *Jeffreys*, the most noted as an unscrupulous and profligate judge in English history, exercised the most unrelenting cruelty. He gloried in his barbarity, and boasted that he had hanged more men than any other judge since the time of William the Conqueror; and his bloody career was styled by James, with unfeeling jocularity, "Jeffreys' campaign."

53. The efforts of James, in favor of the Catholic religion were, for a considerable time, attended with success. But having caused *seven bishops* to be committed to the Tower for refusing to read a declaration to suspend the laws against popery, the passive spirit of the nation disappeared, and a general indignation was roused. *William, Prince of Orange*, who had married *Mary*, the eldest daughter of James, was invited over, and landed at *Torbay*, with an army, in order to assume the government.

54. The principal nobility and officers soon joined his standard, and James, being deserted by the people, and even by his own children, escaped to France, where he passed the remainder of his life. A Convention-Parliament declared the king's flight an abdication, and settled the crown upon *William III. and Mary*. This event is styled by British writers *the glorious revolution of* 1688.

55. The *British constitution* now became, in many important points, fixed and determined. The Protestant succession was secured; religious toleration granted; and Presbyterianism reëstablished in Scotland. A declaration was made, fixing the rights of the subject, and the prerogative of the king. Some of the most important articles are the following: — 1. The king cannot suspend the laws or their execution. 2. He cannot levy money without the consent of parliament. 3. The subjects have a right to petition the crown. 4. A standing army cannot be kept in time of peace but with the consent of parliament. 5. Elections and parliamentary debates must be free, and parliaments must be frequently assembled.

56. Archbishop *Sancroft*, seven other bishops, and a considerable number of the clergy, who held the doctrines of pas

sive obedience and the divine right of kings and bishops, look ing upon James as still their lawful king, refused to take the oath of allegiance to William, and were deprived of their sta tions. From this circumstance they were styled *Non-jurors High Churchmen*, and *Jacobites*.

57. Ireland still adhered to James, and the parliament of that country declared William an usurper. Being assisted by *Louis XIV.* of France, James landed with some French forces n Ireland, where he was joined by a large army; but he was defeated by William at the river *Boyne*, and the country sub mitted to the new king. A large fleet, which Louis XIV. had prepared in favor of James, was destroyed by Admiral *Russell*, off *Cape la Hogue;* and by the peace of *Ryswick*, which followed (1697), the title of William to the crown was acknowledged.

58. William was a man of feeble constitution, but of distinguished talents, especially in war, to which his taste strongly inclined him; and he was esteemed one of the greatest commanders of his age. He was rather fitted to command respect than affection, as he excelled more in the severer, than in the milder, virtues, being wholly devoted to business, and his manners being cold, grave, and reserved: he was a firm friend to civil and religious liberty; but he was less popular with his subjects than some other sovereigns of far less merit. *Mary* his queen, and partner of the throne, who died seven years be fore him, was a woman distinguished for her virtues.

59. On the death of William, the crown devolved upon *Anne* (1702), the second daughter of James II., who was mar ried to *George*, Prince of Denmark. She was respected for her virtues, and she has been honored by the appellation of "Good Queen Anne"; though, according to Lord Mahon, "she was a very weak woman, full of prejudices, fond of flattery,—always blindly guided by some female favorite." Her reign was distinguished not only for military achievements, but also for eminent attainments in philosophy and literature; and is sometimes styled the *Augustan age* of England.

60. In the first year of this reign, Great Britain, Germany and Holland, in alliance with each other, declared war against France. The *Duke of Marlborough*, one of the greatest commanders of modern times, was appointed generalissimo of the allied army; and the imperial general was the celebrated *Prince Eugene*. In this great contest, the Allies had greatly the advantage, effectually checked the ambition and encroachments of *Louis XIV.*, and gained the splendid victories of *Blenheim* (1704), *Ramillies* (1706), *Oudenarde* (1708), and

Malplaquet (1709). The war was terminated by the peace of *Utrecht*, in 1713.

61. An important event of this reign was the *constitutional union between England and Scotland* (1706), which put a period to the contests which had harassed both countries, and included them under one common title of *Great Britain.*

62. The party names of *Whigs* and *Tories*, which are still used to designate parties in England, first became common in the reign of Charles II The Whigs were advocates for the rights of the people; the Tories favored those of the crown The accession of William and Mary was advocated chiefly by the Whigs. During the reign of Anne, parties ran high; the nation was thrown into a ferment by the preaching of *Dr. Sacheverell*, who inculcated the Tory principle of passive obedience; and, towards the close of the reign, the Tories supplanted the Whigs in the queen's favor, and came into power

---

SECTION IX.

House of Brunswick: — *George I.; George II.; George III.; George IV.; William IV.; Victoria.*

1. On the death of Queen Anne (1714), *George I.*, Elector of Hanover, succeeded to the crown, in the 55th year of his age. Before he ascended the throne, he had acquired some reputation as a politician and a general. He was plain in his manners, and not of elevated character or taste; but he was a man of great application to business; and his reign was pacific and prosperous. Some faults in his government were attributed to a venal ministry; and he was esteemed, to the end of his life, in his views and conduct, much more the Elector of Hanover than the King of England.

2. The two parties which had long divided the kingdom now, for a time, changed their titles, the Whigs being styled *Hanoverians*, and the Tories *Jacobites.* The former, being strenuous advocates for the accession of George, received in return from him favor and support, and were restored to power. This circumstance alienated and enraged the Tories to such a degree, that many of them took part with the *Pretender*, son of James II., who was proclaimed king in Scotland, and made an effort to obtain the crown; but the rebellion was suppressed, and the leaders executed.

3. A pacific reign, like that of George I., furnishes few events of importance in history. One, however, of disastrous

19*

consequences, occurred, called the *South Sea Scheme*, a base imposture, by which it was proposed to diminish the burden of the national debt by lowering the interest. It gave a great shock to public credit, and involved thousands in ruin.

4. *George II.*, who succeeded his father in the 44th year of his age, was an able general, of great personal courage, but was too fond of war, and delighted in military parade. His temper was violent, his talents respectable, though little cultivated by education, and his internal administration generally equitable and popular; but his private character was licentious, and the morals of the court, during his reign, were very corrupt. His partialities in favor of his continental dominions are represented as still stronger than those of his father, and he has been censured for involving Great Britain in expensive wars on account of the interests of the electorate of Hanover.

5. The most prominent person in the administration, during a considerable portion of the reign of George I., and during the former part of that of George II., was *Sir Robert Walpole*, a man whose policy was pacific, and who was distinguished for his talents, and not less so for the system of corruption and venality which he practised while in office.

6. The military operations of this reign were extensive and numerous; and the British arms were, for the most part, triumphant. Charles VI., Emperor of Germany, who died in 1740, was succeeded in his dominions by his daughter, the celebrated *Maria Theresa*, who was married to *Francis of Lorraine*. But *Charles*, the Elector of Bavaria, asserted his claim to the throne, and, by the aid of Louis XV., was elected emperor.

7. This gave rise to a war, which involved the principal states of Europe, called the war of the *Austrian Succession;* during which the Allies, under *George II.*, defeated the French in the battle of *Dettingen* (1743); and the French, under *Marshal Saxe*, routed the Allies at *Fontenoy* (1745). Great Britain was the principal support of Maria Theresa, and by the peace of *Aix-la-Chapelle*, in 1748, her claim to the throne was confirmed.

8. While George II. was absent on the Continent, at the head of the British army, *Charles Edward*, the young *Pretender*, assisted by Louis XV. of France, made an effort to recover the throne of his ancestors. Having landed in Scotland, he put himself at the head of an army, and defeated the royal forces in the battles of *Preston-Pans* and *Falkirk;* but was afterwards entirely defeated by the *Duke of Cumberland*, in the decisive battle of *Culloden* (1746). This was the last

battle that has been fought on the soil of Great Britain, and it terminated the last effort of the *Stuart family* to reascend the throne, which had been forfeited by the most egregious folly and the most flagitious attempts.

9. In the latter part of this reign, the war between Great Britain and France was renewed, and in its progress the British took *Louisburg*, *Fort du Quesne*, *Ticonderoga*, *Crown Point*, *Niagara*, and finally, under the command of General *Wolfe*, they gained possession of the city of *Quebec*. These successes were followed by the surrender of all *Canada* on the part of the French to the English, in 1763. During these operations in America, the British also made extensive conquests in India.

10. During the reign of George II., Great Britain made great progress in wealth and general improvement. The national debt, however, was more than doubled during the reign; and at the end of the seven years' war, in 1763, it amounted to nearly £139,000,000. This debt was commenced during the reign of William and Mary, and, at the end of the reign of George III., it amounted to upwards of £800,000,000.

11. George II. was succeeded (1760) by his grandson, *George III.*, who was the first king of the house of Brunswick that was born in England. He commenced his reign at an auspicious period, when the arms of Great Britain were triumphant, and the administration able and popular. The war with France was, not long afterwards, brought to a close; and by the peace of *Paris*, Canada, and other territories in North America, were confirmed to England.

12. *William Pitt* (afterwards *Lord Chatham*) was at the head of the administration during the last years of the preceding reign; and, in the former part of this, he was the most prominent public man in the nation. At this period, oppressive measures were adopted by the British government with regard to the *American Colonies*. These Chatham opposed with his powerful eloquence: but they were persisted in; hostilities were commenced; a declaration of the independence of the *United States* was made, and their independence was finally acknowledged by Great Britain, in 1783. [See *United States*.]

13. The other most important events in the history of England, during this reign, are the extension of the British dominions in India, the Irish rebellion of 1798, the union between that country and Great Britain, in 1800, and the various operations of the unexampled war which grew out of the *French Revolution*. [See *France*.]

14. In 1789, the French revolution broke out, convulsing all Europe; and it was thought to threaten the overthrow of all

established governments. The government of Great Britain alarmed respecting its own safety, embarked zealously in the European war, with a view to check the dissemination of democratic principles both at home and abroad.

15. The system of operations was devised and managed under the direction of *William Pitt*, the son of Lord Chatham who was now at the head of the administration. This calamitous war continued to convulse the Continent for 25 years and, during a part of the time, Great Britain alone had all Europe arrayed against her. But after various fluctuations of failure and success, she came off victorious, yet not without an immense loss of the blood of her subjects, and a vast increase of her national debt. Some of the principal victories, which the *British* obtained during this war, were those of the *Nile* and of *Trafalgar*, by *Nelson;* and those of *Talavera*, *Salamanca*, *Vittoria*, and *Waterloo*, by *Wellington.*

16. The reign of *George III.*, who died in 1820, was longer than that of any other English monarch; and it forms a distinguished period in the history of the kingdom, on account of its military events, and the progress of the nation in commerce, wealth, and the arts. During the last ten years of his life, he was afflicted with insanity to such a degree, as entirely disqualified him for all business, and the *Prince of Wales* acted as *Regent.* His talents were not brilliant, nor were his views, as a statesman, enlarged; but his private character was exemplary, and he was much respected by his subjects.

17. George III. was succeeded, in 1820, by his son, *George IV.*, who was a man of talents and accomplishments, but whose life, during both his youth and his manhood, had been marked by great prodigality and dissipation; and there was little in his character or his conduct, while a sovereign, to entitle him to the affection or respect of his subjects. While a prince, and not in power, he connected himself with the opposition or Whigs; but, both as regent and king, he adhered to the Tories, to the neglect of his former friends.

18. Soon after the accession of George IV., a bill for divorcing and degrading the queen, Caroline, on charges of misconduct, was introduced into the House of Lords, and, after being carried by a vote of 108 to 99, it was abandoned; and the queen soon after died.

19. The Greeks having for some years maintained a sanguinary struggle for independence against the Turks, an interposition in their favor was made by England, France, and Russia; and the united fleets of these three powers obtained in 1827, a great victory over the Turkish fleet at *Navarino.*

20. In 1828 the Corporation and Test Act, which had long operated to exclude Catholics and Dissenters from all corporate offices, was repealed; and it was followed, in 1829, by the still more important measure of Catholic Emancipation. By this act, the laws imposing civil disabilities on Roman Catholics were repealed. In addition to these great national measures, many other important alterations and improvements were made in the laws of Great Britain during the reign of George IV. The penal code was improved by rendering punishment more certain, and much less sanguinary.

21. George IV. was succeeded, in 1830, by his brother, the Duke of Clarence, with the title of *William IV.* In about a month after his accession, a revolution took place in France, which caused the dethronement of Charles X. A wide-spread feeling of uneasiness and disaffection was felt in England, and the country was alarmed by numerous incendiary fires. For many years the subject of a reform of the representation of the people in the House of Commons had been much agitated and it was now more loudly called for than ever before. On the meeting of the new parliament, the *Duke of Wellington*, the prime minister, unexpectedly expressed himself strongly against any reform; but the duke and his colleagues, not finding themselves supported by a majority of the House of Commons, resigned, and were succeeded by a Whig ministry, with *Earl Grey* at the head.

22. On the 1st of March, 1831, *Lord John Russell*, as the organ of the cabinet, brought into parliament the first Reform Bill; but this bill, and also a second one, the ministry failed to carry through both Houses; but a third bill was, after a violent struggle, carried and enacted into a law, in June, 1832. This important measure, which renders the House of Commons a body much more effectually representing the people, occupied the greater part of the first two years of the reign of William, to the exclusion of almost all other measures.

23. The first parliament, elected under the new system, assembled in January, 1833; and the reform of the representation was soon followed by the reform of the Irish church, the abolition of slavery in the British colonies, with a compensation of £20,000,000 paid to the planters; the reform of the poor-laws, and the renewal, with important provisions, of the East India Charter.

24. William IV. was succeeded, in 1837, by Queen *Victoria*, the daughter of the Duke of Kent, the fourth son of George III.; and she was married in 1840 to *Prince Albert* of Coburg.

25. The principal military operations of the British in the present reign have been the wars with *China*, the *Turkish* wars, and the wars in *India*. The Chinese wars have originated mainly in commercial difficulties. The importation of *opium* was forbidden by the Chinese Government, but English merchants smuggled the drug over the frontier. Its seizure led to a war, by which China was compelled (1842) to cede *Hong Kong*, and pay $21,000 000 to Great Britain, and to open *five seaports* to British commerce. In 1857, the Chinese were charged with having broken their treaties; but it was not until the Sepoy Rebellion in India was quelled, that, some massacres having occurred in Chinese waters, France and England formed an alliance against the aggressors. They captured *Canton*, and negotiations were begun; but in 1859 the war was renewed. The allies were at first repulsed on the *Peiho* River; but, the next year, the forts and *Tien-tsin* were taken, and the Chinese, being defeated near *Pekin*, came to terms, and this inglorious war was ended by a commercial treaty.

26. To support the tottering empire of Turkey, and thereby limit the encroachments of Russia, has long been the policy of England and France, in the pursuance of which they have engaged in two wars during this reign. The first was in 1839, when the allies assisted Turkey in putting down the revolt of *Mohammed Ali* in Egypt. The other was the *Crimean War*, which began in 1853 Russia had demanded to be named protector of the *Greek Christians* in the Turkish Empire By the advice of England and France, this demand was refused; and the *Czar* at once occupied the *Danubian Principalities* where these Christians lived The Russians, failing to take *Silistria*, were defeated on the *Danube*, and withdrew from Turkish territory. Meantime, the allied fleets blockaded the Russian fleet in the harbor of *Sebastopol*; and the reduction of this strongly fortified city became the main purpose of the allies, whom *Sardinia* now joined. In the course of this siege were fought the battles of the *Alma*; of *Balaklava*, where the "Six Hundred" made their famous charge; of *Inkermann*; and of the *Tchernaya*; and furious assaults were made on the Russian works, especially upon the battery of the *Malakoff*, which was captured by the French and that of the *Redan*, upon which an attempt of the English failed. After sustaining a siege of eleven months, Sebastopol was evacuated Sept. 9, 1855; and a treaty of peace was signed in the following year.

27. England undertook some naval operations against Russia in the Baltic Sea, but with very small results. The losses to all parties in this war were immense. The allies suffered terribly from disease; and it was by her efforts to improve the hos-

pital service, and relieve the wants of the soldiers in the Crimea, that the name of *Florence Nightingale* became so memorable. *The Order of the Victoria Cross*, open to all ranks, was instituted by the Queen as a reward for special heroic services in this war.

28. The *Afghan* war was between 1838 and 1842. England undertook to support the Afghans against Persia, and finally to place on their throne a prince of a former reigning house, to maintain whose authority a small English force was left in *Cabul*. Violent opposition to the new rule sprung up: these troops, seeing their danger, attempted to cut their way to *Jellalabad*, and were nearly destroyed. A fresh English force in turn destroyed Cabul, but Afghanistan was abandoned. During this war, *Sinde* was annexed to British India. The *Sikhs* invaded the British territories in 1845; and a war followed, which ended in the annexation of their country, the *Punjaub*. In 1852, a war with Burmah resulted in the acquisition of *Pegu;* and, in 1856, the kingdom of *Oude*, long under British protection, was formally annexed on the ground of extreme misgovernment.

29. The English army in India is largely composed of *sepoys*, or native soldiers. Early in 1857, there were signs of a mutinous spirit in the Bengal division, which was by far the largest, and contained many *high-caste* sepoys. The government had resolved to arm the troops with *Enfield Rifles*, in the use of which greased cartridges were employed. A belief spread among the native troops that this was an attempt to make them give up their religion by compelling them to bite the fat of swine and cows, the use of the former being defilement to the *Mohammedan*, and of the latter sacrilege to the *Hindoo*. Although the old cartridges were still used, the greatest excitement prevailed, and the discontent spread like wild-fire.

30. The first outbreaks were quelled; but in May, several regiments mutinied at *Meerut*, killed their English officers, and marched to *Delhi*, where the garrison joined them. The Europeans were massacred, and Delhi became the rallying point of the rebellion. Several thousand sepoys also revolted at *Cawnpore*, and placed themselves under the *Nena Sahib*. Few native regiments could be trusted; and the European troops were too few to check the mutiny, which now spread with frightful rapidity. The scenes at Delhi were repeated at *Benares*, *Allahabad*, *Futtehpoor*, and all over Oude, where many Bengal sepoys had been recruited. The rebels gradually gathered around *Lucknow*, and began to besiege the Europeans there about July 1st.

31. The first movements of the English were against Delhi. The memorable siege of this city lasted from June till Septem-

ber, and it was taken only after the most desperate fighting within, as well as without, the walls. Meantime, *Gen. Havelock* moved with a small force from Allahabad towards Cawnpore, where a few English were besieged by the Nena Sahib, who, on the approach of Havelock, murdered them all with horrible atrocities. He, after defeating the Nena in several battles, marched to relieve Lucknow, where a garrison of less than a thousand was holding out against 10,000 rebels. He fought his way into the city with dreadful loss, and stayed with the besieged until November, when *Sir Colin Campbell* relieved them, and withdrew his troops to Cawnpore, which, after a great battle with the Nena Sahib, was made a centre of operations against Oude. Troops had now arrived from England, and the rebels were followed up with great vigor. Early in 1859, the revolt was at an end. The horrible outrages on men, women, and children, and the relentless punishment of their perpetrators, have no parallel in modern history. One of the most important results of the mutiny was the transfer by Parliament of the government of India from the *East India Company* to the British Queen, the company remaining simply a commercial corporation.

32. The additions made to the Indian possessions of Great Britain, already mentioned, are her principal territorial acquisitions during this reign. The most important event in the history of the *Canadas* is the Union of the two provinces, in 1840, under a constitutional government. The struggles to obtain this result had long kept the country in a disturbed state; and, in 1837, an insurrection broke out, which was put down after some bloodshed and great alarm The discovery of rich gold mines in *New South Wales* and *Victoria*, in 1850, formed an era in the history of the *Australian colonies*. Liberal constitutions were granted to them at about the same time, since which, they have enjoyed a rapid and prosperous growth.

33. The Catholic Emancipation Bill was followed by various minor measures calculated to improve the condition of *Ireland;* but that island was disturbed in 1843 by the agitation of the question of the *Repeal of the Union*. *Daniel O'Connell*, then in Parliament, was the leader of this movement, which ended with the prevention by government of a monster Repeal Meeting, and with the arrest and imprisonment of O'Connell and his friends. In 1846 and 1847, occurred the great *Famine*. In 1848, the Irish agitators appealed to France for aid in establishing the independence of Ireland. Attempts at revolt failed, and the leaders were sentenced to death, but were not executed. The country has since remained politically quiet until now (1866), when the "*Fenians*," a secret organization, is causing great

alarm to England by threats of rebellion and independence. —In 1843, four hundred and seventy-five out of more than twelve hundred ministers of the *Established Church of Scotland* seceded, "in order to free themselves from the interference of the civil courts in ecclesiastical matters," and now, with their congregations, form the "*Free Church of Scotland.*"

34. The leading political parties in England are the *Conservatives* and the *Whigs*, the latter representing the liberal or reform principles. That division of the Liberals which demanded the most radical and extensive reforms, especially in respect to suffrage and Parliament, were called *Chartists*. This name came finally to include the workingmen's leagues and the various advocates of the poorer classes, whose discontents have several times taken the form of riots, or of organizations which force has been employed to put down. The last serious disturbances of this nature were in 1848. The most important legislative enactments are the *Penny Postage Law;* the *Bill* providing that Parliament may dispense with the Christian oath in favor of *Jews* elected to its membership; the *Repeal of the Corn Laws*, or duties on the importation of grain, a measure which the Anti-Corn-Law League, and the Liberals generally, had for ten years steadily labored to bring about; and the repeal of the *Navigation Acts*, and of the *Property Qualification* for members of Parliament.

35. Some threatening difficulties with France arose in 1859; and the defenceless state of England excited such general alarm that a "Volunteer" movement was started, by which a large force was raised to meet the anticipated emergency, and is still retained. Extensive works of defence were begun in the harbors; and the "Warrior," the first English iron-clad vessel of war, was launched in 1860.

36. Among many events of interest, of which only mention can be made, are the laying of the submarine cable across the Straits of Dover in 1851; the proof of the existence of the North-west Passage in 1854, by the meeting of two ships which had entered the Polar Sea respectively from the east and the west; and the Great International Exhibitions of 1851 and 1862. Sir Robert Peel died in 1850, the Duke of Wellington in 1852, Prince Albert in 1862, and Lord Palmerston in 1865. The different Prime Ministers of this reign have been Lord Melbourne, Sir Robert Peel, Lord Aberdeen, the Earl of Derby, Lord Palmerston, and Lord John Russell.

TABLE OF THE HISTORY OF ENGLAND.—*No.* 1.

From the Accession of Egbert, 827, *to the Death of Richard* III., 1485.

A. D.		Kings.	Yrs.	
800	–			
				Saxon Family.
	27	Egbert	11	First sole monarch of England: end of the *Saxon Heptarchy.*
	38	Ethelwolf	20	
9th	57	Ethelbald	3	The *Danes* begin their hostile attacks, and continue, for more than two centuries, to scourge the country.
	60	Ethelbert	6	
	66	Ethelred I.	5	
	72	Alfred	28	An illustrious king; has a prosperous reign.
900	–			
	00	Edward *the Elder*	25	The Danes defeated.
	25	Athelstan	16	Defeats the Danes, Welsh, Scots, &c.
	41	Edmund I.	7	Murdered by the robber *Leolf.*
10th	48	Edred	7	A slave of superstition, and dupe of *Dunstan*
	55	Edwy	4	
	59	Edgar	16	*Dunstan* archbishop: Wolves exterminated.
	75	Edward *the Martyr*	3	Assassinated by order of *Elfrida.*
	78	Ethelred II.	37	Massacre of the Danes at the festival *St. Brice.*
1000	–			
	15	Sweyn, *Dane*	½	Conquers England, and is proclaimed king.
	16	Edmund II., *Ironside*	1	Defeated by the Danes, and murdered.
				Danish Kings
	17	Canute *the Great*	19	Completes the conquest of England.
	36	Harold I., *Harefoot*	4	
	39	Canute II.	3	The power of the *Danes* terminates.
11th				*Saxon Line restored.*
	41	Edward, *Confessor*	24	First king that touched for the *King's Evil.*
	65	Harold II.	1	Defeated and slain at *Hastings.*
				Norman Family.
	66	William, *Conqueror*	21	Conquers England; introduces the *Feudal System* and *Norman Language.*
	87	William II.	13	Is shot while hunting. *Archbishop Anselm.*
1100	–			
	00	Henry I.	35	Usurps the throne of his brother *Robert.*
	35	Stephen (*of Blois*)	19	Usurps, and has contests with *Matilda.*
				Family of Plantagenet.
12th	54	Henry II.	35	Conquers *Ireland;* has long and severe contests with *Becket;* rebellion of his sons.
	89	Richard I.	10	Engages in a *Crusade,* and defeats *Saladin.*
	99	John, *Lackland*	17	Foreign dominions lost: *Magna Charta.*
1200	–			
	16	Henry III.	56	Battles of *Lewes* and *Evesham:* Montfort; First *House of Commons.*
13th	72	Edward I.	35	Subdues *Wales;* battles of *Falkirk,* &c.
1300	–			
	7	Edward II.	20	Defeated by the Scots at *Bannockburn.*
	27	Edward III.	50	A splendid reign: *Chivalry* in its zenith: Victories of *Cressy, Poitiers,* &c.: *Edward* the *Black Prince.*
14th	77	Richard II.	22	Deposed and murdered. *Wickliffe, Chaucer*
				Branch of Lancaster.
	99	Henry IV.	14	Gains the throne instead of the rightful heir.
1400	–			
	13	Henry V.	9	Victory of *Agincourt* *Oldcastle* burnt
	22	Henry VI.	39	Civil wars of the *White* and *Red Roses* *York* and *Lancaster.*
15th				*Branch of York.*
	61	Edward IV.	22	Battles of *Towton, Barnet,* and *Tewksbury.*
	83	Edward V.		Murdered after a reign of 74 days.
	83	Richard III.	2	Defeated and slain at *Bosworth.*

The figures on the left hand of the *kings*, in these tables, denote the *commencement* of their reigns. Thus it appears that *Egbert* began to reign in 827, and reigned 11 years.

TABLE OF THE HISTORY OF ENGLAND.—*No* 2.

From Henry VII., 1485, *to Victoria.*

A. D.		Kings.	Yrs.	
1400	—			*House of Tudor.*
15*th*	85	Henry VII	24	Marries *Elizabeth*, daughter of Edward IV., uniting the Houses of *York* & *Lancaster;* commerce encouraged; the *Feudal System* declines.
1500	—			
	9	Henry VIII	38	A cruel tyrant; victory of *Flodden* by Surrey, introduces the *Reformation;* 2 *queens* divorced, two beheaded; *Wolsey* disgraced; *Bp. Fisher*, *Sir T. More, Cromwell*, and *Surrey* beheaded.
	47	Edward VI.	6	Promotes the *Reformation*, aided by *Cranmer.*
	53	Mary	5	Restores *Cath. relig.;* marries *Philip* II of Spain *Jane Grey* beheaded; many Protestants burnt
16*th*	58	Elizabeth	44	Has an auspicious reign, assisted by *Bacon. Burleigh, Walsingham,* &c.; agriculture, commerce, and literature flourish; the *Church of England* established; *Mary, Queen of Scots,* beheaded; the *Spanish Armada* destroyed.
1600	—		—	*House of Stuart.*
	3	James I.	22	Unites the crowns of *England* and *Scotland;* the Gunpowder Plot defeated; the *Bible* translated; the *Puritans* settle at *Plymouth*, Mass.
	25	Charles I.	24	Despotic; attempts to raise money without consent of Parliament; *civil war* rages; *Strafford* and *Laud* beheaded; *Charles* defeated and beheaded (1649); the *Commonwealth* begins.
17*th*	53	*Cromwell*	5	Dissolves the Long Parliament, and becomes *Protector.* Navigation Act. Dutch war.
	60	Charles II.	25	Profligate; his reign injurious to *liberty* and *morality; Plague* and *Fire* in London; *Clarendon* banished; *Russell* and *Alg. Sydney* executed.
	85	James II.	4	Attempts to establish the *Catholic religion*, and is obliged to abdicate; hence the *Revolution.*
	89	William III. & Mary	13	*Constitution* confirmed: battles of *Boyne* and *La Hogue:* Peace of *Ryswick: Nat. Debt* begins.
1700	—		—	
	2	Anne	12	*Marlborough* & *Eugene's* victories of *Blenheim, Ramillies, Malplaquet,* &c.: *Literat.* flourishes. *House of Brunswick* or *Hanover.*
	14	George I.	13	Rebellion in favor of the *Pretender* suppressed South Sea Scheme. *Walpole* minister.
	27	George II.	33	The Pretender overthrown at *Culloden:* War with *France* carried on in Europe, Asia, and America: Battle of *Dettingen:* Conq. of *Canada.*
18*th*	60	George III.	69	A long and eventful reign: Hostilities with and loss of, the *American Colonies:* long war with *France*, terminated by the battle of *Waterloo*. Possessions in *India* greatly extended: Commerce and the arts flourish; but the *National Debt* greatly increased. *Regency* 1811.
1800	—		—	
	20	George IV.	10	A Bill of Pains and Penalties brought into Parliament against the *Queen* (Caroline), but relinquished: Battle of *Navarino*. *Corporation* and *Test Acts* repealed: *Cathol. Emancipation.*
19*th*	30	William IV.	7	The *Duke of Wellington's Ministry* succeeded by that of *Earl Grey:* the *Reform Bill* passes. Irish Church Reform: *Colonial Slavery* abolished: East India Charter renewed.
	37	Victoria		Married to *Prince Albert* *Melbourne, Peel,* and *Russell*, prime ministers.

CHRONOLOGICAL TABLE OF ENGLISH LITERATURE.

A. D.	Statesmen and Commanders.	*died.*	Poets.	*died.*	Divines.	*died.*	Miscellaneous.	*died.*
1500								
	Wolsey	30	Skelton	29	Tyndale	36	Th. More	35
	T. Cromwell	40	Wyatt	41	Ridley	55	Wyatt	41
	Somerset	52	Earl of Surrey	47	Latimer	55	Th. Elyot	46
	Gardiner	55	Heywood	65	CRANMER	56	Leland	52
	S. Cabot	57	Gascoigne	77	Card. Pole	58	Cheke	57
16th	N. Bacon	79	R. Greene	92	Coverdale	69	R. Ascham	68
	Leicester	88	Marlowe	93	J. Jewel	71	Holingshed	81
	Walsingham	89	Southwell	95	KNOX	72	Buchanan	82
	Drake	96	Peele	97	J. Fox	87	Tusser	83
	Burleigh	98	SPENSER	98	Hooker		P. Sidney	86
1600								
	Essex	1	F. Beaumont	15	Andrewes	26	Napier	17
	Raleigh	18	SHAKSPEARE	16	Chillingworth	44	BACON	26
	Strafford	41	J. Fletcher	25	Usher	56	Camden	28
	Pym	43	Herbert	35	Walton	61	Coke	34
	Hampden	43	Ben Jonson	37	Th. Fuller	61	Wotton	39
	Falkland	43	Massinger	39	Taylor	67	Burton	39
	Blake	57	G. Sandys	43	Barrow	77	Selden	54
17th	Cromwell	58	Quarles	44	J. Owen	83	Harvey	57
	Marvell	78	Donne	62	Leighton	84	Hale	76
	Monk	70	Cowley	67	Pearson	86	Harrington	77
	Clarendon	72	MILTON	74	H. More	87	Hobbes	79
	Shaftesbury	83	Roscommon	84	Bunyan	88	Th. Browne	82
	Russell	83	Otway	85	Cudworth	88	Dugdale	86
	Alg. Sidney	83	Waller	87	Baxter	91	Sydenham	89
	Temple		Butler	88	Tillotson	94	Boyle	91
1700								
	Cavendish	7	DRYDEN	1	Howe	5	LOCKE	4
	Godolphin	12	Farquhar	7	Bull	9	ADDISON	19
	Somers	16	Parnell	17	M. Henry	14	Sir C. Wren	23
	Marlborough	22	Rowe	18	Burnet	15	NEWTON	27
	Walpole	46	Prior	21	South	16	De Foe	31
	Bolingbroke	51	Congreve	28	Clarke	29	Swift	45
	Vernon	57	Gay	32	Watts	48	Fielding	54
	Wolfe	59	POPE	44	Doddridge	51	Richardson	61
	Boscawen	61	Thomson	48	Butler	52	Sterne	68
18th	Anson	62	Collins	56	Berkeley	53	Hume	76
	Cumberland	65	A. Ramsay	58	Sherlock	61	Garrick	79
	Lyttelton	63	Shenstone	63	Lardner	68	Blackstone	80
	Chatham	78	Churchill	64	Whitefield	70	JOHNSON	84
	Cook	79	Young	65	Warburton	79	Ad. Smith	90
	Rodney	92	Akenside	70	Lowth	87	Hunter	93
	North	92	Gray	71	Wesley	91	Robertson	93
	Mansfield	93	Goldsmith	74	Price	91	Gibbon	94
	Burke	97	Burns	96	Campbell	96	Wm. Jones	94
	Amherst	98	COWPER		Blair		Reid	97
1800								
	Nelson	5	Beattie	3	Priestley	4	Sheridan	[illegible]
	Pitt	6	H. K. White	6	Paley	5	Cavendish	10
	Fox	6	Grahame	11	Horsley	6	Playfair	19
	Romilly	18	Shelley	22	Porteus	8	E. D. Clarke	22
	Grattan	20	BYRON	24	Watson	16	Herschel	22
19th	Erskine	23	Crabbe	32	Th. Scott	21	Mitford	27
	Canning	27	W. SCOTT	32	R. Hall	31	Stewart	28
	Huskisson	30	Coleridge	34	A. Clarke	32	Davy	29
	Eldon	38	Southey	43	Arnold	42	Mackintosh	32
	Grey	45	Campbell	44	J. Foster	44	Wilberforce	33
	C. Napier	52	Leigh Hunt	59	Robertson	53	Doug. Jerrold	57
	Wellington	52	Mrs. Browning	62			Macaulay	59
	Cobden	65	W. S. Landor	64			Hallam	59
	Palmerston	65					Thackeray	64

Remarks on the Tables of English History and Literature.

1. Some of the most eminent sovereigns who have occupied the throne of England are the following: — Alfred, William the Conqueror, Henry II, Edward I., Edward III., Henry VII., Elizabeth, and William III.

2. The cause of English freedom has been most effectually promoted during some of the weakest and least prosperous reigns; as those of John, Henry III., Charles I., and James II.

3. Some of the most important political changes, or revolutions, that have taken place in England since the Norman Conquest, are the granting of the *Magna Charta*, or the Great Charter, in the time of King John; the establishment of the House of Commons in the time of Henry III.; the Reformation in religion in the reign of Henry VIII.; the union of the crowns of England and Scotland at the commencement of the reign of James I.; the civil war between Charles I. and the English Parliament, which issued in the defeat and execution of the king, and the establishment of the Commonwealth under Cromwell; the restoration of the monarchy under Charles II.; the dethronement or abdication of James II.; the accession of William and Mary, and the establishment of the principles of the Constitution (1688); the legislative union between England and Scotland in the reign of Queen Anne; the union of Ireland with Great Britain in the reign of George III. (1800); and the Reform of Parliament in the reign of William IV. (1832).

---

1. *Chaucer*, the most celebrated of the early English poets, flourished in the latter part of the 14th century, in the reigns of Edward III. and Richard II.; but English classical literature may be considered as beginning in the latter half of the 16th century, during the reign of Elizabeth, with *Hooker*, a learned divine, *Spenser* and *Shakspeare*, eminent poets, and *Bacon*, the philosopher, who also lived through the reign of James I The reign of Queen Anne was particularly distinguished for men of genius, among whom were *Newton*, *Addison*, *Pope*, and *Swift*.

2. *Wolsey* and *Gardiner*, who are placed in the left-hand column, were both ecclesiastics and bishops, though more distinguished as statesmen than as divines. Of those who are placed in the right-hand column, *Sir Thomas More*, the author of "Utopia," &c., and *Lord Bacon*, the philosopher, were both chancellors of England; *Sir Matthew Hale* was an eminent judge; *Sir Edward Coke*, a great lawyer: — *Sir Philip Sidney*, the author of "Arcadia," &c., *Harrington*, the author of "Oceana," &c., *Sir Henry Wotton*, *John Selden*, and *Sir William Jones*, all eminent scholars, were also distinguished in political life.

3. Some who are classed in the Table among statesmen and commanders are also distinguished as authors, as *Raleigh*, *Clarendon*, *Bolingbroke*, *Lyttleton*, *Temple*, *Marvell*, *Algernon Sydney*, *Burke*, &c.; some classed among the divines and miscellaneous authors are also noted as poets, as *Addison*, *Watts*, *Swift*, &c.; and some of the poets are also eminent as prose writers.

4. *Shakspeare*, the great English dramatist, is eminently distinguished for genius; *Milton* is regarded as the greatest epic poet of modern times *Lord Bacon* pointed out the true mode of philosophizing; the works of *Newton* formed an era in natural philosophy and astronomy, as did those of *Locke* in the philosophy of the human mind.

5. There are many names of much merit in English literature, in addition to those contained in the Table.

EUROPEAN STATES.

The history of the other *States of Europe* is less interesting and important, especially to American readers, than that of *England* and *France*. A brief sketch is here given of the history of several of the other states; and also a tabular view of the succession of the sovereigns of some of the most important of them.

SCOTLAND.

1. The pretensions of Scotland to a regular succession of kings, from so remote a period as the time of Alexander the Great, are not supported by any credible evidence. — When Britain was abandoned by the Romans, A. D. 410, Scotland was divided among a number of hostile tribes, the principal of which were the *Scots* and *Picts;* but, between the years 838 and 843, *Kenneth II.* subdued the latter, and became king of all Scotland.

2. Various contests took place between Scotland and the kings of England, the most memorable of which happened in the reign of *Edward I.*, who conquered the country; but he found able antagonists in the heroic *Sir William Wallace* and *Robert Bruce*, the latter of whom defeated the English in the decisive battle of *Bannockburn*, and established himself on the throne.

3. *James VI.*, the infant son of the celebrated *Queen Mary*, was proclaimed king, after her resignation in 1567, and succeeded to the crown of England in 1603; since which period the two countries have been governed by one and the same monarch; and this connection was rendered perpetual by the *union* of the two kingdoms, in 1706, during the reign of Queen *Anne*. Since that period, the representative peers of Scotland have formed a part of the British House of Lords; and Scotland has also sent members to the British House of Commons

GERMANY

1. In 843, the Empire of the West was divided into three monarchies, France, Germany, and Italy; and at the close of the reign of Charles the Fat, in 887, the imperial dignity was transferred entirely to *Germany*, which, in European history, is styled, by way of eminence, *the Empire*, and its subjects, the *Imperialists*. During more than half of the 10th century, it was governed, successively, by two able sovereigns, *Henry the Fowler*, and his son, *Otho the Great*. The latter reünited Italy to the empire, and was the greatest sovereign of the age.

2. The reign of *Henry IV.*, sometimes called *the Great* during the last half of the 11th century, is memorable for his quarrel with, and humiliating submission to, pope *Gregory VII.* (*Hildebrand*). The election of *Conrad III.* gave rise to two celebrated factions, the *Guelphs* and *Ghibelines*, which harassed Germany and Italy during three centuries; and during this period the imperial authority declined, and the papal increased The Ghibelines were attached to the emperor; the Guelphs to the pope.

3. The reign of *Frederick I.*, surnamed *Barbarossa*, or *Red-beard*, was signalized by his contests with Pope *Alexander III.*, and by a crusade to the Holy Land, during which he was drowned in a small river in Cilicia, in 1190. — After the reign of Conrad IV. succeeded a period of contention and confusion, called the *Great Interregnum*, which, after continuing 19 years, was terminated by the election of *Rodolph*, Count of Hapsburg, in Switzerland, to the imperial throne, in 1273.

4. The principal events in the history of the latter emperors of the *Franconian* line, and of all the princes of the *Swabian* line, were produced by contests between the popes and the emperors. The grounds of these contests were, 1st, the right claimed by the emperors of nominating to vacant bishoprics, and the form of investing the bishops with the temporal possessions of their sees; 2d, the claims of the popes to hold their possessions in Italy, independent of the emperors; 3d, the claim of the popes to supreme dominion, both temporal and spiritual, in every part of the Christian world.

5. The reign of *Louis IV.* was much disturbed by contests with pope *John XXII.* The emperor was excommunicated by the pope, and his election declared void; and the pope was also deposed by the emperor. The princes of the empire assembled at Frankfort, in 1338, and established the famous constitution called the *Pragmatic Sanction*, by which it was de

termined that the pope had no right to approve or reject the election of an emperor.

6. The reign of *Sigismund* is memorable for the meeting of the famous *Council of Constance*, in order to determine the contest respecting the papal authority. *John Huss* and *Jerome of Prague* were condemned (1415) by this council, and delivered over to the secular power to be burnt as heretics. Their adherents in Bohemia took up arms in defence of their religion, and, under their famous leader, *Zisca*, resisted Sigismund in a war of 16 years.

7. *Maximilian I.* (1477) acquired by marriage the sovereignty of the *Netherlands*, divided Germany into *circles*, instituted the *Imperial Chamber* and the *Aulic Council*, and by these means established a perpetual peace among the separate states, and laid the foundation of the subsequent grandeur of the empire.

8. *Charles V.* [Charles I. of Spain], grandson of Maximilian, was the greatest and most powerful sovereign of his age After a reign of nearly 40 years, during most of which he was engaged in war, chiefly with his great rival, *Francis I.* of France, and raised the house of Austria to its highest splendor, he voluntarily resigned the crown of Spain to his son, *Philip II.*, in 1556, left the throne of Germany to his brother, *Ferdinand*, and retired to the monastery of St. Just, in Spain, in order to devote himself to the privacy of monastic life, and forget the cares of government and the temptations of the world. During his reign, the *Reformation* made great progress in Germany, which, however, Charles strenuously opposed.

9. The reigns of *Ferdinand II.* and *Ferdinand III.* were signalized by the *Thirty years' war*, which commenced in 1618, and was terminated by the peace of Westphalia, in 1648. This war grew chiefly out of the religious dissensions of the 16th century: on one side was the Protestant confederacy, styled the *Evangelical Union*, and, on the other, the *Catholic League.* It issued in securing an equal establishment of the Protestant and Catholic religions.

10. By the death of *Charles VI.*, the male line of the house of Hapsburg became extinct; and the circumstance of there being two claimants to the throne gave rise to a war, styled the war of the *Austrian Succession*, which was terminated by the peace of Aix-la-Chapelle, in 1748, by which the claim of the celebrated *Maria Theresa* was acknowledged, and her consort, *Francis of Lorraine*, was invested with the imperial dignity.

11. In 1806, *Francis II.*, who had two years before assumed the title of *hereditary Emperor of Austria*, solemnly resigned

his title as Emperor of *Germany*. Thus ended the German empire, after having lasted, from the commencement of the Western Empire under Charlemagne, 1006 years.

12. The imperial government was *hereditary* during the *Carlovingian* dynasty; afterwards, always elective; but the mode of election was different at different periods. At first, the emperor was chosen by the people at large; then by the nobility and principal officers of state; afterwards, by the five following great officers, namely, the chancellor, the great marshal, the great chamberlain, the great butler, and the great master of the palace. At first they assumed the right of only proposing candidates to the general body of electors; but at length confined the whole right of election to themselves.— After much discontent, this was finally settled in the reign of Charles IV., by the celebrated constitution, called the *Golden Bull*, which fixed the right of election in four spiritual and three temporal electors, namely, the Archbishops of Mentz, of Cologne, and of Treves; the King of Bohemia; the Count Palatine, the Duke of Saxony, and the Margrave of Brandenburg. At subsequent periods, the Dukes of Bavaria and of Brunswick-Lunenburg were advanced to the electoral dignity.

13. In 1848, a grand national congress, composed of 500 deputies from all parts of Germany, assembled at Frankfort-on-the-Maine, with the design of framing a constitution, and uniting all the German states under one confederated government; but the object was not carried into effect.

AUSTRIA.

1. Austria, which was erected into an hereditary empire in 1804 is one of the leading states in Europe; and it has been one of the great pillars for sustaining arbitrary or absolute government. *Prince Metternich*, an able statesman, late prime minister of the empire, had for about 40 years the principal direction of the public affairs, and was a zealous supporter of arbitrary power

2. The revolution which, in 1848, drove Louis Philippe from the throne of France, immediately caused an insurrection at Vienna, and swept Metternich from the seat of power which he had long held. The emperor *Ferdinand* soon fled from Vienna, and, not long after, abdicated in favor of his nephew *Francis Joseph.*

3 The Austrian dominions in the north of Italy soon revolted against Austria, and were assisted by *Charles Albert* King of Sardinia. A sanguinary contest ensued; but the Austrians, under the command of *Marshal Radetsky*, were triumphant.

4. The kingdom of Hungary, which forms a large part of the Austrian empire, though it has long had a distinct constitution, soon afterwards revolted from Austria, on account of its constitution being violated by the latter, declared independence (1849), and established a provisional government, with *Kossuth* at its head.

5. The emperor *Nicholas* of Russia interposed in favor of Austria, sent a powerful army into Hungary, and, after a sanguinary and desolating war, the main division of the Hungarian army, under *Görgey*, was compelled to surrender to *Prince Paskiewitch*, the Russian commander, in August, 1849.

6. In March, 1849, the emperor of Austria issued a liberal constitution, which guaranteed political and religious liberty, freedom of the press and speech, and a legislative body, composed of two houses; but in 1851, this constitution was abolished by a decree of the emperor, and despotism was reëstablished.

SPAIN.

1. In the early part of the 5th century, Spain, after having long been in the possession of the Romans, was invaded by the *Suevi*, *Vandals*, and *Alans*, who were, ere long, subdued by the *Visigoths*, or *Western Goths*. In the early part of the 8th century, the country was invaded by the *Moors* or *Saracens*, who, under their commander *Muza*, gained, in 713, the great battle of *Xeres*, in which *Roderick*, the Gothic king, was slain.

2 In a few years, the Moors overran the most of the country, which, for some time, was governed by viceroys of the *Saracen Caliphs;* but, in 755, *Abderrahman*, of the house of Ommiades, established an independent sovereignty, and assumed the title of *Caliph of Cordova*, which city he made the seat of his empire, and also of arts and magnificence; and his posterity kept possession of the throne nearly three centuries But the territories of the Moors were soon divided into a number of separate sovereignties, of which the most considerable in the earlier part of their residence in Spain, was the caliphate of Cordova, and, in the latter part, the caliphate of Granada.

3. When Spain was first invaded and conquered by the

Moors, the Gothic, or, as they were now styled, the Christian forces, retired into the Asturias, and, under their leader *Pelagio*, founded a kingdom in 718; and they gradually recovered other parts of the country. For several centuries, the history of Spain presents a continued struggle between the Christians and Moors; and the latter part of the 11th century was illustrated by the exploits of the famous Spanish hero, Don Rodrigo Diaz, Count of Bivar, surnamed the *Cid*.

4. Several distinct Christian kingdoms, which subsisted for a long period, were established, the most considerable of which were *Castile and Leon*, *Arragon*, and *Navarre*. In 1479, *Ferdinand II.*, who had been previously married to *Isabella*, Queen of *Castile and Leon*, succeeded to the throne of *Arragon*, and their kingdoms now became united. Granada, the only possession now held by the Moors in Spain, was soon after taken (1492); Navarre was subsequently conquered, and all Spain became, for the first time, united into one monarchy.

5. The reign of Ferdinand and Isabella forms an eventful period in the history of Spain, on account of military exploits, the expulsion of the Moors, the union of the country into one kingdom, and the discovery of America (1492), which brought an immense accession of wealth to the Spanish crown, and laid the foundation for vast colonial possessions in this continent.

6. During the long reigns of *Charles I.* [Charles V. of Germany] and *Philip II.*, Spain acted a conspicuous part in the affairs of the world, and, on account of her extensive possessions in both continents, was regarded as the most formidable power in Europe; but, since that period, her comparative consequence has declined, and she has long held only a secondary rank among the European states. The most flourishing period of Spanish literature was during the time when the kingdom was governed by princes of the house of Austria, in the 16th and 17th centuries.

7. In 1808, Charles IV. was dethroned by *Bonaparte*, who placed on the throne of Spain his brother, *Joseph Bonaparte*. A sanguinary war ensued, which lasted till 1813; and *Ferdinand VII.*, the son of Charles IV., was established on the throne.

8. Within the space of ten years, from 1811 to 1821, all the Spanish colonies on the continent of North and South America revolted from Spain, and declared their independence. Since that time, the kingdom of Spain has been much harassed by civil war and political commotion.

PORTUGAL.

1. This kingdom forms the greatest part of what was anciently called *Lusitania;* and its early history is involved with that of Spain, it having been successively in subjection to the *Romans*, *Suevi*, *Visigoths*, and *Moors*.

2. In the contests between the Moors and Christians, *Henry*, Duke of Burgundy, having rendered important services to *Alphonso*, or *Alonzo*, King of Castile, was rewarded by him, in 1094, with tha part of Portugal which was not in possession of the Moors, to be held with the title of *count* or *earl*. He was succeeded by his son *Alphonso*, who gained a signal victory over the Moors, at *Orique*, threw off the Castilian yoke, and assumed the title of *king*, in 1139.

3. The reign of *John I.*, which began in 1385, is famous for his victories over the Castilians, and his expeditions against the Moors; but still more so for the impulse given by Prince *Henry, the Mariner*, to navigation and the progress of discovery a department of enterprise and skill in which the Portuguese were, for a long time, unrivalled by any other nation.

4. The reigns of *John II.* and *Emanuel* were distinguished for important discoveries. During the reign of the former, *Bartholomew Diaz* reached the *Cape of Good Hope*, in 1486; and during that of the latter, *Vasco de Gama*, in 1497, doubled the same Cape, and sailed to *India*. From that period, the trade between that country and Europe was diverted from its former channel through the *Red Sea* and *Egypt;* and for many years the navigation of the *Cape* was considered as the exclusive property of the Portuguese, on the ground of first discovery; nor was their monopoly effectually invaded till the rise of the *Dutch*.

5. The space intervening between the commencement of the reign of John I. (1385), and the conquest of Portugal by Philip II. of Spain (1580), forms the golden period of the monarchy — a period which was illustrated by the exploits, both in discovery and conquest, of a succession of distinguished heroes, and also by the productions of several men of genius and learning, among whom the poet *Camoens*, the author of the Lusiad, who died in 1579, holds the first rank.

6. In 1580, the male line of the royal family of Portugal having become extinct, and the kingdom having suffered a series of misfortunes, *Philip II.* of Spain seized upon it, and united it to his crown; but, in 1640, the Spaniards were expelled, and *John*, *Duke of Braganza*, the presumptive heir was raised to the throne, in whose family it still remains.

7. Two years after the discovery of the Cape of Good Hope, *Cabral*, a Portuguese, discovered *Brazil*, which was colonized about the middle of the 16th century, and, till lately formed an important part of the territories of the kings of Portugal.

8. In 1807, Portugal being invaded by the French, the roya family removed the seat of government to *Brazil*, where they remained till 1820, when they returned to Lisbon, with the exception of *Pedro* or *Peter*, the king's eldest son, who was left regent. In 1823, Brazil was declared an independent empire, under Pedro, who took the title of emperor; and, in 1825, its independence was acknowledged by Portugal. In 1826, the throne of Portugal became vacant by the death of *John VI.* Pedro, the Emperor of Brazil, resigned his claims to the crown in favor of his daughter, *Maria da Gloria* (*Maria II.*), who was proclaimed queen; but *Miguel*, a younger brother of Pedro, aspired to the throne. After a long struggle he was expelled, in 1832, from the Portuguese territories.

THE NETHERLANDS.

1. This country, during the Middle Ages, comprised various small states, governed by counts or earls. In the 15th century, most of the country, which had then become the seat of extensive manufactures and the centre of European commerce, was possessed by the *Duke of Burgundy;* but, in the latter part of the century, these provinces were transferred, by the marriage of *Maximilian*, to the house of *Austria.*

2. In 1555, they were resigned by Charles V. to his son, Philip II, King of Spain. In 1579, the *Seven United Provinces of Holland* revolted from the tyranny of Philip, and established their independence: part of the others continued in the possession of Spain till the peace of Utrecht, in 1713, when they were again ceded to the house of *Austria*, which held them till 1794, when they were conquered by the French.

3. Soon after the Dutch Provinces had emancipated themselves from Spain, and established their independence and a free government, they rose, by industry and enterprise, to a high degree of prosperity, and became one of the most formidable maritime powers in the world. They stripped the Spaniards of some of their most valuable establishments in the East Indies and America, and extended their commerce in all directions.

4. In 1815, the Seven Provinces, or Holland, and the ten southern or Belgian provinces, were united by the Congress of Vienna, and erected into a kingdom, by the name of the Netherlands, under the government of the Prince of Orange. This union continued 15 years.

5 In 1830, encouraged by the revolution which expelled Charles X. from France, the Belgians revolted, and established a separate kingdom by the name of *Belgium;* and *Prince Leopold* of Saxe Coburg, widower of Princess Charlotte of England, was raised to the throne.

POLAND.

1. Miceslaus, Prince of Poland, introduced Christianity into the country in the 10th century. The most flourishing period of the monarchy was during the 15th and 16th centuries, when Poland ranked among the most formidable states of Europe.

2. *Casimir III.*, surnamed *the Great*, in the 14th century founded the University of *Cracow*, patronized learning, encouraged industry and commerce, and furnished the nation with a code of written laws. In the latter part of the 14th century, *Jagellon* [*Ladislaus V.*], Duke of Lithuania, by his marriage with *Hedwiga*, Queen of Poland, united the two countries.

3. Under the reign of *Sigismund I.* (begun in 1507), the kingdom reached its highest pitch of dominion and splendor. It afterwards declined, but its falling glory was, for a time, upheld by *John Sobieski*, the last great man among its sovereigns

4. Poland was conquered by the sovereigns of *Russia*, *Austria*, and *Prussia*, and subjected by them to three different partitions: the first in 1772; the second in 1793; the third in 1795, when *Stanislaus* was deprived of regal dignity, and his ill fated country, by an act of the vilest tyranny, was blotted out from the list of kingdoms.

5. After the peace of Tilsit, in 1807, the most of Poland that had been taken by Prussia was erected into a sovereign state, under the title of the *Duchy of Warsaw*. In 1815, a part of the duchy of Warsaw was given to Prussia, under the name of the duchy or province of *Posen*. Most of the remainder was erected into the *kingdom of Poland*, a constitutional monarchy, vested in a viceroy, appointed by the Emperor of Russia.

6. The *Grand-Duke Constantine*, brother of the Emperor of Russia, being appointed Viceroy of Poland, administered the government in the most oppressive manner. In 1830, an insurrection broke out, which terminated, after a sanguinary struggle, in the entire subjugation of the Poles; and the kingdom of Poland was incorporated into the Russian empire.

7. The emperor *Nicholas* exercised the utmost severity against the Poles. The Universities of Warsaw and Wilna and many minor schools, were abolished, and public libraries and museums were carried to St. Petersburg.

SWEDEN.

1. This country, together with *Norway*, formed the *Scandinavia* of the ancients, long the seat of the *Goths* and *Vandals*. — In 1388, Sweden became subject to *Margaret* of Denmark, styled the *Semiramis of the North*, who joined the three kingdoms of Denmark, Sweden, and Norway in one, by the *Union of Calmar*, in 1397. But her successor being destitute of her great abilities, this union fell to nothing, and Sweden was, for a long time, disturbed by insurrections and war.

2. In the early part of the 16th century, the Swedes were delivered from the oppression of *Christian II.*, King of Denmark, styled the *Nero of the North*, by *Gustavus Vasa*, a descendant from the ancient kings, and an enlightened prince, who was raised to the throne in 1523, and who promoted the welfare of his subjects, and introduced the *Protestant* religion.

3. The reign of *Gustavus Adolphus*, surnamed *the Great*, forms a distinguished era in the history of Sweden. He was eminent as a statesman and a sovereign, and is ranked among the greatest commanders of modern times. He took part with the Protestants in the *Thirty years' war*, and was their most distinguished general. After having gained a series of advantages, he was slain in the battle of *Lutzen*, in 1632.

4. *Charles XII.*, who possessed an enthusiastic passion for glory, and a romantic spirit to a degree of infatuation, is by some styled the *Alexander*, and by others the *Madman, of the North*. After a brilliant career of victory in his wars with the Danes, Poles, and Russians, he was, at last, entirely defeated by Peter the Great, in the battle of *Poltava*, in 1709 since which, the Swedish territories have been exposed to a progressive reduction by the rising power of Russia.

5. *Gustavus IV.*, having lost *Finland*, which was conquered in 1808, by Russia, and, by his mad schemes, brought his kingdom to the brink of ruin, was, in 1809, deposed, and *Bernadotte*, one of Bonaparte's marshals, was elected crown prince In 1814, the loss of Finland was repaired by the acquisition of *Norway*.

6. On the death of Charles XIII., in 1817, Bernadotte was raised to the throne by the title of *Charles XIV.*, and, after a pacific and prosperous reign of 26 years, was succeeded, in 1844, by his son *Oscar*.

DENMARK.

1. In 1448, the crown of Denmark fell to Christian I., of the house of Holstein or Oldenburg. The monarchy was originally elective, and great power was possessed by the nobility until the year 1660, when, partly in consequence of the unfavorable issue of a war with Sweden, and partly on account of the oppression of the aristocracy, it was changed to an hereditary absolute government.

2. In the beginning of the 18th century, Denmark, during the reign of Frederick IV., waged an unsuccessful war against Charles XII. of Sweden, which was ended in 1720; from which time the country enjoyed almost uninterrupted peace till 1801.

3. During the pacific reigns of *Christian VI.* and *Frederick V.* (1730 to 1766), the kingdom was in a prosperous condition. The latter was assisted by *Count Bernstoff*, a distinguished statesman, whose nephew, of the same name, acted an important and conspicuous part in government, during the reign of *Christian VII.*

4 Christian VII. (1766), a weak and dissolute prince, married *Caroline Matilda*, sister of George III. of England, who was accused of having had improper connection with *Count Struensee*, the minister and favorite of the king. Struensee was condemned and executed, and Matilda, after being imprisoned, was permitted to pass the remainder of her life at Zell, in Hanover.

5. In 1801, Copenhagen was attacked by a British fleet under *Lord Nelson;* and in 1807, when the country was at peace, the city was bombarded by a British armament, under *Lord Cathcart* and *Admiral Gambier*, under pretence that information had been received that Denmark intended to throw herself into the scale of France. The whole Danish fleet, consisting

of 18 ships of the line, and 15 frigates, were surrendered to the British. This unjust transaction has been generally and loudly exclaimed against.

6. In January, 1848, *Frederick VII.* succeeded to the throne of Denmark; the duchies of *Sleswick* and *Holstein* soon revolted; but, after a severe and sanguinary struggle, they were reduced to their allegiance.

PRUSSIA.

1. The foundation of Prussian greatness was laid by *Frederick William*, surnamed *the Great Elector*, who succeeded to the government in 1640, and had a long and prosperous reign. His successor *Frederick*, a weak and vain prince, was raised to the rank, and received the title, of king, in 1701.

2. *Frederick II.*, surnamed *the Great*, after suffering much hard treatment from his father, ascended the throne in 1740; and, being ambitious of conquest and military glory, he immediately invaded *Silesia*, with a fine army, which had been left to him by the late king, and was so successful as to obtain the cession of that valuable province.

3. In 1756, *Frederick* published a declaration of war against *Maria Theresa*, Empress of Germany, who was aided by the French and Russians. The contest, which was carried on with great spirit on both sides, and was signalized by many hard-fought and bloody battles, was terminated by the peace of *Hubertsberg*, in 1763: "and thus, after a seven years' sanguinary struggle, to which his unprincipled projects had given rise, and in which, independent of other sufferers, more than half a million of combatants had fallen in the field, everything was replaced on its ancient footing, and the only gainful result was simply this, that Frederick of Prussia had been furnished with an opportunity of proving himself a consummate commander, animated by an unconquerable spirit of military heroism, and endued with one of the coolest heads and hardest hearts in Christendom."

4. Frederick afterwards applied himself to the internal improvement of his kingdom; rebuilt towns, encouraged agriculture, manufactures, and commerce. In the first partition of Poland, he was the prime mover and the principal agent. He is esteemed one of the greatest commanders of modern times, and was, perhaps, the most indefatigable sovereign that ever

existed. He was fond of literature, and possessed extensive literary acquirements, and considerable merit as an author; but he was despotic in his disposition. and had little sense of justice or humanity.

5. In the European war which followed the French revolution, Frederick William III. suffered a great defeat by the French, under Bonaparte, at *Jena*, in 1806; and at the peace of *Tilsit*, in 1807, he lost nearly one half of his territories. In 1813, he joined the coalition against France, and his army, under *Blucher*, contributed a powerful aid in the overthrow of Bonaparte at the battle of Waterloo; and by the treaty of Vienna, in 1815, he gained a large accession of territory. Since the treaty of Vienna, the condition of Prussia has been in various respects much improved, especially in regard to education; and it is now one of the best educated states in Europe.

6. In 1840, *Frederick William III.* was succeeded by his son, *Frederick William IV.*, whose reign, especially during the years 1848 and 1849, has been characterized by political agitations and convulsions. Earnest and repeated demands were made by the people for a more liberal form of government, and, in 1848, a new constitution was proclaimed, which guarantees political and religious liberty, the freedom of the press, the abolition of all aristocratic privileges, and a legislative body of two houses.

RUSSIA.

1. The importance of Russia, which is now one of the most powerful sovereignties of Europe, is of recent origin. The foundation of its greatness was laid by *Peter the Great*, who reigned from 1696 to 1725, and who was one of the most extraordinary princes that ever appeared. He joined in a coalition against *Charles XII.* of Sweden, and, after suffering some defeats, gained the great battle of *Poltava* (1709), and enlarged and strengthened his empire.

2. *Catharine II.*, who obtained the sceptre, in 1762, by the dethronement and murder of her husband, *Peter III.*, had a long and splendid reign. She displayed extraordinary talents for government; carried on the system of improvement which had been begun by Peter the Great; employed able ministers and generals, among the most celebrated of whom were *Suwarrow* and *Potemkin*; and enlarged her empire by the ad

dition of a part of Poland, the Crimea, and other territories — but her public character was stained by unprincipled ambition, profound dissimulation, and disregard to justice; and her private character was extremely licentious.

3. Catharine was succeeded, in 1796, by her son *Paul*, who, after a short and distracted reign, was assassinated in 1801, and succeeded by his son *Alexander*, a popular and prosperous sovereign, during whose reign the power and dominions of Russia were extended, and objects of public improvement promoted. In 1812, Bonaparte made his disastrous invasion of Russia and here met with the first effectual check to his career of victory and conquest.

4. In 1825, Alexander was succeeded by his brother *Nicholas*, the present emperor, whose reign has been distinguished for the wars carried on against the Turks, Persians, Circassians, Poles, and Hungarians. The war against Turkey was declared in April, 1828, and the Russian army soon after invaded the Turkish dominions, took *Brailow*, *Varna*, and various other important posts. During the campaign of 1829, the Russians, commanded by *Count Diebitsch*, after having taken *Silistria* and other places, crossed the Balkan mountains, took the city of *Adrianople*, and compelled the Turks to accede to their conditions of peace; and in September, 1829, a treaty was signed at Adrianople.

5. In 1830, a general insurrection of the Poles, who were goaded and oppressed by the tyranny of their viceroy, the *Grand-Duke Constantine*, was crushed, by the capture of Warsaw, in 1831. Many thousand Poles were banished to Siberia; the kingdom of Poland was incorporated with Russia, and governed as a conquered province.

6. In 1848, the Emperor of Russia sent a powerful army to assist the Emperor of Austria to put down the insurrection of the Hungarians. Russia is a powerful military despotism, with a standing army of 800,000, a most formidable enemy to free government.

ROME.

1. The *temporal power* of the pope [*Stephen II.*] commenced in 755, and it attained its zenith in the 11th century, during the pontificate of *Gregory VII.* [Hildebrand], who assumed authority over kings and potentates.

2. The first half of the 16th century is a memorable era in

he history of the papacy. Pope *Julius II.*, the projector of the League of Cambray, was distinguished as a statesman and a warrior; and his successor, *Leo X.*, the son of the famous Lorenzo de Medici, was a liberal patron of learning. During his pontificate, the Reformation was begun by Luther, in 1517. Since that event, the power of the Roman pontiff has been greatly diminished.

3. In 1809, Bonaparte united the Ecclesiastical States to the French empire, and the temporal power of the pope was for a while suspended; but, by the Congress of Vienna, he was reinstated in nearly all his former possessions.

4. The Roman government has long been one of the most despotic in Europe. In 1846, *Pius IX.* was elected pope; and he soon manifested a disposition to promote reform, and to grant to his subjects a more liberal government than they had before enjoyed; and he was for a time highly popular.

5. But the revolution in France, and the political movements in other parts of Europe, in 1848, were soon felt at Rome, and the people made more demands on the pope than he was disposed to grant. At length they deposed him from his temporal power, and established a republican government. Pope Pius, disguised as a servant, fled to Gaeta, in the kingdom of Naples.

6. The French government sent an army, which, after a severe bombardment, entered Rome on the 3d of July, 1849, put down the republican government, and prepared the way for the pope to return, and be reinstated in his former authority.

TURKEY.

1. The Turks are a Tartar nation, originally from Asia The first notice of them in history is about the year 800, when, issuing from an obscure retreat, they took possession of a part of Armenia, called, from them, Turcomania. Their dominions, divided for some time into petty states, were united under *Othman*, *Ottoman*, or *Osman*, who assumed the title of *sultan*, and established his empire at *Prusa*, in Bithynia, in 1298.

2. In 1360, the most of Thrace was conquered by them under *Amurath I.*, who made *Adrianople* the seat of his government; his successor, *Bajazet*, conquered most of the Eastern or Greek empire; and, in 1453, *Mahomet II.* took *Constantinople*, which has ever since continued to be the seat of the Ottoman or Turkish empire.

3. The Turks afterwards widely extended their empire in Europe, Asia, and Africa, and gained possession of the greater part of the countries most celebrated in ancient history. During the reign of Selim I., Syria and Egypt were conquered. The reign of Solyman the Magnificent, which began in 1520 was more illustrious than that of any other of the sultans. He took the island of Rhodes from the Knights of St. John besieged Vienna, made the King of Hungary his tributary, reduced Bagdad, conquered the whole of Assyria, Mesopotamia, and Tunis, and established excellent laws in his dominions.

4. Since the reign of Solyman, the Turks have been engaged in various sanguinary wars, particularly with the Austrians, Russians, and also with the Persians under Kouli-Khan.

5. The Turkish power has lately been much weakened, in consequence of the revolt of the Greeks, and also of the calamitous war with Russia, which was terminated by the peace of Adrianople, in 1829.

6. The Greeks commenced an open revolt in 1821. After a war had been for a considerable time carried on, with savage ferocity, between them and the Turks, several European nations interposed in their favor; and, in 1827, the combined fleets of England, France, and Russia, almost annihilated the Turkish naval force in the battle of *Navarino.* In 1828, the Morea, and a part of the Greek islands, being liberated from Turkish thraldom, were formed into an independent government, under *Count Capo d'Istria* as president; and, in 1832, they were erected into a kingdom, and *Otho*, son of the late King of Bavaria, was placed on the throne of the *kingdom of Greece.*

Sovereigns of Germany, Spain, Sweden, Prussia, and Russia,
Since the Beginning of the Fifteenth Century.

A. D.	Germany.	Spain.	Sweden.	Prussia.	Russia.
1400	*Emperors.*	*Kings.*	*Kings.*	*Electors.*	*Czars.*
15th	93 Maximilian I.	79 Ferdinand and Isabella			
1500					
16th	19 Charles V. 58 Ferdinand I. 64 Maximilian II. 73 Rodolph II.	4 Philip and Joanna 16 Charles I. 56 Philip II. 98 Philip III.	23 Gustavus Vasa 60 Eric XIV. 68 John III. 92 Sigismund 99 Charles IX.	35 Joachim II. 72 John George 98 Joachim Frederick	38 John Basil 84 Theodore 97 Boris Godunow
1600					
17th	12 Matthias 19 Ferdinand II. 37 Ferdinand III. 58 Leopold	21 Philip IV. 65 Charles II.	11 Gustavus Adolphus 32 Christina 54 Charles X. 60 Charles XI. 97 Charles XII.	8 Sigismund 19 George Wm. 40 Frederick Wm. 88 Frederick III.	5 Theodore 6 Zuski 13 Michael Theodore 45 Alexis 76 Theodore 82 John *Emperors* 96 Peter I.
1700				*Kings.*	
18th	5 Joseph I. 11 Charles VI. 42 Charles VII. 45 Francis I. 65 Joseph II. 90 Leopold II. 92 Francis II.	Philip V. 24 Louis 46 Ferdinand VI. 59 Charles III. 88 Charles IV.	18 Ulrica Eleonora 41 Frederick 51 Adolphus Frederick 71 Gustavus III. 92 Gustavus IV.	1 Frederick I. 13 Frederick Wm. I. 40 Frederick II. 86 Frederick Wm. II. 97 Frederick Wm. III.	25 Catherine 27 Peter II. 30 Anne 40 John 41 Elizabeth 62 Peter III. 62 Catherine II. 96 Paul
1800	Austria.				
19th	6 Francis 35 Ferdinand 48 Francis Joseph	8 Ferdinand VII. 30 Isabella II.	9 Charles XIII. 18 Charles XIV. (*Bernadotte*) 44 Oscar	40 Frederick Wm. IV.	1 Alexander 25 Nicholas

Germany. — Germany formed a part of the *Empire of the West*, under *Charlemagne*, in 800. In 887, the imperial dignity was transferred to *Germany*, which continued to retain the title of Empire till 1806, when it was dissolved. *Francis* II., emperor of Germany, assumed, in 1804, the title of Emperor of *Austria;* and this title is retained by his successors.

Spain. — *Ferdinand* II., who had previously married *Isabella*, queen of Castile and Leon, succeeded to the throne of Arragon in 1479, and Spain, at that time, became united into one monarchy.

Sweden. — *Gustavus Vasa*, who was descended from the ancient kings of Sweden, was, after a revolution, proclaimed king. In 1818, *Bernadotte*, a French marshal, was raised to the throne, by the title of *Charles* XIV.

Prussia. — Prussia was erected into an *electorate* in 1415, and into a *kingdom* in 1701.

Russia. — The sovereigns were formerly styled *czars;* and the same title is still often applied to them. *Peter the Great*, who succeeded to the throne in 1696, assumed the title of *Emperor.*

Names distinguished in Italian, French, Spanish, German, &c., Literature.

A. D.	Italian.	died.	French.	died.	Spanish and Portuguese.	died.	German, Dutch, &c.	died.
1300								
	*Dante	21			*Lobeira	25		
_14th_	*Petrarch	74	_W. Durana_	33	Juan Manuel	62		
	Boccaccio	75	_W. Occam_	47				
1400								
	§Poggio	59	§Froissart	2	*Ayala	7	_John Huss_	15
	Æneas Sylv.	64	_John Gerson_	29	*Villena	34	Guttenberg	68
_15th_	*Pulci	87	*Chartier	58	*Juan de Mena	56	_Th. à Kempis_	71
	Mirandola	94			*L. de Mendoza	58	Regiomontanus	76
1500								
	†Raphael	20	§P. de Comines	9	_Ximenes_	17	Reuchlin	22
	†Lope de Vinci	20	Budæus	40	*Garcilasso	36	†Alb. Durer	28
	§Machiavel	28	_Bucer_	51	*Boscan	43	_Zuinglius_	31
	*Ariosto	33	Rabelais	53	Loyola	56	Erasmus	36
	†Correggio	34	J. C. Scaliger	58	*Saa de Miranda	58	Paracelsus	41
_16th_	§Guicciardini	40	R. Stephens	59	*Montemayor	61	Copernicus	43
	§Bembo	47	_Castalio_	63	*Camoens	79	_LUTHER_	46
	†M. Angelo	64	_CALVIN_	64	†Morales	86	†Holbein	54
	†Titian	76	Ramus	72	†Vargas	90	Sleidan	56
	Palladio	80	Montaigne	92	*Luis de Leon	91	_Melancthon_	60
	*Tasso	95	H. Stephens	98	*Ercilla		Mercator	94
1600								
	*Guarini	13	_Beza_	5	*Argensola	13	Tycho Brahe	1
	Bellarmine	21	§Thuanus	17	Cervantes	16	_Arminius_	19
	§_Father Paul_	23	*Malherbe	28	§Mariana	24	Buxtorf	21
	§Davila	31	_Jansenius_	38	§Herrera	25	Kepler	31
	*Tassoni	35	Descartes	50	*Góngora	27	†Rubens	41
	Galileo	42	Gassendi	55	*Lope de Vega	35	†Vandyck	41
_17th_	†Guido	42	Pascal	62	*Quevedo	45	_Episcopius_	43
	§_Bentevoglio_	44	†Poussin	65	†Velazquez	60	Grotius	45
	Torricelli	47	*Moliere	73	*Calderon	67	†Rembrandt	68
	L. Socinus	62	†Claude Lor.	82	*Villegas	69	Spinoza	77
	†Bernini	80	*Corneille	84	†Murillo	85	Guericke	86
	Borromeo	94	*La Fontaine	95	§Solis	86	Puffendorf	94
	Malpighi	94	*Racine	99	_Molinos_	96	Huyghens	95
1700								
	F. Socinus	4	§_Bossuet_	4	*Candamo	4	Leibnitz	16
	Cassini	12	§Bayle	6	§Ferreras	35	_Vitringa_	22
	†Maratti	13	*Boileau	11	*Ereiceyra	44	Stahl	34
	Gravina	18	*_Fénelon_	15	*Montiano	53	_Le Clerc_	36
	§_Muratori_	50	_Massillon_	42	Luzan	54	Boerhaave	38
	*Maffei	55	Le Sage	47	Moratin	80	Bernouilli	48
_18th_	Goldoni	72	Montesquieu	55	*Huerta	87	Wolff	54
	*Metastasio	82	*Voltaire	78	*Iglesias	91	§_Mosheim_	55
	Bossovitch	87	Rousseau	78	*Yriarte	91	_Swedenborg_	72
	§Tiraboschi	94	D'Alembert	83	Gonzalez	94	Haller	77
	Beccaria	95	Buffon	88	Ulloa	95	Linnæus	78
	Galvani	98	Condorcet	94	*Forner	97	Lessing	81
	Spallanzani	99	Lavoisier	94	Cruz y Cano		Euler	83
1800								
	*Alfieri	3	Fourcroy	9	*Cienfuegos	9	Lavater	1
	§Denin	3	La Grange	13	Jovellanos	11	*Klopstock	3
	Canova	22	De Staël	17	Melendez	17	Kant	4
_19th_	Volta	27	La Place	27	§Llorente	23	*Schiller	5
	*Foscolo	27	Champollion	32	Moratin	28	*Wieland	13
	*Monti	28	Cuvier	32	Navarrete		*Goethe	32
	§Botta	37	Chateaubriand	48	Escoiquiz		Berzelius	48

* Poets; † Painters; § Historians; those in _Italics_ Divines.

Remarks on the preceding Table.

Italy. In the revival of learning in modern times, Italy has the honor of having taken the lead. The 14th century was illustrated by the celebrated poets, *Dante* and *Petrarch;* and by *Boccaccio*, an eminent prose writer; and, in the 15th and 16th centuries, Italian genius in literature and the fine arts shone forth with great lustre, under the liberal patronage of the wealthy houses of *Medici* and *Este*. This period was illustrated by the poets, *Ariosto* and *Tasso;* by the artists, *Raphael*, *Da Vinci*, *Michael Angelo* &c.; by the historians, *Macchiavel*, *Guicciardini*, and many other men of genius. Of the Italian astronomers, the most eminent is *Galileo*.

France. Literature began to flourish in France in the early part of the 16th century, under the patronage of Francis I. This century was illustrated by the names of *Calvin*, *Scaliger*, *Stephens*, *Ramus*, *Montaigne*, &c.

The most brilliant period of French literature was during the long reign of Louis XIV., in the latter half of the 17th and the early part of the 18th centuries, during which France produced more men, eminent in literature and the arts, than any other country, some of whom are *Pascal*, distinguished for genius and attainments in science; *Molière*, *Corneille*, *Racine*, and *Boileau*, eminent poets; *Fénelon*, author of the Telemachus; *Bossuet*, *Bourdaloue*, and *Massillon*, eloquent preachers.

The most eminent French poet, since Boileau, is *Voltaire*. Some of the greatest French mathematicians and astronomers are *Descartes*, *Gassendi*, *D'Alembert*, *Condorcet*, *La Grange*, and *La Place;* some of the naturalists, *Buffon* and *Cuvier*.

Spain. The principal poetical productions of Spain, before the commencement of the 16th century, were the romances of the Cid, a renowned Spanish hero. The earliest of the classical school of Spanish poets are *Garcilaso* and *Boscan;* the most eminent dramatic poets, *Lope de Vega* and *Calderon;* the most distinguished name in Spanish literature, *Cervantes*, author of Don Quixote; the most eminent historians, *Mariana*, *Herrera*, and *Solis*. — *Camoens*, the author of the Lusiad, is the most distinguished poet of *Portugal*.

Germany. Germany has given birth to a succession of eminent scholars and philosophers since the Reformation; and has, for some time past, produced a greater number of learned authors than any other country. The Germans claim the merit of many important inventions, as gunpowder, printing, watches, the air-pump, and the telescope. *Copernicus* of Thorn, near the borders of Germany, was the restorer of the true *system of the world*. *Luther* is noted as the great reformer. Some of the most eminent German philosophers and men of science, are *Kepler*, *Leibnitz*, *Wolff*, and *Kant;* some of the most eminent poets, *Klopstock*, *Schiller*, and *Goethe*.

Sweden. Some of the eminent men of Sweden may be mentioned, — *Linnæus*, distinguished for his attainments in botany; *Swedenborg*, in science and theology; *Scheele* and *Berzelius*, in chemistry.

Holland. Holland has produced many men of learning, among whom are *Erasmus*, the most celebrated scholar of his age, and one of the principal restorers of learning; *Grotius*, *Vossius*, and *Le Clerc*, eminent scholars; *Huyghens*, a great mathematician; and *Boerhaave*, a distinguished physician.

AMERICA.

DISCOVERY AND SETTLEMENT: — *Columbus, Americus, Cabot &c.; Conquest of Mexico and Peru; — Cortes, Pizarro &c. — From A. D.* 1492 *to* 1600.

1. The discovery of America was the greatest achievement of the kind ever performed by man; and, considered in connection with its consequences, it is the greatest event of modern times. It served to wake up an unprecedented spirit of enterprise; it opened new sources of wealth, and exerted a powerful influence on commerce, by greatly increasing many important articles of trade, and also by bringing into general use many others before unknown: by leading to the discovery of the rich mines of this continent, it has caused the quantity of the precious metals in circulation throughout the world to be exceedingly augmented; it also gave a new impulse to colonization, and prepared the way for the advantages of civilized life, and the blessings of Christianity, to be extended over vast regions, which before were the miserable abodes of barbarism and pagan idolatry.

2. The man to whose genius and enterprise the world is indebted for this discovery was *Christopher Columbus*, of Genoa. He was the son of a wool-comber; was engaged in a seafaring life from the age of 14; was well versed in the sciences of geometry, astronomy, and geography; had more correct ideas of the figure of the earth than were common in his time; was singularly qualified for executing an arduous expedition, being well skilled in naval science, fertile in expedients, patient and persevering, grave and dignified in his deportment, master of himself, and skilful in the government of other men

3. He conceived, that, in order to complete the balance of the terraqueous globe, another continent necessarily existed, which might be reached by sailing to the west from Europe; but he erroneously connected it with India. Being persuaded of the truth of his theory, his adventurous spirit made him eager to verify it by experiment.

4. The passage round the *Cape of Good Hope* not being then known, the merchandise of *India* was, in order to be conveyed to Europe, brought up the *Red Sea*, and transported across the land to *Alexandria*. To find a passage to *China* and the *East Indies* by sea, had long been an object of investigation, and it was in quest of a shorter and easier route by the west that Columbus undertook his voyage of discovery

The riches of the East were the bribe and inducement which he held out to the sovereign or the state that should enable him to execute his design.

5. He first applied for assistance to his countrymen, the Genoese, then to the Portuguese, then to Ferdinand of Spain and then, by means of his brother Bartholomew, to Henry VII. of England, but all without success; and he had the mortification to be considered a visionary projector. At length, after seven years of persevering and anxious solicitation and contemptuous neglect in Spain, and 18 years after he had first conceived the enterprise, he obtained a gleam of royal favor from Queen *Isabella.* By her means he was provided with three small vessels, victualled for twelve months, and having on board 90 men. The expense of building and supplying the whole was only about £4,000. He was appointed admiral of all the seas which he should explore, and governor of all the islands and countries which he should discover and subdue.

6. With the small and ill-appointed fleet which had been furnished, he sailed from *Palos*, in Spain, on the 3d of August, 1492. He steered directly for the Canary islands, where, having refitted, he proceeded on his voyage, on the 6th of September, passing into seas which no vessel had been known to have ever explored, and without a chart to direct his course.

7. He had soon occasion to make use of all his talents and address. After having sailed about 200 leagues from the Canaries, the variation of the magnetic needle from its direction to the polar star, a phenomenon which had never before been observed, excited alarm in his own breast, and filled the sailors with terror and dismay to such a degree, that they were ready to rise in open mutiny. But, with great presence of mind, he made a solution of the phenomenon, which served to silence the murmurs of his crew, though it was unsatisfactory to himself. Having pursued their course for 30 days longer, without discovering land, the murmurs of the crew again broke out, and with increased violence. Columbus made use of encouragement and exhortation; but, according to Oviedo, was compelled to yield so far to their importunity as to propose, that if, after proceeding three days more, no land were discovered, he would instantly return.

8. Strong indications of land had already begun to appear and, in the night of the 11th of October, Columbus, who was standing on the forecastle, discovered a light ahead. The morning displayed the joyful sight of *land!* A hymn of thanksgiving to Almighty God was sung by the whole crew who immediately united in the most ardent expressions of ad-

miration for their commander, with acknowledgments of their rashness and disobedience.

9. The island first discovered was *St. Salvador*, or *Cat Island*, one of the *Bahamas*. He afterwards discovered *Cuba* and *Hayti*, or *St. Domingo*, which he named *Hispaniola*, on which he landed, and left some of his men to form a colony. In conformity with the theory which he had adopted, he connected these islands with *India*, believing them at no great distance from that unexplored region; and, as they had been reached by a western passage, they were denominated the *West Indies*. And, in accordance with this theory, the aborigines of America, from the time of the first discovery, have been designated by the appellation of *Indians*.

10. Having obtained a quantity of gold and some of the natives, he set sail on his return to Spain. During the voyage, a violent tempest arose, which lasted 15 days, and exposed the fleet to extreme danger: and, in order to afford a small chance that the world might not lose the benefit of his discovery, he had the presence of mind to write a short account of his voyage, which he wrapped in an oiled cloth, and inclosed in a cake of wax; and, putting this into an empty cask, he committed it to the sea, in hopes that it might fall into the hands of some fortunate navigator, or be cast ashore. But the storm happily abated, and Columbus entered the port from which he had sailed about seven months before, amidst the acclamations and wonder of the multitude. He proceeded immediately to the court, where he was received with respect and admiration.

11. Columbus afterwards made a second and a third voyage, in the latter of which he discovered, in 1498, the *Continent of South America;* but his successes and honors did not fail to excite envy and intrigues against him in the court of Spain In consequence of false accusations, he was deprived of the government of Hispaniola, and sent home in chains. The captain of the vessel which carried him, impressed with the highest veneration for his captive, and feeling the deepest regret for the indignity which he suffered, offered to release him from his fetters. "No!" said Columbus, in a burst of generous indignation; "I wear these irons in consequence of an order from their majesties, the rulers of Spain. They shall find me as obedient to this as to their other injunctions. By their command I have been confined, and their command alone shall set me at liberty."

12. But he never forgot the unjust and shameful treatment which he had received. Through the whole of his after life, he carried his fetters with him, as a memorial of the ingratitude which he had experienced. He hung them up in his

chamber, and gave orders that they should be buried with him in his grave.

13. Upon the arrival of Columbus in Spain, a prisoner and in fetters, the indignation of all men was highly excited; and Ferdinand, cold, distant, and haughty as he was, felt for a while the emotions of shame. But after detaining him for a long time, in a fatiguing and vexatious attendance, he appointed another person governor of Hispaniola in his stead. Such was the reward which the great discoverer of this western world received, for having devised and carried on to a successful issue one of the noblest and most daring enterprises that ever entered into the mind of man; and such is the account which impartial history is constrained to give of the justice and gratitude of kings!

14. Columbus, intent on finding a passage to India by the west, afterwards made a fourth voyage, examined the coast of Darien, and was shipwrecked on the coast of the island of Jamaica. He here obtained, for a time, an astonishing command over the Indians, by predicting an eclipse of the moon. After having endured a great variety of suffering and calamity, from the mutiny and treachery of his men, from conflicts with the natives, from scarcity of provisions, and from sickness, in this his last and most disastrous expedition, he returned to Spain; and, worn out with fatigue, disappointment, and sorrow, he died at *Valladolid*, in 1506, at about the age of 70 years. His funeral, by the order of Philip II., who had recently ascended the throne, was extremely magnificent, and the following inscription was engraved on his tomb: — "To Castile and Leon, Columbus has given a new world."

15. But this great man was unjustly deprived of the honor of giving his name to this continent by *Americus Vespucius*, a native of Florence, who accompanied *Ojeda* in a voyage, in 1499, and discovered a part of the coast of South America, the next year after the continent had been discovered by Columbus. He wrote an account of this voyage, claiming the honor of being the first discoverer of the *main land;* and from him the continent has been named *America.* But this act of injustice, how much soever it is to be regretted, has done no real injury to the reputation of the one, nor benefit to that of the other; our feelings rather incline us to enhance the merit of Columbus, as one whose noble achievement has been ill requited, and to detract from that of Americus, as one who would usurp the honors of another.

16. In 1497, *Vasco de Gama*, a Portuguese, first doubled the *Cape of Good Hope*, and sailed to India. By this, he effected what was a leading object with Columbus in his enterprise

and what had been, during the preceding century, an object of investigation, namely, the discovery of a more expeditious and convenient passage to the East Indies than through Egypt. In 1519, *Magellan*, a Portuguese in the service of Spain, passed the straits which bear his name, and launched into the vast ocean, which he called *Pacific;* but he lost his life at one of the Philippine islands; yet his officers proceeded on the voyage, and accomplished, for the first time, the *circumnavigation of the globe.*

17. *John Cabot*, a Venetian by birth, but an inhabitant of Bristol, in England, received a commission from Henry VII., and sailed in the beginning of May, 1497, on a voyage of discovery, accompanied by his son, *Sebastian Cabot;* and one or both of them discovered the *continent of North America*, the year before the *main land of South America* had been discovered by Columbus, and two years before it had been seen by Americus.

18. The land first seen was called *Prima Vista*, which is supposed to have been a part of Newfoundland. They proceeded further to the north, in search of a passage to India, but finding no appearance of one, they tacked about, and sailed as far as Florida. They erected crosses along the coast, and took a formal possession of the country in behalf of the crown of England. This was the foundation of the English claim to North America, though no settlements were formed till many years after.

19. Several years passed away, from the time of the first discovery of America by Columbus, before any considerable settlement was formed by the Spaniards, on the continent. In 1519, *Fernando Cortes*, with a fleet of eleven small vessels, having on board 663 men, sailed from Cuba for the invasion of *Mexico*, and landed at Vera Cruz. As fire-arms were not yet in general use, only 13 of the men had muskets, the rest being armed with cross-bows, swords, and spears. Cortes had also 10 small field-pieces, and 16 horses, — the first of these animals ever seen in that country.

20. Cortes proceeded first to *Tlascala*, the capital of a small republic, hostile to Mexico; and here he induced 6,000 warriors to join him, and accompany him to the city of Mexico. On his arrival, he was courteously received by *Montezuma*, the Mexican emperor. Soon after, Cortes perfidiously seized Montezuma in his palace, and carried him to his own quarters, where he was kept more than six months as a prisoner. At length the Mexicans, exasperated by the cruelties of the Spaniards took measures to avenge themselves; and, in the contest which followed, Montezuma was wounded by his own subjects, and

soon afterwards died. The Spaniards, after a sanguinary struggle, were driven from the city, with the loss of half their men and all their muskets and artillery.

21. Cortes, with the shattered remnant of his army, retreated to Tlascala, pursued by an immense host of Mexicans, whom he routed in the great battle of *Otumba*. At Tlascala, he received some reinforcements of Spaniards, and raised a large army of Indians from the nations hostile to the Mexicans. At the head of these forces, he marched against Mexico, where *Guatimozin*, a nephew of Montezuma, had been elected emperor; and, after a siege of nearly three months, he captured the city, and seized Guatimozin, who was treated with the greatest cruelty, and finally put to death. Thus was the great empire of Mexico overthrown by a handful of daring and unprincipled adventurers.

22. In 1518, the Spaniards formed a settlement at *Panama*, on the west side of the gulf of Darien. From this place several attempts were made to explore the regions of South America; and hence *Pizarro* sailed on an expedition, in 1525, and discovered the rich and flourishing kingdom of *Peru*. He afterwards obtained from Charles V., the King of Spain, a commission as governor of the country, and a military force to subdue it; and for this purpose, in 1531, he sailed from Panama, with three small vessels and 180 men.

23. With this little band he invaded the country, marched to the residence of the *inca*, or king, *Atabalipa*, and having invited him to a friendly interview, and attempted to persuade him to embrace the Christian religion, he seized him as a prisoner; and, by his order, his men fell upon the defenceless and unresisting attendants of the monarch, and slew upwards of 4,000 of them.

24. The Peruvian monarch, in order to procure his release caused the room in which he was confined, which was 22 feet by 17, to be filled, for Pizarro, with vessels of gold and silver, as high as he could reach. The treasure, which was collected from various parts of the empire, amounted, in value, to upwards of £1,500,000; and this large sum was divided among the conquerors. But the perfidious Spaniard still held the inca prisoner; and *Almagro* having joined Pizarro with a reinforcement, they brought the monarch to trial, and, on a charge of being a usurper and an idolater, condemned and executed him!

25. The Spanish chiefs not long after quarrelled with each other, and a civil war ensued. Almagro was taken prisoner, condemned, and executed; and, soon after, Pizarro was assassinated. The Indians took advantage of these contentions, and, under their new inca, *Huanca Capac*, rose against the

Spaniards; but they were at last subdued (1532), and Peru became a province of Spain.

26. At the time of the invasion of the Spaniards, the *Peruvians* and *Mexicans* had made considerable progress towards civilization, much more than the rest of the Indians. They understood the arts of architecture, sculpture, mining, and working the precious metals; cultivated their land, were clothed, and had a regular system of government, and a code of civil and religious laws. The *Peruvians* had the superiority in architecture, and possessed some magnificent palaces and temples. They worshipped the sun as the Supreme Deity, and their religion had few of those sanguinary traits which were characteristic of that of the Mexicans.

27. In 1524, *Francis I.* of France, willing to share a part of the new world with his neighbors, commissioned *Verrazano* on a voyage of discovery. This navigator explored a great part of the coast of North America. Ten years afterwards, *James Cartier* set out on a similar expedition, sailed up the gulf of *St. Lawrence*, took possession of the country in behalf of the king, and styled it *New France;* but the name was afterwards changed to *Canada.*

28. In 1584, the celebrated *Sir Walter Raleigh*, under a commission from *Queen Elizabeth*, to discover, occupy, and govern " remote, heathen, and barbarous countries," not previously possessed by any Christian prince or people, arrived in America, entered Pamlico Sound, and proceeded to Roanoke island, near the mouth of Albemarle Sound, and took possession of the country. On his return to England, he gave such a splendid description of the beauty and fertility of the region, that Elizabeth, delighted with occupying so fine a territory, gave it the name of *Virginia*, as a memorial that this happy discovery was made during the reign of a virgin queen.

29. Several attempts were made to form settlements in Virginia, by *Sir Walter Raleigh*, *Sir Francis Drake*, and *Sir Richard Grenville*, but they all proved unsuccessful; and part of the colonists were carried back to England, part of them perished by disease, and part were destroyed by the Indians.

30. It was the practice of Europeans to take possession of the parts of America which they visited, by the pretended right of discovery. The original inhabitants were treated as if they had no rights, and were no more owners of the soil than the beasts of the forest. This example was set by *Columbus* himself. He landed upon St. Salvador, the first island discovered, in a gorgeous dress, with a drawn sword in his

hand, and the royal standard displayed, and took possession of the island for the crown of Castile and Leon; and in conformity to this practice, it was inscribed on his tomb, that to this crown he "had given a new world."

31. The pope, in accordance with principles that were acted upon in an age of ignorance and superstition, granted to the sovereigns of Spain the countries discovered by their subjects in the new world. The propagation of Christianity was held out as the chief reason for taking possession of America and the promotion of a religion which breathes "peace on earth and good-will towards men," was made the pretext for every species of injustice, cruelty, bloodshed, and slavery, which the defenceless inhabitants of America were destined to experience from Cortes, Pizarro, and other unprincipled invaders.

32. The Spaniards who first came to America were stimulated by the desire and expectation of finding the precious metals, gold and silver. So powerful was this passion for gold, that the first adventurers encountered every possible hardship and danger in search of it, and sacrificed millions of the wretched natives, whom they compelled to work in the mines. The unfortunate Indians were distributed, like cattle, into lots of so many hundred heads each, and sold to the colonists. The Indians, who were naturally of a weak constitution, were rapidly wasted away by the hard service to which they were subjected. So great was the mortality among them, that out of 60,000 Indians who were in the island of St. Domingo, in 1508, only 14,000 are said to have remained in 1516; and it was not many years before the race became nearly extinct in most of the islands.

33. This cruelty to the Indians was strongly condemned by Las Casas, and other benevolent persons, and the colonists soon began to look to Africa for a supply of laborers in their mines and on their plantations. It was found that one able-bodied negro could do as much work as four Indians.

34. The first importation of negroes from Africa to the West Indies was made, in 1503, by the Portuguese and a larger one was made by order of Ferdinand of Spain, in 1511; since that time, the inhuman traffic in African slaves has been carried on by most of the European nations; nor has it yet been abandoned by Spain and Portugal, the two European countries which were the first to begin this barbarous traffic and which seem disposed to be last to relinquish it.

THE UNITED STATES.*

SECTION I.

Settlement and Early History of the COLONIES: — *Virginia, New York; Colonies of New England; Indian Wars, Maryland; Pennsylvania.* — *From A. D.* 1607 *to* 1682.

1. The vanity of nations, like that of families, inclines them to lay claim to a high antiquity; and the obscurity in which their early history is, in most instances, involved, affords them an opportunity to indulge this propensity. But with regard to the United States, circumstances are different. The vanity of the people of this country inclines them to dwell upon their recent origin and their rapid growth, and the promise which these afford of future greatness. Of all independent nations of any importance, now existing, this has had the most recent origin, and its early history is the best known; nor do the annals of the world afford another instance of a nation rising, in so short a space of time from its first settlement, to an equal degree of power and freedom.

2. Various circumstances have concurred to promote the rapid increase in population and wealth, and the progress of society, which have been witnessed in this country. The first settlers were emigrants from countries advanced in civilization, and they brought with them the arts of civilized life. A great portion of them were men distinguished for intelligence and enterprise, and were strenuous advocates for civil and religious liberty; and, at the first foundation of their settlements, they paid particular attention to the promotion of education. A vast field of enterprise has been constantly presented before them, with ample rewards to industry. The means of subsistence have been abundant and easily obtained; and extensive tracts of fertile and unoccupied lands, suitable for new settlements, have always been procurable on moderate terms. The political and commercial relations of the inhabitants have connected them with the most enlightened nations in the world;

* The national existence of the *United States*, properly so called, commenced *July 4th*, 1776. Before that period, the inhabitants were in a state of colonial dependence on Great Britain, and were styled the *British Colonies in America*. *Louisiana*, which was formerly a French colony, and *Florida*, formerly a Spanish one, and *Texas*, *New Mexico*, and *California*, all of which formerly formed a part of Mexico, have since been annexed to the United States.

and have afforded them the means of being acquainted with the progress of literature and science, and with the various improvements in the arts of civilized life.

3. The colonization of this country originated either in religious persecution, carried on in England against the *Puritans* and other denominations of Christians, or in visionary schemes of adventurers, who set out for the new world in quest of settlements, and in pursuit of gain. It was the former cause which peopled the colonies of *New England;* and it was to the latter that the colonies of *Virginia* and *New York* owed their origin. These may be considered as the original or parent colonies.

4. They struggled long with the hardships and difficulties incident to all new establishments on barbarous shores, remote from civilized society, and from the means of procuring aid in supplying their wants, and in protecting themselves against the hostilities to which they were exposed. They were, at times, reduced to great extremities by sickness, disease, and want, and by the attacks and depredations of the Indians, insomuch that, in some instances, it was resolved to abandon the settlement of the country as impracticable. All these impediments, however, being gradually overcome by perseverance, industry, and enterprise, the colonies at last began to flourish, and to increase both in wealth and population.

5. The first grant from the crown of England, under which effectual settlements were made in North America, was dated April 10, 1606. By this charter, all the country in America, between lat. 34° and 45° N., was called *Virginia.* But, by this charter, two companies were constituted; one called the *London Company*, the other the *Plymouth Company.* To the former was assigned the territory between lat. 34° and 41° N. called *South Virginia;* to the latter, the part of the territory lying to the north, called *North Virginia.*

6. Some unsuccessful attempts to form a settlement in Virginia, before this charter was granted, have been already mentioned. The first effectual attempt was made in 1607 by a company of 105 adventurers, who came in a vessel commanded by *Captain Newport.* They sailed up the *Powhatan* or *James River*, built a fort, and commenced a town, which, in honor of king *James*, they called *Jamestown.* The government of the colony was, at first, administered by a council of seven persons, with a president chosen from among their number.

7. The name of the first president was *Wingfield;* but the most distinguished member of the council was *Captain John*

Smith, who was the second year chosen president, and who has been styled the Father of the colony. He had commanded a company of cavalry in the Austrian army, in a war with the Turks; and had been taken prisoner and sent to Constantinople as a slave, from which condition he had extricated himself. He was a man of undaunted courage, romantic disposition, and an ardent spirit of enterprise; and to his superior talents the company were greatly indebted for their success.

8. The colonists were soon involved in contests with the Indians, whose hostilities against the English were not unprovoked, as they had been previously treated by them with cruelty. In 1585, *Sir Richard Grenville* burnt a whole Indian town, and destroyed their corn, in revenge for their stealing a silver cup; and *Mr. Lane*, the leader of the adventurers left by Sir Richard, slew a sachem, and killed and took captive several Indians.

9. The year in which the settlement was commenced, an accident is said to have happened to *Captain Smith*, which lent to his history the attraction of romance. According to his own account, while engaged in hunting, he was taken prisoner by a body of 200 Indians; but he so charmed them by his arts and his valor that they released him. Soon afterwards, he was again taken by another party of 300, who carried him in triumph before *Powhatan*, the greatest chief in the region.

10. The sentence of death was pronounced upon him; his head was placed on a stone, and the savages were about to beat out his brains, when *Pocahontas*, the favorite daughter of the chief, who was only about twelve years of age, after having in vain implored mercy for him, rushed forward, and, placing her head upon that of the captive, appeared determined to share his fate. Powhatan relented, and set the prisoner free.

11. Two years afterwards (1609), Pocahontas gave information to Captain Smith of a plot formed by the Indians for the destruction of the colony, which was, by this means, prevented. This extraordinary Indian female was afterwards married, with the consent of her father, to *Mr. Rolfe*, a respectable young planter. Their nuptials were celebrated with great pomp, and Pocahontas was highly useful in preserving peace between the colonists and Indians. She accompanied her husband to England; was instructed in the Christian religion, and baptized. She died when about to return to America, at the age of about 22, leaving one son, from whom are sprung some of the most respectable families in Virginia.

12. During the first year, the colonists suffered severely by the scarcity and badness of provisions; diseases were in consequence introduced, which, in a few months, swept away one

half of their number. But others were added by new arrivals so that, at the end of the year, they amounted to 200.

13. In the latter part of the year 1609, Captain Smith, at once the shield and sword of the colony, returned to England. Soon after his departure, the company was reduced to the greatest extremities. A party of 30 men, under *Captain Ratcliffe*, were all slain by the Indians; and, in consequence of a waste of provisions, a most distressing famine prevailed (1610), which was known, for many years afterwards, by the name of the *starving time.*

14. So dreadful was its effect, that, in the space of six months the colonists were reduced from nearly 500 to 60. This small remainder, being exceedingly enfeebled and disheartened, resolved to abandon the settlement and return to England, and for this purpose they had actually embarked; but, meeting with *Lord Delaware*, who had been appointed governor, under a new charter, with 150 men, and a large supply of provisions they were induced to remain; and the affairs of the company soon began to assume a more auspicious appearance.

15. At the expiration of twelve years from the first settlement, there remained only about 600 persons; but, during the year 1619, the number was increased by the arrival of eleven ships, bringing 1,216 new settlers. The planters were mostly adventurers, destitute of families, and came with the hope of obtaining wealth, intending eventually to return: but with a view to make their residence permanent, and attach them to the country, an expedient was devised for supplying them with wives; and for this purpose, in the years 1620 and 1621, 150 unmarried females, "young and uncorrupt," were sent over from England, to be sold to such as were inclined to purchase. The price of a wife, at first, was 100 pounds of tobacco; but, as the number for sale decreased, the price was raised to 150 pounds, the tobacco being valued at three shillings a pound. In 1620, 20 *negroes* were carried to Virginia in a Dutch vessel of war, and sold for slaves. This was the commencement, in English America, of the unhappy system of *slavery.*

16. The colonists, having turned their attention to agriculture particularly to the cultivation of tobacco, and their numbers being increased yearly by the arrival of new emigrants, began to enjoy a degree of prosperity, when, in 1622, they experienced a stroke which came near proving fatal. *Opecancanough*, the successor of Powhatan, concerted a plan for the destruction of the settlement; and in so artful a manner was the plot devised, that it might have been effectually accomplished, if a large part of the colonists had not been informed of it a few hours before the time appointed for its

execution. The Indians, notwithstanding, succeeded in putting to death, almost instantaneously, 347 persons. A war of extermination followed this massacre; not long afterwards another distressing famine; and in 1624, of 9,000 persons who had been sent from England, only 1,800 remained in the colony. But its severe losses were soon repaired by new arrivals.

17. The colony suffered by restrictions on its trade and by the arbitrary government of *Sir John Harvey;* but, in 1639, *Sir William Berkeley*, a man of superior talents, was appointed governor; and during his administration, which lasted, except during the protectorate of Cromwell, nearly 40 years, it was generally prosperous. The restrictions, however, imposed upon its trade by Charles II., occasioned discontents, and, in 1676, near the end of Berkeley's administration, gave rise to an insurrection, memorable in the history of Virginia, and known by the name of *Bacon's Rebellion*, so called from its leader. Many parts of the colony were given up to pillage; Jamestown was burnt; and all the horrors of a civil war were felt for a time, till at last the rebellion was terminated by the death of Bacon.

18. The population, in 1660, amounted to about 30,000 and, in the 28 succeeding years, the number was doubled. The first adventurers came out with the hope of acquiring wealth by the discovery of the precious metals; and the ships in which they arrived were sent back, one of them loaded by the miners with a glittering earth, which they vainly hoped contained gold; the other, loaded with cedar. About 1616, the cultivation of *tobacco* was commenced, which soon became the chief object of attention with the colonists, and constituted the principal part of their property. It formed the medium of trade, and was received by the government in the payment of taxes.

19. In 1609, *Henry Hudson*, an Englishman in the service of the Dutch, on a voyage in quest of a north-west passage to India, discovered the noble river which bears his name. The first permanent settlements were made by Dutch adventurers, who erected two forts, in or about the year 1614, one at *Albany*, the other on *Manhattan Island*, where the city of *New York* now stands. The country was called *New Netherlands*, and the settlement on Manhattan Island was named *New Amsterdam;* which names they retained till the conquest of the country by the English.

20. The colony was in the possession of the Dutch about 50 years, and the government was administered by three successive governors, namely, *Van Twiller*, *Kieft*, and *Stuyvesant*

The extension of the English settlements gave rise to misunderstandings, and the Dutch governors were engaged in a series of disputes and contests.

21. In 1664, Charles II. of England, being then at war with the Dutch, granted the country to his brother, the Duke of York: Governor Stuyvesant was compelled to capitulate to an English force, under *Colonel Nicholls;* the whole territory became subject to the British crown, and, in honor of the duke, the country and city were named *New York.*

22. The Plymouth Company, to whom the country of *North Virginia* was assigned, commenced a small settlement on the river *Sagadahoc*, or *Kennebec*, in 1607, the same year in which *Jamestown* was founded; but it was soon abandoned. In 1614 *Captain Smith*, having visited the country, and examined its shores and harbors, on his return to England, constructed a map of it, which he presented to Prince Charles, who changed its name from *North Virginia* to *New England;* and a patent was granted by King James, in 1620, to the *Duke of Lenox*, *Ferdinando Gorges*, and others, styled "The Council of Plymouth, in the county of Devon, for settling and governing New England." This patent granted to them the country extending from lat. 40° to 48° N.; and it was the foundation of the subsequent grants of the several parts of the territory.

23. In the year in which this patent was granted, the first permanent settlement was commenced in New England, at *Plymouth*, in Massachusetts, by 101 *Puritans*, a class of dissenters from the Church of England, who were now beginning to become numerous, and who were called *Puritans*, because they were desirous of a *purer* form of discipline and worship. This small colony formed a part of the congregation of *John Robinson*, who is regarded as the founder of the denomination of *Independents* or *Congregationalists.*

24. Being driven from England by persecution, several years before, the congregation, together with their minister, had fled to *Holland;* but a part of them were, at length, induced to seek an asylum, where they might enjoy religious liberty, in the wilds of America. The principle of religious toleration was not, at this period, understood or practised by any denomination of Christians. The Puritans were severely persecuted by the Church of England; but their own principles, also, were intolerant; and, in their turn, they persecuted those who differed from them.

25. The colonists sailed, on the 6th of September, 1620 from Plymouth in England, in the Mayflower, for Hudson's River, in the neighborhood of which they intended to settle

but they were carried, by head winds, farther to the north; and the first land which they discovered was Cape Cod. They arrived on the coast in November; and, as they had not determined on the place for their settlement, parties were despatched to explore the country, who, after incredible suffering from the severity of the weather, found a harbor. Here they landed, *December* 22d, 1620, and began to build a town, which they called *Plymouth*, from the name of the town which they last left in England.

26. The difficulties and sufferings which they had to encounter were sufficient to dishearten men of ordinary resolution. Cast upon an unknown and barbarous coast, in a severe climate, and at an inclement season; worn down with their long voyage, excessive fatigue, the severity of the weather, and the want of comfortable provisions and habitations, they were, soon after their arrival, visited with distressing sickness, and, in three months, reduced to about one half of their original number. The sickness was so general, that, at some times, there were only six or seven well persons in the company.

27. They instituted a republican form of government, and chose *John Carver* for their first governor, who, dying in 1621, was succeeded by *William Bradford.* The governor, who was chosen annually, had at first but one assistant; afterwards five; and the number was, at length, increased to seven. On the opening of the spring, they sowed barley and peas, which produced but an indifferent crop. They were assisted in planting and dressing Indian corn or maize, which they had never before seen, by *Squanto*, a friendly Indian: this afforded them a great part of their subsistence; and it has ever since been a staple production of the country. For several years the whole property of the settlers was held in common.

28. In order to protect themselves against the hostilities of the Indians, they formed a military organization, and *Miles Standish* was chosen their captain. — In March, 1621, they were visited by *Samoset*, a sagamore or petty sachem, who addressed them with the friendly salutation of "Welcome, Englishmen! Welcome, Englishmen!" From him they obtained important information respecting the country, and learned that, not long before, a mortal pestilence had swept off almost all the Indians in the vicinity. By his assistance they entered into a treaty of peace and friendship with *Massasoit*, sachem of the *Wampanoags*, who was the most powerful Indian chief in the region. This treaty, which was of great importance to the colony, was strictly observed till the commencement of Philip's war, a period of 54 years.

29. During subsequent years, there were numerous arrivals

of other persons from England, whose character and views were similar to those of the first settlers at Plymouth. In 1628, the foundation was laid of the colony of *Massachusetts Bay*, by a company of adventurers under *John Endicott*, who formed a settlement at *Naumkeag*, now *Salem;* and in 1630, 1,500 persons, under *John Winthrop*, who was appointed governor, arrived at *Charlestown*, and soon afterwards commenced the settlement of *Boston* and other towns in the vicinity.

30. In 1623, the settlement of *New Hampshire* was commenced at *Dover* and *Portsmouth*, by persons sent out by *John Mason* and *Ferdinando Gorges*, to whom the country had been granted. The former became afterwards sole proprietor of a large part of the country, and the claims of his heirs furnished a fruitful source of contention. The settlements were annexed to Massachusetts in 1641, and so continued till 1679, when a separate government was instituted for New Hampshire.

31. In 1635, the settlement of the colony of *Connecticut* was begun, at *Windsor* and *Wethersfield*, by about 60 persons from Massachusetts; and, in 1638, the colony of *New Haven* was commenced by *Theophilus Eaton*, *John Davenport*, and others. These colonies were united into one in 1665.

32. The settlement of *Rhode Island* was commenced in 1636, at *Providence*, by *Roger Williams*, a minister of the Gospel, who had been banished from Massachusetts on account of his religious opinions.

33. As the quiet enjoyment of religious liberty was the leading cause of the formation of these settlements, the founders of them were particularly solicitous with regard to the support and encouragement of religion. Among the early settlers, there were many men of talents and liberal education; and a wilderness has probably never been planted by a body of men who were more mindful of the interests of learning, or more attentive to the establishment of schools. In ten years after the first settlement of Massachusetts Bay, *Harvard College* was founded at Cambridge.

34. The colonists were possessed of many excellent traits of character. Their enterprise and industry, their love of liberty, their attention to education, their morality and piety entitle them to respect and admiration. They were not, however, without faults, some of which were vices of the age, others belonged more particularly to themselves.

35. With regard to differences in religious opinions, their views were narrow and intolerant. In some instances, it was enacted, that none except members of the church should have a right to vote at elections, or should be eligible to any office. Their rigid principles also appear in the severity with which

they punished many offences, which are not now considered as properly coming under the cognizance of the civil law The close inspection which they practised with regard to every man's principles and conduct, secured, for many years, very strict morals and great uniformity of doctrines. But it was not possible to prevent differences of opinion; and when these arose, the severity with which those were treated, who avowed unpopular sentiments, occasioned many heart-burnings and mutual reproaches.

36. The colonists landed in the country without having obtained the consent of the natives; yet the principle upon which they proceeded was, before taking possession of the lands, to procure them by a regular purchase of the Indians, who were considered as the rightful owners of the soil. The treatment, however, which the Indians in America had generally received from European adventurers, had given them too much reason to distrust the friendly dispositions of white men; and it must be acknowledged, that the New England colonists, in their proceedings with regard to this injured people, were not always pacific or just.

37. In the third year after the formation of the settlement at Plymouth, *Captain Standish*, at the head of a small party, killed a number of Indians who had manifested hostile intentions. When an account of this transaction was sent to *Mr. Robinson*, in Holland, in his next letter to the governor, he exclaimed, in a manner that does honor to his feelings, "O that you had converted some before you had killed any!" The settlers at *Plymouth* and in *Massachusetts Bay*, however, had but little trouble with the Indians for many years. But the colony of *Connecticut*, in 1637, two years after it was first planted, was engaged in a severe contest with the *Pequods*, or *Pequots*, a warlike tribe, inhabiting a district now forming the south-east part of that state. The Pequods had previously made depredations on the infant settlement, and killed several individuals. The Indians were entirely defeated, at their settlement and forts on Mystic River, by the colonists, under *Captain Mason*, with the loss of between 600 and 700 killed and taken prisoners, being about two thirds of their whole number; and 70 of their wigwams were also burnt. Of the English, only 2 were killed and 16 wounded.

38. Not long after this contest, the colonists had strong apprehensions of a general combination of the Indians for extirpating them; the proceedings of the Dutch and the French also created alarm. In order, therefore, to promote their security and welfare, the four colonies of Massachusetts Bay

Plymouth, Connecticut, and New Haven, united in a confederacy, in 1643, by the name of the *United Colonies of New England.* Each one elected two delegates, who were to assemble by rotation, in the different colonies, annually, or oftener if necessary. This union, which subsisted a little more than 40 years, till the colonies were deprived of their charters by James II., was of great service in promoting harmony among themselves, and increasing their means of defence. In it we may see the germ of that grand confederacy which led to American Independence.

39. The most general and destructive Indian war, in which the colonies were ever involved, took place in 1675 and 1676 with *Philip*, king or sachem of the *Wampanoags*, and son of *Massasoit*, whose principal residence was at *Mount Hope*, in Rhode Island. He was the most formidable enemy that the colonists had ever known; a man of great talents and undaunted courage, a shrewd politician, and a great warrior.

40. The Indian tribes, perceiving the English settlements extending in every direction, determined to make one great and combined effort to avoid the loss of their hunting-grounds, their inheritance, their liberty and independence. An extensive combination was accordingly formed among the different tribes, for the purpose of the total destruction of the colonies; and of this combination Philip was the leader.

41. A more immediate cause of the war was the circumstance, that *Sausaman*, a Christian Indian, gave information to the colonists of the plot which had been formed against them, for which three Indians, at the instigation of Philip, murdered him. The murderers were tried and executed by the English. In order to avenge their death, Philip soon commenced his hostile attacks, and, by his agents, drew into the contest most of the tribes in New England.

42. The Indians had now acquired, in some degree, the use of fire-arms. Hostilities were conducted with great spirit and energy on both sides, and with the usual ferocity of savage warfare. The greatest battle, not only during this contest, but in the early history of the country, is known by the name of the *Swamp Fight*, which took place in December, 1675, in the Narraganset country, at the Indian fortress, in a large swamp situated in the western part of what is now the township of South Kingston. The English, who were commanded by *Josiah Winslow*, Governor of Plymouth, obtained a great victory, yet with the loss of 230 men killed and wounded; and among their slain were six brave captains. About 1,000 of the Indians are supposed to have perished, besides many women and children, and 500 or 600 of their wigwams were burnt.

43. The Indians never entirely recovered from the effect of this defeat. They were not, however, subdued, but continued their depredations by massacring the inhabitants and burning the towns. At length, in August, 1676, the great warrior *Philip* was shot by an Indian whom he had offended, and who joined a party under the famous *Captain Benjamin Church.* This was a fatal stroke to the power of the aborigines, and excited the liveliest joy and exultation in the colonies. Most of the hostile Indians soon afterwards submitted, or retreated from the country. After the termination of this conflict, the principal sufferings which the New England colonies endured from the hostilities of the Indians took place during the wars with the *French*, who employed the savages as auxiliaries.

44. This war afflicted almost every family in New England with the most painful privations. The whole English population was computed, at this time, to amount to about 60,000 of which nearly 600 men, comprising a considerable part of the strength of the country, fell during the contest, besides many women and children; and others were led into a miserable captivity. About 600 buildings, mostly dwelling-houses, were consumed; 12 or 13 towns were destroyed, many others damaged, and many cattle killed. The country was in deep mourning, there being scarcely a family or an individual who had not lost either a relative or a friend.

45. The founder of Maryland was *Sir George Calvert, Lord Baltimore*, a Roman Catholic, and an eminent statesman, who had been secretary to James I. He first visited Virginia, with a view to form a settlement of Catholics; but, meeting there with an unwelcome reception, he fixed his attention on the territory to the north of the Potomac, and obtained a grant of it from Charles I. From the queen of Charles, *Henrietta Maria*, the country was named *Maryland.* But, before the patent was completed, Sir George died, and the grant was given to his eldest son, *Cecilius*, who succeeded to his titles, and for upwards of 40 years directed the affairs of the colony, displaying an enlightened understanding and a benevolent heart.

46. *Leonard Calvert*, brother to Cecilius, was appointed the first governor; and he, together with about 200 persons, commenced the settlement of the town of *St. Mary's*, in 1634. The leading features of the policy adopted in this colony do honor to the founders. Universal toleration of religion was established, and a system of equity and humanity was practised with regard to the Indian tribes.

47. In 1681, the celebrated *William Penn* obtained of

Charles II a grant of the tract of country afterwards named from him *Pennsylvania.* It was granted to him in consideration of debts due from the crown of England for services performed by his father, Admiral Penn. In 1682, he arrived in the country, accompanied by about 2,000 associates, who were, most of them, like himself, of the denomination of *Friends* or *Quakers;* and in the next year he laid out the plan of the city of *Philadelphia.*

48. This great man and wise legislator made civil and religious liberty the basis of all his institutions. Christians of all denominations might not only live unmolested, but have a share in the government. In his intercourse with the Indians, he was governed by the strictest principles of equity and humanity, treating them as men and brethren, possessing the same rights as white men. Soon after his arrival, he summoned them to a council, and obtained of them, by fair purchase, a cession of as much land as his exigencies required.

49. The same course was pursued by his followers; the treaties were preserved inviolate on both sides; and a good understanding remained uninterrupted for more than 70 years. It was seen by mankind, with surprise, that kindness and good faith were a better protection than the sword, even to a settlement planted among savages; and that this excellent man, by his humane, equitable, and pacific policy, without any warlike preparations or means of defence, secured to his colony peace, prosperity, and safety, far more effectually than *Lycurgus* secured the same advantages to his country, by rendering the Spartans a nation of soldiers.

50. No one of the other colonies made so rapid advances in population and prosperity as this. The fertility of the soil, the salubrity of the climate, the uninterrupted peace with the natives, and the enjoyment of civil and religious liberty, held out inducements to the Quakers, and other persecuted and oppressed people in Europe, to seek an asylum in Pennsylvania.

51. In the original foundation of *Rhode Island*, by *Roger Williams*, of *Maryland*, by *Lord Baltimore;* and, on a more extended scale, of *Pennsylvania*, by *William Penn*, the free toleration of religion was recognized; and these were the first civil communities in which this liberal and enlightened principle was legally established and acted upon. The inhabitants of the New England colonies, with the exception of Rhode Island, in the early ages of their history, as has already been mentioned, persecuted those who differed from them with regard to religion; and the inhabitants of Virginia harassed those who dissented from the Church of England.

SECTION II.

Oppressive Measures relating to the Colonies: French Wars Capture of Louisburg, Expedition against New England, Conquest of Canada. — *From A. D.* 1682 *to* 1763.

1. From the time of the foundation of the first permanent English settlement in North America, the throne of England had been occupied by sovereigns of the *Stuart Family*, the influence of whose arbitrary principles tended to increase the number of emigrants from Great Britain to America; but this influence was also felt on this side of the Atlantic as well as on the other. The colonies were repeatedly alarmed by the danger of losing their charters, which were at last wrested from them; and several of the governors appointed by the crown occasioned great uneasiness by their oppressive measures.

2. A number of Englishmen, after having visited the colonies, and become, from different reasons, hostile to them, on their return to Great Britain, prejudiced the king and council against them. Of these, no one so much distinguished himself as *Edward Randolph*, who was sent over to America by Charles II., in 1676, and who, according to his own account, crossed the Atlantic 16 times in nine years, chiefly for the purpose of destroying the liberties of New England. This purpose he finally accomplished, and a writ was issued against the several charters in 1683.

3. *Sir Edmund Andros*, who had been for some time Governor of New York, was appointed by James II. governor also of New England. He arrived in Boston, in 1686, and summoned the colonies to surrender their charters. The charter of Massachusetts was given up, but that of Connecticut was concealed, by *Captain Wadsworth*, in the hollow of an oak in Hartford. Sir Edmund began with high professions of his good intentions; but he soon threw off the mask, governed in the most oppressive manner, and attempted to render himself as despotic in America as the king was disposed to be in England.

4. Happily, however, the reign of tyranny was of short duration. the arbitrary proceedings of James II. had rendered him so odious, that he was compelled to flee from his kingdom. The news of the *Revolution* of 1688, in England, and the accession of William and Mary to the throne, was received, in this country, with ecstasy, and was regarded as an event which brought deliverance from despotism to America, as well as to Great Britain. The inhabitants of Boston seized Sir Edmund,

together with Randolph and about 50 others, and put them in close confinement, where they were kept till the leaders were ordered back to England for trial. Connecticut and Rhode Island immediately resumed their charters, and reëstablished their former government.

5. The people of Massachusetts Bay petitioned the king for a restoration of their charter. This was, however, refused but a new charter, less favorable to liberty than the old one was granted. in 1692, by which the colonies of Massachusetts Bay and Plymouth were united into one, by the name of *Massachusetts;* to which were also annexed the provinces of Maine and Nova Scotia.

6. Under the old charter, the governor, together with all the magistrates and officers of state, was chosen annually by the general assembly, the members of which and the assistants of the governor were elected by the freemen of the colony. By the new charter, the appointment of the governor, lieutenant-governor, secretary, and the officers of the admiralty, was taken from the colonists, and was vested in the crown. The right of choosing representatives was the only privilege which was allowed to the people. In order to render the change more acceptable, the king appointed (1692) *Sir William Phips,* a native of Maine, the first governor under the charter.

7. Scarcely had the colonies emerged from one scene of trouble before they were involved in another. The Revolution in England restored, in a great measure, their liberties; but it soon subjected them to the evils of war with the French and the Indians. The war, during the reign of *William and Mary*, lasted from 1690 to the peace of Ryswick, in 1697; that during the reign of *Queen Anne*, from 1702 to the peace of *Utrecht*, in 1713.

8. During the 25 years preceding the peace of Utrecht, he country had enjoyed only four or five years of exemption from war. For several years, not less than a fifth part of the inhabitants, able to bear arms, were in actual service, and sometimes one half of the militia. Those who were not in service were obliged to guard their fields and families at home, and were subject to constant alarms. The resources of the country were greatly diminished; the aspect of affairs gloomy; many fields untilled extensive tracts desolated; the growth of the colonies exceedingly checked; their frontiers laid waste several towns burnt; and the greatest barbarities perpetrated.

9. It has been computed that, during these wars in the colonies of New England and New York, as many as 8,000 young men, the flower of the country, fell by the sword of the enemy

or by diseases contracted in the public service. Most of the families were in mourning for the loss of friends, who were either killed or led into a miserable captivity.

10. After the peace of Utrecht, the colonies enjoyed, for some years, a state of comparative tranquillity. But, in 1744, another war broke out between Great Britain and France, of which the effects were felt in America, and which was here rendered memorable, chiefly by the capture of *Louisburg*, on the island of Cape Breton, by troops from New England, under the command of *General Sir William Pepperell.* Louisburg had been fortified by the French at a vast expense, and was a place of such immense strength, as to be called the *Dunkirk* or *Gibraltar* of America; and the reduction of it was deemed an object of the highest importance to New England.

11. The troops under the command of General Pepperell, amounting to 4,070, the greater part from Massachusetts, arrived at Canso, on the 4th of April, 1745, and, in three weeks after, were joined by *Commodore Warren*, with four ships from England. The siege was soon after commenced, and continued till the 16th of June, when Louisburg, together with the island of Cape Breton, was surrendered by the French commander.

12. The news of this brilliant achievement occasioned great exultation in the colonies, and encouraged them to attempt the conquest of all the French possessions in North America. It also roused the government of France to seek revenge; and, in 1746, an armament, under the *Duke d'Anville*, was sent to America, consisting of 11 ships of the line, and 30 smaller vessels of war, besides transports, with upwards of 3,000 regular troops, and 40,000 stands of arms for the use of the Canadians and Indians. The object of this armament, which was the most formidable that had ever been sent to North America was to recover Louisburg, and to distress, if not to conquer, New England.

13 The first intelligence of the sailing of this fleet filled the colonists with consternation; but they were delivered from their fears in a most extraordinary and providential manner. The fleet had a long and disastrous passage, and sustained so great damages by storms, and losses by shipwrecks, that, on its arrival, the force was reduced more than one half. A mortal sickness prevailed among the troops, which carried off a great part of them; and the two principal commanders died suddenly, one or both of them by suicide, in a fit of despair.

14. The remaining ships returned singly to France, without having accomplished a single object of the expedition; and the whole design against the colonies was frustrated without the

intervention of human aid. — By the peace of *Aix-la-Chapelle* in 1748, Louisburg was given up to France, to the no small mortification of the colonies.

15. The French, having been the first discoverers of the river Mississippi, claimed the country watered by it and its tributaries; and, in the succeeding period of peace, they made great exertions to connect their colonies of Canada and Louisiana, by extending the line of military posts from Lake Ontario to the Ohio, and down that river and the Mississippi to New Orleans.

16. A company of persons belonging to England and Virginia, associated by the name of the *Ohio Company*, obtained from the king a grant of 600,000 acres of land, on and near the Ohio, for the purpose of carrying on the fur trade with the Indians, and settling the country; and they established some trading-houses on the river. But, as the French claimed an exclusive right to this country and its trade, they seized some of the traders, and carried them prisoners to Canada.

17. The company complained loudly of these aggressions on a territory which had been ceded to it as a part of Virginia; and *Robert Dinwiddie*, the governor, having laid the subject before the assembly of that colony, it was determined that it should be demanded, in the name of the king, that the French should desist from designs which were deemed a violation of existing treaties. *George Washington*, then in his 22d year was, in 1753, sent on this service to *M. de St. Pierre*, the French commandant on the Ohio, who stated to Washington, that he had acted according to his orders.

18. The British government, being informed of the designs of the French, directed the Americans to oppose them by force of arms. A regiment was soon formed, and put under the command of Washington, who was appointed colonel. Troops were raised throughout the colonies; naval and land forces were sent from England; and expeditions were, in 1755, sent against *Nova Scotia*, *Crown Point*, and *Niagara.*

19. Another expedition against *Fort du Quesne* [now Pittsburg] was commanded by *General Braddock*, who had two English regiments, and a body of colonial troops under Colonel Washington, the whole amounting to 1,200. Braddock was an officer of reputation, but neither he nor his English soldiers knew anything of savage warfare; and, being attacked by a party of French and Indians in ambush, he was entirely defeated, and himself slain. Of 86 officers, 63 were killed and wounded, and about half of the privates. *Washington* who had two horses shot under him, and four balls shot through his coat, led off the remainder of the troops, remained unhurt, and acquired a high reputation for his good management.

20. The expedition against *Crown Point* was commanded by *General Johnson*, who was met by the French army, under the command of *Dieskau*, on the banks of *Lake George.* A battle ensued, in which Dieskau was repulsed, with the loss of 700 or 800 men, and himself mortally wounded; but no attempt was made upon Crown Point. The expedition against *Niagara* and *Fort Frontenac*, under the command of *Governor Shirley* of Massachusetts, was delayed till it became too late in the season to effect anything; and the campaign closed without any one of the objects of the three expeditions having been attained.

21. The war, which had been carried on two years without any formal proclamation, was at length declared in 1756. The *Marquis de Montcalm* succeeded Dieskau; and the chief command of the English troops was first given to the *Earl of Loudon*, and afterwards to *General Abercrombie.* Montcalm was an able commander, but the British generals were weak and inefficient; and the campaigns of 1756 and 1757 brought reproach both upon them and the British government, and occasioned chagrin and disappointment in the colonies. But a change having taken place (1757) in the English ministry, and *William Pitt* (afterwards *Lord Chatham*) being placed at the head of the administration, everything immediately assumed a new aspect.

22. This great man, who was popular in America, addressed a circular letter to the colonial governors, assuring them that an effectual force should be sent from England, and calling upon them to raise as large bodies of men as the population would allow. The number of men brought into the service was 50,000, of which 20,000 were raised in America. Three expeditions were resolved on for the year 1758; the first against *Louisburg*, the second against *Ticonderoga*, and the third against *Fort du Quesne.*

23. In the expedition against Louisburg, the land forces amounting to 14,000, were led by *General Amherst*, next to whom in command was *General Wolfe;* and a large naval armament was commanded by *Admiral Boscawen.* After a considerable resistance, the fortress was surrendered, with the garrison, consisting of nearly 6,000 men, and a great quantity of military stores. This was the severest blow the French had received since the commencement of the war.

24. The attack on *Ticonderoga* was conducted by *General Abercrombie*, the commander-in-chief; but, owing to his injudicious management, he was repulsed with the loss of about 2,000 men. A detachment of 3,000 men, under *Colonel Bradstreet* took and destroyed *Fort Frontenac.* The expedition

against *Fort du Quesne* was conducted by *General Forbes*, who took possession of the post, and changed its name to *Pittsburg* After the disaster at Ticonderoga, *Abercrombie* fell into contempt, and the chief command was given to *General Amherst.*

25. The campaign of 1759 had for its object the entire conquest of *Canada.* The British army was divided into three parts: the first division, under *General Wolfe*, was to make an attempt on *Quebec;* the second, under *General Amherst*, was to attack *Ticonderoga* and *Crown Point;* and the third, under *General Prideaux*, was to be directed against the stronghold of *Niagara.*

26. On the approach of Amherst, Ticonderoga and Crown Point were evacuated. Niagara was besieged, and, after a severe action, it fell into the hands of the English; but, four days before the conquest, *General Prideaux* was killed.

27. By the taking of these forts, great advantages were gained; but a far more important and arduous enterprise was intrusted to the heroic *General Wolfe.* This was the reduction of *Quebec*, a place of immense strength, both by nature and art, and protected by about 10,000 men, under that able and hitherto successful general, *Montcalm.* But the difficulties which the English general had to surmount served only to inflame his ardent mind, and his military enthusiasm. Having landed his army, consisting of 8,000 men, on the island of Orleans, below Quebec, he made some unsuccessful attempts to reduce the city.

28. He then conceived the bold design of scaling, during the night, a steep precipice on the north bank of the river, and in this way to reach the *Heights or Plains of Abraham* behind the city, where it was least defensible. This he effected before Montcalm was aware of his design, and the whole army was arrayed on the plains before sunrise. A hot battle followed, in which the French were entirely defeated, with the loss of 1,500 men, and their four principal commanders: the English lost 500, together with their two first officers. The two great rivals, *Wolfe* and *Montcalm*, were both mortally wounded before the battle was terminated.

29. *Wolfe*, having received a fatal wound, was carried to the rear; where, at his request, he was raised up, that he might take a view of the engagement. Faint with the loss of blood and his eyes dimmed by the approach of death, he was roused at the words, "They fly, they fly!" "Who fly?" he exclaimed. He was told, "The enemy!" "Then," said the hero, "I die contented"; and, having said this, he expired in the moment of victory. — The same military enthusiasm animated *Montcalm* Being told that he could not continue more

than a few hours, he said, "It is so much the better; I shall not then live to see the surrender of Quebec."

30. Five days after this battle, the city of *Quebec* surrendered to the English army and fleet; and, in the following year (1760), all *Canada* submitted. By the *peace of Paris*, in 1763, the French northern possessions in America — *Canada*, *Nova Scotia*, and the island of *Cape Breton* — were confirmed to Britain. The success of this war, joyful as it was to England, was still more so to the Colonies, who now expected a release from the heavy calamities which they had long suffered from hostilities with the French and Indians.

SECTION III.

Disputes between Great Britain and the Colonies; Commencement of Hostilities; Battles of Lexington and Bunker Hill; Declaration of Independence. — From A. D. 1763 *to* 1776.

1. The colonists, from the time of the first settlement of the country, had been ardently attached to liberty, and extremely jealous of any invasion of their rights. The emigrants from England to America had been induced to leave their native land principally by the idea that they might escape from oppression and arbitrary power, and might enjoy freedom, both civil and religious. They cherished, however, a strong attachment to the parent country as the land of their forefathers, always acknowledged themselves subjects of the crown of Great Britain, and were loyal and faithful subjects.

2. Notwithstanding their various embarrassments, the long and distressing wars with the Indians and French, and the severe restrictions which were imposed by Great Britain upon their trade, and which were borne, in some instances, with extreme impatience, — yet, amidst these difficulties, the Colonies made rapid progress in wealth and population, and in all the arts of civil life; and, at the peace of 1763, they had risen to a high state of prosperity. They abounded in spirited and active individuals of all denominations.

3. After the conquest of Canada had freed them from the distresses occasioned by war with the French and savages, and given them a short interval of repose, troubles assailed them from a new and unexpected quarter. The mother country began speedily to assert her sovereignty over them, and to interfere in their civil concerns in a manner which excited the most serious alarm.

4. The war, which Great Britain had carried on in defence of her American possessions, had made a vast addition to her national debt and greatly increased the burdens of her subjects; and a plan of raising a revenue, by taxing the Colonies, was formed by parliament, under pretext that the mother country might obtain indemnification for the expenses of the war.

5. But it was maintained, on the other hand, by the Colonies, that, if the war had been waged by Great Britain on their account, it was because they were useful to her; that, by the advantages which she derived from the monopoly of their commerce, she was interested in their defence; that, by the happy termination of the war, they derived no benefit which was not a source of ultimate profit to the mother country; and that their own exertions had been greater in proportion to their ability than hers. They also urged their claim to all the rights of English subjects, and maintained that, of these rights, none was more indisputable than that no subject could be deprived of his property but by his own consent, expressed in person or by his representatives.

6. In the beginning of the year 1764, parliament passed an act by which duties were laid on goods imported from such West India islands as did not belong to Great Britain; and *Mr. Grenville*, the prime minister, proposed a resolution, "that it would be proper to charge certain stamp duties on the Colonies," but postponed the consideration of that subject to a future session. These proceedings occasioned great uneasiness and alarm, and were remonstrated against by the Colonies.

7. The system, however, was persisted in by parliament, and, early in the next year, the *Stamp Act* was passed (1765), laying a duty on all paper used for instruments of writing, as deeds, notes, &c., and declaring writings on unstamped materials to be null and void. The news of this measure caused a great sensation throughout the country. The assembly of *Virginia*, being in session when the information arrived, first declared its opposition to the act by a number of spirited resolutions, which were brought forward by *Patrick Henry;* and the assembly of *Massachusetts*, before what had been done in Virginia was known, besides passing resolutions opposed to the claims of the British parliament, took measures to secure the benefit of united counsels in the common cause, and proposed a *General Congress*, from the several Colonies, to be held at New York. In all the Colonies, a determined spirit of resistance was soon manifested.

8. When the news of the stamp act arrived at Boston, the bells were muffled, and rung a funeral peal. The crown officers were insulted; their houses broken open or demolished

and, among other outrages, the populace destroyed a valuable collection of original papers belonging to the governor, *Thomas Hutchinson*, and relating to the history of America. A similar spirit was manifested in the other Colonies; and, in New York, the act was hawked about the streets with a Death's head affixed to it, and styled "The Folly of England and the Ruin of America." The merchants also associated, and agreed to a resolution not to import any more goods from Great Britain until the act should be repealed.

9. A *Colonial Congress*, consisting of 28 delegates, appointed by the assemblies of nine of the Colonies, assembled on the 7th of October, in 1765, at *New York*, and published a declaration of their rights and their grievances, insisting particularly on the right of exclusively taxing themselves, and complaining loudly of the stamp act. The merchants of Boston, New York, and Philadelphia, entered into an agreement not to import or sell any British goods so long as the offensive measure should be continued. So general was the opposition, that the stamp officers, in all the Colonies, were compelled to resign; and the act was never executed. A change took place in the British cabinet, and through the exertions of *Mr. Pitt*, *Lord Camden*, and others, the stamp act was repealed in March, 1766; but the repeal was preceded by a declaration of parliament, "that they had, and of right ought to have, power to bind the Colonies in all cases whatsoever."

10. The favorite project of the British ministry, of taxing America, was still persisted in; and in June, 1767, an act was passed by parliament, imposing a duty on *tea*, *paper*, *glass* and *painters' colors*. To render the act effectual, a custom-house was established in Boston, with a board of commissioners for the Colonies; and in September, 1768, two British regiments arrived in the town. Another most arbitrary measure of parliament, which gave great offence, was a proposition that offenders in Massachusetts should be sent to England for trial.

11. The feelings of the Americans were now greatly exasperated. To a free and high-spirited people, the presence of an insolent soldiery, sent with a design to intimidate them, could not but be extremely odious and provoking. The causes of irritation were numerous; quarrels daily occurred between the soldiers and the populace; and on the 5th of March, 1770, an affray took place between a detachment of troops under *Captain Preston*, and some of the inhabitants of Boston, in which three of the latter were killed, and five dangerously wounded. The funeral of the deceased was conducted with great pomp and ceremony, expressive of the public grief and indignation. After the feelings of the people had, in some

measure, subsided, Captain Preston and his soldiers were brought to trial before a court of the province, and a jury of the neighborhood. They had for their counsel *John Adams* and *Josiah Quincy*, two leaders of the popular party, and were all acquitted, except two, who were convicted of manslaughter

12. During this year (1770), *Lord North* was appointed prime minister of England, and all the duties were repealed except the one of *three pence* per pound on *tea.* By this the British ministry intended to establish their *right* to raise a revenue in the Colonies; but the Americans were determined to resist the principle of taxation in every shape. — The year of 1771, in relation to the matters in controversy, was not distinguished by any important event.

13. In July, 1772, the representatives of Massachusetts passed resolutions, expressing great dissatisfaction with the new regulation of the British government, by which the governor was to have his support from the crown. This measure they declared to be "an infraction of their charter." But the governor defended the measure. The inhabitants of Boston held a town meeting in November, in relation to this subject. A committee of correspondence was appointed; and a report, setting forth the rights and the grievances of the colonists, was printed and circulated through the towns of the province. The towns generally responded to the report, declaring their opinion that their charter had, in many respects, been grossly violated.

14. In 1773, the inhabitants of *New York* and *Philadelphia* returned to England the tea ships which were sent to those cities; but the people of Boston having failed in their attempts to carry into effect the same measure, about twenty persons, disguised like Indians, went on board the vessels, and threw the tea, consisting of 342 chests, into the harbor.

15. — (1774.) — In consequence of these measures, parliament passed further hostile acts; and *Boston*, being regarded as the chief seat of rebellion, was selected as an object of vengeance. By one of the acts, called the "*Boston Port Bill,*" all intercourse by water with that town was prohibited; the government and public officers were removed to Salem; and power was given to the governor to send persons charged with high treason to be tried in Great Britain. A great part of the inhabitants of Boston were suddenly deprived of the means of subsistence; but their sufferings were relieved by contributions forwarded from different parts. All these vindictive measures only served more firmly to unite the Americans in their resistance to the mother country.

16. In May, *General Gage*, the commander-in-chief of the British forces in North America, arrived in Boston, commis

sioned as Governor of Massachusetts, in place of Hutchinson and shortly after, two more regiments landed with artillery and military stores, — events which indicated the determination of the British government to reduce the Colonies to submission by force of arms.

17. When the Americans saw, by these proceedings, that a reconciliation was no longer to be expected, and that their rights were to be defended by an appeal to force, they took measures to prepare themselves for the contest. A committee of correspondence was formed by distinguished men in Massachusetts, who framed an agreement, called a *Solemn League and Covenant*, by which they determined to suspend all intercourse with Great Britain, until their rights should be restored.

18. The general court of Massachusetts resolved that a congress of the Colonies was necessary: they also enrolled a body of men to be prepared for marching at a minute's notice, and therefore called *minute-men;* appointed five general officers to command them; formed a committee of safety; and took measures to collect military stores at Concord and Worcester.

19. On the 4th of September, deputies from eleven of the Colonies met at Philadelphia, and the next day, having formed themselves into a congress, chose *Peyton Randolph*, of Virginia, president, and *Charles Thompson*, secretary. This body, generally known by the name of the *First Continental Congress*, was composed of 55 members, most of whom were men of distinguished character and talents. They published a declaration of the rights of the Colonies; agreed to suspend all commercial intercourse with Great Britain; and drew up an address to the king, another to the people of Great Britain, and a third to the Colonies. These able state papers were highly applauded by Lord Chatham in the British parliament.

20. The disparity between the two contending parties was immense. Great Britain was the first maritime power in the world, and possessed great wealth, vast resources, well-disciplined armies, and experienced and able military and naval commanders. The Colonies possessed none of these advantages, and had no general government to control the contending interests of the different parts. They were almost entirely destitute of experienced officers, of disciplined troops, of arms and munitions of war, of armed ships, and of revenue. Their want of these essential articles, particularly of regular and disciplined troops, of good arms and ammunition, and more especially of *money*, embarrassed all their operations during the continuance of the war. Their resolution to engage in the unequal contest was regarded, in England, with the utmost con

tempt; and it was confidently expected, by the British ministry that their efforts would be speedily and easily crushed.

21. — (1775.) — When the proceedings of the American congress were laid before parliament, a joint address of both Houses was presented to the king, declaring that a rebellion actually existed in Massachusetts, and beseeching his majesty to suppress it. In the winter and spring of 1775, the army in Boston was increased to 10,000, which number was deemed sufficient to reduce the rebellious Colonies to submission.

22 Soon after, a bill was brought forward in parliament by *Lord North*, which he termed a *conciliatory proposition*, the purport of which was, that when any colony should make provision for contributing its proportion to the common defence, and make such provision also for the support of its civil government as should be approved by his majesty and the parliament, the British government would abstain from taxing such colony, and confine itself to commercial regulations. The design of this proposition was to unite Great Britain, and divide America; but it was universally rejected by the Colonies, and by the congress assembled at Philadelphia. It was derided also by the friends of America in parliament as nugatory, since it was the *right*, not the mode, of taxation which the Colonies disputed.

23. In February, *General Gage* sent a party of troops to *Salem*, to seize some cannon which had been lodged there; but finding, on their arrival, that the cannon had been removed, they marched back unmolested. In April, he sent another body of troops, under *Colonel Smith* and *Major Pitcairn*, to seize some military stores at *Concord.* The march, though in the night, was discovered; and early in the morning of the 19th of the month, as they passed through *Lexington*, about 70 men belonging to the minute company of that town, were found on the green, or common, under arms. Major Pitcairn, riding up to them, called out, "Disperse, disperse, you rebels!" Not being obeyed, he discharged his pistol, and ordered his troops to fire Eight Americans were killed, and several wounded. Thus began the sanguinary contest which issued in the establishment of American Independence.

24. Having dispersed the militia at Lexington, the British troops proceeded to Concord, and destroyed some military stores collected in that town. On their return, the passage of a bridge over Concord River was disputed; a skirmish ensued, which was attended with some loss on both sides. The people of the neighborhood were soon in arms, and attacked the retreating troops in all directions; some firing behind stone walls and trees, and others pressing upon their rear, till they had re

turned as far as Lexington, where they were joined by a reinforcement, which secured their retreat to Boston, after a loss of 65 killed and 180 wounded. Of the Americans, 50 were killed and 34 wounded.

25. The affair at Lexington was a signal for war. The forts, magazines, and arsenals, throughout the Colonies, were instantly secured for the use of the Americans. Regular forces were raised; an army of about 20,000 men was collected in the vicinity of Boston, and soon increased by a considerable body of troops from Connecticut, under *Colonel* (afterwards General) *Putnam*. By these forces the British troops were closely blocked up in the peninsula of Boston.

26. An expedition, commanded by *Colonel Ethan Allen* and *Colonel Benedict Arnold*, was sent to *Ticonderoga;* and another commanded by *Colonel Warner*, to *Crown Point;* and both those important fortresses were soon secured.

27. The provincial congress of Massachusetts, which was in session at the time of the affair at Lexington, despatched an account of the transaction to England, with depositions to prove that the British troops were the aggressors. They declared their loyalty to the crown, but protested that they would not submit to the tyranny of the British ministry. "Appealing to Heaven for the justice of our cause," they added, "we determine to die or be free."

28. The second Continental or General Congress met at Philadelphia, in May, and the appellation of the *United Colonies* was assumed. The congress recommended the observance of a day of humiliation, to implore the blessings of Heaven on their sovereign, the King of Great Britain, and the interposition of Divine aid to remove their grievances, and restore harmony between the parent state and the Colonies, on constitutional terms.

29. Towards the end of May, considerable reinforcements of British troops arrived at Boston, together with *Generals Howe*, *Burgoyne*, and *Clinton*, officers who had acquired a high reputation in the preceding war between England and France. Martial law was proclaimed; but a show of reconciliation was still held out by the offer of *General Gage*, in the king's name, of pardon to all such as should return to their allegiance, with the exception of two of the most active patriots in Massachusetts, *John Hancock* and *Samuel Adams*, the former of whom was chosen president of the general congress then in session.

30. It was determined by the Americans to annoy, and, if possible, to dislodge, the British forces in Boston; and, for this purpose, a detachment of 1000 men, under the command of

Colonel Prescott, was ordered, on the 16th of June, to throw up a breast-work on *Bunker Hill*, in Charlestown. They prosecuted the design so silently and expeditiously, that they had nearly completed the redoubt by the return of daylight, without being discovered. Soon after the dawn, the British began to cannonade the works from their ships; and, in the morning, the Americans received a reinforcement of 500 men.

31. About noon (*17th of June*), *General Howe*, at the head of 3,000 men, advanced to make an attack upon the works. The fire of the Americans was dreadful, insomuch that the whole British line recoiled, and was thrown into great disorder; but, from the failure of ammunition, the Americans were obliged to retreat. The loss of the English amounted to 1,054 in killed and wounded; that of the Americans, to 453; and among their killed was the lamented *Major-General Warren*, who hastened to the field of battle as a volunteer. While the British troops were advancing, orders were given to set fire to *Charlestown;* and the whole town, consisting of about 400 houses, was laid in ashes. This barbarous act, which was of no advantage to the enemy, served still further to exasperate the Americans.

32. Congress resolved on measures of defence; drew up a second petition to the king, and addresses to the people of Great Britain and of Canada, setting forth their reasons for taking up arms; and organized a continental army. It was a point of immense importance to select a suitable man for commander-in-chief. Fortunately, their choice, by a unanimous vote, fell upon *George Washington*, a member of their body from Virginia, who, in the late French war, had distinguished himself by his courage and talents. He received from nature a mind of extraordinary capacity, and was endowed with an uncommon degree of perseverance, prudence, and bravery; while the soundness of his judgment, the elevation of his character, and the purity of his motives, were calculated to inspire the highest confidence. He entered immediately upon the duties of his office; and, on the 2d of July, he arrived at *Cambridge*, where he established his head-quarters.

33. Congress, after choosing the commander-in-chief, appointed four major-generals and eight brigadiers for the continental army. The major-generals were *Artemas Ward*, *Charles Lee*, *Philip Schuyler*, and *Israel Putnam;* the brigadier-generals, *Seth Pomroy*, *Richard Montgomery*, *David Wooster*, *William Heath*, *Joseph Spencer*, *John Thomas*, *John Sullivan*, and *Nathaniel Greene*. *Horatio Gates* was appointed adjutant general, with the rank of brigadier.

34 In pursuance of a plan of guarding the frontiers by

taking Canada, an expedition was sent against that province under the command of *Generals Schuyler* and *Montgomery* but the former returning, to hold a treaty with the Indians, was prevented by sickness from again joining the army, and the chief command devolved upon the latter. Having taken *Fort Chamblee* and *St. John's*, he advanced to *Montreal*, which surrendered without resistance; thence he proceeded rapidly to *Quebec*.

35. *Colonel Arnold*, with about 1,000 men, had been sent from Cambridge to penetrate to that city, by way of the Kennebec and the wilderness. After a march, in which he and his troops were exposed to almost incredible sufferings, he joined Montgomery before Quebec, in November. They made a desperate attempt to carry the city by assault, in which, after displaying the highest intrepidity, they were repulsed, with a loss of upwards of 400 killed and wounded; and *General Montgomery* was slain. Early in the next season, the Americans entirely evacuated Canada.

36. While hostilities were thus carried on in the north, the inhabitants of *Virginia*, who had, from the commencement of the controversy, been in the foremost rank of opposition, were engaged in a contest with the royal governor, *Lord Dunmore*, whose intemperate measures advanced the cause which he attempted to overthrow. In the end, he was forced to take refuge with his family on board a man-of-war. For some time, he carried on a predatory warfare against the Colonies, by landing detachments of troops from the ships; and, after having destroyed or taken the military stores of the Colonies at *Norfolk*, he caused that town, on the 1st of January, 1776, to be laid in ashes; but he was finally driven from the coast.

37. In like manner the royal governors of North and South Carolina were expelled by the people; and, before the end of the year 1775, all the old governments of the Colonies were dissolved. Many adherents to Great Britain (styled *Tories*), however, remained in the country; and in some of the Colonies they were numerous and powerful: part of them, being men of principle, remained quiet; others were active in their hostility, and contributed to weaken the opposition to the British arms. — In October, *General Gage* embarked for England, and the chief command of the British forces devolved upon *General Sir William Howe*.

38. — (1776.) — The American army, investing Boston, amounted to about 15,000 men; but it was unaccustomed to discipline, and, in a great measure, destitute of good arms, ammunition, clothing, and experienced officers; and for want of gunpowder, and for other reasons, was rendered inactive during

the summer and autumn of 1775. In the latter part of the winter, General Washington resolved to expel the British from Boston: in order to divert their attention, a severe cannonade was commenced upon them by the Americans, on the 2d of March; and, on the night of the 4th, a battery was erected, with surprising despatch, on *Dorchester Heights*, a position from which the American troops might greatly annoy the ships in the harbor and the soldiers in the town.

39. General Howe prepared to attack the works, but a storm prevented him till they were rendered so strong that it was deemed inexpedient. The only alternative now was to evacuate the town; which having been done, General Washington on the 17th of March, entered triumphantly into Boston, where he was joyfully received, as a deliverer, by the oppressed inhabitants.

40. On the 28th of June, an attack was made by Sir Peter Parker, with a naval force, on the fort on Sullivan's Island, with a design to reduce Charleston, in South Carolina. The fire was returned with great effect from the fort, which was commanded by *Colonel Moultrie*, and the British were compelled to retreat, with much damage to their ships, and with a loss of upwards of 200 men in killed and wounded. The fort, in compliment to the commander, was, from that time, called Fort Moultrie.

41. The news of the battle of Bunker Hill excited astonishment in England. The partisans of the ministry had been accustomed to speak of the American troops in terms of the utmost contempt; but it now appeared that they were engaged in a sanguinary contest of doubtful issue; and *Lord Chatham*, *Burke*, and *Fox*, endeavored, but without success, to produce a change in the measures of government. The ministry determined to employ a powerful force to reduce the Colonies, and obtained an act of parliament, authorizing them to take into pay 16,000 mercenaries, the troops of the *Landgrave of Hesse* and the *Duke of Brunswick*. All trade and intercourse with the Colonies were prohibited; and their property on the high seas was declared to be forfeited to those who should capture it. The whole force, now destined against America amounted to about 50,000 men.

42. The controversy had hitherto been, not for independence, but for constitutional liberty. But the hostile measures of the British government produced a strong sensation in the Colonies, and they soon began to think seriously of dissolving entirely their allegiance to the mother country. A great and sudden change now took place in the public mind, which was, in part, brought about by a series of papers written by Thomas Paine and published under the signature of *Common Sense*, the

design of which was to prove the expediency and necessity of a declaration of independence. On the 7th of June, a motion was made, in congress, by *Richard Henry Lee*, of Virginia, for declaring the Colonies *free and independent.* A committee, consisting of *Jefferson*, *Adams*, *Franklin*, *Sherman*, and *Livingston*, was appointed to prepare a Declaration of Independence and, after a full discussion, the question was carried, by a vote nearly unanimous, on the memorable *4th of July*, 1776.

43. The Declaration thus concludes: "We, therefore, the representatives of the *United States of America*, in general congress assembled, appealing to the Supreme Judge of the world for the rectitude of our intentions, do, in the name and by the authority of the good people of these Colonies, solemnly publish and declare, that these United Colonies are, and of right ought to be, *Free and Independent States;* that they are absolved from all allegiance to the British crown, and that all political connection between them and the state of Great Britain is, and ought to be, totally dissolved; and that, as free and independent states, they have full power to levy war, conclude peace, contract alliances, establish commerce, and to do all other acts and things which independent states ought to do. And for the support of this declaration, with a firm reliance on the protection of Divine Providence, we mutually pledge to each other our lives, our fortunes, and our sacred honor."

SECTION IV.

Revolutionary War continued; — Battles of Brooklyn, White Plains, Trenton, Princeton, Bennington, Brandywine, Germantown, Stillwater; Surrender at Saratoga; Battles of Monmouth, Rhode Island, Camden, Cow-Pens, Guilford, Eutaw Springs; Surrender at Yorktown; — Independence acknowledged. — From A. D. 1776 *to* 1783.

1 Before the evacuation of Boston by Sir William Howe, it had occurred to General Washington, that the occupation of the important and central position of the city of New York would be a favorite object with the British; and he had detached *General Lee*, from Cambridge, to put Long Island and New York in a posture of defence. Soon after the evacuation he followed with the most of his army.

2. Sir William Howe, after having evacuated Boston, sailed with his army to Halifax, where he waited about two months, and then directed his course towards New York, and arrived

in June, off Sandy Hook. He was soon after joined by his brother, *Admiral Lord Howe*, with a reinforcement from England. General Clinton arrived about the same time, with troops brought back from the south. The British troops, which were soon collected, amounted to upwards of 24,000, by some stated as high as 30,000. To meet this formidable army, Washington had only between 11,000 and 12,000 men, many of them militia, unaccustomed to military duty.

3. Lord Howe, being commissioned by the king to offer terms of peace before military operations were commenced, sent a circular letter on shore, directed to the royal governors of the Colonies. This paper came to the hands of General Washington, who forwarded it to the president of congress. The terms, which amounted to nothing more than a promise of pardon and favor to those who should return to their allegiance, and assist in restoring public tranquillity, were not listened to. The Americans felt, that, having taken up arms to defend their indisputable rights, they were conscious of no guilt, and wanted no pardon. Lord Howe despatched a letter to General Washington, directed to *George Washington, Esq.;* and another was sent by General Howe, directed to *George Washington, &c. &c. &c.;* but Washington declined to receive them, or any writing, unless directed to him in his proper character.

4. Both sides prepared seriously for action. On the 27th of August, an engagement took place between *Brooklyn* and *Flatbush.* The Americans, under the command of *Generals Putnam* and *Sullivan*, being surrounded, and exposed to the fire of the Hessians in front, and of the British troops in the rear, were totally defeated, with a loss, according to their own statement, of upwards of 1,000, and according to that of the British, of 3,000. Three American generals, *Sullivan*, *Lord Stirling*, and *Woodhull*, fell into the hands of the enemy, whose loss was only about 300 or 400. During the heat of the engagement, General Washington crossed over from New York to Brooklyn, and made an admirable retreat, on the night of the 29th. It was effected under the cover of a thick fog, with such silence, order, and secrecy, that the British army, which was encamped only a quarter of a mile distant, did not discover it till it was too late to annoy the Americans.

5. Washington, with a part of his army, retired to *White Plains*, where, on the 28th of October, an engagement took place, in which several hundred fell. General Howe soon after reduced *Fort Washington*, on the Hudson, containing a garrison of upwards of 2,800 men, under *Colonel Magaw.* This was the severest blow that the American arms had yet sustained. The British were now in possession of the city of New York Long Island, and Staten Island.

6. Washington, having crossed the Hudson, retreated through New Jersey, by Newark, New Brunswick, Princeton, and Trenton, thence he crossed over to the Pennsylvania side of the Delaware, being closely pursued by the British army, under *Lord Cornwallis*, who arrived at the river just after the American army had effected the passage. The British troops, in the full career of success, were ordered into winter cantonments.

7. The aspect of American affairs was now exceedingly gloomy. The army was greatly reduced by the loss of men in killed, wounded, and taken; and by the departure of those whose enlistments had expired. To add to the disasters, *General Charles Lee* had been surprised and taken prisoner at Baskenridge; and the British had seized upon Rhode Island. The whole number of troops under Washington, on the west side of the Delaware, amounted to only about 3,000, many of whom were without shoes or comfortable clothing. In this darkest hour during the war, General Howe issued a proclamation, offering pardon to all who would submit to royal authority; and many persons abandoned the American cause and joined the British.

8. Washington, aware of the importance of striking some successful blow, in order to animate the expiring hopes of the country, on the night of the 25th of December, crossed the Delaware, fell on the enemy, at *Trenton*, by surprise, and took the whole body, consisting of about 1,000 Hessians, whose commander, *Colonel Rahl*, was slain. He then proceeded to *Princeton*, and on the 3d of January, 1777, defeated a party of British troops, who lost about 100 men; and forced about 300 to surrender, who had taken refuge in the College. In this action, *General Mercer*, of Virginia, was killed. These bold and decisive measures of Washington revived the drooping spirits of the Americans, and surprised and confounded the enemy.

9. During the gloomy period of the latter part of the year 1776, congress manifested the greatest firmness; they increased the power of Washington, investing him with supreme and unlimited command; took measures for raising an army for three years, or during the war; sent agents to Europe to solicit the friendship and aid of foreign powers; endeavoured to rouse the people by an impressive address; and, in 1777, formed Articles of Confederation between the Thirteen States.

10. — (1777.) In March, General Howe sent up the Hudson a detachment to destroy some stores at *Peekskill*; and in April, another detachment of 2,000 men, under *General Tryon*, proceeded to *Danbury*, in Connecticut, destroyed valuable stores collected there, and burnt the most of the town. During

their return, there took place, between the British and the Connecticut militia, some skirmishes, in one of which the American commander, *General Wooster*, was killed.

11. On the opening of the campaign in the spring, the principal American army was increased to but little more than 7,000 men. General Howe, after having attempted in vain to provoke Washington to an engagement, retired from New Jersey to Staten Island; afterwards embarked with 16,000 men on board his ships; entered the Chesapeake, and landed at the head of navigation on Elk river. It being obviously his object to occupy *Philadelphia*, Washington put his army in motion, in order, if possible, to prevent it. On the 11th of September a battle was fought on the *Brandywine*, in which the American forces, after a brave resistance, were obliged to yield to superior numbers and discipline, with the loss of about 1,000 men in killed, wounded, and taken. Among the wounded was the young *Marquis de Lafayette*, who had recently entered as a volunteer in the American service, and had been appointed a major-general. The loss of the British was about 500 men.

12. Immediately after this battle, General Howe took possession of *Philadelphia;* and the principal part of his army was stationed at Germantown, seven miles from the city. It now became necessary for him to take the forts on the Delaware, in order to open a communication with the Atlantic. This was effected after having cost the British a loss of three or four hundred men. While a detachment was absent to accomplish this purpose, Washington attacked the army at *Germantown*, on the 4th of October, but was repulsed, with a loss of about 1,200 men in killed, wounded, and prisoners; while the loss of the enemy was only about half as great. After these transactions, the British army went into winter-quarters in Philadelphia.

13. During these inauspicious operations in the Middle States important events were taking place in the north. Early in the spring, it was determined in England to invade the States through Canada; and, in June, a British army, amounting to 7,000 men, besides Canadians and Indians, commanded by *General Burgoyne*, passed up Lake Champlain, and laid siege to *Ticonderoga*, which was abandoned by the Americans under *General St. Clair*. General Burgoyne proceeded to *Skeensborough* [now *Whitehall*], and destroyed the American flotilla and stores; and from thence he led his army to Fort Edward on the Hudson.

14. While remaining here, he sent a detachment of 500 English troops and 100 Indians, under *Colonel Baum*, to destroy a collection of stores at *Bennington*, in Vermont. On

the 16th of August, *General Stark*, with about 800 Vermont and New Hampshire militia, killed and took prisoners the most of this detachment. The next day, a reinforcement of 500 Germans, under *Colonel Breyman*, arrived, and was also defeated by General Stark. The loss of the British in these two engagements was about 600. A few days before this battle, *General Herkimer* was defeated, on the Mohawk, by the British, under *Colonel St. Leger*, with considerable loss.

15. *General Burgoyne*, having collected his forces and stores, crossed the Hudson, and encamped at *Saratoga*. *General Gates*, who had recently taken the chief command of the American army in the northern department, having concentrated his troops, advanced towards the enemy, and on the 19th of September, an obstinate but indecisive engagement took place at *Stillwater*, in which the Americans lost between 300 and 400, and the British about 600. The British army was soon after confined in a narrow pass, having the Hudson on one side, and impassable woods on the other; a body of Americans in the rear, and an enemy of 13,000 men in front.

16. In this exigency, Burgoyne resolved to ascertain whether it were possible to dislodge the Americans, and sent a body of 1,500 men to reconnoitre the left wing, when a second severe engagement took place, in which the British were worsted, and *General Fraser* was killed; and the American generals, *Lincoln* and *Arnold*, were wounded. Burgoyne, after having made ineffectual attempts to retreat, finding his provisions nearly exhausted, his troops worn down with incessant toil, and his situation becoming every hour more critical, called a council of war, in which it was unanimously resolved to capitulate; and, on the 17th of October, the whole army, consisting of 5,752 men, exclusive of sick and wounded, surrendered at *Saratoga*, as prisoners of war, to General Gates.

17. The surrender of Burgoyne excited the liveliest joy among the Americans, and inspired them with confidence with regard to their ultimate success in establishing their independence. In 1776, congress had sent *Dr. Franklin*, *Silas Deane* and *Arthur Lee*, commissioners to France, to solicit assistance, but though it was evident that the French court secretly wished success to the Americans, yet they would give no open countenance to their agents, till the news of the surrender of Burgoyne. That event decided the negotiation; and in February, 1778, treaties of alliance, and of amity and commerce, were signed at Paris. The news of this alliance was received with great joy in America.

18. — (1778.) — The British ministry, after hearing of the fate of their northern army, began to speak of American

affairs with more moderation; and, on receiving intelligence of the alliance between France and the United States, their fears were increased. In February, Lord North laid before parliament bills for conciliating America; and commissioners were appointed, who arrived in June, bringing terms of accommodation, which, a few years before, might have effected the object. But the day of reconciliation was past; congress had now proceeded too far, and were too sanguine with regard to ultimate success, to listen to any terms short of an acknowledgment of independence.

19. At the opening of the campaign of 1778, *General Howe* went to England, and *General Sir Henry Clinton* succeeded him as commander-in-chief. It was now determined by the British to concentrate their forces in the city of *New York;* and with this view the royal army left Philadelphia in June, and crossed the Delaware. General Washington, penetrating their design, attempted to interrupt their progress. The two armies met on the 28th of June, near *Monmouth* court-house, in New Jersey, where a smart action took place, in which the Americans lost about 230, in killed and wounded, and the British about 400. This day was remarkable for excessive heat which occasioned great suffering and many deaths in both armies. The British troops retreated, after the battle, to New York, and remained inactive during the summer.

20. A French fleet of 12 ships of the line and 4 frigates under the command of *Count d'Estaing*, arrived at the entrance of the Delaware in July; and a plan was concerted to attack the British troops at *Newport*, but it proved unsuccessful. A short but obstinate engagement took place on *Rhode Island*, on the 29th of August, between the British under *General Pigot*, and the Americans under *General Sullivan*, in which each lost upwards of 200 men. The next day, the Americans retreated from the island. At the close of the season, the French fleet, without having accomplished anything of importance, sailed to the West Indies. — In the autumn, General Clinton sent an expedition to Georgia; and on the last of December, the British, after defeating the American force, took possession of *Savannah*.

21. — (1779.) — Near the close of the year 1778, *General Lincoln* was appointed by congress to take the command in the southern department; and, during the year 1779, the principal theatre of the war was changed from the north to the south. The operations, however, were not of any decisive consequence, though they gave rise to various expeditions, in which much valor and skill were displayed. The exertions of the Americans were enfeebled from the depreciation of their bills

of credit, and from their not deriving the benefit which they had expected from the French fleet, which was unsuccessful in all its enterprises.

22. Early in the season, *Sir George Collier* and *General Matthews* were sent from New York to Virginia, on a predatory expedition. They landed at *Portsmouth*, and destroyed the shipping and valuable stores in that vicinity, together with many houses. A similar expedition was afterwards sent against the maritime parts of Connecticut, under the command of *General Tryon*, who plundered *New Haven*, and burnt *Fairfield* and *Norwalk*.

23. The British troops having taken and fortified *Stony Point*, an eminence on the Hudson, an expedition, under the command of *General Wayne*, was sent, in July, to reduce it, which was conducted with great heroism, and the whole garrison surrendered. A similar expedition, under the command of *General Lovell*, was sent against a British post at *Penobscot*, but it was unsuccessful. *General Sullivan*, with a strong force, invaded the country of the *Six Nations of Indians*, who had been induced to take part with the British against the Americans, destroyed 40 of their villages, with all their corn and fruit-trees, and returned with little loss.

24. *General Lincoln* sent a detachment of 1,500 men to cross the Savannah, under the command of *General Ash*, who was surprised and defeated at *Briar Creek*, by *General Prevost*, with a loss of about 300 men, in killed and taken. This success emboldened General Prevost to make an attempt on Charleston, but it was unsuccessful. *Count d'Estaing* having arrived with his fleet from the West Indies, an attack was made on the British under the command of *General Prevost*, in *Savannah*, by a united force of French and Americans; but they were repulsed, with the loss of about 1,000 men, among whom was *Count Pulaski*, a Polish officer in the American service. The French fleet soon after departed from the American coast.

25.—(1780.)—In 1780, *South Carolina* was the principal theatre of the war. *Sir Henry Clinton* sailed from New York with a large force, and arrived at Savannah in January. Proceeding thence to *Charleston*, he laid siege to the city in April. and, having prepared to storm it, *General Lincoln* was, on the 17th of May, compelled to capitulate. The garrison, consisting of about 2,500 men, together with all the adult male inhabitants, were surrendered as prisoners of war. General Clinton leaving about 4,000 troops for the southern service, under the command of *Lord Cornwallis*, returned to New York. A proclamation was issued, inviting the Carolinians to the royal standard; several recruits were, in consequence, procured; but the great body of the people remained true to the cause of liberty and independence.

26. Charleston being now in the possession of the British, measures were taken to secure the obedience of the interior country. For this purpose, a considerable force was sent to *Camden*, under the command of *Lord Rawdon*. Several severe skirmishes took place between small parties, in one of which *Colonel Buford* was defeated by a body of British cavalry, under *Colonel Tarleton;* in others, the American *General Sumter* distinguished himself.

27. *General Gates*, who had been appointed to the chief command of the southern army, in place of General Lincoln, arrived at the American camp, in South Carolina, in the latter part of July, and troops were collected in order to oppose the progress of the British. Lord Cornwallis, hearing of these movements, repaired to *Camden*, to reinforce Lord Rawdon. On the 16th of August, a severe engagement took place between the two armies, in which the Americans were defeated, with the loss of 700 or 800 men, among whom was the *Baron de Kalb*, a Prussian in the American service, and the second officer in command. The British lost about half as many. The greater part of the American force consisted of militia, who fled at the first fire, and could not be rallied. General Gates, with the feeble remains of his army, retreated to Hillsborough, in North Carolina; and Lord Cornwallis, for some time after the battle of Camden, remained inactive.

28. In July, *M. de Ternay*, with a French fleet, consisting of seven ships of the line, besides frigates, and 6,000 land troops, commanded by *Count de Rochambeau*, arrived at Rhode Island. This gave new life to the American counsels and arms; but the fleet suddenly returned to France, and all hope of naval assistance vanished. The land forces, however, remained, and coöperated in the final reduction of the British army.

29. The most flagrant instance of treachery during the war occurred this year. This was the plot of *General Benedict Arnold* for delivering into the hands of the enemy the important fortress of *West Point*, on the Hudson. Arnold had distinguished himself at the siege of Quebec, and also at Saratoga, where he was severely wounded. He was afterwards appointed to a command in Philadelphia, where his oppressive conduct had subjected him to a trial by a court martial, by which he was sentenced to be reprimanded. By these proceedings he was highly exasperated, and determined on revenge. General Washington still valued him for his bravery and former services, and, at his request, not suspecting his in-

tentions, intrusted him with the command of West Point. He soon entered into a negotiation with General Clinton for the surrender of that post; but happily the plot was discovered in season to prevent the disastrous consequences which must have followed from its execution.

30. The unfortunate *Major Andre*, the British agent in this negotiation, being apprehended and convicted as a spy, his life was forfeited by the laws of war, and he was condemned and executed. The fate of this heroic and amiable young officer was deeply regretted by the Americans, as well as by the English. Arnold escaped to the enemy, and received, as a reward of his treason, an appointment to the office of brigadier-general in the British army.

31. — (1781.) — The operations of the war, during the campaign of 1781, were chiefly in the south, and were of great importance. In January, the traitor *Arnold*, with about 1,500 men, made a descent upon Virginia, and committed extensive depredations on the unprotected coast of that State.

32. In the autumn of 1780, *General Greene* was appointed to the chief command of the American southern army. The first action, after he assumed the command, was fought at the *Cow-Pens*, by the Americans under *Colonel Morgan*, against the English under *Colonel Tarleton*, who was defeated, with the loss of 300 killed, and 500 taken prisoners. The loss of the Americans, in killed and wounded, was only 72.

33. The two armies, under *Greene* and *Cornwallis*, met near *Guilford* court-house, in North Carolina, and, on the 15th of March, a battle was fought, in which the British lost upwards of 400 men, yet they remained masters of the field. The loss of the Americans, who were mostly militia, was about equal. After this battle, General Greene marched to *Camden* where *Lord Rawdon* was fortified with 900 men. The British commander sallied out and attacked him. The loss on each side was between 200 and 300 men; but the British had the advantage. — In September, *General Greene* obtained an important victory over the British, under *Colonel Stuart*, at the *Eutaw Springs*. The loss of the enemy in killed, wounded, and captured, amounted to about 1,000; that of the Americans to 550. This action nearly finished the war in South Carolina.

34. After the battle of Guilford, *Lord Cornwallis* proceeded towards *Virginia*, to join the British army under *General Phillips;* and, arriving at *Petersburg* in May, he took the command of the united forces. After some predatory warfare, he encamped with his army on York River, at *Yorktown* and *Gloucester Point*, where he fortified himself in the best manner he was able.

35. A plan of combined operations against the British had been previously concerted by *Generals Washington, Knox Rochambeau*, and other officers. The point of attack was not absolutely determined on; but, after Lord Cornwallis had collected a large army in Virginia, Washington resolved to concentrate his forces against him. At the same time, it was given out that New York was to be the point of attack, in order to induce the Eastern and Middle States to exert themselves in furnishing supplies, as well as to deceive Sir Henry Clinton, and prevent him from sending reinforcements to Cornwallis. Washington wrote letters to General Greene and others, stating his intention to attack New York, and contrived that these letters should be intercepted by the British commander. The project was successful, and by a variety of military manœuvres, in which he completely out-generalled Clinton, he increased his apprehensions about New York, and prevented his sending assistance to Cornwallis.

36. Having, for a considerable time, kept Clinton in perpetual alarm in New York, Washington suddenly quitted his camp at White Plains, crossed the Hudson with his army, and, passing rapidly through New Jersey and Pennsylvania, arrived at Elk river, the head-quarters of a considerable army under the *Marquis de Lafayette*. A part of the forces embarked and sailed for Virginia; the rest marched by land.

37. Clinton was not informed of the movements of Washington till it was too late to pursue him. He then sent a strong detachment under the traitor *Arnold*, who had recently returned from Virginia, against *New London* in Connecticut. *Fort Griswold*, which stood on a hill in Groton, nearly opposite, was taken by a party of the British, and the most of its garrison, together with *Colonel Ledyard*, the commander, were killed or wounded; and New London was afterwards set on fire and consumed.

38. At Chester, Washington heard the cheering news of the arrival of 24 French ships of the line, under *Count de Grasse*, in the Chesapeake. Admiral *Graves*, with 19 British ships of the line, arrived soon after. The two fleets had a slight engagement, in which the French had the advantage, and were left masters of the navigation of the bay. A body of French troops was landed to coöperate with the Americans. The whole combined force, under Washington, closely investing the British army at *Yorktown*, including continentals, French and militia, amounted to about 16,000.

39. The British army being blockaded by land and sea, the American forces opened the first batteries upon them early in October, with such effect as to silence a part of their artillery

Two British redoubts were taken. The second parallel was begun on the night of the 11th; and such was the tremendous effect of the American artillery, that the British works were demolished, their guns silenced, and no hope of relief or escape remained. On the 17th of October, Lord Cornwallis proposed a cessation of hostilities; and, on the 19th, articles of capitulation were signed, by which the British army, military stores, and shipping, fell into the hands of General Washington. The whole number of prisoners, exclusive of seamen amounted to 7,073; but many of them, at the time of the surrender, were incapable of duty.

40. As the reduction of this division of the British forces was considered as deciding the war, and establishing the independence of the United States, the news was everywhere received with emotions of inexpressible joy. Divine service was performed in all the American brigades; and the commander-in-chief recommended that all who were not on duty should join in the worship, "with a serious deportment and that sensibility of heart which the recollection of the surprising and particular interposition of Divine Providence in our favor claims." A day of public thanksgiving was recommended by congress and observed throughout the United States; and General Washington liberated all persons under arrest, that all might partake in the general joy.

41. As no rational expectation, on the part of the British, of conquering the United States, now remained, the military operations which succeeded were of little consequence. In March, 1782, Lord North resigned his office as prime minister, and a new cabinet was formed, that advised the king to discontinue the further prosecution of the war. *General Carleton* was appointed to the command of the British forces in America; and, on the 30th of November, provisional articles of peace were signed, by which the independence and sovereignty of the United States were acknowledged. On the 3d of September, 1783, there was concluded, at *Versailles*, by *Adams Franklin Jay*, and *Laurens*, on the part of the Americans, and *Oswald*, on the part of the British, a definitive treaty of peace by which the thirteen United Colonies were admitted to be "Free, Sovereign, and Independent States."

42. Thus ended the revolutionary war; a war which began in the injudicious and tyrannical endeavor to procure a revenue from the Colonies, and which terminated in their freedom and sovereignty; a war which cost Great Britain, in addition to the loss of her Colonies, the sum of about £100,000,000 sterling, and about 50,000 subjects; a war in which America lost many lives and much treasure, and endured every hardship and suf

fering incident to so arduous a struggle, for which she was so ill prepared; a war, the issue of which will remain an encouragement to the oppressed to endeavor to rid themselves of oppression, and a lesson to those who, unmindful of the rights of the people, would lift against them the arm of power, and force them to a compliance with their unjust demands; a war to use the language of *Mr. Pitt* (the younger), "which was conceived in injustice, nurtured in folly, and whose footsteps were marked with slaughter and devastation. The nation was drained of its best blood and its vital resources, for which nothing was received in return but a series of inefficient victories and of disgraceful defeats; victories obtained over men fighting in the holy cause of liberty, or defeats which filled the land with mourning for the loss of dear and valuable relations, slain in a detested and impious quarrel."

SECTION V.

The Army disbanded: The Constitution formed: Washington's Administration: Adams's Administration. — *From A. D.* 1783 *to* 1801.

1. When the American army was to be disbanded, new and serious difficulties arose concerning the payment of the arrears of their wages and rations. The want of resources to carry on the war, and of supreme power to lay and collect taxes had driven congress to the expedient of emitting vast sums in bills of credit, which depreciated so much as to be of scarcely any value; and, on account of the interruption of commerce and the vast quantities of paper money which had been issued gold and silver were, for a time, almost wholly banished from circulation. The depreciated currency, in which the troops were paid, deprived them of a great part of what was really their due; and neither officers nor soldiers could make a decent appearance in point of dress, while the families of many were suffering at home.

2. The officers of the army, reposing confidence in the faith of their country, remained quiet till the close of the war, but much agitation and alarm were, at length, excited among them, by the apprehension that they were to be disbanded without having a settlement of their accounts, or any provision for the payment of what was due to them. In this state of feeling, that portion of the army, that was stationed at *Newburg* was thrown into alarming agitation by an address to the officers

privately circulated among them, appealing to their passions, and designed to stir them up to violent measures.

3. At this crisis, the virtues of *Washington* shone forth with peculiar and unrivalled lustre. He assembled the officers exhorted them to moderation in demanding their arrears; promised to exert all his influence in their favor; and conjured them, "as they valued their honor, as they respected the rights of humanity, and as they regarded the military and national character of the American States, to express their utmost detestation of the men who were attempting to open the flood-gates of civil discord, and deluge their rising empire with blood."

4. These words, coming from one whom they had been accustomed to reverence, were weighty and decisive. After his speech, the officers voted him an address of thanks, and resolved that they continued to have an unshaken confidence in the justice of congress and their country. Congress had but little money, and no effectual means of raising it; but they put the accounts of the army in a train for settlement; and decreed, that the officers should receive, after the end of the war, five years' additional pay, and each soldier eighty dollars besides his wages.

5. The 3d of November was fixed upon for disbanding the army: the day preceding, *Washington* issued his farewell orders to his troops, replete with friendly advice and affectionate wishes for their present and future welfare. Having afterwards taken an affecting leave of his officers, he repaired to *Annapolis*, where congress was then sitting, delivered to the president his military commission, and declared that he was no longer invested with any public character. After this declaration, he retired, followed by the gratitude of his country and the applause and admiration of the world, to his estate at *Mount Vernon*, and addicted himself to his favorite pursuit of agriculture.

6. At the close of the war, when the States were released from the presence of danger, the government, under the *Articles of Confederation*, was found to be weak, and wholly insufficient for the public exigencies. The authority of congress was reduced to a mere name; a large public debt had been contracted, but no provision had been made for paying either the principal or the interest. As congress had no revenue, they could give no effectual value to their paper currency; and the public securities fell to a very small proportion of their nominal value, as it was regarded as extremely doubtful whether the government would ever be able to redeem them.

7. In this state of affairs, most of the army notes were sold

for about a sixth or an eighth of their nominal value, so that the brave men who had fought the battles of their country, and endured hardships, cold, and hunger, and who had repeatedly received of congress solemn assurances of recompense for their toils and dangers, were at last forced to sell their securities for a mere trifle, in order to keep their families from distressing want.

8. The necessity of a more efficient general government was, at length, extensively felt; and, in accordance with a proposition of the legislature of Virginia, commissioners from several of the States met, in 1786, at *Annapolis*, to form a general system of commercial regulations. But, judging that their authority was too limited to accomplish any desirable purpose, they adjourned, with instructions to advise the States to appoint delegates with more ample powers to meet the next year at *Philadelphia*.

9. Accordingly, delegates from the different States assembled in that city, in May, 1787, and elected *General Washington*, who was a member of their body from Virginia, for their president. After four months' deliberation, the *Federal Constitution* was, on the 17th of September, unanimously agreed to by the members of the convention; and, being presented to congress, it was, by that body, transmitted to the several States for their consideration. Being accepted and ratified, in 1788 by eleven members of the confederacy, it became the constitution of the United States. The two dissenting States were North Carolina and Rhode Island; the former adopted it in 1789 the latter in 1790.

10. According to the constitution, the several States elected their delegates to congress; and, by a unanimous vote, *Washington* was chosen the first president. When the appointment was officially announced to him, although unwilling to leave his retirement, he yielded to the unanimous voice of his country; and bidding adieu to Mount Vernon, to private life, and to domestic felicity, he proceeded, without delay, to *New York*, where congress was assembled. In his progress to that city, he was met by numerous bodies of people, who hailed him as the father of his country; triumphal arches were erected to commemorate his achievements; aged women blessed him as he passed; and virgins, strewing flowers in his way, expressed their hope that he, who had defended the injured rights of their parents, would not refuse his protection to their children.

11. On the 30th of April, he was inaugurated President of the United States. The ceremony was performed in the open gallery of the City Hall, in *New York*, where the oath was administered to him in the presence of a countless multitude

of spectators. The importance of the act the novelty of the scene, the dignity of the general's character, the gravity of his manner, and the reverence with which he bowed to kiss the sacred volume, impressed upon the transaction a solemnity never before witnessed in America.

12. The joy of the nation at the establishment of the new government, with Washington at its head, was scarcely exceeded by that of any preceding event. His personal influence was such as to give the government a character both at home and abroad; and he possessed the inestimable talent of collecting the wisest counsellors, and of selecting the best opinions for the direction of his own conduct. At the same time that he was elected president, *John Adams*, who had borne a distinguished part in the revolution, was chosen vice-president. The other principal officers, at the first organization of the government, were *Thomas Jefferson*, Secretary of State; *Alexander Hamilton*, Secretary of the Treasury; *Henry Knox*, Secretary of War; *Edmund Randolph*, Attorney-General; *Samuel Osgood*, Postmaster-General; and *John Jay*, Chief Justice of the United States.

13. The beneficial effects of the new government, as administered by Washington and his assistants, were soon felt. Public confidence was restored; commerce revived; the national debt, incurred during the revolutionary war, was funded, and brought, at once, to its par value; and the United States suddenly rose from a state of embarrassment and depression to a high degree of national prosperity.

14. In 1790, the country was involved in a sanguinary war with the Indians to the north of the Ohio, who obtained a victory over *General Harmer*, and another in the following year (1791) over *General St. Clair;* but *General Wayne*, who succeeded to the command of the army, completely routed the savages, and negotiated a treaty of peace, in 1795, at *Greenville.*

15. While the United States were engaged in war with the Indians, they were also involved in new difficulties by the convulsions of Europe. The French revolution had commenced, and that nation was under the wild misrule of the *Directory*. Claims were made on this country for assistance; the feelings of a large portion of the community were warmly enlisted on the side of France, and would have urged the nation into hostilities with England. But it was the policy of Washington's administration to remain neutral; yet this course of the government met with opposition, and increased the hostility of the two parties into which the country had begun to be divided.

16. Washington, having been twice unanimously elected president and having administered the government with great

advantage to the country, near the close of his second term of four years, declined a reëlection, in a valedictory address to the people, replete with maxims of political wisdom, and breatning sentiments of the warmest affection for his country. At the expiration of his term, he again withdrew to his residence at Mount Vernon, and was succeeded in office, in 1797, by *John Adams*

17. During Mr. Adams's administration, the French revolutionary government, disappointed in its object of engaging the United States in the war with England, pursued a course of insult and aggression towards them, which ended in open hostilities. The American government, at length, adopted measures of defence and retaliation; the navy was increased and a provisional army was raised, of which *General Washington* was appointed commander-in-chief. A few months afterwards, the directory government of France was overthrown, and the disputes between that country and this were amicably adjusted.

18. Not long after, having accepted the command of the army, *Washington* died suddenly, at Mount Vernon, on the 14th of December, 1799, in the 68th year of his age. The news of the death of the great American general, statesman, and patriot, produced an impression that is without a parallel in America. The people of the United States, in accordance with the recommendation of congress, wore crape on the left arm thirty days, as a token of spontaneous and unaffected grief; eulogies were delivered, and funeral processions celebrated, throughout the country, — thus exhibiting the affecting and sublime spectacle of a nation in mourning for the loss of one whom they had been accustomed to regard as the father of his country.

19. For several years, the nation had been much agitated by the conflicts of parties. At the time of the adoption of the federal constitution, those in favor of it were styled *Federalists*, and those against it, *Anti-federalists;* but the two parties were afterwards generally designated by the names of *Federalists* and *Democrats* or *Republicans.* These parties differed from each other, both with regard to the foreign relations of the country, and on various subjects of domestic policy. The federalists accused the republicans of an undue partiality for France; and the latter charged the former with a similar partiality for Great Britain. A commercial treaty with Great Britain, negotiated by *Mr. Jay*, in 1794, was severely censured by the republicans, and increased the animosities of the parties.

20. Many of the measures of Mr. Adams's administration relating both to foreign and domestic policy, met with much

opposition. Some of the acts which excited the most dissatisfaction, were those of raising a standing army, imposing a direct tax, and enacting the "alien and sedition laws." In 1801, a revolution took place in the administration of public affairs; and the republican party, having become the majority, succeeded in elevating their candidate, *Thomas Jefferson*, to the presidency, in opposition to Mr. Adams.

SECTION VI.

Jefferson's Administration: Madison's Administration, War with Great Britain: — Monroe's Administration. Adams's Administration. — From A. D. 1801 *to* 1829.

1. The great measure of the first term of Mr. Jefferson's administration was the acquisition and annexation to the United States of the great country of *Louisiana*, which was purchased of France for the sum of $ 15,000,000. This country was first colonized by the French in 1699. In 1762, it was ceded by France to Spain; and, in 1800, it was ceded back by Spain to France.

2. At the time when Mr. Jefferson was raised to the presidency, the state of the country was highly prosperous, and it so continued during his first presidential term. The conflicts between the two great political parties, which had greatly agitated the country during the preceding administration, still continued; but the party which sustained Mr. Jefferson increased in strength to such a degree, that he was reëlected by an almost unanimous vote.

3. The war which had, for a number of years, been raging between Great Britain and France, had involved nearly all the nations of Europe. America endeavored to maintain a neutrality towards the belligerents, and peaceably to carry on a commerce with them. Being the great neutral trader, she had an interest in extending the privileges of neutrality, which the belligerents, on the contrary, were inclined to contract within the narrowest limits.

4. In May, 1806, the British government declared all the ports and rivers, from the Elbe in Germany to Brest in France to be blockaded, and all American vessels, trading with these interdicted ports, were liable to seizure and condemnation. In the ensuing November, 1806, the Emperor of France issued his *Berlin Decree*, declaring the British islands in a state of blockade, and prohibiting all intercourse with them. Next

followed, in November, 1807, the *British Orders in Council* by which all neutral vessels, trading with France, were compelled to stop at a British port and pay a duty. In consequence of this measure, Bonaparte issued, in December, 1807, the *Milan Decree*, by which every vessel, which should submit to British search, or consent to any pecuniary exactions whatever, was confiscated.

5. In the same month (December, 1807), on the recommendation of Mr. Jefferson, congress laid an *embargo* on all the shipping of the United States. This measure was designed to retaliate on both England and France, and also to put the United States in a better state of defence, by retaining their vessels and seamen at home; but, inasmuch as it annihilated all foreign commerce, it operated with great severity on the interests of the people, and became unpopular; and in March, 1809, the embargo was removed, and *non-intercourse* with France and Great Britain was substituted.

6. While matters continued in this state, new causes of provocation continually occurred. The trade of the United States was harassed by both of the belligerents; and the government was accused in Britain of partiality to France, and in France of pusillanimously submitting to the insults of Britain.

7. But one species of injury, which was keenly felt and loudly complained of in this country, the United States suffered exclusively from Britain. This was the impressment of her seamen, on board the American vessels, by British men-of-war. The similarity of language renders it difficult to distinguish American from British seamen; but there is reason to believe, that, on some occasions, the British officers were not anxious to make the distinction, being determined, at all hazards, to procure men; and American seamen were compelled to serve in the British navy, and fight the battles of Britain.

8. The British, on the other hand, complained that their seamen escaped on board American vessels, to which they were encouraged, and where they were carefully concealed; and they contended for the right of searching American merchant vessels for their own runaway seamen. This custom had been long practised; was a fruitful source of irritation and was submitted to, with extreme reluctance, on the part of the Americans, who maintained that, under British naval officers, it was often conducted in the most arbitrary manner, with little regard to the feelings of those against whom it was enforced; and that, under the color of this search, native seamen were frequently dragged on board British vessels.

9. The custom of searching for British seamen had hitherto been confined to private vessels; but, in 1807, it was ascer

tained that four seamen had deserted from the British service, and entered on board the *Chesapeake*, an American frigate, commanded by *Commodore Barron*, and carrying 36 guns. *Captain Humphreys* of the *Leopard*, an English frigate of 50 guns, in compliance with the orders of *Admiral Berkeley*, followed the Chesapeake beyond the Capes of Virginia, and, after demanding the deserters, fired a broadside upon the American frigate, and killed and wounded about 20 men. The Chesapeake struck her colors, and the four seamen were given up.

10. This outrage occasioned a general indignation throughout the country, and was deemed, by many, in conjunction with other causes, a sufficient ground for declaring war. The president issued a proclamation, ordering all British vessels of war to quit the waters of the United States, and forbidding all intercourse between them and the inhabitants. The British government disavowed the attack on the Chesapeake; yet the measures taken with regard to the affair were far from being satisfactory to the government of this conntry.

11. In 1809, Mr. Jefferson, having declined a reëlection, was succeeded by *James Madison*, who had held the office of secretary of state in the late administration, and who pursued the same general policy. At the commencement of the new administration, an arrangement was made with *Mr. Erskine*, the British minister, by which the American government was induced to renew the trade with England; but this arrangement was afterwards disavowed on the part of Great Britain. The succeeding negotiator, *Mr. Jackson*, having, soon after his arrival, used offensive language, the president declined having any further correspondence with him. An unhappy rencounter between the American and English ships of war, the *President* and the *Little Belt*, served to increase the unfriendly sentiments of the two countries.

12. — (1812.) — The prospect of an amicable adjustment of existing difficulties, between the United States and Great Britain, continuing to become daily more dark and unpromising, congress met, pursuant to adjournment, on the 25th of May 1812; and, on the 1st of June, the president sent a message to that body, strongly recommending a declaration of war. The principal grounds for it, as stated in the message, were the impressment of American seamen by the British; the blockading of the ports of their enemies; the orders in council; and a suspicion that the Indians had been instigated to acts of hostility by British agents.

13. The bill for declaring war passed the house of representatives by a vote of 79 to 49, and the senate, by one of 19

to 13; and on the 18th of June, the day after it passed the senate, it was signed by the president. Five days after the declaration of war, the British orders in council were repealed, in consequence of the decrees of Berlin and Milan having been revoked.

14. The minority of congress opposed the declaration of war, on the ground of its being, in their view, unnecessary and impolitic; they maintained, also, that the aggressions of the French had been greater than those of the English; and they entered a solemn protest against the measure. A considerable proportion of the people of the United States sympathized, in their views, with this minority; and the war was, consequently, prosecuted with much less energy and success than it might have been, if there had been a unanimity in its favor.

15. Notwithstanding the length of time during which hostilities had been meditated, they were commenced in a very imperfect state of preparation on the part of the American government; and, in consequence, the operations of the American armies, by land, during the first year, were wholly unsuccessful and disastrous.

16. On the 12th of July, *General Hull*, with an army of upwards of 2,000 men, invaded Canada; and, on the 16th of August, he surrendered, with the whole of his troops, to the British. A second attempt to invade the province was made by *General Van Rensselaer*, who, with about 1,000 men, crossed the Niagara, in November, and attacked the British at *Queenstown:* after an obstinate engagement, he was obliged to surrender with his army. In this engagement the British commander, *General Brock*, was killed.

17. While the operations of the troops of the United States, in Canada, were so extremely unfortunate and mortifying, brilliant success attended the American flag on the ocean. In August, the frigate *Constitution*, commanded by *Captain Hull*, captured the British frigate the *Guerriere*. In October, the frigate *United States*, commanded by *Captain Decatur*, took the British frigate the *Macedonian*. In November, the British sloop the *Frolic*, was captured by the sloop *Wasp*, under *Captain Jones;* but the Wasp was immediately after taken by the Poictiers, a British seventy-four. In December, the *Constitution*, commanded by *Captain Bainbridge*, captured the British frigate the *Java*. In these four engagements, the total loss of the British, in killed and wounded, was 423; that of the Americans, only 73.

18. — (1813.) — The operations of the war during this year were productive of alternate successes and reverses. In January, a detachment of about 800 men, under *General Winchester*

was surprised and defeated by the British and Indians under *General Proctor*, at Frenchtown, on the river Raisin Those who had not fallen, amounting to about 500, surrendered prisoners, a great part of whom were inhumanly massacred by the Indians.

19. In April, a detachment of 1,700 American troops, under *General Pike*, after some severe fighting, took possession of *York*, in Upper Canada, and destroyed a large quantity of public stores. By the explosion of a mine, prepared for the purpose, General Pike, together with about 100 Americans, was killed. The British lost about 700 in killed, wounded, and captured. — *Colonel Dudley*, being detached from *Fort Meigs*, with 800 men, to attack the enemy's battery, was surrounded by a large army of Indians, under *Tecumseh*, and was defeated, with the loss of most of his troops.

20. In May, an attack was made upon *Sackett's Harbor* by about 1,000 British troops, under *Sir George Prevost*, who was repulsed, with considerable loss, by the Americans under *General Brown*. Two days before this event, *Fort George*, in Canada, was taken by the Americans under *General Boyd* and *Colonel Miller*. The British, who were commanded by *General Vincent*, lost nearly 1,000 in killed, wounded, and captured. A few days afterwards, *Generals Chandler* and *Winder*, who had advanced with a considerable force, were surprised in the night, not far from the fort, by the British under *General Vincent*, and were both taken prisoners.

21. The most brilliant achievement, during this year, was the defeat of the British naval force on *Lake Erie*, in September, by *Commodore Perry*. The British fleet consisted of 6 vessels, having 63 guns; that of the Americans, of 9 vessels, with 56 guns. The conflict, which lasted three hours, was tremendous; but the victory was complete. The British force, being reduced to almost a total wreck, fell entirely into the hands of the Americans, who were, by this achievement, rendered masters of the lake.

22. After this victory, *General Harrison* embarked his main army on board the American squadron, landed on the Canadian shore, and in October, near the *Thames*, defeated and dispersed the British army under *General Proctor*. In this action the enemy sustained a severe loss, and the celebrated Indian chief *Tecumseh* was killed. But the Americans were afterwards repulsed at *Williamsburg*.

23. Great preparations had been made for the conquest of Canada, under *Generals Wilkinson* and *Hampton*; but nothing of importance was effected; and a disagreement between the two generals prevented that concert which was necessary to

insure success. The village of *Newark*, in Canada, being burnt by the Americans, the British crossed over, and, in retaliation, burnt *Buffalo*, which was then a small town, and some other villages. During this year, the British, under *Admiral Cockburn*, committed various depredations in the south, and on the shores of the Chesapeake; but they were repulsed at *Craney Island*, near Norfolk.

24. The English were more successful on the ocean during this year, than during the preceding. The American flag however, was not, in any instance, disgraced; nor were the American ships and men found inferior to those of Britain of equal force. In February, the *Hornet*, commanded by *Captain Lawrence*, captured the British sloop the *Peacock*. In June, the *Chesapeake*, under *Captain Lawrence*, was captured by the *Shannon*, commanded by *Captain Broke*. In August, the *Argus* was captured by the English sloop the *Pelican*; and, in September, the British brig the *Boxer* surrendered to the *Enterprise*.

25. — (1814.) — The campaign of 1814 was distinguished by more severe fighting in Canada than had before occurred. On the 2d of July, the Americans under *General Brown*, having taken *Fort Erie*, proceeded to attack the British under *General Drummond*, at *Chippewa*, where, on the 5th, an obstinate engagement took place, which terminated in favor of the Americans. On the 25th of the month, a more sanguinary and warmly contested battle was fought, at *Bridgewater*, by the Americans under *Generals Brown* and *Scott*, and the British under *Generals Drummond* and *Riall*. The British were forced to retreat, with the loss of about 900 in killed, wounded, and taken. The American army was also so much weakened that it fell back to *Fort Erie*, which the British afterwards attempted to storm; but they were repulsed with a severe loss This was the last important operation of the war on this frontier.

26. *Sir George Prevost*, having received large reinforcements from the troops which had been employed under the *Duke of Wellington*, in Spain, now advanced with an army of 14,000 men, to carry offensive war into the United States; and his first attempt was on *Plattsburg*. The operations of this army were accompanied by those of the British naval force on *Lake Champlain*, consisting of 95 guns and 1,050 men, commanded by *Commodore Downie*. This force was totally defeated by the American fleet, having 86 guns and 826 men, under the command of *Commodore Macdonough*. During the engagement between the fleets, *Sir George Prevost* attacked the forts of *Plattsburg*, but was effectually repulsed by the Americans under *General Macomb*. The loss of the Brit

ish, in killed, wounded, and deserters, was estimated at 2,500 while that of the Americans, both on the land and water, was only 231.

27. In August, a British fleet of about 60 sail arrived in the Chesapeake, and an army of about 5,000 men, under *General Ross*, landed in the *Patuxent*, about forty miles from the city of *Washington*. Having easily put to flight the American militia, under *General Winder*, at *Bladensburg*, the enemy entered *Washington*, burnt the capitol, the president's house, and other public buildings, and retired without molestation. In September, about a fortnight after this transaction, the British army, to the number of about 7,000, under *General Ross* and *Admiral Cockburn*, made a similar attempt on *Baltimore*; but, after gaining some advantages, they were finally repulsed. In this attempt *General Ross* was killed.

28. On the ocean, the American flag maintained its reputation, and in no instance yielded to an inferior or an equal force. The American frigate the *Essex*, however, was captured by the British frigate the *Phœbe* and the sloop *Cherub* of a superior force; and the frigate *President*, by a squadron of the enemy; but the British vessels of war the *Epervier*, *Avon*, *Reindeer*, *Cyane*, *Levant*. and *Penguin*, were taken by the Americans.

29. As the war between the United States and Great Britain was a branch of the great European quarrel, it naturally fell to the ground when that quarrel ceased. The matters in dispute between the two countries related to maritime and neutral rights; but, with regard to these subjects, there was no longer any cause of difference, as the world was at peace. On the restoration of peace in Europe, both parties began to think seriously about ending the war; and the Emperor of Russia offered his services as mediator, which were, however, declined by the British government, and a direct negotiation at London or Gottenburg was proposed. In April, 1813, commissioners, on the part of the United States, were appointed to meet others from England at Gottenburg; but the place of meeting was afterwards changed to *Ghent*, where a treaty was finally signed on the 24th of December, 1814.

30. While the negotiation was in progress, a large armament, under the command of *Sir Edward Packenham*, was fitted out by Great Britain for an attack on *New Orleans*, with the intention, apparently, of ending the war with some eclat, but the design met with a most signal and fatal defeat. The British, after enduring great fatigues and numerous difficulties, and sustaining some desperate encounters, assaulted the works

thrown up for the defence of the city, on the 8th of January 1815, when they were dreadfully cut to pieces and repulsed by the Americans under *General Jackson.* The loss of the enemy in killed, wounded, and captured, amounted to about 2,600: among the slain were the commander-in-chief, *General Packenham*, and other principal officers. The loss of the Americans was only seven killed and six wounded. This was the last important operation of the war.

31. In 1814, the northeastern States were in a very exposed condition, being destitute of protection from the national troops, and great alarm was excited among the people. At this juncture, the legislature of Massachusetts proposed a conference, by delegates from the legislatures of the New England States and of any of the other States that might accede to the measure, in order to devise and recommend to these States measures for their security and defence. A *convention*, composed of distinguished men, delegates from the New England States, accordingly met at *Hartford*, in Connecticut, on the 15th of December; and, after a session of three weeks, they published the result of their deliberations. The commissioners of the convention, who were sent to confer with the national government, and the treaty of peace with Great Britain, arrived at Washington about the same time; so that the war and all proceedings relating to its continuance were, at length, happily terminated.

32. In the treaty of Ghent, no allusion is to be found to the causes of the war; nor was any attempt made to settle the vexed question respecting the right of Great Britain to impress her seamen on board American vessels, or any of the other points in dispute, each party being left, precisely as it was before the war, in possession of all its real or imaginary rights. In case, therefore, that Great Britain should be engaged in another European war, the questions between the two countries, which were, for a time, set at rest by peace, might be again revived, and lead to new difficulties. But it is to be hoped that both nations will see, that it is their interest, as well as duty, to cultivate friendly relations, to avoid every cause of hostile contention, and to draw closer every tie, whether of consanguinity, religion, or interest, which may firmly unite them in a lasting peace.

33. When the waste of life and of property, the amount of crime and of suffering, which *war* always occasions, and the little chance there is, that, by an appeal to arms, the wrongs of an injured nation will be properly redressed, are duly considered, every Christian patriot and every philanthropist must

desire that some better method of settling national disputes may be established and carried into practice; — some method which would not only be free from the multiplied evils of war but by which an adjustment of the points in dispute might be made more on a basis of law and equity.

34 Mr. Madison, after having filled the office of president eight years, was succeeded, in 1817, by *James Monroe*, who had held the office of secretary of state during most of the time of Mr. Madison's administration. In 1821, Mr. Monroe wanted only a single vote of a unanimous reëlection.

35. During Mr. Monroe's administration, the United States were at peace, with the exception of a war with the Seminole and Creek Indians; and the prosperity of the country, which had been interrupted by the war with England, was gradually restored.

36. In 1821, Florida was ceded by Spain to the United States, for the sum of $5,000,000.

37. The admission of the State of *Missouri* into the union, which took effect in 1821, gave rise to a very spirited discussion of the question of *slavery*, — a subject which has ever since continued to occasion political excitement. The bill for its admission, without restriction of slavery, passed the house of representatives, after a long and exciting debate, by a vote of 90 to 86. It was accompanied by a declaration prohibiting slavery in the territories north of lat. 36.30 N. This is what has been since called "the Missouri compromise."

38. In August, 1824, *General Lafayette*, having received an invitation from congress, landed at New York, on a visit to the United States; passed through twenty-four of the States; was everywhere enthusiastically received as the nation's guest was present, on the 17th of June, 1825, at the celebration of the 50th anniversary of the battle of Bunker Hill; and, in September, sailed for France. In the following December, congress made him a grant of $200,000, and a township of land in Florida, in consideration of his revolutionary services.

39. In 1825, Mr. Monroe was succeeded by *John Quincy Adams*, who had held the office of secretary of state during Mr. Monroe's administration. In the presidential election of 1824, there were four candidates for the presidency, — *John Quincy Adams*, *Andrew Jackson*, *William H. Crawford*, and *Henry Clay*. Of the electoral votes, Jackson received 99, Adams 84, Crawford 41, and Clay 37. There being no choice by the people, the election devolved upon the house of representatives; and Adams was elected, having received the votes of 13 States Jackson 7, and Crawford 4.

40. During Mr. Adams's administration, the country was at peace and in a highly prosperous condition; and advantageous treaties of peace and commerce were negotiated with various foreign nations. The policy of Mr. Monroe's administration was continued and greatly extended, in strengthening every arm of the national defence, by erecting light-houses, arsenals, fortifications, &c.; by increasing the naval establishment; and especially by improving the intercommunication between the different parts of the country. In these internal improvements more was effected by the aid of the government, during Mr. Adams's administration, than during the administrations of all his predecessors.

41. The national government had agreed to extinguish, for the benefit of Georgia, the Indian title to the lands held by the *Cherokees* and *Creeks* in that State. In the last year of Mr. Monroe's administration, the Creeks, in a national council, refused to part with their territory. After the council broke up, however, a few of the chiefs remained, and were induced to make a treaty, ceding the lands to the United States. This treaty was repudiated by the Creek nation as an act of fraud; but the governor of Georgia determined to act upon it as valid.

42. At this juncture, the Indians appealed for protection to the president of the United States, who interposed to protect them from gross injustice. It was, however, deemed expedient to obtain the lands in question by fair purchase. This was subsequently accomplished; and, in a few years, the Indians were removed to territories west of the Mississippi.

43. In 1828, a new *tariff law* was enacted, imposing duties on imports, with a view to afford protection to American manufactures. The principle of a *protective tariff* has met with strong opposition, especially in the southern States; and it has, ever since the passage of this act of congress, unhappily continued to be a subject of contention between opposite political parties.

44. On the *4th of July*, 1826, *John Adams* and *Thomas Jefferson* died; the former in his 91st year, and the latter in his 84th. These distinguished men stood first and second on the committee of five appointed by congress to prepare the Declaration of Independence in 1776; and, of this instrument, Mr. Jefferson was the writer, and Mr. Adams the most powerful advocate. They afterwards held, in succession, the office of President of the United States, and were also at the head of the two opposite parties, into which the country was long divided; and they finally passed out of the world together, on the 50th anniversary of the day which their Declaration had rendered illustrious as the era of American Independence.

SECTION VII.

Jackson's Administration: Van Buren's Administration: Harrison; — Tyler's Administration: Polk's Administration; War with Mexico: Taylor; — Fillmore's Administration. — *From A. D.* 1829 *to* 1853.

1. In 1829, Mr. Adams was succeeded by *Andrew Jackson*, who had been principally known for his military achievements and who, in the battle of New Orleans, and in conducting a war with the Seminole and Creek Indians, had acquired a high reputation as a military commander.

2. General Jackson's administration was signalized by a more extensive removal of office-holders than had been practised by any of his predecessors; by a persevering hostility to the United States Bank, which terminated in the overthrow of that institution; and by opposition to the policy of making appropriations for internal improvements. Several bills making such appropriations, and also a bill for the renewal of the charter of the United States Bank, which passed both houses of congress, he returned with his veto.

3. In November, 1832, a convention of delegates, called by the legislature of South Carolina, assembled at Columbia, and pronounced the acts of congress of 1828 and 1832, imposing duties on foreign imports, for the protection of domestic manufactures, unconstitutional, void, and not binding upon the citizens of that State. The remedy proposed was termed *nullification*

4. In the December following, President Jackson issued a proclamation, containing an exposition of the principles and powers of the general government, and expressing a determination to maintain the laws. The Governor of South Carolina issued a counter-proclamation, calling on the people to resist any attempt to enforce the tariff laws. The president then addressed a message to congress, recommending such measures as would enable the executive to suppress the spirit of insubordination, and sustain the laws of the United States.

5. Everything, for a time, wore a threatening aspect; but more moderate counsels at length prevailed. An appeal was made to South Carolina by the general assembly of Virginia · Mr. Clay introduced a new bill, modifying the tariff, called the "compromise act," which was enacted into a law on the 1st of March, 1833; and the convention of South Carolina assembled on the 11th of March, and repealed the nullifying ordinance.

6. In March, 1833, President Jackson, having been reëlected

entered on his second term; and, in the following September he directed the secretary of the treasury, Mr. Duane, to remove the public funds or deposits from the United States Bank. This Mr. Duane having declined to do, he was removed; and Mr. Taney was appointed in his place. By the latter the deposits were removed and placed in several State banks. A resolution, strongly censuring the president for this measure was passed by the senate in 1834; and, in 1837, the senate voted to expunge this resolution from their journal.

7. In 1834, the country was disturbed by an apprehension of a hostile collision with France. The French government, by a treaty negotiated in 1831, had agreed to make indemnity for spoliations made on American commerce during the reign of Napoleon; but it had failed to fulfil its engagements. The president recommended (1834) reprisals upon French commerce. The measure, however, was not adopted by congress; and the danger of open hostility was happily removed by the action of the French government in making, in the following year, provision to fulfil its stipulations.

8. On the 16th of December, 1835, a great fire broke out in the city of New York, which destroyed the most of that part of the city which is the seat of its principal commercial transactions. This was the most destructive fire that ever took place in this country; and the loss was estimated at upwards of $17,000,000.

9. The *public debt* of the United States in 1816, after the close of the war with Great Britain, amounted to upwards of $127,000,000. After the return of peace, the debt was rapidly reduced; and, in 1836, it having been all paid off, it was computed, that, on the 1st of January, 1837, there would remain in the treasury a surplus revenue of $27,000,000. An act was passed by congress (1836) for distributing this surplus (reserving $5,000,000), to be paid, in four instalments, to the several States, in proportion to their representation in the senate and house of representatives.

10. Near the close of the year 1835, a conflict commenced with the *Seminole Indians*, who refused to remove from Florida to lands appropriated to them west of the Mississippi, and the United States became involved in a long and expensive war with them; but, in 1842, having been finally subdued, they were removed. The expenses of this war, from 1836 to 1840 inclusive, as officially stated, amounted to upwards of $15,000,000, more than three times as much as was paid to Spain for the country of Florida.

11. Andrew Jackson was succeeded, in 1837, by *Martin Van Buren*, who had held the office of vice-president the pre

ceding four years, and who, in his administration, continued the same general policy as that of his predecessor.

12. In the spring of this year (1837) commenced the greatest commercial revulsion ever known in this country. A spirit of extravagant speculation had, for some years, prevailed; a multitude of State banks had been chartered, by means of which there was a great expansion of paper currency; numerous and very expensive public works, as canals, railroads, &c., were undertaken by States and incorporated companies; immense importations of foreign goods were made; and real estate, especially in cities and villages, was raised far above its intrinsic value. At length the crisis came, with tremendous effect. The panic extended throughout the country, and all confidence and all credit were at an end.

13. On the 10th of May, all the banks in the city of New York suspended specie payment; and the suspension soon became general throughout the country. The mercantile classes were subjected to the greatest embarrassments, and failures were numerous in all the commercial cities. In the city of New York alone, the list of failures, including only the more considerable ones, exhibited an amount of upwards of $60,000,000.

14. The national government became involved in the general embarrassment, inasmuch as the banks in which the public deposits were placed, had, like the rest, suspended specie payment. In this state of affairs, the president convoked an extra session of congress, to meet on the 4th of September. Congress passed an act postponing, to the 1st of January, 1839, the payment to the States of the fourth instalment of the surplus revenue, and authorized an issue of treasury notes to the amount of $10,000,000, to be receivable in payment of public dues. A bill for placing the public money in the hands of receivers-general, called the *sub-treasury* or *independent treasury bill*, was recommended by the president, and passed the senate, but was lost in the house. This bill, after repeated failures, was finally passed and enacted into a law in June 1840.—In August, 1838, the banks throughout the country generally resumed specie payment.

15. In 1837, a rebellion against the British government broke out in *Canada*. It was sustained by some men of talents and influence, and disturbed the peace of that country through the following year (1838). A considerable number of citizens of the United States, belonging to the parts of Vermont and New York which border on Canada, unhappily took part with the insurgents. Their course was condemned by the general government; and the president issued a proclamation, exhorting

27*

such citizens of the United States, as had violated their duties, to return peaceably to their respective homes, and warning them that the laws would be rigidly enforced against such as should render themselves liable to punishment.

16. In 1841, Mr. Van Buren was succeeded by *William Henry Harrison*, who had been somewhat distinguished in political life, but more for his military services. He was inaugurated on the 4th of March, and died on the 4th of April, just one month after his inauguration. He was the first president of the United States that died in office, and his death was greatly lamented.

17. General Harrison was the candidate of the Whigs, and Mr. Van Buren of the Democrats; and the electioneering contest was carried on with an excitement and enthusiasm never before witnessed in this country. Of the 294 electoral votes given for president, Harrison received 234; and *John Tyler* received the same number of votes for vice-president. On the death of President Harrison, John Tyler, in accordance with the provisions of the constitution, became president. But he refused to carry out the principles of the party by which he was elected; nor did he become popular with any party.

18. On the 31st of May, congress met in an extra session, which had been called by President Harrison, and, besides other acts, they repealed the sub-treasury bill, and passed two different bills, establishing a *Fiscal Bank*, or *Fiscal Corporation of the United States*, both of which were vetoed by the president. The establishment of such an institution was a favorite measure of the whigs, and the action of the president, in relation to it, caused much excitement; and all the members of the cabinet resigned, with the exception of the secretary of state, *Mr. Webster*, who fortunately retained office till after the settlement of the difficulty with England in relation to the northeastern boundary.

19. In 1842, a new *tariff law* was enacted, which made provision for the public revenue, and afforded protection to American manufactures and other branches of national industry, and which was a favorite measure of the whig party. This measure, as it was maintained by its friends, had a powerful influence in restoring a high state of prosperity to the country; but it caused great dissatisfaction in some parts, especially in the southern States.

20. The *northeastern boundary* of the United States, between the State of Maine and the British provinces of Lower Canada and New Brunswick, had been for some years a subject of negotiation and controversy; and at length it threatened

to become a subject of serious national dispute. The difficulty however, was amicably adjusted by the treaty of Washington concluded in September, 1842, by Lord Ashburton and Daniel Webster.

21. One of the last acts of Mr. Tyler's administration was the annexation of the republic of Texas to the United States — a measure which was greatly promoted by the exertions of *John C. Calhoun*, the secretary of state, and which excited a spirited controversy. Joint resolutions for the annexation of that republic to the United States, as one of the States of the Union, passed the house of representatives, on the 25th of January, 1845, by a vote of 120 to 98; and the senate, on the 1st of March, by a vote of 27 to 25; and, on the same day, they were approved by the president.

22. In 1845, Mr. Tyler was succeeded by *James Knox Polk.* Mr. Polk was the democratic candidate; and, after a very exciting electioneering contest, he received 170 electoral votes for president; and *Henry Clay*, the whig candidate, received 105 votes.

23. The party by which Mr. Polk was supported took strong ground in favor of the *annexation of Texas*, and of the claim of the United States to the whole of the *Oregon Territory*, and Mr. Polk, in his inaugural address, sustained the views of his party on both of these questions; one of which threatened to involve the nation in hostilities with Mexico, and the other with Great Britain.

24. The settlement of the northwestern boundary, between the United States and the North American territories of Great Britain, involving the claims of both parties to the *Oregon Territory*, had long been a subject of negotiation; and it now assumed a threatening aspect. But it was happily adjusted by a treaty, concluded at Washington, in June, 1846, fixing on the 49th degree of north latitude as the boundary-line.

25. On the recommendation of the president, congress passed, in July, 1846, a new *tariff law*, having a primary view to the interests of the public revenue, and withdrawing, in a great measure, the protection to domestic industry afforded by the tariff of 1842.

26. The *war with Mexico* grew out of the annexation of Texas to the United States. Texas, which was formerly a province of Mexico, declared its independence in 1836; and, from that time, it had maintained a separate republican government; but its independence had not been acknowledged by Mexico. In March, 1845, immediately after the passage of the resolutions of congress in favor of the annexation, *General*

Almonte, the Mexican minister to the United States, remonstrated against these resolutions, and demanded his passports and all diplomatic intercourse between the two governments was immediately broken off.

27. The boundaries of Texas were never definitely settled. The government of Texas and of the United States maintained that the southwestern boundary of that country was formed by the *Rio Grande;* but the Mexicans contended that that boundary was formed by the river *Nueces*. The country between these two rivers was disputed territory, both parties claiming it: it was on this disputed territory that hostilities were commenced; and each party charged the other with being the aggressor.

28. In July, 1845, the legislature of Texas ratified the resolutions of congress, by which that republic was annexed to the United States, and requested President Polk to take immediate measures to defend the new State against an apprehended attack from Mexico. An American squadron was accordingly despatched to the Gulf of Mexico, and *General Zachary Taylor* was ordered to proceed to the southern frontier of Texas, with a sufficient force for its defence.

29. In March, 1846, General Taylor, having previously concentrated an army of about 4,000 men at *Corpus Christi* received orders from the United States government to move forward, into the disputed territory, to the *Rio Grande*. He accordingly took a position on the left bank of that river, opposite to *Matamoras*, where he erected a fort; and, at the same time, he established a depôt of supplies at *Point Isabel*, upwards of twenty miles in his rear, near the coast.

30. A Mexican force of about 8,000 men was soon assembled on the Rio Grande, at and near Matamoras, under the command of *Generals Ampudia* and *Arista*, who declared the advance of General Taylor with his army to be a hostile movement. On the 24th of April, General Arista informed General Taylor that "he considered hostilities commenced, and should prosecute them." On the same day, a party of 63 American dragoons, under *Captain Thornton*, who had been despatched to reconnoitre, were surprised by a large Mexican force, 16 being killed and wounded, and the rest taken prisoners.

31. A few days afterwards, the greater part of the Mexican army crossed the river, and General Taylor being informed that they intended to attack Point Isabel, where his military stores were deposited, marched to the relief of that place, which he reached unmolested. The garrison there having been strengthened by a reinforcement of 500 sailors and marines, from the American squadron in the Gulf of Mexico, he began, on the 7th of May, to retrace his steps to the Rio Grande.

32. About noon the next day, he encountered the Mexican army of 6,000 men, at *Palo Alto* ; and, after an action of five hours, he drove them from the field, with the loss of nearly 400 in killed and wounded. The Americans, whose number was about 2,300, lost about 50 in killed and wounded, and among the former was the lamented *Major Ringgold.*

33. On the following day, after advancing three miles, the American army again met the Mexicans, strongly posted at *Resaca de la Palma*, and completely routed them, killing and wounding about 600, taking a large number of prisoners among whom was *General La Vega*, and capturing all the cannon and military stores of the enemy. A few days after this battle, General Taylor crossed the Rio Grande, and took possession of Matamoras, which had been left by the Mexican troops.

34. —— Early in May, the news of Captain Thornton's disaster reached Washington, accompanied by exaggerated statements of the peril to which General Taylor's army was exposed, and it produced great excitement. The president, in a special message, on the 11th of May, announced to congress, which was then in session, that the Mexicans "had invaded our territory and shed the blood of our fellow-citizens on our own soil." Congress, after an animated debate of two days, declared, that, "by the act of the republic of Mexico, war existed between that government and the United States"; and, at the same time, authorized the president to accept the services of 50,000 volunteers for twelve months, and appropriated $10,000,000 to carry on the war. The whig members of congress proposed to strike out the preamble to the bill, in which it is asserted that the war existed by the act of Mexico, but without success; and the bill, with the preamble, passed the house by a vote of 142 to 14, and the senate by a vote of 40 to 2.

35. It is proper to remark, that there was a strong feeling in a great part of the country against the war, and a large portion of the citizens, especially in the northern States, condemned it as unnecessary, unjust, and made for unworthy purposes Such views were expressed by the legislatures of some of the northern States, and repeatedly by the whig members of congress. And notwithstanding the above vote relating to the war, in the house of representatives, the same body, in January, 1848, declared, by a vote of 85 to 81, that it was "a war unnecessarily and unconstitutionally made by the President of the United States." ——

36. General Taylor's force was soon after increased by a large number of volunteers from Texas and the adjacent States. The Mexican towns on the Rio Grande were seized and occu-

pied, and camps formed to muster and drill the new levies, preparatory to an invasion of the interior of Mexico.

37. After three months' preparation, General Taylor, with an army of between 6,000 and 7,000 men, proceeded to attack the strongly fortified city of *Monterey*, the capital of the State of New Leon, which was garrisoned by about 10,000 Mexican troops, commanded by *General Ampudia.*

38. The American army reached Monterey on the 19th of September, 1846, and, on the 21st, assaulted the city with the view of taking it by storm; and, after a severe and sanguinary struggle of three days, they became masters of the principal defences, and the greater part of the city. On the 24th, General Ampudia proposed terms of capitulation, which were accepted, and the Mexican army evacuated Monterey. At the same time, General Taylor agreed to an armistice of eight weeks, subject to the ratification of the governments at Washington and Mexico.

39. While these events were taking place near the Rio Grande, *General Santa Anna*, ex-president of Mexico, and the most distinguished military commander of that country, had returned from exile, and had overthrown the government of *President Paredes*, who was at the head of the party supposed to be most in favor of prosecuting the war with the United States. Strong hopes were entertained by the American government that the influence of Santa Anna, on his restoration to power, would be exerted in favor of peace; and the president accordingly had given orders to the naval commander in the Gulf of Mexico to throw no obstacle in the way of his return But these expectations proved to be ill-founded; and, under his administration, the Mexicans were roused to greater efforts, than they had hitherto made, to repel their invaders.

40. Under these circumstances, the American government resolved to strike a decisive blow, by attacking *Vera Cruz*, the principal Mexican port and fortress, with the intention of thereby gaining access to the heart of the country, and to the capital of the republic, for the avowed purpose of "conquering a peace.' *General Winfield Scott* was accordingly ordered to take the chief command of all the forces in Mexico, and to conduct the expedition against Vera Cruz.

41. The armistice, which General Taylor had concluded at Monterey, was not approved by the authorities at Washington; and, in November, his army resumed offensive operations, and speedily overran and subdued the States of Coahuila and Tamaulipas. About this time, however, General Scott arrived at the seat of war, and withdrew from General Taylor the principal part of his army, including nearly all the regular troops to augment the forces destined to besiege Vera Cruz

42. In February, 1847, General Taylor formed a camp of about 5,000 men, mostly volunteers, at *Agua Nueva*, near the city of *Saltillo*. On the 20th of the month, he learnt that Santa Anna, with 20,000 troops, had arrived within 30 miles of him, by a series of forced marches from *San Luis Potosi*, 300 miles distant, across a barren country, almost destitute of water. General Taylor immediately broke up his camp, and fell back 11 miles to *Buena Vista*, where he posted his army in a very strong position, protected by deep ravines and rugged mountainous ridges.

43. On the 22d of February, the Mexican army appeared in front of the American lines, and Santa Anna summoned General Taylor to surrender, which the latter declined to do. Some skirmishing ensued; but the battle did not begin until the 23d, when the Mexicans attempted, by repeated charges, to force the American lines. Notwithstanding some partial successes, achieved by their immense superiority of force, they were, at length, completely repulsed; and, after a fierce and sanguinary contest, which lasted throughout the day, the Americans remained masters of the field. During the night, the Mexicans abandoned their camp, and retreated, in a state of great disorder, towards San Luis Potosi, from whence they had advanced. The American loss, in this battle, was 723 in killed and wounded, and that of the Mexicans amounted to about 2,000.

44. On the 9th of March, 1847, *General Scott* landed near *Vera Cruz*, with an army of about 12,000 men. The city was immediately invested, and after a furious bombardment of several days, during which the destruction of life and property was very great, the Mexican commander, on the 29th of March, capitulated and surrendered the city, and also the famous fortress of *St. Juan d'Ulloa*, together with 5,000 prisoners and 400 pieces of artillery.

45. Early in April, the American army began its march from Vera Cruz to the city of Mexico. At the mountain pass of *Cerro Gordo*, about 50 miles from Vera Cruz, it encountered the Mexican army, commanded by *President Santa Anna*, consisting of 12,000 or 15,000 men, strongly entrenched in an almost impregnable position.

46. On the 18th of April, the Americans, who numbered 8,500, began the assault, and in a few hours carried by storm all the batteries and entrenchments of the Mexicans, who fled in confusion, leaving in the hands of the victors about 3,000 prisoners, 4,000 or 5,000 stand of arms, and 43 pieces of artillery. Among the prisoners were five generals, one of whom, *La Vega*, had before been captured in the battle of Resaca de

la Palma. The American loss in this engagement was 431 in killed and wounded; the Mexican loss, about three times as many.

47. The victory of Cerro Gordo was followed by the immediate surrender of the city of *Jalapa*, and the strong fortress of *Perote;* and, on the 15th of May, the Americans entered *Puebla*, the most important city of Mexico, next to the capital. Here, the army, which had been diminished by death, sickness, and the departure of volunteers, to about 5,000 effective men, remained nearly three months, waiting for reinforcements and supplies.

48. On the 7th of August, 1847, reinforcements having arrived, General Scott began his march from Puebla to the city of Mexico, at the head of about 11,000 men. On the 18th, the army reached the hamlet of San Augustin, 10 miles south of the capital; and, on the 20th, two sanguinary battles were fought with a Mexican force of more than 30,000 men, who were stationed in and around the strongly fortified posts that defended the approaches to the city. In the first battle, that of *Con'reras*, 4,500 Americans assaulted, and, in less than twenty minutes, drove from their entrenchments, 7,000 Mexicans, killing 700 and taking 813 prisoners, besides many colors and standards, and 22 pieces of artillery. In the second battle, that of *Churubusco*, the disparity of force was even greater, and the Mexican loss still more severe,—about 6,000 Americans engaging and completely routing almost the whole Mexican army. General Scott thus speaks of the achievements of the army under his command on this occasion:—"It has in a single day, in many battles, as often defeated 32,000 men; made about 3,000 prisoners, including 8 generals (two of them ex-presidents) and 205 other officers; killed or wounded 4,000 of all ranks, besides entire corps dispersed and dissolved; captured 37 pieces of ordnance,—more than trebling our siege train and field batteries,—with a large number of small arms, a full supply of ammunition of every kind, &c.—Our loss amounts to 1,053: killed, 139, including 16 officers, wounded, 876, including 60 officers."

49. These rapid and decisive victories caused such consternation among the Mexicans, that General Scott might at once have forced his way into the city; but he forebore to do so, not wishing to drive the people to desperation, and, to use his own words, "willing to leave something to the republic on which to rest her pride and recover temper." Accordingly, he acceded to a request made by President Santa Anna for an armistice, the terms of which were agreed upon and signed on the 23d of August.

50. *Mr. Nicholas Trist*, a commissioner appointed by the President of the United States, had arrived in Mexico some months before, and was now in General Scott's camp. Negotiations for peace were immediately commenced between him and commissioners appointed by the Mexican government. But as the latter proposed terms that were not satisfactory, and the Mexican military commanders were violating the terms of the armistice by erecting and strengthening fortifications, General Scott recommenced hostilities on the 7th of September.

51. On the following day, a division of the American army, 3,200 in number, commanded by *General Worth*, carried by storm the strong position of *El Molino del Rey*, which was held by above 14,000 Mexicans, under the command of *President Santa Anna.* The Mexican loss in this action, which was perhaps the most fiercely contested of the whole war, amounted to 3,000 in killed, wounded, and captured. The Americans lost, in killed and wounded, nearly 800, about one fourth of the number engaged.

52. Five days afterwards, the fortress of *Chapultepec*, situated on a steep, rocky hill, 150 feet in height, was stormed, and the army which supported it was routed and driven into the city · the victorious Americans followed, and, by nightfall, one division of their army was within the gates of Mexico, while another occupied the suburbs.

53. During the night, the shattered remnant of the Mexican army, and the members of the federal government and congress, fled from the city, of which the Americans took full possession the next day, September 14th, 1847.

54. The total loss of General Scott's army, in these battles before Mexico, amounted to about 2,700 in killed and wounded. The number of American troops, that entered and took possession of this city of 140,000 inhabitants, was less than 6,000.

55. Besides the invasions of Mexico by the armies commanded by Generals Taylor and Scott, another was conducted by *General Kearny*, who, in the latter part of June, 1846, set out from Missouri, at the head of 1,600 men, mostly volunteers from that State, for the purpose of conquering *New Mexico.*

56. After a fatiguing march of about 1,000 miles across the prairies, General Kearny arrived at *Santa Fe*, of which he took possession, without opposition, on the 18th of August. He immediately declared himself Governor of New Mexico, and issued a proclamation absolving the people from their allegiance to the Mexican government, and constituting them citizens of the United States.

57 In December, 1846, *Colonel Doniphan* a volunteer from

Missouri, departed from Santa Fe, at the head of 900 men, to invade the Mexican State of *Chihuahua.* At *Bracito*, on the Rio Grande, a division of his force, 500 in number, encountered 1,200 Mexicans, whom they put to flight, with a loss of about 200 in killed and wounded; while the Americans had none killed, and only seven wounded.

58. Two months later, on the 28th of February, 1847, at the *Pass of Sacramento*, Colonel Doniphan's little army met and defeated 4,000 Mexicans, commanded by the governor of the State, and occupying a strong position, defended by heavy artillery. On the following day, March 1st, they took possession of the important city of Chihuahua.

59. In the summer of 1846, *Captain* (afterwards Colonel) *Fremont*, who, with a party of about 60 men, was exploring California by order of the President of the United States, became involved in hostilities with the Mexican governor of that province. With the aid of a few American settlers, Fremont defeated the Mexican forces, which were much superior in number; and, on learning that war existed between the United States and Mexico, he raised the American flag, and in conjunction with *Commodore Stockton*, who commanded the United States fleet in the Pacific, prosecuted the conquest of the country with such success, that, by the end of August, the whole of California was in possession of the Americans.

60. Soon after the conquest of the city of Mexico by General Scott, negotiations for peace began, which resulted in a treaty concluded on the 2d of February, 1848, at the city of *Guadalupe Hidalgo*, and ratified, with some modifications, by the American senate, on the 10th of the following March.

61. By the provisions of this treaty, Mexico ceded to the United States the provinces of *New Mexico* and *Upper California*, and agreed to accept the *Rio Grande* as the boundary between her territories and Texas. — The territory acquired from Mexico, by this treaty, including *Texas*, as well as *New Mexico* and *California*, amounts, according to the statement of President Polk, in his message to congress in December, 1848, to 851,598 square miles.

62. The United States, in return, stipulated to pay Mexico 15,000,000 of dollars, and to assume the debts due to citizens of the United States by the Mexican government, to the amount of 3,500,000 dollars.

63. Soon after the acquisition of California, important *gold mines* were discovered on the Sacramento, which have been found to extend over a large tract of country, and to exceed in richness any other gold mines known in any part of the world

These mines caused a sudden emigration to California of great numbers of persons, not only from the United States, but also from various foreign countries. The quantity of gold obtained from the mines during the first year (1848), notwithstanding the insufficiency of means and the want of system and experience in operation, was estimated to amount in value to upwards of $4,000,000.

64. Such was the progress and such the issue of the Mexican war, — a war presenting a series of remarkable victories, under the able management of Generals Scott and Taylor, and other American officers, and terminating in a great accession of territory to the United States. Still the important question may be asked, Can the war be justified on moral or religious principle? But however this question may be answered, it is to be hoped that a beneficent Providence will bring good out of evil, and cause, in the final result, an advancement of human freedom and human happiness, of good government and of true religion.

65. In 1849, Mr. Polk was succeeded by *Zachary Taylor*, most of whose life had been spent as an officer in the army, and who, in the Mexican war, had acquired a high reputation as a military commander. *General Taylor* was the whig candidate and he received 163 electoral votes for president; and *General Lewis Cass*, the democratic candidate, received 127 votes. *Millard Fillmore*, the whig candidate, received 163 votes for vice-president.

66. *President Taylor* died suddenly at Washington, during the session of congress, on the 9th of July, 1850, greatly lamented; and *Millard Fillmore*, in accordance with the provision of the Constitution, became President of the United States.

67. Soon after the accession of Mr. Fillmore, a series of important acts were passed by congress, which have been styled "*compromise measures.*" These acts consisted of the admission of *California* into the Union as a State, the establishment of the boundary of *Texas*, the organization of the territories of *New Mexico* and *Utah*, the suppression of the *slave-trade* in the *District of Columbia*, and the law for the *rendition of fugitive slaves.*

68. The act for the rendition of fugitive slaves, which was passed in the house of representatives, on the 12th of September, 1850, by a vote of 109 to 75, contains some provisions which were very offensive to the whig party generally, and to most of the people in the free States, and its execution has in a few cases, been attended with much opposition.

69. In 1849, *General N. Lopez*, a native of Venezuela, came to the United States, and organized a hostile expedition against the island of Cuba; and in 1850, a second expedition. In these enterprises he was aided by some distinguished Southern men; but both of these expeditions failed.

70. In April, 1851, President Fillmore, having been informed of another attempt to invade Cuba by lawless citizens of the United States, under the command of Lopez, issued a proclamation warning them of the consequences.

71. The expedition, however, comprising several hundred men, a part of them foreigners, sailed from New Orleans in August, landed in Cuba, and were captured. Lopez suffered capital punishment on the 1st of September, in the Spanish form, by the *garrote*. Many of his followers were executed, and some of them were ultimately pardoned.

72. Although Mr. Fillmore, by signing the fugitive slave law bill, lost the support of many of his party, yet most of the measures of his administration were popular, some of the most noted of which were the reduction of inland *postage* to 3 cents on each single letter when prepaid, and an expedition to *Japan*, in 1852, under the command of Commodore Perry, which resulted in a favorable treaty with that empire, which was ratified by the senate in 1854; and when he retired from office, he left the country at peace, and in a high state of prosperity.

SECTION VIII.

Pierce's Administration:—Kansas: Buchanan's Administration:—Lincoln.—Secession.—From A. D. 1853 *to* 1861.

1. In 1853, Mr. Fillmore was succeeded by *Franklin Pierce*, the democratic candidate, who received 254 electoral votes; *General Winfield Scott*, the whig candidate, received 42 votes. President Pierce, in his inaugural address, maintained the recognition of slavery by the constitution, and the constitutionality of the fugitive slave law; and he denounced, in strong terms, political agitation on the subject of slavery; yet public measures were soon adopted, which tended greatly to increase this agitation.

2. After the termination of the war between the United States and Mexico, several lawless military expeditions (commonly styled *filibustering expeditions*) were made against *Nicaragua*, and some of the other countries of *Central America*.

3. These expeditions were regarded with favor by many of the people of the Southern States, and pecuniary aid was furnished by some of their wealthy men. The pretended object was to rescue those countries from tyranny, domestic and foreign; and it was also designed to introduce slavery.

4. The most noted leader in these enterprises was *William Walker*, a native of Tennessee; and the most considerable of the expeditions was made in 1855, against Nicaragua. Walker made himself master of the country, and after holding it for some time, he was finally expelled by the union against him of the other States of Central America. In this expedition, more than three thousand men miserably perished.

5. In Walker's last expedition, he landed near Truxillo, in Honduras, took the fort on the 6th of August, 1860, and he was shot on the 12th of September.

6. At the assembling of the 34th Congress, on the 3d of December, 1856, there was an unprecendented struggle for the choice of a *speaker*, which lasted till the 2d of February (nine weeks), and, after 133 ballotings, resulted in the choice of Nathaniel P. Banks, who was elected by 103 votes,—100 votes being cast for William Aikin.

7. In October, 1854, a conference was held at *Ostend*, at which Mr. Buchanan, American minister to England, Mr. Mason, minister to France, and Mr. Soulé, minister to Spain, were present; and it was proposed by them to purchase the island of *Cuba* from Spain, for the sum of $120,000,000, and in case of her refusal to sell the island, to take it by force. This proposition was favored by the people of the Southern States, but was strongly disapproved by the people of the free States.

8. Two important measures of this administration were the *Reciprocity Treaty* between the United States and Great Britain, providing for a commercial reciprocity between this country and the British American Provinces, and the establishment of a *Court of Claims* at Washington.

9. In January, 1854, Mr. Douglas, chairman of the senate committee on Territories, introduced a bill for the organization of the Territories of *Kansas* and *Nebraska*, in the country west of the State of Missouri, and north of the parallel of 36° 30′. By the *Missouri Compromise* (noticed on page 313) slavery had been formally and forever excluded from this region; but by this bill, which was supported by the administration, the *Missouri Compromise* was repealed, and slavery was permitted to enter these Territories.

10. The introduction of this bill soon excited the strong opposition, throughout the free States, of those who were opposed to the further extension of slavery; and in the month of March following, a memorial protesting against its passage, signed by 3,000 New England clergymen of different religious denominations, was presented to the senate; but it was passed by that body, on the 26th of May, by a vote of 35 to 12. It was passed in the house of representatives by a vote of 113 to 100.

11. This measure caused great excitement in the free States; it was denounced as a flagrant breach of faith, and a violation of what was regarded as a sacred compromise; and it led to a disastrous and sanguinary contest between those who advocated and those who opposed the establishment of slavery in these Territories. This unhappy contest continued during the administration of Mr. Pierce and that of his successor, Mr. Buchanan.

12. Soon after the passage of this act, large emigrations were made from the free States, with the design of making Kansas a free State. At the same time, great efforts were made to establish it as a slave State, by emigrants chiefly from the State of Missouri, many of them taking their slaves with them. A violent and sanguinary contest soon ensued between the advocates and the opponents of slavery; and the grossest frauds were committed in several of the subsequent elections for the choice of public officers, and also for the choice of delegates for the formation of a constitution.

13. Large bodies of armed men from Missouri, who have commonly been styled "*Border Ruffians*," formed into regiments, entered the Territory, in order to frustrate, by military force, the purpose of those emigrants who designed to establish Kansas as a free State, and a considerable number of lives were sacrificed in the conflict.

14. The first governor of the Territory was *A. H. Reeder*, of Pennsylvania, who arrived in October, 1854; and an election for a delegate to congress was held in November, but a great part of the votes were cast by persons from Missouri, who were not residents of the Territory, and a majority of the votes was found to be illegal.

15. In March, 1855, another election was held for choosing members of the territorial legislature, and it was found that, out of 6,218 votes cast, only 1,310 were legal, and of these 791 were given for the free-state candidates.

16. *Wilson Shannon*, of Ohio, was appointed governor in place of Reeder, and assumed office on the 1st of September. Delegates were chosen to a constitutional convention that assembled at *Topeka*, and, in November, promulgated a con-

stitution in which slavery was prohibited; but the *Topeka Constitution* was never carried into effect.

17. In August, 1856, Shannon was succeeded in office by *John W. Geary*, of Pennsylvania, who found the Territory in a very disturbed condition, and after various conflicts, and ineffectual endeavors to restore order, he demanded the removal of *Lecompte*, the district judge of Kansas, for gross misdemeanor; but Lecompte, being sustained by a majority of the United States senate, Governor Geary resigned his office in March, 1857, and *Robert J. Walker*, of Mississippi, was appointed in his place, by *Mr. Buchanan*, who had now become President.

18. In June, 1857, the delegates to another convention for forming a constitution were elected, but the free-state men, feeling that they had no security for a fair election, generally took no part in it. This convention met at *Lecompton*, and formed a constitution in which slavery was established. The promulgation of this constitution caused great excitement. It was strongly condemned by Governor Walker, who proceeded immediately to Washington to remonstrate against its adoption; but, before his arrival, it had been adopted by congress, and received the approval of the President. Governor Walker soon after resigned his office, and *James W. Denver*, of California, was appointed in his place.

19. The *Lecompton Constitution*, when submitted to the people, in 1858, was rejected by a majority of upwards of 10,000 votes. Soon after this rejection, *Denver* resigned his office, and *Samuel Medary*, of Ohio, was appointed governor.

20. Delegates to another constitutional convention were elected, who met in July, 1859, at *Wyandot*, and formed a constitution in which slavery was prohibited. This constitution was ratified by the people by about 4,000 majority. A State election was held under it, on the 6th of December, 1859, and *Charles Robinson* was elected governor.

21. *Kansas*, after a long, calamitous, and sanguinary conflict, in which the grossest frauds were committed, and the vilest passions exhibited, was finally admitted, by congress, into the Union, in January, 1861, as a *free State*.

22. In 1857, Franklin Pierce was succeeded by *James Buchanan*, the democratic candidate, who received 174 electoral votes. *John C. Fremont*, the republican candidate, received 114 electoral votes.

23. The two great political parties into which the people of the United States had, for a considerable number of years, been divided, were the *democratic* and the *whig* parties; but after the repeal by congress of the Missouri Compromise, a

party styled the *republican* party was formed, composed chiefly of those citizens who had before belonged to the whig party. The leading principle of this new party was opposition to the further extension of slavery into free territory; yet it maintained that congress had no right to interfere with slavery as it existed in the slave States.

24. The subject of slavery continued unhappily to disturb the peace of the country during Mr. Buchanan's administration, as it had done during that of Mr. Pierce; and his administration was noted for the continuation of the troubles in Kansas, for the raid of John Brown in Virginia, and, towards its close, for the manœuvres and preparations for the great rebellion which soon followed. Three of the members of his cabinet, Cobb, Thompson, and Floyd, ultimately took an active and prominent part in the secession of the slave States, and much was done by them, while in office, to aid it, especially by *Floyd*, the secretary of war, by sending the United States arms and munitions of war to the Southern States.

25. On the 16th of October, 1859, *John Brown*, with fifteen white men, two of them his sons, and five men of color, made a foolhardy invasion into the State of Virginia, with the avowed object of freeing the slaves, took possession of the United States Arsenal at Harper's Ferry, and a considerable part of the town, and seized and held some of the citizens as hostages. Four of the inhabitants were killed in the conflict.

26. A great panic was soon raised in the neighborhood, and in a great part of the State of Virginia; and the next day some of the federal troops and of the Virginia militia arrived, and 1,500 armed men were on the ground to suppress the insurrection.

27. Brown and his men, with the hostages, took refuge in the armory buildings, which were seized by the troops; twelve of the invaders were killed, Brown and four of his men were taken prisoners, and two of them escaped, but they were afterwards captured. Brown and the six other prisoners were brought to trial, and were hanged.

28. This mad enterprise caused a great sensation throughout the country, and it was generally condemned, as wholly unjustifiable, in the free, as well as in the slave States.

29. Brown was a native of Connecticut, but had passed most of his life in Ohio, and he had sustained, from early life, the character of an upright and religious man. He had long been a zealous abolitionist, and, together with six sons, had taken an active part in the contest to prevent the establishment of slavery in Kansas; and in this contest one of his sons was killed.

30. His hostility to slavery became a sort of monomania, and he was thought by some persons to be insane. But Mr. Wise, the governor of Virginia, who had interviews with him, said of him, "They are mistaken who take him to be a madman. He is a man of clear head, cool, collected, indomitable.—He inspired me with great trust in his integrity as a man of truth."

31. After his condemnation, he maintained unwavering firmness, serenity, and cheerfulness; corresponded much with his family and friends,—regarding himself as a martyr who had sacrificed his life in a good cause; and he met his fate in such a manner as excited the admiration even of those who condemned his course.

32. At the time of the adoption of the federal constitution, and long afterwards, there was little difference of opinion between the Northern and the Southern States on the subject of *slavery*. In both parts of the country, it was regarded as a "social, moral, and political evil."

33. This was the opinion of Washington, Jefferson, Madison, Patrick Henry, Marshall, Pinckney, and some of the other eminent Southern statesmen; and it was a common expectation that the institution would, before long, be abolished.

34. But after the invention of the *cotton-gin* by Mr. Whitney, in 1794, the cultivation of *cotton* became a very important business, the value of slaves and of slave labor was greatly increased, and to extend and perpetuate the institution of slavery soon became a leading object in the Southern States. Since that time, slavery has unhappily been a disturbing political question, which has caused much dissension and hostile feeling between the free and the slave States.

35. This feeling was strongly manifested when the State of Missouri was admitted into the Union, and the Missouri Compromise was formed; and it was greatly increased by the repeal of this Compromise by the bill for the organization of the Territories of Kansas and Nebraska.

36. In 1860, the 16th President of the United States was elected. Previous to this election, the country was in a state of great prosperity, being at peace at home and abroad; yet it was convulsed by fierce party contentions in relation to this election. The two principal parties into which the country was divided, were the *democratic* and the *republican;* and *slavery* was the great cause of strife.

37. The democratic party, which was strongly supported in the slave States, and which had long had the ascendency in the country, being unable to unite on a candidate for the Pres-

idency, was divided into two sections. The Southern section, which was the most strenuous to promote the interests of slavery, took *John C. Breckenridge* for its candidate; the other section took *Stephen A. Douglas;* the candidate of the republican party was *Abraham Lincoln;* and the candidate of a fourth party, styled the *Union party*, was *John Bell.*

38. The election, which was conducted without violence, took place on the 6th of November, 1860, and resulted in the choice of *Abraham Lincoln,* who received 180 electoral votes; Breckenridge had 72; *Bell,* 39; and *Douglas,* 12.

SECTION IX.

Lincoln's Administration:— Secession:— The War of the Rebellion.— From A. D. 1861 *to* 1866.

1. The Southern leaders declared that the election of Mr. Lincoln, a candidate whom they called "sectional," so menaced the security of their local institutions that *Secession*, long claimed by them as a State right, had become a necessity; and so successful were their machinations, that, on the 20th of December, 1860, South Carolina, by a convention, declared that "the union then subsisting between herself and other States, under the name of the 'United States of America,' was dissolved." Her example was soon followed by Mississippi, Florida, Alabama, Georgia, Louisiana, Texas, Virginia, Arkansas, North Carolina, and Tennessee.

2. On the 4th of February, 1861, delegates from the then seceded States met at Montgomery, Ala., and formed a *provisional government* for the "Confederate States of America," of which *Jefferson Davis* of Mississippi was appointed President, and *Alexander H. Stephens* of Georgia Vice-President. This provisional government was soon superseded by a "permanent" one, under whose constitution the same chief officers were re-elected to serve for six years from Feb. 22, 1862.

3. A *Peace Congress*, composed of delegates from twenty states, held a session of three weeks at Washington, in February; but its recommendations were not adopted by Congress. In March, a *Commission* was also sent to Washington, by the Confederate Government, to obtain recognition from the authorities there, and to negotiate for the settlement of difficulties; but the President declined any official intercourse.

4. In the midst of the excitement produced by these events,

Mr. Lincoln was inaugurated. His Inaugural Address, though mild and conciliatory in tone, expressed his firm determination to maintain the integrity of the Union, and to enforce obedience to the laws.

5. The senators and representatives from the seceded States had withdrawn from Congress, but many of the public offices were still held by avowed secessionists. Affairs had been so managed that few vessels of the navy were available at home, and the army was scattered on the Western frontier, while many officers of both joined the traitors. The Confederate States had seized the entire government property within their then limits, consisting of *mints*, *custom-houses*, *post-offices*, *dock-yards*, *revenue cutters*, *arsenals*, and *forts*. Of the latter there were excepted *Forts Pickens*, *Taylor*, and *Jefferson*, near the Florida Coast, and *Fort Sumter* in Charleston Harbor. The national finances had been seriously tampered with by Southern members of the late Cabinet; and these circumstances, together with the prevalent feeling of uncertainty and distrust at the North, made the position of the Government extremely embarrassing.

6. An unsuccessful attempt to convey supplies to Fort Sumter had been made in January. Mr. Lincoln gave notice that the attempt would be repeated, but before this was done, *Gen. Pierre Beauregard*, Confederate Commander at Charleston, summoned the fort to surrender. *Major Robert Anderson*, then in command with a garrison of 70 men, refused; and on April 12, a bombardment was begun, by which, after two days, he was compelled to capitulate, evacuating the fort on the 15th.

7. The North was aroused to the greatest enthusiasm, and the President's call for 75,000 men (April 15) was answered by immediate volunteers from all the loyal States. The first bloodshed was in *Baltimore*, April 19, when a mob attacked a body of troops passing through that city to the defence of Washington, and killed two Massachusetts men. This was just 86 years after the battle of Lexington.

8. In April, the Confederates seized the *Armory* at *Harper's Ferry*, and the *Navy Yard* at *Norfolk;* and soon after, their forces were mainly distributed across Virginia, between these two places, being heaviest at *Manassas*. Lieut. Gen. Scott collected the Federal troops about Washington, occupying and fortifying the *Heights* opposite that city.

9 A force sent out from *Fortress Monroe*, where *Gen. B. F. Butler* was in command, was defeated, June 10, at *Big Bethel*. *Col. Wallace* dispersed a body of Confederates at *Romney*, Va. June 11, and early in July, *Gen. Patterson* drove another up the *Shenandoah Valley*. In the meantime, *Gen. Geo. B. McClellan*, having gained the battles of *Philippi* and *Rich*

Mountain, and having received the surrender of a force at *Beverly* in June, obtained entire possession of West Virginia.

10. Under Gen. Scott's orders, *Gen. Irwin McDowell* advanced from Washington to dislodge the enemy at Manassas. A reconnoisance having been made from *Centerville*, the whole force met the enemy under Gen. Beauregard, at *Bull Run*, where a severe battle occurred July 21. The rebels were at first driven back, but were re-enforced by *Gen. Joseph E. Johnston*, whom Gen. Patterson, in the Shenandoah Valley, had failed to hold in check. The Union forces gave way, and fled in panic to Washington, suffering great loss.

11. The rebels, who had now made *Richmond* their capital, were greatly encouraged by the results of this battle; while the North, aroused by it to the reality of the war, made vigorous efforts to raise and equip fresh troops. Gen. McClellan was called, July 22, to the command of the Union Army in East Virginia, and spent the autumn and winter in preparations for the spring campaign. Various engagements occurred, of which the chief were the defeat of the rebel *Gen. Floyd*, at *Carnifex Ferry* by *Gen. William S. Rosecrans*, and the failure, with heavy loss, of *Gen. N. P. Banks* to throw Federal troops across the Potomac at *Ball's Bluff*.

12. Missouri, by her Convention and Legislature, had refused to secede, but the Confederates sent in troops from Arkansas and Texas to aid her governor in attempting to force her out of the Union. *Col. Franz Sigel* won a battle at *Carthage*, July 5, but was compelled to fall back, leaving the rebels to overrun South-western Missouri. *Gen. Nathaniel Lyon*, in May, really saved the State by securing the arsenal at *St. Louis*. Having waited in vain at *Springfield* for re-enforcements, he at last attacked the advancing rebels at *Wilson's Creek*, Aug. 10, where he fell; and his men, unable to hold the field, retreated under Sigel. *Col James A. Mulligan*, after a brave resistance, surrendered *Lexington* to the rebel *Gen. Sterling E. Price*, but the place was retaken in October. In November, *Gen. John C. Fremont*, who had for some time been in command of this department, was relieved by *Gen. Robert Hunter*.

13. During the summer of 1861, naval preparations were made on an immense scale. Many steamers were built or purchased, and stationed along the coast to enforce the *blockade* declared April 19. The year is memorable in naval history for the change effected in warfare by the extensive building of iron or *iron-clad* vessels of war. An expedition, under *Commodore Silas H. Stringham* and Gen. Butler, took the forts at *Hatteras*, Aug. 29; and another, under *Commodore S. F. Dupont* and *Gen. T. W Sherman*, took *Port Royal*, Nov 7, thus securing two important footholds upon the coast.

14. In accordance with a call of the President, Congress met in *special session*, July 4, and authorized the enlistment of 500,000 men, and appropriated $500,000,000 to defray the expenses of the War. Towns, counties, and States contributed large sums to be variously applied to war purposes.

15. — (1862.) At the beginning of this year the Confederate forces numbered not far from 350,000. They occupied half of Missouri, Kentucky, and West Virginia, nearly all East Virginia and Florida, with the whole of the other Southern States, their strongest force being at Manassas, under Gen. Johnston. They also held the Mississippi and its chief branches.

16. The Federal forces numbered about 450,000, of which 200,000 were near Washington, under Gen. McClellan, Gen. Scott having retired; a large body was at Fortress Monroe, under Gen. Wool; one in West Virginia, under Rosecrans; one in Kentucky, under *Gen. Don Carlos Buell;* and one about *Cairo*, under *Gen. Ulysses S. Grant*, *Gen. Henry W. Halleck* being Commander-in-Chief of the Western Department. A strong *flotilla* of *gun* and *mortar boats*, designed to operate on the Western rivers, was also at Cairo, under *Commodore A. H. Foote.* A considerable naval force was already in the Gulf of Mexico, while preparations were making for formidable expeditions to various points on the coast.

17. In January, one of these, under *Gen. A. E. Burnside* and *Commodore L. M. Goldsborough*, entered Hatteras Inlet, and, after encountering heavy storms, captured *Roanoke Island* by severe fighting. Soon after, Gen. Burnside took *Newbern* and *Beaufort*, N. C. *Fort Pulaski*, the main outer defence of Savannah, was taken by an expedition from Port Royal, in April; and *Pensacola* also fell into Federal possession.

18. The rebels, having iron plated the frigate "Merrimac" at Norfolk, and fitted her with a ram, on March 8th attacked the fleet at the mouth of the *James River*, sunk the "*Cumberland*" and the "*Congress*," after the bravest resistance on their part, and then retired. On that night, the "*Monitor*," the first of a class of *iron-clads* invented by Ericsson, opportunely arrived from New York, and the next day attacked the "Merrimac," and drove her back disabled to Norfolk.

19. President Lincoln had ordered a general movement of troops to be made on the 22d of February. The rebels fell back upon Richmond before Gen. McClellan, who prepared to approach the city by the peninsula lying between the York and James Rivers. Moving his troops by way of Fortress Monroe to *Yorktown*, he besieged that city for a month, taking possession May 4th, and the next day defeated the confederates at

Williamsburg. Gen. Wool, from Fortress Monroe, occupied Norfolk on the 10th; and the next day, the rebels blew up the "Merrimac," leaving James River open to Federal gun boats.

20. By the 25th of May, Gen. McClellan had crossed the *Chickahominy,* near which occurred the severe battle of *Fair Oaks.* Neither side won a decided advantage, although the rebels suffered the heavier loss, and Gen. Johnston was wounded. He was succeeded in command by *Gen. Robert E. Lee,* before employed in West Virginia. The rebel Generals *Thomas J. Jackson* and *Richard Ewell,* in the Shenandoah Valley, had overpowered the Federal forces under Gens. Fremont and Banks, and thus threatened Washington. This prevented the sending of re-enforcements to McClellan, who now decided to change his base from the York River to the James

21. This movement brought on a series of desperate encounters, known as the "*Seven Days' Battles,*" which lasted from June 25 to July 1 Among the most bloody of these were *Mechanicsville, Cold Harbor, Savage Station, White Oak Swamp,* and *Malvern Hill.* On the evening of July 1, the rebels, worn out in the conflict, retired to Richmond, and the Federal troops, equally exhausted, took position at *Harrison's Landing,* under cover of the gunboats, having lost 15,000 men, in killed, wounded, and missing.

22. The President now called for 600,000 troops, and soon after ordered that 300,000 of these should be raised by *draft,* to serve for nine months. Gen. Halleck became Commander-in-Chief; and the troops about Washington, and in West Virginia, were consolidated into the "Army of Virginia," under *Gen. John Pope.* McClellan was ordered to withdraw from the Peninsula to join Pope in opposing Lee, who had taken the offensive, and who, early in August, marched rapidly northward.

23. The rebels reached the *Rapidan River,* and Generals Jackson and Ewell with the advance were checked by Gen. Banks at *Cedar Mountain;* but the coming up of the main army compelled Gen. Pope to retreat towards Washington, fighting on the old battle-fields of *Manassas* and *Bull Run,* and at *Chantilly* where Gens. *Stevens* and *Kearney* fell. Sept. 3d found his exhausted army within the intrenchments of the capital, and he himself was relieved of his command by McClellan.

24. Gen. Lee crossed the Potomac, occupying *Frederic* and *Hagarstown.* The battle of *South Mountain,* Sept. 14, compelled him to fall back to *Antietam Creek,* where he was joined by Jackson, who had just received the surrender of *Harper's Ferry,* with its garrison and munitions of war. On the 17th was fought the great battle of *Antietam,* in which Lee

was defeated, but was allowed to retreat into Virginia, having lost 30,000 men in this campaign.

25. The national army remained in Maryland until the last of October, the rebel *Gen. Stuart* meantime making a *raid* completely round it. It next moved into Virginia, and *Gen. Burnside*, succeeding Gen. McClellan, attempted to approach Richmond by *Fredericsburg*. He crossed the Rappahannock with some opposition, attacked, Dec. 13, the strong position of the rebels, and was repulsed with fearful loss. He recrossed the river, and his plan was abandoned.

26. During this year (1862), the military movements in the West were numerous and important. In January, a confederate force was routed in Eastern Kentucky, by *Col. Garfield;* and *Gen. Geo. H. Thomas* won a brilliant victory at *Mill Springs*, where the rebel *Gen. Zollicoffer* was killed. In February, Gen. Grant, aided by Foote with his gunboats, captured *Fort Henry* on the Tennessee River, and *Fort Donelson* on the Cumberland, with many stores and provisions. These Federal successes obliged the rebels to withdraw from Kentucky.

27. Gen. Grant now pushed up the Tennessee, and was attacked at *Pittsburg Landing*, April 6, by a superior force under *Gens. A. S. Johnston* and *G. T. Beauregard*. He was compelled to retreat with heavy loss; but Gen. Buell coming up with re enforcements the same night, the enemy were pursued the next day, and completely routed, the federals recovering what they had before lost. This was the battle of *Shiloh*, one of the bloodiest of the war. The rebels retreated to *Corinth*. Miss., where they were besieged by *Gen. Halleck*, who came down from St. Louis after the battle of Shiloh, and took command in person After severe fighting, Corinth was evacuated, May 26 *Gen. O. M. Mitchell* had meantime taken *Huntsville*, Ala., thus severing one of the chief rebel lines of railroad communication.

28. During the summer, the confederates made a vigorous attempt to regain Kentucky; but, after exciting great alarm in that State and in Ohio, they were compelled to fall back to Tennessee, carrying, however, many spoils When *Gen. Halleck* was made Commander in-Chief, Gen. Grant took command of the Army of the Tennessee. Early in the autumn, *Gen Price* made a vigorous attempt to drive him from Corinth, but was defeated by Gen. Rosecrans in the battle of *Iuka*. Several battles followed, resulting in the rescue of West Tennessee from the rebels. In December, Gen. Grant failed in an attempt to penetrate Mississippi for the purpose of cutting railroads east of *Vicksburg;* and, at about the same time, *Gen W. T. Sherman* was repulsed in an attack upon that place. Gen

Rosencrans, in October, went to the Ohio to organize a new army, with which he afterwards encountered *Gen. Braxton E. Bragg* in East Tennessee, and defeated him in the severe battle of *Murfreesborough*, Dec. 31 and Jan. 1, 1863.

29. At *Pea Ridge*, Ark., March 8, 1862, the confederates, under *Gens. Early, Van Dorn, Price*, and *Mc Cullough*, were defeated by *Gens. Samuel R. Curtis* and *Sigel*, after three days' fighting; and *Mc Cullough* was killed. *Columbus*, Ky., was abandoned early in the year by the rebels, who then fortified *Island No.* 10, in the Mississippi. Gen. Pope, having driven a strong force from *New Madrid*, Mo., opposite the island, co-operated with Com. Foote, for its capture. After 23 days' bombardment, the rebels withdrew; but Pope cut off their retreat, taking many prisoners. Their fleets were soon after destroyed at *Fort Pillow* and at *Memphis*, which surrendered to Commodore *Charles H. Davis*.

30. *Flag-Officer David G. Farragut* was sent to the Gulf in command of a squadron designed to co-operate with land forces under Gen. Butler for the capture of *New Orleans*. *Forts Jackson* and *St. Philip*, below the city, were attacked April 18, and six days' bombardment proving vain, Farragut ran past the forts with part of his fleet, destroyed the rebel fleet above, and reached the city on the 25th. The forts surrendered to *Commander D. D. Porter*. Butler took command in New Orleans, and Farragut proceeded up the river, capturing Natchez, May 12.

31. During 1862, the Government made liberal appropriations and strenuous exertions for the prosecution of the war. Treasury notes and interest-bearing bonds were issued to a large amount; taxes were imposed on incomes and manufactures; duties increased; and revenue stamps required upon various *papers* and *articles*. — The year closed gloomily. The Rebellion was in full strength, party spirit was running high at home, commerce was crippled, credit impaired, and foreign interference was seriously threatened; while the successes of the year seemed balanced by its reverses and disappointments. — West Virginia was admitted to the Union in 1862.

32. — (1863.) The 1st of January, 1863, is memorable as the date of the "*Emancipation Proclamation*," in which President Lincoln, by virtue of the power vested in him as Commander-in-Chief, and in pursuance of notice given Sept. 22, 1863, declared that all persons held as slaves within any State or designated part of a State, the people whereof are in rebellion against the United States, "are, and henceforward shall be, free." In 1862, slavery in the District of Columbia had been abolished by Congress, and forever prohibited in the terri-

tories of the Republic. In March, the "*Conscription Act*" became a law; and the preparations made to enforce it caused great excitement. In New-York City, the commencement of the draft, July 13, was followed by a three-days' *riot*, in which a great amount of property was destroyed, and many persons, chiefly negroes, were killed. The draft nowhere else met serious opposition, as military power was employed when necessary to insure its quiet enforcement.

33. In January, Gen. Burnside was succeeded by *Gen. Joseph Hooker* in the command of the "*Army of the Potomac*," still lying opposite Fredericsburg. Hooker crossed the *Rappahannock* early in May, and fought the severe battle of *Chancellorsville*, in which the rebels defeated him, but lost their able general, "*Stonewall Jackson.*" At the same time, *Gen. Stoneman* made a cavalry raid into Northern Virginia, cutting rebel communications in every direction.

34. In June, Gen. Lee attempted a second invasion of the North. He took *Winchester* and *Martinsburg*, and, crossing Maryland, nearly reached *Harrisburg*. The Army of the Potomac, under *Gen. Geo. G. Meade*, to whose command it had been transferred the last of June, pressed forward to cut off the advance of the enemy; and on the 1st, 2d, and 3d of July was fought the bloody battle of *Gettysburg*. This decisive victory may be considered the turning point of the war, and had a most encouraging effect upon the country, accompanied as it was with great successes in the South-west. Gen. Lee, thoroughly defeated, escaped to the Rapidan, followed by *Meade;* and the two armies confronted each other throughout the year, with occasional skirmishing or minor engagements. Simultaneously with Lee's invasion, *Gen. Morgan* made a cavalry raid into *Indiana* and *Ohio* for purposes of plunder. His band was scattered and mostly captured, he himself being taken prisoner.

35. The rebels, early in this year, made vigorous efforts to recover North Carolina; but the Federals, under *Gen. John G. Foster*, secured a stronger hold than ever in that State. *Rear-Admiral Dupont* made an attack upon Fort Sumter in April, which proved the inability of the navy to capture it without cooperating land forces. These were sent out under *Gen. Q. A. Gillmore*, who landed troops on *Folly Island*, and succeeded in planting on Morris Island batteries which commanded *Fort Sumter* and *Charleston*. The fire of *Fort Wagner* and *Battery Gregg* on *Morris Island* was silenced by the fleet, which, with the land batteries, kept up a fierce bombardment of Sumter from the 17th to the 24th of August, laying one side of it in ruins. Several *assaults* were made on *Fort Wagner*, the second of which, noted for its desperate bravery, was one of the earliest occasions of bringing colored troops to the

test of battle. The fort was taken in September The first shell was thrown into *Charleston*, Aug. 22, and its bombardment continued at intervals until its final surrender.

36. The movements of Grant in Mississippi, and Sherman at Vicksburg, already mentioned, were part of a plan for the capture of that stronghold, which was still (1863) the object of Gen. Grant, who now commanded the united armies of the Tennessee and the Mississippi. While awaiting his arrival from Memphis, Gen. Sherman and Commodore Porter captured *Arkansas Post*, the key of the Arkansas River. The forces were collected on the Mississippi, above Vicksburg. An attempt to cut a new channel for the river, which should leave Vicksburg inland, failed; as well as another to get in its rear by the *Yazoo River;* and Grant then moved his army down the west side of the Mississippi, while Porter ran his fleet past the batterries, and met Farragut, who had passed *Port Hudson* in the same way. Grant now recrossed the river, and by rapid movements, and a series of brilliant victories (*Port Gibson*, *Raymond*, *Jackson*, *Champion Hill*, and *Black River Ridge*), drove the rebels, under *Gen. John C. Pemberton*, within their intrenchments at Vicksburg, and secured to himself a secure position in the rear of the city. Meanwhile, *Col. Grierson* made a daring and destructive raid from *Lagrange*, Tenn., to *Baton Rouge*.

37. Two assaults on Vicksburg were unsuccessful; but the siege was kept up with incessant bombardment until July 4 (the very day of Lee's retreat from Pennsylvania), when Pemberton, *Johnston* being unable to reach him with supplies from the interior, surrendered his whole garrison with his munitions of war, to Gen. Grant. Four days later, Port Hudson surrendered to Gen. Banks; and the whole Mississippi was thus opened.

38. After his victory at Murfreesborough, Gen. Rosecrans remained there, sending out occasional expeditions, or repelling those of the enemy, until June, when he moved southward, and drove the confederates, under Gen. Bragg, from *Duck River* across the *Cumberland Mountains* to *Chattanooga*, Ga., which they began to fortify, but deserted it on the further approach of Rosecrans. Bragg was soon re-enforced by *Gen. James Longstreet* from Virginia, and Johnston from Mississippi, with many paroled men from Vicksburg, and on the 19th September attacked Rosecrans at *Chicamauga Creek*, Ga., where, after fighting furiously for two days, the latter fell back to Chattanooga.

39. Reinforcements were hastened to his relief by Gen. Grant, who had assumed command of the consolidated departments of the *Tennessee*, *Cumberland*, and *Ohio;* and vigorous preparations were made to force Bragg to raise the siege of

Chattanooga. Gen. Sherman joined Grant in November; and on the 23d they began the series of conflicts which included the battles of *Lookout Mountain* and *Missionary Ridge*, and lasted until the 25th, when the confederates, completely routed, fled into Georgia. At the same time, Gen. Burnside was struggling for the possession of East Tennessee, being besieged at *Knoxville* by Longstreet, who had moved northward after the battle of Chicamauga; but Sherman hastened to his relief from Chattanooga, and Longstreet, raising the siege Dec. 3, crossed the mountains, and rejoined Lee in Virginia.

40. In January, 1863, the rebels were repulsed at *Springfield* and *Hartsville*, Mo., at *Cape Girardeau* in April, and at *Helena*, Ark., July 4; on the 10th of September *Gen. Frederick Steele* entered *Little Rock*, and almost the whole State of Arkansas was thus restored to the Federal Government. Late in 1862, Gen. Banks had succeeded Gen. Butler in the Department of the Gulf. Before May, 1863, he had taken possession of the rich country between New Orleans and *Alexandria*, La., after which he invested Port Hudson, whose fall has been already mentioned. This siege was remarkable for the great number of fierce and fruitless assaults made upon the enemy's works. Gen. Banks afterwards sent two expeditions to *Texas*, which, though partial failures, secured several points on the coast, and the *Rio Grande* as far as *Brownsville*.

41. The Navy, besides its memorable deeds on the Mississippi and the attack on Charleston, this year rendered effective service in blockading the coast. Two marked exploits were the capture of the "*Nashville*" by the "*Montauk*," and of the ram "*Atlanta*" by the "*Weehawken*," both on the coast of Georgia.

42. The 37th Congress terminated March 4, 1863. It had put the entire resources of the country at the disposal of the President, had authorized the enlistment of colored troops, and had removed the distinctions between the *regular* and the *volunteer* service. The great progress of the national arms in this year, by which Missouri, Arkansas, Kentucky, Tennessee, a large part of Louisiana, Mississippi, and Florida, the Rio Grande frontier of Texas, and the control of the Mississippi had been won from the confederates, gave just cause of rejoicing; and the year 1864 opened with a reasonable prospect of an early and successful close of the war.

43. — (1864.) Gen. Sherman, leaving Vicksburg with a strong force, Feb. 2, made an invasion into Mississippi, as far as *Meridian*, destroying the railroads about that place; but a detachment under *Gen. A. J. Smith*, expected from *Memphis*, failing to meet him there, he returned to Vicksburg, with a great

amount of property and several thousand liberated slaves. At about the same time, an expedition sent by *Gen. Gillmore* from Hilton Head into Florida, under *Gen. Seymour*, defeated the rebels at *Jacksonville*, but was in turn defeated at *Olustee*.

44. The disastrous "*Red River Expedition*," designed to capture *Shreveport*, La., was undertaken early in this year by Gen. Banks. He led a heavy force from New Orleans to Alexandria, where he was joined by Gen. Smith from Vicksburg, and Admiral Porter with his fleet. Above *Natchitoches*, the army, being separated from the gunboats, was drawn into ambuscade near *Mansfield*, and routed. The attack was renewed at *Pleasant Hill;* but the rebels were at last repulsed by Gen. Smith, and the army reached the river greatly disorganized. The fleet, which had gone up nearly to Shreveport, turned back, passing the rapids at Alexandria with great difficulty, and the whole expedition returned to the Mississippi.

45. Gen. Steele, in Arkansas, had attempted to join in this movement, but, hearing of its failure, returned to Little Rock with considerable loss. The employment of these forces in Louisiana gave opportunity to *Gen. Forrest*, commanding the rebel forces on the Mississippi, to make a fresh attempt on Western Tennessee and Kentucky. He captured *Union City*, Tenn., attacked *Paducah*, Ky., and, on April 12, perpetrated an inhuman massacre of the garrison, consisting partly of colored troops, at *Fort Pillow*. In April, *Plymouth, N. C.*, was taken by the rebel *Gen. Hoke*, assisted by the ram "*Albermarle*," which in October was sunk by *Lieut. Cushing*, and the place was recaptured.

46. But the great interest of 1864 centers about the main Federal armies, whose movements now displayed a unity of purpose not hitherto apparent. The grade of *Lieut.-General*, made extinct by the retirement of Gen. Scott in October, 1861, was revived by Congress, and conferred in full, March 3, upon Gen. Grant, who became Commander-in-Chief in place of Halleck. Gen. Grant turned over to Sherman the military division of the Mississippi, comprising the Departments of the *Ohio* under *Gen. John M. Schofield*, of the *Cumberland* under *Gen. Geo. H. Thomas*, and of the *Tennessee* (late Sherman's) under *Gen. James B. McPherson*. The Lieut.-General made his headquarters with the "*Army of the Potomac*," which was still commanded by Gen. Meade; the cavalry corps being under *Gen. Philip H. Sheridan*. To Gen. Sigel was assigned the department of West Virginia; to Gen. Foster that of the South; and Gen. Butler held a large force at Fortress Monroe.

47. In the month of April, vast preparations were made for a simultaneous advance upon Richmond from the Potomac, and upon Atalanta from Chattanooga, by the respective Eastern and

Western armies; and on May 3, the great forward movement was ordered. *Gen. Lee*, strengthened by the corps of Longstreet, was entrenched in *Orange County, Va.* The army of the Potomac left its position near *Culpepper Court House*, crossed the *Rapidan* May 4, and, moving southward to the right of Lee, compelled him to fight. Then followed the terrible battles of the *Wilderness* and *Spottsylvania Court House*, which resulted in the continued retreat of Lee, who, followed by Grant, with constant flanking, fell back to the defences of Richmond.

48. Meantime, Gen. Butler had taken up the James River a strong expedition designed to capture and hold Petersburg. This he failed to do, as well as to prevent Beauregard from joining Lee; but he fortified *City Point* and *Bermuda Hundred*, at the junction of the *Appomatox* and *James Rivers*, thus securing a foothold for Grant, whose entire army was by the middle of June transferred to the south side of the James, and who then began the siege of Petersburg. To defend this city, on whose safety that of Richmond depended, Lee threw his main army into its fortifications The siege was vigorously pushed during the year, with frequent engagements, among which the most important was that at *Ream's Station*, by which the *Weldon Railroad* was seized; an attempt to capture Richmond by an attack from the North; and the battle of *Hatcher's Run*.

49. Frequent cavalry raids were made about Richmond; and two co-operating movements, designed to cut the *Virginia and Tennessee Railroad* and capture *Lynchburg*, failed. On the retreat of Hunter, successor of Sigel, who conducted the second, the rebels again occupied the Shenandoah Valley, whence, in July, Early made a third invasion of Maryland, and threatened Philadelphia, Baltimore, and Washington. The invaders retreated, but remained about the Upper Potomac until autumn, when Sheridan, who had taken command in this department, routed them in the battle of *Cedar Run*, Oct. 19, and Early remained quiet through the next winter.

50. Gen. Sherman's Army at Chattanooga was put in motion, May 5, towards *Atlanta*, distant 140 miles. This whole route was contested by *Johnston* in a series of battles, among which the most severe were at *Resaca*, and around *Dallas* and *Kenesaw Mountain*. By the middle of July, Sherman's army was before Atlanta, where furious fighting occurred on the 20th, 22d, and 28th. Here, *Gen. McPherson* was killed. The siege continued until Sept. 1, when *Gen. John B. Hood*, who had superseded Johnston, withdrew from the city. Sherman at once occupied it, and spent September in accumulating supplies and recruiting his army. Meanwhile, Hood seriously threat-

ened the Federal communications with *Chattanooga* and *Nashville*, but finally moved into Alabama, severing his own with the Eastern coast. Sherman, leaving Thomas in Tennessee to watch Hood, at once abandoned Atlanta, and set out on his celebrated "*March to the Sea*," which constitutes one of the most remarkable military movements on record.

51. He left Atlanta, Nov. 15, with a well organized and equipped force of almost 60,000 picked men. The right wing, under *Gen. O. O. Howard*, followed the railroad towards *Macon*, and the left, under *Gen. Henry W. Slocum*, that towards *Augusta*. Avoiding both places, and taking *Milledgeville*, the two wings met at *Millen*, and thence marched to *Savannah*, which was reached about the 10th of December; *Fort McAllister* was soon carried by assault, and Gen. Sherman was thus enabled to communicate with the fleet off the coast, and the Federal lines closing about the city, the rebel commander, *Gen. William J. Hardee*, evacuated it on the night of the 20th, and escaped to Charleston with his troops.

52. Meantime, Gen. Hood, tempted by Sherman's withdrawal from Atlanta, attacked *Schofield* at *Franklin*, Tenn., and after a severe battle, Nov. 3, forced him to retreat to *Nashville*, which Hood then besieged; but he was driven from his intrenchments, and completely routed, by Thomas. Several successful Federal raids were made in Louisiana and Texas during the autumn; *Price* failed in making one from Arkansas into Missouri, and *East Tennessee* was the scene of frequent minor conflicts.

53. The navy, largely increased and thoroughly organized, did most important service in 1864 in blockading the coast and co-operating in the movements of land forces. The plan of operations inaugurated early in this year included the capture of seaports remaining in rebel possession. In carrying out this design, one of the most notable naval exploits was performed in *Mobile Bay*, Aug. 5, by *Rear-Admiral Farragut*, who ran the batteries of *Forts James and Morgan*, and attacked the rebel fleet above, destroying, among other vessels, the "*Tennessee*," the most formidable ram ever fitted out by the confederates. Afterwards, aided by *Gen. Gordon Granger* with troops, he obtained the surrender of these forts, which constituted the outer defences of Mobile. Farragut was made *Vice-Admiral* by Congress in December, 1864.

54. Three rebel piratical cruisers terminated their career of destruction in this year. The "*Alabama*," which had been the scourge of American commerce, was sunk off *Cherbourg*, June 14, by the "*Kearsarge*," after a fight of an hour and a half. The "*Florida*" was captured in the neutral harbor of *Bahia*, by the "*Wachusett*;" and the "*Georgia*," by the "*Niagara*," off the coast of Portugal.

55. In November, Mr. Lincoln was re-elected to the Presidency. Gen. McClellan was the candidate of the opposite party. *Nevada*, having become a State, Oct. 31, the votes of 28 States were cast in this election; all but those of *New Jersey*, *Delaware*, and *Kentucky* being for Mr. Lincoln. The close of 1864 found the strength of the South shattered by its immense losses in men and property, and by the severance of the Gulf States from those on the Atlantic, although the area of territory actually occupied by the Federal armies was about the same as the year previous.

56. — (1865.) The field of operations was now reduced to three States, and both sides prepared for a desperate and decisive struggle. Lee was made General-in-Chief at Richmond; Johnston was ordered to South Carolina, and *Richard Taylor* succeeded Hood in Alabama and Mississippi. Gen. Schofield was placed in command in North Carolina, and Gen. Gillmore, who had been in Virginia, relieved Gen. Foster in South Carolina.

57. The earliest operations of 1865 were in North Carolina. *Rear-Admiral Porter*, with the most formidable fleet ever collected, had made, Dec. 25, 1864, a fierce bombardment of *Fort Fisher*, situated at the mouth of Cape Fear River, and one of the main defences of *Wilmington;* but Gen. Butler, who commanded the land forces, considered an assault impracticable; and the attempt was abandoned until Jan. 15, when the terrific bombardment from the fleet was renewed, and the works were carried by troops under *Gen. Alfred H. Terry.* The surrender of Fort Fisher was followed by that of the other forts; Wilmington itself was soon after taken, and the last harbor was closed to blockade running.

58. Gen. Sherman now began an invasion of the Carolinas. He left Savannah, Jan. 22, and, completely deceiving the enemy as to his real object, reached *Orangeburg* Feb. 2, and *Columbia* on the 17th. He thus divided the rebel forces, and caused the evacuation of Charleston by Gen. Hardee, of which Gen. Gillmore took possession with colored troops. Sherman pushed on, reaching *Cheraw* March 3, *Fayetteville*, N. C., on the 12th, and *Goldsborough* on the 23d. Here he was met by Gen. Terry from Wilmington, and Gen. Schofield from Newbern. He spent the month of March in resting his army for co-operation with Grant, who, during Sherman's march, was completing his preparations for the final conflict with Lee.

59. Gen. Sheridan left Winchester Feb. 27, and, passing up the Shenandoah Valley, pursued *Early* from *Staunton*, over the mountains to *Charlottesville*, and having destroyed railroads and canals on his way, joined Grant March 28. Grant's army

now occupied a line of 30 miles, extending from *Chapin's Farm*, a point north of the James and near Richmond, through *Bermuda Hundred*, and around *Petersburg* to *Hatcher's Run*. The main force and strongest fortifications were on the left of this line; and one of the latter, *Fort Steadman*, was surprised and captured, but retaken after great slaughter. Attacks on the rebel works were made daily from some part of the line, with heavy losses on both sides, until April 1, when Gen. Sheridan, on Grant's left, broke through the rebel right, and, after fearful fighting, virtually decided the contest for Richmond. The struggle continued through the next day, on the night of which Lee evacuated Petersburg and Richmond, and they were at once occupied by National troops. Lee retreated towards Danville, pursued by the Federal army; and on the 9th of April he formally surrendered his entire army to Grant.

60. Gen. Sherman, after recruiting at Goldsborough, prepared to capture or destroy the rebel forces under Johnston, who, April 6, was at *Smithfield*, North Carolina. On the 10th, Sherman's army was in full pursuit towards *Greensborough;* but, on learning of Lee's surrender, the two generals agreed upon a suspension of hostilities, which resulted in Johnston's capitulation on the 26th of this month.

61. About the same time *Selma*, *Montgomery*, and other points in Alabama, surrendered to *Gen. J. H. Wilson*, sent out by Gen. Thomas from Nashville. An important movement was also in progress for the capture of the city of Mobile, then strongly defended by Gen. Taylor; Gen. Canby commanded the Federal land forces, while a fleet co-operated in the Bay. The city was approached from the east, and severe fighting occurred at *Spanish Fort* and *Blakely River*. On the 18th of April, the evacuation of Mobile was begun; and, two days after, it was surrendered to Gen. Canby and *Acting Rear-Admiral Thatcher*. On 4th of May, were surrendered all the land and naval forces in the Mississippi department to the same officers. The last battle of the war was at *Brazos*, Texas; and the surrender of the Texan army was made by *Gen. Kirby Smith*, on the 26th of May.

62. The rejoicings caused by these successes were suddenly interrupted by an event that filled every heart with grief and horror. This was the *assassination* of *President Lincoln*. On the evening of April 14, while at the theatre, he was shot in the head, and died in a few hours. The immediate assassin was one of a band of *conspirators*, whose design was to cripple the government by destroying its chief officers. The *President* was the only victim; although *Secretary Seward* was, at the same time, attacked in his own house, and severely wounded. Mr Lincoln was an honest, patient, clear-headed, and large-

hearted man; and these qualities, as displayed in his wise and firm administration of affairs in such perilous and difficult times, had won for him a respect and love rarely accorded to any ruler or any man. He was carried to his burial amid the tears of a nation; and his memory will be cherished forever by the American people, and kept equally sacred with that of Washington.

63. The *Vice-President, Andrew Johnson*, took the oath of office, and was inaugurated as President, April 15. On the 29th of May, he issued a *Proclamation of Amnesty*, granting, with certain exceptions, conditional pardon to persons who had engaged in the Rebellion; and he also took measures to restore civil government to the seceded states. Jefferson Davis, who had fled from Richmond on the approach of Grant, was captured May 10, 1865, at *Irvinsville*, Ga. He was placed in Fortress Monroe, where he is still confined (April 1866), awaiting trial for *treason*. An *Amendment*, providing that slavery shall not exist under the United States Government, having been duly adopted and ratified, became part of the Constitution early in 1866. On the 2d of April, 1866, President Johnson issued a proclamation, declaring the country no longer in a state of war.

64. Throughout the war, France and England showed little sympathy with the national cause, and adopted a general policy hostile to its success. England declared her neutrality, and very early accorded to the confederates belligerent rights: their privateers were built and fitted out in her harbors, while the supplies brought in by blockade runners came largely from English ports. The seizure of *rebel envoys* from a British steamer by a United States cruiser in 1861, and a raid made upon *St. Albans*, Vt., by rebels from Canada in 1864, caused great excitement in England and America; but, in both cases, due reparation was rendered on demand.

65. The previous pages contain only an outline of the most important events of the war. The entire frontier of the "*Confederacy*" was the constant theatre of lesser conflicts, of incursions from either side, and of a cruel *guerilla* warfare. Great difficulty attended the exchange of prisoners, of whom 130,000 or more were held by each side for various periods. Confederate prisoners at the North were comfortably housed and fed; but the inhuman treatment and horrible suffering of Federal soldiers in Southern prisons form one of the most shocking chapters in the history of the Rebellion. In bright relief to its horrors, stand out the charities called forth by the war. From the humblest country towns, as well as from the great cities, money and stores were freely poured out; while men and women, working under the various "organizations" which were the agents of this liberality, rendered most invaluable service to the national

cause. The *Sanitary* and *Christian Commissions* penetrated with their supplies and aid to every camp and hospital in the Federal army; while the *Union* and various *Freedmen's Commissions* were devoted to the special wants of the distressed Unionists and destitute freedmen of the South.

66. The enormous expenses of the war left upon the country a *debt* of about $2,800,000,000. It is worthy of notice, that no foreign *loans* were made by the United States Government: market for its *notes* and *bonds* being found at home, chiefly among the loyal people of the North. The banks early suspended specie payment; and the withdrawal of gold and silver from circulation created a necessity, which was met by the issue, in 1862, of *postage-currency* of all the denominations of smaller silver coins. *Legal tender* notes were also issued in the same year, which, from the color of the ink used in printing them, were called *greenbacks*. In 1863 a *National Banking System* was put in operation, by which any bank, on depositing government bonds with the United States Treasurer, receives from him, for issue, 90 per cent of said deposit, in notes, the payment of which is guaranteed by the United-States Government. —Gold was at its highest premium in July, 1864, when a dollar sold for $2.85 in currency.

67. At the close of the war, the *Federal Army* nominally contained 1,000,000 men. The *navy* contained 51,000 men, with 700 vessels of all descriptions. The whole number of soldiers enlisted is estimated at about 2,000,000, of whom 179-000 were colored. The losses, in battle and disease, are estimated at a little less than 300,000. Material changes in the art of war will, doubtless, follow from the experiences of this war, in respect to improved *ordnance*, the employment of *torpedoes* and *floating batteries*, and the value of *iron-clad* war-vessels, and of *earth-works* as defences.

68. Time enough has not yet elapsed for a just summing up of the results of the Great Rebellion. The abolition of slavery, the inevitable social changes in the South, the wonderful development of the resources and strength of the country, the settlement of the question of the "Integrity of the Union," the higher position of the nation before the world, are established facts; but in their working and final adjustment are involved problems that will require a long time for solution.

A. D.		Chronological Table of the History of the U. States.
1600	7	Virginia settled by the *English*.
	14	New York " " *Dutch*.
	20	Massachusetts " " *English Puritans*.
	23	New Hampshire " *English Puritans*.
	24	New Jersey " " *Dutch*.
	27	Delaware " " *Swedes* and *Fins*.
	30	Maine " " *English*.
	34	Maryland " " *Irish Catholics*.
17th	35	Connecticut " " *English Puritans*.
	36	Rhode Island " " *English* under *Roger Williams*.
	43	*Confederation* of the Colonies of *New England* for mutual defence
	50	North Carolina settled by the *English*.
	64	*New York* surrendered by the *Dutch* to the *English*.
	65	The Colonies of *Connecticut* and *New Haven* united.
	70	South Carolina settled by the *English*.
	82	Pennsylvania settled by *English Quakers* under *William Penn*
	92	The Colonies of *Plymouth* and *Massachusetts Bay* united.
1700	2	*East* and *West Jersey* united, and styled *New Jersey*.
	33	Georgia settled by the *English* under *General Oglethorpe*.
	63	*Peace of Paris: French war* ends: *Canada* confirmed to Engl.
	75	The *Revolutionary War* begins: *Peace* restored in 1783.
	76	*Declaration* of the INDEPENDENCE of the *United States*.
	88	The *Constitution of the United States* adopted.
18th	89	GEORGE WASHINGTON, 1st President of the U. States.
	91	Vermont admitted into the Union as a State.
	92	Kentucky " " "
	96	Tennessee " " "
	97	JOHN ADAMS, 2d President of the United States.
	98	Hostilities with *France*.
1800	1	THOMAS JEFFERSON, 3d President of the United States.
	2	Ohio admitted into the Union as a State.
	3	*Louisiana* purchased of France by the United States.
	7	General *Embargo* laid in all the ports of the U. S.; repealed 1809.
	9	JAMES MADISON, 4th President of the United States.
	11	Louisiana admitted into the Union as a State.
	12	Declaration of *War* against England, June 18: ends Dec. 24, '14.
	16	Indiana admitted into the Union as a State.
	17	JAMES MONROE, 5th President of the United States.
	17	Mississippi; in 1818, Illinois; in 1819, Alabama; in 1820, Maine; in 1821, Missouri; admitted into the Union as States
	21	*Florida* ceded to the United States by Spain.
	25	JOHN QUINCY ADAMS, 6th President of the U. States.
	28	The *Tariff Law* enacted, imposing protecting duties on imports.
	29	ANDREW JACKSON, 7th President of the United States
19th	32	*South Carolina* passes an act to *nullify* the laws of the U. S.
	37	MARTIN VAN BUREN, 8th President of the U. States.
	41	WM. H. HARRISON, 9th, & John Tyler, 10th Pres. of U.S.
	45	Texas annexed, and admitted into the Union as a State.
	45	JAMES K. POLK, 11th President of the United States.
	46	War with *Mexico* begins: — Peace restored in 1848.
	48	*New Mexico* and *California* annexed to the United States.
	49	ZACHARY TAYLOR, 12th President of the United States.
	50	MILLARD FILLMORE, 13th President of the U. States.
	53	FRANKLIN PIERCE, 14th President of the United States.
	57	JAMES BUCHANAN, 15th President of the United States.
	61	ABRAHAM LINCOLN, 16th President of the United States.
	61	*Secession* of eleven Southern States. — Civil War.

EVENTS OF THE REVOLUTIONARY WAR.

Year	Event / Battle	Victor	Loss	Defeated	Loss
1765	The *Stamp Act* passed by the British Parliament.				
"	Resolutions against the Stamp Act passed by the Assemblies of Virginia and Massachusetts.				
"	First *Colonial Congress*, from nine Colonies, meets at New York.				
66	The Stamp Act repealed by the British Parliament.				
67	Act of Parliament imposing duties on tea, paper, glass, and painters' colors.				
68	British troops arrive at Boston.				
70	Affray between the British troops and the inhabitants of Boston three of the latter killed.				
73	British tea thrown into the harbor at Boston.				
74	The *Boston Port Bill*, shutting up the harbor, passed.				
"	First *Continental Congress* meets at Philadelphia.				
75	The REVOLUTIONARY WAR begins by a skirmish at *Lexington*.				
"	Ticonderoga and Crown-Point taken by the Americans				
	Battle.	*Victor.*	*Loss.*	*Defeated.*	*Loss.*
"	1. Bunker Hill,	Howe,	1,054	Prescott,	453
"	Congress meets; *George Washington* chosen commander-in-chief.				
"	Boston evacuated by the British, and Canada by the Americans.				
76	*Declaration of* INDEPENDENCE; July 4.				
"	2. Flatbush, or Brooklyn,	Howe,	400	Putnam & Sullivan,	2,000
"	3. White Plains,	Howe,	3 or 400	Washington,	3 or 400
"	Fort Washington, on the Hudson, containing a garrison of upwards of 2,800 men, taken by the British.				
"	Gen. Washington retreats through N. Jersey over the Delaware.				
"	4. Trenton,	Washington,	9	Rahl,	1,000
77	5. Princeton,	Washington,	100	Mawhood,	400
"	6. Bennington,	Stark,	100	Baum & Breyman,	600
"	7. Brandywine,	Howe,	500	Washington,	1,000
"	8. Germantown,	Howe,	600	Washington,	1,200
"	9. Stillwater,	Gates,	350	Burgoyne,	600
"	Burgoyne surrenders to Gen. Gates, at *Saratoga*, with 5,752 men.				
"	*Articles of Confederation* and perpetual Union between the Thirteen United States.				
78	Treaty of Alliance between the United States and France.				
"	10. Monmouth,	Washington,	230	Clinton,	.00
"	11 Rhode Island,	Sullivan,	211	Pigott,	260
79	12 Briar-Creek,	Prevost,	16	Ash,	300
80	Charleston, S. C., surrendered to Sir Henry Clinton.				
"	13. Camden,	Cornwallis,	325	Gates,	730
"	Treachery of *Arnold* in attempting to deliver up West Point.				
81	14. Cow-pens,	Morgan,	72	Tarleton,	800
"	15 Guilford, N. C.	Cornwallis,	523	Greene,	400
"	16. Eutaw Springs,	Greene,	550	Stewart,	1,000
"	New London taken and burnt by Arnold.				
"	Cornwallis surrenders to Washington at *Yorktown*, with 7,073 men, the last important event of the Revolutionary War.				
83	*Treaty of Peace* with England; the Independence of the United States acknowledged.				

Note. — The numbers 1 (*Bunker Hill*), 2, 3, &c., to 16 (*Eutaw Springs*), are prefixed to the places where the principal battles were fought, with the names of the victorious commanders, with their loss in killed and wounded, as stated by the best authorities, placed on the left of the defeated commanders. But the exact amount of loss, in many instances, was never ascertained. The two events most important to the American cause were the surrenders at *Saratoga* and *Yorktown*.

EVENTS OF THE WAR OF THE REBELLION.

1861.

Attack on Fort Sumter,	Apr. 12
Bloodshed in Baltimore,	" 19
Philippi,	June 3
Big Bethel,	" 10
Rich Mountain,	" 11
Bull Run,	July 21
Wilson's Creek,	Aug. 10
Forts at Hatteras taken,	" 29
Carnifex Ferry,	Sept. 10
Lexington surrendered,	" 20
Ball's Bluff,	Oct. 21
Port Royal taken,	Nov. 7

1862.

Mill Springs,	Jan. 19
Fort Henry taken,	Feb. 6
Roanoke Island taken,	" 9
Fort Donelson "	" 16
Pea Ridge,	March 6, 7, 8
Merrimac and Monitor,	Mar. 8
Newbern taken,	" 14
Slavery abolished in D. C.,	April
Pittsburg Landing,	April 6
Shiloh,	" 7
Island No. 10 taken,	" 7
Fort Pulaski "	" 11
Beaufort "	" 25
New Orleans "	" 28
Yorktown "	May 4
Williamsburg,	" 5
Pensacola taken,	" 9
Natches "	" 12
Corinth evacuated,	" 28
Fair Oaks,	" 31
Memphis taken,	June 6
Mechanicsville,	" 26
Cold Harbor,	" 27
Savage's Station,	" 29
Frazier's Farm,	" 30
Malvern Hill,	July 1
Cedar Mountain,	Aug. 9
Bull Run,	" 30
Chantilly,	Sept. 1
South Mountain,	" 14
Antietam,	" 17
Iuka,	" 19
Fredericsburg,	Dec. 13
Murfreesboro',	" 31

1863.

Emancipat'n Proclamat'n,	Jan. 1
Arkansas Post,	" 4
The Nashville destroyed,	Feb. 27
Port Gibson taken,	May 1
Chancellorsville,	May 2, 3
The Atlanta destroyed,	June 17
Gettysburg,	July 1, 2, 3
Vicksburg surrendered,	July 4
Helena,	" 4
Port Hudson surrendered,	" 8
Sumter bombarded,	Aug. 17
Charleston "	" 22
Little Rock taken,	Sept. 10
Chicamauga,	" 19
Lookout Mountain,	Nov. 24
Missionary Ridge,	" 25
Chattanooga occupied,	" 26
Siege of Knoxville raised,	Dec. 3

1864.

Olustee,	Feb. 20
Mansfield,	April 8
Pleasant Hill,	" 9
Massacre at Fort Pillow,	" 12
Plymouth captured,	" 18
The Wilderness,	May 5, 7
Spottsylvania C. H.,	" 10, 14
Resaca,	" 14, 15
Dallas,	" 27, 28
Kenesaw Mountain,	June 14, 31
Kearsarge and Alabama,	June 19
Battles before Atlanta,	July 20, 22, 28
Mobile Bay,	Aug. 5
Ream's Station,	" 18
Atlanta evacuated,	Sept. 1
Cedar Run,	Oct. 19
Hatcher's Run,	" 27
Fort McAllister taken,	Dec. 13
Battles before Nashville,	Dec. 16 & 17
Savannah evacuated,	Dec. 20

1865.

Fort Fisher taken,	Jan. 15
Charleston evacuated,	Feb. 18
Wilmington taken,	" 22
Fort Steadman,	March 2
Richmond evacuated,	April 2
Spanish Fort,	" 3
Blakely River,	" 9
Lee surrendered,	" 9
Mobile surrendered,	" 12
Lincoln assassinated,	" 13
Johnson inaugurated,	" 15
Johnston surrendered,	" 26
Davis captured,	May 10
Brazos,	" 13
Grand Review,	May 22, 23
Amnesty Proclamation,	May 29

1866.

Peace declared,	April 2

A. D.		Chronology of Improvements and Events indicating the Progress of Society.
1600		
	16	*Tobacco* first cultivated by the English in Virginia.
	38	*Harvard College* founded at Cambridge, Mass.
	39	First *Printing Press* in the Colonies, at Cambridge, Mass.
	48	Cambridge Platform adopted.
17*th.*	61	Eliot's *Indian Testament* (*Bible* in 1664) printed at Cambridge.
	93	*William and Mary College* founded at Williamsburg, Va.
	95	Cultivation of *Rice* introduced into South Carolina.
		Population of the Colonies about 260,000.
		Yale College, the third in the Colonies, founded.
1700	4	*Boston News Letter*, the first American *Newspaper*, published.
	10	First *Post-Office* in America, at New York.
	19	First *Philadelphia Newspaper* published.
	20	*Tea* begins to be used in New England.
	25	First *New York Newspaper* published.
	33	First Lodge of *Freemasons* in America, at Boston.
	46	*College of New Jersey* founded.
	49	*White Population* of the Colonies 1,046,000.
	64	First *Medical School* in the Colonies, at Philadelphia.
	69	*American Philosophical Society* instituted at Philadelphia.
	74	The streets of Boston first lighted with lamps.
	75	*Population* of the Colonies about 2,600,000.
18*th.*	75	The number of *Newspapers* in the Colonies 37.
	80	*American Academy of Arts and Sciences* instituted at Boston.
	81	*Bank of North America*, first American bank, instituted.
	82	First American 74 *gun ship* built at Portsmouth, N. H.
	84	Bishop Seabury, first *Bishop* in the United States, consecrated.
	84	First American *voyage to China* from New York.
	90	Bishop Carroll, first *Catholic Bishop* in the U. S., consecrated.
	90	First *Census* of the U. S. taken: — Population 3,929,326.
	91	First *Quarto Bibles* printed in the U. S., at Worcester, Mass.
	91	United States *Mint* established at Philadelphia.
	94	The *Cotton-Gin* invented by E. Whitney. *Cotton* soon afterwards became an important article of produce.
	96	First *Turnpike* corporation in Massachusetts established
	98	*Transylvania University*, first west of the Alleghanies, instituted.
1800	1	About 200 *Newspapers* published in the United States.
	3	*Merino Sheep* first imported.
	4	*Middlesex Canal*, the first large canal, completed.
	7	*Steamboats* first used on the Hudson.
	8	*Andover Theological Seminary*, first of the kind in the U. States.
	1	Number of *Newspapers* published in the United States 359.
	11	First Steamboat on the Mississippi and Ohio. — Navigation by steam was soon afterwards extensively introduced.
	15	The *American Education Society* instituted.
19*th.*	16	The *American Bible Society* instituted.
	25	The *Erie Canal* completed.
	26	The *American Temperance Society* instituted.
	32	The *Ohio Canal* completed.
	34	The *Columbia Railroad;* and in 1835, the *Boston and Lowell*, *Boston and Providence*, *Boston and Worcester*, and *Chesapeake and Ohio Railroads*, opened. — Many other important railroads were soon afterwards completed.
	9	Number of *Newspapers* and other *Periodicals* in U S. 1,555.
	46	The *Electric Telegraph* first used for conveying intelligence.

DISTINGUISHED AMERICANS.

A. D.	Statesmen and Civilians.	died.	Warriors and Commanders.	died.	Divines.	died.	Miscellaneous.	died.
1600								
	John Carver	21			F. Higginson	30		
	John Smith	31			John Harvard	38		
	Lord Baltimore	32			Thomas Hooker	47	A. Hutchinson	43
	John Winthrop	49			Thomas Shepard	49	W. Brewster	44
	Edward Winslow	55			John Cotton	52		
	Wm. Bradford	57	Miles Standish	56	Nathaniel Ward	53		
17th	Theophil. Eaton	57			John Norton	63		
	John Endicott	65			Richard Mather	69		
	Charles Calvert	76	John Mason	73	John Davenport	70	Edw. Johnson	72
	Philip. *King*,	76			Charles Chauncy	72	Nath. Morton	85
	Sir W Berkeley	77			Urian Oakes	81	Samuel Gortor	87
	W. Coddington	78	Josiah Winslow	80	Roger Williams	83	Daniel Gookin	87
	Sir Wm. Phips	95			John Eliot	90		
1700								
	Sir Edm. Andros	14	Benj. Church	18	William Hubbard	4	R. Beverly	17
	William Penn	18	Sir W. Pepperell	59	Samuel Willard	7	Thomas Godfrey	49
	William Burnet	29	John Winslow	74	Increase Mather	23	James Logan	51
	William Shirley	71	Joseph Warren	75	Cotton Mather	28	Z. Boylston	66
	Josiah Quincy	75	R. Montgomery	75	Benj. Colman	47	Jona. Mitchell	72
	Peyton Randolph	75	John Thomas	76	David Brainerd	47	John Clayton	73
	Phil. Livingston	78	Hugh Mercer	77	John Callender	48	Cadw. Colden	76
	Rich. Stockton	81	David Wooster	77	Jona. Edwards	58	John Bartram	77
	James Otis	83	Count Pulaski	79	Thomas Prince	58	John Winthrop	79
	Jona. Trumbull	85	Charles Lee	82	Samuel Davies	61	T. Hutchinson	80
18th	Joseph Reed	85	Lord Stirling	83	Gilbert Tennent	64	Jona. Carver	80
	W. Livingston	90	Nathaniel Greene	86	Jona. Mayhew	66	Ant. Benezet	84
	James Bowdoin	90	Ethan Allen	89	Thomas Clap	67	John Ledyard	89
	Henry Laurens	92	Israel Putnam	90	Samuel Johnson	72	Tho. Hutchins	89
	John Hancock	93	Baron Steuben	94	Charles Chauncy	87	John Morgan	89
	Roger Sherman	93	John Sullivan	95	Mather Byles	88	Benj. Franklin	90
	Richard H. Lee	94	Francis Marion	95	Joseph Bellamy	90	F. Hopkinson	91
	Patrick Henry	99	Anthony Wayne	96	J. Witherspoon	94	D. Rittenhouse	96
	Geo. Washington	99	Thomas Mifflin		Ezra Stiles	95	James Wilson	
	John Rutledge		Artemas Ward		Jer. Belknap	98	John Bard	99
1800								
	Samuel Adams	3	Philip Schuyler	4	Jona. Edwards	1	George R. Minot	2
	Alex. Hamilton	4	William Moultrie	5	John Ewing	2	Robert Morris	6
	George Wythe	6	Henry Knox	6	Samuel Hopkins	3	John Dickinson	8
	Oliver Ellsworth	7	Horatio Gates	6	Joseph Willard	4	Ch. B. Brown	9
	Fisher Ames	8	Edward Preble	7	John B. Linn	4	Joel Barlow	12
	Theoph. Parsons	13	William Eaton	7	Buckminster	12	Joseph Dennie	12
	Samuel Dexter	15	Benj. Lincoln	10	Abp. J. Carroll	15	Benjamin Rush	13
	Caleb Strong	20	James Clinton	12	H. E. Muhlenberg	15	Count Rumford	14
	Elias Boudinot	21	George Clinton	12	Bp. Theo. Dehon	17	Robert Fulton	15
	Wm. Lowndes	22	Zebulon M. Pike	13	Timothy Dwight	17	David Ramsay	15
	William Pinkney	22	James Lawrence	13	Sam. S. Smith	19	B. S. Barton	15
	C. C. Pinckney	25	William Heath	14	Jesse Appleton	19	Caspar Wistar	18
	John Adams	26	Arthur St. Clair	18	Joseph Lathrop	20	Eli Whitney	25
	Thomas Jefferson	26	Oliver H. Perry	20	Benj. Trumbull	20	Gilbert Stewart	28
	Rufus King	27	Stephen Decatur	20	Sam. Worcester	21	Stephen Elliott	30
19th	De Witt Clinton	28	John Stark	22	J. Heckewelder	23	William Tudor	30
	Tim. Pickering	29	Thomas Truxton	22	Jedediah Morse	26	Isaiah Thomas	31
	John Jay	29	J. Wilkinson	25	Edward Payson	27	John Trumbull	31
	James Monroe	31	J. Macdonough	25	John M. Mason	29	S. L. Mitchell	31
	John Randolph	33	Thos. Pinckney	28	Bp. J. H. Hobart	30	Nathan Dane	35
	William Wirt	34	Jacob Brown	28	J. P. Wilson	30	William Rawle	36
	John Marshall	35	Thomas Sumter	32	John H. Rice	31	E. Livingston	36
	Aaron Burr	36	Wm. Bainbridge	33	C. H. Wharton	33	Philip S. Physic	37
	James Madison	36	G. M. Lafayette	34	Ebenezer Porter	34	Nat. Bowditch	38
	Wm. H. Harrison	41	Wade Hampton	35	Bp. Wm. White	36	J. A. Hillhouse	41
	Jeremiah Smith	42	John Rogers	38	Abiel Holmes	37	Noah Webster	43
	Joseph Story	45	S. Van Rensselaer	39	Noah Worcester	37	Wash. Allston	43
	James Kent	47	John Armstrong	43	Nath'l Emmons	40	P. S. Duponceau	44
	John Q. Adams	48	Isaac Hull	43	John T. Kirkland	41	John Pickering	46
	Albert Gallatin	49	Andrew Jackson	45	W. E. Channing	42	Henry Wheaton	48
	John C. Calhoun	50	Edm'd P. Gaines	48	Samuel Miller	50	Jas. F. Cooper	51
	Henry Clay	52	Wm. J. Worth	48	Moses Stuart	52	Wm. H. Prescott	59
	Daniel Webster	52	Zachary Taylor	50	Leonard Woods	54	Wash. Irving	59

POPULATION OF THE UNITED STATES. — *Eight Official Enumerations.*

States.		1790.	1800.	1810.	1820.	1830.	1840.	1850.	1860.
New Hampshire		141,899	183,762	214,360	244,161	269,328	284,574	317,976	326,272
Massachusetts		378,717	423,245	472,040	523,287	610,408	737,699	994,914	1,231,065
Rhode Island		69,110	69,122	77,031	83,059	97,199	108,830	147,545	174,621
Connecticut		238,141	251,002	262,042	275,202	297,665	309,978	370,792	460,151
New York		340,120	586,756	959,949	1,372,812	1,918,608	2,428,921	3,097,394	3,880,735
New Jersey		184,139	211,949	249,555	277,575	320,823	373,306	489,555	672,031
Pennsylvania		434,373	602,365	810,091	1,049,458	1,348,233	1,724,033	2,311,786	2,906,370
Delaware		59,098	64,273	72,674	72,749	76,748	78,085	91,532	112,218
Maryland		319,728	341,548	380,546	407,350	447,040	470,019	583,034	687,034
Virginia		748,308	880,200	974,642	1,065,379	1,211,405	1,239,797	1,421,661	1,596,079
North Carolina		393,751	478,103	555,500	638,829	737,987	753,419	860,039	992,667
South Carolina		249,073	345,591	415,715	502,741	581,185	594,398	668,507	703,812
Georgia	*Adm.*	82,548	162,101	252,433	340,987	516,823	691,392	906,185	1,057,329
Vermont	1791	85,416	154,465	217,713	235,764	280,652	291,948	313,120	315,116
Kentucky	1792	73,077	220,955	406,511	564,317	687,917	779,828	982,405	1,155,713
Tennessee	1796	30,791	105,602	261,727	422,813	681,904	829,210	1,002,717	1,109,847
Ohio	1802	. .	45,365	230,760	581,434	937,903	1,519,467	1,980,329	2,339,599
Louisiana	1812	. .	. .	76,556	153,407	215,739	352,411	517,762	709,290
Indiana	1816	. .	4,875	24,520	147,178	343,031	685,866	988,416	1,350,941
Mississippi	1817	. .	8,850	40,352	75,448	136,621	375,651	606,526	791,396
Illinois	1818	. .	. .	12,282	55,211	157,455	476,183	851,470	1,711,753
Alabama	1819	. .	. .	20,845	127,901	309,527	590,756	771,623	964,296
Maine	1820	96,540	151,719	228,705	298,335	399,955	501,793	583,169	628,276
Missouri	1821	. .	. .	20,845	66,586	140,445	383,702	682,044	1,182,317
Michigan	1836	. .	. .	4,762	8,896	31,639	212,267	397,654	749,112
Arkansas	1836	. .	. .	. .	14,273	30,388	97,574	209,897	435,427
Florida	1845	. .	. .	. .	. .	34,730	54,477	87,445	140,439
Texas	1845	. .	. .	. .	. .	. .	. .	212,592	602,432
Iowa	1846	. .	. .	. .	. .	. .	43,112	192,214	674,948
Wisconsin	1848	. .	. .	. .	. .	. .	30,945	305,391	775,873
California	1850	. .	. .	. .	. .	. .	. .	165,000	380,016
Oregon	1858	. .	. .	. .	. .	. .	. .	. .	52,464
Dist. of Columbia		. .	14,093	24,023	33,039	39,834	43,712	51,687	75,076
Territories		. .	. .	. .	. .	. .	. .	. .	220,143
Total,		3,929,827	5,305,925	7,239,814	9,638,131	12,866,920	17,063,353	23,263,485	31,443,790

SLAVES IN THE UNITED STATES.

States.	1790.	1800.	1810.	1820.	1830.	1840.	1850.	1860.
Maine	0	0	0	0	0	0	0	0
New Hampshire	158	8	0	0	0	1	0	0
Vermont	17	0	0	0	0	0	0	0
Massachusetts	0	0	0	0	0	0	0	0
Rhode Island	952	381	103	48	17	5	0	0
Connecticut	2,759	951	310	97	25	17	0	0
New York	21,324	20,343	15,017	10,088	75	4	0	0
New Jersey	11,423	12,422	10,851	7,657	2,254	674	236	0
Pennsylvania	3,737	1,706	795	211	403	64	0	0
Delaware	8,887	6,153	4,177	4,509	3,292	2,605	2,299	1,798
Maryland	103,036	105,635	111,502	107,398	102,294	89,737	90,368	87,188
Virginia	203,427	345,796	392,518	425,153	469,757	448,987	472,528	490,887
North Carolina	100,572	133,296	168,824	295,117	235,601	245,817	288,548	331,080
South Carolina	107,094	146,151	196,365	258,475	315,401	327,038	384,984	402,541
Georgia	29,264	59,404	105,218	149,656	217,531	280,944	381,682	462,232
Florida	. .	. .	. .	. .	15,501	25,717	39,310	61,753
Alabama	. .	. .	. .	41,879	117,549	253,532	342,844	435,132
Mississippi	. .	3,489	17,088	32,814	65,659	195,211	309,878	436,696
Louisiana	. .	. .	34,660	69,064	109,588	168,452	244,809	332,010
Missouri	. .	. .	3,011	10,222	25,081	58,240	87,422	114,965
Arkansas	. .	. .	. .	1,617	4,576	19,935	47,100	111,104
Tennessee	3,417	13,584	44,535	80,107	141,603	183,059	239,459	275,784
Kentucky	11,830	40,343	80,561	126,732	165,213	182,258	210,981	225,490
Texas	. .	. .	. .	. .	0	0	58,161	180,382
Ohio	. .	. .	. .	. .	0	3	0	0
Indiana	. .	135	237	190	0	3	0	0
Illinois	. .	. .	168	117	747	331	0	0
Michigan	. .	. .	24	. .	32	0	0	0
Wisconsin	. .	. .	. .	. .	. .	11	0	0
Iowa	. .	. .	. .	. .	. .	16	0	0
Dist. of Columbia	. .	3,244	5,395	6,377	6,119	4,694	3,687	3,181
Total,	697,897	893,041	1,191,364	1,538,064	2,009,031	2,487,355	3,204,296	3,953,524

1866. Slavery abolished throughout the United States.

Remarks. — The *Population* of the several States, and also the number of *Slaves* in each State, according to eight censuses, or official enumerations, are exhibited on the preceding page.

The *census* is not as correct as it should be. According to the census of 1840, there were a few slaves in the States of *New Hampshire*, *Rhode Island*, *Connecticut*, *New York*, *New Jersey*, *Pennsylvania*, *Ohio*, *Indiana*, and *Illinois*, though there were none in these States, slavery in them being prohibited by law. In New Jersey, however, there were a few colored persons, styled *apprentices* by the State act to abolish slavery, of April 18, 1846.

The first *thirteen States* in the table are the States which existed at the time of the forming of the Constitution of the United States The other States are arranged in the order in which they have been admitted into the Union.

Maine formed a part of the State of *Massachusetts* till 1820, when it was admitted into the Union as an independent State.

By the table it will be seen that the *Population* of the United States has increased, from 1790 to 1860 (70 years), from less than 4 millions to upwards of 31 millions.

The number of *Slaves* has increased from a little less than 700,000 to upwards of 3,950,000.

The population of the United States, since 1790, has doubled once in about 24 years.

Post-Offices.

The number of *Post-Offices* in the United States, in 1790, was 75 in 1810, 2,300; in 1830, 8,450; in 1840, 13,468; in 1850, 18,417 in 1860, 28,498.

Railroads.

The first considerable *railroads* for conveying passengers in the United States were opened in 1834 and 1835. — The number of miles of railroad in use, in 1849, was upwards of 6,000; in 1859 upwards of 27,000.

Literary Seminaries.

Colleges. — The first *college* in the Colonies was founded at Cambridge, in 1638. The number of Colleges existing, in 1700, was 3 the number of colleges and universities in the United States, in 1800 26; in 1860, 122.

Medical Schools. — The number of *medical schools* in the United States, in 1800, was 3; in 1860, 40.

Theological and Law Schools. — Almost all the *theological schools* in the United States have been established within the last forty years, and the *law schools* are of still later date.

The number of *theological schools* in 1860 was 50; *law schools*, 19

CHART OF HISTORY.

DESCRIPTION AND ILLUSTRATION.

1. This Chart affords means of facilitating the study of History similar to what are afforded by maps in the study of Geography. It supposes time to be flowing, in a stream, from the left hand to the right; and represents, at one view, the principal States and Empires which have existed in the world, together with their origin, revolutions, decline, and fall.

2. Those who may make use of this Chart are supposed to be conversant with the common principles of Geography, and to understand the relative situation and importance of the different countries which are represented. It will be readily seen, that the spaces, which represent the several countries on the Chart, do not give any exact idea of the *extent* of those countries, but of the revolutions which they have undergone, and, in some degree, of their comparative importance in history. Those parts of the world which are almost unknown in history (as, for example, all *Africa* except Egypt and the Barbary States) are not represented at all on the Chart.

3. In the arrangement of the countries, the geographical order is generally followed. It unavoidably happens, that, owing to conquests, and other acquisitions, the several parts of an empire or state cannot always be placed in a contiguous position. To remedy this inconvenience, recourse has been had to coloring the different parts of the same empire with the same color, by means of which the eye can embrace, at one view, the various territories of which it was, at any given period, composed. The colors fit for this purpose are so few, that a repetition of some of them has been necessary; but they are applied in such a manner as not to be likely to mislead the student.

4. The scale of the main body of the Chart comprises a period of 2,700 years; namely, from the year B. C. 800, to the end of the 19th century. This interval is divided into 27 equal parts, by *perpendicular lines*, extending from the top to the bottom, each space between the lines denoting the period of 100 years.

5. To the left hand of that portion of the Chart appropriated to *America*, are represented the principal states that flourished in remote antiquity, from the time of the *Deluge* to the year 800 before the *Christian Era*.

6. The several countries of which the history is delineated are represented by spaces included between *horizontal lines* The *slant lines* denote the gradual conquest of a country ; as, for example, the conquest of the *Britons* by the *Romans* was commenced A. D. 43, but not completed till 84.

7. In order to ascertain the date of any event or revolution in the history represented on the Chart, add the figures at the line denoting the event to the next century, if *before* Christ, on the *right* hand, and if *after* Christ, on the *left* hand, and the sum will give the date before or after Christ, as the case may be.

8. Thus it appears, that *Egypt* dates from 2188 B. C. ; the *Calling of Abraham*, 1921 ; the foundation of *Rome*, 753 B. C., that *Macedonia* was annexed to the *Roman Empire* 168 B. C , that the *Heruli* conquered *Italy*, and put an end to the *Western Roman Empire*, in the year 476 after Christ ; and that the *Turks* put an end to the *Eastern Empire* in 1453.

9. By carrying the eye *horizontally* upon the Chart, from the left hand to the right, one may see the succession of states and empires ; their rise, progress, and fall ; of what states they were composed, and what states rose from their ruins.

10. By carrying the eye *vertically* upon the Chart, from the top to the bottom, one may see what states and empires were flourishing at any given era. At the period of 500 years B. C., it will be seen that the *Persian Empire* was much the most considerable then existing ; that it had swallowed up the Babylonian empire, and various other countries in Asia, and also *Egypt ;* that the *Grecian States* existed separate and independent ; that the republic of *Rome* was of very small extent ; and that the nations of the middle and north of Europe were unconquered and independent.

11. At the period of A. D. 100, it will be seen that the *Roman Empire* embraced almost all the then known world ; that the *Britons* had been recently subdued, but that the *Irish*, *Scots*, and the *northern nations* of Europe, and also the *Parthians*, *Arabs*, *Hindoos*, and *Chinese* (nations then little known), were not conquered.

12. At the period of A. D. 800, it will be seen that the three principal empires were those of the *Saracens* and the *Franks*, and the *Eastern* or *Greek Empire ;* that the *Western Empire* of the Romans had been, for upwards of three centuries, extinct ; and that the kingdom of the *Lombards* had been recently terminated ; that *England* was under the government of the *Saxon Heptarchy ;* that *Wales*, *Scotland*, and *Ireland* were independent, and the northern kingdoms not yet formed ; that the temporal dominion of the *Pope* had commenced ; that the *Saracens* were in possession of the greater part of *Spain*, the

whole of *Arabia* and *Persia*, a great part of the *Eastern* or *Greek Empire*, all *Egypt*, and *Barbary*.

13. At the period of A. D. 1300, it appears that the three kingdoms of *Sweden*, *Norway*, and *Denmark* were separate and independent; that a large part of the country, which now forms the *Russian Empire*, was in the possession of the *Moguls;* that *Poland* was an independent kingdom, but that *Lithuania* was separate; that *England* was in possession of *Wales* and *Ireland*, but not of *Scotland;* that *Bohemia* and *Hungary* were independent; that a considerable portion of *France* belonged to *England;* that *Lorraine*, *Alsace*, and *Burgundy* were independent of *France;* that *Italy* and *Spain* comprised various states, the latter being partly in possession of the *Moors;* that *Portugal* had become an independent kingdom; that the *Eastern Empire* was still in existence; that the *Moguls* were in possession of *Persia*, a part of the *Eastern* or *Greek Empire* (modern *Turkey*), and *China*, as well as a part of *Russia*; that the kingdom of *Jerusalem* had fallen into the possession of the *Mamelukes;* and that the Mamelukes also possessed *Egypt*.

14. At the period of 1800, it appears that *Denmark* was in possession of *Norway*, which was soon after annexed to *Sweden;* that the kingdom of *Poland* had been dismembered between *Russia*, *Austria*, and *Prussia*, all of which had now become important sovereignties; that *Holland*, the *Netherlands*, and a great part of *Italy*, had been recently annexed to *France*, but were soon after again separated from it; that *Naples* had become an independent kingdom; that the *Turks* were in possession of a great part of the countries most celebrated in ancient history; that the *Wahabees* had got possession of a great part of *Arabia*, and the *English* of *Hindostan;* that the *English* possessed *Canada;* that the *United States* had become independent of England; that the *Spanish Provinces* in America belonged still to Spain, and *Brazil* to *Portugal*, but that soon afterwards they all became independent.

15. The figures on the left hand of the *American States* denote the time of the conquest or settlement of each; those on the right hand, the time when each became independent. Thus it appears, that *Virginia* was settled by the English in 1607, and *New England* in 1620; that the *United States* became independent in 1776; that *Mexico* was conquered by the Spaniards in 1521, and became independent in 1821.

16. The four great empires of antiquity, as may be seen by the Chart, were the *Assyrian* or *Babylonian*, the *Persian*, the *Macedonian*, and the *Roman*.

7. The *Assyrian* or *Babylonian Empire* was the most an

cient, and was succeeded, in 536, by the *Persian Empire*, which was swallowed up, 330 B. C., by the *Macedonian Empire*. This latter empire, which, in its extensive form, was of short duration, was dissolved 301 B. C.

18. The *Roman Empire* was much the most powerful empire of antiquity, and from about half a century before Christ, to the latter part of the 5th century after Christ, when the *Western Empire* was conquered by the *Heruli*, embraced the greater part of the then known world.

19. The *Heruli* were supplanted by the *Ostrogoths*, that is, *Eastern Goths*, the latter by the *Greeks*, and these by the *Lombards*, who retained possession of Italy till 774, when they were conquered by the *Franks*, whose empire, during several centuries, was the most formidable in Europe. In 843, it was divided into three monarchies, *France*, *Germany*, and *Italy*.

20. After the fall of the Western Empire of the Romans, the *Franks*, *Goths*, *Vandals*, *Huns*, *Lombards*, and other barbarous nations, obtained possession of the principal part of Europe.

21. The empire of the *Saracens* commenced before the middle of the 7th century, and continued through that and the 8th and the 9th centuries, flourishing and powerful; but was at length broken into various parts, and, in 1258, the *Caliphate of Bagdad* terminated.

22. The empire of the *Moguls* was widely extended, in the early part of the 13th century, under the mighty conqueror *Genghis-Khan;* and, in the latter part of the 14th century *Timur Bek*, or *Tamerlane*, a *Tartar*, ran a similar career of conquest.

23. By the Chart, it appears that, before the Christian era, England was inhabited by the *Britons*, who were conquered by the *Romans* in the first century after Christ, and continued subject till 410; that the *Saxon Heptarchy* was commenced in 455, completed in 585, and continued till 827, when England became one kingdom, under *Saxon* monarchs; that the *Danes* were possessed of the kingdom from 1013 to 1041; that the *Saxons* then regained possession, and held it till 1066, when they were conquered by the *Normans*, under William the Conqueror; that *Ireland* was annexed to England in 1172, *Wales* in 1283, and *Scotland* in 1603; and that England held possessions in *France* from 1066 to 1588.

[*The changes of other states and kingdoms, delineated on the Chart will be easily understood.*]

QUESTIONS ON THE CHART OF HISTORY.*

1. What are some of the states and empires that flourished from the *Deluge* to 800 B. C.? 2. How long before Christ was the *Deluge*?

3. When was *Babel* built?

4. From what period does *Babylon* date? 5. *Egypt?* 6. *Siçyon*, in Greece? 7. What other cities in Greece were founded before 1400 B. C.? 8. What is the date of the *Argonautic Expedition?*

9. What is the period of *Lycurgus?* 10. When did the kingdom of *Troy* end? 11. What is the date of the *Calling of Abraham?*

12. When were the *Israelites in Egypt?* 13. When did they enter *Canaan?* 14. When were they first governed by a *king*?

15. When was the kingdom divided into the *Ten Tribes of Israel* and *Judah?*

16. When was *Israel* incorporated with the *Assyrian Empire?*

17. When was *Judah* added to the *Babylonian Empire?*

18. When was *Phœnicia* annexed to the *Babylonian Empire?*

19. When did the *Babylonian Empire* end? 20. What empire succeeded it? 21. When did the *Persian Empire* begin and end?

22. By what empire was it succeeded? 23. When was *Egypt* conquered by the *Persians?* 24. When by the *Macedonians?*

25. When were *Athens*, *Sparta*, *Thebes*, &c., annexed to the *Macedonian Empire?* 26. When was the *Macedonian Empire* dissolved?

27. When was the kingdom of *Macedonia* annexed to the *Roman Empire?* 28. When did the *Ptolemies* govern *Egypt?*

29. When did the *Seleucidæ* govern *Syria?* 30. When did the *Ptolemies* govern *Judea?* 31. When the *Maccabees?*

32. What is the date of the foundation of *Rome?*

33. What is the date of the commencement of the *Republic?*

34. What were some of the nations first conquered by the Romans?

35. When were the *Cisalpine Gauls* conquered? 36. *Macedonia?* 37. *Greece* or the *Achæan League?* 38. The *Carthaginians?* 39. The *Gauls?* 40. The *Helvetii?* 41. *Syria?* 42. *Judea?* 43. *Egypt?* 44. The *Britons?*

45. During what centuries was the *Roman Empire* most extensive?

46. When did the *Roman dominion* over the *Britons* end?

47. When did the *Suevi* obtain possession of *Spain?*

48. When did the *Heruli* conquer Italy?

49. When did the empire of the *Franks* begin?

50. During what centuries was it most extensive?

51. When did the kingdom of the *Lombards* in Italy begin and end?

52. In what century did the *Saracen Empire* commence?

53. In what three centuries was it most flourishing?

54. What are the modern names of the countries which it embraced?

55. When did the *Caliphate of Bagdad* terminate?

56. When did the *Greek Empire of Nice* terminate?

57. In what century was the Eastern or Greek Empire governed by *French Emperors?* 58. When did the *Eastern* or *Greek Empire* end?

59. By whom was it conquered?

MODERN PART.

1. In what centuries was the empire of the *Moguls* most flourishing?

2. When were the *Tartars* in possession of Persia, &c.?

* By the Chart, it appears that *Babylon* was founded 2227 B. C.; *Siçyon*, 2089 B. C.; *Argos*, 1856 B. C., &c.

3 Who anciently inhabited Sweden, Norway, Denmark, and Russia
4. When were Sweden, Norway, and Denmark all united together?
5. With what country was Norway connected from 1448 to 1814?
6. In what centuries did the Moguls or Tartars possess a part of Russia
7. When was Poland divided between Russia, Austria, and Prussia?
8. Who were the ancient inhabitants of England?
9. In what centuries were the Romans in possession of Britain?
10. In what centuries did the *Saxon Heptarchy* exist?
11. When did the *Saxon Heptarchy* end, and the kingdom under the *Saxon* monarchs begin? 12. When did the *Danes* obtain possession of England? 13. When the *Normans?*
14. When was Ireland added to England? 15. Wales? 16. Scotland?
17. In what centuries did England hold possessions in France?
18. When was Bohemia annexed to the House of Austria? 19. When Hungary?
20. When was the empire of the Franks divided into the three sovereignties of Germany, France, and Italy?
21. When did the empire of Germany end?
22. When did the republic of Holland begin and end?
23. What nation held possessions in France from 1066 to 1558?
24. What countries were annexed to France a little before 1800?
25. When did the republic of Switzerland commence?
26. In what centuries did Naples belong to Spain?
27. When did Naples become independent?
28. When did the dominion of the Moors in Spain cease?
29. How many centuries has Spain been united in one kingdom?
30. When did the kingdom of Portugal commence?
31. During a part of what centuries was it united with Spain?
32. When did the empire of the Turks commence?
33. How many centuries have their dominions been as extensive as at present?
34. When did the *Sophis* or *Shahs* get the possession of all Persia?
35. What different people have been in possession of Persia since the downfall of the ancient Persian Empire?
36. When did the dominion of the *Wahabees* in Arabia commence?
37. When did the *English* dominion in India begin?
38. When did the *Mantchew Tartars* gain possession of *China?*
39. What different nations have possessed *Egypt* since 800 B. C.?
40. When did the Turks get possession of Egypt?
41. What nation first settled Canada?
42. When did the English gain possession of Canada?
43. When and by whom was Virginia settled? 44. New York? 45 New England? 46. Pennsylvania?
47. When did the United States become independent?
48. Which country on the continent of America was first settled by Europeans? 49. When was Mexico conquered by the Spaniards?
50. What other countries were soon after colonized by the Spaniards?
51. By whom was Brazil colonized?
52 Which of the countries in South America first became independent?
53 What others soon followed?
54 How long did Spain possess Mexico?

CHRONOLOGY.

CHRONOLOGY is a science which treats of the natural and artificial divisions of time; and it refers to certain points or eras the various events recorded in history.

Various eras have been adopted in different ages, and by different nations, in the computation of time, and in adjusting the dates of events recorded in history. Some of the most important only of these eras can be here mentioned.

1. THE OLYMPIADS. The Greeks computed their time by the era of the Olympiads, which date from the year 776 B. C. being the year in which Corœbus was successful at the Olympic games. This era differed from all others, in being reckoned by periods of four years instead of single years. Each period of four years was called an Olympiad, and, in marking a date, the year and the Olympiad were both mentioned.

2. THE FOUNDATION OF ROME. The Romans reckoned their time from the date assigned for the founding of Rome, corresponding to the year 753 B. C. This era is designated by the letters A. U. C., or *ab urbe conditâ*, "from the building of the city."

3. THE CHRISTIAN ERA. The Christian era, which is used by Christian nations, is reckoned from the birth of Christ, which, according to the Hebrew text of the Old Testament, took place A. M. (in the year of the world) 4004; according to the Samaritan text, A. M. 4700; and, according to the Septuagint, A. M. 5872. The computation according to the Hebrew text is followed in this work; and it is generally adopted in English literature. The birth of Christ is supposed to have taken place about four years earlier than the period assigned to it in the vulgar era.

The computation by the Christian era first began to be used in the 6th century. The Roman or Julian year was followed consisting of 365 days and 6 hours, which exceeded the true time of the solar year by a little more than 11 minutes. This erroneous computation had, in the year 1582, occasioned a deviation of 10 days from the true time; and in that year (1582) Pope Gregory introduced a reform into the calendar, by taking 10 days from the month of October. The calendar thus reformed (called *New Style*) was immediately introduced into all Catholic countries. The reckoning according to the Julian year (called *Old Style*) continued to be used in England till the year 1752, when 11 days were omitted in September, the day after the 2d being accounted the 14th. — The Greeks and Russians still use the Old Style.

4. The Era of the Hegira. The era of the Hegira, which dates from the flight of Mahomet from Mecca to Medina, is used by Mahometan nations, and corresponds to the 16th of July, A. D. 622.

5. The American Era. The era most used in this country, next to the Christian era, is that of the Declaration of the Independence of the United States, which took place on the 4th of July, 1776.

Comparison of Different Eras.

	Year.	
The Era of the Olympiads corresponds to	3228	of the Creation of the World
	23	before the Foundation of Rome.
	776	before Christ.
	1398	before the Hegira.
The Foundation of Rome corresponds to	3251	of the Creation of the World.
	4	of the 6th Olympiad.
	753	before Christ.
	1375	before the Hegira.
The Christian Era corresponds to	4004	of the Creation of the World
	1	of the 195th Olympiad.
	753	of the Foundation of Rome.
	622	before the Hegira.
The Hegira corresponds to	4626	of the Creation of the World
	3	of the 348th Olympiad.
	1375	of the Foundation of Rome
	622	of the Christian Era.

CHRONOLOGICAL TABLE.

In the following table the most important epochs are given together with a system of *Artificial Memory*, to facilitate the recollecting of dates. This system is derived chiefly from Dr. Grey's *Memoria Technica.*

In order to facilitate remembering dates, a word is formed of the *name* recorded, or of the first syllables of it, together with one or more syllables added to it, and made up of *numeral letters.* For this purpose, a vowel and a consonant are assigned to each digit, and *a* or *b* denote 1; *e* or *d* 2; *i* or *t* 3; *o* or *f* 4; and so on, in the following series: —

a	*e*	*i*	*o*	*u*	*au*	*oi*	*oo*	*ou*	*ai*
1	2	3	4	5	6	7	8	9	0
b	*d*	*t*	*f*	*v*	*s*	*p*	*k*	*n*	*z*

These letters may be easily remembered by considering that the first five vowels represent 1, 2, 3, 4, 5; that the diphthong *au*, which is composed of *a* 1 and *u* 5, denotes 6; that *oi*, for the same reason, denotes 7, *oo* 8, and *ou* 9. The diphthong *ai* is put for the cipher 0, but without any similar reason.

The *first* consonant, *b*, denotes 1; *d*, the first letter of *duo*, the Latin for *two*, denotes 2; *t*, the initial of the word *three*, is put for 3; *f*, for the same reason, for 4; *v* (V being the Roman numeral for *five*) denotes 5; *s*, the initial of *six*, is put for 6; *p*, from se*p*tem, the Latin for *seven*, denotes 7; *k*, from the Greek o*k*to, *eight*, is put for 8; *n*, the initial of the word *nine*, denotes 9; and *z*, the final letter, is put for 0.

Having perfectly learned the foregoing series, the student may proceed to exercise himself in the formation and resolution of dates, in the following manner: —

10	189	342	390	659	1492	1776	1830
az	*boon*	*tod*	*tonz*	*sun*	*afne*	*apois*	*bkoiz*

The system may be extended at pleasure; and, by the formation of words in the manner described, it will be easy to fix in the mind the time of the death of illustrious men, the commencement of the reigns of kings, and other events, of which it is desirable to remember the date. It will be easy to remember whether the event took place *before* or *after* Christ. — Besides the series of letters already explained, *g* may denote a hundred and *th* a thousand.

Table.

4004	*Creation* of the world	Cre-*faizo*
2348	*Deluge*	Del-*etok*
2247	*Babel* built; mankind dispersed	Babel-*edop*
2188	The kingdom of *Egypt* commences	Egypt-*ebook*
921	Calling of *Abraham*	Abrah-*aneb*
1556	*Athens* founded by Cecrops	Ath-*avus*
1493	*Cadmus* brings letters into Greece and builds Thebes	Cadmus-*bont*
1491	*Israelites* brought out of Egypt by Moses	Israel-*bona*
1263	*Argonautic* expedition	Argonaut-*best*
1184	*Troy* taken and burnt by the Greeks	Troy-*bako*
1095	*Saul* king of Israel	Saul-*azpu*
1012	The *Temple* of Solomon founded	Templ-*azad*
884	*Lycurgus* reforms the laws of Lacedæmon	Lycurg-*ooko*
776	The first *Olympiad* begins	Olym-*pois*
753	*Rome* founded by Romulus	Rom-*put*
536	*Cyrus* founds the Persian empire	Cyru-*vis*
509	*Tarquin* expelled from Rome	Tarquin-*vai*[illegible]
490	Battle of *Marathon*	Marath-*onz*
400	*Socrates* put to death	Socrat-*ozai*
324	*Alexander* the Great dies at Babylon	Alexand-*ido*
312	The era of the *Seleucidæ*	Seleucid-*ibe*
146	*Greece* reduced to a Roman province	Greece-*bos*
31	Battle of *Actium*; end of Roman commonwealth	Actium-*ta*
	Birth of Christ; 4 years before the vulgar era.	
70	*Jerusalem* taken and destroyed	Jerusal-*oiz*
98	*Trajan* emperor of Rome	Trajan-*noo*
306	*Constantine* emperor of Rome	Constan-*tais*
476	End of the Western *Roman* empire	Rom-*fois*
622	Era of the *Hegira*, or Flight of Mahomet	Hegira-*sed*
800	*Charlemagne* emperor of the West	Charlemag-*oozat*
827	The kingdom of *England* begins under Egbert	England-*kep*
1066	*William* the Conqueror king of England	Will-*baisau*
1096	*First Crusade* to the Holy Land	Crusad-*azous*
1227	*Genghis-khan's* conquests in Asia	Genghis-*bedoi*
1258	End of the *Caliphate* or Saracen empire	Caliphat-*aduk*
1340	*Gunpowder* invented at Cologne, by Schwartz	Gunpowder-*atoz*
1370	*Wickliffe* propagates his doctrines in England	Wickliff-*atoiz*
1398	*Timur Bek* or *Tamerlane's* conquests	Timur-*bink*
1440	The art of *Printing* invented	Print-*afoz*
1453	*Eastern Empire* ends; *Turks* take Constantinople	Turks-*afut*
1492	*America* discovered by Columbus	America-*bone*
1517	The *Reformation* in Germany begun by Luther	Reform-*avap*
1603	Union of England and Scotland under *James I.*	Jam-*asait*
1620	*Plymouth*, Mass., settled by the Puritans	Plymouth-*bausa*
1688	*Revolution* in England	Revolut-*ascok*
1776	*Independence* of the United States declared	Independen-*apois*
789	First French *Revolution*	Revolut-*apoon*
1804	*Bonaparte* crowned emperor of France	Bonapart-*boozo*
1815	Battle of *Waterloo*	Waterl-*akbu*
1848	France declared a *republic*	Republ-*akok*

SACRED HISTORY.

THE historical parts of the Bible treat chiefly of the history of the *Israelites* or *Jews*. The other principal source of information, in addition to the Scriptures, relating to the ancient history of the Israelites, is to be found in the writings of *Josephus*, a Jewish historian, who lived in the time of the destruction of Jerusalem by the Romans. The Old Testament history of the Israelites ends with the book of Nehemiah, about 440 years B. C., and, from this time to the birth of Christ, Josephus is the principal authority for Jewish history.

The Israelites were descended from *Abraham*, who was called, according to the common computation, 427 years after the Deluge, and 1921 B. C., to separate himself "from his kindred and his father's house" [see Genesis xii.], and who received a promise that the *Messiah* should be of his posterity.

They were called *Hebrews*, as is commonly supposed, from *Eber* or *Heber*, an ancestor of Abraham ; *Israelites*, from *Jacob*, who was surnamed *Israel;* and *Jews*, from *Judah*, one of the twelve sons of Jacob, the head or patriarch of the principal of the Twelve Tribes.

Jacob, with his sons and their families, consisting of 70 persons, migrated from Canaan to Egypt, 1706 B. C., and their posterity were, in that country, reduced to slavery. After a residence, according to Calmet, of 215 years, they were liberated from Egyptian bondage by *Moses*, the great Hebrew Lawgiver.

After wandering 40 years in the wilderness, they took possession of Canaan, under the direction of *Joshua*.

From the entrance into Canaan to the commencement of the reign of Saul, a period of 356 years, they were governed by a succession of *Judges* — A view of the succession of the *Kings of Israel* and *Judah*, during the continuance of the monarchies, is given in the *Tables I.* and *II.* on the following pages.

The most flourishing period of the Israelitish monarchy was during the reigns of *David* and *Solomon*.

The sceptre of *Judah* descended regularly, except during the usurpation of *Athaliah*, from *father* to *son*, in the family of *David*, till the death of *Josiah*, three of whose sons were, for a short time, raised to the throne.

During nearly all the period of the Old Testament history of the Israelites, the nation manifested a strong tendency to forsake the worship of the true God, and to fall into *idolatry*. Many of the kings of *Judah*, and all the kings of the *Ten Tribes*, were promoters of idolatrous worship

The history of the *Ten Tribes*, subsequent to their captivity by Shalmaneser, is buried in utter obscurity. The *Jews*, or subjects of the kingdom of Judah, after the 70 years' Babylonish captivity, returned, 536 B. C., by permission of *Cyrus*, under *Zerubbabel* their governor, and rebuilt *Jerusalem* and the *Temple*.

After this period, they were subject successively to the *Persians*, the *Ptolemies of Egypt*, the *Syrians*, and the *Maccabees*, till 63 B. C., when they were subjected to the *Romans* by *Pompey*. A. D. 70, Jerusalem was taken and destroyed by the Romans, under *Titus*, and since that event, the Jews have been dispersed in all parts of the world.

B. C.	Chronological Table of Kingdoms of Israel and Judah.			
1100	Kings.	ys.	Kingdom of Israel: 3 *Kings*: 120 *Years*.	Prophets.
95	Saul	40	The son of *Kish*, the first king of Israel; is engaged in war with the *Philistines*, *Amalekites*, &c.; persecutes *David*, who is anointed by *Samuel* in his stead; *Saul* and *Jonathan* slain by the Philistines	Samuel
55	David	40	The son of *Jesse*, of the tribe of *Judah*; is first proclaimed king of Judah, afterwards of all Israel; makes *Jerusalem* the seat of his kingdom; subdues the *Philistines*, *Edomites*, *Amalekites*, *Moabites*, &c.	Nathan Gad
14	Solomon	40	Celebrated for wisdom; has a pacific, prosperous reign; builds the *Temple*. After the death of Solomon, ten Tribes revolt from his son Rehoboam, and two separate kingdoms are formed, *Judah* and *Israel*.	
1000			Kingdom of Judah: 19 *Kings*: 387 *Years*.	Ahijah
75	Rehoboam	17	Revolt of the *Ten Tribes*.	Iddo
58	Abijah	3	Gains a great victory over Jeroboam.	Shemaiah
55	Asa	41	A religious king; suppresses idolatry; has a prosperous reign.	Azariah
14	Jehoshaphat	25	A religious king; a prosperous reign; joins Ahab in a war against Syria.	Micaiah Elijah
900				
89	Jehoram	4	An idolater; slays his six brothers.	
85	Ahaziah	1	Is slain by Jehu.	Elisha
84	(Athaliah)	6	Usurps; slays all the royal family.	
78	Joash (or	40	*Jehoash*) defeated by the Syrians.	Jehoiada
39	Amaziah	29	Defeats the Edomites; is defeated by Joash; is slain in a conspiracy.	Zachariah
10	Uzziah	52	Defeats the Philistines and Arabians; is smitten with leprosy.	Jonah Amos
800				
58	Jotham	16	Has a prosperous reign.	Oded
42	Ahaz	16	Defeated by *Pekah* with great loss.	Hosea
26	Hezekiah	28	An excellent king; has a prosperous reign. — *Sennacherib's* repulse.	Micah Nahum
700				
98	Manasseh	55	An impious king; is carried by *Esarhaddon* in chains to Babylon.	Isaiah Joel
43	Amon	2	An idolatrous king; is murdered.	
41	Josiah	31	An excellent king; great reform; slain.	Zephaniah
9	Jehoahaz (or	¼	*Shallum*); carried captive into Egypt.	Habakkuk
9	Jehoiakim (or	11	*Eliakim*); is carried in chains to Babylon.	
600				
98	Jehoiachin (or	½	*Jeconiah*); is carried to Babylon.	Obadiah
98	Zedekiah	11	The king and the nation carried captive to Babylon. The city and temple destroyed by *Nebuchadnezzar*, 588 B. C. **The captivity lasted 70 years, from 606 B. C. to 1st year of Cyrus, 536 B. C.**	Jeremiah Ezekiel Daniel Haggai Zechariah

Malachi, the last of the Old Testament prophets, lived after the rebuilding of the Temple. The political condition of the Jews from the time of Zerubbabel, the first governor after the return from captivity, was very variable. Jerusalem was taken by a Roman army under Pompey, 63 B. C., and Judea was afterwards reduced to a Roman province.

Chronological Table of the Kingdom of Israel, or the Ten Tribes: — 19 *Kings:* — 254 *Years.*				
B. C.		Kings.	Length of Reign.	
1000	75	Jeroboam I.	21	Son of *Nebat*, becomes king of the *Ten Tribes;* resides first at *Shechem*, afterwards at *Tirzah;* institutes the worship of *golden calves* one at *Bethel* and another at *Dan*, and seduces the people to idolatry; overcome by *Abijah*, and 500,000 Israelites slain.
	54	Nadab	1	Son of *Jeroboam;* slain by *Baasha*.
	53	Baasha	24	Usurps the throne, and destroys all the family of Jeroboam; at war with Asa.
	30	Elah	1	Son of Baasha; is slain by Zimri.
	29	Zimri		Usurps the throne; destroys the race of Baasha; after a reign of 7 days is overcome by *Omri*.
	29	Omri	12	Founds *Samaria*, and makes it the capital.
	18	Ahab	21	Son of Omri; notorious for impiety, as well as his queen *Jezebel;* seizes the vineyard of *Naboth;* wars against *Ramoth Gilead;* is slain.
900	97	Ahaziah	1	Son of Ahab; wounded by a fall, and dies.
	96	Jehoram	12	*Samaria* besieged by *Benhadad*, king of Syria; the inhabitants in great distress.
	84	Jehu	28	Destroys *Jezebel* and all the family of *Ahab*, and the priests of *Baal*, but maintains the worship of Jeroboam's *golden calves*.
	56	Jehoahaz	17	Oppressed by *Hazael*, king of Syria.
	39	Joash	14	Defeats Benhadad II., king of Syria; also *Amaziah;* takes *Jerusalem*.
	26	Jeroboam II.	41	A warlike sovereign; has a prosperous reign.
800				After this reign the kingdom hastens to its downfall; and its subsequent history is replete with treason, disorder, and misrule.
				An *Interregnum* of 11 years.
	73	Zechariah	½	Is slain by *Shallum*, who usurps the throne.
	73	Shallum		After a reign of 1 month is killed by *Menahem*.
	63	Menahem	10	Becomes tributary to *Pul*, king of Assyria.
	61	Pekaiah	2	Is murdered by *Pekah*, one of his captains.
	59	Pekah	20	Unites with *Rezin*, king of Syria, and besieges *Jerusalem;* defeats *Ahaz*, slays 120,000 men, and takes 200,000; is overthrown by *Tiglathpileser*, who carries a part of the Israelites to Syria: slain by *Hoshea*.
	39	Hoshea	18	Becomes tributary to *Shalmaneser*, king of Assyria, but applies to *So*, king of Egypt, and revolts. Shalmaneser besieges, takes, and demolishes Samaria, carries the Israelites captive into *Assyria* and *Media*, and puts an end to the kingdom, B. C. 721.

The subsequent history of the *Ten Tribes* is buried in obscurity. The country was afterwards repeopled by colonies from Assyria, whose descendants adopted the Law of Moses as contained in the Pentateuch, which they regarded as the only inspired book and they were called *Samaritans*, from the chief city of the country. The Samaritans built a temple on *Mount Gerizim*. They were always at variance with the Jews, by whom they were despised and hated as heretics.

A. D.		Eras in Modern History.
800		New Empire of the West under *Charlemagne* formed.
9th	27	The *Kingdom of England* begins. The *Saxon Heptarchy* **ends.**
900		
10th	12	The Normans under *Rollo* take possession of Normandy.
	64	*Otho the Great*, emperor of Germany, conquers Italy.
1000		
	66	*William the Conqueror* (battle of *Hastings*) conquers England.
11th	96	FIRST CRUSADE to the Holy Land: Peter the Hermit.
1100	47	*Second Crusade*, excited by St. Bernard.
12th	88	*Third Crusade*, under Richard I. of England and Philip Augustus of France.
1200	2	*Fourth Crusade*, under Baldwin, who takes Constantinople.
	12	*Magna Charta* signed by King John of England.
13th	27	Genghis-Khan, emperor of the Moguls, overruns the **Saracen** [empire.
	58	End of the Caliphate of Bagdad.
	70	*Last Crusade*, under St. Louis IX. of France.
1300	14	*Robert Bruce* defeats Edward II. of England at *Bannockburn.*
	46	*Edward* III. of England gains the battle of *Cressy.*
14th	47	*Great Plague* in Europe; said to carry off ¼ of the inhabitants.
	58	*Timur Bek* or *Tamerlane* commences his reign and conquests.
1400	53	TURKS take *Constantinople;* end of the *Eastern Roman Empire.*
	55	The *York and Lancaster War* begins in England; lasts 30 years
	79	Arragon and Castile united, forming the kingdom of *Spain.*
15th	86	The *Cape of Good Hope* discovered by Bartholomew Diaz.
	92	AMERICA discovered by *Columbus.*
	97	*Vasco de Gama* reaches India by way of the *Cape of Good Hope.*
1500	17	Reformation by *Luther.*—1519. *Charles* V. emp. of Germany.
	21	*Mexico* conquered by Cortes.
16th	22	The *Globe* first *circumnavigated* by Magellan's squadron: by *Drake* in 1580.
	60	The *Civil Wars* in France begin, conducted by Condé and Guise.
	79	The *Republic of Holland* begins by the union of Utrecht.
	82	The *Calendar* reformed by Pope Gregory XIII.
1600	3	Union of the crowns of *England* and *Scotland.*
	7	First English settlement in *America*, at Jamestown, Virginia.
	12	First English establishment in *Hindostan.*
17th	48	*Peace of Westphalia* or *Munster:* end of the 30 Years' War.
	49	*Charles* I. of England beheaded: the *Commonwealth* begins.
	88	*Revolution* in England; abdication of James II.
1700	13	*Peace of Utrecht* between France and the Allies.
	48	*Peace of Aix-la-Chapelle;* end of the war of the Austrian Suc- [cession
18th	52	*New Style* introduced into England.
	63	*Peace of Paris; Canada* ceded by France to England
	76	The INDEPENDENCE of the United States declared.
	89	The FRENCH REVOLUTION;—completed in 1792–93.
1800	2	*Peace of Amiens*, between England, France, Spain, and Holland
	4	NAPOLEON BONAPARTE emperor of France.
	6	End of the *German Empire.*
	12	War between the U. States and England begins: ends in 1814
	15	The Battle of WATERLOO; the empire of *Bonaparte* overthrown; Congress of European sovereigns at Vienna.
19th	29	*Peace of Adrianople* between Russia and Turkey.
	30	*New Revolution* in France; *Charles* X. dethroned.
	32	The *Reform Bill* passes the British Parliament.
	33	Act for the abolition of *Slavery* in the British Colonies.
	48	New *Revolution in France: Louis Philippe* dethroned.
	60	The kingdom of Italy established. — *Victor Emanuel* king.

A. D.		CHRONOLOGICAL TABLE OF INVENTIONS.
900		
	91	The *Figures of Arithmetic* brought into Europe by the Saracens.
10th	96	*Clocks* with toothed wheels invented in France by Gerbert.
1000	—	*Paper* made of cotton rags in use.
11th		*Surnames* begin to be used by the nobility.
1100		
	37	The *Pandects of Roman Law* discovered at Amalfi.
12th	57	The first regular *Bank* at Venice.
1200		
	53	*Linen* first made in England.
	60	*Glass Mirrors* and *Magnifying-Glasses* invented by R. Bacon.
13th	80	to 1311. *Spectacles* invented by Bacon, Salvinus, Armatus & Spina.
	90	*Tallow Candles* begin to be used.
1300	—	*Chimneys* and *Glass Windows* begin to be used in private houses.
	2	The *Mariner's Compass* improved by Flavio Gioia.
	20	to 40. GUNPOWDER invented at Cologne by Swartz.
14th	42	*Cannon* used at the siege of Algeziras: *Muskets* in use in 1370.
	50	*Clocks* in use: first made in England in 1568.
	90	*Playing-Cards* invented: first *Paper-Mill* in Germany.
1400		
	10	*Painting* in oil-colors invented at Bruges by Van Eyck.
	40	Art of PRINTING invented by Coster, Guttenberg, &c.
	64	*Post-Offices* established in France: in England in 1581.
15th	71	*Printing* introduced into England by William Caxton.
	77	*Watches* made at Nuremberg: in use in England in 1597.
	89	*Maps* and *Charts* brought into England by Barthol. Columbus.
1500		
	30	The *Spinning-Wheel* invented at Brunswick by Jurgen.
	32	The true SOLAR SYSTEM revived by Copernicus.
	45	*Needles* first made in England.
16th	82	First treatise on *Decimal Arithmetic* published at Bruges.
	86	*Potatoes* introduced into England from America.
	90	to 1620. The *Telescope*, by Porta, Jansen, Drebell, and Galileo.
1600		
	10	The *Thermometer* invented by Sanctorius, Drebell, and Galileo.
	14	*Logarithms* invented in Scotland by Napier.
	19	The *Circulation of the Blood* discovered by Harvey.
	30	The first *Gazette* or *Newspaper* at Venice: in England in 1665.
	41	*Coffee* first brought into England: *Tea* in 1666.
17th	43	The *Barometer* invented by Torricelli and Pascal.
	54	The *Air-Pump* invented at Magdeburg by Guericke.
	55	The *Steam-Engine* invented: improved by Watt in 1768.
	59	*Saturn's Ring* discovered by Huyghens.
	87	The *Newtonian Philosophy* published in England.
1700		
	21	*Inoculation* introduced into England from Turkey.
	25	*Stereotype Printing* invented by *Ged;* introduced by *Didot*, 1789.
	52	The identity of *Lightning* and *Electricity* ascertained by Franklin.
	69	The *Spinning-Jenny* invented by Arkwright.
18th	81	The planet *Uranus* or *Herschel* discovered by Herschel.
	94	The *Cotton-Gin* invented by Whitney.
	98	VACCINATION discovered and introduced by Dr. Jenner
	98	*Galvanism* discovered by Galvani.
		Lithography invented at Munich by Sennefelder.
1800		
	7	The first STEAMBOAT on the Hudson.
	16	The *Safety-Lamp* invented by Sir Humphrey Davy.
	30	The *Liverpool and Manchester Railroad* opened; the first on which *locomotive steam-carriages* were used.
19th.	38	The Great Western, *Steamship*, makes her first voyage, crossing the Atlantic, from Bristol, England, to New York.
	53	The Caloric Engine invented by Ericsson.

QUESTIONS.

N. B. The *numbers* prefixed to the following *Questions* correspond to the *paragraphs* in the *Volume*; so that the student will readily see where to seek for every answer. It will be perceived that, in many instances, the answers to three or four questions are to be found in one paragraph.

USES OF HISTORY.

1. What is history? What is said of the study of it?
2. What is said of history, compared with novels and romances?
3 On what is the general taste for history founded? What view does it afford of human nature?
4. What is a higher use of history? What has it been styled? What does it add to our own experience?
5. With what does it make us acquainted? From what does it serve to free the mind?
6. To what class of persons is history indispensable? Of what do we gain a knowledge by history?
7. What further does history show and teach us?
8. What influence has it on the character? How does it make virtue appear, — and vice? What does the reader of history learn to connect with true glory?
9 What does history teach us has been often done under the direction of Providence?
10. Why does a knowledge of history tend to render us contented with our condition in life?

THE SOURCES OF HISTORY.

1. What is the first source of history? Who derived his history chiefly from this source?
2. What is the second source? What instances are mentioned?
3. What is the third source? 4. The fourth? 5. The fifth? 6. The sixth? To what century do the most ancient coins that have been found belong?
7. What is the seventh source of history? What is the most celebrated collection of marbles of this kind?
8. What is the most important of these inscriptions? What is said of it?
9 What is said of hieroglyphics, paintings, and sculptures?

DIVISIONS OF HISTORY.

1. How is history divided with respect to time?
2. What is Ancient History? Modern History?
3. What other eras do some historians adopt for the dividing points?
4. What is a third division of history? What does this period comprise

5. What is said further of the Middle Ages?
6. By what is Ancient History distinguished?
7. By what are the Middle Ages characterized? By what has the last half century been characterized?
8. By what is Modern History distinguished?
9. How is history divided with regard to subject?
10. What is Sacred History? Profane History? Ecclesiastical History? Civil History?
11. How far back does Sacred History go, and what was the length of time from the creation to the Christian era?
12 What is said of Geology?
13 Who is the earliest profane historian? When did he write, and of what nations?
14 What is said of the history of the world before the time when the history of Herodotus begins?
15. What is said of our knowledge of the early history of the world? What is the only source of this information?
16. What are some of the most remarkable events respecting the early history of the world recorded in the Bible?
17. What are the most important portions of profane history?
18. What is said of the history of the Middle or Dark Ages?
19. What portions of history are the best known?

EGYPT.

1. Why does Egypt hold a conspicuous place in history? What nation derived its information chiefly from it?
2. What is said of the ancient history of Egypt?
3. What are some of the works of ancient grandeur?
4. What is said of the glory of Thebes?
5. What city supplanted Thebes? What is said of the description given of Thebes by Strabo and Diodorus?
6. How was the place of alphabetic writing supplied?
7. What is said of the researches of Champollion and other learned men?
8. What is said of the inhabitants of Egypt?
9. What of the government and the kings?
10. What is said of the laws and customs?
11. To what was every person subject after his death?
12. What is said of the armies and weapons of the Egyptians?
13. Who was the first king that is known? What is said of his successors?
14 Who was the most distinguished king?
15 What other kings are mentioned?
16 Who is the next distinguished sovereign? What is said of him?
17. Who conquered Egypt, 525 B. C.? In what manner?
18. By whom was it wrested from Persia? What was its situation after the death of Alexander?

THE PHŒNICIANS.

1 What is said of the Phœnicians and their history?
2 What are they styled in the Scriptures, and what were their chief cities?
3. Of what were they the reputed inventors?
4. To what places did they send colonies? By whom did Tyre suffer memorable sieges?

ASSYRIA AND BABYLON.

1. What is said of Assyria? Who founded Babylon? What is said of their history?
2. What is commonly supposed respecting Assyria and Babylon? What is the opinion of Dr. Gillies?
3. What is said of Ninus and Semiramis?
4. How is Ninus represented? How is Semiramis described?
5. What is said of the history of the empire from the time of Ninyas to Sardanapalus?
6. What is said of Sardanapalus? Who excited a rebellion against him?
7. What took place with regard to the empire?
8. Who were the four successors of Pul?
9. Who put an end to the Assyrian monarchy?
10. By whom was Nabopolassar or Nebuchadnezzar succeeded?
11. What took place during the reign of Belshazzar?
12. What is said of Babylon after the conquest? What is its present state?
13. What is said of Nineveh? What has lately been discovered on its site?

PERSIA.

1. What is said of Persia? What is the state of its history prior to the reign of Cyrus? What was it originally called? Who was the founder of the great Persian empire? What countries did it comprise?
2. To whom are we indebted for the history of Persia? What is said of the Persian historians? Which are entitled to most credit?
3. What is said of Cyrus? What did he perform?
4. What ancients have written accounts of Cyrus? Who have followed Xenophon? What was Xenophon's supposed design?
5. What is said of Cambyses? Of Smerdis? Darius?
6. Who succeeded Darius? What is said of him? To whom did he leave the empire?
7. Who were the other two principal sovereigns?
8. When did Cyrus begin to reign? Darius Hystaspes? Darius Codomanus?

GREECE.

Section I.

What was the extent of Greece? How was it bounded? What is its general aspect?
2. What is said of this country? For what were the inhabitants renowned?
3. What did Greece comprise? How did these states differ? How were they united?
4. What was the form of government in the early ages? What form afterwards prevailed?
[illegible] What is said of the history of these republics? Why does their history excite interest?
6. What were Greece and the inhabitants called by the natives? What do the poets style the Greeks? From whom were the original inhabitants descended?
7. Who brought to Greece the first rudiments of civilization?

Section II.

1. Into how many general periods may the history of Greece be distinguished? What is the first? What the second?
2. How many years does the first period comprise? What is said of it?
3. Into how many subdivisions may this period be distinguished? When does the first period begin and end, and what may it be termed? The second? The third? The fourth?
4. What does the second general division (the period of authentic history) comprise? What is said of its history?
5. Into how many parts may this period be divided? When does the first begin and end, and what is said of it? The second? The third? The fourth?

Section III.

1. What does the fabulous age comprise?
2. By whom was Sicyon founded? Argos? Athens? Thebes? Corinth? Mycenæ? Lacedæmon?
3. What are some of the memorable events of this period? What else does it embrace?
4. What was the first great enterprise recorded of the Greeks? By whom was it commanded? Who were some of the heroes who accompanied Jason?
5. Why were they called Argonauts? What was their object? What is said of the fleece?

Section IV.

1. To what has the heroic age been compared? What difference is mentioned between the Greeks and the Gothic nations?
2. On whose authority does the history of the Trojan war rest? What is said of the Iliad?
3. What is said of Helen? To what oath did her father bind her suitors? Who was the favored individual?
4. What is said of Paris? What did he do on visiting Sparta?
5. What was the effect of this treachery? How many vessels and men were conveyed to the Trojan coast? Who was chosen commander-in-chief? Who were some of the other most celebrated princes?
6. By whom were the Trojans commanded? What was the final result of the siege?
7. When did the return of the Heraclidæ take place?
8. What is said of Hercules? How long was it after his banishment when his descendants returned? What was the consequence of it?
9. What was the effect of this revolution?

Section V.

1. What were the two leading states of Greece, and how were they distinguished? How were their different characters formed?
2. Of what was Sparta the capital? How was the government administered?
3. Who was Lycurgus? With what duty was he intrusted?
4. What did he accomplish? What senate did he institute? What did he do respecting the two kings? How did he divide the territory?
5. What measure did he take respecting commerce, &c.? How did the citizens take their food?
6. What was the situation of every citizen? What was the regulation respecting infants?
7. What was the fact respecting letters? How were the Spartans distinguished? For what were they noted?

8. What were the young especially taught? What further regulations were made respecting them?

9 What were the institutions of Lycurgus adapted to form? What was considered the great business of life? What virtues were cherished, and what were sacrificed?

10. What is said of the women? What was their education calculated to give them? What charge did a mother give her son?

11. How long did the institutions of Lycurgus continue in force? What is said of the power and influence of Sparta?

12. What took place in process of time? How were changes introduced?

Section VI.

1. What is said of Athens? For what is it distinguished?

2. Who was the last king of Athens? What took place after his death? What is said of the office of the archons?

3. By whom was the first code of written laws prepared for Athens? What is said of these laws? What reason did Draco give for the severity of his punishments?

4. Who afterwards framed a new system of laws? What did Solon attempt to do? What did he say of his laws?

5. In whom did he vest the supreme power? What was done by this assembly? Of what number did the senate consist?

6. What did he encourage? What further is said respecting his laws?

7. What effects did the different laws of Athens and Sparta produce? What were the differences at the two cities? How were an Athenian and a Spartan characterized?

8. What happened before the death of Solon? How long did Pisistratus and his sons continue in power? What is said of his government?

9. To whom did Pisistratus transmit the sovereignty? By whom were they dethroned? What was their fate?

Section VII.

1. What period is esteemed the most glorious age of Greece? What is said of the victories of the inhabitants over the Persians?

2. What was the state of Persia at this period? What colonies and countries were subject to it?

3. What gave offence to Darius? What did he resolve to do?

4. What step did Darius first take? How were his heralds received?

5. How did Darius begin his hostile attack? What was the fate of the first Persian fleet? What was done by a second fleet? How numerous was the army that invaded Attica? By whom was it commanded?

6. Where and by whom was this host met? What was the loss on each side?

7. How was the merit of Miltiades repaid? What happened to him?

8. What were the parties into which the Athenians were divided? Who were the two leaders?

9. What is said of Aristides? What happened while the people were giving their votes for his exile? What did Aristides do?

10. What caused a discontinuance of the Persian war? By whom was it renewed? How large an army is Xerxes said to have collected?

11. Of what did his fleet consist? What canal and bridges were formed?

12. Why did Xerxes shed tears on viewing the vast assemblage?

13. What course was taken by the Persians? Who was leader of Athens? What states took part with Athens?

14. What did Leonidas undertake? What reply did he give to the

herald of Xerxes, who commanded him to deliver up his arms? What followed?

15. What course did Leonidas take? What was the result? What inscription was written on the monument erected on the spot?

16. What did the Persians now do? What course did the Athenians take?

17. For what were preparations now made? Of what did the two fleets consist? Who commanded the Grecian fleet? Where did the engagement take place? What was the issue?

18. Who was left by Xerxes to complete the conquest of Greece? Where and by whom was this army met? What was the issue?

19. What took place on the same day of the victory of Platæa? What happened to Xerxes?

20. What course did the Greeks pursue? By whom were the Spartans and Athenians commanded? What did they accomplish?

21. What is related of Pausanias?

22. What is related of Themistocles?

23. Who took the direction of affairs in Athens after the banishment of Themistocles?

24. What victories did Cimon gain?

25. What afterwards happened to Cimon? Who succeeded him?

26. What further is related of Cimon?

27. How long did the Persian war last? What were the conditions of peace?

28. What took place after the death of Cimon?

29. What is said of the government of Pericles?

30. What is said of the time of the Persian war? What took place after the war with Persia? What is related of Athens and Sparta?

31. What was the effect of the war on the Athenians? By what means did they reach the summit of political influence and military power?

32. On what did the politics of Greece, after this, turn? What is said of Athens and Sparta, and how did they differ?

33. What took place from this period? What was the effect of an acquaintance with Asia? How was this luxurious spirit directed by the Athenians?

Section VIII.

1. What was the origin of the Peloponnesian war?

2. What is said of this war? How was it carried on?

3 Of what were the Athenians accused?

4 What state took the lead? By what states was she joined? What allies had Athens? What did the forces of each amount to?

5. What was done in the first year of the war? What took place in the second year? Was the war arrested by the plague?

6 Who governed Athens after the death of Pericles? What is said of Cleon? What happened after his death?

7 What is said of Alcibiades?

8. Who commanded the expedition against Sicily? What was the issue of it?

9. What is said of Lysander? What was next done by the Lacedæmonians?

10. On what conditions were the Athenians spared? How did the Peloponnesian war terminate?

11. What did Lysander do after the reduction of Athens? How many citizens did the thirty tyrants sacrifice in the space of six months? What was done by Thrasybulus?

12. What is said of pure democracy at Athens? How were the Athenians characterized?

13. Who is at once the glory and the reproach of Athens? What is said of this philosopher?
14. What is related of him during his imprisonment?
15. What is said of the philosophy of Socrates? What did he do respecting philosophy?
16. In what contest were upwards of 10,000 Greek mercenaries employed? Who commanded the Greeks in their retreat?
17. What is said of this retreat?
18. How did the Spartans become involved in the war? What did the king of Persia effect by means of bribes? What course did Agesilaus take?
19. How was the war ended? What were the conditions of peace?
20. What state now rose into importance? What was done by the Spartans? By whom was the citadel recovered?
21. What then ensued? What were the losses of each in the battle of Leuctra?
22. What was then done by the Thebans? How long had it been since the country of Laconia had been ravaged?
23. What course did the Theban commander then take? What other victory did he gain?
24. What is said of Epaminondas?
25. By what was the battle of Mantinea followed? In what did the Spartans next engage? What was the issue?

Section IX.

1. What is said of the history of Greece after the death of Agesilaus? What was the situation of the Grecian affairs?
2. What is said of Athens at this time? What of Sparta? What project did Philip form?
3. What is said of the kingdom of Macedon? Who were the inhabitants?
4. What is said of the Macedonian empire? Why is it sometimes called the Grecian empire?
5. Under whom was Philip educated? What is further said of him? What measures did he adopt to bring the states of Greece under his dominion?
6. What was the cause of the Sacred War? What states took part in the contest?
7. What course did Philip adopt? What was he styled? What course did the Athenians take?
8. What circumstance again drew Philip into Greece? What was the occasion of it? What states resisted Philip? What was the result of the contest?
9. What measures did the conqueror adopt?
10 What did Philip next project? What happened to him?
11 By whom was Philip succeeded? What is said of Alexander?
12. What was done by Demosthenes? What course did Alexander take? What was the fate of the Thebans? What was the effect of these acts?
13. What were Alexander's next measures? Who were his companions in arms?
14. With what force did he cross the Hellespont? To what place did he first proceed? What did he say respecting Achilles?
15. Where did the Persian satraps meet him? What were the losses on each side in the battle of the Granicus? What is here mentioned respecting Alexander?
16 What were the consequences of this victory?

17. What battle was fought in the next spring? What was the number of the Persian army? What were the losses? Where did the engagement take place?

18. Who fell into the hands of the conqueror? What offer did Darius make Alexander, in consequence of his generous conduct?

19. What did Parmenio say of the offer? What was Alexander's reply? What answer did he return to the proposal?

20. What was his next course? What was the consequence of the Tyrians refusing his demand? What piece of cruelty did he exercise?

21. What was the next exploit?

22. Whither did he then proceed? What did he accomplish? What city did he found?

23. What proposal did he receive from Darius on his return? What answer did he return?

24. With how large an army did he cross the Euphrates? What losses were sustained in the battle that followed? Where was this battle fought, and what is it called?

25. What was the consequence of this battle? What has since been the fact with regard to Europe? What happened to Darius and the empire?

26. What was Alexander's next procedure? What course did his soldiers take?

27. To what city did Alexander then march his army? What did he do here? Where and in what manner did he die?

28. What is said of Alexander and his course?

29. What is said of his abilities and traits of character?

30 For what was he distinguished in the early part of his career? What afterwards took place?

31 Of what acts of ingratitude and injustice was he guilty?

32. What does his history show?

Section X.

1. What did Alexander do respecting a successor? By what was his death followed?

2. Who was appointed by his generals? How was the empire divided? What followed? What was the new division after the battle of Ipsus?

3. What was the end of the kingdoms of Thrace and Macedonia? What is said of Syria and Egypt?

4. What was done by the Grecian states during Alexander's conquests?

5 What effect did the news of Alexander's death have at Athens? By whom was Demosthenes opposed? What was the language of Phocion?

6 How far did the counsels of Demosthenes prevail? What was the fate of Demosthenes?

7. By whom was Antipater succeeded? What took place at Athens? What is related of Phocion?

8 By whom was Polysperchon succeeded? What is said of the government of Demetrius Phalereus?

9. What was the state of Athens afterwards?

10 What was the condition of the Grecian states from this period? By whom was the country ravaged?

11. Who next invaded Peloponnesus? What happened to him?

12. By what confederacy was the last effort made in favor of Greece? To whom was the government of this confederacy committed? What design did he form?

13 By whom was Aratus succeeded? What is said of him?

14. What is related of the Romans? What was accomplished by their

army under Quintius Flaminius? What took place nearly thirty years afterwards?

15. What part did the Romans take, with respect to the Achæan league? Who sought the assistance of the Romans? What was done by Metellus? What afterwards took place?

16. What is said of Greece after she became subject to the Romans? Where were the most distinguished Romans educated?

17. What do we see in reviewing the history of the Greeks? In what were they unrivalled?

18. What circumstance must impress the readers of the history of Athens? Who were victims of this injustice? What was done respecting them?

19. What is said respecting the supposed virtuous age of Greece? What is said of the morality of the Greeks?

20 What is stated by Mitford?

21 How were the earlier times characterized? How was it in a later age? What had the history of the world demonstrated?

Section XI. — Grecian Antiquities.

Among whom did the most of the ancient sects of philosophy have their origin? When did Grecian literature flourish most?

What is said of the Ionic sect? The Italian or Pythagorean sect? The Socratic School? The Cynics? The Academic sect? The Peripatetic sect? The Sceptical sect? The Stoic sect? The Epicureans?

What does Tytler say respecting the Greek philosophy? What course did its teachers pursue?

Who were most illustrious Grecian poets?

Who were famous statuaries? Painters? Historians?

Who were the seven wise men of Greece?

By whom is the council of the Amphictyons supposed to have been instituted? Of what was it composed? Of how many deputies did it consist? When and where did they meet?

What were the objects of this assembly?

On what occasions were the Greeks in the habit of consulting oracles? What were their most celebrated oracles?

What were the four public games in Greece? What exercises were practised at these games?

What is said of running, leaping, and boxing?

In honor of whom were the Olympic games instituted? Where and when were they celebrated? What did they draw together? What preparation was required?

What oath were the contenders obliged to take? What was the prize bestowed on the victor? What is said of it? How was the victor treated?

How did the Greeks compute their time?

What is said of the Pythian games? With what were the victors crowned?

Where and how often were the Nemean games celebrated? With what were the victors crowned?

Why were the Isthmian games so called? What is said of them? What was the reward of the victors?

Into what classes were the inhabitants of Athens divided?
Who were the citizens? Into how many tribes were they divided
What is said of the privilege of citizenship?
What was the condition of the sojourners?
What is said of the slaves or servants?
In what was the supreme executive power vested? What garlands did they wear? What was the first of the nine called? What was his office? For what crime was he punished with death?
What were the duties of the second archon? What did the third archon superintend?
What were the duties of six other archons?
Into what three sorts were the Athenian magistrates divided?
What rights had the poor citizens? What were the candidates for office obliged to do? To what were the magistrates liable while in office? What were they obliged to do after their office had expired?
Of whom were the assemblies of the people composed? How often and where were they held?
Of how many citizens must the assembly consist, in order to transact business? How was the decision made?
How often was the senate elected, and of how many did it consist? What were the duties of the senate?
From what was the name of Areopagus taken? What is said of this court? Of what were the Areopagites guardians?
What is said of the ostracism? Was it necessary that any crime should be alleged against the exile? What is remarked of this institution?

Of what two classes did the inhabitants of Sparta consist?
Into what two classes were the citizens divided?
Which were the more numerous, the slaves or the freemen? What did the slaves perform?
What were the two chief magistrates? What were their duties?
Of what did the senate consist? What was its authority? Who were admitted to this assembly?
What were the Ephori? What was their duty?
What were the two public assemblies of Sparta? When was the general assembly convened? When and for what purposes was the lesser assembly held?

Chronological Table of Grecian History.

When did the first Olympiad begin?
When did Solon form his code of laws?
When did the Persian war begin? The Peloponnesian war?
When did Alexander invade Persia?
When was the battle of Ipsus? Pydna?
When was Greece reduced to a Roman province?
What are some of the events mentioned in the 8th century B. C? What in the 7th? The 6th? &c.

Chronological Table of Grecian Literature.

What statesmen and warriors flourished in the 7th century B. C.? The 6th? &c.
What philosophers in the 6th century B. C. The 5th? &c.
What poets and artists in the 7th century B. C.? The 6th? &c
What historians in the 5th century B. C.? The 4th? &c.

SYRIA UNDER THE SELEUCIDÆ.

1. Who obtained possession of the principal possessions of Alexander in Asia, after his death? Who defeated Antigonus? How long did the kingdom of Syria or Syro-Media last? By what kings was it governed?

2. What is said of Seleucus and his exploits? What is said of Antioch?

3. What was the end of Seleucus? By whom was he succeeded?

4. What is said of the reigns of Antiochus Theos and Seleucus Callinicus?

5. Who was one of the most distinguished of this race of sovereigns? What is related of his reign?

6. By whom was Antiochus visited? What did he undertake? By whom and where was he defeated?

7. Who were the next two kings? What was done by the latter? What did the Jews perform?

8. What is said of the succeeding reigns?

9. When did Seleucus I. begin to reign? Antiochus the Great? Who was the last of the Seleucidæ?

EGYPT UNDER THE PTOLEMIES.

1. What is said of the prosperity of Egypt? How long did the dynasty of the Ptolemies last?

2. Who was Ptolemy Lagus? What is said of his history and his abilities?

3. What important public services did he perform?

4. By whom was Ptolemy Soter succeeded? What is related of Ptolemy Philadelphus? What is said of his court? What celebrated version was made during his reign?

5. What is said of Ptolemy Evergetes? With what did his reign commence? What vow was made by his queen?

6. How was the hair regarded? What is said of that of Berenice? What took place respecting it?

7. By whom was Ptolemy Evergetes succeeded? For what was his reign distinguished? What excited his resentment against the Jews?

8. What decree did he publish? What effect did it produce? What did he then command? What was the consequence?

9. What is said of the first three Ptolemies? What of the others?

10. Why was Ptolemy Soter so named? Ptolemy Philadelphus? Ptolemy Evergetes? Ptolemy Philopater? Ptolemy Epiphanes? &c.

11. Who was the last of the Ptolemies? Who was his queen? With whom is her history connected? What was the manner of her death? What was the condition of Egypt afterwards?

12. What is related respecting the queens of the Ptolemies?

13. When did Ptolemy Lagus begin to reign? Who was the last of these sovereigns? When did she die?

ROME.

Section I

1. What state becomes the leading object of attention, after the conquest of Greece? What is said of its rise and importance? What is remarked of its history? What is involved in its history?

2. What was its extent during its early history? What change afterwards took place? How long did the empire continue?

3. What is said of the early history of the Romans? What reasons are there for supposing there must be a mixture of fiction?

4. How is the length of time comprised in the reigns of the seven kings regarded? What happened to several of these kings? What was the average length of their reigns?

5. What is remarked respecting the histories of the early ages? Of Romulus, of the seven kings, and early ages of the commonwealth?

6. What account do the poets give of Æneas? How long was the succession continued in his family?

7. Of whom was Rhea Sylvia the mother? What is related of the brothers? What did Romulus do after he had built the city of Rome?

8. How is Romulus said to have divided the people? Of how many members did the senate consist? From whom were they chosen? How did he attach the two classes to each other? What duties did the patron and client perform to each other?

9. By what persons was the king attended?

10. Who was the second king of Rome? Of what town was he a native? How is he represented? What did he do?

11. Who was the third king? For what is his reign memorable? What was the issue of this combat?

12. Who was the fourth king? What did he do?

13. Who was the successor of Ancus Martius? What was done by him?

14. What is related of Servius Tullius? What did he establish? By what was the census closed?

15. What were the characters of the two daughters of Servius? What measure did he take with regard to them, in order to secure the throne? How did he attempt to correct their defects? What was the issue?

16. How did Tarquin the Proud begin his reign? What was the consequence? What is related of Sextus? What course did Lucretia take?

17. What measures were taken to excite the indignation of the people against the Tarquins? What was done with Tarquin?

Section II.

1. What government was established instead of the regal authority? To whom did the supreme power belong? What two new officers were chosen? What is said of their power? Who were the first consuls?

2. What measures were taken by Tarquin? What partisans had he in Rome? In what plot were the sons of Brutus concerned? What course did Brutus take? What remark is made by an ancient author upon his conduct?

3. What took place after the insurrection in the city was suppressed? What notice was taken of the death of Brutus? Who was the first that enjoyed the reward of a triumph?

4 What course did Valerius adopt to regain his popularity? What was the effect of this law?

5 How long were the Romans involved in hostilities on account of Tarquin? What was the most remarkable of these wars? Who distinguished themselves in it?

6. What other troubles were added to those of war? What course did the plebeians take? Why was the authority of the consuls of no avail?

7. What new magistrate was now created? In what cases was he appointed? What was his authority? Who was chosen dictator? What was the issue? What other occasion was there for a dictator?

8. What troubles followed after the return of peace? What course did the plebeians adopt on an alarm of war? What was their language? What step did they at length take?

9. What was the consequence of this procedure? What was done by

Menenius Agrippa? What was granted to the plebeians? How often were tribunes elected, and what was their number? What two other magistrates were appointed?

10. What did a neglect of agriculture occasion? In what manner did Coriolanus excite the resentment of the people? What was the consequence?

11. What law was proposed that caused dissension? Who demanded such a division of the public lands?

12. What was the law which Volero caused to be enacted? What was the effect of this law?

13 What is related of Cincinnatus? What did he do after his victories?

14 What was the fact respecting the laws of the Romans? Who administered justice? What is said of their proceedings? What measures were taken to provide a code?

15. For what were the decemvirs appointed? Of what statutes was this the origin?

16. With what were the decemvirs invested? How did they govern? What caused a termination of the office?

17. What was one of the crimes of Appius Claudius? What was the other?

18. What decree did he pronounce? What was done by Virginius? What was the effect? What took place respecting the decemvirs and decemvirate?

Section III.

1. What were the barriers which still separated the patricians and plebeians? Which was repealed? What was the effect?

2. What officers were chosen instead of consuls? Did this institution continue long?

3. What was prevented by the disorders of the republic? What officers were appointed to remedy this neglect? What was their duty? What is said of this office?

4. What practice was introduced to avoid the evils arising from the people's refusing to enlist in the army? What changes took place after this?

5. What decree was made respecting Veii? What followed?

6. How did Camillus proceed? How was he rewarded?

7. What is related of the Gauls? In what did they engage? What reply did Brennus make to the ambassadors from the senate? What did Brennus do in consequence of the ambassador's having assisted the inhabitants of Clusium?

8. What steps did the Gauls take after the battle of Allia? What enterprise did a body of Gauls perform? What was the issue?

9. On what condition did the Gauls agree to quit the city? What was done by Camillus?

10 What afterwards happened to Manlius?

11. Against whom did the Romans next turn their arms? How long did this contest last, and how was it carried on? What disgrace did the Samnites cause the Romans to undergo? What was the effect?

12. What war broke out during the consulship of Torquatus Manlius? What is related respecting the son of Manlius?

13. What course did the Tarentines take? With how large an army did Pyrrhus land? What was the issue of the battle? What exclamation did Pyrrhus make?

14. What generous conduct is related of Fabricius? What effect did this have on Pyrrhus?

15. What course did Pyrrhus afterwards take? Of what did the Romans now become masters?

SECTION IV.

1. With what states does the history of Rome now become connected?
2. By whom was Carthage founded? What was the government? What was the religion?
3. What was the situation of Carthage in the time of the Punic wars? What had it under its dominion? What is said of the character of the Carthaginians?
4. Did Carthage produce many philosophers? What generals did it produce?
5 By whom was Sicily colonized? What is said of Syracuse? How was it governed?
6 What is said of Gelon and his successors? By whom was the regal government restored? By whom was Dionysius the Younger dethroned?

SECTION V.

1. What were the Romans desirous of, after having become masters of all Lower Italy? What conquests had they not yet made? What is said of Carthage? How are the Carthaginians and Romans compared?
2. How was the first Punic war brought on? What was the object of both parties?
3. What course did the Romans take? What was their success? What part did the Syracusans act?
4. What further advantages did the Romans gain? What course was adopted by Regulus? What was the issue? What is further related of Regulus?
5. What was the final issue of the war? To what terms did the Carthaginians agree? What was the state of Sicily and Syracuse? What conquest did the Romans next make?
6. How long did peace last? How long was it since the temple of Janus had been shut?
7. What is said of Hamilcar? What of Hannibal? How did Hannibal commence the second Punic war?
8. What design did Hannibal now form and execute? What is said of the victory of Cannæ, and of the losses of the Romans?
9. For what has Hannibal been censured?
10. By whose counsels were the Romans now guided? What were Fabius and Marcellus styled? What was the subsequent fortune of Hannibal?
11. What is related respecting Syracuse? What did it now become? What was the fate of the Carthaginians under Asdrubal?
12. What was done by Scipio the Younger? What course did the Carthaginians adopt? What engagement followed? What were the conditions of peace? How long did the war continue?
13. Where did Hannibal pass the rest of his life? With whom did he hold friendly conversations? What reply did he make to the question, whom he thought the greatest general?
14. How did the first Macedonian war terminate? What victory did the Roman army under Scipio Asiaticus gain? How did the second Macedonian war terminate?
15. What was the pretext with the Romans for commencing the third Punic war? What is stated of Porcius Cato?
16. What was offered on the part of the Carthaginians? What did the Romans require of them? How was the demand received?
17. What was the duration and issue of the siege? What is related respecting the destruction of the city?
18. By what other event was the same year signalized? What other conquest did the Romans soon after make?

Section VI.

1. How had the Romans been hitherto characterized? What changes were now introduced?

2. What was now the condition of Rome? What took place after there ceased to be danger from a foreign enemy?

3. What is related of Tiberius and Caius Gracchus? What did Tiberius attempt? What was the issue?

4. What is related of his brother Caius?

5. How did Jugurtha attempt to obtain the crown of Numidia? What were his further proceedings?

6. Who commanded the Roman army in the war against Jugurtha? What was the issue? What victory did Marius afterwards gain?

7. What gave rise to the Social war? How many men were destroyed in it? How was it ended?

8. What design did Mithridates form? How did he begin the Mithridatic war? What Romans bore a distinguished part in it?

9. What is related respecting Sylla? What of his rival Marius?

10. What course did Sylla take? What became of Marius? What was performed by Cinna? What is further related of Marius and Cinna?

11. What was done by Sylla after returning from his campaign? How did he proceed after he had wreaked his vengeance on his enemies? What epitaph did he write for himself? How many were slain in the civil war between Sylla and Marius?

12. What took place after the death of Sylla? By whom was the party of Marius supported?

13. By what war was Rome next harassed? What was its termination?

14. What took place a few years after the defeat of Spartacus? What plan was concerted?

15. By whom was this conspiracy detected and crushed? How was it ended?

Section VII.

1. Why was Pompey surnamed the Great? What did he perform? How was he received on returning to Rome?

2. Who were now the most considerable men in Rome? What is related of Julius Cæsar? What was done by Pompey, Crassus, and Cæsar?

3. How did they distribute the provinces? What was the course of Crassus? What took place with regard to Cæsar and Pompey?

4. What course did Cæsar take after the division of the provinces? What is said of his career? How did he continue to give a color of justice and humanity to his operations? What did he acquire?

5. What is related of Pompey? What took place when the term of Cæsar's government was about to expire? What then followed? Who were friends of Pompey? Who were on the side of Cæsar?

6. What preparations had Pompey made? What reply did he make when asked with what troops he expected to oppose Cæsar?

7. What course did Cæsar adopt? What river formed the limits of his command? What did he do on arriving at the banks of this river?

8. What effect did the news of this movement have at Rome? What course did Pompey adopt? By whom was he followed?

9. What success did Cæsar meet with? For what purpose did he say that he had entered Italy? What was his next course?

10. What part did the monarchs of the East take? By whom was Pompey joined?

11. What were Cæsar's movements after staying eleven days at Rome? What is said of the importance of the contest?

12. What force had each of the parties? What was the feeling on the side of Pompey? What was the issue of the engagement?

13. What acts of clemency did Cæsar perform? What is related of him on viewing the field of battle?

14. What is related of the course and fate of Pompey? What inscription was placed over his ashes? What anecdote is related respecting Cæsar?

15. By whom was the throne of Egypt now possessed? What is mentioned respecting Cleopatra? What war ensued? What called Cæsar away from Egypt? How did Cæsar express the rapidity of his victory over Pharnaces?

16. What was Cæsar's next proceeding? Over whom did he gain a victory at Thapsus in Africa? What is related of Cato?

17. What triumph did Cæsar celebrate on returning to Rome? What else did he do to please the army and people? What effect did these acts produce on the multitude and senate?

18. What expedition was he next obliged to undertake? What was the issue?

19. How did he use his power after having subdued all who opposed his usurpation? What did he say respecting his designs? How did he proceed, and what did he perform?

20. What rumor was circulated respecting Cæsar's designs? What is said of the feelings of the people? What design was formed against him? What is said of Brutus and of Cassius?

21. What time did the conspirators fix upon for executing their designs? How did he defend himself, and what was the result? What particulars are mentioned respecting his age and career?

22. What threefold character did Cæsar unite? What is said of his claims to regard?

23. What is remarked of his career and disposition? What apology has been made for him? What Roman patriots lived in the same age?

24. What remark did he make in passing a village among the Alps? What sentiment of Euripides did he often repeat?

25. What is said of his military character, and his popularity with his troops? How are Alexander and Cæsar compared?

26. What summary does Müller give of Cæsar's exploits?

27. How did the murder of Cæsar affect the Roman people? What was done by Mark Antony, and what was the effect?

28. What is related of Mark Antony, Lepidus, and Octavius?

29. What did they stipulate? Who were some of the persons consigned to death? What is related respecting the death of Cicero? What persons were sacrificed in the proscription?

30. What is related of Brutus and Cassius? By whom were they pursued? What was the issue? What course did Brutus and Cassius take?

31. What is mentioned respecting the triumvirs? What is related of Antony and Cleopatra?

32. What was the effect of the battle of Actium? What course did Antony and Cleopatra take?

Section VIII.

1. What is said of the battle of Actium? What is said of Augustus What did Agrippa, and what did Mæcenas advise him to do?

2. To which did Augustus give the preference? How did he proceed?

3. What is said of his reputation? What of his reign, and what did he effect?

4 In what year of his age, and after how long a reign, did he die? What is said of him?

5. Of what were Augustus and Mæcenas patrons? What is said of the Augustan age?
6. By what is the reign of Augustus rendered memorable? When did the birth of our Saviour take place? When did he suffer crucifixion?
7. By whom was Augustus succeeded? How did he commence his reign? How did he afterwards proceed?
8. How did the successes of Germanicus affect Tiberius? Whom did he then take into his confidence? What did Sejanus persuade him to do? What finally happened to Sejanus and Tiberius?
9. Whom did Tiberius adopt for his heir and successor? What is related of him and his proceedings? What does Seneca say of him?
10. What took place after the death of Caligula? Who was raised to the throne? What is said of him?
11. What enterprise did he undertake? What is said of Caractacus? What exclamation did he make on being led through the streets of Rome?
12. What is related of Messalina? What of Agrippina?
13. By whom was Nero educated? How did he commence his reign? What is said of his character? Who were some of the victims of his cruelty?
14. Why did he cause Rome to be set on fire? How did he attempt to divert the public odium from himself?
15. What is said of Nero? By whom was the conspiracy against him headed? What crimes did Galba enumerate? What took place respecting him?
16. Who was declared emperor after the death of Nero? What is said of Galba? Whom did he adopt for his successor, and what was the consequence? What does Tacitus say of him?
17. Who was then proclaimed emperor? What afterwards took place? What course did Vitellius take on being proclaimed emperor? What afterwards took place?
18. How was Vespasian received after being declared emperor? What is said of him and his acts?
19. For what is his reign memorable? What was done to Jerusalem? How many perished, and how many were taken prisoners? What became of the survivors?
20. By whom was Vespasian succeeded? What is related of Titus? What event happened during his reign? By whom was he succeeded?
21. What is said of Domitian, his character and habits?
22. What was the manner of Domitian's death? By what was his reign signalized?
23. Who was the last and who the first of the twelve Cæsars?

Section IX.

Who succeeded Domitian? What is said of Nerva? Whom did he adopt for his successor?
2. What is said of Trajan? For what has he been commended? What is said of him as a general? What charge did he give to the pretorian prefect on presenting the sword? What surname did the senate confer upon him, and how were they accustomed to hail every new emperor?
3. What was the extent of the empire in the reign of Trajan? What conquests did he make? How were his victories commemorated?
4. What is said of him with respect to literature? What is remarked of his death? By what was his character tarnished?
5. By whom was Trajan succeeded? What is said of Adrian? To what did he devote himself? What expedition did he undertake? What was done by him in Britain?
6. What did he do respecting Jerusalem? What course did the Jews

33*

take? What destruction was made by the emperor's army? Whom did Adrian adopt for his successor?

7. What is said of Titus Antoninus and his reign? What was his favorite maxim?

8. Who succeeded Antoninus Pius? What is said of him? To what was he attached?

9. Did the Antonines permit the persecution of the Christians? What was presented to the former of the two? What happened to the army under the latter?

10 What are the last five emperors styled? What took place after this period?

Section X.

1. By whom was Aurelius succeeded? What is said of Commodus? By whom was he succeeded? What was his fate?

2. What was now done with the empire? Who was proclaimed emperor instead of Didius Julianus? Who were his competitors? What is said of Severus? What did he do in Britain?

3. To whom did Severus leave the empire? What is related of them? Who succeeded Macrinus?

4. What is said of Heliogabalus? What was his fate?

5. By whom was Heliogabalus succeeded? What is said of Alexander Severus? By whom was he murdered and succeeded? What is said of Maximin?

6. How many reigns were there between Alexander Severus and Diocletian? What was the length of this period? What is said of these reigns?

7. By whom was Valerian taken prisoner? How was he treated?

8. What is said of the reign of Aurelian? For what was he distinguished? What exploits did he perform? What took place on his return to Rome?

9. What is said of Diocletian? What did he do after he had reigned awhile? How was the empire divided?

10. What happened during this reign? What is said of this persecution?

11 What did Diocletian experience in the latter part of his reign? What course did he take? What did he say of his situation?

Section XI.

1. Where did Constantius die? Who succeeded him? What extraordinary circumstance is related by historians?

2. What did Constantine become? To what did he put an end? What is remarked of his reign?

3 What important event took place during his reign? What is thought to have been the effect of this measure? What is said of the character of Constantine?

4. How did Constantine divide the empire? Who became sole emperor? What is said of the reign of Constantius?

5 By whom was Constantius succeeded? What is said of him? What did he undertake to do, and what was the issue? How was he killed?

6. By whom was Julian succeeded? Who was next chosen emperor? What course did he adopt? What people settled in Thrace?

7. Who succeeded Valentinian? Who became sole emperor after the death of Gratian and Valentinian II.? By what was his reign signalized? What is said of him? By whom was he succeeded?

8. What happened through the weakness of the emperors? What was done by the Goths? Who defeated Alaric? What did Alaric afterwards perform? To what was the city reduced?

9. What took place after the ravages of famine? What was the address of Alaric to his army? What is said of the devastation?

10. What did the Goths do after the death of Alaric?

11. What took place after the sacking of Rome by Alaric? What defeat did Attila suffer? What did he do afterwards?

12. What was the occasion of the invasion of Genseric? What was performed by him?

13. What took place with regard to the Western Empire after the death of Valentinian III.?

14. What is said of the rise and fall of the empire?

Section XII.

1. How long did the kingdom of the Heruli continue? By whom was it terminated? Where was the residence of Theodoric? Who defeated Theodotus? What afterwards took place?

2. What was done by Narses after he was recalled by Justin? What was done by Alboin? How long did the kingdom of the Lombards last? By whom was it overthrown? What is said of the period from Theodosius to the establishment of the Lombards in Italy?

3. What is said of the Goths? Why were the Ostrogoths and Visigoths so called? Who were the Heruli and Lombards?

4. What is said of the Eastern Empire?

5. When was this empire in the meridian of its glory? What is said of the code of Justinian?

6. What was performed by Belisarius and Narses? What church was built by Justinian? What is remarked of him and his successors?

7. What happened after the removal of the seat of empire? How did this controversy terminate?

8. What was done by the Crusaders in 1204? How long did their dominion continue? What was the seat of the Greek emperors during this time?

9. When and by whom was an end put to the Eastern Empire?

Section XIII. — Roman Antiquities.

2. To whom has the whole structure of the Roman constitution under the monarchy been attributed? What was doubtless true?

3. What three divisions of the people are attributed to Romulus? Who added a fourth tribe? How were the tribes named?

4. What other division was made by Servius? How were the classes formed? How many centuries were there?

5. What order was added to those of patricians and plebeians? Of whom were the knights composed?

6. Who were the *nobiles?* The *homines novi?* The *ignobiles?* The *ingenui?* The *liberti* or *libertini?*

7. Of whom did the Roman *citizens* consist?

8. Who were the *slaves?* How were they considered? How did men become slaves?

9. What is said of the *kings?* What could they not do of themselves? What were their badges? In what did they sit, and by whom were they attended?

10. Of how many members did the *senate* consist? How were they chosen? How often did they meet? What was a *senatûs consultum?* Why were the senators styled *patres?* Why did the patricians derive their name from them?

11. Why were the magistrates previous to their election styled *candidati?*

12. How were the Roman *magistrates* divided? Who were the ordinary magistrates? The extraordinary? The provincial?

13. What is said of the *consuls?* What was done respecting them in dangerous conjunctures? What age was requisite in order to be a consul?
14. What is said of the *pretor?* What were his duties?
15. What is said of the office of *censor?* How many censors were there, and what were their duties?
16. For what purpose was the office of the *tribunes* instituted?
17. What were the duties of *ediles?* What two kinds were there?
18. What duties did the *questors* perform? What were the duties of the military questors? The provincial questors?
19. What were the *comitia?* How many kinds were there? For what purpose were the *comitia* summoned?
20. Of what did the *comitia curiata* consist?
21. What is said of the *comitia centuriata?* What was done by them? Where did they meet?
22. What were the *comitia tributa?* For what were they held?
23. How long did the *comitia* continue to be assembled? Who discontinued them?
24. What is said of the *priests* or ministers of religion? What priests were common to all the gods?
25. What is said of the *pontifices?* Of the *pontifex maximus?*
26. What is said of the *augurs?* What of their office? In what five ways did they divine?
27. Who were the *haruspices?* From what did they derive their omens?
28. Who were the *quindecimviri?* What were the Sibylline books supposed to contain?
29. Who were the *septemviri?*
30. What were the priests of particular deities called? Who were the chief of them?
31. Where did the Romans worship their gods? Of what did their worship consist?
32. What *festivals* were there among the Romans? Which were the most celebrated?
33. What *games* or *shows* were exhibited?
34. Who were the *gladiators?* When were these combats introduced? Of whom were the combatants composed? What took place in these exhibitions? What is related of the spectacles exhibited after the triumph of Trajan over the Dacians?
35. What was a *triumph?* On whom was the honor bestowed? What is said of the procession? Of whom was it composed?
36. What were the most distinguished parts of the Roman *dress?* What was the *toga?* By whom was the *toga virilis* assumed? What was the *tunica?*
37. What was the principal *meal* among the Romans? On what did the early Romans chiefly live? How was it afterwards? How did they place themselves at their meals? What was their ordinary drink.
38. What was the *Forum?* By what was it surrounded?
39. What was the *Campus Martius?* By what was it adorned?

Chronological Table of Roman History.—No. 1.

Who was the first king of Rome? Who the last? When did Romulus found Rome? When was the regal government abolished? What was done by Romulus? Numa? &c.

When did the contests between the patricians and plebeians begin? When was Rome burnt by the Gauls? When did the first Punic War begin? The second? The third? What were Hannibal's victories?

When did the Mithridatic war begin? The civil war between Marius and Sylla? Between Cæsar and Pompey? Battle of Actium?

What events took place in the fourth century B. C.? The 3d? &c

Chronological Table of Roman History. — No 2.

Who was the first emperor of Rome?

Who the last sole emperor of the West and East? Who the last of the Western Empire?

When did Augustus begin to reign? Trajan? Diocletian? Constantine the Great? Who was the last of the twelve Cæsars?

When was the empire divided into Western and Eastern?

When did the Western Empire terminate?

What is said of Augustus or his reign? Tiberius? &c.

Chronological Table of Roman Literature.

What public men flourished in the 5th century B. C.? In the 4th? &c.

What poets flourished in the 2d century B. C. In the 1st? What ones in the 1st century A. D.? The 2d?

What historians in the 1st century B. C.? In the 1st A. D.?

What philosophers, orators, &c., in the 1st century B. C.? In the 1st A. D.?

What Jews in the 5th century B. C.? In the 1st A. D.?

What Christians in the 1st century A. D.? The 2d? &c.

THE MIDDLE AGES.

1. What do the Middle Ages comprise? What was the state of Europe during these centuries?

2. When did the migration of the Goths, Vandals, Huns, &c., take place? Of what did they possess themselves? What followed? At what time did literature begin to decline? When was the darkest period?

3. What is related respecting these times? To what was the learning which existed confined?

4. What was the state of morals and of Christianity? What was the political state of Europe?

5 What methods of discovering guilt or innocence were used?

6. What was the most considerable empire that existed in Europe during the Middle Ages? What impostor appeared in these ages? At what period did the Saracens cultivate literature?

7 What are some of the most remarkable circumstances which characterized these ages?

THE ARABS OR SARACENS.

1. What is said of the Arabians before the time of Mahomet?

2. What is related of the Saracens?

3. What is said of the introduction of Christianity into Arabia? What kind of Christianity was it?

4. What is said of Mahomet? How was the Koran formed? On what did Mahomet rely as proofs of his inspiration?

5. What were his two leading doctrines? What other persons did he admit to have been inspired? What did he adopt and retain? To what did he chiefly owe his success?

6. How did he propagate his religion, and stimulate his followers What was inculcated as a fundamental doctrine? What do the Saracens term their religion?

7. How did Mahomet at first succeed? Who were his first converts?

8. What was he compelled to do? What is said of his Flight or Hegira? How did he enter Medina? What was his subsequent career?

9. What is said in favor of Mahomet? What further is said of his character?

10. By whom was Mahomet succeeded? What is the meaning of *caliph*? What is related of Abu-bekir? Who was his successor?

11. What conquests did Omar make?

12. What answer did Omar give, when requested to spare the Alexandrian library? How many volumes did the library contain?

13. What did Omar perform in the space of ten years? By whom was he succeeded? Who was elected after the death of Othman? What is said of him?

14. What is related of the progress and extent of the Saracen empire

15. For what is the reign of Ali remarkable? What is said of the partisans of Ali? What of the Sunnites? Who belong to each?

16. To what place did Ali remove the seat of the sovereigns? To what place was it afterwards removed? What caliphate ranked next to that of Bagdad? What is related of Walid?

17. What was the first race of the caliphs styled? The second? What is related of Almansor?

18. What is said of the reign of Haroun al Raschid? By what did he render himself illustrious? What are to be referred to these times? What sciences were cultivated? What is said of the successors of Haroun al Raschid?

19. What took place with respect to Arabia after the seat of government was removed to Bagdad?

20. What is remarked of the Saracens and their states? How did Spain, Egypt, Morocco, and India regard the caliph of Bagdad?

21. How many caliphs did the house of Abbas furnish? How long did Bagdad continue the seat of empire? When and by whom was the caliphate abolished?

22. What is said of the immediate successors of Mahomet? What were their manners? How did they proceed after their power was established?

23. What is said of the power of the caliphs? Was there any privileged order? By what were they bound to observe the duties of humanity and justice? What office did theirs resemble?

THE FEUDAL SYSTEM.

1. What was the origin of the Feudal System? By what sovereigns was it adopted?

2. How did the northern barbarians dispose of their conquered lands? Who had the largest portion? What were those who received lands bound to render?

3. How did the courtiers manage? How is a feudal kingdom described?

4. What is said of the barons or lords?

5. What was the fundamental principle of this system? What were the grantor, and those to whom he made grants, styled? How was the service esteemed?

6. What was the condition of the great mass of the people?

7. What is said of the feudal government? What did a kingdom resemble?

8. What did a kingdom often exhibit? In what period was Europe in a state of anarchy and war?

9. What were the principal causes of the overthrow of the Feudal System? In what countries do relics of it still exist?

THE CRUSADES.

1 What were the Crusades? What nations engaged in them? What is related of the Saracens? What of the Turks? What is said of the dangers of pilgrimage?

2 What is related of Peter the Hermit?

3. What course did Pope Urban II. take? How was the project opened? Why were these expeditions termed *Crusades?* What was granted to all who devoted themselves to the service?

4. What description of persons took the cross? What were their inducements? What was done by Peter the Hermit? By what was Peter's army followed? What was their fate?

5. What is said of the other part of the expedition? Who were the commanders? To what did the force amount?

6. What did they accomplish? What was the fortune of Godfrey?

7. How did the conquerors divide Syria and Palestine? What afterwards took place? What was the fate of the army under Hugh?

8. By whom was the second crusade preached, and who engaged in it? What was the issue?

9. What is related of Saladin?

10. Who united in the third crusade? What happened to Frederick? What is said of the French and English?

11. What did Richard perform? What happened to him on his return?

12. Who engaged in the fourth crusade? What was his fortune?

13. What was performed by John de Brienne?

14. What is said of St. Louis IX.?

15. What was his success? How did his crusade against the Moors terminate?

16. To what did the crusades owe their origin? What is said of them? What character did they assume? What were some of their effects? How many Europeans were buried in the East while they lasted? What became of those who survived?

17. Of what beneficial effects were they productive? In what were these effects observable?

18. What system prevailed in Europe at this period? What were the barons who engaged in the crusade obliged to do? What was the effect? How did kings raise money?

19. What is said of the manners and mode of life that prevailed in Europe? With what did the crusaders become acquainted in the East? To what institutions did the crusades give rise?

20. What was the effect of the crusades on commerce and the arts? How had commerce before this period been carried on? What changes afterwards took place?

21. What was the effect of the crusades on literature and religion? What is said of the period of their commencement and duration? What took place after two centuries of disaster?

22. Were these benefits designed by the projectors?

CHIVALRY.

1. What is said of Chivalry? What does it constitute with regard to the Middle Ages? What were its distinguishing features?

2. What is said of the early history of chivalry? When did it originate? Where were its principles found before? By what was it imbodied into form? What was the effect of the crusades upon it?

3. In what countries did chivalry prevail?

4. How were the sons of noblemen destined for chivalry disciplined? What was the place of their education? What were their different titles?

5. How were they managed? By whom were they surrounded? What were they taught?

6. What were they taught by the ladies of the castle? What were they accustomed to do in order that they might have opportunity to practise the instructions which they received?

7. What was the proper age for admission to the honors of knighthood? How did the candidate prepare himself?

8. What did he do after having performed the preliminary rites?

9. What were the insignia of chivalry which he received from the knights and the ladies? In what manner was he dubbed?

10. What was the most important part of the equipments of a knight? What were his weapon and arms? What was his dress?

11. What virtues and endowments were necessary to form an accomplished knight?

12. In what estimation was chivalry held? What did one become on being dubbed? What had he a right to do?

13. What was he authorized to do? How did he proceed in relation to his mistress? What was the injunction of a sovereign when he led his army to the attack?

14. What is said of the influence of chivalry on the female sex? What was the duty of the knights with regard to the ladies?

15. What is said of the behavior of a knight with regard to the fair sex.

16. Of what were the knights and ladies ambitious?

17. What virtues did chivalry enjoin? How was a chevalier treated on entering the castle of another? If he arrived wounded, how was he received?

18. What were the favorite amusements and exercises of the knights? What does Hallam say of the tournaments?

19. What is said of the reward of the victor?

20. What is said of the influence of chivalry? What effects are mentioned?

21. With what did chivalry rise and fall? What put an end both to the feudal system and to chivalry?

22. What does Dr. Robertson say of the exploits of the knights, and of the effects of chivalry? During what centuries were the effects of chivalry most felt?

23. What is said of the morals of chivalry? What productions afford evidence of dissolute morals?

24. What was professed and what performed by the knights? What did chivalry nourish? To what did it give birth?

25. To whom is the original of the duel traced? How far did it prevail among the Germans, Danes, and Franks?

26. What is related respecting its regulations? For what purpose was it then resorted to? For what end is it now practised?

MODERN HISTORY.

1. What different periods have been adopted for the commencement of Modern History?

2. What is the most convenient method in treating of the history of the several European States? What European sovereignty traces its origin farther back than the 9th century?

3. What is said of the period that succeeded the downfall of the Eastern Empire? What do we see on casting an eye back to this period?

4. What were some of the causes of the beneficial changes?

5 What is said of the Hanse Towns? When was the League formed, and what towns were associated? Where were its depôts?

6. When was the League most flourishing? What is said of its decline?

7. When had Venice, Genoa, and Pisa the management of European commerce? What states took the lead in the maritime discoveries of the 15th and 16th centuries?

8. By what states have Spain and Portugal been succeeded in maritime enterprise?

9. What are now the most powerful European States? What are the countries of which the history is most important to Americans?

FRANCE.

SECTION I.

1. What is said of the history of France and of England? How long did the kings of England hold possessions in France?

2. Who were the ancestors of the French? What did ancient Gaul comprehend? By whom and when was it conquered? From what people did it receive its modern name?

3. What is related of the Franks? What is the first race of French kings styled? Who is regarded as the founder of the monarchy? What did he perform?

4. What is said of the Merovingian kings? What is related of Pepin d'Heristel and Charles Martel?

5. How did Pepin obtain the crown? Of what race of kings was he the founder? How did Pepin reward the pope?

6. By whom was Pepin succeeded?

7. What is related of Charlemagne? When was he crowned Emperor of the West? What did his empire comprise?

8. What is said of Charlemagne's services to literature? How did he manifest his zeal for religion?

9. What is related of his private character and habits?

10. By whom was Charlemagne succeeded? What great battle was fought by the rival brothers? What division of the empire followed?

11. By whom was Charles the Bald succeeded? Who was elected after the short reign of his sons, Louis III. and Carloman? What event followed?

12. To whom was the crown next given? What took place during the reign of Charles the Simple?

13. What took place during the reigns of Louis IV. and Lothaire? What is related of Hugh Capet?

Section II.

1. By whom was Hugh Capet succeeded?
2. What law was enacted during the reign of Henry I.?
3. By what was the reign of Philip I. signalized? What may be dated from the invasion of France by William the Conqueror?
4. What is said of Louis VI.?
5. What three eminent men flourished during the reign of Louis VI?
6. What act of violence did Louis perform? To what did the remorse which he felt give rise?
7. Who was the wife of Louis, and what is related of her?
8. What is said of Philip Augustus? How did he signalize the commencement of his reign?
9. Of what did Philip accuse John, king of England, and of what did he deprive him?
10. By whom was Philip succeeded?
11. What is said of Louis IX.? For what was he distinguished What was his principal weakness?
12. By whom was St. Louis succeeded? What event took place during his reign?
13. What is said of Philip IV.? How was he involved in a quarrel with Pope Boniface?
14. What took place after the death of Boniface? What is the removal of the seat of the papacy to Avignon called? What other acts did Philip perform?
15. By whom was Philip succeeded? For what was the reign of Philip V noted?

Section III

1. What is said of the children of Philip the Fair? On whom did the throne devolve after the death of Charles the Fair?
2. Who claimed the crown? To what did this claim of Edward give rise? What did Edward perform? What favorable event happened to Philip in the midst of his misfortunes?
3. By whom was Philip succeeded, and what happened to him?
4. Who next ascended the throne? What measures did Charles V adopt, and what was performed?
5. What is said of Charles? How large a library did he collect?
6. By whom was Charles V. succeeded? What is said of him and of his reign? Who was his queen?
7. What advantages did Henry V. of England gain?
8. Who next succeeded to the throne? What place did the English besiege, and with what success?
9. By whom was the power of England overthrown? Who was this heroine?
10. How did she execute her exploit? How did Charles succeed? What course did Joan then take, and what was her fate?
11. What was the success of the French? What is further related of Charles?
12. What is said of the character and reign of Louis XI.?
13. In what war was he involved with the nobles?
14. What is said of Charles VIII.? In what expedition did he engage?

Section IV

1 By whom was Charles VIII. succeeded? What was the character of Louis XII. What did he say with respect to those ministers who had treated him ill before he came to the throne?

2. What is related of his exploits and success?

3. What is said of the republic of Venice? Who projected the League of Cambray against it? What was the issue?

4. What victory did the French gain? What took place after the death of Gaston de Foix?

5. Who succeeded Louis XII.? What is said of Francis?

6. For what were Francis and Charles rival candidates? What did Francis say with respect to the object of competition?

7. What was the issue, and how did it affect the two rivals?

8. For what is the reign of Charles V. distinguished? What is said of Charles and other contemporary sovereigns?

9. What was the commencement of the contest between the two rivals? What is related respecting the Constable of Bourbon? What happened to the king of France at Pavia?

10. What course did Charles take with regard to Francis? What did the French king do after being set at liberty? What is said of the conduct of the two sovereigns?

11. How did the two monarchs treat each other, when they met at Aigues Mortes, after having been at war for 20 years? What afterwards took place?

12. What was the occasion of the renewal of the war? What was the issue?

13. How did Francis leave his kingdom? What did he patronize? What did the French court acquire at this period?

14. What qualities did Francis possess? What was his character?

15. Who was the successor of Francis, and what is said of Henry II.? What is said of his reign? What great events took place during this war?

16. How was this war terminated? By what other events was the reign of Henry signalized?

17. Who was the successor of Henry? Who succeeded Francis II.?

18. What was now the state of Protestantism in France?

19. Who was at the head of the Catholics? For what purpose was the conspiracy of Amboise formed? What was the issue of it?

20. What public conference was held? What edict was published? What followed?

21. What is said of the contest? What is said of the treaty of peace?

22. What is related respecting the marriage of Henry of Navarre? What massacre was planned? What is related respecting the massacre on St. Bartholomew's day?

23. How many are said to have been murdered? What does De Thou say of it?

24. What is related respecting Charles?

25. What was done at Rome on hearing the news? What is further said of Charles and his reign?

26. By whom was Charles succeeded? What was the effect of the massacre of St. Bartholomew? What did Henry do for the Protestants? What course did the Catholics take?

27. What measure was the king persuaded to adopt? How did he find himself situated, and what did he do? What was the consequence?

SECTION V.

1. To whom did the throne pass after the death of Henry III? What is said of the mother of Henry IV., and of himself?

2. What is said of the army of the League? In what battle did Henry defeat it?

3. Why did Henry change his religion? What followed? What did he do in favor of the Calvanists?

4. To what did Henry turn his attention after being quietly seated on the throne? By whom was he assisted? What change was effected?

5. What romantic scheme did Henry form? What happened to him before he executed his design?

6. What is said of the character of Henry? What was his reply when asked what the revenue of France amounted to?

7. What were the defects of his character? How many persons were killed in duels during the first eighteen years of his reign?

8. By whom was Henry succeeded? What is said of Mary de Medicis? What is related of Cardinal Richelieu, his policy, and objects?

9. What course did the Protestants take? What measure did Richelieu adopt? What was the issue?

10. What is further related respecting the proceedings of Richelieu? By whom was a rebellion excited? What did Richelieu effect?

11. What is said of the character of Louis?

12. Who next succeeded to the throne? Who was chosen minister? What is said of Mazarin? By what was his administration signalized?

13. What took place after the death of Mazarin? What is related of Louis and his exploits?

14. Who were some of his chief men in the cabinet and in the field?

15. What success did Louis meet with? What is related respecting the two devastations of the Palatinate?

16. What events afterwards took place? What were the consequences of Louis's conquests and of his ambition?

17. What states united against him in the League of Augsburg? What alliance was formed in 1701? Against whom had the armies of Louis now to contend? What victories did Marlborough and Prince Eugene gain?

18. What was one of the worst measures of Louis? What was done by this act? What did France lose by it?

19. How long was the reign of Louis? What is said of it?

20. What is said of the person and manners of Louis?

21. What is said of his talents and character? What did he patronize, and how is his reign regarded?

SECTION VI.

1. Who succeeded Louis XIV.? For what is the regency of the Duke of Orleans remarkable?

2. Whom did Louis XV. choose for his minister after coming of age? What is said of the administration of Fleury?

3. In what war was France involved after the death of Fleury. Who were the two claimants for the imperial throne? By whom were they supported? Where were the French defeated, and what battle did they gain? How were hostilities terminated?

4. What war broke out in 1775? How was it terminated? How was the remainder of this reign chiefly occupied?

5. What is said of Louis? What title was conferred upon him by his subjects? What induced them to retract it? What is further said of him and his reign?

6. Who succeeded to the throne? What is said of Louis XVI.? What were the difficulties of his situation?

7. What was one of his first measures? Who were appointed to office? What was the effect?

8. What is said of Necker? What followed after he was displaced?

9. What took place after the war broke out between Great Britain and her American colonies? What was the state of affairs after the return of peace?

10. What were some of the principal causes of the French Revolution? What was the more immediate cause?

11. What measure did Louis adopt by the advice of Calonne? What was proposed to the Assembly of the Notables? How did they receive it?

12. By whom was Calonne succeeded? What body was next assembled? Of what orders was the States General composed?

13. What did Necker propose respecting the States General? What was the result?

14. How did the king address the States General? What difficulties arose?

15. What measure did the commons adopt? Who were leading members in the National Assembly?

16. What is said of their measures? In what situation were the king and nobility placed?

17. What is said of the dismissal of Necker? What outrages were committed? What is said of the king and royal family?

18. What is said of the progress of the revolution and changes which were effected?

19. What was the next great design of the Assembly? What is related of Louis? What of the constitution?

20. What was the next Assembly styled? What is related of the Jacobin Club?

21. What new body next met? What was done at their first sitting? What is related respecting the king?

22. What were some of the remarks of Desèze in defence of Louis?

23. By what majority was the king condemned? What is further related of him?

Section VII.

1. When was the constitution completed, and in what was the executive power now lodged? What is the domination of Robespierre and his associates styled? What two parties arose in the National Convention? Who were the leaders?

2. What did the Mountain party do? What is related of the Duke of Orleans?

3. To what further excesses did the Convention proceed? What was done to the churches?

4. How was the Convention divided anew? What followed? In what was the executive power afterwards vested? How many constitutions were formed from 1791 to 1799? In whom was the executive power vested by the fourth?

5. What was the French Revolution at first? What did it become? What change did it effect?

6. What course was taken by many of the nobility and clergy before the execution of the king? What was the effect? Of what was this the origin? What states declared war against France after the death of the king?

7. What is said of the Duke of Brunswick?

8 What was the issue of the invasion? What advantages did France

gain? To whom was the command of the army in Italy given? What did Bonaparte accomplish?

9. When was the Second Coalition formed? What had Bonaparte done before this event?

10. What advantages were gained over the French in 1799? What did Bonaparte do at this crisis?

11. What change now took place in the affairs of France?

12. What achievements did Bonaparte then perform? To what events did the victories of Marengo and Hohenlinden lead?

13. What is said of the limits of France and power of Bonaparte? What measure did the Convention adopt with regard to religion?

14. To what office was Bonaparte now raised? By whom was a conspiracy formed against him? What became of the conspirators? What were Bonaparte's next elevations?

15. When and by what powers was the Third Coalition formed? What course did Bonaparte then take, and with what success? What followed the victory of Austerlitz?

16. What victory was gained by Lord Nelson a little before the battle of Austerlitz?

17. What course did Bonaparte take with regard to Naples and Holland? What with respect to the German empire? What was done by Francis II.? What electors did Bonaparte raise to the rank of kings?

18. How and by whom was the Fourth Coalition formed? What battles did Bonaparte gain? What did he do on entering the capital of Prussia? What other battle did the French army gain?

19. What were the next proceedings of Bonaparte? What treaties were made with Russia and Prussia? What was done with the provinces conquered from Prussia?

20. What course did the British government take in retaliation of the Berlin Decree? What was done by the emperor after the peace of Tilsit?

21. How did Bonaparte seem to be affected by his success? What did he do respecting Spain and Portugal?

22. How did he dispose of the throne of Spain?

23. What part did the Spaniards take? How long did the war last? Who commanded the forces of England and Spain? What were some of the principal exploits?

24. With what empire was France again involved in war? What successes did Bonaparte gain?

25. To what terms was the emperor of Austria compelled to submit by the treaty of Vienna? What followed in consequence of this treaty?

26. To what did Alexander accede by the treaty of Tilsit, and what were its consequences? How was the year 1811 spent? What measures did Bonaparte adopt?

27. Whither did he direct his march? What events followed? Why was Moscow burnt?

28. How did this transaction affect Bonaparte, and what had he expected? What course was he compelled to adopt?

29. What is said of his retreat? What losses were sustained?

30. What course did the French emperor pursue? How large an army did he now raise? By what was he opposed?

31. What were the next events? What is said of the battle of Leipsic?

32. What course did Bonaparte now take? What was done by the Allies?

33. What measure was Bonaparte now compelled to adopt, and what place was fixed upon for his residence? What followed?

34. For what purpose was the Congress of Vienna assembled? What did Bonaparte now undertake? How did he proceed? What is said of his progress?

35. What measures did he take to strengthen his authority?
36. What was done by the Congress of Vienna? What events followed?
37. What is said of the battle of Waterloo? What course did Bonaparte now take? What was done with him by the allied sovereigns? When did Bonaparte die, and at what age?
38. What is said of the career of Bonaparte? At what age was he raised to his several elevations? What is said of his power?
39. Why may he be called a king-maker? What is remarked of the last four kings?
40. What did he unite in his own person? What is said of his deeds? For what is France indebted to him?
41. Of what beneficial measures was he the author? What was his ruling passion? What is said of his opportunity of being useful? What did he choose to be?
42. What is further said of him and his career?

Section VIII.

1 What took place after the second dethronement of Bonaparte? What measures were taken in relation to France? What relating to the officers who sided with Bonaparte?
2. What is said of Louis XVIII., his situation, and policy? What was one of the principal events of his reign?
3. Who succeeded Louis XVIII.? What is said of him?
4. By what enterprises was his reign distinguished?
5. What is said of the contests of parties? What course did Charles take?
6. What was done by the Chamber of Deputies? What events followed, and what measures were adopted?
7. What occurrences then took place?
8. What course did the citizens take? Who commanded the National Guards? What was done by the Chambers?
9. What became of Charles?
10. What is said of Louis Philippe? What was his course? Who were some of his ministers?
11. What is said of his foreign policy, and of the condition of France during his reign? What is further said of him, and of his fate?
12. What was the most considerable foreign achievement?
13. What is said of the state of the country and the feeling of the lower classes? What is said of these classes?
14. What classes were favored by the government? What did these classes do for the government?
15 What is said of the system of obtaining venal support? With what was the government charged? What were other causes of dissatisfaction?
16 To whom were these offensive measures ascribed? What impression gained ground among the people?
17. What occurrence promoted discontent? What course did the opponents of the government take?
18. When was a Reform Banquet proposed to be held in Paris? What course did the king's ministers take? What was the result?
19. What took place on the day the banquet was to have been held? What was done by the people?
20. What was done on the two following days? What was done by the king, and by Guizot?
21 What course was taken by the insurgents? What followed?
22 What was done by the provisional government? What decrees were issued?

23. What was done by the National Assembly?
24. What took place in June? What followed?
25. What was done by the National Assembly, after a session of six months? For what does the constitution provide?
26. Who was elected President? By how many votes? What is said of Louis Napoleon? For what has he been chiefly distinguished?
27. When did a new National Assembly commence a session? How have elections resulted? What has been the course of the government?
28. What took place, in 1848, at Rome? What was done by the French? What did the French army accomplish?

Chronological Table of French History.—No. 1

Who were the first two kings of the Carlovingian Race?
Who was the first of the Capetian Race? Of the Branch of Valois?
When did Charlemagne begin to reign? Hugh Capet? St. Louis? Philip VI.? Francis I.?
What is said of Pepin and his reign? Charlemagne? &c.

Chronological Table of French History.—No. 2.

Who was the first king of the House of Bourbon?
When did Henry IV. begin to reign? Louis XIV.? Louis XVI.? Bonaparte? Louis XVIII.? Louis Philippe?
When did Louis Napoleon become President of the republic of France?
When was France first declared a republic? When the last time?
What is said of Henry IV. and his reign? Louis XIII.? &c.

ENGLAND.

Section I.

1. What is said of the history of England?
2. What conflicts have been maintained in England?
3. Why is the history of England interesting to the citizens of the United States?
4. Why do we feel an interest in the conflicts which civil and religious liberty has had with despotism and bigotry in England?
5. When did Julius Cæsar invade Britain? Who defeated Caractacus? By whom was the Roman dominion completely established?
6. What sort of people were the Britons at the time of the conquest? What were their habits and their religion?
7. What three walls did the Romans build across Britain? When did they entirely abandon the country?
8. By whom was the southern part of the island afterwards invaded? To whom did the Britons apply for assistance? What was the result?
9. What course did the Saxons take? From whom is the name of England derived?
10. What is related of Arthur? How long did the Heptarchy subsist? Who united the seven kingdoms into one monarchy?
11. How was Christianity introduced? What was the state of society

Section II.

1. What is related of the Danes?
2. What is said of Alfred and of his contest with the Danes What was he compelled to do?
3. What stratagem did he use? What was his success?
4 How did he employ himself after tranquillity was restored! What measures are attributed to him?
5. What is said of the character of Alfred?
6 By whom was he succeeded? What is said of Edward?
7 What is related of Athelstan?
8. What is related of Edmund? Of Edred? Of Dunstan?
9. What is mentioned of Edwy or Edwin?
10 For what is the reign of Edgar remarkable?
11. By whom was Edgar succeeded? What is said of Edward?
12. What outrage was committed by Ethelred that exasperated the Danes?
13. What did the Danes accomplish? Who succeeded Ethelred?
14. What took place after the death of Sweyn? What did Canute accomplish? What is said of him?
15. What two other Danish kings succeeded to the throne?
16. Who was then raised to the throne? What is said of Edward? With what privilege was he said to be favored? How long was the practice of touching for the king's evil, by the English kings, continued?
17. To whom did Edward bequeathe the crown? Who was elected by the nobility?
18. What did William resolve to do? What followed? What losses were sustained? What was the issue?

Section III.

1. What is said of William? What does Mr Burke say of him?
2. In what way did he disgust the English? What changes did he introduce?
3. What did he do by his forest laws? How did he form the New Forest? What was one of the most useful acts of his reign?
4. What is said of William II. and his reign?
5. In what way did Henry I. obtain the crown? What more did he do respecting his brother?
6. How were the Saxon and Norman families united? What affliction did Henry suffer, and what is said of him?
7. Who was the rightful heir to the crown after the death of Henry? Who usurped the throne? What followed?
8. What was done by Henry? What followed? What is said of Stephen's reign?

Section IV.

1. What is said of Henry II.? Why is he called Shortmantle? What did he possess besides England?
2. By what had the countries of Europe been agitated? When did this contest reach its height? What is said of Thomas à Becket?
3. What is said of the power of the clergy? What of their morals?
4. What did Henry resolve to do? What course did he adopt? What

was enacted in these Constitutions? What was Becket's course? What was said by Henry? What was the consequence?

5. What was the effect of this transaction? What was done by the Pope? What followed?

6. What penance did Henry do for his offence? What became of the assassins?

7. What is said of the latter part of Henry's reign? What is said of his sons?

8. What is related of Queen Eleanor? What alienated the queen?

9. What is said of Henry's attachment to his children? What did he do when he found that his son John had joined the confederacy against him?

10. What is said of the character of Henry?

11. For what is his reign remarkable? What is related respecting the arts and conveniences of life?

12. What is related respecting the magnificence of Becket?

13. How did Richard I. commence his reign? With whom did he unite in a crusade? What was achieved?

14. What happened to him as he was returning home? How was he ransomed?

15. What has Richard been styled, and what is said of him?

16. What crime is John, Richard's brother and successor, supposed to have committed? What course did Philip Augustus of France take? What followed?

17. What is related of Pope Innocent III.? In what way did John make peace?

18. What was done by the barons? What followed? What is said of Magna Charta? What other charter did the king grant?

19. What is said of John and his reign?

20. What is said of Henry III. and his reign?

21. What is said respecting the cause of freedom and the prosperity of the nation?

22. What was done by the barons? What measure did the twenty-four barons adopt?

23. What was the effect of this measure? Where did Leicester defeat the royal army? What did he afterwards do? Of what was his summoning deputies from the principal boroughs the commencement?

24. What did Prince Edward perform? What was the issue?

25. What did Edward I. do to the Jews? What did he afterwards accomplish? What did he create his eldest son?

26. What effect had the conquest of Wales on Edward? What took place with regard to Scotland?

27. What took place in consequence of Baliol's renouncing his allegiance? What did Edward accomplish?

28. Who roused the Scots to recover their independence? What was the issue? What happened to Wallace? Who was the second Scotch champion? What further was done by Edward?

29. What is said of Edward? What of his reign? What important clause did he add to Magna Charta?

30 What enterprise did Edward II. undertake? What was the issue?

31. What is said of Edward? How was his reign characterized?

32. What is said of Isabella? What was done to the king?

33. Who had the chief control during the minority of Edward III? What is said of Edward on his coming of age? What became of Mortimer and Isabella?

34. What victory did Edward gain over the Scots? What measure did he adopt with regard to France?

35 What naval victory did he gain?

36. What account is given of the battle of Cressy? For what is this battle memorable? What further advantage did he gain?
37. What took place in England while Edward was in France?
38. What account is given of the battle of Poictiers? What was done with King John?
39. What is said of Edward in the latter part of his reign? What is mentioned of the Black Prince and of Charles V. of France? What is said of the death of the Black Prince?
40. What is said of Edward and his reign? What is said of his wars?
41. What is mentioned respecting chivalry in this reign?
42. What is said of Richard II.? To whom was the administration of the government intrusted during his minority? What is said of John of Gaunt?
43. What tax was imposed, and what was its effect? What is related respecting a tax-gatherer? What events followed?
44. What account is given of the battle of Otterburn? What ballad is founded on this battle?
45. What did Richard do respecting his cousin Henry? How did Henry revenge himself? What became of the king?
46. Who was the true heir to the crown? What contests followed this transaction? What is said of Chaucer?

Section V.

1. What is said of Henry's situation? What account is given of the battle of Shrewsbury?
2. What was supposed respecting Henry while a subject? How did he proceed after he came to the throne?
3. What is said of Henry and his reign?
4. By what was the latter part of his life imbittered? What is related of the Prince of Wales?
5. What did the king say respecting the circumstance?
6. What course did Henry V. take on succeeding to the throne? What is said of this conduct?
7. What account is given of Sir John Oldcastle?
8. In what war did Henry engage, and what battle did he gain? What was the loss of the French? What followed?
9. What is said of the reign and character of Henry?
10. At what age was Henry VI. proclaimed king of England and France? To whom was his education intrusted, and who were protectors of his dominions?
11. What is related of Charles VII. and his success?
12. What is said of Henry on coming of age? Whom did he marry? What is said of her?
13. What is related of Jack Cade's rebellion?
14. What is mentioned respecting the Duke of Gloucester? What was the consequence of his death?
15. What was the origin of the Houses of York and Lancaster? How were the parties distinguished, and what were the wars styled?
16. What is related of this quarrel?
17. In what battles were the Lancastrians defeated? What was done by the queen? What did the son and successor of the Duke of York accomplish?

Section VI.

1. What battle took place between the two parties, soon after Edward IV. was raised to the throne? How many were slain? What became of Henry?

2. What became of the queen? What is related of her deliverance by a robber?

3. By whom had the House of York been hitherto supported? What course did the Earl of Warwick take in consequence of Edward's offending him? What followed?

4. What was the issue of the battle of Barnet? Of Tewksbury? What became of the queen and her son?

5. What course did Edward afterwards pursue? What did he do to his brother, the Duke of Clarence? What is said of him?

6. Who succeeded to the throne? What is related of Richard Duke of Gloucester? What was done with the young princes?

7. In whom did Richard III. find an avenger? What followed? What was the effect of the battle of Bosworth?

8. What is said of the character and person of Richard?

Section VII.

1. How did Henry VII. strengthen his claim to the crown? What was Henry's descent? What is said of the Tudor family?

2. What was the policy of Henry? What was attempted by Lambert Simnel? What by Perkin Warbeck? What is said of him?

3. To what did the adventurers aspire? What was the destiny of Simnel? What of Perkin? Who was executed near the same time?

4. What is said of the character and habits of Henry? What did he accumulate by his frugality and exactions?

5. What is said of his reign? What was the effect of his regulations?

6. What was the consequence of his permitting the nobles to alienate their lands? What was the commencement of the English navy?

7. What advantages had Henry VIII. on succeeding to the throne?

8. What was the character which he developed? What does Sir Walter Raleigh say of him?

9. What is said of his government? What of his ministers?

10. What became of the treasures which he inherited? What were the military operations of his reign?

11. How did he obtain the title of Defender of the Faith?

12. What are the most memorable transactions of his reign? Who was his first wife? What is said of this connection?

13. What is related of Cardinal Wolsey in relation to this matter?

14. What course was taken to disannul the marriage? What afterwards took place in England?

15. What is remarked respecting the separation of England from the Church of Rome? What course did Henry now pursue? Who were beheaded for refusing to acknowledge his supremacy?

16. What was the fate of Anne Boleyn? Who were Henry's other queens, and what was their destiny?

17. What three children did Henry leave? Who succeeded him? What is said of his reign? What is said of the Reformation?

18. What is related of Edward? To whom did he bequeathe the crown?

19. By whom was Edward succeeded? What is said of Mary?

20. What is related of Jane Grey and her husband?

21. What message did Jane Grey send to her husband on the day of her execution?

22. What course was taken with regard to religion? Who were some of the most eminent martyrs? What effect was produced by these proceedings?

23. To whom was Mary married? What happened in the last year of her reign? What is related respecting her death?

24. How was the accession of Elizabeth received? What is said of her reign? By what names was it illustrated?

25. What is related of the changes with respect to religion? Of 9,000 clergymen, how many gave up their preferments on the accession of Elizabeth?

26 With what is Elizabeth charged in her treatment of Mary, Queen of Scots? Who was Mary? What had she been persuaded to do?

27. What had taken place at the period of Mary's return to Scotland?

28. What is related of Mary's second and third marriages? What effect did her conduct produce?

29. What course did Mary then take? What was her fate?

30. How did Elizabeth offend Philip II. of Spain? How did he attempt to avenge himself?

31. Of what did the Armada consist? By what force and what commanders was it met? What was the result?

32. By what eminent statesmen was Elizabeth assisted? Who were her chief personal favorites?

33. What is said of the close of her life? To what has her unhappiness been ascribed? What anecdote is related respecting Essex?

34. What is said of Elizabeth and her public character? What were her three leading maxims of policy? What is further said of her reign and character?

35. What is said of her private character, manners, &c.?

Section VIII.

1. Whom did Elizabeth nominate for her successor? What title did James assume? What is said of the Stuart family?

2. What conspiracy was formed against James? What is related of Sir Walter Raleigh?

3. What was the design of the Gunpowder Plot? Who was taken with matches in his pocket?

4. What was James's characteristic weakness? Who were his chief favorites?

5. When did the Puritans first make their appearance? For what were they advocates? Were their hopes realized on the accession of James? What settlement did they begin?

6. What was James's leading characteristic? What was his favorite topic? What was the best part of his character?

7. What is said of his private character, talents, and manners? What does Bishop Burnet say of him?

8. What circumstances had conspired to diffuse the spirit of liberty? How was the current of public opinion directed?

9. Under what circumstances did Charles I. ascend the throne? What was the state of feeling of many of his subjects? Of what did he soon give proof? Whom did he marry?

10. Why did Charles visit Madrid? What was the result? Why was Charles offended with the Parliament? What course did he pursue?

11. What taxes did he levy? How was the tax of ship-money levied? What did Charles claim? What is said of this tax?

12. Who opposed this tax? How was the cause decided?

13. Who were Charles's chief counsellors after the assassination Buckingham? What course did Laud pursue?

14. What measure did the king undertake with respect to Scotland? What effect did it produce? What took place at one of the churches in Edinburgh?

15. What success did the prelates meet with in other parts? What is said of the National Covenant? What other bond was formed?

16. When, after eleven years' intermission, the king convoked a Parliament, what measures did the House of Commons adopt? What was done by a Parliament afterwards assembled?

17. How had Charles already violated the privileges of Parliament? Into what act of greater indiscretion was he afterwards betrayed? What answer did Lenthal, the Speaker, make, when the king ordered him to point out the five men?

18. How did the king then proceed? What was now the feeling of the Parliament towards him?

19. By whom, in the civil war, was the cause of the king supported? By whom that of the Parliament? What were the supporters of each styled?

20. What formed the characteristic of most of the leaders in Parliament? On whom did the charge of license and excess chiefly fall? What is remarked by Mr. Baxter?

21. How long was it since England had been but little engaged in war? Who were the chief commanders in the royal army? Who in the Parliamentary army? What two men were killed in an early part of the contest? In what battles had the royalists the advantage? In what ones were they defeated?

22. What happened to the king? What measure was adopted respecting him? What sentence was passed?

23 What is said of Charles on this occasion, and how did he conduct himself?

24. What lesson does the fate of Charles furnish? What is said of the feelings of the people respecting his execution? What has been the effect of it on his reputation?

25. What were the misfortunes of Charles's condition? What was his greatest defect?

26. What is said of his talents, private character, and manners?

27. What is said of the proceedings of Charles? What does Mr. Hume say respecting the Puritans?

28. What is said of those who opposed the king?

29. What measures were adopted after the death of the king?

30. What was done respecting episcopacy? Who soon after gained the ascendency? To what body was the power transferred from the Parliament? Of whom was that part of the Parliament called the Rump composed?

31 What course was adopted by the Parliament of Scotland? Where did Cromwell defeat the royalist Covenanters? What account is given of the battle of Worcester?

32. What adventures did young Charles meet with?

33. What is said of the Navigation Act? Of what war was this act the cause? How did this war terminate, and who took a distinguished part in it?

34. How many years had the Long Parliament been in session? What course did it adopt? What did Cromwell resolve upon? What did he do while in a council of officers?

35. What was his next proceeding?

36. In what manner was the Little Parliament assembled? What is said of it?

37. What title did Cromwell assume at the dissolution of the Little Parliament? What is further related of him?
38. How did he administer the government? What is said of his reign and the state of England? How did he pass the latter part of life?
39. What is said of his talents and career?
40. To what did he owe his elevation? What is said of the officers and soldiers? How did Cromwell manage while toiling up the ascent to greatness?
41. To what has the name of Cromwell been subjected? What is said of the treatment he has received from history? Why is it so?
42. What is said of his private character?
43. What is said of Richard Cromwell? What was done by General Monk? When was Charles II. restored?
44. How did the nation suffer him to assume the crown? What do his reign and that of James II. exhibit? What is said of the new king?
45. What change now took place? What measures were adopted respecting the regicides? What principles and doctrines came in vogue? What acts were passed respecting religion?
46. What was done with Dunkirk? With what nation did Charles engage in war? What calamities visited London?
47. Why did the government become unpopular? On whom was the odium cast? What were the five ministers, who conducted the government after Clarendon was banished, termed?
48. What was the religion of Charles and James? For what purpose did Charles receive a pension from Louis XIV. of France? What is said of the latter part of Charles's reign?
49. Whose execution was occasioned by the pretended Popish Plot? What is said of the Rye-House Plot?
50. What was the character of the court? How was the reign characterized? What is said of Charles II.?
51. What is said of James II. and his reign? What course did he take on assuming the government? Who were his counsellors, and what did he attempt to do?
52. What is related of the Duke of Monmouth? How were those who favored him treated? What is related of Jeffreys?
53. How did James succeed in his designs? What act of his roused the general indignation? Who was invited to England to assume the government?
54. What followed? What was done by the Convention-Parliament? What is this event styled?
55. What was now done respecting the British constitution? What regulations were made respecting religion? What are some of the most important articles in the declaration of the rights of the subject?
56. What is related of Archbishop Sancroft, &c.? What were they styled?
57. What course did Ireland adopt? Where was James defeated by William? What naval battle was fought? What peace followed?
58 What is said of William? What is said of Mary his queen?
59. Who succeeded William? What is said of Anne? For what was her reign distinguished?
60. What states united in an alliance against France? Who were the commanders of the allied army? What victories did the Allies gain? When was the war terminated?
61. What is said of the constitutional union between England and Scotland?
62. When did the party names of Whigs and Tories first become common? What is said of the two parties? Who advocated the accession of William and Mary? What is said of the state of parties during the reign of Anne?

SECTION IX.

1. Who succeeded Anne? What is said of George I.? To what are some faults in his government attributed?

2. What change took place in the names of the two parties? Who were favored by George? What part did the Tories take?

3. What is related of the South-Sea Scheme?

4. What is said of George II., and of the court? What is said of his partialities in favor of his continental dominions?

5 What is related of Sir Robert Walpole?

6. What is said of the military operations of this reign? Who succeeded to the dominions of Charles VI., emperor of Germany? Who asserted his claim to the throne?

7. To what war did this give rise? What battle did the Allies gain, and in what were they routed? How was the contest decided?

8. What took place in Britain while George II. was on the Continent? Where did the Pretender defeat the royal forces? Where was he finally defeated?

9. What advantages did the British gain over the French in America? By what were they followed?

10. What is said of Great Britain during the reign of George II.? What is said respecting the national debt?

11. In what circumstances did George III. commence his reign? How was the war with France closed?

12. What is said of William Pitt? What was the consequence of the oppressive measures respecting the American Colonies?

13. What were the other most important events during the reign of George III.?

14. What is said of the French revolution? What course did the government of Great Britain take?

15. Who devised the system of operations? What is said of this war? What were some of the victories gained by the British?

16. What is said of the reign of George III.? What was his condition during the last ten years of his life? What is said of George III.?

17. By whom was George III. succeeded? What is said of his character and his course?

18. What bill was introduced into the House of Lords? What was the result?

19. What is stated in relation to the Greeks?

20. What is said of the Corporation and Test Act? By what was this repeal followed? What was the effect? What other improvements in the laws are mentioned?

21. By whom was George IV. succeeded? What took place soon after his accession? What was the state of feeling in England? What subject had been long agitated in England? What was done by the Duke of Wellington? What was the consequence?

22. What was done by Lord John Russell? What was the result? What is said of the measure?

23. What important acts were passed by the first reformed parliament

24. By whom was William IV succeeded?

25. Principal military operations of the British in Victoria's reign? Time, cause, and results of first Chinese war? Of the second?

26. Policy of France and England in respect to Turkey? What is said of first Turkish war? Time, cause of, and party to, the Crimean war? What is said of the Siege of Sebastopol? Battles connected with it?

27. Naval operations of England? Losses? Florence Nightingale? Order of Victoria Cross?
28. Time, cause, and result of Afghan War? Territory in India annexed to Great Britain?
29. What was the Sepoy Rebellion? Time and cause?
30. Relate what is said of the outbreak? Who was Nena Sahib?
31. When, and by whom made, was the Siege of Delhi? Massacre at Cawnpore? Relief of Lucknow? Result of the revolt? What is said of the East-India Company?
32. Important event in the history of the Canadas? Of the Australian Colonies?
33. What agitations have taken place in Ireland? When and how originated the Free Church of Scotland?
34. Political parties in England? Who are "Chartists?" Important legislative enactments?
35. Effect of threatened difficulties with France? What other events are mentioned? Distinguished persons who have died? Prime ministers of this reign?

General Questions for English History.

What sovereign of England has had the longest reign? The shortest? Which have been the most warlike reigns? The most peaceful?

In which reigns have occurred wars with Scotland? With France? In America? Which are noted for revolutions at home? Which for rapid progress in civilization?

Date, parties, cause, and result of the Wars of the Roses? Of the great civil war? Of the war of Independence in America? Of the Crimean War?

General result of wars with Scotland? With France?

When and how did England acquire Wales? Scotland? Canada? Australia? Her Indian possessions?

Who was Sir Robert Peel? John Wickliffe? Sir Walter Raleigh? Oliver Cromwell? Joan of Arc? Duke of Marlborough? William Pitt? William Shakspeare? Cœur de Lion? Geoffrey Chaucer? Thomas Cromwell?

What was the Gunpowder Plot? The Invincible Armada? The Long Parliament? The Corporation and Test Act? The Magna Charta?

Chronological Table of the History of England. — No. 1.

Who was the first king of the Saxon Family? Who were the Danish kings? Who was the first of the Norman Family? The Plantagenet? The Branch of Lancaster? The Branch of York?

When did Egbert begin to reign? Canute? William the Conqueror? Henry II.? Edward III.? Henry V.?

What is said of Egbert or his reign? Alfred? William the Conqueror? &c.

Chronological Table of the History of England.—No. 2.

What kings were of the House of Tudor? Stuart? Brunswick?
When did Henry VII. begin to reign? Henry VIII.? Edward VI? &c
How long did Henry VII. reign? Henry VIII.? Edward VI.? &c
What is said respecting Henry VII. or his reign? Henry VIII? &c

Chronological Table of English Literature.

What statesmen and commanders flourished in the 16th century? The 17th? &c.

What poets flourished in the 16th century? What divines? The 17th? &c.

EUROPEAN STATES.

Scotland.

1. What is said of the pretensions of Scotland to a regular succession of kings from the time of Alexander the Great? What were the principal tribes that anciently inhabited Scotland? Who was the first king of all Scotland?

2. In whose reign did the most memorable contests happen between Scotland and the kings of England? Who were Edward's antagonists? In what battle did Robert Bruce defeat the English?

3. What took place in 1603? What in 1706?

Germany.

1. Into what three monarchies was the Empire of the West divided in 843? What afterwards took place? What two sovereigns governed Germany in the 10th century?

2. For what is the reign of Henry IV. remarkable? To what factions did the election of Conrad III. give rise? To whom were the Ghibelines, and to whom the Guelphs attached?

3 By what was the reign of Frederick Barbarossa signalized? By what was the reign of Conrad IV. followed? Who was elected emperor after the Great Interregnum?

4 What is said of the principal events in the history of the latter emperors of the Franconian line and those of the Swabian line? What were the grounds of these contests?

5. What quarrel took place between Louis IV. and Pope John XXII.? What was determined by the Pragmatic Sanction?

6. For what is the reign of Sigismund memorable? Who were burnt by the Council of Constance? What was done by the adherents of Huss and Jerome in Bohemia?

7. What is related of Maximilian I.?

8. What emperor was the most powerful sovereign of his age? What is related of Charles V.? What is said of the Reformation?

9 By what were the reigns of Ferdinand II. and Ferdinand III. signalized? What account is given of this war? How did it issue?
10. What took place on the death of Charles VI.? How was the war of the Austrian Succession terminated?
11. When and how did the German empire terminate?
12. When was the imperial government hereditary? How was it afterwards? What was the mode of election at first? How afterwards?
13. What took place in 1848?

Austria.

1. When was Austria erected into an empire? What is said of it?
2 What effect did the French revolution of 1848 produce at Vienna What was done by the Emperor Ferdinand?
3. What took place in the Austrian dominions in Italy?
4 What is related respecting Hungary?
5 What was done by the emperor of Russia? What was the issue?
6 What measure was taken by the emperor of Austria in 1849?

Spain.

1. By whom was Spain invaded in the 5th century? What took place in the 8th century?
2. What was done by the Moors? What was accomplished by Abderrahman in 755? What is said of the Moorish states?
3. What course did the Gothic or Christian forces pursue? What does the history of Spain present?
4. What Christian kingdoms were formed? How did the kingdoms of Castile, Leon, and Arragon become united?
5. What is said of the reign of Ferdinand and Isabella?
6. What is said of Spain during the reigns of Charles I. and Philip II.? What has since taken place? When was the most flourishing period of Spanish literature?
7. What took place in 1808? What was the result?
8. What took place in relation to Spain from 1811 to 1821? What has been the condition of Spain since?

Portugal.

1. What is related of the early history of Portugal?
2. How was Henry, Duke of Burgundy, rewarded for his services to Alphonso, king of Castile? What did his son and successor Alphonso accomplish?
3. For what is the reign of John I. famous?
4. For what were the reigns of John II. and Emanuel distinguished? What was done during their reigns? What took place with respect to trade after the discovery of a passage to India round the Cape of Good Hope? Who first shared with the Portuguese the navigation of the Cape?
5 What is said of the period from John I. to the conquest of Portugal by Philip II. of Spain?
6. What took place in 1580? When were the Spaniards expelled?
7. What is said of the discovery and colonization of Brazil?
8. What took place in 1807? What measure was adopted with respect to Brazil? What happened in 1826?

The Netherlands.

1. What was the situation of the Netherlands in the Middle Ages? What is said of the country in the 15th century?
2. To whom did Charles V. resign these provinces? What afterwards took place respecting them?
3. What is said of the prosperity of the Dutch Provinces?
4. What measure was adopted in relation to the Seventeen Provinces by the Congress of Vienna? How long did this union last?
5. What took place in 1830? What was the result?

Poland.

1. When and by whom was Christianity introduced into Poland? When was the monarchy in its most flourishing state?
2. What is related of Casimir III.? What took place in the latter part of the 14th century?
3. Under whose reign did the kingdom rise to its greatest height? What took place afterwards?
4. By whom and when was Poland conquered and partitioned?
5. What was done after the peace of Tilsit in 1807? What in 1815?
6. What is said of the Grand Duke Constantine? What took place in 1830?
7. What is related of the Emperor Nicholas?

Sweden.

1. What did Sweden and Norway anciently form? What took place in the latter part of the 14th century? What followed?
2. What is related of Gustavus Vasa?
3. What is said of Gustavus Adolphus and his reign?
4. What is said of Charles XII.? What was his career?
5. What is related of Gustavus IV.? By whom was he succeeded? By what has the loss of Finland been repaired?
6. What took place on the death of Charles XIII.?

Denmark.

1. To whom did the crown of Denmark fall in 1848? What is said respecting the monarchy?
2. With whom was Denmark engaged in war in the beginning of the 18th century? How long afterwards did the country enjoy peace?
3. What was the condition of the kingdom during the reigns of Christian VI. and Frederick V.? By what statesman was the latter assisted?
4. Whom did Christian VII. marry? What is said of Matilda?
5. By whom was Copenhagen attacked in 1801? What was the pretence for bombarding it in 1807? How large a fleet was surrendered to the British?
6 What took place in 1843?

Prussia.

1. By whom was the foundation of Prussian greatness laid? What is related of his successor?

2. What is said of Frederick II.?

3. Against whom did Frederick declare war in 1756? How was the contest carried on, and how terminated? What was the only gainful result of this sanguinary struggle?

4. What did Frederick afterwards do? What is said of him?

5. What did the king of Prussia lose by war with the French? What course did he take in 1813? What did he gain by the treaty of Vienna? What is said of the condition of Prussia since?

6. By whom was Frederick William succeeded? How has his reign been characterized? What has been done?

Russia.

1. What is said of the importance of Russia? What is related of Pete the Great?

2. What is said of Catharine II.? What further is related of her char acter and exploits?

3. By whom was Catharine succeeded? What is said of Alexander?

4. By what has the reign of Nicholas been distinguished? When was the war against Turkey declared? What is related of it, and how did it terminate?

5. What took place in 1830? What followed?

6. What was done by the emperor in 1848? What is said of Russia?

Rome.

1. When did the temporal power of the pope commence? When did it attain its zenith?

2. What is said of the first half of the 16th century? What is related of Popes Julius II. and Leo X.? What took place during the pontificate of the latter? How has the power of the pope since been diminished?

3. What was done by Bonaparte in 1809? What was done by the Congress of Vienna?

4. What is said of the Roman government? What of Pius IX.?

5 What took place at Rome after the French revolution of 1848?

6 What was accomplished at Rome by the French?

Turkey.

1. What are the Turks? What is the first notice of them in history? By whom were their dominions united?

2. What conquest was made by Amurath? What by Bajazet? What by Mahomet II.?

3. How did the Turks afterwards succeed? What countries were conquered by Selim? What is said of the reign and exploits of Solyman the Magnificent?

4. With whom have the Turks been engaged in war since the time of Solyman?

5. By what has the Turkish power been lately weakened?

6 When did the Greeks revolt? What took place afterwards? What was done in 1828 and 1832?

Sovereigns of Germany, Spain, Sweden, Prussia, and Russia.

When did Charles V. of Germany begin to reign? Ferdinand and Isabella of Spain? Gustavus Vasa of Sweden? Frederick I. of Prussia? Peter I. of Russia? Francis of Austria?

Who were the emperors of Austria in the 16th century, &c.

Table of Italian, French, Spanish, German, &c., Literature

What distinguished men did Italy produce in the 14th century? In the 15th? &c.

Remarks on the Table.

What is said of Italy respecting the revival of learning? Who were some of the distinguished men?

What is said of France? What was the most brilliant period of French literature? Who were some of the most eminent men? What is related of Spain? Germany? Sweden? Holland?

AMERICA.

1. What is said of the discovery of America? What were some of the effects of this discovery?
2. To whom is the world indebted for this discovery? What is related of Columbus?
3. What did he conceive was necessary in order to complete the balance of the terraqueous globe?
4. How was the merchandise of India conveyed to Europe before the passage round the Cape of Good Hope was known? For what purpose did Columbus undertake his voyage of discovery?
5. To whom did he apply in succession for assistance? From whom did he gain some favor after seven years' solicitation? With what was he provided for the expedition? What appointment did he obtain?
6. From what place and when did he sail? How did he proceed?
7. What circumstance alarmed both him and his men? How did he manage? What took place thirty days after? How far was he compelled to yield to his crew?
8. When did Columbus first discover a light? What satisfaction did the crew now make to Columbus?
9. What island was first discovered? What islands were discovered afterwards? Why did he name these islands the *West Indies*?
10. What did he procure before he set sail for Spain? What happened during the voyage? What method did he take to preserve an account of his discovery? What favorable occurrence took place? Whither did he proceed?
11. When did Columbus discover the continent of South America? What was caused by his successes? What was done to Columbus? What did he say when the captain offered to release him from his fetters?
12. What did he afterwards do with his fetters?
13. What was the feeling upon Columbus's arriving thus in Spain? How was he treated?
14. How did Columbus obtain command over the Indians in his fourth voyage? What afterwards happened to him? What is said of his funeral? What inscription was engraved on his tomb?

15. By whom was Columbus deprived of the honor of giving his name to the continent? What did Americus claim? What is said of this act of injustice?

16. Who first sailed to India round the Cape of Good Hope? What is said of this enterprise? What is related of Magellan?

17. When and by whom was the continent of North America first discovered?

18. What land was first seen? Which way did they proceed? In what manner did they take possession of the country?

19. When and with what force did Cortes invade Mexico? How were his men armed? With what else was he furnished?

20. What was his first course? How was he received by Montezuma? How did Cortes requite his hospitality? What followed?

21. What assistance did Cortes obtain? What was the success of the Spaniards?

22. When did the Spaniards form a settlement at Panama? With what force did Pizarro sail from this place in order to conquer Peru?

23. In what manner did he proceed with the Inca Atabalipa?

24. What did Atabalipa do in order to procure his release? To what did this treasure amount, and what was done with it? What was then done to the inca?

25. How did the Spanish chiefs then proceed? What followed?

26. What is said of the Peruvians and Mexicans? What arts did they understand? In what did the Peruvians excel? What is said of their religion?

27. What was done, in 1524, by Francis I. of France? What is related of James Cartier?

28. What enterprise was performed by Sir Walter Raleigh? What took place on his return to England?

29. What Englishmen made unsuccessful attempts to settle Virginia?

30. By what right did Europeans take possession of the parts of America which they visited? How were the original inhabitants treated? Who set this example? How did he proceed?

31. What was done by the popes? What was held out as the chief reason for taking possession of America? Of what was this made the pretext?

32. By what were the Spaniards stimulated? What is said of their passion for gold? How were the Indians treated? What was the result?

33. By whom was this cruelty condemned? Where did the colonists look for a supply of laborers? What is said of them?

34. When and by whom was the first importation of negroes from Africa made? What has been since done?

THE UNITED STATES.

Section I

1. To what are nations inclined to lay claim? How is it with regard to the people of this country? What is said of the early history and growth of this country?

2. What is said of the first settlers, and of what were they the advocates What circumstances have favored their growth? With whom have their political and commercial relations connected them?

3. In what did the colonization of this country originate? What Colonies were peopled by these causes?

4. What were their early condition and sufferings? What was the ultimate issue?

5. When did the crown of England grant the charter under which the first effectual English settlements were made in North America? What two companies were constituted? What territories were assigned to them?

6. When and by whom was the first effectual attempt to form a settlement? Where was it begun? How was the government administered?

7 Who was the first president? Who was chosen the second year? What is related of Smith?

8. In what contests were the colonists involved? What provocations had the Indians before received?

9. What happened to Captain Smith? Before what chief was he carried?

10. What measures were taken respecting him? By whose influence was he delivered?

11. What service did Pocahontas, two years after, perform for the colonists? What is further related of her?

12. What diminution did the colonists suffer in a few months? What did their number amount to at the end of the year?

13. To what sufferings were the colonists afterwards subjected?

14. What was the effect of this famine? What course did those who survived it, take? What induced them to remain?

15. What was the number of colonists at the end of twelve years? What addition was made in 1619? What is said of the planters? What method was adopted for supplying them with wives? What price was paid for a wife? What was the commencement of slavery?

16. What plot was concerted against the colonists in 1622? How many of them were put to death? What calamities followed the massacre? What number of inhabitants did the colony contain in 1624?

17. By what other circumstances did the colony suffer? What is said of Sir William Berkeley and his administration? To what did the restrictions on the trade of the colony give rise? What was the consequence?

18. What was the population in 1660? What was the increase in the 28 succeeding years? With what views did the first adventurers come? To what did they turn their attention in 1616? What use was made of tobacco?

19. By whom and when was Hudson's River discovered? When and where were the first permanent settlements made by the Dutch? What were the country and the settlement on Manhattan Island named?

20. Who were the three successive Dutch governors? To what did the extension of the English settlements give rise?

21. To whom did Charles II. of England grant the country? What afterwards took place?

22. Where did the Plymouth Company commence an unsuccessful settlement? By whom was the name of the country changed? To whom was a patent granted by King James? Between what degrees of latitude did the country granted lie?

23 When and by whom was the first permanent settlement begun in New England? Why were they called Puritans? Of whose congregation did they form a part?

24. To what country had they before fled? Why did they come to America? What is said of the principle of toleration at this period?

25. To what river did they propose to sail? What was the first land that they discovered? When did they land at Plymouth?

26. To what sufferings were they subjected?

27. What kind of government did they institute? Who were the first two governors? What articles of food did they raise? How was their property for several years held?

28. What method did they adopt to protect themselves against the Indians? What is related of Samoset? What of Massasoit? How long was the treaty made with him observed?

29 When and by whom was the Colony of Massachusetts Bay begun? By whom were Boston and other places near it first settled?

30 What is mentioned respecting the first settlements in New Hampshire? How long did they continue annexed to Massachusetts?

31. When and where was the Colony of Connecticut commenced? The Colony of New Haven? When were these united?

32. When, where, and by whom was the settlement of Rhode Island commenced?

33. What is said of the attention of the colonists to religion and learning? How long after the first settlement of Massachusetts Bay was it before Harvard College was founded?

34. For what virtues were the colonists distinguished?

35 On what subjects were their views narrow? What is related of their principles and habits.

36. In what way did the colonists get possession of the land? How had the Indians been treated by Europeans?

37 What is related of Captain Standish and of Mr. Robinson? What Colonies suffered little from the Indians for many years? What is related respecting the Colony of Connecticut? What was the issue of this contest?

38. What measure did the four Colonies of Massachusetts Bay, Plymouth, Connecticut, and New Haven, adopt to promote their security and welfare? How many delegates were elected by each? What is said of this union?

39. What was the most destructive Indian war in which the Colonies were ever engaged? What is said of Philip?

40. What did the Indians determine to do? What measure was adopted?

41. What was the immediate cause of war? What next took place?

42. How were hostilities conducted? What is the greatest battle called? Where was it fought? Who commanded the colonists? What was the loss on each side?

43. What was the condition of the Indians after this defeat? What happened to Philip? What is said of his death? In what wars were the colonists afterwards annoyed by the Indians?

44. To what was the English population of these Colonies at this time computed to amount? What losses were sustained? How many buildings and towns were destroyed?

45. Who was the founder of Maryland? Where did he first project a settlement? From whom was the country named? By whom was Lord Baltimore succeeded?

46. Who was appointed the first governor? When and where did he begin a settlement? What measures were pursued?

47. To whom was the country of Pennsylvania granted? Why was it granted to Penn? When and with whom did he arrive?

48. What did he make the basis of his institutions? How did he manage in his intercourse with the Indians?

49. How long were the treaties preserved inviolate?

50. What is said of the prosperity of this colony? What inducements were held out to settlers?

51. What were the first civil communities in which the free toleration of religion was recognized?

Section II.

What sovereigns had hitherto occupied the throne of England since the commencement of the Colonies? What was the effect of their principles? With what were the Colonies alarmed?

2. What was done by Edward Randolph in order to destroy the liberties of New England?

3. Who was appointed by James II. governor of New England? What measure did Sir Edmund Andros adopt? What was done with the charters? How did Sir Edmund then proceed?

4. What took place in England at this time? How was the news of the Revolution of 1688 received in this country? What measures were adopted by the Colonies?

5. What was done with regard to the Colonies of Massachusetts Bay and Plymouth?

6. How were the magistrates under the old charter elected? What change was made by the new charter? Who was appointed the first governor?

7. To what evils did the revolution in England subject the Colonies? How long did the war during the reign of William last? How long did that during the reign of Anne continue?

8. How much of the time, for 25 years preceding the peace of Utrecht had the country been exempted from war? What number of the inhabitants were in actual service? What was the condition of the rest? What was the state of the country?

9. How many young men, belonging to New England and New York, are supposed to have been lost in the public service?

10. When did another war break out between Great Britain and France? By what was this war rendered memorable in America? What is said of Louisburg?

11. How many troops had General Pepperell? By whom was he joined? What was the issue?

12. What effect did the news of this achievement of the Colonies have on the government of France? What armament was sent by the French to America? What was the object of it?

13. What disasters happened to this fleet?

14. What became of the ships that remained? What was done with Louisburg at the peace of Aix-la-Chapelle?

15. Who claimed the country watered by the Mississippi and its tributaries? What measures did the French take with regard to it, in the succeeding period of peace?

16. What grant was obtained by the Ohio Company? What course did the French take with respect to the traders?

17. What measures were adopted by the Company and by the Colony of Virginia? Who was sent to the French commandant?

18. What course was taken by the British government? What warlike preparations were made?

19. On what expedition was General Braddock sent? What did his force amount to? What is said of Braddock and his fate? What loss was sustained? What is related of Washington?

20. By whom and where was General Johnson met in his expedition against Crown Point? What was the issue? What is said of the expedition against Niagara and Fort Frontenac?

21. How long was the war carried on before a formal declaration was made? Who succeeded Dieskau? Who had the chief command of the English troops? What is said of the commanders, and of the campaign? By whose means was a favorable change effected?

22. What measure was pursued by Mr. Pitt? What number of men was brought into the service? What three expeditions were resolved on?

23. What forces and what commanders were sent against Louisburg? What was the issue?

24. What was the result of the attack on Ticonderoga by Abercrombie? What was done by Colonel Bradstreet and General Forbes?

25 To whom was the chief command given after the disaster at Ticon

deroga? What was the object of the campaign of '759? What three divisions were now made of the British army?

26. What was the success of the expeditions against Ticonderoga, Crown Point, and Niagara?

27. To whom was the expedition against Quebec intrusted? What is said of this place? What effect had the difficulties of the enterprise on the English general? With what force did he approach the city?

28. What enterprise did he accomplish during the night? What was the issue of the battle that followed?

29. What is related of Wolfe on his viewing the engagement, after he had received a fatal wound? What is said of Montcalm?

30. By what was this battle followed? What was done by the peace of Paris in 1763? How did the success of this war affect the Colonies?

Section III.

1. What is said of the colonists? Why did emigrants leave England? How did they regard the parent country?

2. What was their condition at the peace of 1763?

3. What troubles assailed them after the conquest of Canada had freed them from the hostilities of the French and Indians?

4. What had been the effect of the war which Great Britain had carried on in defence of her American possessions? What was the pretext for taxing the Colonies?

5. What was maintained respecting this matter by the Colonies? What did they maintain was a right of British subjects?

6. What measures were adopted by parliament in 1764? How were these proceedings regarded by the Colonies?

7. What act was passed the next year? On what did the Stamp Act lay a duty? What was done by the Assembly of Virginia? What by Massachusetts?

8. What took place in Boston when the news of the Stamp Act arrived? What in New York? What was done by the merchants?

9. When and where did a Colonial Congress meet? What measure did this Congress adopt? What was done by the merchants? What was the issue respecting the Stamp Act? What was done by parliament after a change in the British cabinet?

10. What act was passed by parliament in 1767? What was done to render the act effectual? What was another arbitrary measure of parliament?

11. What were now the feelings of the Americans? What affray took place on the 5th of March? How was the funeral of the deceased conducted? What was the result of the trial of Captain Preston and his soldiers?

12. Who was appointed prime minister of England in 1770? What did the British ministry intend to do by retaining the duty of three pence on tea? What were the Americans determined to do? What is said of the year 1771?

13. What was done in 1772 by the representatives of Massachusetts? What by the inhabitants of Boston and the towns generally?

14. What was done with the tea in New York and Philadelphia? In Boston?

15. What place was considered the chief seat of rebellion? What was the act called the Boston Port Bill? What was its effect?

16. With what authority did General Gage arrive in Boston? What soon followed?

17. What measures were adopted in Massachusetts to prepare for the contest?

18. What was done by the General Court of Massachusetts?

19. When and where did the Continental Congress meet? Of whom was this Congress composed? What measures did they adopt?

20. What is said of the power of Great Britain? What was the condition of the Colonies? By what were their operations especially embarrassed? How was their resolution to engage in the contest regarded in England?

21. What was done when the proceedings of the Congress were laid before parliament? To what number was the British army increased?

22. What was the purport of Lord North's *conciliatory proposition?* What was the design of it? How was it received?

23. For what object did General Gage send a party of troops to Salem? Who were sent to seize the military stores at Concord? What account is given of the affair at Lexington?

24. What was done by the British troops after having dispersed the militia at Lexington? What took place on their return?

25. What was now done by the Americans? What army was raised?

26. What fortresses were secured, and by whom?

27. What was done by the Provincial Congress of Massachusetts?

28. When and where did the second Continental Congress meet? What did they recommend?

29. What generals arrived with British troops? What measure was now adopted? Who were excepted from the offer of pardon?

30. For what purpose was Colonel Prescott ordered to throw up a breastwork on Bunker Hill? How far had the work proceeded before it was discovered?

31. With what force did General Howe make an attack on the works? What is said of the defence of the Americans? What losses were sustained on each side? What was done by the British while their troops were advancing?

32. What measures were now adopted by Congress? Who was chosen commander-in chief of the army? What is said of Washington? Where did he establish his head-quarters?

33. What other chief officers were appointed?

34. Who were sent on an expedition to Canada? On whom did the chief command devolve?

35. What was accomplished by Arnold? What was the issue of the attack on Quebec?

36. What took place in Virginia during these operations in the north? What was done by Lord Dunmore?

37. From what other States were the royal governors expelled? What were the adherents of Great Britain called? What is said of them? By whom was General Gage succeeded?

38. What is said of the American army investing Boston? What did Washington resolve to do in the latter part of the winter? What measures were adopted?

39. What prevented Howe from attacking the works? What took place?

40. What attack was made by Sir Peter Parker? What was the result?

41. What was the effect produced in England by the news of the battle of Bunker Hill? What measures did the ministry adopt? To what did the force destined to America amount?

42. What had hitherto been the object of the controversy? What did the Colonies now begin to think of doing? What publication contributed to bring about a great change in the public mind? By whom was the

motion in Congress made for declaring the Colonies free and independent? Of whom did the committee for preparing the Declaration consist? How and when was the vote carried?

43. How does the Declaration conclude?

Section IV.

1. What did Washington suppose would be a favorite object with General Howe? What measure was adopted?

2. Whither did Sir William Howe sail, after evacuating Boston? What soon after took place? What is said of the number of the British troops? What of the American army?

3. What attempt was made to bring about a reconciliation? What terms were proposed? What other occurrences took place?

4. Where did an engagement take place? By whom were the Americans commanded? What were the issue and the losses? How was the retreat of the Americans effected?

5. What was Washington's next movement? What fort was reduced by Howe? Of what were the British now possessed?

6. What retreat did Washington now make? What was now done by the British troops?

7. What was now the aspect of American affairs, and the state of the army? What other misfortunes had occurred? How large an army had Washington? What else took place unfavorable to the American cause?

8. What account is given of Washington's attack on Trenton? What was his next exploit? What was the effect of these measures?

9. What measures did Congress adopt at this period?

10. What was done by General Howe in March and April of 1777?

11. Of what did the American army now consist? What measure was adopted by Howe? What movement was made by Washington? What battle followed? What were the losses?

12. What was done by Howe after this battle? What account is given of the battle of Germantown? What was then done by the British army?

13. Who invaded the States through Canada? What advantages did General Burgoyne gain?

14. For what purpose did he send a detachment to Bennington? What was the issue? What took place on the Mohawk?

15. Where did Burgoyne encamp with his forces? Who had now the command of the American army in the north? What losses were sustained in the battle of Stillwater? How was the British army soon after situated?

16. What did Burgoyne do in this exigency? What measure was he next compelled to adopt? What number was surrendered?

17. What was the effect of the surrender of Burgoyne? Who had been sent, in 1776, to France, to solicit assistance? What was their success? What was done after the surrender of Burgoyne?

18. How were the British ministry affected by these events? What measures were adopted? What was the issue?

19 Who succeeded General Howe as commander-in-chief of the British army? What did the British now determine to do? What events followed?

20. How large was the French fleet under Count d'Estaing? What plan was now concerted? What account is given of the engagement on Rhode Island? What was done by the French fleet? What town was taken by the British in December?

21. What change was made in the theatre of the war in 1779? What is said of the operations? By what were the exertions of the Americans enfeebled?

22. What was done by Collier and Matthews? What by Tryon?

23. What account is given of the achievement of General Wayne? Of General Lovell? Of General Sullivan?

24. What measure was taken by General Lincoln? What was the result? What was the issue of the attack made on the English in Savannah?

25. What State was the principal theatre of the war in 1780? What account is given of the siege of Charleston by Clinton? Who was left to command the British troops in the south?

26. What measures were taken to secure the obedience of the interior country to the British? What events took place?

27. Who now took the command of the southern American army in place of General Lincoln? What account is given of the battle of Camden?

28. What French fleet and army arrived? What is said of them?

29. What treacherous plot did General Arnold form? What facts are related respecting Arnold? How was his design frustrated?

30. What is said of Major Andre? What became of Arnold?

31. What is said of the operations of the war in 1781? What was done by Arnold?

32. Who was now appointed to command the southern American army? What is related respecting the battle of the Cow-Pens?

33. What account is given of the battle near Guilford court-house? What took place at Camden? What account is given of the battle of Eutaw Springs?

34. What course did Cornwallis take after the battle of Guilford? Where did he encamp and fortify himself?

35. What measure had been concerted by the American officers? On whom was it finally resolved to make an attack? How was Sir Henry Clinton prevented from sending assistance to Cornwallis?

36. What course did Washington now pursue?

37. What measure was adopted by Clinton? What was done in Connecticut?

38. What good news did Washington hear at Chester? What was the issue of the engagement between the English and French fleets? To what did Washington's force now amount?

39. What was the effect of the attack of the Americans on the British army? When did Cornwallis propose a cessation of hostilities? What was the number of prisoners that surrendered?

40. How was the news of this surrender received? What expressions of gratitude were made by the army and by Congress?

41. What is said of the subsequent military operations? What changes were made in the British cabinet and in the command of the British army? When were provisional articles of peace signed? When, where, and by whom was the definitive treaty of peace concluded?

42. What is said of the war? What did it cost Great Britain?

SECTION V.

1. What difficulties arose when the American army was about to be disbanded? To what expedient had Congress been driven? How had the army been paid, and what was their condition?

2. Why had the officers remained quiet, and why were they now alarmed? What took place with regard to that portion stationed at Newburg?

3. What did Washington do at this crisis?

4. What effect had this speech upon the officers? What measures did Congress adopt?

5 In what manner did Washington resign his command?

6 After the return of peace, how was the government under the Articles of Confederation found? What was the state of the paper currency?

7. In what proportion to their nominal value were the army notes sold? Who were the sufferers by this depreciation?

8. When and where did commissioners meet to form a system of commercial regulations? What measure did they adopt?

9. When did the delegates meet at Philadelphia? When was the Constitution unanimously agreed to by them? What measure was then taken respecting it? When was it ratified by eleven of the States? By what States was it not at first adopted?

10. Who was unanimously chosen first president? What is said of his journey to New York?

11. When was he inaugurated? What is said of the ceremony?

12. How was the nation affected by this event? What is said of his qualifications? Who was elected vice-president? Who were the other principal officers?

13. What beneficial effects were soon felt?

14. Over whom did the Indians north of the Ohio obtain victories in 1790 and 1791? Who routed them, and negotiated a treaty at Greenville?

15. In what other difficulties were the United States now involved? What were the feelings of a large portion of the community? What was the policy of Washington's administration?

16. What did Washington do near the end of the second term of his administration? By whom was he succeeded?

17. What course was pursued by the French revolutionary government? How did the American government act? What soon after took place?

18. What particulars are mentioned respecting Washington's death? What effect was produced by the news? How was his death noticed throughout the country?

19. What parties arose at the time of the adoption of the Federal Constitution? How were they afterwards generally designated? How did these parties differ? What is said of the treaty negotiated by Mr. Jay?

20. What measures of Mr. Adams's administration excited most dissatisfaction? What change took place in 1801?

Section VI.

1. What was the great measure of the first term of Mr. Jefferson's administration? What sum was paid for Louisiana? What is said of the history of Louisiana?

2. What was the state of the country when Mr. Jefferson became president? What is said of parties, and of his reelection?

3 What is said of the war between Great Britain and France? How was America affected by it?

4. What measure did the British government adopt in 1806? What did the French Berlin Decree declare? What was the effect of the British Orders in Council? What was the import of Bonaparte's Milan Decree?

5. What measure was recommended by Mr. Jefferson, and adopted by Congress? What was the design of this measure? What was the effect? What was substituted in its stead?

6. What was the condition of the trade of the United States?

7. What species of injury did the United States suffer exclusively from Britain? What is said on this subject?

8. What complaint did the British make? What is said of this practice?

9. To what vessels had the custom of searching for British seamen been confined? What account is given of the attack on the American frigate Chesapeake?

10. How was this outrage regarded? What measures were adopted?

11. By whom was Mr. Jefferson succeeded? What took place at the commencement of Mr. Madison's administration? What is related of Mr. Jackson? Between what vessels of war did a rencounter take place?

12. Under what circumstances did Congress meet in May, 1812? What did Mr. Madison state as the principal grounds of war?

13. How was the bill passed? What took place five days after the declaration?

14. On what ground did the minority oppose the war? How was it with the people?

15. Under what circumstances was the war commenced?

16. What is related respecting General Hull's invasion of Canada? What is said of General Van Rensselaer's attempt?

17. What is said of the success of the Americans on the ocean? What naval victories were gained?

18. By whom was General Winchester defeated? What became of about 500 prisoners?

19. What is related of General Pike? What of Colonel Dudley?

20. By whom were the British repulsed at Sackett's Harbor? By whom was Fort George in Canada taken? What followed?

21. What is related of Perry's achievement on Lake Erie?

22. What was done by General Harrison? What is stated respecting this action?

23. What is said of the preparations against Canada under Wilkinson and Hampton? What villages were burnt? What is related of Admiral Cockburn?

24. What naval engagements took place this year?

25. What is said of the campaign of 1814? What is related of the battle of Chippewa? What of the battle of Bridgewater?

26. With how large an army did Sir George Prevost advance to Plattsburg? Who commanded the British naval force on Lake Champlain? By whom was Downie defeated? By whom was Sir George Prevost repulsed? What were the losses?

27. How numerous an army under General Ross landed in the Patuxent? What was accomplished by them? By whom was an attempt made on Baltimore? What was the issue?

28. What naval operations took place?

29. What is said respecting the connection of this war with that which had been raging in Europe? When and where was a treaty of peace signed?

30. What was done by the British while this negotiation was in progress? By whom were the British repulsed? What losses were sustained?

31. What was the condition of the Northeastern States in 1814? What was proposed by the legislature of Massachusetts? What convention met? What was the result?

32. What is related of the treaty of Ghent? What might occur in case Great Britain should be again engaged in a European war?

33. What is said respecting war as a method of settling national disputes?

34. By whom was Mr. Madison succeeded? What is said of his reëlection?

35. What was the state of the country during Mr. Monroe's administration?

36. When, and for what sum, was Florida ceded to the United States?

37. What is said of the admission of the State of Missouri into the Union? How did the bill pass? What declaration accompanied it?

38. What is related of the visit of General Lafayette? What was done for him by Congress?

39. By whom was Mr. Monroe succeeded? Who were the candidates for the presidency? How many votes did each receive?

40. What was the state of the country during Mr. Adams's administration? What is said of the policy pursued?

41. What is related respecting the Cherokee and Creek Indians?

42. What course did the Indians take? What was afterwards done?

43. What is said of the new tariff law, and the principle of a protective tariff?

44. What is related respecting John Adams and Thomas Jefferson

Section VII.

1. By whom was Mr. Adams succeeded? For what had General Jackson been distinguished?

2. By what was Jackson's administration signalized? What bills did he return with a veto?

3. What measures were adopted in South Carolina?

4. What was then done by President Jackson? What by the governor of South Carolina? What was the next measure of the president?

5. What afterwards took place, and what was the result?

6. What was done by President Jackson soon after he was elected for a second term? What course was taken by Mr. Duane and by Mr. Taney? What was done by the Senate?

7. What is said of the difficulties with France? What was done by France?

8. What is related respecting the fire in New York?

9. What did the debt of the United States amount to in 1816? When was it all paid off? What surplus revenue was there in the treasury in 1837? What was done with it?

10. What is related respecting the Seminole Indians? What did the expenses of this war amount to?

11. By whom was Jackson succeeded? What is said of Mr Van Buren?

12. What is said of the commercial revulsion, causes, and effects?

13. What course did the banks take? What was the condition of the mercantile classes?

14. How was the government involved in the embarrassment? What measures were taken by the president and by Congress? When did the banks resume specie payment?

15. What is said of the rebellion in Canada? What American citizens took part in it? What was done by the president?

16. By whom was Mr. Van Buren succeeded? What is said of General Harrison?

17. What is related respecting the election of Harrison? Who succeeded to the presidency on the death of Harrison? What is said of President Tyler?

18. What acts were passed by Congress in an extra session? What course was taken by the president? What was the consequence?

19. What law was enacted in 1842? What is said of it?

20. What is said respecting the northeastern boundary of the United States? When and how was the matter adjusted?

21. What was one of the last measures of Mr. Tyler's administration? How was Texas annexed, and by what vote?

22. By whom was Tyler succeeded? What is said of the election?

23. What measures were strongly favored by the party that supported Mr. Polk? What course did the president take?

24. What is said of the northwestern boundary? How was the matter adjusted?

25. What tariff law was passed on the president's recommendation?

26. What did the war with Mexico grow out of? What is related respecting Texas? What was done by the Mexican minister?

27. What is said of the boundaries of Texas? What were the boundaries contended for by the different parties? What took place on the disputed territory?

28. What was done by the legislature of Texas in 1845? What was then done?

29. Where was General Taylor with his army in March, 1846? Where was he ordered to proceed? What were his next movements?

30. What is said of the Mexican force that was assembled? What was done by General Arista on the 24th of April? What took place on the same day?

31. What was done a few days afterwards by the Mexicans and by General Taylor? What was the result?

32. What is related of the battle of Palo Alto, and the losses?

33. What took place the following day? What next followed?

34. What is said of the effect produced by the news of Captain Thornton's disaster at Washington? What course did the president take? What did Congress do? What did the whig members attempt to do? By what vote did the bill pass?

35. What is said of the feeling against the war? What vote was passed by the House of Representatives?

36. How was General Taylor's force increased? What measures were taken?

37. What is related respecting the attack on Monterey?

38. When was the city assaulted? What was the result? What next followed?

39. What is related respecting General Santa Anna? What course was it expected he would take? What was done, and what was the result?

40. What course did the American government now resolve to take? Who was ordered to take the chief command?

41. What is said respecting the armistice concluded by General Taylor? What then followed? What was done by General Scott?

42. What was now done by General Taylor? What did he soon learn respecting Santa Anna? What course did General Taylor then take?

43. What is related respecting the battle of Buena Vista? What were the losses on both sides?

44. What is related respecting General Scott's attack on Vera Cruz, and its result?

45. What course did the American army then take? What took place at Cerro Gordo?

46. What was the issue of this assault? What were the losses of the Mexicans, and the Americans?

47. By what was the victory of Cerro Gordo followed? What is said of the state of the army?

48 When and with what force did General Scott march from Puebla? What two battles were fought? What is stated respecting the battle of Contreras? What of Churubusco? What does General Scott say of the achievements of the American army?

49. What was the effect of these victories? What course was then adopted?
50. What is said of Mr. Trist, and what was done by him? What was the result, and what followed?
51. What military operation took place the following day? What was the loss on each side?
52. What is said of the storming of the fortress of Chapultepec? What was then done by the Americans?
53. What was then done by the Mexican army, and by the Americans?
54. What was the total loss of General Scott's army in these battles? What was the number of American troops that took the city of Mexico?
55. What expedition was conducted by General Kearny?
56. What is said of his march and conquest? What measures did he then adopt?
57. What is related of Colonel Doniphan? What of the contest at Bracito?
58. What took place at the Pass of Sacramento? What followed?
59. What is related respecting Colonel Fremont? What was done when the existence of the war with Mexico was heard of?
60. What was done soon after the conquest of the city of Mexico by General Scott? What was the result?
61. What provinces were ceded by Mexico to the United States? What does the territory acquired amount to?
62. What sum did the United States engage to pay to Mexico?
63. What is said of the discovery of gold mines? What consequence has followed this discovery?
64. What is said of the progress and issue of the war? What beneficial results may be hoped from it?
65. By whom was Mr. Polk succeeded? What is said of General Taylor? What of the election?
66. What is said of the death of President Taylor? By whom was he succeeded?
67. What important acts were passed soon after the accession of Mr. Fillmore?
68. What is said of the act for the rendition of fugitive slaves?
69. What is related of General Lopez?
70. What was done by President Fillmore?
71. What is related concerning this expedition? What of Lopez and his followers?
72. What is said of the administration of Mr. Fillmore?

SECTION VIII.

1. By whom was Mr. Fillmore succeeded? What is said of the election, and of the inaugural address of President Pierce?
2. What military expeditions were made after the termination of the Mexican war?
3. What is said of these expeditions and their object?
4. Who was the most noted leader? What the most considerable of these expeditions?
5. What is said of Walker's last expedition?
6. What is related concerning the choice of a speaker for the 34th Congress?
7. What conference was held at Ostend? What proposition was made? How was it regarded?
8 What two important measures of President Pierce's administration?
9. What is related respecting the bill for organizing the Territories of Kansas and Nebraska? What was the effect of this bill with respect to the Missouri Compromise?

10. What is said of the introduction of this bill? What was done by New England clergymen? By what vote was the bill passed?
11. How was this measure regarded in the free States? To what did it lead?
12. What was done soon after the passage of this act?
13. What is related respecting bodies of armed men from Missouri?
14. Who was the first governor of Kansas? When did he arrive, and what followed?
15. What is related concerning an election in March, 1855?
16. Who was appointed governor in place of Reeder? What constitution was formed?
17. By whom was Shannon succeeded? What is related respecting Geary? By whom was he succeeded?
18. What is related respecting the formation of a constitution? What course did Governor Walker take? By whom was he succeeded?
19. What was done with respect to the Lecompton Constitution? By whom was Governor Denver succeeded?
20. When and where was another constitution formed? By what majority was it ratified by the people? Who was elected governor?
21. What is further said respecting Kansas?
22. By whom was Franklin Pierce succeeded? What is said of the election?
23. By what political parties had the people of the United States been long divided? What new party was now formed? What was its leading principle?
24. What is said of Slavery? For what was Mr. Buchanan's administration noted? What is related respecting some members of his cabinet?
25. What is related respecting John Brown and his followers?
26. What effect did it produce, and how many armed men were collected to oppose him?
27. What course did Brown pursue? What was the fate of Brown and his followers?
28. What is said of this enterprise?
29. What is related respecting the life and character of Brown?
30. What is said of his hostility to Slavery? What was said of him by Governor Wise?
31. How did he appear after his condemnation?
32. What is said respecting Slavery at the time of the adoption of the Federal Constitution?
33. What eminent men regarded it as a bad institution?
34. What change took place after the invention of the cotton-gin?
35. At what times has a hostile feeling or dissension between the free and slave States been strongly manifested?
36. When was the 16th President of the United States elected? What was the state of the country at the time? What the parties?
37. What is related respecting the democratic party? Who were the candidates of the different parties for President?
38. What is said of the election? What was the result?
39. What is related respecting South Carolina and other Southern States? What course did South Carolina take?
40. What further measures were taken by South Carolina?
41. When and where did the delegates of the seceding States meet? What measures did they adopt? What States were styled Confederate States?
42. What took place on the 4th of March, 1861?
43. When and how was the rebellion or war begun?
44. What was done by President Lincoln?

SECTION IX.

1. What is said of secession? What States seceded?
2. What provisions for government were made by the seceded States? Who were their chief officers?
3. What was done by a Peace Congress? A Confederate Commission?
4. What is said of Mr. Lincoln's inauguration and address?
5. What circumstances embarrassed the position of the Federal Government?
6. Relate the circumstances of the attack on Fort Sumter.
7. Effect of the news at the North? First bloodshed?
8. Military movements of the Confederates in April? Of the Federals?
9. Engagements in June and July? How was West Virginia secured?
10. Give an account of the battle of Manassas, or Bull Run.
11. Effects of this battle? Other engagements about the Potomac?
12. What is said of secession in Missouri? What battles occurred in Missouri? Give an account of Wilson's Creek and its results.
13. Naval preparations in 1861? Expeditions sent out?
14. What provision was made to carry on the war?
15. Number and position of rebel forces at the beginning of 1862?
16. Same of Federal forces? Naval preparations?
17. Give an account of Burnside's Expedition. Forts taken?
18. Relate the affair of the "Merrimac" and "Monitor."
19. Movements of McClellan in spring of '62? Norfolk taken, when?
20. Battle of Fair Oaks? Why did McClellan change his base?
21. What, where, and when, were the "Seven Days' Battles"?
22. What followed immediately after these battles?
23. What battles occurred on Pope's retreat, and with what results?
24. What is said of Lee's invasion? Of the battle of Antietam?
25. What and when was Stuart's raid? What is said of Fredericksburg?
26. What successes were obtained in the West? Their result?
27. Give an account of the battle of Shiloh. Of the siege of Corinth.
28. Efforts of the Confederates to regain Kentucky? Battle of Iuka? What attempts were made by Grant and Sherman? Give an account of the battle of Murfreesborough.
29. Battle of Pea Ridge? Siege of Island No. 10? What followed?
30. Give an account of the capture of New Orleans.
31. Means employed by Government to carry on the war? Situation at the close of the year? State admitted?
32. What is said of the Emancipation Proclamation? Other acts relating to slavery? Riot in New York? Enforcement of draft?
33. What is said of the battle of Chancellorsville? Stoneman's raid?
34. What is said of Lee's second invasion? O the battle of Gettysburg? Of Morgan's raid?
35. Effect of rebel efforts to recover North Carolina? Give an account of the attack on the defences of Charleston.
36. What is said of Arkansas Post? Of fruitless efforts to take Vicksburg? How did Grant finally secure a position in its rear? Grierson's raid?
37. What is said of the siege and surrender of Vicksburg?

38 Movements of Rosecrans? Battle of Chicamauga?

39. What was done by Grant? What battles around Chattanooga? What is said of Knoxville?

40. How was Arkansas recovered to the Federals? What was done by Gen. Banks? Siege of Port Hudson?

41. What is said of the Navy in 1863?

42. What was done by the Thirty-seventh Congress? Prospects of the war?

43 Sherman's expedition to Meridian? The Florida expedition?

44 Give an account of the "Red River Expedition."

45. Gen. Steele's movement? Forrest's raid? Plymouth, N.C.?

46 Two great armies in 1864. Their divisions and officers.

47 What advance was proposed? Describe that of Grant, and its results.

48. What is said of Gen. Butler? Of the beginning of the siege of Petersburg? Engagements during it?

49. Attempts to take Lynchburg? Relate the account of the third rebel invasion.

50. What is said of Gen. Sherman's progress to Atlanta? Of the siege of Atlanta? Movements of Hood? Of Sherman?

51. Relate the account of Sherman's "March to the Sea."

52. Battle of Franklin? Siege of Nashville? Various raids?

53. Naval operations? Relate the exploit of Farragut in Mobile Bay. New rank created for Farragut?

54. What is said of rebel privateers?

55. Re-election of Mr. Lincoln? Prospects at close of '64?

56. Field of operations for 1865? Changes in commanders?

57. Relate the circumstances of the capture of Wilmington.

58. March of Gen. Sherman from Savannah to Goldsborough?

59. What movement was made by Sheridan? Position of Grant's army? Movements towards the capture of Richmond? Final struggle? Surrender of Lee?

60. Movements of Sherman and Johnston? Surrender of Johnston?

61. What was done by Wilson in Alabama? Relate the circumstances of the capture of Mobile. What surrenders were made in the South-west? Last battle of the war?

62. Death of Mr. Lincoln? His character and the mourning for him?

63. Who succeeded Mr. Lincoln? Early acts of the President? Capture of Jefferson Davis? Amendment to the Constitution? Peace declared?

64. What was the attitude of France and England? Causes of irritation between England and the United States?

65. What is said of the border warfare? Of prisoners? Of charitable associations?

66. Cost of the War? Money raised how? What was postage-currency? What were greenbacks? National Banks? Premium on gold?

69. Numbers of army and navy? Losses? Improvements in art of war?

68. Results of the Rebellion?

TABLES

History of the United States.

Which were some of the first settled colonies?
When was Virginia settled, and by whom? New York? &c.
When was the Peace of Paris, and the end of the French war?
When did the Revolutionary War begin? When was peace restored?
When was the Declaration of Independence? When was the Constitution adopted?
Who was the first president of the United States? Who have been his successors?
When did Washington become president? Adams? &c.

Events of the Revolutionary War.

When was the Stamp Act passed? What other events took place before the meeting of the first Continental Congress?
When did the Revolutionary War begin?
What other events took place the same year?
When was the Declaration of Independence made?
What battles in 1776? In 1777? In 1778? In 1779? In 1780 In 1781?
When was the surrender at Saratoga? At Yorktown?
When was peace with England, and independence acknowledged?

Chronology of Improvements, &c.

When and where was the first college in the Colonies founded?
What other colleges were founded in the 17th century?
When and where was printing introduced into the Colonies?
When and where was the first newspaper published?
When and where was the first medical school established?
When and where was the first quarto Bible printed?
When was the first census of the United States taken?
When was the first steamboat used on the Hudson?
When was the Erie Canal completed? The Ohio Canal?
When were several important railroads opened?
When was the use of the magnetic telegraph introduced?

Distinguished Americans.

Most of the men enumerated in the Table, in the 17th century, and some of those in the 18th, were born in England. Some who are classed as warriors were known also as statesmen, and some classed as statesmen were likewise distinguished as military commanders.

The persons enumerated in the fourth column were men of science or literature, physicians, historians, poets, artists, &c.

Population of the United States.—Remarks.

Which were the thirteen original States? What States added?
From what, to what, number did the population of the United States increase from 1790 to 1860?
From what, to what, number did the slaves increase in the same time?

In about how many years has the population doubled?
How many post-offices were in the United States in 1790? In 1860?
When were the first considerable railroads for conveying passengers opened in the United States?
How many miles of railroad were in use in 1859?

CHRONOLOGY.

What is chronology? What is said respecting eras?
1. How did the Greeks compute time? What is said of the Olympiads?
2. How did the Romans reckon time? How was their era designated?
3. What is said of the Christian era? In what year of the world, according to different computations, did the birth of Christ take place? Which is generally adopted in English literature? When did computation from the Christian era begin to be used? What is said of the Roman or Julian year? How great a deviation from the true time had been occasioned in 1582? What was done by Pope Gregory XIII.? When was the New Style first used in England? What change was occasioned by it?
4. What is said of the era of the Hegira?
5. What era, next to the Christian era, is most used in this country?

SACRED HISTORY.

Of what do the historical parts of the Bible chiefly treat? What is the other principal source of information respecting the ancient history of the Israelites? When does the Old Testament history end?
What is said of the descent of the Israelites?
Why were they called Hebrews, Israelites, and Jews?
What is related respecting their residence in Egypt?
How long did they wander in the wilderness?
How long were they governed by Judges?
When was the most flourishing period of the monarchy?
How long did the sceptre of Judah continue in the family of David?
What is said of the tendency of the Israelites to idolatry?
What is said of the history of the Ten Tribes subsequent to their captivity by Shalmaneser? When did the Jews return from Babylon?
By whom were they afterwards governed? When were they subjected to the Romans? When was Jerusalem destroyed?

Chronological Table of the Kingdoms of Israel and Judah

How long did the kingdom of Israel continue undivided? How long did the kingdom of Judah continue?
What is said of Saul and his reign? David? Solomon?
How many years did Saul reign? David? &c.
Who was the first king of Judah? Who the last?
What is said of Rehoboam, or of his reign? Abijah? &c.
What prophets flourished between 1100 and 1000 years B. C.?
Between 1000 and 900? Between 900 and 800? &c.

Chronological Table of the Kingdom of Israel, or the Ten Tribes.

How long did the kingdom of Israel continue?
Whc was the first king? Who the last?
How long did Jeroboam I. reign? What is said of him and his reign? Nadab? &c.
What is said of the history of the Ten Tribes after their captivity?

Eras of Modern History.

This Table exhibits some of the most important eras in Modern History, but the chronology of the rise and fall of states and empires may be best learned from the *Chart of History*.

When was the New Empire of the West formed? &c.
What eras or events are mentioned in the 9th century? The 10th? &c.

Chronological Table of Inventions.

When was gunpowder invented? Printing? The solar system revived? The telescope invented? Thermometer? Logarithms? The steam-engine? Inoculation? Stereotype printing? Vaccination? The steamboat? Railroads? The magnetic telegraph?
What inventions or improvements were made in the 10th century? In he 11th? &c.

THE END

www.ingramcontent.com/pod-product-compliance
Lightning Source LLC
LaVergne TN
LVHW021128110826
845150LV00005B/965

9781425550882